SOCIAL PSYCH OLOGY

SOCIAL PSYCHOLOGY

FOUNDATIONS, ADVANCES AND APPLICATIONS

Edited by

Stefania Paolini
Rhiannon N. Turner
Milica Vasiljevic
& Richard J. Crisp

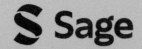

1 Oliver's Yard
55 City Road
London EC1Y 1SP

2455 Teller Road
Thousand Oaks
California 91320

Unit No 323-333, Third Floor, F-Block
International Trade Tower
Nehru Place, New Delhi – 110 019

8 Marina View Suite 43-053
Asia Square Tower 1
Singapore 018960

Editor: Amy Maher
Editorial assistant: Hanine Kadi
Production editor: Imogen Roome
Copyeditor: Sarah Bury
Proofreader: Leigh Smithson
Cover design: Wendy Scott
Typeset by: C&M Digitals (P) Ltd, Chennai, India
Printed in the UK by Bell & Bain Ltd, Glasgow

Library of Congress Control Number: 2024933132

British Library Cataloguing in Publication data

A catalogue record for this book is available from the British Library

ISBN 978-1-5264-2813-4
ISBN 978-1-5264-2814-1 (pbk)

CONTENTS

ONLINE RESOURCES

Social Psychology is supported by a wealth of online resources which are available at https://study.sagepub.com/paolini

- **Teaching Guide** includes teaching tips for each chapter.
- **PowerPoints** to accompany each chapter.
- **Multiple choice questions** to accompany each chapter, for formative assessment.

THE EDITORS

EDITOR BIOGRAPHIES

Stefania Paolini is Professor of Social and Intercultural Psychology at Durham University. She is a social psychologist with expertise in intergroup dynamics, prejudice, stereotyping, discrimination, and social cohesion. At the core of her work, Stefania explores with mixed methods 'when' and 'why' experiences with individual members of stigmatised groups affect responses to the stigmatised group as a whole, in conflict societies as well as peaceful settings. Stefania has published extensively, and her work on the topics of intergroup contact, intergroup friendship, intergroup emotions, motivation for contact, and negative contact is highly cited and has demonstrated an impact beyond academia in high-profile policy reports. Stefania is passionate about equality, diversity and inclusion (EDI) issues in science and broader society and has received numerous science, service, and community awards for her work, including the Most Influential Article Awards from the Academy of Management and the Asian Journal of Social Psychology, the Australian Psychology Society's Peace Research Award, and the Distinguished Service to SPSSI Award. She has been a Fellow of the Society of Experimental Social Psychology since 2013.

Rhiannon N. Turner is Professor of Social Psychology at Queen's University Belfast, and is founder and Director of the Centre for Identity and Intergroup Relations. Her research focuses on intergroup relations, prejudice, and prejudice-reduction. She has published over 100 articles on these topics, and has received numerous awards for her research, including the British Psychological Society Award for Outstanding Doctoral Research Contributions to Psychology, the Society for Personality and Social Psychology's Robert B. Cialdini Award for excellence in field research, and the Gordon Allport Intergroup Relations Prize. Rhiannon was also part of the team that made the Channel 4 show *The School That Tried to End Racism*, which won several awards, including a BAFTA. Rhiannon is currently President of the psychology section of the British Science Association.

Milica Vasiljevic is Professor of Behavioural Science at Durham University. She uses her training in social psychology to investigate how cues in the environment impact health behaviours, and how this knowledge can be translated into more effective and acceptable behaviour change interventions to improve health and reduce inequalities. Milica specialises in large-scale population-level, field experiments evaluating the impact of behavioural interventions. Her expertise in designing and evaluating population-level interventions of health behaviour change have been recognised by an Early Career Award from the Society of Behavioural Medicine. Milica's work on reduced alcohol strength labelling, food calorie labelling, and e-cigarette advertising has been used by national and international policy teams working in these domains. Currently, she is an Associate Editor of the *British Journal of Health Psychology*, and former Associate Editor of the *Journal of Applied Social Psychology* and *Frontiers in Personality and Social Psychology*.

Richard J. Crisp is Professor of Social Psychology at Durham University. A prolific scholar, writer, and educator, his scientific contributions have provided novel insights into how other people shape our behaviour, beliefs, attitudes, and values. He has published over 150 academic papers and is the author of several books, including *Social Psychology: A Very Short Introduction, The Social Brain: How Diversity Made the Modern Mind*, and the introductory textbook *Essential Social Psychology* (5th ed.). He is Editor-in-Chief of the *Journal of Applied Social Psychology* and his scientific achievements have been recognised with numerous awards, including the British Psychological Society President's Award for Distinguished Contributions to Psychological Knowledge. He is a Fellow of the British Psychological Society, the Academy of Social Sciences, and the Association for Psychological Science.

PREFACE

Social Psychology: Foundations, Advances and Applications is an entirely new undergraduate introduction to the science of social behaviour. Designed to meet the needs of students across their entire undergraduate journey into social psychology, it provides an inclusive and authoritative overview for UK, European, and Australasian degree courses.

Departing from other social psychology textbooks, this book is written by chapter contributors who are experts in their respective research fields and experienced teachers of undergraduate social psychology and behavioural science – this is particularly important to meet the needs of second- and third-/fourth-year undergraduate psychology students who may be encountering complex concepts and models for the first time. Each chapter, written through the lenses of the expert contributor, provides a state-of-the-art summary of the particular social psychology topic it covers.

Notably, the text is distinguished by a fresh, new, and distinctive narrative through contributors' *personal journeys* into their field, opening each chapter with a personalised perspective from the start. These sections illustrate *why* each chapter is so important, exciting, and engaging for the writer, and highlight how the student reader may themselves become passionate about this area, or why this topic may impact on their lives. The journey is further built on throughout the chapter: Other *guest personal journeys* are included to showcase the vibrant social psychology family, spanning from early career researchers to key thinkers, and through to investigators from other social sciences who have made an impact in social psychology through interdisciplinary perspectives.

To ensure the book encompasses a degree's worth of social psychology, we have adopted a unique *three-part structure* to each chapter. The first part covers *foundations* and includes all of the core content required for an undergraduate introduction to the topic. The second part is an *advances* section, targeted at more advanced years of study. The *advances* sections may focus on cutting-edge theoretical or empirical developments in the field or on recent debates, or present more complex theories or approaches than in the first part of the chapter. The third part focuses on the *application* of the topic area to address real social, economic, and cultural issues. Social psychology is a scientific discipline with profound implications for the personal and the professional, for policy and practice, in all aspects of life, and we wanted, uniquely, to make this a core aspect of our new textbook. The textbook goes beyond other texts on social psychology to cover a wide array of new and exciting real-world applications using theories, models, and tenets from social psychology.

It's also important to note that the contributors have deliberately written the *advances* and *application* sections to specifically cater for the UK's levels 2, 3, and 4 and Europe's/ Australasia's 3-plus-2 undergraduate and Master's levels, and give instructors flexibility in how they choose to use the book (the latter sections can be used interchangeably across these levels). We want to hand instructors and students the *only* book they will ever need, but also the *flexibility* to use the book how they see fit. We don't think there is any other text out there like this, and we hope it helps to introduce a whole new generation of students and instructors to the wonderful world of social psychology.

1
HISTORY AND RESEARCH METHODS
PADDY ROSS, MILICA VASILJEVIC, & STEFANIA PAOLINI

Contents

1.1 AUTHORS' PERSONAL JOURNEYS

The three of us (Paddy, Miki, and Stefania) are working at the same university and in the same Psychology Department together at Durham University.

Paddy's Journey

Source: © Paddy Ross

The summer before I went to university, I was working at a 24-hour garage. During one particularly long night shift a colleague of mine asked me what I was doing after the summer. I told him proudly, 'I'm going to study psychology'. He stared at me for a bit and then said, 'Is that the one to do with ghosts?'. I laughed for a moment, thinking he was winding me up, before realising he was deadly serious. 'No', I said, with probably a little too much condescension in my voice. 'What is it then?', he asked. 'It's eh … it's to do with … erm … the brain and stuff', I garbled. He looked unimpressed.

What I learned very quickly is that psychology is a vast subject. The degree at my institution consists of modules in Social Psychology, Developmental Psychology, Evolutionary Psychology, Cognitive Psychology, Clinical Psychology, Forensic Psychology, to name a few. But the one thing that is always present is research and investigation. Empirical investigation leads to theories. Theories lead to hypotheses. Hypotheses lead to empirical investigations. The 'circle of life' in the scientific community if you will. Research makes science go round. My area of expertise is the development of emotion recognition in children. But the 'research methods' that I use to answer my questions in that area are exactly the same as my colleagues whether they're studying new brain cells used for navigation, the ability of blind participants to echolocate and 'see' or how empathy develops in humans and great apes. Actually, come to think of it, 'it's to do with the brain and stuff' turned out to be a pretty accurate description of psychology in the end.

Miki's Journey

Source: © Milica Vasiljevic

I (Miki) have always been passionate about using social psychological theories, models, and methods to study human nature and human behaviour. I have, in particular, always been interested in changing human behaviour for the better, which has led me to investigate how we can devise the most effective interventions and policies for human and societal thriving. I have written Chapter 11 of this textbook on the topic of behaviour change, so hop on to Chapter 11 to find out more about my personal journey into Social Psychology.

Stefania's Journey

I (Stefania) first studied psychology at the University of Padova, which with the University of Bologna, also in Italy, claims to be the oldest university in the world. My interest in social and intergroup psychology started early in my undergraduate studies. What immediately struck me was the possibility it offered to combine the study of complex human behaviour with methodological rigour and elegance. Upon completing a psychology degree with a social/organisational specialisation, I worked as a research consultant for governmental and private organisations, but the need to feed my inquisitive mind eventually brought me back to academia, first as an international

Source: © Stefania Paolini

ERASMUS student and eventually for a PhD at Cardiff University. That is where I overlapped in my research training with Richard Crisp, also an editor of this textbook. There, I used both survey methods and experiments to investigate the process of *social induction*, which refers to how and when an experience with a discrete number of members of a social group shapes impressions of their group as a whole. Over 20 years later, I still love using an eclectic toolkit for my work and I am still driven by the same intellectual passion for complex behaviour and rigorous psychological investigation of topics in intergroup dynamics and the science of social cohesion. But more and more these days, I also like to take this knowledge and my curiosity to the service of social justice, towards a more inclusive and equitable society.

We hope you will enjoy this journey about complex human behaviour, rigorous social psychological investigation, and its application, which we have prepared for you in this textbook.

1.2 CHAPTER OUTLINE

Gordon Allport, a father figure in social psychology, once defined social psychology as the scientific investigation of how the thoughts, feelings, and behaviours of individuals are influenced by the actual, imagined or implied presence of others (Allport, 1935). The aim of this chapter is to introduce you to some key research methods that can be used to ask questions in social psychology, and some key statistical tests that may help to answer those questions, within their historical and cultural context. First, we'll give a history of social psychology. We will then introduce some basic analysis techniques, then build upon that knowledge by introducing some more complex research designs, and thus some more complex statistical tests. Throughout, we will be using classic social psychology studies and will explore what research designs and statistical techniques they used to produce their famous findings. There'll be no formulae, and only a few numbers. The aim is not to teach you statistics, but rather to give some insight into the toolkit that is available to us; to get you thinking about not only *what* those famous findings were, but also *how* they came about.

1.3 INTRODUCTION

> **Key concept – Study design:**
> A research (study) design is the structured framework that serves as the skeleton for an investigation. The study design is made up of the methods and procedures used to collect data on variables specified to answer a particular research problem.

If you want to contribute to social psychology, you need to study the research designs and methods employed by social psychologists. How is research conducted? Which **study design** should you use, and which type of data should you gather? Which tests could or should you use to answer your question? Which participants should you recruit? What does it mean to have statistically non-significant results? What on earth is a p-value?

Figure 1.1, which shows a graphic of the study wheel, helps you to think about social psychology from the perspective of the research methods the field employs. Typically, research starts with a research question or hypothesis. This leads to deciding upon the most suitable design or methods to be used to collect our data. Then, this in turn informs our **theories** and models, and once again helps to generate new hypotheses, research methods, and so on. According to Karl Popper, a very influential epistemologist or philosopher of sci-

> **Key concept – Theory:** An integrated set of principles that explain and predict an observed phenomenon or aspect of the world. These principles should be testable and falsifiable. A seminal theory developed and used by social psychologists is the social identity theory (Tajfel & Turner, 1979) discussed in more detail throughout this textbook.

ence, scientific progress reflects an iterative process whereby the scientist interfaces the 'world of theory' with the 'world of data'. Scientific investigation therefore means checking the fit or match (vs mismatch) between our expectations about reality and what data tells us reality is like. The identification of a mismatch between these two worlds – or 'empirical falsification' as Popper calls it – provides the impetus to adjust the theory towards an improved fit to the data. And this progress would repeat over and over again (Camiller & Popper, 2013) in a kind of cyclical manner because, according to Popper, no theory can ever be proven but only falsified by evidence.

Although quite neat, the 'study wheel' always struck me (Paddy) as a little static in two dimensions. Nearly as if the same research is being done again and again, over and over. A more apt visualisation of doing research in science for me wouldn't be a circle, but rather something three-dimensional like a spiral, forever turning forwards through time. Imagine that study wheel turning, but coming out of the page towards you like a corkscrew. Always the same shape, but also always moving and growing, with its trajectory always towards the future, pushing forwards.

I once heard science described as being this sphere that expands as we learn new things. Every researcher pushes out their own little bit with every bit of research they do, expanding

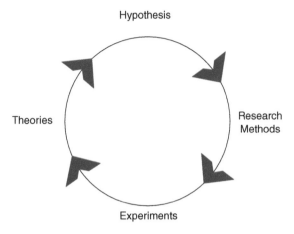

Figure 1.1 The study wheel

it just a smidge so that when everyone does a little bit, our cumulative knowledge grows, and the sphere of knowledge gets bigger. Everyone works together to expand science with their research spirals, pushing into the unknown. In this chapter (indeed in this book) we want to give you the tools to be able to start your own research spiral and learn not only how to ask interesting questions, but crucially, how to go about answering them.

With this chapter, we aim to give you the basic knowledge to create your own social psychology studies. The aim is also to give you a lens through which to view and critique the theories and research that social psychologists have used to address important and specific research questions about how, as Gordon Allport put it, people's feelings and behaviours are influenced by their personal experience of others.

1.4 LEARNING OBJECTIVES

By the end of this chapter, you will:

- Know more about the history of social psychology;
- Know more about different research methods used by social psychologists;
- Know more about the statistical tests used to analyse the data gathered in social psychology studies;
- Better understand the choices you need to make in conducting social psychological research;
- Understand more about how seminal studies in social psychology used different research methods;

- Learn about the latest methodological innovations and the move towards open and transparent science in the field of social psychology.

1.5 PART 1: FOUNDATIONS

In this section we will explore the foundations of research, beginning with basic research designs, exploring the methods available to us to answer our questions and how they apply to social psychology.

1.5.1 Types of Design and Methods

In research, everything starts with a question, a curiosity about, for instance, the relationship or difference between two aspects of our reality. You might want to know whether extroversion goes together with hosting lots of parties, or whether extroverts and introverts vary in the kind of people they socialise with. Once a question, or more formally a 'research hypothesis', emerges, we must attempt to **operationalise** the question and be ready to embark on searching for an answer. A question, a curiosity about something, is the bedrock of any research investigation.

In designing a study, to use perhaps one of the English language's most baffling and unpleasant metaphors, 'there is more than one way to skin a cat'. It's also necessary here to define a research design and a research method, as I've seen them used interchangeably in the past. A research design is your plan of how to answer your research question. The research method is the procedure you use to collect and analyse your data.

> **Key concept – Operationalisation:** Turning concepts that are not easily measured (e.g., attitudes, anxiety) into measurable observations. By operationalising your experiment, you can gather data on cognitive and behavioural phenomena that aren't directly observable.

> **Key concept – Research hypothesis:** A statement of expectation or prediction that will be tested by research. For example, a research hypothesis might be about the relationship or difference between two aspects of our social experience.

The method one uses depends on the type of design chosen. Some designs will be better than others at addressing the question you want to answer; some will come with logistical issues. The best one is rarely the most practical, and the easiest one is rarely the best. There is a kind of balancing act you must perform to effectively answer your question, but in a way that is practical as well.

The nature of the thing you want to know about (e.g., extraversion, partying) will usually determine whether you will be doing quantitative or qualitative research. If the thing you want to know about can be 'quantified' (e.g., number of parties, accuracy in a task, reaction times, scores on a questionnaire, etc.), then it's more likely you will need to use a quantitative study design. If what you're after can't be quantified (e.g., people's personal account of a significant experience), then you've got a qualitative study design. This distinction has implications for the ways you will analyse your data to answer your question, but we'll get into all that later. So first, some examples of the main types of quantitative designs and methods are discussed next.

Quantitative Designs and Methods

One important thing to keep in mind about quantitative designs is the distinction between correlational and experimental approaches. In a correlational cross-sectional survey design, for example, researchers may ask their participants to rate where they sit on the political continuum (Left to Right) and which of the current candidates running for political office they endorse. This design would allow the researchers to see how strong the relationship is and in what direction the variables are related (positively or negatively). However, the downside to this design is that it cannot help us infer causation. It only allows us to draw conclusions regarding the relationship between a set of two variables of interest.

> **Key concept – Independent variable:** An independent variable (often denoted as 'x') is an aspect of reality that is manipulated, controlled, varied, or simply measured in a study to explore its effects. The label 'independent' is to say that it is not influenced by other variables within the study.

Another type of design commonly used by social psychologists is the experimental design in which we manipulate one variable and measure its effect on another variable. For example, we may be interested to find out whether hunger levels affect mood. In an experimental design, we would manipulate levels of hunger among participants (e.g., we would feed one group of participants but deprive a second group of food prior to

> **Key concept – Dependent variable:** A dependent variable (often denoted as 'y') is an aspect of reality being measured in a research study. The label 'dependent' is to say that it depends on the independent variable.

completing the other tasks in the experiment), while trying to keep all other variables constant. Once we have manipulated levels of hunger, we would then administer mood tests to examine the effect hunger has on mood. In an experiment, the variable that is being manipulated is commonly referred to as the **independent variable** (IV) and the variable that is hypothesised to be affected by the changes in the independent variables is referred to as the **dependent variable** (DV). Importantly, experimental designs, unlike correlational designs, allow us to infer causation. Below, we first cover correlational types of study designs (longitudinal and cross-sectional studies), before turning our attention to different types of experimental studies (laboratory, field, and quasi-experiments).

Longitudinal and Cross-Sectional Studies

Imagine you want to know whether and to what extent attachment (or lasting psychological connectedness) to mothers in early childhood affects confidence in later childhood. Attachment is considered an independent variable, causing changes on the dependent variable, confidence. Ideally, to answer this question, we would track all the children in the country from birth until late childhood, constantly taking measurements of attachment and confidence in real-life settings over a period of a decade, and then come up with a definitive answer to that question.

This would be a study using a longitudinal design, one in which lots of data are repeatedly gathered from the same individuals over a (long) period. An example of a longitudinal study in this textbook is Rosenberg and colleagues' (1989) study examining the relationship between students' self-esteem and grades over time (for more details see Chapter 2). This design type allows us to track patterns and changes in behaviour over time. However, it would also likely be one of the longest, most intrusive, and most expensive studies one could do. So, what alternative and more efficient approaches are there?

First, your participant numbers are going to have to come way down. We have statistics so that we can get participants (your sample) and then generalise your results to everyone else (your population). Therefore, you do not need the entire population to address your question.

Now that your participant numbers have been reduced, what else can be changed to make your research into a workable study? Well, instead of tracking participants longitudinally, we can attempt to get attachment and confidence measurements from a range of participants from as many ages as possible within the limits of our resources. Thus, we can obtain a snapshot or 'cross-section' of participants, where we are looking at many different participants at one point in time.

KEY STUDY 1.1

An Election Poll Gone Wrong

One issue psychology and social psychology tend to run into when looking for participants is that the samples in our studies are often undergraduate students, predominantly Caucasian females (in psychology departments!), aged between 18 and 23. Then we're using those results to generalise about how people behave – or at least, we used to (we return to this later). With the rise of the internet in the late 1990s, it is now possible to reach huge samples instantaneously and have participants' responses come back within the hour. The key challenge remains that of achieving a **representative sample**. Are you simply surveying the people you have asked (convenience sample), or can those results be applied to the general population as a whole? (See the concept of external validity below.)

A classic example of survey sampling bias is the cautionary tale of the American election predictions made by *The Literary Digest* in 1936. A weekly publication, *The Literary Digest* had been surveying opinion on presidential elections since 1916 and had never got one wrong. In 1936, Franklin D. Roosevelt was up against Alfred Landon, and the *Digest* confidently predicted a landslide victory for Landon. If President Landon doesn't ring a bell, that's because Roosevelt won every single state except two, and won the popular vote by nearly 25%! Despite surveying an incredible 2.27 million people, *The Literary Digest* had made some catastrophic sampling errors. To administer the survey, they first turned to their own subscriber list, then to the telephone book, and finally to the list of registered automobile owners in the country. But one must remember that this was 1936, in the middle of the Great Depression, and the people on all three of those lists had something that the average American did not: a healthy disposable income. If you could afford a car, a telephone, or even a subscription to a weekly magazine, you were unlikely at the time to be voting for the Democrat candidate. Thus, by excluding less affluent Americans from their survey, *The Literary Digest* made a huge front-page error. The error was also cited as one of the key factors in the demise of the publication, and it folded two years later. So, generating a representative sample is critical, but also very difficult.

The main and important drawback of cross-sectional designs is that they do not allow us to make confident causal inferences about our results. This issue is also where the next type of research design can be very handy!

Experimental Studies

In an experiment, the researcher directly controls or manipulates the independent variable by randomly allocating participants to different treatment conditions or levels of the independent variable, and then checks these treatments' effects on the dependent variable. This approach and high degree of control provides great confidence in causal interpretations of the IV–DV relationship.

For example, we might want to know how people score on a video game (DV) as a function of screen resolution (IV). Our hypothesis is that the higher the screen resolution, the better the score. To test this idea, we randomly allocate people into three groups (**between-subjects design**), such that (a) one group plays the game in SD, (b) one group in HD, and (c) one group in 4K resolution.

Key concepts – Between-, within-subjects designs and counterbalancing: Allocation of participants to experimental treatments can take two main forms. In between-subjects designs, each participant is randomly allocated to one level of the independent variable or treatment. In a within-subjects design, each participant is allocated to all levels of the independent variable or treatments in turn, often in a 'counterbalanced order', which means in a randomly varied order across participants to limit the impact of order effects on the results.

With this approach, however, we are taking some risks: individual differences. What if, by chance, we had a couple of participants in the SD group who were brilliant at the game and a few in the 4K group who were just dreadful. These individual differences would affect the results of the experiment in ways that have little to do with our interest in screen resolution! (See below the concept of internal validity.) By randomly assigning participants to the different experimental groups (conditions) we are minimising the potential for individual differences to affect our dependent variable. Another way in which we can ensure our experiment doesn't suffer from the potential effects of the individual differences between our participants is to increase our sample size. The larger our sample is, the greater our confidence that the impact of individual differences will be mostly levelled out across conditions and reduce any biasing effects on the results. One good example of a social psychology laboratory experiment is the minimal group paradigm experiment that you will read about more in Chapter 10.

Finally, we might decide to employ a **within-subjects design**. The experiment remains identical, but in this design every participant does the experiment under every condition. Thus, they all play the game three times (in SD, HD, and 4K) and we do a slightly different statistical analysis (more on that later). By doing this, we are effectively taking individual differences out of the experiment. If someone just happens to be rubbish at the game, they'll be rubbish under all conditions, so it doesn't skew one condition's scores and it's fine. Also, to ensure this works best, we need to **counterbalance** the order of the treatments across participants. For clarity of results, we don't want the situation where everyone does all three resolution conditions in the same order and is gradually getting better at the game at the same time. If every participant gets the resolutions in a random order, we can completely disregard order of presentation as a factor impacting our results.

Of course, these examples are a tiny snapshot of designs and methods but they illustrate how important a good design is. If your design is flawed, your results are flawed. And once you've collected your data, it's too late. To use another metaphor, you can't put the toothpaste back in the tube.

Field Experimental and Quasi-experimental Studies

Laboratory experiments give you excellent control over key variables in your research design because you can closely orchestrate what your participants are required to do and when. But is behaviour you see in the lab really how someone would behave in the real world? In the field, we have much less ability to control key variables, but individuals are likely to display more genuine behaviours. When designing research, a constant trade-off that needs to be made is that between **internal**, **external**, and **ecological validity**.

Field experiments are a useful tool within the methodological toolkit used by social psychologists, enabling us to increase the external and ecological validity of our findings. Of course, this comes with the added drawback of reduced internal validity. A famous example of a social psychology field experiment is the Robbers Cave study by Sherif et al. (1961), which divided boys into two different groups and instigated competition between the two groups. This field experiment was the basis for the development of the influential realistic conflict theory (for more details on the experiment and the theory it inspired see Chapter 10).

Sometimes it is not possible to randomly assign people to conditions in the field. In those cases, we may run a field quasi-experiment, where membership of certain groups is predetermined. An example of a field quasi-experiment is Dutton and Aron's (1974) study, described in Chapter 3, where men were approached by an attractive female experimenter before going on a wobbly, high-suspension bridge and asked to write their impressions of an unrelated photograph shown to them.

> **Key concept – Validity:** **Internal validity** in research describes the extent to which a cause-and-effect relationship established in a study cannot be explained by other factors. This type of validity is easier to achieve under high control of key variables in the study. **External validity** indicates the extent to which you can generalise your findings to other situations, people, settings, and measures. **Ecological validity** examines whether the results of a study can be generalised to real-life settings.

KEY STUDY 1.2

Balancing Internal and Ecological Validity in Eye-Witness Research

There are several well-known experiments into eye-witness testimony conducted by Elizabeth Loftus which nicely highlight this trade-off. In 1974, Loftus and Palmer were investigating the impact of leading questions on eye-witness testimony. In a lab experiment, they showed participants video footage of various car crashes and asked them afterwards what speed they thought the cars were going. Crucially, they altered the verb used (between-subjects), so one group were asked 'About how fast were the cars going when they *hit* each other?', while another group were asked 'About how fast were the cars going when they *smashed* each other?'. They showed that, on average, the verb used in the question systematically affected the participants' memory of the accident, with nearly a 10 miles per hour difference between the highest and lowest estimates!

The Loftus studies have great internal validity: they are well controlled and show largely repeatable results. However, anyone who has ever been unfortunate enough to witness a real car crash knows that the reality is probably quite different. Instead of being prompted to look at a crash, it happens suddenly and unexpectedly. It can be traumatic, and the lack of context means you are unlikely to make a conscious effort to remember anything in particular.

(Continued)

But how could you perform a similar study in the field? Staging a car crash or crime would be quite a nightmare to get past an **ethics** advisory board. And again, you would run into the same problem of not being able to control where your participants are looking/ how much they see/how involved they are in the incident. Finding the 'correct' balance of internal and external validity is therefore extremely difficult, and a lack of either should always be considered when reading research and considering its impact.

Qualitative Research

So far, we have looked at methods in which we are investigating things that can be easily quantified. However, sometimes social psychologists and other researchers are interested in examining particular phenomena in depth in their naturalistic settings. Sometimes we are really interested in observing and interpreting the behaviours as they occur, without quantifying them. This calls for the use of qualitative methods.

However, most often nowadays, social psychologists are part of large interdisciplinary teams that use a mixture of qualitative and quantitative methods, and this is often referred to as mixed methods research design. Next, we'll take a brief look at some qualitative methods, to hopefully give you an idea of what can be done with this research method.

Interviews

Interviewing is an essential tool for many types of social psychology research. The flexibility interviews offer is vast, and by allowing the method to be participant-led, you can generate a huge amount of data. Interviews can range from simple question-and-answer sessions (structured and semi-structured) to fully unstructured open-ended conversations. You may try to quantify responses to a structured interview (e.g., 'Do you think that discrimination takes place in your organisation?'; count 'yes' and 'no'). On the other hand, following up a 'yes' answer there by asking 'Can you describe the discrimination and how it made you feel?' will yield an answer that cannot be quantified in the same way.

Interviews provide us with rich data that can contextualise phenomena that we have observed or recorded. Another great thing about interviews as a qualitative technique is that there aren't really any right or wrong answers (flexibility). However, this comes hand-in-hand with significant variability in interpretation. In other words, the knowledge and experience of the researcher might make a big difference in terms of interpretation.

Focus Groups

What's not so great about interviews is that they take a lot of time. Think of the amount of transcribing you need to do before you even have the raw information to analyse! They can also sometimes be somewhat stilted as their one-to-one setting can be awkward. A slightly different method to combat these issues is to use a focus-group design. By getting people in a room and asking an open question, or again some semi-structured questions, you can record their interactions and their verbal contents. Maybe they agree, or disagree, or challenge each other, or argue. The way that they develop and extend each other's views and ideas can be a very rich well of data that the researcher can mine for meaning. They typically shouldn't consist of more than six people so that everyone can interact and any wallflowers aren't left out of the conversation. The researcher will also be keeping a keen ear open in order to steer the conversation back on topic if things start to go a little off-piste. As with our other designs and methods, there is again a trade-off here. Sensitive topics or conversations about intimate personal experiences are unlikely to be appropriate in a focus-group setting, as people may actually be *less* likely to share what they think within a group.

Study Designs Providing Both Quantitative and Qualitative Data

In addition to the quantitative and qualitative study designs reviewed above, the social psychologists' repertoire consists of designs that straddle both and may provide us with both quantitative and qualitative data. We describe two types of such designs below: observational and archival studies.

Observational Studies

Let's imagine I (Paddy) am working with children. I have a one-way mirror in my lab and I want to do an observational study. In this study I'm looking at children's social interactions with strangers and I want to know how a child behaves when interacting with a stranger who has a new toy. So, what am I actually measuring? First, I'm going to need some coding schema – a kind of framework with which to carry out my observations. So, I'm noting down behaviours (e.g., approaches the stranger, plays passively, is aggressive) and vocalisations (e.g., is questioning, speaks quietly, cries). Using my coding schema, I might turn all of this qualitative observational data into something quantifiable (e.g., the number of times a child approaches the stranger; the number of crying episodes recorded). In such instances, we use descriptive and inferential statistics, as for the other quantitative research designs that we will discuss in Part 2.

But my measurements for these schemas are open to subjectivity. Do I code that little movement away from the stranger as shyness? When the child started to speak louder, was that extroversion? You can see how easily interpretation errors (experimenter bias) can slip into data like this unless we have a robust coding protocol in place. In good observational studies, the behavioural correlates of the concepts of interest will be theoretically and empirically grounded. In these cases, the links between the behaviour I'm observing and the coding protocol are clear and less susceptible to subjective interpretation. We can also overcome this by having two or more observers (who are possibly unaware of or 'blind' to the research hypotheses) who collate observations to check for inter-rater reliability or agreement.

In the last example, we had children and possibly their parents in the lab. They knew they were taking part in a study of some kind, and so were, literally, 'participants'. The researcher was behind the two-way mirror so as not to interfere with the behaviour observed (non-participatory observation). In some observation studies in the field, however, people do not know that they are research participants. So, you conduct your experiment like a 'fly on the wall'. This allows you to view social behaviour while keeping people in their natural environments, but also creates various ethical problems. What if they wouldn't have wanted to take part? Can they opt-out? Does it matter if they don't even know they are being observed? These difficult-to-answer ethical dilemmas are perhaps further amplified (and thus need to be managed with even more care) in participatory observational studies, where the researcher interacts with the people they are observing and thus potentially influences their behaviours. Luckily, psychologists have developed rigorous research protocols that help them to collect valid information while minimising risks for their participants.

Archival Studies

Another powerful way of studying human behaviour without observing behaviours as they occur is to perform archival analyses. This doesn't mean being holed up in a library poring over old books under one of those green desk lamps like in the movies (although it can be!). Rather, it can be the analysis of any archive of cultural artefacts, such as music lyrics, movie posters, advertising, popular television shows, novels, newspaper articles, census data, and more recently even memes and tweets (posted on Twitter, renamed X). All these human products can tell us a great deal about a society, our psychology, and attitudes. Archival data can provide us with both rich quantitative and qualitative data.

Performing an archival analysis into the cultural attitudes of a society, for example, through their changing media trends, is a fascinating insight into changing *Zeitgeists* and moral standards. The main challenge of this kind of research, however, is that it is retrospective. What is observed was not originally created for the purpose of being studied. This means that some important information might be missing for our understanding or that it might be difficult to extrapolate reliable and valid information as it would be for prospective research, which is research that is designed to look into the future for the purpose of testing specific research hypotheses and clearly defined concepts.

This is by no means an exhaustive list of the different types of quantitative or qualitative (or both) research methods used by social psychologists. But we think you will have a sufficiently good idea of the methodologies you will encounter in the rest of the book and throughout your degree.

1.5.2 Social Psychology's Early Positioning Around Methods

We'll now be moving away from research design slightly to briefly focus on the history of these methods in social psychology and how they have impacted on the direction of the discipline.

The Historical Schism Between Quantitative and Qualitative Research Designs

The distinction between quantitative and qualitative methods is not merely technical; it is not simply about using different tools and methods for research. As the history of social psychology in the 20th century illustrates, it reflects quite distinct ways of thinking of the social world and people's mental processes. When I (Stefania) was doing my bachelor degree at the University of Padova, Italy, in the late 1980s, I remember these alternative ways being regarded as 'separate' and incompatible. The tension of approaches was so palpable that it led to a real crisis of confidence in the discipline and a real rupture between scholars.

Drawing from the natural sciences, scholars in the quantitative camp have traditionally aspired to make psychology, and by implication, social psychology, a hard science. Quantitative social psychologists bolstered a positivistic and perhaps at times reductionist view of the social reality and the social brain. In this tradition, society, relationships, social groups, social structures, and the mental processes that reflect on them (e.g., thoughts, emotions, memories, attention, schemas, etc.) have a life of their own. They exist and are independent of the observer contemplating them and are often reduced to asocial, acontextual, individual-level intra-psychic processes in people's heads (Moscovici, 2001). From this standpoint, the (social) psychologist, as the scientist with the white lab coat, was charged with the important task of objectively quantifying mental constructs and processes, and with equal detachment dispassionately measuring people's impressions of the external reality. Fellow humans in this world were defined as 'subjects' to stress their passive and objectified nature, which was very apt to empirical investigation.

The qualitative tradition starts from a profoundly different position, a constructivist view of reality. Here, the world – as well as the brain – is inseparable from its observer and the very act of interpreting and making sense of reality (Gergen, 1973). From this stance, the social reality loses its essentialised nature and instead becomes the continuously changing product of the mind. The literal 'objects' of interest of quantitative social psychologists here become social constructions, or mental artefacts like arts, culture, and similar, amenable to ever-changing transformation and negotiations of meaning by a multiplicity of participants with their agency, power, and agendas. In this camp, the social psychologists immerse themselves in this place of meaning making and subjective and symbolic experiences that transcend crude quantification (Antaki et al., 2003; Edwards, 1996; Harré, 2005).

In the 1960s and 1970s, social psychology as a discipline experienced a deep crisis, which took the form of a schism between the 'quant' and 'qual' camps (e.g., Gergen, 1976; Rosnow, 1981). The two groups regarded the tension between their two views as too profound for peaceful co-existence. Hence, for several decades they went their separate ways. They established their own journals in which to report their own research, and they funded their own professional societies and associations, which screened for like-minded scholars and excluded those with 'suspicious' opinions. Within the Western world, the quant scholars were concentrated in North American and English-speaking countries, including the UK; the qual scholars became more prevalent in Australasia and continental Europe, such as in France.

These times have now long since passed, and scholars with different philosophical views and toolkits work together again. Quantitative and qualitative methods are no longer regarded by most scholars as incompatible or mutually exclusive. In fact, you can easily imagine a modern programme of research in which you perform non-participatory observation, followed by one-to-one interviews, and maybe even some quantitative tests and surveys. This eclectic approach is called 'mixed methods' because it literally mixes and matches different kinds of designs and methods into often a more powerful and inclusive method of inquiry. Pragmatically, these mixed methods are seen as a rich and flexible toolkit, there to be used to design your study.

GUEST PERSONAL JOURNEY

John Dixon

Source: © John Dixon

My career has been deeply marked by my experiences growing up in Northern Ireland and South Africa. Both societies have a troubling history of intergroup division, inequality, and violence, and both have witnessed profound changes over the 30-year span of my career. Understanding the lived experience and consequences of such changes has driven most of my work.

My early research focused on the dynamics of contact and desegregation during South Africa's transition from a society based on the principle of racial apartheid to a society based on the principle of racial justice and inclusion. This work examined, among other themes, white resistance to social change, the tenacity of segregation as a 'micro-ecological' system for organising everyday contact between groups, even in contexts where desegregation is institutionally supported, and the limits of the prejudice reduction model of change that dominates social psychology. My thinking at that time, and since, was enriched by collaborations with Kevin Durrheim (now Professor of Psychology at the University of Johannesburg) and Colin Tredoux (now Professor of Psychology at the University of Cape Town), with whom I spent many productive hours of dialogue and debate. This experience also taught me that supportive collaboration is key to overcoming the inevitable stresses, failures, and disappointments of an academic career.

More recently, I have discovered the joys of interdisciplinary collaboration, working with colleagues with backgrounds in GIS [geographic information system], anthropology, Irish

Studies, and geography. The Belfast Mobility Project (see https://belfastmobilityproject.org/) has sought to develop a new approach to understanding segregation, exploring how, when, and why everyday mobility practices may shape segregation in historically divided cities. This work has combined traditional psychological methods, such as questionnaire surveys, with data gathered using methods rooted in other disciplines, including walking interviews, GNSS [Global Navigation Satellite Systems] movement tracking, and GIS analytics. It brought me into exciting new conversations with colleagues who bring entirely different assumptions, perspectives, and skills, including Dr Jonny Huck. Some of these more recent, cutting-edge methodologies will be described in Part 3 of this chapter and there you will also learn how psychology met human geography in Dr Jonny Huck's career pathway.

A Frequent Neglect of Culture and Cultural Variations

We touched earlier on the challenges of generalising social psychological findings from non-representative samples of Caucasian, mostly female undergraduates from affluent back-grounds, the so-called WEIRD samples (samples from Western, Educated, Industrialised, Rich, Democratic societies; Henrich et al., 2010). The problem is twofold: Can these people be representative of many other populations and human groups? Can a focus on any human group lead to real understanding of the human mind? Let's delve into each of these issues in turn.

In the late 1990s, Smith and Bond looked at the most popular social psychology textbooks and found that only a small percentage of the studies that are cited in them have been conducted outside the United States (for a discussion, see Smith et al., 2013). These studies were conducted in less than a dozen of the 200 or more nations in the world. A similar conclusion was drawn by a survey of all the published papers between 1965 and 2000 in the history of the *Journal of Personality and Social Psychology*, the flagship journal of social and personality psychology (Quiñones-Vidal et al., 2004).

These disconcerting data suggest that most of what social psychologists currently know is based on a particular view of humankind, the so-called Western view (Markus & Kitayama, 1991). Also, it starts from the implicit premise that WEIRD samples can provide a window on the psychology of humans more generally. This premise is obviously easily questionable, but it perhaps hides a more fundamental one: Can we even think of a single psychology, or social psychology, for all humans?

Social psychologists appreciate that there is variability in the behaviour of people around the world (e.g., what people wear, eat, etc.). However, traditionally we have embraced what Berry (1969) calls an 'etic approach' to cultural differences. We often assume that there are *general* psychological processes; hence the variability in what people do is just a red herring, some noise to get rid of to discover the fundamental commonalities in the social psychological processes we share. For example, in a very influential article published by Henrich and colleagues in *Nature* in 2010, these scholars demonstrated that much research on human behaviour and psychology assumes that everyone shares fundamental cognitive and affective processes, and that findings from one population apply across the board. A growing body of evidence in social psychology and psychology in general, however, now indicates that this is not the case.

Henri Tajfel, a brilliant social psychologist who had a firm grasp of the limitations of the discipline of psychology, and was responsible for a theory (social identity theory) that we discuss many times in this book, much earlier on pointed out that 'the general case', that is the generalisation of results from specific individuals to humankind as a whole, is an impossible myth. He noted that human beings behave as they do because of the social expectations with which they enter social psychological studies, in other words their culture. From this revised standpoint, the observed regularities in any social psychological study (aka their findings) will inevitably result from the interaction between general processes and the social context in which these processes operate (check Tajfel, 1981, in Tajfel, 2010).

This means that research studies do not take place in a 'cultural vacuum' (Tajfel, 1981, in Tajfel, 2010). Governments, ideologies, the public, and therefore culture, all influence what we pay attention to in our research, and even what receives research funding and what does not. Researchers' cultural worldviews shape the way we construct our studies and our research plans. Similarly, participants interpret and respond to our research materials and equipment in terms of their culture. In a nutshell, culture always influences the instigation and interpretation of (social) psychological theory and research (Farr, 1996). Therefore, it is important that we keep this in mind when we read any of the research discussed in this textbook and elsewhere.

1.6 PART 2: ADVANCES

So, let's assume that you have nailed your design, and now you have an unintelligible spreadsheet of data in front of you. What now? Well, now it's time to decide which data analysis technique to use. In the following section we will learn more about the analytical tools and statistical tests you can use for analysing the various types of research designs we have discussed in the Foundations section.

1.6.1 Introduction to Simple Statistics

Statistics shouldn't be scary. I know, however, that they are some students' worst nightmare. I (Paddy) certainly wasn't aware of the statistics that would be involved when I started my psychology degree. And yet, here I am writing about it. I sometimes think that the *thought* of statistics is worse for some students than the reality. But when learning something, if you *think* it's going to be something you're not going to enjoy or get your head around, it can become a self-fulfilling prophecy.

Statistics are a tool, that's all. A tool to be used to answer a question. Understanding which tool to use in any given situation is the skill. It's not about memorising formulae or being a human calculator. It's about applying the right tool for the problem at hand to get an appropriate answer. When viewed like this, statistics can just be seen as learning how to use a nice shiny new toolkit instead of doing tricky maths problems.

So, what's the point? Why do we need statistics at all? In a nutshell, statistics can be used to make sense of very complicated things. In this section, I (Paddy) will outline content analysis, correlation, the difference between descriptive and inferential statistics, and use a classic social psychology study to explore t-tests and ANOVA.

1.6.2 Content Analysis

We saw in Part 1 many of the ways in which qualitative data can be gathered and how studies can be designed using qualitative methods. But what do we do in the analysis stage if we have no numerical data?

One common method is content analysis. This is, as you'd expect, an analysis of the content of your non-numerical data. This data can be nearly anything – books, media, interview transcripts. In Part 1 we talked about interviews and focus groups so we'll stick with those for now. Let's imagine we are studying sleep quality. We invite several people in for an interview to share their experiences of sleeping. Some are brilliant sleepers, but others couldn't fall asleep in a pillow factory. You're interested in the types of things associated with good and bad sleep. So, you might conduct a semi-structured interview, with some set questions and some open-ended ones that allow your participant to talk freely. 'How did you sleep last night? What do you feel like when you go to bed? What is your bedtime routine?', etc.

Then you have *a lot* of content, usually recorded. So, after transcribing the interviews, you must now read them and become familiar with them. This is the first step of content analysis. In reading the words of your participants, you notice some patterns. The word 'stress' comes up often, as does 'mobile phone'. Or that mentions not of a single word, but of a topic, like exercise, comes up. These are your coding units. They are driven by you, the researcher. Someone else may read the transcripts and come up with different coding units, but you are interested in sleep quality, and these are what you have noticed.

Now we can analyse the data applying these coding units. How often did your participants mention 'stress'? Or whether they read on their phone before bed? Did they report themselves to be good or bad sleepers? We can now start to build a picture of our data using the coding units. We might find that people who said they were poor sleepers reported reading on their phones before bed or were stressed in their day-to-day life. Likewise, we might notice that references to all kinds of exercise turn up in the transcripts of those who said they were good sleepers. So, by using some guided searching through all your data using coding units, you've found something out that may have otherwise been buried in the data.

KEY STUDY 1.3

Weitzman's Sex Roles in Children's Books

In the 1970s, just after the sexual revolution, the effect of sex stereotyping was examined in America. Primarily, this was how children learnt about sex-role distinctions. There were some scary results coming out in the 1960s that showed that by the time children were four years old, they were describing the main feminine role as the housekeeper, while the masculine role was wage earner (Hartley, 1960). It was found that girls started to fall behind boys in terms of academic achievement as they got older and took on the social roles they thought they were meant to ascribe to (Maccoby, 1966).

Lenore Weitzman and colleagues (1972) wanted to use a very specific type of media to explore these rigid sex-role portraits that children held: children's picture-books. More specifically, preschool picture-books. Even more specifically, the preschool picture-books that had won the awards for being the best preschool picture-books in America. They ought to be pretty good. Well....

They conducted a large-scale content analysis of several hundred books, but focused mainly on the 18 prize-winners. By looking through these books using coding units of sex-roles and sex representation, they were able to distil thousands of pages and pictures to reveal some quite shocking results at the time. In the prize-winning books, for example, they found that when looking for female representation in the pictures, there were hardly any. In fact, there were 261 pictures of males compared to only 23 pictures of females, a ratio of about 11:1. But as these are children's picture-books, sometimes the characters are anthropomorphic animals (think of the three bears in Goldilocks). When they looked at animal pictures with obvious sex identities, the ratio of male to female representation was 95:1! The very titles of the books themselves had a male to female ratio of 2:1.

Boys in the books were active, girls were passive. Boys went on adventures, girls either 'loved', 'watched' or 'helped'. Boys spent their time outdoors, girls indoors. Boys worked together to solve problems, girls spent time by themselves and were rarely seen with other girls. Boys walked dogs, girls got pulled off their feet by them. Boys led, girls followed. Boys rescued, girls were rescued.

It's a depressing picture. And one that doesn't get any better in the depictions of the adults. Fathers were never seen bothering themselves with anything as trivial as childcare or housework. No, no, it was a pipe and a paper in a nice armchair for them, while the mother was swept off her feet doing all the housework. Just to reinforce in children the stereotypes that the main characters show, you can aspire to grow up and be like the adults in the books too.

But 'this is the 1970s, it gets better', I hear you say. Well, no, not really. In the 100 best-selling children's books of 2018 in the UK, *The Guardian* newspaper found that male leads still outnumbered females 3:2, female characters were far less likely to speak, and in one in every five books there were no female characters at all! Even more recently (this will date this textbook), a very similar pattern of sex inequality in children's books was found in Australia and America (Adam & Harper, 2023).

It doesn't look like a problem that's going away anytime soon unfortunately, but at least by using content analysis in a creative way to flag a real societal issue, we are able to turn thousands of pages into something understandable, even if the picture it paints is an ugly one.

1.6.3 Qualitative Approaches to Data Analysis

While content analysis aims to provide a quantifiable dimension to non-numeric data, social scientists also use other qualitative approaches to summarise the data obtained from qualitative research designs such as interviews and focus groups. One such approach is thematic analysis, which involves iterative reading through a set of qualitative data (e.g., transcribed interviews) and looking for patterns in the meaning of the data to identify themes. The researcher then uses the identified themes to make further interpretations of the data.

Another approach for analysing qualitative data is discourse analysis, where language obtained from conversations, interviews, and text (such as in magazines) is analysed. Proponents of discourse analysis argue that language constructs people's social and psychological lives, thereby making language-based data particularly important in the quest of understanding social psychological processes. The text used for discourse analysis is analysed and interpreted in the context where it was produced, enabling the researcher to draw conclusions regarding the communicator's experiences, feelings, and thoughts. A subset of discourse analysis is conversational analysis (CA) where conversational interactions are examined and classified. CA doesn't solely focus on the content of people's interactions, but also analyses how people conduct the conversation (turn-taking, pausing, interruptions, and so on) and uses verbal and non-verbal elements for analysis. Naturally occurring conversations such as between medical professionals and patients are commonly analysed using CA.

1.6.4 Correlations to Detect Relationships Between Variables

In correlation studies we want to know whether two variables are related in some way. What we want to find out is whether there is a relationship between one set of scores and another set. Crucially, most of the time we are *not* going to find out if one set of scores *causes* the changes in another set, only that there is a relationship. Correlation (usually) does not equal causation, unless the data is generated as part of an experiment.

In talking about correlations, here we will focus on linear correlations. In other words, relationships that can be described by a straight line. All a linear correlation is trying to do is to draw a straight line through your data in such a way that it minimises the distance between each data point and the line. This is called the 'line of best fit'. Let's pretend we have a theory that Maths ability and Music ability are related in some way (this is in no way inspired by the fact that my (Paddy) three A-levels were Maths, Music, and Media Studies ...). We have some data and we want to see whether there is a correlation between scores in Maths and Music exams. We can plot the data in a scatter graph, as shown in Figure 1.2, where each dot shows the scores of a particular participant:

Maths Score vs Music Score

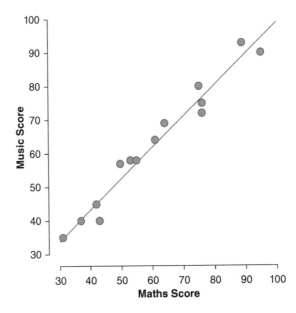

Figure 1.2 An example of a correlation line of best fit

We can see from this data that the line of best fit looks a very good fit indeed. There is very little deviation from the line and we can see that as Maths scores increase, so do Music scores. The statistics we can do on this depend on the types of data, but usually you will do Pearson's *r* test. This gives you a couple of numbers. An *r*-value and a *p*-value (we will learn more about *p*-values later in this chapter). The *r*-value will be a number between −1 and 1. The data in Figure 1.2 gives a value of 0.97, which is a strong positive correlation (as one variable goes up, the other goes up as well), 0 would be no correlation, and −1 would be a perfect negative correlation (as one value goes up, the other goes down).

Correlations can be a really useful way of associating variables with each other and allow a researcher to interpret the results with a little freedom. For instance, with the above example, I might make some link between music and maths from a logical thinking point of view. Composing and musical theory is a system much like mathematics, in which there are rules that can be followed to arrive at a certain outcome. Therefore, there is some connection between how the brain processes the information in these two subjects, resulting in this positive correlation. Or I could say, well, if you're better at Maths, you're more likely to be a good student and therefore will be good at any other subject at school. The point is that because correlation does not equal causation (again, unless the data was generated by an experiment!), you can be a little inventive in your interpretation. This is fine when you have a nearly perfect correlation like we have here, but this type of correlation is actually quite rare. Consider this example: We want to re-run our school subjects experiment but this time choose Maths and History, and we get the graph shown in Figure 1.3.

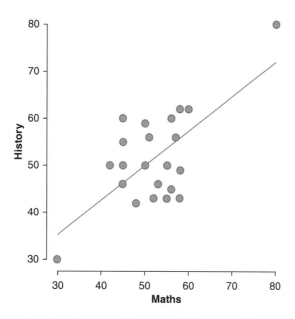

Figure 1.3 An example of a strong positive correlation caused by two outliers

Now Pearson's *r* gives us a significant correlation with an *r* of 0.65, which is still a really strong positive correlation. So, we leave it there and write a report about how maths and history ability are related and speculate on why that may be.

But look at that graph. Is there *really* a strong positive correlation there? We appear to have two fairly substantial outliers: one student who is really good at both subjects, and one student who is quite poor at both subjects. There does not appear to be much going on in the middle. In fact, if you removed those two outliers, you could nearly draw a line any way you wanted through that middle cloud of data and it would look right.

This is a real problem with interpreting correlation, and something to keep a very keen eye on. Correlation lines, just like means, are very sensitive to outliers. A cloud of data like that acts like the centre of a compass, the needle not knowing what to point at. Throw in two outliers in a line and the needle will swing round and be drawn to them, creating this false impression of a strong correlation. Let's remove those two students and see what happens (Figure 1.4).

Removing our two outliers, we can see that all we are left with is our cloud of data in the middle, and the line of best fit is nearly horizontal. The *r* is now 0.108 and we have a non-significant *p*-value. There is nothing going on here, but the presence of just two students in a group of 22 was enough to create the impression that there was. Let's see if we can create the opposite effect with just one outlying student. Maybe someone who was good at Maths but rubbish at History (me, for instance ...) (Figure 1.5).

Now look what's happened. See how the needle has been swung downwards by just one pesky outlier. This is now a significant negative correlation with an *r* of –0.44, so a fairly strong effect. So now I could write an interpretation that says that maths has objective truth but history can be very subjective. Objective thinkers therefore wouldn't be expected to be good at subjective subjects, therefore this explains our strong negative correlation. And you might read that in an abstract and take it at face value, use it as a basis of your research, and now a whole new theory

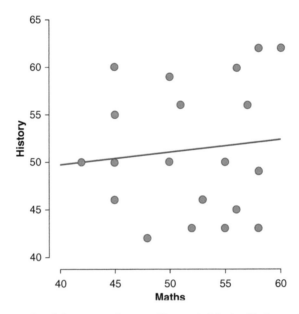

Figure 1.4 An example of the same data as Figure 1.3 but with the outliers removed. There is now no correlation

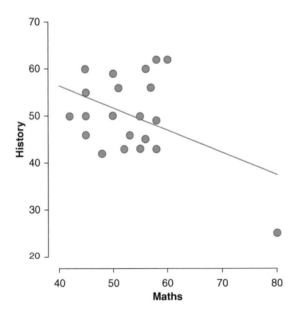

Figure 1.5 An example of a negative correlation caused by a single outlier

has been born from one student being really good at maths and really bad at history! So, in your research cycle, or theory to hypothesis to research methods to experiments, one would hope that this would 'come out in the wash'. In other words, by performing further research based on this negative correlation theory, you would be able to tell that something was wrong.

1.6.5 Descriptive versus Inferential Statistics

In order to illustrate some of the key statistical tests and terms described in this section, we will use a key classic social psychology study. In 1951, Solomon Asch published 'Effects of group pressure upon the modification and distortion of judgments' as part of a book titled *Groups, leadership and men: research in human relations*. The study is more commonly known as the 'Conformity Experiment'. I'll outline it briefly here.

Asch asked participants to come into the lab to take part in a 'vision test'. The participant sat at the end of a long table with seven other participants. They were then presented with two pictures. One of a target line (a line of a certain length), and another picture of three comparison lines. The task was simply to say out loud which of the three comparison lines matched the target line. The answer was always pretty obvious (Figure 1.6).

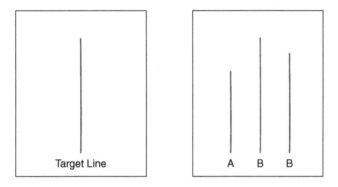

Figure 1.6 Example of the stimuli used in Asch's conformity experiments
Source: based on Asch (1956).

However, as with all great social psychology experiments, there was a twist. The other seven participants weren't actually real participants at all (dun dun DUUUUN), they were stooges working with Asch. The study had a total of 18 trials, but in 12 of them the confederates would all give the wrong answer (called the 'critical trials'). The real purpose of the experiment was to see whether the real participant, who was seated at the end of the table (and thus went last every time), would conform to this majority (and objectively wrong) view, or whether they would give the right answer. There was also a control condition in which instead of saying your answer out loud, you would simply write it down. This took any need to 'fit in' out of the equation.

They found that 33% of all answers in the critical trials were in line with the distorted estimate of the confederates. They also found that over the 12 critical trials, 75% of the participants conformed at least once, with 25% never conforming. They also performed some follow-up questionnaires to find out why they had conformed. Most said that they didn't really believe that their answer was correct, but they didn't want to be ridiculed and wanted to fit in with the majority for social reasons (distortion of judgement and action), while others reported that they truly believed that the group was better informed than them and that they themselves must have been mistaken (distortion of perception).

So, let's look at this design. Our dependent variable is the number of times the participant went with the erroneous group answer in the critical trials. Our independent variable is whether you had to state your answer out loud or not. Table 1.1 demonstrates the way the data is presented in the original paper.

Table 1.1 Data from Asch's (1956) conformity experiment

Number of critical errors	Critical group ($N = 50$)	Control group ($N = 37$)
0	13	35
1	4	1
2	5	1
3	6	0
4	3	0
5	4	0
6	1	0
7	2	0
8	5	0
9	3	0
10	3	0
11	1	0
12	0	0

Source: based on Asch (1956)

Now personally I found this a little hard to get my head around originally, but what this is showing is the total number of people who fit into each category: those who made 0 errors (13 in the critical groups and 35 in the control group), those who went with the group once, twice, etc., all the way down to those who followed the group the full 12 times.

This is where statistics come in. There are primarily two things we can do: descriptive statistics and inferential statistics. Using descriptive statistics, we can summarise these raw scores in different ways; we are 'describing' the data in some way. In contrast, using inferential statistics we are going to 'infer' something from the data. This is where we can find support (or not) for our hypothesis.

Let's talk briefly about descriptive statistics. There are lots of ways to summarise data, but there are some 'big hitters' in terms of describing the 'central tendency' and 'spread' of the data. Measuring the central tendency just means describing some aspect of the middle of the data. The most common are the **mean** (the average: all numbers added up and divided by the number of data points), the **median** (the middle number when all data points are put in order from smallest to largest), and the **standard deviation** (a measure of how far, on average, each data point you have lies from the mean) (Table 1.2).

Table 1.2   Descriptive statistics for Asch's (1956) conformity data

	Descriptive statistics	
	Critical group	Control group
Mean	3.84	0.08
Median	3	0
Std. Deviation	3.52	0.36

Eyeballing this data, we can see that the critical group has a higher mean score (3.84) than the control group (0.08). This means that, on average, people in the critical group (saying their answer out loud) made an error 3.84 times, compared to nearly no errors (0.08) in the control group (writing down their answer). So, can we just finish here and say that we've found what we were looking for? Predictably, no.

So, let's backtrack a little. We have Asch's **hypothesis**: 'People in the Critical Group will make more errors than the Control Group'. We have our **independent variable**, which is the thing we manipulate or change: in this case whether the participant answers out loud or not. And we have our **dependent variable**, which is the thing we are measuring: whether they make an error in the line they choose. So, using descriptive statistics, we can describe the numbers we got, say which group made more errors, etc., but we can only address our hypothesis using inferential statistics.

Now, by creating a hypothesis, we have also created what is called the 'null hypothesis'. The null hypothesis always states that there is no difference between your groups, or relationship between your variables. Our hypothesis is that the group participants are assigned to will make a difference to the scores, the null hypothesis is that the group participants are assigned to will make no difference. Your inferential statistics will provide you with the tools to either accept or reject the null hypothesis. Remember that you can never 'prove' your hypothesis, only find support for it (us scientists are a cautious bunch who shy away from talking in absolute certainties, for reasons that will become apparent below).

What your inferential statistics will likely give you is a ***p*-value**. Please do not glaze over and skip to the next page, this is important! The *p*-value is a probability value between 0 and 1. So $0 = 0\%$ probability and $1 = 100\%$ probability. And what it is measuring is the probability of you getting the results you got, *if* the null hypothesis is true. So, *if* there actually is no difference between your groups, what are the chances that you will get the data that you did? The lower this number, the more confident you can be in rejecting the null hypothesis and the more support you have for your hypothesis.

We have an arbitrary cut-off in psychology of 0.05. If the *p*-value is less than 0.05, it means that there is less than a 5% chance we got our data *if* the null hypothesis is true; i.e., a small chance of thinking we have an effect when actually there is nothing going on. Therefore, if we get a *p*-value of less than 0.05, we say that we have enough evidence to reject the null hypothesis and support our hypothesis. We call this a 'statistically significant' result, or a 'statistically significant' difference.

One thing I see a lot that I'd like to flag here is an issue of semantics around the term 'statistically significant difference'. In my experience, students tend (understandably so) to equate 'significance' in the statistical sense with the finding being of some value. Or somehow intrinsically good. It isn't. One can have a very significant (or important) non-significant result, for example. It's all about how well justified your question is, and how well put together your methods are. If those two things are in place, then you can have confidence in the answer you get. And if that answer is a non-significant difference between two groups, for example, then that is still the answer to your question. And therefore it is still of some importance. The pitfall some students fall into is to think that if they get non-significant results they have done something wrong. Or that it's just a really bad thing. It isn't. It's just the answer to your question.

So back to the Asch study. We can see using descriptive statistics that it looks like groups make a difference to scores, but now we want to do some inferential statistics to find out. We want to know whether we have a statistically significant difference between our two groups and whether there is sufficient evidence to allow us to reject the null hypothesis. We will pick this up again in the 't-tests' section below.

1.6.6 T-tests

T-tests are the building blocks of lots of statistics. They are the basis of most of my own (Paddy's) research and, from a student point of view, once you can get to grips with what a t-test is doing and what it can and cannot do, the experimental world is your oyster. If you want to compare two groups, or compare two different conditions, or compare one group against a known baseline number, then different variations of the t-test are what you will need.

Going back to our Asch data in Table 1.1, we had two groups: Critical Group and No Group. We won't go into details of the formula here, but a t-test is a test that uses the means, standard deviations, and number of data points in both your groups to determine whether there is a large overlap between groups, which then gives us a *p*-value. Remember that your *p*-value is the chance of you getting this data if your null hypothesis is true (that there is no difference between your groups), so a number under 0.05 is what you're looking for to say you have support for your hypothesis.

An independent t-test here shows a significant difference between the critical group and the control group ($p < 0.001$). More interesting perhaps is the data in the critical group. There looks to be a pretty even spread of data across the error cases (i.e., of the 75% of participants who made at least one error, eyeballing the data, there looks to be no real difference between whether they did this once or 11 times). There's another thing that one must remember with this data as well, that it is error data. So, the four participants who made one error and 'conformed' with the group means that they didn't conform 11 times out of 12. Is this really informative? Did they conform or did they just get the answer wrong? One might split this data further and only be interested in those participants who went with the majority most of the time. So, if we take those who made errors six times or more, what do we find?

Running the statistics on that, we find that there are only 15 participants who went with the majority most of the time, and made on average 8.53 errors. The other group, however, who went with the majority fewer than half of the time (or never), made on average 1.8 errors. Is it possible that the low error individuals were guessing/didn't know a couple of the answers? Maybe. Although 75% of participants made at least one error, only 30% made errors a majority of the time. Furthermore, using many more participants, subsequent studies were unable to replicate this effect (Perrin & Spencer, 1980). So, statistics aside, the effect itself could be caused by its own time and place: America in the 1950s. In a time of McCarthyism and communist witch-hunts, the idea of sticking out and looking different was much more unpalatable than it is today. Personally, I do not think this is the explanation, and Asch's conclusions are correct, but I think this really illustrates the different pictures you can paint (if you want) by the use of statistics.

And that's it! Given all that information we can answer our question and reject the null hypothesis! We can therefore accept our alternative hypothesis that people in the critical group made significantly more errors than those in the control group. However, what if we tweaked our design? We have done a between-subjects design here (i.e., there were different people in each group). Is this the best design Asch could have employed? What if the people in the critical group just so happened to be really bad at judging the length of lines? It may seem a slightly facetious argument, but it's a really important consideration to make when designing a study with groups. Could the case be made that a design in which a single participant was in *both* groups (e.g., sometimes wrote their answers down and sometimes said them out loud) might have been a better design? That way it wouldn't matter if they were good or bad at judging line length. We will imagine this is the case when we expand this experiment now using ANOVA.

1.6.7 ANOVA

In our t-test section we did a t-test when we had two groups. We used Asch's data. Well, Analysis of Variance (ANOVA) is used when we have more than two groups. So, let's start there and gradually make a more complex design.

One-way ANOVA

Let's assume that we performed a within-subjects version of the Asch experiment, i.e., the same people are in both the critical group/condition (where everyone says their line choice out loud) and control group/condition (where they write it down). What would happen, however, if we had a third condition? Let's say we added a condition in which the participant answers out loud, but only to the experimenter. This way we can test whether it's the physical presence of the other people or the fact that you have to say it out loud that affects line choice. For ease, we'll also say that we have 50 people doing the experiment, and they each do all three conditions. The data might look like that in Table 1.3.

Table 1.3   A reimagined version of Asch's (1956) conformity study with a third experimental condition

Number of critical errors	Critical group	Control group	Experimenter group
0	13	45	25
1	4	3	5
2	5	1	5
3	6	1	2
4	3	0	2
5	4	0	3
6	1	0	3
7	2	0	2
8	5	0	1
9	3	0	1
10	3	0	1
11	1	0	0
12	0	0	0

Source: based on Asch (1956)

So now we can't perform a t-test because we have more than two groups. We can, however, conduct a one-way ANOVA. It is called a 'one-way' because in this experimental design we have one factor (type of group). This factor has three levels (Critical, Control and Experimenter), but that doesn't really matter here. I've illustrated the results in the graph in Figure 1.7 by plotting the means.

Now, as we know, this pattern or the results could still just be noise, which is why we're doing our inferential test. What this will do is analyse all conditions and give us a 'main effect'. If we have a significant main effect, it means that there is a difference between our conditions *somewhere*. It doesn't, however, tell us where that difference is. So, let's run an ANOVA first and see if there is a main effect. Again, I won't go into the statistics, but this does give a significant main effect of group type ($p < 0.001$), meaning that these conditions are different.

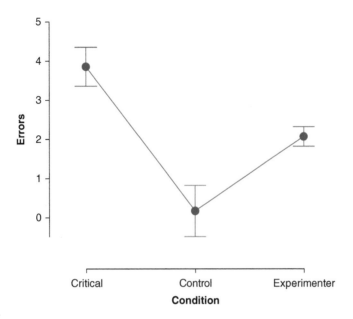

Figure 1.7 Mean errors of the three groups in our reimagined Asch experiment

So now we have to work out where that difference is. To do this we will use 'post-hoc' t-tests. Post-hoc simply means 'after the event'. So, we will do t-tests comparing all possible combinations between our conditions: Critical vs Control, Control vs Experimenter, and Critical vs Experimenter. Doing this, we find that there are significant differences between all groups.

So, we can conclude here that there is a significant main effect of type of group, and this is driven by people's scores when speaking their line judgements out loud containing significantly more errors than both when just telling the experimenter and when writing the judgements down. We've come to this conclusion by going back to the descriptive numbers, in order to interpret the direction of the significant post-hoc t-tests. The test just tells us there is a significant difference. We then need to go and see which number is bigger than which other number.

KEY STUDY 1.4

The Dead Salmon fMRI Study

Before we make this experiment a little more complicated, it's worth touching on an interesting problem that ANOVA throws up. Here we only had three groups. But one could imagine an experiment where we have several groups, maybe even hundreds of groups.

(Continued)

In this situation, something very interesting happens. If you recall from earlier, the *p*-value is the chance that you get your data if you assume that the null hypothesis is true. So, if the *p*-value is 0.05 and you say this is significant, there is a 5% chance that you would get this data if the null was true. But you've said that it's significant, rejected the null hypothesis and accepted your alternative hypothesis. Now if you did this 100 times, each time you would think you were right. But the more you do that, the greater the chance that you will reject the null hypothesis when actually it *is* true. If there's a 5% chance that you'd get that data when the null hypothesis was true, and you did it 100 times claiming significance every time, five times out of the 100 you would be claiming significance when the null *was* true. You might want to read that section again just to make sure it makes sense. I usually get a few blank faces in lectures when I bust that one out for the first time. This is the problem of multiple comparisons. Here in the ANOVA post-hoc tests we are doing multiple comparisons by doing several t-tests in a row. What we should do (and what most statistical software does for you) is correct for multiple comparisons. This means applying a formula to the *p*-value to change it, making it harder for us to accidentally reject the null hypothesis when it is true.

One very famous example of multiple comparisons in action (or a real lack thereof!) is the case of the dead salmon. There was an academic poster presented in 2009 to the Human Brain Mapping conference by Bennet and colleagues showing fMRI activity in the brain of a dead salmon when shown social interactions. Now this was all very tongue in cheek (in gills?) as what they were really illustrating is what happens when you don't properly correct for multiple comparisons. The way fMRI works is by dividing your brain into tens of thousands of tiny cubes called voxels (think pixels, but in 3D). Then it takes the first one and compares it to *all* of the others. Then the next one, and the one after that, etc. This is an absolutely enormous number of comparisons, and if we don't correct for that, as we can see above with just three comparisons, we run the risk of false positives. So, by scanning a dead salmon's brain, not applying multiple corrections and showing 'activity', Bennet et al. deliberately demonstrated some very bad scientific practices. And probably stank out a very expensive fMRI machine …

Two-way ANOVA

Let's make things a little more complicated then. We previously had one factor (type of group). But what if we also wanted to look at something else? We currently have a within-subjects ANOVA where every participant takes part in every condition. But now we also want to know whether there are variations in error (dependent variable) dependent on age (old vs young). So now we have added a between-subjects factor (old vs young participants).

This is now a two-way 3 × 2 ANOVA. It is two-way because we have two factors (Type of Group and Age), and 3 × 2 because we have three levels of the first factor (Critical, Control and Experimenter) and two levels of the second factor (Old Age and Young Age). It is also now a Mixed ANOVA, as we have a within-subjects element and a between-subjects element. Running an ANOVA on this data will give us a lot more output than a one-way ANOVA, and can be daunting when you do it yourself, but sticking to a logical (or methodical) way of going through the results will help to get your head around it.

We start off just like we did before, with our main effects. When we have a two-way ANOVA like this, the main effects of each factor do *not* take into account the other factor. So the ANOVA will generate a main effect for Group Type, just like before. This is significant, so we know that, ignoring people's ages, there is a difference in error count across group type. We run our post-hoc tests to see where the significant difference arises and get a similar result to the last time.

We then look at the results for our other main effect, in this case the main effect of age. We find a significant main effect of age ($p < 0.001$), which means that ignoring what condition the participants were doing, there is a difference between the number of errors made by older versus younger participants. Here, we don't need to do any post-hoc tests, however, as we only have two groups, so we can just look at the means and see which is larger! In this case, older participants make significantly fewer errors compared with younger participants. However, in a two-way ANOVA, unlike a one-way ANOVA, we must check whether the two factors interact. An interaction tells us when or for whom an effect occurs or is more pronounced. So, we must be cautious when interpreting main effects because the interaction also has something to say about the differences between our groups.

So what exactly does the interaction tell us that we don't get by looking at the main effects only? That is a little more complicated to explain. You will find a significant interaction

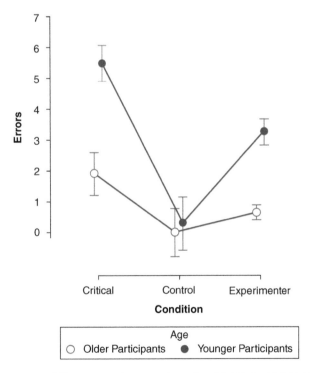

Figure 1.8 Mean errors of the groups in our reimagined Asch experiment, split by age

if the *difference* between levels *is different* between factors. I told you it was a little more complicated ... . Let me break that down a little because interactions are among those things that as soon as your brain gets them, you can nearly hear it clicking. Let's take the difference between old and young age. We will have an interaction if the difference between old and young age is different under the Critical, Control, and/or Experimenter conditions. This is much easier to see than it is to imagine. So let's see our data (Figure 1.8).

Looking just at the critical condition, it appears that younger people are making many more errors than older people. When participants write down their line judgements, it looks like there's no difference. And when they tell the experimenter, again it looks like younger participants are making more errors than older participants. So here the difference in scores between the levels of one factor (age) appears to be different at different levels of the other factor (group type). We can see that it looks like this: big difference for the Critical, no difference for the Control, big difference for the Experimenter condition. To formally check this, we can do t-tests to check for significant differences. We can do a t-test just looking at the differences between old and young at the Critical, then at the Control, and finally at the Experimenter condition. These are called simple main effects. If we do that, we do indeed find there is a significant difference ($p < 0.001$) between old and young under the Critical and Experimenter conditions, but no significant difference between old and young in the Control condition.

Interactions can be tricky because they can be 'broken down' in different ways. In our example, you could also check for the effects of Type of Group separately for young and old participants. This would likely reveal that among young participants the effect of group type is more pronounced than for older participants. After you've reported your main effects, any post-hoc tests you have to do to understand the main effects, and any interactions and simple effects arising from any significant interactions, you're done!

You can even go deeper than this as well, with three-way, even four-way ANOVAs, but trying to work out the interactions between those is a nightmare, and frankly, you probably should have designed your study a little better if you need to do a four-way ANOVA! For the most part, a two-way ANOVA will be as complicated as it gets, and remember you only have to delve deeper into your post-hoc and simple main effects if you actually find significant results in the first place. Don't have a significant interaction? Then there is no need to look at simple main effects as the data is telling you that the effects of your experimental factor don't differ depending on the level of the other factor (and vice versa).

I (Paddy) use ANOVAs a lot, and I like them a lot. They allow you to add in a grouping factor (like age in this case) that really adds depth to your results. In my work, my grouping factor would usually be age (young children, adolescents, adults, for example), and then a within-subjects variable such as type of emotion or something. Like this imagined extension of Asch's work, this allows me to see any age differences in the different conditions that everyone took part in. From a fairly simple experimental design, by analysing it in this way, it allows you to paint a rich picture with the data and, as we'll see later in this book, has been used by some of the most famous experiments in social psychology. Experimental designs that allow for the testing of potential interactions between multiple factors are of special interest to social psychologists, since they allow us to examine whether an effect occurs in certain contexts more than others and whether an effect works differently among different groups of people.

1.7 PART 3: APPLICATIONS

As you will have gathered from the previous sections in this chapter, social psychologists have historically been at the forefront of methodological innovation in the field of psychology. In Part 3, we will take a forward-looking tour of some of the state-of-the-art novel methodologies social psychologists have started engaging with and which are expected to shape our future research landscape. Then, we will discuss an important recent innovation in our research practices that emerged in part as a response to a 'new' crisis of confidence we touched upon in Part 1, namely that of keeping our research practices open and transparent for everyone, a movement known as the Open Science movement.

1.7.1 Novel Advances in Research Methods

Experience Sampling Methods

Experience sampling methods (ESM) is an umbrella term reserved for methods using repeated (longitudinal) collection of real-time data of people's behaviours and experiences within their natural environments. ESM is also sometimes referred to as ecological momentary assessment (EMA), ambulatory assessment, intensive longitudinal assessment, and real-time data capture. Sometimes you may hear these types of studies referred to as diary studies.

As you will have gathered in the previous parts of this chapter, much of psychology, including social psychology, has historically relied on global, summary, or retrospective self-report measures of behavioural and psychological states (e.g., how much you like this person, what your mood is like at present, how much experience you have with environmental action, and so on). However, such global and retrospective measures are limited. ESM/EMA methods are better suited to capture the dynamic changes in behaviour over time and across situations, allowing us to understand how behaviour varies and is governed by context and other people in our environments (variables that are especially important for understanding social psychological phenomena).

ESM originated in clinical psychology where clinicians and practitioners found it helpful to track patients' behavioural responses and psychological states as they are happening (see Shiffman et al., 2008). Among the first investigations to use these methods were studies of smokers undergoing treatment for smoking cessation, enabling clinicians to examine craving and relapse in real time as well as delineate the type of contextual and situational cues within participants' environments that were either supportive or detrimental to their quitting attempts. Some of these early studies were able to show that craving and relapse occurred more often in social situations, for example when participants were together with their friends or in a pub/club environment which they had previously associated with smoking behaviours (Shiffman et al., 2015).

Some of the original studies using these methods relied on palm-top computers provided by the researchers and were quite expensive and time-consuming, and required high levels of technological know-how. However, with recent innovations in mobile and wearable technology, it has become possible to provide more fine-grained and varied data as well as simplify the data collection process, while making it more affordable for a wider array of researchers. However, the use of ESM/EMA methods with their large data outputs across multiple points per day and across multiple days have also necessitated social psychologists to engage with complex statistical techniques, such as multi-level modelling and growth-curve analysis (that are beyond the scope of this textbook), which might limit the widespread uptake of these methods.

With the advent of new technologies, social psychologists have started using ESM to examine topics as diverse as how desire and temptation fluctuate over time (Hofmann et al., 2012); how moral acts unfold across our daily lives (Hofmann et al., 2014); what emotions we experience across time and situations and how we regulate said emotions (Blanke et al., 2020); what the time-course is that can help us to explain sexual objectification in real-life contexts (Holland et al., 2017); and many other phenomena. Many of these insights have then been used to develop and evaluate the effectiveness of behaviour change interventions and policies (see also Chapter 11) in varied domains, including weight management, sustainability, organisational human resource policies, diversity initiatives, and many others.

GUEST PERSONAL JOURNEY

Elise Kalokerinos

Source: © Elise Kalokerinos

I finished my undergraduate degree in psychology with no particular idea of what to do with myself. I'd always loved learning about research, and after going to an event on doing a PhD, I decided it was for me with no real idea of what I was in for. In retrospect, I'm very lucky it all worked out!

For my PhD, which I started in 2010, I was drawn to social psychology. I loved all the fun experimental paradigms and wacky research findings I'd learned about in some of my undergraduate subjects. But, as I began my PhD, the replication crisis kicked into gear, and we learned that many of those cute findings were not methodologically sound. I became disillusioned with the tricky lab work I had initially loved, and increasingly interested in taking my research outside the lab. In my PhD, I was investigating emotions using experimental stimuli, and I was excited to get closer to emotions outside the lab, where we could track personally meaningful consequences. I was also very keen to go abroad: I am Australian, and had completed all my training in Australia, which was starting to feel very far away from the rest of the world.

After my PhD, I moved halfway across the world to start a postdoctoral position at KU Leuven in Belgium, based on a single Skype interview: in retrospect, I'm very lucky it all worked out! In this position, I was working with large experience sampling data sets of emotions in daily life. I was also a social psychologist in a department composed of mostly quantitative psychologists. I found this a bit overwhelming at first, and I felt very out of place going to talks about statistical methods! I had never thought of myself as a particularly strong statistician, and suddenly, I was learning to work with complex multilevel data sets. It took me a while to find my feet, but I fell in love with experience sampling. I loved the rich data sets, and the insight into what people were doing in their everyday lives.

After I finished my postdoc, Australia was calling: I wanted to find something more permanent closer to my family. I took a position at the University of Newcastle, followed by my current job at the University of Melbourne. As part of my current job, I've spent a lot of time thinking about how best to teach the complex set of skills I've learned to students. This is important to me, because I think experience sampling data are valuable, but collecting and analysing these data sets often require skills that undergraduates aren't exposed to, and sometimes find a bit scary and overwhelming. Given my career, I feel like it's particularly important to help psychology students realise that complex stats are achievable.

Virtual Reality (VR)

With recent strides in technology, social psychologists have also started using virtual reality (VR) to study social interactions and other social psychological phenomena. Virtual reality or immersive virtual environments provide realistic and compelling experimental settings while allowing researchers to maintain a high degree of experimental control. VR is a simulated three-dimensional environment where users can explore and interact with a virtual surrounding in a way that approximates reality. VR technology relies to a different extent on incorporating perceivers' senses for immersing participants into the virtual world. There are three types of VR that are commonly used by psychologists for their studies. The first type is non-immersive, where participants interact with the virtual world on a computer screen (e.g., playing a video game). The second type is semi-immersive, where participants interact with the virtual world via a computer screen or some form of headset/glasses, thus focusing primarily on the visual 3D aspect and not incorporating physical movement in the way that full immersion does (e.g., the flight simulator). The final type is fully immersive, where sight, hearing, touch, smell, and proprioception are incorporated. Participants wear special equipment, such as helmets, goggles, and gloves, and are able to fully interact with and move within the virtual world. Immersive VR worlds sometimes also incorporate equipment as treadmills or stationary bicycles to provide users with the experience of moving through the 3D space (such as in Figure 1.9).

These methods are particularly suited for studies that cannot be done easily in the real world due to, for example, ethical constraints, such as replicating Stanley Milgram's seminal

Figure 1.9 A person in a wheelchair being motion-tracked in an immersive virtual environment via VR headsets simulating boat paddling

Source: RDNE Stock Project on Pexels.com

studies involving the purported administration of an electric shock to another participant (in this case, a confederate of the researcher) (for a discussion of Milgram's studies, see Chapter 10). Since it would be unethical to expose participants to the stress of believing they are administering real electric shocks to actual human beings, Mel Slater and colleagues pioneered early VR studies replicating the effects of Milgram's experiments with virtual avatar confederates (see Slater et al., 2006). Other VR studies have circumvented ethical constraints by placing participants in an immersive virtual environment where a violent altercation between two football avatar fans ensued (Slater et al., 2013). In such studies, researchers were able to measure whether participants are more likely to intervene when the VR avatars were from the ingroup (a person with whom the participant shares the same group membership, e.g., both fans of Arsenal FC) versus the outgroup (a person with whom the participant does not share the same group membership). As it happens, participants were more likely to help when the avatar victim of the altercation was an ingroup member.

KEY STUDY 1.5

The Impact of Non-Verbal Behaviour and Power Cues in Immersive Virtual Reality

Virtual reality methods have also allowed researchers to examine topics such as non-verbal behaviour which would ordinarily present challenges in the real world. For example, in a series of studies by Mario Weick and colleagues (2017), researchers were able to examine the impact of power and threatening eye-gaze on actual approach and avoidance behaviours between participants and a VR avatar. Power is an important construct that guides people's everyday behaviours when they interact with others, and when they carry out their day-to-day tasks. Power is defined as a person's actual or perceived control over others. While power has usually been manipulated in the laboratory by asking participants to recall a time in their lives when they felt powerful, within the virtual world it is possible to use other ways to manipulate power, as demonstrated by Study 2 reported by Weick and colleagues (2017). In this study, the researchers were able to manipulate participants' height in the virtual world (height is a known proxy of power). Furthermore, the use of virtual worlds enabled researchers to measure threatening eye-gaze behaviour and how this affected the approach/avoidance of the human participants towards the avatar. This novel approach to studying power relations and non-verbal behaviour showed that sustained, direct gaze led to spontaneous avoidance in low-power perceivers and spontaneous approach in high-power perceivers. Without novel techniques in VR methods, the researchers would not have been able to accurately measure approach/avoidance behaviours in immersive virtual worlds approximating our real world.

Other Methodological Innovations

In addition to ESM/EMA and VR studies, social psychologists have more recently also engaged with already existing **Big Data**. For instance, analysis of posts on X (formerly Twitter) has revealed that the language used by Democrats (more swearing and anxiety-related words) and Conservatives (fewer words related to feelings) on this social media platform is associated with enduring differences in psychological states between these two political groups (Sylwester & Purver, 2015). Other studies have begun answering questions of interest to social

> **Key concept – Big Data:** Large, hard-to-manage volumes of data that cannot be processed or analysed using traditional data-processing software or statistical techniques. Big Data is wide-ranging and encompasses messages, updates, images, and videos posted on social networks; patient records; readings from sensors (including Smartwatches); GPS signals from mobile devices, and so on.

psychologists using social media platforms such as Facebook and Google Trends, and, where possible, linking this data with either participants' own data elsewhere (existing cohort surveys, shopping data, etc.) or global data at the level of the region/state/country in which the participant resides.

Other innovations have included linking GIS (geographic information system) data from people's anonymised mobile phone signals with other pertinent variables, such as the number of people who have been diagnosed with COVID-19 and the number of people who have died of the infection across locations (see Oishi et al., 2021).

GUEST PERSONAL JOURNEY

Jonny Huck

Source: © Jonny Huck

My journey to research in (or at least adjacent to) Psychology began when I joined Lancaster University to study Geography in 2004. I became particularly interested in the computational aspects of the subject when Duncan Whyatt (now Professor of GIS at Lancaster University) introduced me to Geographical Information Science (GIS). After completing my degree, I went on to study an MSc in GIS at the University of Leeds, where I met Andy Evans, who taught me to write software using a programming language called Java. Though I had relatively little experience with computers and the learning curve was very steep, this proved to be a pivotal moment for me, as writing software became a constant theme throughout the rest of my career.

Towards the end of my Master's, Duncan Whyatt contacted me with the details of a Lancaster-based wind farm developer who wanted a student to do some GIS programming work for them. I ended up spending over five years working there, initially writing GIS software for them and latterly as Technical Manager, responsible for a team of GIS and technical staff. During this time, I provided a series of 'industry' placements to Duncan's MSc students, and he eventually persuaded me to start a PhD in 2011, which I self-funded and did part-time alongside my full-time job.

Around 2013, I left my career in the wind industry and moved to work at Lancaster University as a researcher, during which time Duncan introduced me to John Dixon (in the sports centre changing room!) to talk about the Belfast Mobility Project (see his profile in Part 1 of this chapter). They invited me to join the project, allowing me to contribute the GNSS tracking application and the Participatory GIS software. The tracking application was a particular success, in which we collected around 1,000 hours of high-resolution movement data from over 200 people – an unprecedented data set! In 2015, I moved to a lectureship in GIS in the Department of Geography at The University of Manchester, where I continued my research on the Belfast Mobility Project. This led to a series of publications, providing new insights into the geography and psychology of segregation, and leading to new collaborations with international psychology researchers.

Powerful technological advances have also simplified the job of conducting time-consuming searches and analysis of data on the same topic. For example, **data mining** has successfully been used to uncover the most robust relationship satisfaction predictor among an array of 43 existing longitudinal studies of couples (see Joel et al., 2020). Data mining in this case was able to show that people's own

> **Key concept – Data mining:** The process of extracting and discovering patterns and relationships in large data sets involving methods at the intersection of machine learning, statistics, and database systems.

judgements about the relationship itself (e.g., how satisfied and committed they perceived their partners to be, and how appreciative they felt towards their partners) was the best predictor of their current relationship satisfaction.

1.7.2 Reproducibility Crisis and Open Science

Doing research is great. It is challenging, rewarding, and sometimes very impactful (both for the progression of scientific knowledge and for improving human and societal outcomes). It is exciting for the investigator, but it can also be quite hard to take when your research hypotheses turn out to be wrong.

This was the situation in which many researchers found themselves in the mid-2010s. In a major project which attempted to replicate behavioural science studies (Open Science Collaboration, 2015), approximately half of the replications yielded similar results to the original studies. Some explained this as reflecting the multi-determined and context-sensitivity of most psychological findings, which limit our capacity to carry out true replications. Some blamed bad practice, as psychology studies sometimes have small sample sizes, thus leading to unreliable findings. Some blamed 'cherry-picking' and 'p-hacking' – the dark arts of statistical analysis. If you are close to a significant result and have one participant who is a bit of an outlier (performing differently from your other participants), what would happen if, say, they were to disappear from the study? A significant result, you say? Get that participant in the bin, then. That's cherry picking and p-hacking.

Others blamed publication bias (the failure to publish the results of a study based on the direction or strength of the study findings). Some discussed the pressures academics face to produce results that count towards their career progression. Furthermore, for a long time there was a bias in academic publishing to favour the cool, new, and statistically significant results (in both senses of the word). What is publication bias? So, let's say I work in a psychology lab with five other people, and we all run the same study, but where I found a significant difference, they didn't. Guess who's getting published? Even though five out of six times there is no difference in our samples, the one time it just so happened that there was a difference, that one is getting published. Now what if you want to check that and replicate it? Tough luck, the journal will tell you that your work isn't novel anymore as it's already been done. So now you have a dodgy result that cannot be replicated. This was the case for many years, not just in psychology but in many scientific disciplines (for a discussion see Ioannidis, 2005).

So, what can be done to combat these practices? There has been a big and very welcome push in the last few years for what is known as 'Open Science'.

If you write some computer code to run an experiment, when you publish your study should you also publish your computer code for people to check or use themselves? Open Science would say absolutely! If someone finds that you have made a mistake, isn't that a good thing? The same goes for your raw data. Shouldn't that be available for people to scrutinise or re-use? And any research material you made – couldn't other researchers use that for their own studies? Sharing data and resources (especially when they were paid for by taxpayers money!) equates to transparency, and with the need to be transparent come better research practices and robust planning and execution.

Open Science also applies to the whole act of publishing your studies in academic journals. We spoke briefly about publication bias earlier, in which only statistically significant results were getting published, and a whole host of results that did not reach the statistical threshold for significance were just gathering dust in drawers (commonly known as the 'file-drawer effect'). But those results are also interesting and valuable. Did you predict a difference between two groups but found that they performed the same? Cool! Why might that have happened? Maybe there was no difference to be found. Maybe the theories you used to justify hypothesising there would be a difference between the two groups were flawed. But without publishing null results (where there is no significant difference or a lack of a relationship between variables) how would the scientific community ever know about the lack of difference or relationship between these two groups and why such a lack of difference or relationship may occur?

As we've said before, just because results aren't *statistically* significant doesn't mean they are not *scientifically* significant. So how do we make sure these results get published as well? By entering pre-registered reports. Under this relatively new publishing method, researchers submit half of an academic paper, a section justifying the research question or hypothesis (an introduction) and a section outlining the method and planned analyses they will use to test this hypothesis (a methods section). Based on the strength of these two sections (is this an interesting and well-justified question and is this a solid method to answer it?) the journal will agree to publish the results *regardless* of whether the results are statistically significant or not. That way researchers are not able to cherry-pick, or p-hack, or change their hypotheses after seeing the results. It maintains scientific integrity, while helping to combat publication bias at the same time! Research plans and data, stimuli, code, and all other pertinent study materials are then made public. Thus, it is truly open science, for all to see, warts and all.

The practice of pre-registering manuscript reports with journals before the conduct of the study or analyses has gained traction across social psychology and beyond. Many journals nowadays have special sections dedicated to studies that have been pre-registered. One example from our own work (Paddy and Miki) is a paper in which we pre-registered two competing hypotheses to be explored in an existing big data set, including implicit and explicit measures of attitudes (for more on implicit and explicit measures see Chapter 6 and Chapter 9). The paper examined whether communal attitudes peak among those from medium socioeconomic groups using existing data to explore this novel hypothesis (Weick et al., 2022). The data analysis plan, together with the hypothesis, was pre-registered. The paper found no support for the pre-registered hypothesis.

But pre-registering a research report is not the only way in which Open Science has changed our practices. Nowadays many social psychologists pre-register their research protocols on the Open Science Framework (OSF), which was founded by fellow social psychologist Brian Nosek. The OSF allows researchers to share their protocols and all study materials for free and in perpetuity, separately from their published manuscript (with links to all these resources provided within the published manuscript). This is another way in which the practices of social psychologists have become more open and transparent, which has paved the way to more reliable scientific endeavours.

1.8 SUMMARY

In this chapter we have given you a crash course through some of the research methods you can use to explore social psychology. You will be introduced to a lot of exciting theories and empirical studies in this book, and what we want you to have in the back of your mind is a thought on not only *what* the theories and studies can tell us, but *how* they came about. What was the study behind the theory and, vice-versa, what was the theory behind the study and the sociocultural context that has generated it? How did the researchers design their studies, gather data, and analyse them? What was the make-up of the sample they used and were there any limitations that could be relevant?

Understanding how these empirical studies are seen through from hypothesis to operationalisation and finally interpretation is a key skill that will help you to become a better scientist and social psychologist. Being able to understand and critique work that leads to theory generation will in turn lead to better understanding and critiques of the theories themselves and scientific progress. Also, you will likely be designing your own studies as part of your degree soon, and knowing what others have done, the techniques, research methods and analyses they have used, will help to inform your own research.

It should inspire you to use Open Science practices, implement certain design features, and help to move your own research spiral or sphere forwards just a little bit. You'll find your research niche and, indeed, maybe even come across or use some of the techniques in this chapter. As we mentioned at the start of the chapter, by finding your area, you will likely end up knowing a lot about a little, but by understanding what other people have done and are doing, it also won't hurt for you to know a little about a lot.

1.9 REVISION

1   Explain why a mismatch between the 'world of theory' and the 'world of data' is important for scientific progress according to Popper's epistemology.
2   If you were interested in finding out the nature of the relationship between two different variables, what kind of research design and data analytic technique should you be using?
3   Describe the different ways in which qualitative data can be analysed.
4   Describe the models of humans and social reality that underpinned traditional quantitative/positivist and qualitative/constructivist approaches to social psychology. Explain why they were regarded as incompatible during the discipline's crisis of confidence and schism, whereas they often coexist in modern investigation.
5   Explain why it is problematic for psychological understanding to infer regularities about the functioning of the human mind, relying almost exclusively on data from Western, Industrialised, Educated, Rich, Democratic (WEIRD) samples.
6   Explain why at parity of sample size a within-subjects design has more statistical power than a between-subjects design. Identify topics in social psychology that are typically not amenable to within-subjects manipulations. Explain why that would be the case.
7   Describe and evaluate some of the methodological innovations in research methods used by social psychologists.
8   What is Open Science and how has it been utilised by social psychologists?

1.10 FURTHER READING

Rubin, M. (2023, September 10). The replication crisis is less of a 'crisis' in the Lakatosian approach than it is in the Popperian and naïve methodological falsificationism approaches. *Critical Metascience: MetaArXiv*. https://doi.org/10.31222/osf.io/2dz9s

This article compares and contrasts alternative philosophies of science, including Popper's and Lakatos', and links them to contemporary analyses of the replication crisis, arguing that different epistemologies might be differently equipped to address different types of replication failures.

Gergen, K. J. (1973). Social psychology as history. *Journal of Personality and Social Psychology,* *26,* 309–320. https://doi.org/10.1037/h0034436

This paper was born out of the profound crisis of confidence in social psychology in the 1970s and 1980s, reflecting polarised views about the implied assumptions behind quantitative and qualitative approaches/methods. In this paper, Gergen articulates their positioning in the qualitative camp, underscoring their view of an intimate relationship between psychological knowledge, methods, history and culture. It contributed to the Qualitative manifesto during the acute stages of that early disciplinary schism.

Markus, H. R., & Kitayama, S. (1991). Cultural variation in the self-concept. In J. Strauss & G. R. Goethals (Eds.), *The self: Interdisciplinary approaches* (pp. 18–48). New York: Springer.

This article, co-authored by prominent researchers from the West and the East, played a key role in revealing the mono-cultural nature of early (US-dominated) social psychological knowledge, American intellectual imperialism in science, and the implication for psychological understanding of assuming that other human groups share a similar individualistic outlook to the human nature. This critical analysis will pave the road for more modern criticisms of WEIRD-dominated samples and knowledge generation (see next entry).

Henrich, J., Heine, S. J., & Norenzayan, A. (2010). Most people are not WEIRD. *Nature, 466,* 29. https://doi.org/10.1038/466029a

This is a seminal review by Henrich and colleagues demonstrating the pervasive sampling bias prevalent in most psychology studies. They found that the majority of psychological studies have sampled highly educated, Western, university undergraduates, thus limiting the potential generalisability of much of what has been published in the field.

Ioannidis, J. P. (2005). Why most published research findings are false. *PLoS Medicine, 2,* e124. https://doi.org/10.1371/journal.pmed.0020124

In this classic paper, which has been cited circa 13,000 times to date, John Ioannidis argues that most published research findings are false. He showed that small-scale studies with small samples and a great number of hypotheses with flexible analytic plans were more likely to yield false positive results. This paper is considered a turning point in the Open Science movement for more transparent design, conduct, and reporting of research studies.

Open Science Collaboration. (2015). Estimating the reproducibility of psychological science. *Science, 349,* aac4716. https://doi.org/10.1126/science.aac4716

This is the paper that reports the results of a large-scale multi-laboratory replication effort of psychological effects carried out soon after the drive for Open Science began. It replicated about 40% of original effects reported in published psychology studies.

Weitzman, L., Eifler, D., Hokada, E., & Ross, C. (1972). Sex role socialization in picturebooks for preschool children. *American Journal of Sociology, 77,* 1125–1150. https://doi.org/10.1086/225261

In this now classic archival content analysis of children's picture books for preschool children, Weitzman and colleagues showed that women and men were largely portrayed in sex-stereotypical roles.

Friehs, M. T., Bracegirdle, C., Reimer, N. K., Wölfer, R., Schmidt, P., Wagner, U., & Hewstone, M. (2024). The between-person and within-person effects of intergroup contact on outgroup attitudes: A multi-context examination. *Social Psychological and Personality Science, 15*, 125–141. https://doi.org/10.1177/19485506231153017

This article shows how social psychologists are often at the forefront of analytical innovation. It shows how the application of traditional statistics to analyse longitudinal panel data consistently returns significant cross-lagged longitudinal that do not allow the situational fluctuations by the individual (within-person variations) and stable differences between individuals (between-person variations) to be distinguished. When new generation statistics capable of discriminating are used, in this article it is evident that the old findings are driven almost exclusively by the between-person component.

Gollwitzer, M., & Schwabe, J. (2022). Context dependency as a predictor of replicability. *Review of General Psychology, 26*, 241–249. https://doi.org/10.1177/10892680211015635

This article advances the very interesting argument (from a social psychological perspective) that unsuccessful replications, and heterogeneous effect sizes more generally, may reflect an underappreciated influence of context characteristics. The article presents a conceptual and analytical framework that allows researchers to empirically estimate the extent to which effect size heterogeneity is due to conceptually relevant versus irrelevant context characteristics.

1.11 REFERENCES

Adam, H., & Harper, L. J. (2023). Gender equity in early childhood picture books: A cross-cultural study of frequently read picture books in early childhood classrooms in Australia and the United States. *The Australian Educational Researcher, 50*, 453–479. https://doi.org/10.1007/s13384-021-00494-0

Allport, G. W. (1935). Attitudes. In C. Murchison (Ed.), *A handbook of social psychology* (pp. 798–844). Worcester, MA: Clark University Press.

Antaki, C., Billig, M., Edwards, D., & Potter, J. (2003). Discourse analysis means doing analysis: A critique of six analytic shortcomings. *DAOL Discourse Analysis Online* [electronic version], *1*(1). https://doi.org/10.4135/9781473983335

Asch, S. E. (1951). Effects of group pressure upon the modification and distortion of judgments. In H. Guetzkow (Ed.), *Groups, leadership and men: research in human relations* (pp. 177–190). Pittsburgh, PA: Carnegie Press.

Asch, S. E. (1956). Studies of independence and conformity: I. A minority of one against a unanimous majority. *Psychological Monographs: General and Applied, 70*, 1–70. https://doi.org/10.1037/h0093718

Bennett, C. M., Miller, M. B., & Wolford, G. L. (2009). Neural correlates of interspecies perspective taking in the post-mortem Atlantic Salmon: An argument for multiple comparisons correction. *NeuroImage, 47*(Suppl. 1), S125. https://doi.org/10.1016/S1053-8119(09)71202-9

Berry, J. W. (1969). On cross-cultural comparability. *International Journal of Psychology, 4*, 119–128. https://doi.org/10.1080/00207596908247261

Blanke, E. S., Brose, A., Kalokerinos, E. K., Erbas, Y., Riediger, M., & Kuppens, P. (2020). Mix it to fix it: Emotion regulation variability in daily life. *Emotion, 20*, 473–485. https://doi.org/10.1037/emo0000566

Camiller, P., & Popper, K. (2013). *All life is problem solving.* Abingdon: Routledge.

Dutton, D. G., & Aron, A. P. (1974). Some evidence for heightened sexual attraction under conditions of high anxiety. *Journal of Personality and Social Psychology, 30,* 510–517. https://doi.org/10.1037/h0037031

Edwards, D. (1996). *Discourse and cognition.* London: Sage.

Farr, R. M. (1996). *The roots of modern social psychology, 1872–1954.* Oxford: Blackwell Publishing.

Gergen, K. J. (1973). Social psychology as history. *Journal of Personality and Social Psychology, 26,* 309–320. https://doi.org/10.1037/h0034436

Gergen, K. J. (1976). Social psychology, science and history. *Personality and Social Psychology Bulletin, 2,* 373–383. https://doi.org/10.1177/014616727600200409

Harré, R. (2005). The discursive turn in social psychology. In D. Schiffrin, D. Tannen, & H. E. Hamilton (Eds.), *The handbook of discourse analysis* (pp. 688–706). Oxford: Blackwell.

Hartley, R. E. (1960). Children's concepts of male and female roles. *Merrill-Palmer Quarterly of Behavior and Development, 6,* 83–91. www.jstor.org/stable/23082570

Henrich, J., Heine, S. J., & Norenzayan, A. (2010). Most people are not WEIRD. *Nature, 466,* 29. https://doi.org/10.1038/466029a

Hofmann, W., Vohs, K. D., & Baumeister, R. F. (2012). What people desire, feel conflicted about, and try to resist in everyday life. *Psychological Science, 23,* 582–588. https://doi.org/10.1177/0956797612437426

Hofmann, W., Wisneski, D. C., Brandt, M. J., & Skitka, L. J. (2014). Morality in everyday life. *Science, 345,* 1340–1343. https://doi.org/10.1126/science.1251560

Holland, E., Koval, P., Stratemeyer, M., Thomson, F., & Haslam, N. (2017). Sexual objectification in women's daily lives: A smartphone ecological momentary assessment study. *British Journal of Social Psychology, 56,* 314–333. https://doi.org/10.1111/bjso.12152

Ioannidis, J. P. (2005). Why most published research findings are false. *PLoS Medicine, 2,* e124. https://doi.org/10.1371/journal.pmed.0020124

Joel, S., Eastwick, P. W., Allison, C. J., Arriaga, X. B., Baker, Z. G., Bar-Kalifa, E., ... & Wolf, S. (2020). Machine learning uncovers the most robust self-report predictors of relationship quality across 43 longitudinal couples studies. *Proceedings of the National Academy of Sciences, 117,* 19061–19071. https://doi.org/10.1073/pnas.1917036117

Loftus, E. F., & Palmer, J. C. (1974). Reconstruction of automobile destruction: An example of the interaction between language and memory. *Journal of Verbal Learning and Verbal Behavior, 13,* 585–589. https://doi.org/10.1016/S0022-5371(74)80011-3

Maccoby, E. E. (1966). *The development of sex differences.* Stanford, CA: Stanford University Press.

Markus, H. R., & Kitayama, S. (1991). Cultural variation in the self-concept. In J. Strauss & G. R. Goethals (Eds.), *The self: Interdisciplinary approaches* (pp. 18–48). New York: Springer.

Moscovici, S. (2001). *Social representations: Essays in social psychology.* Albany, NY: NYU Press.

Oishi, S., Cha, Y., & Schimmack, U. (2021). The social ecology of COVID-19 cases and deaths in New York City: The role of walkability, wealth, and race. *Social Psychological and Personality Science, 12,* 1457–1466. https://doi.org/10.1177/1948550620979259

Open Science Collaboration. (2015). Estimating the reproducibility of psychological science. *Science, 349,* aac4716. https://doi.org/10.1126/science.aac4716

Perrin, S., & Spencer, C. (1980). The Asch effect: A child of its time? *Bulletin of the British Psychological Society*, *32*, 405–406.

Quiñones-Vidal, E., Loźpez-García, J. J., Peñarañda-Ortega, M., & Tortosa-Gil, F. (2004). The nature of social and personality psychology as reflected in *JPSP*, 1965–2000. *Journal of Personality and Social Psychology*, *86*(3), 435–452. https://doi.org/10.1037/0022-3514.86.3.435

Rosenberg, M., Schooler, C., & Schoenbach, C. (1989). Self-esteem and adolescent problems: Modeling reciprocal effects. *American Sociological Review*, *54*, 1004–1018.

Rosnow, R. L. (1981). *Paradigms in transition: The methodology of social inquiry*. Oxford: Oxford University Press.

Sherif, M., Harvey, O., White, J. B., Hood, W. R., & Sherif, C. W. (1961). *Intergroup Conflict and Cooperation: The Robbers Cave Experiment [1954]*. Norman, OK: University of Oklahoma Book Exchange.

Shiffman, S., Li, X., Dunbar, M. S., Ferguson, S. G., Tindle, H. A., & Scholl, S. M. (2015). Social smoking among intermittent smokers. *Drug and Alcohol Dependence*, *154*, 184–191. https://doi.org/10.1016/j.drugalcdep.2015.06.027

Shiffman, S., Stone, A. A., & Hufford, M. R. (2008). Ecological momentary assessment. *Annual Review of Clinical Psychology*, *4*, 1–32. https://doi.org/10.1146/annurev.clinpsy.3.022806.091415

Slater, M., Antley, A., Davison, A., Swapp, D., Guger, C., Barker, C., ... & Sanchez-Vives, M. V. (2006). A virtual reprise of the Stanley Milgram obedience experiments. *PLoS One*, *1*, e39. https://doi.org/10.1371/journal.pone.0000039

Slater, M., Rovira, A., Southern, R., Swapp, D., Zhang, J. J., Campbell, C., & Levine, M. (2013). Bystander responses to a violent incident in an immersive virtual environment. *PLoS One*, *8*, e52766. https://doi.org/10.1371/journal.pone.0052766

Smith, P. B., Fischer, R., Vignoles, V. L., & Bond, M. H. (2013). *Understanding social psychology across cultures: Engaging with others in a changing world*. London: Sage.

Sylwester, K., & Purver, M. (2015). Twitter language use reflects psychological differences between democrats and republicans. *PLoS One*, *10*, e0137422. https://doi.org/10.1371/journal.pone.0137422

Tajfel, H. (Ed.). (2010). *Social identity and intergroup relations* (Vol. 7). Cambridge: Cambridge University Press.

Tajfel, H., Turner, J. C., Austin, W. G., & Worchel, S. (1979). An integrative theory of intergroup conflict. *Organizational identity: A reader*, *56*, 9780203505984-16.

Weick, M., Couturier, D. L., Vasiljevic, M., Ross, P., Clark, C. J., Crisp, R. J., ... & Van de Vyver, J. (2022). Building bonds: A pre-registered secondary data analysis examining linear and curvilinear relations between socio-economic status and communal attitudes. *Journal of Experimental Social Psychology*, *102*, 104353. https://doi.org/10.1016/j.jesp.2022.104353

Weick, M., McCall, C., & Blascovich, J. (2017). Power moves beyond complementarity: A staring look elicits avoidance in low power perceivers and approach in high power perceivers. *Personality and Social Psychology Bulletin*, *43*, 1188–1201. https://doi.org/10.1177/0146167217708576

Weitzman, L., Eifler, D., Hokada, E., & Ross, C. (1972). Sex role socialization in picturebooks for preschool children. *American Journal of Sociology*, *77*, 1125–1150. https://doi.org/10.1086/225261

2
SELF AND IDENTITY
KIMBERLY RIOS & ALYSSON E. LIGHT

Contents

2.1 AUTHORS' PERSONAL JOURNEYS

Alysson Light

When I was in high school, it seemed vitally important to me to understand who I was, and by that I mean which of several social categories or social cliques I fell into. I think a lot of people can relate to the experience of wondering which lunch table they belong to.

A particularly confusing one for me had to do with being a 'girly girl' or not. I loved a cute dress but knew nothing about make-up. I avoided team sports at all costs but loved a good knock-down debate. The fact that I couldn't easily classify myself as feminine or not bothered me – to me, it was a question that needed to be answered, rather than something I could simply leave alone. I found myself turning this question over to other people, and even initiating a debate at one point between my friends about how girly I was! (They concluded I was a 'granola girl'. Problem solved!)

The questions of self-definition didn't stop there. As a college student, I was a committed political activist, but had interests beyond politics. Was this OK? Could I be devoted to my ideals without having them define *everything* I did?

As a social psychologist, I am fascinated by self and identity, and particularly moments like these when people question who they are. In a lot of ways, I find that the answer is less important than the question itself, and the processes people like me have used to try to answer it. Why was it so important to define myself? Why would I turn to other people in my attempt to answer that question? Why would consistency be so vital to identity? Is it possible for the self to be more variable and nuanced?

When I was younger, I asked myself 'Why can't I be more consistent? Why am I not one thing or the other? Why don't I understand myself?' These days, I flip those questions on their heads. Given the sheer amount of information we have about ourselves – every conscious moment of our lives, in total – how can we perform the amazing cognitive feat of summarizing all of that information into something singular, coherent, consistent? Indeed, why would we *want* to? As many of the chapters in this textbook will reveal, people's behavior can be very inconsistent across social environments. Wouldn't our self-knowledge be more accurate if that kind of inconsistency was baked into our self-concepts? These are the types of issues we explore in this chapter.

Kimberly Rios

Reflecting on my life thus far, it is no wonder I study topics related to self and identity! I come from a multicultural family – my mother was born in Puerto Rico, and my father in Wisconsin – and grew up in a suburb of San Diego, California, no more than 15 minutes from the US–Mexico border. My hometown and the schools I attended were remarkably diverse, with no clear racial/ethnic majority group, and I often found myself questioning where I fit in demographically. At school, my friends and teachers inevitably categorized me as White due to my fair skin and blue eyes; but at home, where my maternal grandparents (who lived next door) regularly spoke to me in Spanish, my experiences felt somewhat different from those of most of my White friends. As a college student, once I began taking courses in both psychology and racial/ethnic studies, my confusion compounded, as did my curiosity about identity-relevant topics. Did I need to 'pick a side' in terms of how I personally identified? If I claimed to be part Puerto Rican, was I doing a disservice to my Latino(a) friends and relatives who, by virtue of their darker skin tone and/or accented speech, self-identified in a way that matched up with the way others perceived them? What factors determine the social identities and group memberships that people deem more versus less central to their sense of self, in general?

It wasn't until the summer between my second and third years of college, while studying abroad in Beijing, China, that I began to understand the answer is not clear-cut ... Indeed, as many social psychologists will joke, their response to everything is 'It depends!'. During those two months, I had the experience of being a visible racial/ethnic minority – and being subjected to associated stereotypes and misconceptions – for the first time in my life. Now, as a researcher and instructor, I convey to my students that identity is not static, but rather can shift according to the contexts in which we find ourselves, and that having multiple identities does not make any one of our identities any less authentic or legitimate. Uncovering how our different identities can coexist and sometimes conflict is, for me, one of the most exciting parts of social psychology!

2.2 INTRODUCTION

Who doesn't like thinking about themselves? As it turns out, we are not the only people who have spent a lot of time thinking about who we are, how others perceive us, and who we want to be in the future. If you find yourself thinking about yourself a lot, this doesn't necessarily mean you're a narcissist – studies of what people think about when their minds freely wander show that the majority of the time, if our attention wavers from the task at hand, it's probably because we're thinking about ourselves (Baird et al., 2011).

Psychologists are also fascinated by self and identity, and the topic can be an important nexus for many areas of psychology. For example, your self-concept is clearly informed by your memories, so an understanding of memory and cognition can inform our understanding of the self (Conway, 2005). As we will discuss, the self-concept changes in consistent ways over the lifespan, meaning that developmentalists, too, study the self (McAdams & Cox, 2010). Personality psychologists consider the self-concept and our personal 'autobiography' to be key parts of our personality (McAdams & Pals, 2006). And clinical psychologists have commented that many mental illnesses are characterized by differences or disruptions to the self-concept (Westen & Heim, 2003).

At this point, you might be wondering why a chapter in a book on *social* psychology is focusing on the self, something that belongs to just one individual. Could there be anything less social than the self? Well, as it turns out, the self is influenced by all kinds of social factors.

Other people can be some of the most important sources of information about ourselves. They can serve as comparisons by which we understand ourselves. They are often the most crucial aspects of situations we find ourselves in, which can shape how we view ourselves in any given moment. And they contain the social groups we belong to, which frame our social identities.

Indeed, as you'll see, self and identity are often much broader than we initially assume. Psychologists describe the self as a rich knowledge structure that connects beliefs about our personal characteristics (e.g., 'I am generous') to our personal memories (e.g., 'One time I gave my friend some money when she needed it'), to our personal relationships (e.g., 'I am Nicki's friend'), to our personal values (e.g., 'It is important to me to take care of other people'), and even potentially including other people (e.g., 'My parents are an important part of me'), our social groups (e.g., 'I am part of the queer community'), and our possessions (e.g., 'I own over 100 books').

While we often think of people as having only one singular, cohesive, coherent self that stays consistent over time and across situations, many psychologists focus on the ways in which the self changes to reflect the situations in which we find ourselves, and can be divided into divergent self-aspects that describe who we are in different areas of our lives. As you read this chapter, we encourage you to indulge in the question 'Who am I?', and to consider that the answer likely depends on where you are and what other people are around when you answer it. Throughout this chapter, we will also include personal examples and anecdotes, with parenthetical references to indicate who (Kim or Aly) is the narrator in each instance.

2.3 LEARNING OBJECTIVES

By the end of this chapter, you will be able to:

- Explain how the self is influenced by other people, and by our social groups;
- Identify common self-enhancement strategies, and how they contribute to the 'better-than-average effect';
- Describe how and why people strive for high self-esteem;
- Understand why people choose to identify with particular social groups;
- Explain how self and identity vary across contexts, and how this impacts affect and behavior.

2.4 PART 1: FOUNDATIONS

In this section, we introduce classic theories and contemporary empirical research on the social psychology of the self-concept and self-esteem.

2.4.1 The Looking Glass Self

One classic insight from social psychological theory is that we understand who we are, in part based on information we get from other people. The process by which these interactions impact our self-concept is colorfully referred to as the 'looking glass self' (Cooley, 1902; Mead, 1934), the idea being that other people often serve as our mirrors when we try to determine who we are. Others' impressions of us are referred to as appraisals. Like when a jeweler appraises the value of a gem, other people form appraisals of us based on our appearance, our behavior, our reputation, and so on (see Chapter 5 on social cognition for more about how this process occurs). These appraisals are then reflected to us in the words and actions of other people. For example, someone might give direct feedback about our traits, strengths, and weaknesses (e.g., a boss saying 'You're such a hard worker!'), or their words and actions may imply what they think of us (e.g., seeing someone's eyes light up when they see us conveys that this person likes us).

This information we glean about how others see us is known as **reflected appraisals**, reflected because other people are acting as our mirrors, giving us information about ourselves. We can then internalize these appraisals (or not), at which point they become part of our self-concept. Importantly, we aren't necessarily consciously aware that we are

> **Key concept – Reflected appraisal:** Also sometimes called a metaperception, reflected appraisals are our impressions of what specific people think of us. They are formed partly based on direct feedback, partly from observations of others' behavior toward us, and partly by projecting our own beliefs about ourselves, and assuming that others see us the same way.

internalizing these reflected appraisals. While we might sometimes consciously integrate feedback from others into our definition of who we are, we may internalize appraisals without being aware of it, and may even internalize things that we are uncomfortable with (Figure 2.1).

Does this mean that anyone we interact with has the potential to change how we view ourselves? Any interaction has the potential to lead us to internalize a new reflected appraisal, but some people are definitely more impactful than others. Not surprisingly, we're more likely to internalize reflected appraisals from people whose opinions we value (Baldwin et al., 1990). We might imagine that the people whose opinions matter the most would be the people we are closest to – our best friends, or our close family members. But in fact, our self-concepts are often more influenced by people who are a little more distant, though still valued (Wallace & Tice, 2012). One explanation is that we tend to assume the people we're closest to are biased in our favor. In other words, we are not alone in taking effusive praise from our parents with a grain of salt! And this means that people we are a little less close to can have greater power to influence how we feel about ourselves.

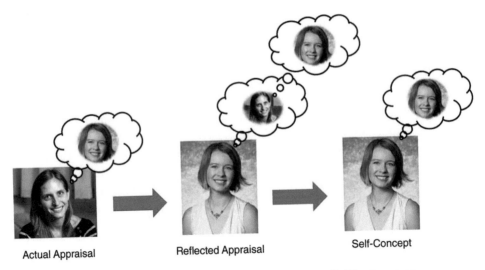

Actual Appraisal   Reflected Appraisal   Self-Concept

Figure 2.1 Symbolic interactionism, or the looking glass self: Kim forms an impression or *appraisal* of Aly. Influenced by her words and behavior towards Aly, Aly forms a *reflected appraisal* of Kim's impression of her. Aly may then internalize that appraisal such that it influences her self-concept

KEY STUDY 2.1

My Advisor and the Pope are Watching Me from the Back of My Brain!

Social scientists had theorized, since the early 20th century, that we internalize the reflected appraisals of others into our self-concepts, but a key experimental test of this theory was reported by Baldwin et al. (1990). In two studies, they used priming techniques to manipulate the reflected appraisal people would have in mind, and then had them evaluate themselves. In Study 1, the participants were psychology graduate students who were asked to evaluate their research ideas (something that is central to graduate students' sense of self.) This study was a within-subjects design, in that participants completed trials related to all three study conditions (approving reflected appraisal, disapproving reflected appraisal, and control), though the order of the conditions was randomly assigned and varied.

Participants were asked to think about one of their research ideas. They then were, beyond their conscious awareness, exposed to either (a) a picture of Robert Zajonc, the director of their program, scowling at the camera (disapproving reflected appraisal), or (b) a picture of John Ellard, then a young, postdoctoral researcher in the department, smiling at the camera (approving reflected appraisal). After the prime, participants evaluated the quality of the research idea they'd been thinking about. The 'looking glass self' predicts that participants would internalize the reflected appraisal they had been primed with, thus leading them to evaluate their research ideas more negatively after seeing Zajonc's frown than after seeing Ellard's smile. And that's exactly what the results showed! Participants gave their research ideas roughly a B grade after the approving reflected appraisal, but roughly a D+ after the disapproving reflected appraisal.

Research on the looking glass self shows that it is a normal characteristic of human psychology to be influenced by what others think of us. This highlights the fact that as we are seeking to know ourselves better, the people around us who know us well can be a good place to start.

EXERCISE 2.1

Develop Your Critical Thinking

Listen to *This American Life*'s podcast story, 'The Answer to the Riddle is Me' (www.thisamericanlife.org/399/contents-unknown/act-three). As you listen, try to answer the following questions:

a   How does Dave, the narrator, construct reflected appraisals of how others view him?
b   How do those reflected appraisals impact how Dave sees himself?
c   When do other people have the greatest influence on how we see ourselves?
d   How do our self-concepts shape our behavior?

2.4.2 Social Comparison Theory

In addition to information we receive from others, we sometimes learn about ourselves by observing our thoughts, feelings, and actions. This might seem like something we are capable of doing independently, but once again, constructing self-knowledge ends up being highly social. An important insight is that the information we get about ourselves is most informative when compared to other people (Festinger, 1954). For instance, it takes me (Aly) about 10 minutes to walk from my office to my favorite lunch spot. Does that make me fast or slow? To answer that question, I need to compare my

> **Key concept – Social comparison:** The process in which we interpret and evaluate information about ourselves by comparing ourselves to other people. A key distinction is between upward and downward social comparisons: upward social comparisons are when we compare ourselves to someone who is better than us on a given dimension, and downward social comparisons are when we compare ourselves to someone who is worse than us.

speed to that of other people walking a similar route. So to understand even something as objective as my walking speed, I need to engage in **social comparison** – comparing myself to other people in order to make sense of myself.

As might already be apparent, this means that the conclusions that I draw will be heavily influenced by who I compare myself to. Returning to the example of my walking speed, I never thought much about how fast I walked growing up, because I seemed to walk about the same speed as my parents. My parents served as the reference group for my judgments about myself – that is, they were the group against which I implicitly compared myself in order to understand myself. However, since growing up and venturing out into the world, I've noticed that I tend to walk a lot faster than most other people. In fact, 'walking fast' has become part of my identity (just ask all my psychologist friends who see me zipping around the convention center at psychology conferences!). This information, which has become part of my self-concept, importantly depends on the reference group I used for social comparison. Relative to my family (all fast walkers themselves), my walking speed didn't seem to be anything special. Relative to other people, though, my walking speed seems very fast.

An important insight from social comparison theory is exactly this phenomenon: that our understanding of ourselves can be changed depending on the reference group we're implicitly comparing ourselves to. One common way to think about this influence is to focus on whether we're comparing ourselves to people who are better than us at something, or worse than us at something. We call these upward social comparisons and downward social comparisons, respectively, which one might visualize by using the image of competitors standing on a medals platform. The people who came in second place can look up at the first-place winner to make an upward social comparison, or down at the person in third place to make a downward social comparison.

Perhaps not surprisingly, the type of social comparison we engage in can change how we feel about ourselves. For example, a lot of students experience a drop in their academic self-esteem when they arrive at university. Previous classrooms may have offered a lot of opportunity for downward social comparison (i.e., lower performing students), leading students to feel good about their academic abilities. The more elite university environment, however, might mean that upward social comparisons are easier to find, resulting in a drop in students' perceptions of their abilities. Of course, nothing has changed about the students' abilities – they are simply comparing themselves to a different reference group!

What kinds of things affect the reference group we compare ourselves to? There are several factors that can influence who we choose to compare ourselves to. One is *similarity* – we tend to compare ourselves to others whom we believe to be somewhat similar to ourselves. If we begin learning Spanish and want to get a sense of how we're progressing, it makes sense that we would compare our abilities to other beginning students, and not compare ourselves to a native speaker. Another factor, though, is the motive to maintain a positive self-image – in other words, the motive *to have high self-esteem*. Self-esteem motives can lead people to selectively choose reference groups that result in flattering, downward social comparisons. So, for example, if we want to feel good about ourselves and our language-learning abilities, we might compare our knowledge of Spanish to that of someone who hasn't studied the language at all. This comparison would highlight everything that we've already mastered, allowing us to feel better about ourselves.

However, upward social comparisons do not always make us feel worse about ourselves, and downward social comparisons do not always make us feel better (Buunk et al., 1990). Consider the impact of having a role model. Many education and workplace programs to boost performance involve highlighting potential role models. If these upward social comparisons led people to feel bad and demoralized, surely they wouldn't be achieving their goals. How can upward social comparisons sometimes make us feel deflated, but sometimes make us feel inspired?

The key difference seems to be whether we believe we can attain the same glory as our role models (Lockwood & Kunda, 1997). In one study, newly entering accounting students and graduating accounting students read about a 'stellar' graduating accounting student, who had balanced outstanding academic performance with a variety of extracurricular activities and community engagement. After reading about this student, all participants completed a measure of self-esteem. Control participants simply rated themselves without reading about the star student. The consequence of reading about this star student on self-esteem depended on the participant's year in their program. First-year students, who had a lot of time to achieve everything that this positive role model had, rated themselves more positively after they read about the superstar than when they had not read about them. By contrast, graduating students, who were out of time to achieve the things the superstar had achieved, rated themselves more negatively after reading about the superstar compared to participants who had not read about them.

2.4.3 Theories of Self-esteem

As might be evident from learning about social comparison theory, a major focus of research on self and identity concerns how we evaluate and feel about ourselves – in other words, our **self-esteem**. Of all the theories and constructs related to the self-concept that psychologists have developed, perhaps none has experienced such widespread attention as self-esteem. Self-esteem refers to an individual's overall evaluation of themselves: a person who likes

> **Key concept – Self-esteem:** A person's attitude toward themselves. People with high self-esteem feel positively toward themselves in general, like themselves, and feel that they are competent. People with low self-esteem generally have negative attitudes toward themselves, dislike themselves, and believe they are incompetent.

themselves and believes they have value has high self-esteem, while a person who views themselves harshly and thinks negative things about themselves has low self-esteem.

As noted previously, most social psychologists believe that people are motivated to strive for high self-esteem (Deci & Ryan, 2000; Fiske 2008). As with other core motives, our success at attaining self-esteem impacts our emotions, with things that raise our self-esteem, such as receiving positive feedback and praise, eliciting positive emotions, and things that lower our self-esteem, such as social rejection, eliciting negative emotions (Coleman, 1975). Motives for self-esteem also impact our behavior. For example, people are more likely to engage in downward social comparisons after their self-esteem has been threatened by recent negative feedback (Hakmiller, 1966), suggesting that people are doing so to counteract the threat.

Why might we be motivated to have high self-esteem? Social psychologists have proposed two major theories addressing this question, Sociometer Theory and Terror Management Theory.

Sociometer Theory

Sociometer Theory proposes that self-esteem is an indicator of one of our most important motives, namely, our level of belonging (Leary et al., 1995). As discussed in Chapter 3 on affiliation, friendship and love, humans have a fundamental need to belong. It has been proposed that humans are evolved to take advantage of living in group settings by cooperating on basic tasks related to survival and reproduction (Baumeister & Leary, 1995). Some consequences of this need are that we feel bad when we are rejected, and we seek to strengthen our social connections, or initiate new ones, when we do not feel like our belonging needs are met. But how can we check to see if we are sufficiently included? Sociometer Theory proposes that self-esteem is our gauge for our level of inclusion. Much like a fuel meter in a car tells us whether the car needs more fuel, self-esteem functions as the 'sociometer' to tell us when we need to seek more inclusion.

Supporting this idea, self-esteem does seem to be greatly impacted by experiences of exclusion versus inclusion (Leary et al., 1995). In one study, participants came into the lab with four other participants, and were told they'd either be working in a group of three on an assignment (included condition), or they'd work alone (excluded condition). Importantly, half of the participants were told their assignment was made at random by the experimenter, but the other half were told it was based on the decisions of the other participants: if they were included, it was because the other participants had asked to work with them, but if they were excluded, it was because none of the other participants wanted to work with them. When participants reported their self-esteem afterward, those who had been excluded because of the group's choice reported lower self-esteem than those in the other conditions. So at least in many instances, self-esteem does seem to reflect how included (vs excluded) we are, meaning its function could be as our sociometer.

GUEST PERSONAL JOURNEY

Mark Leary

I first became interested in psychology while taking a psychology class in high school, but I didn't settle on social psychology until late in college. I chose social psychology both because I was intrigued that social psychologists conduct controlled experiments on human behavior and because I could see that most problems we face – within ourselves, in our relationships with other people, and in society – are caused by people. Most problems are *people problems*, and the people who cause our problems are often us. Thus, solving these problems requires understanding human social behavior.

In graduate school, I gravitated toward the topic of self-presentation (also called impression management) – the ways in which behavior and emotions are affected by people's concerns about other people's impressions of them. Much of our behavior,

Source: © Mark Leary

both good and bad, is influenced by our desire to be viewed in certain ways by other people. Although we manage our impressions for many reasons, one goal is to get other people to like and accept us, which led me to study the ways that concerns with acceptance and belonging affect human behavior and emotion.

For the first 15 years of my career, I avoided the topic of self-esteem like the plague because no one seemed to have a good grasp on what self-esteem actually does. But after our research consistently found that rejection lowers people's self-esteem, I developed *Sociometer Theory* (discussed in this chapter), which proposed that self-esteem is part of the psychological system that monitors social acceptance and rejection.

More recently, I also became interested in the personal and social problems caused by our tendency to think too much about ourselves and for our self-thoughts to be biased in both positive and negative directions.

Terror Management Theory

Terror Management Theory (TMT) (Solomon et al., 1991) focuses on the uniquely human experience of contemplating one's own mortality. It is believed that humans are the only species that have awareness that they will one day die. If that thought makes you a little uncomfortable, you are not alone! Terror Management Theory argues that death is the ultimate threat to all of our other motives – the limits of our personal control, of our ability to plan for the future, to pursue our personal goals, and to stay connected to people we care about. This is a fairly bleak prospect that can lead us to feel overwhelmed, and incapable of taking any effective action.

However, while we are aware of our mortality, most of us are not constantly paralyzed by thoughts of our own death. How do we manage? One way that Terror Management Theory proposes we cope with the threat of death is by striving for what they call symbolic immortality. There are a variety of ways to do this, but a primary one is to align ourselves with our culture. Although each of us individually will die someday, cultures last much longer, and even retain some level of memory for many people who have passed away. By aligning with their culture, a person can symbolically live on after their death as that culture lives on.

According to TMT, self-esteem is an indicator of whether we are living up to our culture's expectations. People who embody cultural ideals will have high self-esteem, and people who do not embody cultural ideals will have low self-esteem. With this in mind, the reason why TMT proposes we strive for high self-esteem is that having high self-esteem provides reassurance that we will achieve that symbolic immortality mentioned earlier. If I am a good representative of my culture's values (as indicated by my high self-esteem), and my culture persists after my death, then I will symbolically live on with it. Consistent with this claim, participants with low self-esteem react to reminders of their own mortality by aligning themselves more strongly with their country and culture, presumably as a way of bolstering their symbolic immortality. But participants with high self-esteem, who may already feel like they are living up to their culture's standards, are not affected by thinking about their own death (Harmon-Jones et al., 1997).

Which theory is correct? There is supporting evidence to back both theories. However, recently, some carefully conducted studies have been unable to replicate some of the other evidence supporting Terror Management Theory (Klein et al., 2022). While the failed replications were not related to self-esteem, they might reduce confidence about other aspects of the theory, including its claims about self-esteem motives. We encourage you to explore this scientific debate for yourself, and consider which theory you think has the strongest supporting evidence.

2.4.4 Self-enhancement

> **Key concept – Self-enhancement:** The general tendency for people to perceive themselves in positive and often self-flattering ways.

Regardless of which theory a psychologist believes, all agree that high self-esteem generally feels good and low self-esteem generally feels bad. Because of this, we are often motivated to think about ourselves in self-flattering ways. We call this our tendency for **self-enhancement**, and it can be expressed in a variety of ways. Suppose you receive a poor exam grade in one of your courses. Failing at something feels bad and can threaten our perception of ourselves as a competent, capable person. How can you cope with this threat? As discussed earlier, you might engage in downward social comparison, by finding someone who did worse than you on the exam and thinking 'At least I did better than them!'

Alternatively, you might engage in self-serving attributions. Attributions refer to our explanations for what caused a particular outcome. We typically differentiate internal attributions, in which the cause is attributed to something inside of us, like our ability or personality, from external attributions, in which the cause is attributed to something outside us, like the situation we are in. Self-serving attributions describe a pattern in which we tend to make internal attributions for our successes, and external attributions for our failures (Miller & Ross, 1975). So thinking back to that poor exam grade, you might attribute the failure to the exam being unreasonably hard, or to the fact that your roommate distracted you from studying beforehand – both external attributions – rather than to a lack of skill on your part – a potentially painful internal attribution.

These kinds of self-serving attributions are pervasive, impacting how athletes explain the outcomes of games, how employees explain experiences at work, and how drivers perceive car accidents versus near-misses (Shepperd et al., 2008). People tend to make self-serving attributions even when they think they are undergoing a lie detector test, suggesting that they really believe them to be true (Riess et al., 1981). Even psychotherapists tend to make self-serving attributions when a patient terminates treatment, thereby avoiding the possibility that they hadn't done a good job of treating the patient (Murdock et al., 2010). So when you blame your bad grades on an unfair test, but believe your good grades are due to your natural intelligence, you are not alone!

We don't always avoid responsibility for our failures, though. For example, I (Aly) make no excuses for failing at sports questions during pub trivia. I won't claim the questions are unnecessarily obscure, or that the announcer didn't read them loud enough – I just don't know the answers. What makes this failure roll off my back where other failures might sting is that the domain of athletics and sports trivia is not one that I personally value. Indeed, the more we value a domain or consider it central to our identity, the more we tend to self-enhance in that domain (Gebauer et al., 2013). This even applies to values related to humility, charity, and having a 'small' sense of self. For example, Christians exaggerated their knowledge of the Bible (Gebauer et al., 2017), and meditators boasted about their superior mindfulness (Gebauer et al., 2018) to the extent that those domains were central to their sense of self. The converse of this is that we can escape the pain of failure by *disengaging* from a domain when we perform poorly in that domain (Leitner et al., 2014) – that is, reduce the extent to which we value or determine our self-worth by performance in that domain.

And if we are especially concerned about failure, we may engage in self-handicapping. When people self-handicap, they take actions that create or amplify possible external attributions for their outcomes, thereby setting up excuses that can be made for potential failure (Berglas & Jones, 1978). For example, a student could knowingly under-prepare for an exam, and stay out late with friends the night beforehand. If the student receives a poor mark, they can easily attribute the failure not to their lack of intelligence, but to the fact that they didn't really try. In other words, people sometimes self-sabotage as a means of protecting their self-esteem. Interestingly, the same barriers that can be used to excuse failure can also be capitalized on for self-enhancement following success. If that same student receives a good mark on the exam they didn't prepare for, they can say 'And I did it without even trying – I must be a genius!'

People are especially likely to self-handicap when they feel uncertain about their self-esteem or level of performance (Harris & Snyder, 1986). In one classic study by Berglas and Jones (1978), participants in one condition were made to feel uncertain about their competence by having them work on unsolvable problems, only to give them unexpectedly positive feedback. Participants in the other condition received feedback consistent with their actual performance. Participants were then told that they could choose to take one of two drugs that would impact cognitive performance – either a drug that enhanced cognitive performance, or a drug that undermined cognitive performance – before completing another set of problems. Nearly 59% of participants chose the drug that would undermine their performance in the uncertain condition, while only about 18% chose it in the certain condition.

Many students engage in self-handicapping by avoiding studying, not prioritizing good sleep, procrastinating, and using drugs and alcohol, which in turn leads to poorer academic performance (Schwinger et al., 2014). If you're among them, one way to reduce the motivation to self-handicap is to reframe academic performance as something that reflects your current mastery of material right now, rather than as a reflection of your stable intrinsic abilities (Schwinger & Stiensmeier-Pelster, 2011).

> **Video:** Do You Do More Housework Than Your Roommates? www.youtube.com/watch?v=MTWXHu9jO78

EXERCISE 2.2

Applying Theory to Your Own Life

Reality shows and other trashy TV can be great places to see self-enhancement in action! Why not indulge in a guilty pleasure while practicing identifying different strategies people use to flatter themselves? Watch a reality show of your choice – preferably one in which people participate and are judged on some kind of challenge. See if you can see examples of:

a   Downward social comparisons
b   Self-serving attributions
c   Disidentification/disengagement
d   Self-handicapping

Do you observe any other self-enhancing behaviors that don't fall into these categories?

2.4.5 The Better-Than-Average Effect

So far, you have learned about how people are motivated to both feel better about themselves and compare themselves to others. As noted earlier in this chapter, downward social comparisons (i.e., comparing oneself to somebody who is perceived as inferior or worse-off in some domain) can help people to self-enhance and maintain their view that they are overall good, worthy individuals. One way that people use social comparisons as self-enhancement tools is through the **better-than-average effect** (BTAE). The BTAE is exactly what it sounds like: it refers to people's tendencies to rate themselves as above-average compared to their peers.

In an initial investigation of the BTAE, Alicke (1985) had college student participants rate how characteristic each of over 150 traits was of (1) themselves, and (2)

> **Key concept – Better-than-average effect:** The pervasive tendency for people to rate themselves as possessing desirable traits (e.g., friendly, intelligent) to a greater extent, and undesirable traits (e.g., rude, lazy) to a lesser extent, than the average person.

'the average college student.' The traits varied in terms of whether they were desirable (e.g., cooperative, intelligent) or undesirable (e.g., hostile, lazy). The results indicated that participants consistently rated the desirable traits as more characteristic of themselves than the average college student. By contrast, they consistently rated the undesirable traits as more characteristic of the average college student than themselves.

The BTAE has been offered as an explanation for many somewhat humorous phenomena. To cite just a few examples, 94% of university professors in one study rated themselves as having above-average teaching abilities (Cross, 1977), 77% of Swedish and 88% of American college-aged drivers in a different study rated their driver safety as above-average (Svenson, 1981), and 85% of US students who took the Scholastic Aptitude Test (SAT) in 1976 reported that they were above average in their ability to get along well with others (College Board, 1976–1977).

Are there any situations in which we do *not* claim to be better than average, or at least claim to be above average to a lesser extent than we normally would? After all, self-enhancement isn't the only self-related motive that people might possess. Not only do individuals want to feel positively about themselves, but they also strive to be accurate in how they evaluate their traits, characteristics, and abilities. A case in point: I (Kim) have never been able to draw much more than stick figures, but before my third year of high school, I briefly contemplated enrolling in Advanced Placement Art because several of my friends – who had won local drawing contests and had assembled elaborate portfolios of their work – planned to take the class. Upon raising this possibility with my mother (who erroneously sees me as above-average on just about everything), she responded 'AP Art? Really, Kim?' Instead of insisting that I had the artistic prowess to succeed in the course, I was grateful for the reality check. At least in the domain of art, both my mother and I saw myself in terms of my actual (limited!) abilities.

Why, though, was I not particularly inclined to perceive myself as more artistically talented than my peers? According to research on the BTAE, there are at least two possibilities. First, people are less likely to claim they are above average when they have objective indicators of how they stack up in comparison to others. Participants in one study (Allison et al., 1989), all college students, rated themselves as above average on social and moral traits (e.g., friendly, honest) to a greater extent than they did on intelligence. Presumably, this was because, in everyday life, they had encountered fewer clear signals of whether they were more friendly or honest, relative to signals of whether or not they might be smarter, than their peers. In my case, I had plenty of indicators of my probable artistic skills by observing my friends' artistic abilities; put simply, they had won art contests and I hadn't.

Second, people are less likely to claim they are above average when comparing themselves to particular individuals, especially those they have more information about or with whom they have had direct contact. On the other hand, it is relatively easy for us to view ourselves as better than 'the average person' because our conception of such a person is so abstract and thus open to interpretation (Alicke et al., 1995). Going back to the art example, I wasn't judging my artistic abilities in relation to the average high-school student; my standards of comparison were specific peers (in fact, friends whom I knew very well). As a result, I would have had a more difficult time convincing myself that I could outperform these peers in an advanced art class.

Despite the limitations of the BTAE, it is a highly robust psychological phenomenon. An analysis of 124 published articles on the BTAE, with over 950,000 participants in total, found that the BTAE held across studies and populations (Zell et al., 2020). What's more, researchers recently replicated Alicke's (1985) classic BTAE study (reviewed above) in two pre-registrations, studies in which the methods, expected results, and planned analyses are documented ahead of time to increase transparency and minimize the chances that the authors' own biases will impact their analyses and reporting of the findings (Ziano, Mok, & Feldman, 2020). But a particularly remarkable demonstration of the BTAE was conducted with a population whose members we might least expect to rate themselves as above average: prisoners.

KEY STUDY 2.2

The BTAE Among Prisoners

Although the better-than-average effect provides valuable information about people's tendencies to perceive themselves as superior to peers on a variety of dimensions, it is by nature subjective. In other words, it can't speak to whether people's ratings of themselves are objectively accurate. However, one study suggestive of the idea that people *inappropriately* consider themselves above average was conducted by Sedikides and colleagues (2014) on a sample of incarcerated individuals in the south of England.

All participants were convicted offenders, mostly for crimes involving violence against people and robbery. Participants indicated where they felt they stood relative to both the average prisoner and the average member of the community on several morally relevant traits (e.g., kind, honest, generous), as well as on law-abidingness, using scales with *I am much less than ...* and *I am much more than ...* as endpoints. As in Alicke's (1985) original study, the order in which participants compared themselves to the average prisoner versus the average community member was randomized.

The researchers reasoned that prisoners are, by nature, less law-abiding than the general population and are probably also lower on morality-related traits. Thus, how prisoners compare themselves to community members on these dimensions should be particularly telling. Consistent with the BTAE, participants rated themselves as higher on every morally relevant characteristic than both the average prisoner and the average community member. And perhaps most strikingly, the prisoners rated themselves as equally law-abiding compared to the average community member, despite strong evidence to the contrary (their being incarcerated for breaking the law)! Overall, these findings indicate that even when people have received clear feedback that they are *not* superior to others, they can still fall prey to the BTAE.

> **Video:** Criminals Think They're Better Than You www.youtube.com/watch?v=8JjVwsmpObM

KEY THINKER

Mark Alicke

Mark Alicke (1955–2020) became renowned in social psychology for his research on self-enhancement and social comparison. Even outside professional settings, his fascination with these topics was apparent. He enjoyed reading and quoting 19th-century philosophy in his spare time (to each their own!), and he never ceased to tie philosophical concepts back to notions of the self and how people find meaning in their lives. A few months before he unexpectedly passed away, he emailed me (Kim), asking about my 'five greatest hits' – that is, the five life events I would relive if given the opportunity. Upon sharing his biggest moments, he (among the humblest individuals I've ever known) was somewhat chagrined to realize that a good number of them involved personal achievements and comparisons with others. I smile to myself as I write this, thinking that in his case, the mantra 'We are what we study' could not have been more applicable.

In addition to self-enhancement, we will learn about self- and social identity complexity throughout this chapter. There is perhaps no better epitome of these concepts than Dr Alicke, who juggled many seemingly contradictory identities with ease. Despite being raised in one of the largest metropolitan areas in the US (New York–Newark–Jersey City), he fully embraced life in rural southeastern Ohio. He was an outspoken atheist, but his Jewish cultural heritage rendered him willing to discuss all things religion with friends and colleagues. He could, amazingly, make color-coordinated tracksuits – which he regularly

(Continued)

wore to the office and to his 500-person lecture classes – look fashionable and even fancy. Although he is no longer with us, Dr Alicke's work will continue to influence the field for years to come. Now that you have read a bit about him personally, you might come away with a newfound appreciation of how a person's own idiosyncrasies can impact their chosen career path.

2.4.6 Self-Uncertainty and Self-Concept Clarity

I (Aly) have been known to contradict myself, and one of my most glaring contradictions is this: when arguing in support of self-report measures (see Chapter 1), I often make the point that people can be 'their own best experts.' You presumably have access to more information about yourself than anyone else. But as we've seen, the self isn't a straightforward, easily understood object. It is not a table, with dimensions that stay the same every time it's measured. It changes depending on the situation, depending on the people we're interacting with, which goals we're currently pursuing. So it's normal for people to have difficulty taking the measure of who they are, given that, as we've discussed, the self-concept has so many varied dimensions, and also changes over time. In other words, self-uncertainty is pretty normal and widespread.

> **Key concept – Self-concept clarity:** A person's subjective sense that they know themselves well. They feel certain and clear about their self-concept, and perceiving the self-concept as being consistent both over time and across situations.

In fact, feelings of uncertainty about the self are an area of study themselves. People can experience momentary or state self-uncertainty, but people also differ in the extent to which they feel like they know themselves in general. This is captured by the variable **self-concept clarity**, which assesses how clear people feel their self-concepts are, how consistent the content is, and how stable they are over time and across situations. As you might expect, self-concept clarity is lower during adolescence and emerging adulthood than it is during middle age, but you might be surprised to learn that self-uncertainty increases again for many people with advancing age (Lodi-Smith & Roberts, 2010).

While the reasons are not fully known, these findings may be partly explained by social role transitions over the lifespan. Social roles, such as being a student, a parent, a worker, or a book club member, provide information about who we are by structuring our activities and facilitating relationships with other people. For that reason, exiting social roles tends to predict lower self-concept clarity compared to entering social roles (Light & Visser, 2013). Given that aging brings with it many role exits that are not counteracted by role entries (e.g., retirement, bereavement, etc.), and that physical aging can reduce people's ability to take part in regular activities (Lodi-Smith & Roberts, 2010), self-concept clarity may decline with age because older adults have fewer and less structured social roles in which to engage.

While self-uncertainty seems to be fairly common, people often find self-uncertainty uncomfortable or aversive (Morrison et al., 2012), and as a result, are motivated to reduce that uncertainty. There are a variety of ways that people can increase their certainty about themselves; for example, by turning to friends who can bolster their confidence (Slotter & Gardner, 2014), or by focusing on concrete reminders of their identity, such as personal fashion and other possessions (Morrison & Johnson, 2011). But as we will discuss later, a key way that people address self-uncertainty is by turning to our social identities as sources of clarity.

Many studies show that low self-concept clarity is associated with more stress, less happiness, and more symptoms of depression. Low self-esteem and lower psychological well-being are some of the closest correlates of low self-concept clarity (see Light, 2017, for a review). Why might this be the case? There are multiple theories connecting self-concept clarity to well-being. One explanation is that having clear, consistent self-knowledge is valued by some cultures, and so in order to live up to such cultural standards, it is important to have high self-concept clarity. This is supported by evidence that people from interdependent cultures, in which people are expected to shift their identity fluidly to accommodate social roles and social situations (see Chapters 8 and 10), do not suffer poorer well-being as much when their self-concepts are uncertain or ambivalent (Spencer-Rodgers et al., 2009).

Another possibility is that having high self-concept clarity makes people less vulnerable to threats to their self-worth by decreasing the extent to which such threats impact the self-concept. Imagine that an acquaintance calls you unreliable for arriving a few minutes late to a meeting. If you are certain that you generally arrive punctually, and this is a one-off occurrence, you may feel frustrated that this person has judged you inaccurately, but you're unlikely to start thinking of yourself as an unreliable person. Conversely, generally feeling uncertain or unclear about oneself can increase the extent to which people accept and internalize feedback from others, including negative feedback, which can undermine well-being (Lee-Flynn et al., 2011). A third possibility is that feeling certain about who we are helps us to effectively make decisions (Schlegel et al., 2013) and pursue our goals (Light, 2017), which in turn enables us to earn higher self-esteem, reduce stress related to poor goal attainment, and better maintain important relationships.

Regardless of which perspective is correct (and indeed, all may operate simultaneously), research on self-concept clarity helps to explain why questions about who we are feel so important and impactful in our daily lives. When as a teenager I (Aly) was trying to resolve the question of how 'girly' I was, this was part of a broader pattern of human behavior in which we strive for self-knowledge and clarity about who we are.

2.4.7 Self-Affirmation

From time to time, we are confronted with information that calls our sense of self into question. I (Kim) might consider myself a great cook but then completely forget to add flour to a cake recipe (yep, this actually happened to me). You might generally think of yourself as a giving person but decline to round up to the nearest pound/euro/dollar when the grocery store

> **Key concept – Self-affirmation:** A process by which people affirm a valued part of their self-concept, such as by reflecting on an important personal value (e.g., social relationships, aesthetics/art, science). People who have been self-affirmed subsequently exhibit less defensiveness in response to self-threats.

cashier asks if you'd like to do so in support of your local food bank. In both these situations, we would likely wonder whether we really are the type of person we claim to be, or whether we really are as skilled in a particular area as we think. How do we cope with these threats to the self? One possible answer lies in self-affirmation theory.

According to **self-affirmation** theory, people can restore their self-image in the face of threat by affirming their value, worth, or integrity in a different domain that is unrelated to the threat (Steele, 1988). As a personal example, math was my (Kim's) favorite subject in high school, and I was devastated when I failed a particularly difficult calculus exam. That evening, I lamented to my mother through tears that perhaps I wasn't cut out for a career that required strong quantitative skills after all. Her response (very different from when I considered taking that advanced art course) was 'I would rather you get a mediocre grade in calculus and be as kind as you are, than get straight As but be a mean person.' Although in this case it was my mother who had affirmed my character, her comment made it far easier for me to accept my exam grade and to remind myself of my worth in other areas. In essence, I could reason that I may not have done as well on the exam as I would have liked, but at least my character was intact ... and in the grand scheme of things, *that* was what mattered most.

Self-affirmation theory has been supported in numerous studies since its inception in the 1980s. In one of the first tests of the theory (Steele & Liu, 1983), college student participants were given the opportunity to help the researchers by freely choosing to write an essay in support of tuition increases at their university. Given that many if not most college students oppose tuition increases, agreeing to write a pro-increase essay – especially when they are not forced to do so – is likely to induce a sense of psychological discomfort referred to as cognitive dissonance. (You will learn more about cognitive dissonance theory in Chapter 6) In other words, they may wonder, 'Why did I agree to write this essay when I am against tuition hikes? What kind of person does this make me?'

Importantly, after writing the essay, participants also completed a survey about the importance of a particular value (i.e., aesthetics/artistic orientation) to their self-concept. Among participants who saw aesthetics as central to their sense of self, the survey enabled them to self-affirm in an area unrelated to the threat. Thus, these participants did not feel a need to change their attitudes to be more consistent with the essay they had just written (i.e., more positive toward tuition increases). By contrast, participants who saw aesthetics as unimportant to their sense of self had no opportunity to self-affirm and reported feeling more positively about tuition increases after writing the essay, so as to align their attitudes with their behavior.

One of the most common ways to get participants to self-affirm is by having them select their most important value from a list (e.g., social relationships, aesthetics, business/economics) and write about why that value is important to them personally. A control group of participants will instead select their least important value from the same list and write about why that value might be important to somebody else. Such a method uses true random assignment to either the self-affirmation or control group, rather than grouping participants according to whether or not they espouse a particular value in the first place (as in Steele & Liu, 1983).

Experiments conducted with this manipulation have revealed that self-affirmation reduces people's defensiveness to potentially threatening information about their health (e.g., it makes female coffee drinkers less likely to dismiss an article linking caffeine consumption to breast cancer; Sherman et al., 2000), increases people's openness to political views that do not conform to those of their party (Binning et al., 2010), and reduces people's expressions of prejudice against stigmatized group members (Fein & Spencer, 1997; Hoorens, Dekkers, & Deschrijver, 2021). Self-affirmation can even have long-term effects on achievement and feelings of belonging among students from marginalized backgrounds, including women in STEM (science, technology, engineering, and mathematics) (Walton et al., 2015), racial/ethnic minorities (Goyer et al., 2017), and those whose families are low in socioeconomic status (Hadden et al., 2020). Key study 2.3 highlights how self-affirmation can impact minority secondary school students' educational outcomes several years later.

KEY STUDY 2.3

Self-Affirmation and Academic Achievement Over Time

Recent studies have demonstrated that the effects of self-affirmation can persist over time. In one such study (Goyer et al., 2017), African American and White American middle school students (ages 12–14) completed a 15-minute writing exercise three to five times throughout the academic year. Specifically, they were randomly assigned to write about a personally important value or a topic unrelated to their personal values (i.e., a value that was unimportant to them but might be important to others, their daily routine). The researchers tracked these students until they graduated high school, at which point they assessed (1) whether or not each student enrolled in university, and (2) for those who enrolled in a four-year university, how selective the university was (as indicated by admitting a low percentage of applicants).

Strikingly, 92% of self-affirmed African American students (i.e., who had written about a personally important value) enrolled in university, compared to 78% of African American students who had not written about a self-affirming topic. There was no difference in likelihood of university enrollment among White American students who had and had not self-affirmed (80% versus 86%). Further, self-affirmed African American (but not White American) students attended more selective four-year universities than did their unaffirmed counterparts. These results demonstrate not only that a brief self-affirmation writing task can impact students' educational choices four to five years later, but also that with appropriate interventions, students from stigmatized backgrounds are just as capable as their more advantaged peers of gaining admission to university.

2.4.8 Social Identity

Given the key study on self-affirmation and group membership, you might wonder where we can draw the line between our self-concepts and the groups to which we belong. That is, when and why do our social identities (i.e., group memberships, connections with others) become integrated into our personal identities (i.e., sense of self as unique individuals)? As social identity theory and the later theoretical perspectives that it inspired have demonstrated, the boundary between self and group is not always clear-cut. You will learn more about these theories in Chapters 8 and 10.

One function of social identities is to reduce uncertainty about the world around us, especially uncertainty pertaining to ourselves. Indeed, our lives are fraught with many sources of uncertainty. People might, for instance, be unsure about what they want to pursue as a long-term career, whether they should stay in their current relationship, or whether they are a 'girly girl' or not (as in the example from one of our personal journeys). Such uncertainty can be uncomfortable.

As we learned earlier in this chapter, self-concept clarity – or having a clear, consistent, and coherent sense of self – is associated with positive psychological outcomes, including greater well-being (Ritchie et al., 2011) and fewer depressive symptoms (Bigler et al., 2001). Thus, when our sense of clarity or certainty with respect to the self is shaken, we seek to resolve the uncertainty. According to uncertainty-identity theory (Hogg, 2007), one way of resolving self-uncertainty is through identifying with groups. In doing so, we can effectively say to ourselves, 'I don't know everything about who I am or what path my life will take, but at least I know I am part of a meaningful group.'

But what makes a group 'meaningful'? Uncertainty-identity theory posits that people are most likely to turn to groups with clearly defined characteristics when they feel uncertain about themselves. In an initial test of this idea (Hogg et al., 2007), participants in a laboratory experiment were told that they would complete a group task with several other people in their session. Participants received one of two types of bogus information, allegedly based on a battery of personality assessments everyone had taken: that the members of their group were very similar to one another and the group task would be clearly structured, or that the members of their group were very different from one another and the group task would not have a clear structure. Next, they were assigned to write about three aspects of themselves, their lives, and their futures that made them feel either uncertain or certain about themselves. Finally, they completed a measure of identification with their group – that is, how attached they felt to the group and how important the group was to their sense of self. Participants who had written about self-uncertainty and whose group supposedly had clearly defined properties (e.g., similarity among members, structure) demonstrated the highest levels of group identification, suggesting that affiliating with meaningful groups can in fact help people to resolve their personal uncertainties (Hogg et al., 2007).

Indeed, groups have many important functions, including resolving uncertainty about the self. That said, losing oneself in one's group memberships isn't necessarily a good thing for the self-concept. Even though we are fundamentally social beings and strive to affiliate with others, we are also motivated to develop and maintain a unique sense of self.

These competing needs for similarity and distinctiveness, and how we resolve them, are the focus of Optimal Distinctiveness Theory (Brewer, 1991; Leonardelli et al., 2010). If you remember reading the story of 'Goldilocks and the Three Bears', the core idea behind the theory is a lot like that story. Much like Goldilocks tried out different parts of the bears' house (e.g., the beds, the chairs, the porridge) to see what felt 'just right' to her, Optimal Distinctiveness Theory argues that we want to feel neither too similar to nor too different from other people.

As a result, we look for groups that feel 'just right' to us in terms of their ability to satisfy both motives. When we feel overly similar to others (e.g., in a long line to renew our vehicle registration), we may gravitate toward groups or situations that enable us to stand out. Conversely, when we feel overly distinct from others (e.g., being the only woman in a large group of men, or vice versa), we may gravitate toward groups or situations that enable us to blend in. These motives can shift according to the context; it is unlikely that we will always feel too similar (or too different) from our peers. We thus may be motivated to join either large or small groups, groups that are considered either 'mainstream' or 'non-mainstream,' and groups that make up either the numerical

> **Video:** Identity Politics –
> How All Your Identities Sway Your
> Vote www.youtube.com/watch?
> v=78RhBJAEAtk

majority or a numerical minority in society, depending on whether our need for uniqueness or similarity is most pressing at the moment (Hornsey & Jetten, 2004). We revisit Optimal Distinctiveness Theory in the Advances and Applications sections later in this chapter.

2.5 PART 2: ADVANCES

In this section, we introduce cutting-edge research that builds upon and extends foundational perspectives on the self-concept and self-esteem.

2.5.1 Contingencies of Self-Worth

As we noted earlier when discussing self-enhancement, not all failures impact self-esteem equally – it depends on how much we value the domain in question. The domains that are important to us, on which we 'stake' our self-esteem, are called our **contingencies of self-worth** (Crocker & Wolfe, 2001). The term points to the fact that our self-esteem is thought to be 'contingent on' or to depend on success or positive feedback in domains that we personally value. These contingencies differ from person to person, and help to determine how much a given experience impacts our self-esteem. For example, people differ a great deal in the extent to which their self-esteem is contingent on physical attractiveness. For someone whose self-esteem is contingent on attractiveness, a bad hair day outbreak might make them feel terrible about themselves. For someone for whom this is not a contingency, these same experiences will have less of an impact on their global self-esteem.

> **Key concept – Contingencies of self-worth:** Valued domains that a person draws on to assess their personal worth or esteem. These vary from person to person. Self-esteem is said to be contingent on these, in that having high self-esteem is contingent on evaluating oneself positively in the domains that are personal contingencies of self-worth.

While we may differ on what our self-esteem is contingent on, we all have such contingencies. Our particular contingencies of self-worth are relatively stable over time, and are thought to reflect our personal life experiences, including what we have been rewarded versus punished for, where we have found comfort, success, and support, and the values we have internalized from our families, cultures, social environments, and social roles. For example, one study found that students increasingly based their self-worth on academic performance over their years at university (Hallsten et al., 2012). This may be because being a student means that people are reinforced for good academic performance (and punished for bad performance!). In addition, fellow students, professors, and other members of the university community may communicate that academic performance is valuable. Thus, the longer a student is in this environment, the more they are likely to internalize these values, and perceive their value as being contingent on academic performance.

Your personal contingencies can include just about anything, but some common ones that psychologists have explored include general social approval, physical appearance, competence/academic success, family support, competition (i.e., outperforming other people), virtue (i.e., living up to your moral standards), and having a relationship with (or love from) a god or gods (for people who are religious).

Contingencies can differ in terms of how easily one succeeds at 'earning' self-worth in that domain versus how often one might experience threats and setbacks to self-esteem from that contingency. For example, consider self-esteem that is contingent on others' approval. In my (Aly's) life, the people I encounter give me approval for different and sometimes contradictory things. My fellow professors care about the rigor of my courses, and want me to demonstrate that my students are held accountable for learning the material. Thus, they will give me approval if I cover more topics in my course, and uphold stringent standards in my grading/marking. My students, by contrast, are generally more approving when I reduce the amount of material they need to learn, and grade more leniently. Thus, no matter how I teach, some important people will approve, and some important people will disapprove! If my self-esteem is contingent on everyone's approval, then I'd necessarily suffer some loss to self-esteem with whatever teaching decisions I make. Perhaps because of situations like this, people whose self-esteem is more contingent on others' approval generally have lower self-esteem (Cambron et al., 2010; Crocker & Wolfe, 2001).

To better clarify which contingencies are associated with higher self-esteem, psychologists often sort these contingencies into external and internal sources of self-esteem. Internal sources of self-esteem are largely within our personal control, and include domains like virtue/personal moral standards, and relationship to a god or gods. External sources of self-esteem, by contrast, depend heavily on things outside our control. These include approval from others, physical appearance, and competition. You may be surprised to hear that academic performance is considered an external contingency. While a student's abilities and actions certainly impact their performance, academic performance can also be influenced by many external factors, like stringency of grading standards, the quality of the instructors, and other demands on students' time. Consistent with the idea that relying on external/uncontrollable sources of self-worth makes it more difficult to achieve high self-esteem, basing one's self-worth on external sources predicts poorer well-being, while internal sources of self-worth are unrelated to well-being, or predictive of higher well-being (Crocker et al., 2008).

The consequences associated with academic self-worth contingencies may be of particular interest. As a student, it may seem natural for your self-esteem to rise and fall based on your school performance. It may even seem adaptive to be so personally invested in academic success – after all, wouldn't that motivate an individual to work harder? Indeed, there is some evidence that academically contingent self-worth impacts motivation. For example, high school students who base their self-worth on academics go on to spend more time studying during their first semester of college (Crocker et al., 2003). But tying self-worth too strongly to one's grades seems to have many negative consequences. As noted previously, academics are an external source of self-worth, and as with other external sources, academically contingent self-worth predicts higher levels of depression (Burwell & Shirk, 2006).

Even more concerning, people who base their self-worth on academic performance are especially prone to 'choking' and underperforming on tests that are described as diagnostic of academic ability (Lawrence & Williams, 2013). This appears to be caused by increased anxiety. If failing a test means experiencing a major drop in self-esteem, it makes sense that taking the test would evoke a lot of anxiety, which in turn can impair cognitive functioning, resulting in poorer performance. Thus overall, while valuing academics and striving for high performance certainly promote academic success (Richardson et al., 2012), it seems advisable to feel like your self-worth is not tied to your grades.

KEY THINKER

Jennifer Crocker

Jennifer Crocker (1952–) is an American social psychologist. She grew up in Plymouth, Massachusetts, where she graduated from high school first in her class and was voted 'most likely to succeed.' She attended Reed College in Portland, Oregon, as a math major for a year before dropping out to work at a Vermont ski area, then transferred to Michigan State University where she majored in psychology and received a Bachelor of Science degree in 1975. She received her PhD in Psychology and Social Relations from Harvard

Source: © Jennifer Crocker

(Continued)

University in 1979, with Shelley Taylor as her major advisor. She held faculty positions at Northwestern University, the State University of New York at Buffalo, the University of Michigan, and the Ohio State University, where she is now Emerita Professor of Psychology. Crocker's research has explored the self and self-esteem, stereotyping and stigma, social motivation, and close relationships. She has authored more than 200 articles and chapters. Crocker served in many leadership roles in professional societies and received numerous honors and awards for her research and service. She currently resides in Portland, Oregon, in the US.

2.5.2 The Working Self-Concept and Multiple Self-Aspects Framework

At this point, you might have noticed that a lot of situational factors impact how we view ourselves. One implication of this is that the self-concept isn't a fixed, stable, singular thing. In order for it to shift in response to our social environment, it must be something that changes with the situations in which we find ourselves.

Many psychologists think about this through the lens of the **working self-concept**. This idea draws on the concept of working memory – that is, information that we temporarily hold in conscious awareness. Similar to working memory, the working self-concept describes how you view yourself in a given moment. Just as working memory has a smaller capacity than long-term memory, the working self-concept includes only a small subset of information about the self. For example, you certainly know what your hometown is, and can include that information in an autobiographical statement. But you likely aren't always thinking of that information when you think about yourself, meaning that it is not always part of your working self-concept.

> **Key concept – Working self-concept:** How one currently identifies/perceives oneself in a given moment. This is thought to be a subset of the self-concept, reflecting traits, values, goals, and identities that are relevant to the current social situation, but not those that are irrelevant or in conflict with the demands of the current situation.

To some extent, the working self-concept is idiosyncratic. Since every experience is somewhat unique, each experience will have a unique influence on exactly what information about ourselves is called to mind. However, most of us encounter certain kinds of situations repeatedly in our lives, which may habitually activate certain pieces of self-knowledge in that context. For example, *attending class* may lead you to think about your academic interests, your career goals, your intelligence, your study skills, and your extraversion as it impacts your comfort speaking up in class discussions. Borrowing another principle from cognitive psychology, repeatedly activating these pieces of information together may build linked associations between them, so that they come to form a *self-aspect* – in this case, we might label it as your student self-aspect.

You likely have many self-aspects reflecting different situations that you regularly encounter in your life, with each self-aspect becoming active when you are currently in or when you think about that context. One implication of this is that being in situations associated with a given self-aspect will cause that self-aspect to become 'active' – that is, we will automatically view ourselves in line with the self-aspect associated with that situation. But sometimes self-aspects will be activated by more subtle cues – for example, thinking about that situation, or being exposed to subtle reminders of it.

One interesting application of this is to the concept of transference. In the context of psychotherapy, transference refers to a client using a schema about a significant other (e.g., a romantic partner, or a parent) as a way to understand the relationship to the therapist. They may feel emotions toward the therapist that are evoked by the significant other, or speak in therapy as they would toward the significant other. But transference is actually something that happens in everyday life, outside therapy – we develop schemas about important people in our lives, and sometimes we 'transfer' these schemas to people who remind us of them. Interestingly, this kind of transference doesn't just affect how we view the person in question, it also impacts how we view ourselves when we are around them. Because we typically have developed a self-aspect that describes how we see ourselves around a significant other, meeting a new person who reminds us of that significant other can activate that relational self-aspect, leading us to view ourselves as (and possibly act like) we do when we are around the significant other (Hinkley & Andersen, 1996).

KEY STUDY 2.4

Transference and Relational Self-Aspects

Have you ever had the uncanny experience of meeting someone who resembles your best friend, or a family member? Did you find yourself automatically liking this person, and feeling strangely comfortable around them? You may have experienced transference, in which the perceptions and self-aspects associated with a significant other are transferred to a stranger who is similar to them! Michael W. Kraus and Serena Chen (2010) explored this phenomenon by having a group of college students think about someone they knew and liked well, and who was important to them – in other words, a 'significant other'. Participants then answered questions about what they were like when they were around this person. Finally, they viewed hundreds of pictures of different faces, and rated how much those faces resembled their significant other.

Two weeks later – presumably after they'd forgotten what all those faces they'd viewed looked like – participants came to the lab for a follow-up lab session. They were told that they had been paired with another student and would interact with them later in the lab session. But before doing that, they were shown a picture of the person they had supposedly been paired with. For participants in the 'own' condition, the picture of their new partner happened

(Continued)

to be the picture that two weeks prior they had rated as most closely resembling their significant other. For participants in the 'yoked' condition, the picture was of the face that another participant had rated as most resembling their significant other, but not one that resembled their own significant other. In other words, for half of participants the picture resembled their significant other, and for half of participants it did not.

After viewing the picture and answering questions about what they anticipated it would be like to work with them, participants rated how they saw themselves *at that moment* using the same personality inventory they had used two weeks prior. Kraus and Chen then calculated how similar those self-ratings were to the relational self-aspect the participants had described two weeks earlier. Sure enough, participants in the 'own' condition, whose partner resembled their significant other, described themselves in that moment as being more similar to the relational self-aspect associated with the significant other than did participants in the 'yoked' control condition. The researchers reasoned that the partner merely physically resembling their significant other activated the relational self-aspect associated with the significant other, changing their working self-concept.

GUEST PERSONAL JOURNEY

Serena Chen

Source: © Serena Chen

My personal journey to becoming a social psychologist began with US History. I had a hugely influential high school history teacher who pushed me to think more deeply than I had ever been asked to think before. His class made me decide to major in US History when I entered Cornell as a first-year undergraduate. But taking Introductory Psychology alongside my history courses, I quickly discovered that it wasn't history *per se* that I loved, but rather thinking analytically about any topic that I found intriguing. And the topics that most gripped my attention had to do with people, who they are, what drives them, who they form bonds with, how these bonds shape them, and so forth – topics that were the focus of my social psychology course at Cornell, co-taught by Professors Tom Gilovich and Dennis Regan. By my latter years at Cornell, Professor Gilovich, Tom, would become a research mentor and then honors thesis advisor. Fast forward 20 years, and I would be invited to join Tom and two other co-authors (Dick Nisbett and Dacher Keltner) as a co-author on a social psychology textbook, now in its fifth edition.

I went to graduate school at NYU and was blessed to work with multiple faculty mentors there, but chief among them were Shelly Chaiken and Susan Andersen. Both of them, in their own unique ways, had an enormous impact on who I am today as a scientist, teacher, and mentor. Though I grew up on the East Coast, I eventually made my way to UC Berkeley, where I've been now for almost 23 years. And true to what social psychology is all about, it is my relationships with mentors, colleagues, and now over two decades' worth of graduate and undergraduate students who have largely defined my journey – what topics I've chosen to work on, how I teach and relate to students, what I have learned about the field, the profession, and myself along the way. I wouldn't have had it any other way.

Thinking of the self-concept as made up of multiple self-aspects raises the question, how do we create unity out of this multiplicity? Are people really completely different across all domains of their lives? Or are there commonalities across their self-aspects? Research describing the structure of people's self-concepts has noted that people vary both in the number of distinct self-aspects they have, and the similarity between self-aspects. These two variables in combination are known as self-complexity (Linville, 1985). People high in self-complexity have many self-aspects that are very distinct from each other, while people low in self-complexity have fewer self-aspects with more overlap in content. Importantly, differences in how self-aspects are structured – whether they overlap or are distinct from one another – can impact how intense positive and negative events feel, by impacting how much of the self-concept as a whole is threatened.

We like to use the analogy of the ship *Titanic*, which was made with many separated, watertight compartments. These compartments were what supposedly made the *Titanic* 'unsinkable.' If there are watertight barriers between the compartments, a single compartment can be breached and filled with water, but the ship as a whole will not be compromised, and can continue sailing. If there are connections between the compartments, then breaching one means that water can rush into all connected compartments, flooding a greater portion of the ship and risking its integrity as a whole. Similarly, if a person has many self-aspects that are very distinct from one another, feedback that is threatening to one of them threatens relatively little of the self-concept as a whole. But if there are similarities between self-aspects, threats to one self-aspect can spill over to other self-aspects, threatening a greater proportion of the self, and leading to bigger emotional impacts (Figure 2.2).

Consistent with this, people who are higher in self-complexity generally have more muted impacts of emotional events on their lives (Linville, 1985), and are less prone to depression and poor health in response to life stressors (Linville, 1987). In one study (McConnell et al., 2009), participants who had both a *student* self-aspect and a *dating/relationship* self-aspect completed a task in which they described their self-aspects, which were then scored for similarity (i.e., use of overlapping adjectives to describe the two self-aspects). Participants then completed a bogus personality quiz and were randomly assigned to receive either positive or negative feedback relevant to either their student or their dating self-aspect. Participants then rated how positively or negatively they felt about each of their self-aspects. Not surprisingly, getting positive feedback made participants rate the targeted self-aspect more positively, and negative feedback made them rate it more negatively.

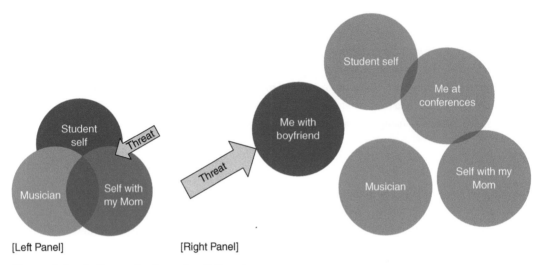

[Left Panel]   [Right Panel]

Figure 2.2 Self-complexity and self-threat

The image on the left depicts the self-structure of someone with low self-complexity. If this person experiences a threat to one of their self-aspects, the degree of overlap between their self-aspects means the threat may easily 'spill over' and impact overlapping self-aspects (illustrated by self-aspects depicted in red.). As a result, a greater portion of their overall self-concept is threatened, leading them to feel worse.

The image on the right shows the self-structure of someone with high self-complexity. Because their self-aspects don't overlap as much, a threat to one self-aspect is less likely to threaten other self-aspects. Moreover, they have more self-aspects. Together this means that less of their self-concept is threatened, reducing the impact of the threat on their overall sense of self-worth.

But how did the feedback affect ratings of their other self-aspects? This depended on the degree of overlap with the targeted self-aspects. If there was little overlap between the two self-aspects, evaluations of the non-targeted self-aspect weren't really affected by the feedback. But if the two self-aspects were very similar, then evaluations of the non-targeted self-aspect were impacted by the feedback for the targeted self-aspect – the feedback 'spilled over' from the targeted self-aspect to the non-targeted self-aspect. Moreover, this moderated the impact of the feedback on participants' overall mood. For people with low self-complexity, negative feedback put people in worse moods, and positive feedback improved moods. But for people with high self-complexity, the feedback had minimal impact on their mood, presumably because a smaller proportion of their self-concept was impacted by the feedback.

This may make it seem like high self-complexity is better than low self-complexity, and indeed, the more even-keeled response to stress and negative feedback means that people with high self-complexity can fare better in some circumstances. But low self-complexity has its benefits, too. Just as high self-complexity makes negative experiences feel less bad, it also makes positive experiences feel less good. When stress is low, and when people have ample social support, people with low self-complexity actually report higher self-esteem and better well-being than people with high self-complexity (McConnell et al., 2009).

On top of that, negative emotions can be important in guiding adaptive behavior sometimes. For example, the motivation to avoid experiencing guilt or shame is part of what motivates ethical behavior. So if people with high self-complexity experience muted shame and guilt, they may be more willing to act unethically. Indeed, Maferima Toure-Tillery and I (Aly) found that perceiving less overlap between self-aspects led people to be more willing to cheat and lie to get more rewards, and less willing to donate money to charity (Toure-Tillery & Light, 2018). Similarly, other research found that people with high self-complexity were more comfortable with their own hypocrisy and didn't shift their attitudes to align with their behavior when discrepancies between the two were highlighted (McConnell & Brown, 2010). You will have to decide for yourself whether the benefits of high self-complexity outweigh the drawbacks!

2.5.3 Multiple Social Identities

Just as we have multiple self-aspects or self-schemas that comprise our personal identities, we all belong to multiple groups that comprise our social identities. What determines which of these social identities are most prominent or influential to us? One of the first social psychologists to investigate this question was William McGuire, who argued that, put simply, we are what makes us distinctive (McGuire & McGuire, 1988). In other words, we tend to define ourselves according to the traits, characteristics, and group memberships that set us apart from other people.

McGuire and Padawer-Singer (1976) conducted an initial study with a sample of primary school students, who answered two open-ended questions: 'Tell us about yourself' and 'Describe what you look like.' The students were especially likely to spontaneously mention both general characteristics (e.g., hometown, age, hobbies/activities) and physical attributes (e.g., height, weight, hair color, eye color) that they did *not* have in common with most of their peers. For example, students with red hair brought up their hair color more frequently than did those with brown hair.

McGuire and colleagues extended this phenomenon beyond personal attributes to social identities: racial/ethnic minority students in majority-White classrooms in the US listed their race/ethnicity more often in their self-descriptions than did White counterparts, and although White students were unlikely to list their race/ethnicity at all, they were more likely to do so when their classrooms had higher proportions of non-White students (McGuire et al., 1978). Similarly, boys from majority-female households and girls from majority-male households mentioned their gender identity more frequently than did boys from majority-male households and girls from majority-female households, respectively (McGuire et al., 1979).

Relating this back to my (Kim's) personal journey of negotiating my White and Puerto Rican identities, my White identity becomes particularly salient to me when I visit extended family in Puerto Rico, many of whom have darker skin and hair than I do (and are much more fluent in Spanish than I am). By contrast, my Puerto Rican identity becomes particularly salient to me when I interact with extended family on my dad's side, who generally don't have strong ties to cultures outside the continental US and speak little, if any, Spanish. These shifts in identity salience tend to happen regardless of how I would ideally like to define myself.

> **Key concept – Optimal Distinctiveness Theory:** A theory proposing that people have competing motives to be both similar to and different from their peers. When people's similarity needs are threatened (e.g., they feel too different from others), they will respond by joining larger groups or exaggerating their group's size. When people's differentiation needs are threatened (e.g., they feel too similar to others), they may respond by joining smaller groups or downplaying their group's size.

That said, **Optimal Distinctiveness Theory** posits that if we ever feel *too* distinctive (e.g., being the only student with red hair or the only racial/ethnic minority student in a 100-person lecture hall), we will engage in strategies designed to highlight our similarities to others. For instance, we might remind ourselves that even though we are only one red-haired person out of 100, we are one woman out of 50 in the lecture hall. Thus, we can override our tendencies to define ourselves by what makes us different from others if the extent or nature of the difference is uncomfortable.

By now, it should be clear that we all have multiple social identities, and that each social identity may be more or less salient to us at any given time (or in any given situation). However, it is also important to understand how our different social identities operate in relation to one another, and the concept of **social identity complexity** helps shed light on this question (Roccas & Brewer, 2002). Earlier in this chapter, we discussed what it means to have a simple versus complex self-concept: a self-concept low in complexity consists of a small number of self-aspects that tend to overlap and have similar characteristics, whereas a self-concept high in complexity consists of a larger number of self-aspects that do not overlap and have distinct characteristics (Linville, 1985, 1987). Social identity complexity works in much the same way, except that it pertains to group memberships and identities rather than to personal traits and characteristics.

According to Roccas and Brewer (2002), social identity complexity refers to the perceived overlap between both the members themselves and the prototypical characteristics of each group to which we belong. As a concrete example, we (Kim and Aly) are both women and university professors. If we perceive most university professors to be male, or to embody characteristics that are more typical of how men rather than women are expected to behave (e.g., assertive, independent), then we will likely not see much overlap between our female and university professor identities. Therefore, we will be relatively high in social identity complexity. By contrast, if we perceive most university professors to be female, or to embody characteristics that are more typical of how women rather than men are expected to behave (e.g., nurturing, cooperative), then

> **Key concept – Social identity complexity:** The extent to which people construe their multiple identities in simple (low-complexity) versus complex (high-complexity) ways. A person with high social identity complexity sees little to no overlap, whereas a person with low social identity complexity sees much overlap, between the members and prototypical characteristics of the groups to which they belong.

we will likely see a lot of overlap between these two identities and thus be relatively low in social identity complexity.

Research on social identity complexity has demonstrated that people whose identities are complex (versus simple) tend to feel more distinctive from others. That is, they are less inclined to perceive themselves as too similar to their peers. One reason is that people high in identity complexity are harder pressed to find many others who have the same particular combination of social identities as they do (Maloku et al., 2019). Consider my (Kim's) own social identities. If I'm thinking only of my gender (woman) and occupation (professor), I may not see myself as particularly distinctive – at least not within my discipline or university, both of which are fairly gender balanced. But if I add my racial/ethnic background to the mix, I know many fewer female university professors with one White parent and one Puerto Rican parent, and so this extra layer of complexity renders me more different from my colleagues than I otherwise would be.

Put differently, and linking this back to Optimal Distinctiveness Theory, having a complex social identity is a potential way for people to satisfy their motives to be both similar to and different from others. Indeed, social identity complexity has been linked to a variety of positive outcomes. For instance, in response to feelings of uncertainty about themselves, people are more likely to identify with groups that do not overlap with their other social identities, compared to groups that do overlap (Grant & Hogg, 2012). Additionally, in a study of female PhD students, participants who saw themselves in terms of multiple, non-overlapping identities (e.g., 'I am a PhD student, an engineer, and a teacher') perceived their desired future professional outcomes as more attainable than did those who saw themselves in terms of just one identity (e.g., 'I am a PhD student') (Bentley et al., 2019). Taken together, these findings suggest that social identity complexity can help people to cope with life's major stressors.

EXERCISE 2.3

The Twenty Statements Test

Take out a blank sheet of paper and write 'I am' on the first 20 lines. Next, complete each 'I am ...' sentence with a word, phrase, or concept that comes to mind to describe yourself. Try to go with your first instinct.

Once you have completed your list of 20 statements, review them and think about how they relate to each level of the self-concept in Brewer and Gardner's (1996) model. How many statements are related to the personal self? To the relational self? To the collective self? Are there any statements that could be categorized into more than one level of the self-concept? Overall, what does this exercise tell you about 'who you are'?

2.6 PART 3: APPLICATIONS

In this section, we introduce practical applications of some key theories related to the self-concept.

2.6.1 Uncertainty-Identity Theory and Radicalism

As discussed earlier in this chapter, uncertainty-identity theory (Hogg, 2007) offers an account for why people are motivated to see groups as an important part of their self-definitions. Recall the central premise of the theory: that when people are feeling uncertain about themselves, their lives, and their futures, they attempt to resolve this self-uncertainty by identifying with groups that have meaningful, clearly defined characteristics (e.g., structured leadership, similarity among members) (Hogg et al., 2007). We can likely think of several groups in our own lives with these properties – cliques with which we might have associated in high school, extracurricular organizations whose members all share a common interest (e.g., chess, football), and even close-knit families, to name a few. But one particularly interesting application of uncertainty-identity theory has to do with why people might choose to join radical groups, such as cults.

Radical groups aren't just characterized by having strong leaders and members who are similar to one another; they also often involve closed boundaries (i.e., its members have limited contact with those outside the group), intolerance of opinions or behaviors that deviate from what group members usually think or do, and engagement in extreme activities (e.g., harming oneself or others for the sake of the group). In other words, radical groups take group membership and loyalty to the next level, which may appeal to people whose sense of uncertainty about themselves is extreme. Radical groups also encourage identity fusion, or a sense of oneness and willingness to make personal sacrifices on behalf of the group, among their members (Gómez et al., 2021).

Perhaps one of the most well-known historical examples of self-uncertainty and radicalism can be seen in the Jonestown Massacre. In November 1978, over 900 members of the People's Temple cult who had followed their leader, Jim Jones, from San Francisco, CA, to a remote village in Guyana (Jonestown) to build a new community died by cyanide poisoning as part of what Jones deemed a 'revolutionary suicide.' Although evidence later emerged that the tragedy could be more aptly described as a mass murder than a mass suicide, we will focus here on what prompted so many individuals to join the People's Temple and move thousands of miles away from their former lives in the first place.

Several characteristics of both the cult members themselves and the sociocultural context in which the People's Temple rose to prominence point to self-uncertainty as a plausible explanation. Approximately 70% of People's Temple members (and those who perished at Jonestown) were African American, and many belonged to the working class (Moore, 2017). Furthermore, the 1970s were a period fraught with race- and class-based tensions in the United States, given that the Civil Rights movement had ended just a decade earlier.

To racial/ethnic minorities and working-class individuals, Jones, who advocated for racial and socioeconomic integration, and the People's Temple may have represented a welcome break from the uncertainty that plagued this era and their own lives. Such self-uncertainty could also help to account for why People's Temple members tended to overlook, and in some cases even embrace, Jones's more toxic characteristics (Mergen & Ozbilgin, 2021). For instance, Jones often forbade members from maintaining contact with friends or family outside the cult and required members to donate nearly all of their earnings and savings to the People's Temple. Once Jones and his followers relocated to Guyana, he became still more controlling: members were forced into a schedule of grueling work with little sleep, could not leave the compound without special permission, and even encountered restrictions on the extent and nature of their communication with one another. It is likely that being in a remote, unfamiliar territory exacerbated the cult members' sense of personal uncertainty and hence made them more susceptible to the group's radical characteristics and the whims of their leader than otherwise would have been the case (Dittman, 2003).

KEY STUDY 2.5

Self-Uncertainty and Identification with Radical Groups

We read about how self-uncertainty may have been an underlying factor explaining why Jim Jones's followers were drawn to the People's Temple, but is the connection between self-uncertainty and identification with radical groups supported in actual research? The answer is yes, at least according to the results of one experiment (Hogg et al., 2010).

Australian university students watched one of two videos about a campus organization formed in opposition to a (very unpopular) proposal that students should pay their tuition upfront rather than after graduating from university. The first video depicted an organization with radical characteristics: the leadership was strict and controlling, members had to be fully committed to the group, there was no tolerance for disagreement among members, and members engaged in extreme protest actions such as large/loud rallies and classroom walkouts. The second video depicted an organization with moderate characteristics: the leadership was more relaxed, members had varying degrees of commitment to the group, diversity of opinions among members was encouraged, and members engaged in less extreme protest actions, such as writing letters to newspapers and attending meetings. After watching their assigned video, students wrote down three things about the tuition proposal that made them feel either personally uncertain or personally certain. They then completed measures of how much they identified with the group in the video and how willing they were to participate in various behaviors (e.g., signing a petition, acting as a representative) on behalf of the group.

(Continued)

The findings demonstrated that students exhibited greater identification with and were more willing to act on behalf of the radical group when they felt personally uncertain, compared to when they felt personally certain. By contrast, self-uncertainty did not increase students' identification with and willingness to act on behalf of the moderate group. If anything, students exhibited *less* commitment to the moderate group when they felt personally uncertain (versus personally certain). Self-uncertainty therefore pushes people, even university students who tend to be fairly moderate at baseline, toward groups characterized by extreme leaders and behaviors.

Other work related to uncertainty-identity theory has suggested that feelings of self-uncertainty can lead people not only to identify with radical groups, but also to embrace radical belief systems. In one set of studies, participants randomly assigned to write about a personal dilemma they were currently facing (e.g., whether to break up with a romantic partner, whether to change one's major) subsequently reported greater conviction and extremity in their attitudes toward several social issues (e.g., abortion, capital punishment) than did participants randomly assigned to write about a dilemma their friend was currently facing. Presumably, the former group of participants felt more uncertain about themselves compared to the latter, and they attempted to compensate for these feelings by claiming certainty in a different area of their lives (McGregor et al., 2001).

Of course, holding extreme positions on social issues is not necessarily the same as espousing truly radical beliefs. However, later research demonstrated that inducing people to feel self-uncertain triggers religious zeal in the form of heightened agreement with statements like 'I would support a war that defended my religious beliefs' and 'If I really had to, I would give my life for my religious beliefs' (McGregor et al., 2010). Based on both our case study of the Jonestown Massacre and research in this area, then, self-uncertainty does seem to fuel radicalism in terms of the groups people choose to join as well as the beliefs they hold.

GUEST PERSONAL JOURNEY

Michael Hogg

Source: © Michael Hogg

I trace my interest in social psychology to my peripatetic background, which created an enduring fascination with cultural difference and human similarity.

I was born in India, spent my childhood in Sri Lanka, and moved to the UK in my mid-teens. Although a cultural outsider in Sri Lanka, I also initially felt an outsider in Britain. However, I quickly fitted in and to this day consider myself British (more precisely European). Bristol became my home town, where I attended school and discovered that I loved and was good at physics and mathematics. So, in 1973 I went to Birmingham University to study physics.

The 1970s were a period of social turmoil that refocused me on social change. I also missed the cultural exposure (and sunshine) of my Sri Lanka days, so I travelled extensively throughout Europe, North Africa, India, and Southeast Asia. I wanted to become a sociologist but the nearest I could get to this at Birmingham was transferring from physics to psychology. In 1974, this is what I did – and the social psychology of intergroup relations and social identity became my passion.

I graduated in 1977 and spent a year travelling through South and Central America. On returning to the UK, I knew I wanted to be a social psychologist and research social identity. So, in 1978 I started my PhD at Bristol University, which at the time was the leading centre for social identity research. I consider this the greatest break I could ever have had; and my 'arrival' as a social psychologist.

In 1981, I was appointed assistant professor of psychology at Bristol, and in 1985 I moved to Australia where I remained for 20 years, working at universities in Sydney, Melbourne, and Brisbane. Finally, in 2006, I moved to Claremont Graduate University in Los Angeles.

2.6.2 Optimal Distinctiveness Theory and Fashion

Fashion trends tend to ebb and flow over time. In the late 1960s and early 1970s, bell-bottom pants were extremely popular among young adults – particularly those who identified with the counter-cultural 'hippie' movement – in Europe and North America. As the 1970s progressed, however, bell-bottoms receded into obscurity and remained there until their revival in the 1990s. This is far from the only instance of a recycled fashion trend. I (Kim) was a pre-teen in the early- to mid-1990s, when hair scrunchies, friendship bracelets, oversized T-shirts, and 'mom jeans' were all the rage among girls in my peer group. Fast forward 25 years, when I learned that my niece Ruby (then 12 years old) and her friends had adopted a 'new' style called VSCO. I immediately Googled the term, only to find that most of the search results were spitting images of my pre-teen peer group!

Optimal Distinctiveness Theory (Brewer, 1991; Leonardelli et al., 2010) can help explain these sudden revivals (and declines) in fashion trends. Recall the central premise of the theory: that people seek to balance their competing needs to both fit in with and stand out from others. In the domain of fashion, individuals often want to adopt their own personal style but, at the same time, don't want to be *too* different from others, especially during adolescence and young adulthood when peer pressure is rampant. As a result, a style that has been met with approval in the past (e.g., bell-bottoms in the 1990s, VSCO clothes in the late 2010s and early 2020s) may at first be viewed as a safe yet relatively cutting-edge choice. Yet as time goes on and the style becomes 'too trendy,' they will eventually be abandoned. This is perhaps most likely to happen when the style is adopted by members of a group we do not wish to identify with.

In one illustrative field study (Berger & Heath, 2008), researchers distributed yellow wristbands to students living in a particular dorm on campus, as part of a campaign to raise cancer awareness. A week later, the researchers distributed identical wristbands to students living in the adjacent dorm, which had a reputation for being 'geeky.' Both before and after wristbands were given to students in the 'geeky' dorm, the researchers asked students in the original dorm whether they regularly wore their wristbands. Remarkably, the proportion of these students who reported wearing the wristbands declined by 32% once the 'geeky' students had also adopted the trend.

A control group of students in a dorm on the other side of campus did not report such a decline over time, which suggests that rather than simply getting tired of the wristbands, students stopped wearing them *because* a different group had started to wear them.

Even within groups we value, our fashion choices can still be influenced by our motives for both similarity and distinctiveness. Sometimes, as with the wristband example, it involves abandoning trends altogether once they become too widespread in our peer group. Consider my niece Ruby's reaction once her mother (my sister) told her there was an actual name for her friends' new style and showed her pictures and articles of 'VSCO girls' from the internet. Instead of being pleased to take part in such a popular movement, Ruby became agitated and stuffed all her VSCO clothes into the back of her closet, proclaiming that she didn't want to be 'a stereotype.' For Ruby, VSCO lost its appeal once she realized how many girls her age had adopted the trend.

In other cases, our needs to both fit in and stand out can be satisfied by finding some way to distinguish ourselves while still conforming to the general trends of our group. We might wear a particular type of clothing or shoes that our group embraces, but opt for a brand that is less popular within the group. For instance, if we belong to a group whose members tend to wear Nike sneakers, we might also wear sneakers but choose Converse or Adidas instead of Nike. Alternatively, our fashion choices could differ from those of other group members in just one aspect, such as style, color, or fabric, as would be the case if we were part of a group in which skinny blue jeans were popular but we decided to wear bootcut blue jeans or skinny khaki pants instead. Indeed, a study by Chan et al. (2012) demonstrated that people who are motivated to be unique from others will adopt fashion trends that differ from those of their peers on one dimension but not on another.

Overall, the above examples and studies suggest that Optimal Distinctiveness Theory can enhance our understanding of why people may find particular fashion trends more (or less) appealing than others, why people's fashion preferences may shift over time, and how people use trends to inform their personal sense of style.

2.6.3 The Self-Esteem Movement: Should Schools Teach High Self-Esteem?

In this chapter, we've discussed what self-esteem is, and described multiple theories for why we are motivated to maintain high self-esteem. Although they differ on key points, both Terror Management Theory and Sociometer Theory argue that self-esteem is a key indicator of psychological motives, which themselves serve to promote our survival (either literally or symbolically.) Thus, they both suggest that things that threaten our self-esteem can feel like a life or death situation.

With that in mind, should we as a society work to increase people's self-esteem? That was the position taken by the so-called Self-Esteem Movement. Inspired by research that showed positive correlations between self-esteem and good outcomes like school performance (Hansford & Hattie, 1982), leadership ability (Chemers, Watson, & May, 2000), and happiness (Diener & Diener, 1995), and negative correlations with bad outcomes, such as romantic break-ups (Hendrick et al., 1988), delinquency (Neumark-Sztainer et al., 1997), adolescent smoking (Pederson et al., 1998), drug and alcohol abuse (Steffenhagen & Burns, 1987), and disordered eating (French et al., 2001), a coalition of government officials, educators, and mental health professionals argued that increasing self-esteem should be a major priority for governments and institutions. One oft-cited example of this is the California Task Force on Self-Esteem and Personal Responsibility, launched in 1986, which reviewed some of the available research on self-esteem, argued that low self-esteem was a causal factor in many problems facing the state, and proposed strategies for raising and maintaining self-esteem in schools and workplaces (California Task Force, 1990).

One of the areas where the Self-Esteem Movement has had the greatest impact is in education. Many schools and school districts adopted self-esteem development as a part of their curriculum (e.g., New York State Education Department, 2018), in addition to academics. As a result, students in these schools would often complete class activities and assignments intended to raise their self-esteem. For example, one activity used in many elementary school classrooms instructed the teacher to ask students 'Who do you think is the most important person in the world?' They would then tell students to look inside a 'magic box' they'd brought in to reveal the answer; this was a box that contained a mirror in which students would see themselves when they opened the box (Canfield & Wells, 1976)! Teachers, administrators, and other school staff were also trained to promote students' self-esteem in all teaching (e.g., Aknin & Radford, 2018), and schools would sometimes evaluate students' self-esteem as standard in assessing the quality of their education.

But does increasing students' self-esteem through such interventions lead to real benefits? For many of the outcomes of interest, the answer appears to be ... no! For example, school and extracurricular interventions designed to increase self-esteem generally do not improve academic performance (Scheirer & Kraut, 1979), or may even backfire. In one experiment done with college students (Forsyth et al., 2007), low-performing students were sent weekly emails including review questions on the weeks' material. In addition to the review questions, some students were randomly assigned to receive messages intended to boost either their self-esteem or their sense of personal responsibility. Neither the self-esteem message nor the personal responsibility message improved performance, and in fact the lowest-performing students actually did worse on the course's final exam if they received such messages, compared to students who only received the review questions.

Why do such interventions fail so spectacularly, given the correlations between self-esteem and positive outcomes? The answer may be found in that old cliché,

'Correlation does not equal causation.' As discussed in Chapter 1, the fact that two variables are associated does not mean that there is a causal relationship between them. It is possible that some third variable is having a causal impact on both variables, leading them to appear associated with one another. In the case of self-esteem and life outcomes, other variables such as socioeconomic status, parental involvement, and early life stress are likely to be 'third variables.' Children who experience a lot of stressors, such as neglect, poverty, housing instability, or violence, may have lower self-esteem (Godrich et al., 2019) and poorer academic performance (Barnett et al., 1996) because the stressors and lack of support children experience are causing lower self-esteem *and* poorer academic achievement.

Moreover, even if there is a causal relationship between two correlated variables, correlational studies cannot tell us the direction of that relationship. In other words, a correlation between high self-esteem and positive life outcomes could indicate that positive life outcomes cause high self-esteem, not the other way around! Indeed, some evidence suggests that this is the case. Longitudinal studies often show that your self-esteem this year doesn't predict the grades you will earn next year, but the grades you earn this year do predict your self-esteem next year (Rosenberg et al., 1989).

Does this mean that self-esteem as a construct is worthless, and psychologists and educators alike should focus on something else? Well, not completely. Self-esteem does seem to have crucial impacts on happiness and mental health, and low self-esteem is particularly associated with development of depression and eating disorders (Diener & Diener, 1995; Heatherton et al., 1992; Murrell et al., 1991). For this reason, self-esteem may continue to be an important area of concern for the science of well-being. But many have argued that even if we are interested in promoting well-being and preventing mental illness, focusing narrowly on raising self-esteem may not be an effective strategy. Consider the theories we have discussed for why people value self-esteem in the first place. Whether self-esteem indicates that we are socially included, or live up to our culture's values, or are living in accordance with our personal standards, most major theories consider self-esteem to be an indicator of where we stand on basic psychological needs. To disrupt this indicator, then, would be like artificially shifting your fuel meter so that your tank appears full. While it might be comforting, it does not mean you can actually drive any further!

Thus, many psychologists argue that if we want the benefits of high self-esteem, we should focus on addressing those psychological needs directly (Baumeister et al., 1996). And in line with this new understanding, many schools that previously dedicated class time to developing self-esteem have shifted their socioemotional development curriculums to addressing bullying (Divecha & Bracket, 2019), persistence in the face of adversity (sometimes called grit or resilience; Park et al., 2018), and, as you read earlier, self-affirmation (Goyer et al., 2017). The benefit of focusing on these non-cognitive skills is that experimental research suggests they can support students in achieving outcomes like strong friendships, good relationships with teachers, and academic success, which will allow them to earn high self-esteem.

2.7 SUMMARY

As we've discussed in this chapter, identity can be a major source of motivation. People are motivated to develop self-knowledge and reduce uncertainty about themselves. To this end, we elicit and internalize feedback from others, compare ourselves to other people, and identify with social groups and social roles that can give us information about ourselves. We are also motivated to view ourselves positively. Although psychologists differ as to why they believe we desire self-esteem, most agree that it is tied to broader psychological needs. As a result of this motivation, people will often self-enhance, or see themselves through rose-colored glasses. However, which personal characteristics or social groups are most salient to our identity varies depending on a given situation. As a result, most people shift their identities across social contexts, which in turn can have consequences for how we see ourselves and how we behave. We've focused a lot on how social contexts, cognition, and motivation impact self and identity. In Chapter 3, you will learn more about how social motivations like these operate in close relationships.

2.8 REVISION

1   What is a reflected appraisal, and what factors influence whether a reflected appraisal is internalized into the self-concept?
2   Describe at least *two* strategies that people use to maintain high self-esteem.
3   Describe the two major theories for why people value high self-esteem. How are they similar? How do they differ?
4   What is *one* potential explanation for why self-affirmation helps to reduce defensive responses to threats?
5   Identify *at least two* ways in which joining or identifying with a group can alter one's self-concept.
6   According to Optimal Distinctiveness Theory, what is *one* strategy people might employ to satisfy their need to be different from others?

2.9 FURTHER READING

Foundations

Khanna, N. (2004). The role of reflected appraisals in racial identity: The case of multiracial Asians. *Social Psychology Quarterly*, *67*(2), 115–131.

This article explores how reflected appraisals impact social identities, looking particularly at multiracial Asian participants to explore how others' perceptions impact how people view themselves.

Suls, J., Martin, R., & Wheeler, L. (2002). Social comparison: Why, with whom, and with what effect? *Current Directions in Psychological Science, 11*(5), 159–163.

This paper is a brief, accessible review of the literature on social comparison, including some important nuances about who engages in downward vs upward social comparison, and how different kinds of comparison affect the choice of who to compare to.

Crocker, J., Niiya, Y., & Mischkowski, D. (2008). Why does writing about important values reduce defensiveness? Self-affirmation and the role of positive other-directed feelings. *Psychological Science, 19*(7), 740–747.

The studies in this paper demonstrate that self-affirmation can reduce defensive responses to threat through increases in other-focused emotions.

Ziano, I., Mok, P. Y., & Feldman, G. (2020). Replication and extension of Alicke (1985) Better-than-Average Effect for desirable and controllable traits. *Social Psychological and Personality Science, 12*(6).

This paper reports a successful replication of Alicke's (1985) classic Better-than-Average Effect study, in which participants rated desirable traits as more characteristic of themselves than the average person, and undesirable traits as more characteristic of the average person than themselves.

Advanced

Andersen, S. M., Tuskeviciute, R., & Przybylinski, E. (2017). Coherent variability: The self with significant others in memory and context. *Social Cognition, 35*(2), 107–126.

This paper reviews research on relational self-schemas. It illustrates one way in which social contexts lead to the development of distinct self-aspects, and describes how these impact on how we think, feel, and act.

Brewer, M. B. (1991). The social self: On being the same and different at the same time. *Personality and Social Psychology Bulletin, 17*(5), 475–482.

This paper introduces Optimal Distinctiveness Theory, which posits that people strive to be both similar to and different from others, and therefore will avoid affiliating with groups that are either too personalized/small or too inclusive/large.

Hornsey, M. J., & Jetten, J. (2004). The individual within the group: Balancing the need to belong with the need to be different. *Personality and Social Psychology Review, 8*(3), 248–264.

Building upon Optimal Distinctiveness Theory, this paper reviews the ways in which people can satisfy their motives to be both similar to and different from others by either identifying with certain types of groups (e.g., subgroups, numerical minorities) or adjusting their perceptions of the groups to which they belong (e.g., underestimating the size of their group, seeing their group as non-mainstream).

Roccas, S., & Brewer, M. B. (2002). Social identity complexity. *Personality and Social Psychology Review, 6*(2), 88–106.

This review introduces the concept of social identity complexity, defined as whether people construe their multiple identities in either simple terms (i.e., little or no overlap between groups in terms of their members and prototypical characteristics) or complex terms (i.e., much overlap between groups in terms of their members and prototypical characteristics).

Applications

Lisjak, M., Lee, A. Y., & Gardner, W. L. (2012). When a threat to the brand is a threat to the self: The importance of brand identification and implicit self-esteem in predicting defensiveness. *Personality and Social Psychology Bulletin, 38*(9), 1120–1132.

In this chapter, we discussed how fashion and other possessions can be used as markers of identity. This article explores how consumer brands can become so linked to the self-concept that people react defensively when the brands are threatened, just as they would do if their self was threatened.

Baumeister, R. F., & Vohs, K. D. (2018). Revisiting our reappraisal of the (surprisingly few) benefits of high self-esteem. *Perspectives on Psychological Science, 13*(2), 137–140.

This brief article reflects on the history of research on the relationship between self-esteem and life outcomes. The authors describe why early research suggested that improving self-esteem might be desirable, how they changed their perspectives based on a review of the evidence, and what this might mean for research on self-esteem in the future.

2.10 REFERENCES

Aknin, I., & Radford, L. (2018). Exploring the development of student self-esteem in urban schools. *Contemporary Issues in Education Research, 11*(1), 15–22.

Alicke, M. D. (1985). Global self-evaluation as determined by the desirability and controllability of trait adjectives. *Journal of Personality and Social Psychology, 49*(6), 1621–1630.

Alicke, M. D., Klotz, M. L., Breitenbecher, D. L., Yurak, T. J., & Vredenburg, D. S. (1995). Personal contact, individuation, and the better-than-average effect. *Journal of Personality and Social Psychology, 68*(5), 804–825.

Allison, S. T., Messick, D. M., & Goethals, G. R. (1989). On being better but not smarter than others: The Muhammad Ali effect. *Social Cognition, 7*(3), 275–295.

Baird, B., Smallwood, J., & Schooler, J. W. (2011). Back to the future: Autobiographical planning and the functionality of mind-wandering. *Consciousness and Cognition, 20*(4), 1604–1611.

Baldwin, M. W., Carrell, S. E., & Lopez, D. F. (1990). Priming relationship schemas: My advisor and the Pope are watching me from the back of my mind. *Journal of Experimental Social Psychology, 26*(5), 435–454.

Barnett, D., Vondra, J. I., & Shonk, S. M. (1996). Self-perceptions, motivation, and school functioning of low-income maltreated and comparison children. *Child Abuse & Neglect, 20*(5), 397–410.

Baumeister, R. F., & Leary, M. R. (1995). The need to belong: Desire for interpersonal attachments as a fundamental human motivation. *Psychological Bulletin, 117*(3), 497–529.

Baumeister, R. F., Smart, L., & Boden, J. M. (1996). Relation of threatened egotism to violence and aggression: The dark side of high self-esteem. *Psychological Review, 103*(1), 5–33.

Bentley, S. V., Peters, K., Haslam, S. A., & Greenaway, K. H. (2019). Construction at work: Multiple identities scaffold professional identity development in academia. *Frontiers in Psychology, 10*, 628.

Berger, J., & Heath, C. (2008). Who drives divergence? Identity signaling, outgroup dissimilarity, and the abandonment of cultural tastes. *Journal of Personality and Social Psychology, 95*(3), 593–607.

Berglas, S., & Jones, E. E. (1978). Drug choice as a self-handicapping strategy in response to noncontingent success. *Journal of Personality and Social Psychology, 36*(4), 405–417.

Bigler, M., Neimeyer, G. J., & Brown, E. (2001). The divided self revisited: Effects of self-concept clarity and self-concept differentiation on psychological adjustment. *Journal of Social and Clinical Psychology, 20*(3), 396–415.

Binning, K. R., Sherman, D. K., Cohen, G. L., & Heitland, K. (2010). Seeing the other side: Reducing political partisanship via self-affirmation in the 2008 presidential election. *Analyses of Social Issues and Public Policy, 10*(1), 276–292.

Brewer, M. B. (1991). The social self: On being the same and different at the same time. *Personality and Social Psychology Bulletin, 17*(5), 475–482.

Brewer, M. B., & Gardner, W. (1996). Who is this "We"? Levels of collective identity and self representations. *Journal of Personality and Social Psychology, 71*(1), 83–93.

Burwell, R. A., & Shirk, S. R. (2006). Self processes in adolescent depression: The role of self-worth contingencies. *Journal of Research on Adolescence, 16*(3), 479–490.

Buunk, B. P., Schaap, C., & Prevoo, N. (1990). Conflict resolution styles attributed to self and partner in premarital relationships. *The Journal of Social Psychology, 130*(6), 821–823.

California Task Force (1990). *Toward a state of esteem: The final report of the California Task Force to Promote Self-Esteem and Personal and Social Responsibility.* https://eric.ed.gov/?id=ED321170

Cambron, M. J., Acitelli, L. K., & Steinberg, L. (2010). When friends make you blue: The role of friendship contingent self-esteem in predicting self-esteem and depressive symptoms. *Personality and Social Psychology Bulletin, 36*(3), 384–397.

Canfield, J., & Wells, H. C. (1976). *100 ways to enhance self-concept in the classroom.* Englewood Cliffs, NJ: Prentice-Hall.

Chan, C., Berger, J., & Van Boven, L. (2012). Identifiable but not identical: Combining social identity and uniqueness motives in choice. *Journal of Consumer Research, 39*(3), 561–573.

Chemers, M. M., Watson, C. B., & May, S. T. (2000). Dispositional affect and leadership effectiveness: A comparison of self-esteem, optimism, and efficacy. *Personality and Social Psychology Bulletin, 26*(3), 267–277.

Coleman, R. E. (1975). Manipulation of self-esteem as a determinant of mood of elated and depressed women. *Journal of Abnormal Psychology, 84*(6), 693–700.

College Board. (1976–1977). *Student descriptive questionnaire.* Princeton, NJ: Educational Testing Services.

Conway, M. A. (2005). Memory and the self. *Journal of Memory and Language, 53*(4), 594–528.

Cooley, C. H. (1902). *Human nature and the social order.* New York: Scribners.

Crocker, J., Niiya, Y., & Mischkowski, D. (2008). Why does writing about important values reduce defensiveness? Self-affirmation and the role of positive other-directed feelings. *Psychological Science, 19*(7), 740–747.

Crocker, J., & Wolfe, C. T. (2001). Contingencies of self-worth. *Psychological Review, 108*(3), 593–623.

Cross, P. (1977). Not can but will college teachers be improved? *New Directions for Higher Education, 17,* 1–15.

Deci, E. L., & Ryan, R. M. (2000). The 'what' and 'why' of goal pursuits: Human needs and the self-determination of behavior. *Psychological Inquiry, 11*(4), 227–268.

Diener, E., & Diener, M. (1995). Cross-cultural correlates of life satisfaction and self-esteem. *Journal of Personality and Social Psychology, 68*(4), 653–663.

Dittman, M. (2003, November). Lessons from Jonestown. *Monitor on Psychology, 34*(10). www.apa.org/monitor/nov03/jonestown

Divecha, D., & Brackett, M. (2019). Rethinking school-based bullying through the lens of social and emotional learning: A bioecological perspective. *International Journal of Bullying Prevention, 2,* 93–113.

Fein, S., & Spencer, S. J. (1997). Prejudice as self-image maintenance: Affirming the self through derogating others. *Journal of Personality and Social Psychology, 73*(1), 31–44.

Festinger, L. (1954). A theory of social comparison processes. *Human Relations, 7*(2), 117–140.

Fiske, S. T. (2008). Core social motivations: Views from the couch, consciousness, classroom, computers, and collectives. In J. Y. Shah & W. L. Gardner (Eds.), *Handbook of motivation science* (pp. 3–22). New York: The Guilford Press.

Forsyth, D. R., Lawrence, N. K., Burnette, J. L., & Baumeister, R. F. (2007). Attempting to improve the academic performance of struggling college students by bolstering their self-esteem: An intervention that backfired. *Journal of Social and Clinical Psychology, 26*(4), 447–459.

French, S. A., Story, M., & Jeffery, R. W. (2001). Environmental influences on eating and physical activity. *Annual Review of Public Health, 22*(1), 309–335.

Gebauer, J. E., Nehrlich, A. D., Stahlberg, D., Sedikides, C., Hackenschmidt, A., Schick, D., ... & Mander, J. (2018). Mind-body practices and the self: Yoga and meditation do not quiet the ego but instead boost self-enhancement. *Psychological Science, 29*(8), 1299–1308.

Gebauer, J. E., Sedikides, C., & Schrade, A. (2017). Christian self-enhancement. *Journal of Personality and Social Psychology, 113*(5), 786–809.

Gebauer, J. E., Wagner, J., Sedikides, C., & Neberich, W. (2013). Agency-communion and self-esteem relations are moderated by culture, religiosity, age, and sex: Evidence for the "self-centrality breeds self-enhancement" principle. *Journal of Personality*, *81*(3), 261–275.

Godrich, S., Loewen, O., Blanchet, R., Willows, N., & Veugelers, P. (2019). Canadian children from food insecure households experience low self-esteem and self-efficacy for healthy lifestyle choices. *Nutrients*, *11*(3), 675.

Gómez, Á., Bélanger, J. J., Chinchilla, J., Vázquez, A., Schumpe, B. M., Nisa, C. F., & Chiclana, S. (2021). Admiration for Islamist groups encourages self-sacrifice through identity fusion. *Humanities and Social Sciences Communications*, *8*(1), 1–12.

Goyer, J. P., Garcia, J., Purdie-Vaughns, V., Binning, K. R., Cook, J. E., Reeves, S. L., ... & Cohen, G. L. (2017). Self-affirmation facilitates minority middle schoolers' progress along college trajectories. *Proceedings of the National Academy of Sciences*, *114*(29), 7594–7599.

Grant, F., & Hogg, M. A. (2012). Self-uncertainty, social identity prominence and group identification. *Journal of Experimental Social Psychology*, *48*(2), 538–542.

Hadden, I. R., Easterbrook, M. J., Nieuwenhuis, M., Fox, K. J., & Dolan, P. (2020). Self-affirmation reduces the socioeconomic attainment gap in schools in England. *British Journal of Educational Psychology*, *90*(2), 517–536.

Hakmiller, K. L. (1966). Threat as a determinant of downward comparison. *Journal of Experimental Social Psychology*, *1*, 32–39.

Hallsten, L., Rudman, A., & Gustavsson, P. (2012). Does contingent self-esteem increase during higher education? *Self and Identity*, *11*(2), 223–236.

Hansford, B. C., & Hattie, J. A. (1982). The relationship between self and achievement/ performance measures. *Review of Educational Research*, *52*(1), 123–142.

Harmon-Jones, E., Simon, L., Greenberg, J., Pyszczynski, T., Solomon, S., & McGregor, H. (1997). Terror management theory and self-esteem: Evidence that increased self-esteem reduced mortality salience effects. *Journal of Personality and Social Psychology*, *72*(1), 24–36.

Harris, R. N., & Snyder, C. R. (1986). The role of uncertain self-esteem in self-handicapping. *Journal of Personality and Social Psychology*, *51*(2), 451-458.

Heatherton, T. F., Herman, C. P., & Polivy, J. (1992). Effects of distress on eating: The importance of ego-involvement. *Journal of Personality and Social Psychology*, *62*(5), 801–803.

Hendrick, S. S., Hendrick, C., & Adler, N. L. (1988). Romantic relationships: Love, satisfaction, and staying together. *Journal of Personality and Social Psychology*, *54*(6), 980–988.

Hinkley, K., & Andersen, S. M. (1996). The working self-concept in transference: Significant-other activation and self change. *Journal of Personality and Social Psychology*, *71*(6), 1279–1295.

Hogg, M. A. (2007). Uncertainty-identity theory. In M. P. Zanna (Ed.), *Advances in experimental social psychology* (Vol. 39, pp. 69–126). San Diego, CA: Academic Press.

Hogg, M. A., Meehan, C., & Farquharson, J. (2010). The solace of radicalism: Self-uncertainty and group identification in the face of threat. *Journal of Experimental Social Psychology*, *46*(6), 1061–1066.

Hogg, M. A., Sherman, D. K., Dierselhuis, J., Maitner, A. T., & Moffitt, G. (2007). Uncertainty, entitativity, and group identification. *Journal of Experimental Social Psychology*, *43*(1), 135–142.

Hoorens, V., Dekkers, G., & Deschrijver, E. (2021). Gender bias in student evaluations of teaching: Students' self-affirmation reduces the bias by lowering evaluations of male professors. *Sex Roles*, *84*(1), 34–48.

Hornsey, M. J., & Jetten, J. (2004). The individual within the group: Balancing the need to belong with the need to be different. *Personality and Social Psychology Review*, *8*(3), 248–264.

Klein, R. A., Cook, C. L., Ebersole, C. R., Vitiello, C., Nosek, B. A., Hilgard, J., & … Ratliff, K. A. (2022). Many Labs 4: Failure to replicate mortality salience effect with and without original author involvement. *Collabra: Psychology*, *8*(1), 35271.

Kraus, M. W., & Chen, S. (2010). Facial-feature resemblance elicits the transference effect. *Psychological Science*, *21*(4), 518–522.

Lawrence, J. S., & Williams, A. (2013). Anxiety explains why people with domain-contingent self-worth underperform on ability-diagnostic tests. *Journal of Research in Personality*, *47*(3), 227–232.

Leary, M. R., Tambor, E. S., Terdal, S. K., & Downs, D. L. (1995). Self-esteem as an interpersonal monitor: The sociometer hypothesis. *Journal of Personality and Social Psychology*, *68*(3), 518–530.

Lee-Flynn, S. C., Pomaki, G., DeLongis, A., Biesanz, J. C., & Puterman, E. (2011). Daily cognitive appraisals, daily affect, and long-term depressive symptoms: The role of self-esteem and self-concept clarity in the stress process. *Personality and Social Psychology Bulletin*, *37*(2), 255–268.

Leonardelli, G. J., Pickett, C. L., & Brewer, M. B. (2010). Optimal distinctiveness theory: A framework for social identity, social cognition, and intergroup relations. In M. P. Zanna (Ed.), *Advances in experimental social psychology* (Vol. 43, pp. 63–113). San Diego, CA: Academic Press.

Leitner, J. B., Hehman, E., Deegan, M. P., & Jones, J. M. (2014). Adaptive disengagement buffers self-esteem from negative social feedback. *Personality and Social Psychology Bulletin*, *40*(11), 1435–1450.

Light, A. E. (2017). Self-concept clarity, self-regulation, and psychological well-being. In J. Lodi-Smith & K. DeMarree (Eds.), *Self-concept clarity*. Cham, Switzerland: Springer International.

Light, A. E., & Visser, P. S. (2013). The ins and outs of the self: Contrasting role exits and role entries as predictors of self-concept clarity. *Self and Identity*, *12*(3), 291–306.

Linville, P. W. (1985). Self-complexity and affective extremity: Don't put all your eggs in one basket. *Social Cognition*, *3*(1), 94–120.

Linville, P. W. (1987). Self-complexity as a cognitive buffer against stress-related illness and depression. *Journal of Personality and Social Psychology*, *52*, 663–676.

Lockwood, P., & Kunda, Z. (1997). Superstars and me: Predicting the impact of role models on the self. *Journal of Personality and Social Psychology*, *73*(1), 91–103.

Lodi-Smith, J., & Roberts, B. W. (2010). Getting to know me: Social role experiences and age differences in self-concept clarity during adulthood. *Journal of Personality*, *78*(5), 1383–1410.

Maloku, E., Derks, B., Van Laar, C., & Ellemers, N. (2019). Stimulating interethnic contact in Kosovo: The role of social identity complexity and distinctiveness threat. *Group Processes & Intergroup Relations, 22*(7), 1039–1058.

McAdams, D. P., & Cox, K. S. (2010). Self and identity across the life span. In R. M. Lerner, M. E. Lamb, & A. M. Freund (Eds.), *The handbook of life-span development.* Hoboken, NJ: John Wiley & Sons.

McAdams, D. P., & Pals, J. L. (2006). A new Big Five: Fundamental principles for an integrative science of personality. *American Psychologist, 61*(3), 204–217.

McConnell, A. R., & Brown, C. M. (2010). Dissonance averted: Self-concept organization moderates the effect of hypocrisy on attitude change. *Journal of Experimental Social Psychology, 46*(2), 361–366.

McConnell, A. R., Rydell, R. J., & Brown, C. M. (2009). On the experience of self-relevant feedback: How self-concept organization influences affective responses and self-evaluations. *Journal of Experimental Social Psychology, 45*(4), 695–707.

McGregor, I., Nash, K., & Prentice, M. (2010). Reactive approach motivation (RAM) for religion. *Journal of Personality and Social Psychology, 99*(1), 148–161.

McGregor, I., Zanna, M. P., Holmes, J. G., & Spencer, S. J. (2001). Compensatory conviction in the face of personal uncertainty: Going to extremes and being oneself. *Journal of Personality and Social Psychology, 80*(3), 472–488.

McGuire, W. J., & McGuire, C. V. (1988). Content and process in the experience of self. In L. Berkowitz (Ed.), *Advances in experimental social psychology* (Vol. 21, pp. 97–144). San Diego, CA: Academic Press.

McGuire, W. J., McGuire, C. V., Child, P., & Fujioka, T. (1978). Salience of ethnicity in the spontaneous self-concept as a function of one's ethnic distinctiveness in the social environment. *Journal of Personality and Social Psychology, 36*(5), 511–520.

McGuire, W. J., McGuire, C. V., & Winton, W. (1979). Effects of household sex composition on the salience of one's gender in the spontaneous self-concept. *Journal of Experimental Social Psychology, 15*(1), 77–90.

McGuire, W. J., & Padawer-Singer, A. (1976). Trait salience in the spontaneous self-concept. *Journal of Personality and Social Psychology, 33*(6), 743–754.

Mead G. H. (1934). *Mind, self and society.* Chicago, IL: The University of Chicago Press.

Mergen, A., & Ozbilgin, M. F. (2021). Understanding the followers of toxic leaders: Toxic illusion and personal uncertainty. *International Journal of Management Reviews, 23*(1), 45–63.

Miller, D. T., & Ross, M. (1975). Self-serving biases in the attribution of causality: Fact or fiction? *Psychological Bulletin, 82*(2), 213–225.

Moore, R. (2017). An update on the demographics of Jonestown. https://jonestown.sdsu.edu/?page_id=70495

Morrison, K. R., & Johnson, C. S. (2011). When what you have is who you are: Self-uncertainty leads individualists to see themselves in their possessions. *Personality and Social Psychology Bulletin, 37*(5), 639–651.

Morrison, K. R., Johnson, C. S., & Wheeler, S. C. (2012). Not all selves feel the same uncertainty: Assimilation to primes among individualists and collectivists. *Social Psychological and Personality Science, 3*(1), 118–126.

Murdock, N. L., Edwards, C., & Murdock, T. B. (2010). Therapists' attributions for client premature termination: Are they self-serving? *Psychotherapy: Theory, Research, Practice, Training, 47*(2), 221–234.

Murrell, S. A., Meeks, S., & Walker, J. (1991). Protective functions of health and self-esteem against depression in older adults facing illness or bereavement. *Psychology and Aging, 6*(3), 352–360.

Neumark-Sztainer, D., Story, M., Toporoff, E., Himes, J. H., Resnick, M. D., & Blum, R. W. (1997). Covariations of eating behaviors with other health-related behaviors among adolescents. *Journal of Adolescent Health, 20*(6), 450–458.

New York State Education Department. (2018). *Mental health education literacy in schools: Linking to a continuum of well-being.* www.nysed.gov/common/nysed/files/programs/curriculum-instruction/continuumofwellbeingguide.pdf

Pederson, L. L., Koval, J. J., McGrady, G. A., & Tyas, S. L. (1998). The degree and type of relationship between psychosocial variables and smoking status for students in grade 8: Is there a dose–response relationship? *Preventive Medicine, 27*(3), 337–347.

Richardson, M., Abraham, C., & Bond, R. (2012). Psychological correlates of university students' academic performance: A systematic review and meta-analysis. *Psychological Bulletin, 138*(2), 353–387.

Riess, M., Rosenfeld, P., Melburg, V., & Tedeschi, J. T. (1981). Self-serving attributions: Biased private perceptions and distorted public descriptions. *Journal of Personality and Social Psychology, 41*(2), 224–231.

Ritchie, T. D., Sedikides, C., Wildschut, T., Arndt, J., & Gidron, Y. (2011). Self-concept clarity mediates the relation between stress and subjective well-being. *Self and Identity, 10*(4), 493–508.

Roccas, S., & Brewer, M. B. (2002). Social identity complexity. *Personality and Social Psychology Review, 6*(2), 88–106.

Rosenberg, M., Schooler, C., & Schoenbach, C. (1989). Self-esteem and adolescent problems: Modeling reciprocal effects. *American Sociological Review, 54*, 1004–1018.

Scheirer, M. A., & Kraut, R. E. (1979). Increasing educational achievement via self concept change. *Review of Educational Research, 49*(1), 131–149.

Schlegel, R. J., Hicks, J. A., Davis, W. E., Hirsch, K. A., & Smith, C. M. (2013). The dynamic interplay between perceived true self-knowledge and decision satisfaction. *Journal of Personality and Social Psychology, 104*(3), 542–558.

Schwinger, M., Wirthwein, L., Lemmer, G., & Steinmayr, R. (2014). Academic self-handicapping and achievement: A meta-analysis. *Journal of Educational Psychology, 106*(3), 744–761.

Schwinger, M., & Stiensmeier-Pelster, J. (2011). Prevention of self-handicapping— The protective function of mastery goals. *Learning and Individual Differences, 21*(6), 699–709.

Sedikides, C., Meek, R., Alicke, M. D., & Taylor, S. (2014). Behind bars but above the bar: Prisoners consider themselves more prosocial than non-prisoners. *British Journal of Social Psychology, 53*(2), 396–403.

Shepperd, J., Malone, W., & Sweeny, K. (2008). Exploring causes of the self-serving bias. *Social and Personality Psychology Compass, 2*(2), 895–908.

Sherman, D. A., Nelson, L. D., & Steele, C. M. (2000). Do messages about health risks threaten the self? Increasing the acceptance of threatening health messages via self-affirmation. *Personality and Social Psychology Bulletin, 26*(9), 1046–1058.

Slotter, E. B., & Gardner, W. L. (2014). Remind me who I am: Social interaction strategies for maintaining the threatened self-concept. *Personality and Social Psychology Bulletin, 40*(9), 1148–1161.

Solomon, S., Greenberg, J., & Pyszczynski, T. (1991). Terror management theory of self-esteem. In C. R. Snyder & D. R. Forsyth (Eds.), *Handbook of social and clinical psychology: The health perspective* (pp. 21–40). Oxford: Pergamon Press.

Spencer-Rodgers, J., Boucher, H. C., Mori, S. C., Wang, L., & Peng, K. (2009). The dialectical self-concept: Contradiction, change, and holism in East Asian cultures. *Personality and Social Psychology Bulletin, 35*(1), 29–44.

Steele, C. M. (1988). The psychology of self-affirmation: Sustaining the integrity of the self. In L. Berkowitz (Ed.), *Advances in Experimental Social Psychology* (Vol. 21, pp. 261–302). San Diego, CA: Academic Press.

Steele, C. M., & Liu, T. J. (1983). Dissonance processes as self-affirmation. *Journal of Personality and Social Psychology, 45*(1), 5–19.

Steffenhagen, R. A., & Burns, J. D. (1987). *The social dynamics of self-esteem: Theory to therapy.* Westport, CT: Praeger.

Touré-Tillery, M., & Light, A. E. (2018). No self to spare: How the cognitive structure of the self influences moral behavior. *Organizational Behavior and Human Decision Processes, 147,* 48–64.

Wallace, H. M., & Tice, D. M. (2012). Reflected appraisal through a 21st-century looking glass. In M. R. Leary & J. P. Tangney (Eds.), *Handbook of self and identity* (pp. 124–140). New York: The Guilford Press.

Walton, G. M., Logel, C., Peach, J. M., Spencer, S. J., & Zanna, M. P. (2015). Two brief interventions to mitigate a 'chilly climate' transform women's experience, relationships, and achievement in engineering. *Journal of Educational Psychology, 107*(2), 468–485.

Westen, D., & Heim, A. K. (2003). Disturbances of self and identity in personality disorders. In M. R. Leary & J. P. Tangney (Eds.), *Handbook of self and identity* (pp. 643–664). New York: The Guilford Press.

Zell, E., Strickhouser, J. E., Sedikides, C., & Alicke, M. D. (2020). The better-than-average effect in comparative self-evaluation: A comprehensive review and meta-analysis. *Psychological Bulletin, 146*(2), 118–149.

Ziano, I., Mok, P. Y., & Feldman, G. (2020). Replication and extension of Alicke (1985) Better-than-Average Effect for desirable and controllable traits. *Social Psychological and Personality Science, 12*(6), 1005–1017.

3
AFFILIATION, FRIENDSHIP, AND LOVE
JENNY L. PATERSON

Contents

3.1 AUTHOR'S PERSONAL JOURNEY

'Love, sex, and relationships? In Hawaii?! You've got to be kidding me!'

While I'm sure my mum was very proud that I had been accepted on a Master's course in Hawaii, as you can see from her reaction, she was a little unimpressed with my choice of topic. She, like many others, assumed that my younger self had been lured to the tropical island to study sex tips while drinking Mai-Tais on Waikiki Beach. It turns out, she was (partly) wrong. Although the cocktails were delicious, I was drawn to study interpersonal relationships under the guidance of the legendary Professor Elaine Hatfield because I firmly believe they are a crucial part of our lives: they help to shape and define who we are, while enabling us to experience utter joy and, at other times, complete devastation.

So, how did a lass from Leeds end up in Hawaii, sipping cocktails, and getting hooked on interpersonal relationships research? Like many academics, my route into my career was not particularly straightforward. My first passion was, in fact, football. I was also quite good at it, managing to make the England Under 18s squad with future England legends Fara Williams and Alex Scott. But, because there were (disgracefully) no opportunities for women to play professionally in England at that time, I headed to the US to pursue my dreams and was awarded a full scholarship at Berry College, Georgia. As football was my main priority, the key reason why I chose to major in Psychology was because I believed it would give me a psychological edge on the field! However, once I started, I loved it. I was fascinated by every aspect of the subject, especially social psychology. I was blown away by how the presence of others, real or even imagined, can have such a huge, and often underappreciated, influence on what we do, what we think, and how we feel.

Interpersonal relationships, in particular, amazed me. Along with seemingly all the poets and musicians who have ever lived, I was fascinated with love – in all its forms. From the love and attachment we (hopefully) have with our caregivers, to the invaluable bonds we build with our friends, to the often immensely passionate feelings we have with our romantic partners. I was absolutely riveted – and still am. It is these relationships that we generally maintain, develop, and talk about on a day-to-day basis. It is these relationships that shape our life, bringing us the happiest days of our lives, yet they have the potential to cause us the most distress. It is this importance, along with the fascinating research that we will explore in this chapter, that made my career choice a no-brainer – I just had to become a social psychologist!

3.2 INTRODUCTION

The interpersonal relationships we forge with our friends and lovers often consume our lives. We spend an inordinate amount of time seeking out, developing, and maintaining these important relationships, which are often pivotal to our happiness – and even our survival. In this chapter, we will examine the importance of these relationships by reflecting upon our innate and enduring *need to belong* and our *attachment styles*, and by discussing the often-catastrophic consequences of when we are unable to form these affiliations due to being socially *ostracised*.

In discussing *interpersonal attraction* (or liking), we will look at who we choose to affiliate with and why, by examining the roles of physical features and psychological characteristics, including proximity, similarity, and familiarity. From there, we will see how *friendships* develop from this initial attraction and how these deep relationships are vital to our mental and physical health.

We will then turn our attention to *romantic love* and explore the different types of love, including the distinction between the all-encompassing, thrilling form of *passionate love* and the more subdued, but longer-lasting, *companionate love*. We will explore how *fairness, equity,* and *trust* are key components to satisfying romantic relationships, and examine why romantic relationships end, discussing both the positive and negative consequences of *relationship dissolutions*.

The second part of the chapter delves further into the age-old debate of nature versus nurture by examining the theories explaining *gender differences in attraction*. We then highlight the need for further research into *singlehood* – the state of not being in a long-term relationship – and identify the stigma, as well as the satisfaction, felt by the growing number of single people in modern societies. We will also focus on how *technology* has revolutionised relationships, bringing positive advances which enable us to develop relationships with many more people with greater ease, but also negative consequences, including technology-enabled abuse.

In the final section, we discuss how research can have a real impact on individuals, societies, policies, and practices. We show how a more inclusive research agenda can reduce heteronormativity and *promote equality for LGBTQ+ relationships*. We also examine how social psychological research can inform interventions that are shown to reduce *loneliness*, and how big businesses utilise social psychological concepts to make *matchmaking* very much a money-making endeavour.

3.3 LEARNING OBJECTIVES

After this chapter, you will be able to explain:

- *Why we affiliate with others.* You will be able to define the need to belong, explain attachment styles, and describe the consequences of social ostracism.
- *Why we like people.* You will be able to identify physical cues of interpersonal attraction, including facial symmetry and averageness, and explain the role of psychological characteristics, including proximity, familiarity, and similarity.
- *The development and benefits of friendships.* You will be able to recognise the importance of self-disclosure in friendships and describe how friendships can improve mental and physical health.

- *The factors that make or break romantic relationships.* You will be able to describe how perceived equity and trust increase satisfaction in romantic relationships. You will also be able to describe the Investment Model and how it explains whether relationships persist or end.
- *The consequences of relationship dissolution.* You will be able to provide a balanced view of the impacts of break-ups, outlining the negative consequences, including guilt, shame, and depression, *and* the benefits, including feelings of relief, empowerment, and growth.
- *The diverse perspectives on significant issues.* You will be able to critically engage with existing research to provide a balanced perspective on (1) gender differences in attraction, (2) the experiences of being single, and (3) how technology influences relationships.
- *How interpersonal relationships research is applied to the real world.* You will be able to describe how research helps to promote equality, reduce loneliness, and can even make you money!

3.4 PART 1: FOUNDATIONS

To start, we will explore a whole host of groundbreaking theories and riveting studies that have shaped our knowledge of interpersonal relationships. We will learn key concepts and hear from leaders of the field to discover the importance, predictors, and consequences of affiliation, friendships, and love.

3.4.1 Affiliation

In general, people are social beings: we tend to need and want to form relationships with others. While we all differ in how many affiliations we make, and the type of bonds we form with others, these relationships are vital for our survival and happiness. In this section, we will reflect on why and how we form affiliations, as well as what happens when we are ostracised and are deprived of these affiliations.

> **Key concept – The need to belong:** The fundamental need to affiliate with others and to be accepted by them. This universal basic desire motivates individuals to develop relationships throughout their lives which helps ensure safety and survival.

When thinking about our **need to belong**, it is easy to conjure up the image of a newborn baby. These helpless human infants are unable to feed, shelter, or protect themselves; they are entirely reliant on others for their survival from the outset. To help ensure their survival, newborns instinctively employ behaviours to help form bonds that will provide them with the food, protection, and warmth they need. Newborns, for example,

Figure 3.1 A newborn baby and toddler

Source: J. Paterson (2016)

prefer looking at faces compared to other stimuli, presumably in an effort to form – and benefit from – interpersonal bonds with caregivers who cannot help but be enamoured by such a tiny, cute human (Mondloch et al., 1999). This reliance on others, however, does not stop in infancy: the innate need to belong is both powerful and enduring (Baumeister & Leary, 1995). We purposefully seek out other individuals across our lifespans for friendship, cooperation, and copulation. Doing so brings many evolutionary and psychological advantages, including the basics of survival, such as obtaining food and protection, as well as enabling us to thrive by enhancing self-esteem through forming important and rewarding identities and social ties.

Variations in the Need for Affiliation

The need to belong seems to be universal, but the extent to which we need to affiliate does vary across people and contexts. Extroverts, for example, seek more social stimulation than introverts (Johnson et al., 1999). Furthermore, contexts that elicit fear and anger also seem to have a big influence. In a famous study, Schachter (1959) found that participants who expected to receive an electric shock preferred contact with others who shared a similar fate rather than being alone. Those in the control group, however, showed no such preference for affiliation. This increased need for contact was not solely for comfort; the affiliation helped participants engage in social comparison: they could look to similar others to better understand and react to the given situation.

Exemplifying this process in real life, Kulik et al. (1996) found that cardiac patients talked more about their upcoming surgery to other cardiac (versus non-cardiac) roommates, especially if the roommate had already undergone the surgery. Importantly, this study not only showed social comparison in action; it showed that when people engaged in social comparison, they were less anxious (as measured by the amount of anxiety-reducing medication taken) and recovered quicker (as measured by discharge date). It seems that seeking out others when fearful can provide clarity and comfort that aid our survival.

Attachment Theory

We now know that we all have the need to belong, and various factors determine the extent to which we are motivated to affiliate (e.g., personality, fearful contexts). But what about the *way* in which we affiliate? Not only do individuals vary in the *quantity* of affiliations they desire, but they also differ in the *nature* of those affiliations. Although initially focused on the mother–child bond, **attachment theory** (Bowlby, 1969) has since developed into an encompassing theory that attempts to explain *how* we relate to other people within meaningful relationships throughout our lives. Below, we detail the initial findings related to children and how these have evolved to explain attachment *style* in adulthood.

> **Key concept – Attachment theory:**
> A theory that suggests that the emotional bond between a caregiver and child has a lasting influence on subsequent relationship behaviours. Dependent upon the caregiver's consistency and responsivity to the infant's needs, the child will develop either a *secure*, *avoidant*, or *anxious/ambivalent* attachment with the caregivers, which will then be replicated in relationships with others later in life.

Expanding on Bowlby's (1969) insight into the importance and lasting influence of the emotional, instinctive bonds (or lack thereof) between caregiver and infant, Ainsworth and colleagues (1971) argued that these bonds could be grouped into three categories which influence how the infant forms subsequent relationships (Ainsworth, 1989). **Secure attachments** are exemplified by harmonious interactions in which the caregiver is responsive to the infants' needs. These infants believe they are worthy of love and, thanks to the caregiver's sensitivity and responsiveness, believe that others can be trusted in relationships. Other infants, however, may have caregivers who are unavailable or even reject their advances. Consequently, the infant develops an **avoidant attachment style** in which they have learnt not to trust or rely on others, preferring instead to be independent. Sometimes, the caregiver is between these two extremes, providing an inconsistent response to the needs of the infant: sometimes loving and doting, at other times rejecting. In this case, the infant becomes somewhat confused and forms an **anxious/ambivalent attachment style** in which they are eager to form relationships, but do not feel they are worthy of the love.

Supporting Bowlby's (1969) suggestion that attachment styles are with us 'cradle to grave' (p. 127), Bartholomew and Horowitz (1991) found young adults to have similar attachment styles to those of Ainsworth's infants. However, they specified that attachment patterns are determined by two dimensions: the extent to which we view *ourselves* as worthy of love and support or not (positive vs negative), and the extent to which we view *others* as trustworthy and available or not (positive vs negative). Table 3.1 shows how the combination of these two dimensions results in four different attachment outcomes.

Table 3.1   Attachment styles in adulthood. Adapted from Figure 1, Bartholomew and Horowitz (1991)

		View of self	
		Positive	Negative
View of others	Positive	**Secure** Comfortable with intimacy and autonomy.	**Preoccupied** Consumed with relationships.
	Negative	**Dismissing** Dismissing of intimacy. Counter-dependent.	**Fearful** Fearful of intimacy. Socially avoidant.

Those who are *secure* have a sense of 'lovability' and trust others to reciprocate. Those who are categorised as *preoccupied* believe others to be trustworthy, but that they, themselves, are not good enough for love. *Fearful-avoidant* individuals share this same low self-esteem, but also anticipate rejection from untrustworthy others so avoid relationships. *Dismissing-avoidant* individuals also avoid relationships, but do so because, although they believe themselves to be lovable, they do not trust others with intimacy.

If all this discussion of attachment styles has left you wondering whether your parents have ruined your chances of love, fear not! Although there is evidence of stability in attachment styles (Brumbaugh & Fraley, 2006), there is a weak correlation between infant attachment and later adult attachment (see Fraley, 2019, for a review). Indeed, basic ageing seems to be correlated with less attachment anxiety (Chopik et al., 2013), and certain life events can change attachment styles. For example, relationships with secure partners who engender trust can help people develop more secure attachments (Kirkpatrick & Hazan, 1994), while therapy can help lower anxiety and increase security (Taylor et al., 2015). Together, these findings show that although attachment styles are relatively stable, experiences can alter the way we view ourselves and others, consequently altering – and potentially improving – our attachment styles.

Social Deprivation: When Affiliation Does not Happen

We've talked at length about how affiliation, in terms of both quantity and quality, is important, but what happens when we cannot affiliate? Or when we are shunned by others? The effects are dramatic and underline just how important our need to affiliate is.

One of the most haunting examples of the psychological consequences of social deprivation was Spitz's scathing (1945) report on hospitalism – a state of apathy and depression in infants caused by a lack of close contact with a caregiver in an institution. Spitz noted that, compared to institutions where infants had contact with a caregiver, infants in overcrowded institutions who were fed but deprived of human contact were less mentally and socially advanced. They also had a devastatingly high mortality rate (e.g., up to 75% in the first year).

Research with rhesus monkeys provides further evidence of the impacts of social isolation. In a now infamously unethical series of experiments, Harlow and colleagues (1965) took newborn monkeys from their mothers and placed them in different contexts, including total isolation for three months, six months, or a year. Once the monkeys were removed from isolation, the results were horrific. Two out of the six monkeys who were isolated for three months attempted to starve themselves. One was successful. The monkeys who were isolated for six months showed extreme behaviours in which they would rock back and forth repeatedly and bite themselves. Those isolated for a year fared even worse. The '12 months of isolation almost obliterated the monkeys socially' (Harlow et al., 1965, p. 94), so much so that the experiment was cut short for fear that the control monkeys would kill the helpless monkeys who had been isolated. Quite clearly, this experiment revealed that contact with others is essential for development and survival.

> **Video:** Harlow's monkeys – 'He may die for the want of love'. Please note the video contains footage of the actual study which may be upsetting https://www.youtube.com/watch?v=_O60TYAlgC4

Social Ostracism

While social deprivation is the extreme lack of affiliation, we are all likely to experience instances of **social ostracism** from time to time, for example, being overlooked, simply ignored, or even flat out rejected (Nezlek et al., 2012). Instances of ostracism that are seemingly trivial, such as an averted gaze, can upset us, threaten our self-esteem, and even cause us physical pain (Wirth et al., 2010). If we are repeatedly excluded, we can feel alienated and depressed, and it does not matter who is excluding us; exclusion by anyone, even those we despise, can leave us feeling devalued and disappointed (Gonsalkorale & Williams, 2007). This suggests that our need to belong is so strong that threats to it, even when perpetrated by people we do not actually *want* to affiliate with, can have harmful consequences.

> **Key concept – Social ostracism:** When someone is ignored or excluded by an individual or group, thereby causing distress.

KEY STUDY 3.1

Cyberball

Imagine you are with two people and you start playing a friendly game of catch. Except, in this game, after a few turns, the two other people do not throw the ball to you. How do you feel? Even if you do not particularly like playing catch, you are probably going to feel a bit left out, frustrated, and perhaps even a little resentful towards the other players. Such a simple technique for inducing feelings of ostracism (being ignored and excluded) has been studied extensively by Kip Williams and colleagues (2000) with the programme 'Cyberball'.

The basic premise of Cyberball is that participants play a computer game of catch with people they believe are other participants. However, the game is rigged. The 'other participants' are, in fact, a computer program that 'throws' the ball to the participant a predetermined number of times: either a reasonable number of times (inclusion condition) or not at all (exclusion condition). Following the 'game', participants' reactions are measured, for example, their self-esteem, their emotions, and even whether they believe life is meaningful.

You may think that being 'ignored' on a computer game would not have a significant influence, but people really do get upset: Functional magnetic resonance imaging (fMRI) studies show that the social pain caused by ostracism in Cyberball maps onto the same brain regions of physical pain (Eisenberger et al., 2003). Our bonds with others, then, are so important to us that fears of breaking them is akin to experiencing physical pain.

> **Video:** Kip Williams explaining the inspiration behind cyberball
> https://www.youtube.com/watch?v=A3UTXsJzAj4

3.4.2 Interpersonal Attraction

Hopefully the previous section has convinced you that we all need to affiliate with others. We may differ in the extent to which we *want* to socialise and vary in *how* we socialise, but it is clear that we, as social animals, desperately need contact with others. Having firmly established this, we now turn to the question of *who* do we choose to socialise with and *why* do we choose those people?

Interpersonal attraction, or liking, is the desire we have to interact with individuals, to form friendships with them, and, sometimes, romantic relationships. It is often difficult to pinpoint what it is we are exactly attracted to, but interpersonal research, as we will discover, has identified a range of factors that explain why we may become interpersonally attracted to certain people.

Physical Attraction: 'What is Beautiful is Good'

Typically, one of the first things we notice about people is their physical appearance. Even though we may tell ourselves that 'beauty is only skin deep', a person's appearance has a significant influence on how much we like them – or *think* we will like them. Research consistently shows that beautiful people are viewed more positively (Dion et al., 1972) and are desired more (Lemay Jr et al., 2010). In their seminal work, for example, Dion, Berscheid and Walster (also known as Hatfield – see Key Thinker box) asked undergraduate students to evaluate the personalities of unknown people in pictures that varied on attractiveness. Compared to those who were perceived as less attractive, attractive people were rated as being more successful, intelligent, possessing better social skills, and more likely to have better futures; for instance, being better parents and experiencing deep personal fulfilment. Beautiful people were perceived to have it all.

But do beautiful people have it all? To a certain extent, yes. Attractive people are not only *perceived* more favourably, they *are* given preferential treatment and *feel* better about themselves than unattractive people (Langlois et al., 2000). It even starts in childhood, with attractive children being more popular, better adjusted, and receiving higher grades. Even when attractive children transgress, they are treated more leniently. Dion (1972), for example, asked adults to read a description of a report of a 7-year-old who had allegedly been throwing stones at a cat. When the description was accompanied by a picture of an attractive child, the behaviour was excused as a one-off and atypical of the child. But, when the exact same description was accompanied by a picture of an unattractive child, the behaviour was seen as more typical of the child and that the transgressions were likely to happen again. This suggests that the attractiveness, rather than the behaviour of the child, was being judged.

Similar results are found for adults. Attractive people are rewarded for their beauty with higher essay marks (Landy & Sigall, 1974), higher earnings (Judge et al., 2009), as well as more dates and sexual experiences (Langlois et al., 2000). Attractive criminals also receive more lenient sentences for less serious crimes (Downs & Lyons, 1991). Highlighting how it pays to be beautiful, Frieze et al. (1991) obtained pictures and salaries of 700 MBA graduates. They found that attractive male graduates' starting salaries were $2,200 more than those rated below average in attractiveness. The starting salaries for female graduates were not influenced by attractiveness but their later salaries were. The more attractive females received $4,200 more in their average salary than females rated as below average in attractiveness.

Are Beautiful People Actually Better?

So, attractive people are perceived more positively and are more successful, but why is this the case? How does being attractive make you more intelligent? More worthy of a pay rise? And less culpable of a crime? A possible reason is based around the self-fulfilling prophecy. When we *believe* people to be more pleasant, more intelligent, more successful, we *treat* those people as if they are better, helping them to extol the virtues that we have placed upon them. Indeed, in a meta-analysis of 90 studies, Feingold (1992) found no significant correlation between attractiveness and mental ability. Tellingly, though, attractiveness was correlated with the more socially oriented characteristics – those that can be shaped by what others think and respond to, for instance, being more popular, socially skilled, less lonely, and less socially anxious.

In support of this argument, Snyder et al. (1977) conducted an ingenious experiment in which men talked to women over the phone. The men were given a picture of a person whom they believed they were talking to, which was of either an attractive or an unattractive woman. Neither picture was the real woman who, importantly, was not aware of this experimental manipulation. The conversations were recorded and subsequently coded by independent observers. Naïve to the study's aims, the observers rated the men more outgoing and sociable when those participants thought they were talking with an attractive woman. Crucially, and providing evidence for the self-fulfilling prophecy, the observers also rated the woman as more attractive, animated, warm, and confident in the condition when the men thought they were speaking to an attractive woman rather than an unattractive woman. This suggests that attractive people are more sociable and charming *because* others enable them and treat them as if they are more sociable and charming.

What *is* Beautiful?

OK, so, perceived beauty influences liking and has many positive consequences for those deemed attractive, but how do we define beauty? Who do we consider physically attractive? Does it vary from person to person, culture to culture? Is it in the eye of the beholder? To get a very rough and ready answer, think about your friends' past and present romantic partners (try not to be *too* judgemental here). They clearly must have thought them somewhat attractive, but what about you? Can you 'see it'? Or do you gag a little at the thought of seeing that person again?

Facial Attractiveness

As the question above alludes to, we do not always have the same 'taste' in people and typically there are individual differences in who is perceived as attractive, as well as some differences across cultures (Penton-Voak et al., 2004). That is, we all have our unique preferences and our socialisation likely plays a pivotal role in who we find attractive. Nevertheless, there also seem to be near universal preferences in what we find attractive in faces. Babies, for example, will look at attractive faces (as rated by adults) more than they will look at those rated as unattractive.

Further highlighting these cross-cultural commonalities, Zebrowitz et al. (2012) recruited participants from the very isolated Bolivian Amazon and asked them to rate the facial attractiveness of 55 men from their ethnic group (Tsimane'), as well as the attractiveness of 40 white US men. The researchers then compared these ratings with those reported by undergraduate students in the US. They found that all participants generally agreed which faces were attractive, no matter what ethnic group they or the faces belonged to, thereby suggesting that what we consider attractive in a face is relatively universal and not based entirely on socialisation processes.

But what makes a face attractive? One factor is facial symmetry: we generally prefer faces that are symmetrical, those in which the right-hand side closely matches the left-hand side. As previous research has shown that facial symmetry is positively related with genetic, physical, and mental health, this symmetry serves an important adaptive, evolutionary function as it indicates the absence of things you may want to avoid for yourself and any future kids you may want, such as harmful pathogens and genetic mutations (Thornhill & Gangestad, 1999). It seems, then, if the eyes are the window to the soul, the face is the window to our genetic health and, even, reproductive potential.

Another key factor to being ridiculously good-looking is, ironically, averageness. Although distinctive faces can be attractive, faces that are more prototypical of the human face are likely to be judged more attractive. Key study 3.2 outlines how research using composite images tests this averageness effect.

KEY STUDY 3.2

The Averageness Effect

Adding to the centuries-old debate of 'What is beauty?', Langlois and Roggman (1990) suggest a deceptively simple answer – we prefer averageness. This does not mean we prefer *average-looking* people; instead, we prefer faces that represent the *mathematical* average of faces we have seen. To test this assumption, Langlois and Roggman took grayscale photographs of young adults with neutral expressions and created composites. These composites were created with meticulous care, averaging the greyscale of each pixel in a 512 × 512 digitised photograph. They made composites with 2 images, 4 images, 8 images, 16 images, and 32 images. Participants then rated the attractiveness of the composites plus the original, individual photographs. Images made from the average images were consistently rated as more attractive than the original images. Moreover, the *more* images used to make the composite (i.e., 32 images), the *more* attractive it was perceived to be.

So, why do we prefer this mathematical average face? What is so special about averageness? A possible reason is that the faces typify the prototype of what we expect a face to look like. That is, throughout our life, we see a lot of faces and form a schema (mental representation) of what a face *generally* looks like, and so we develop a facial prototype of in our minds eye – our own facial composite. When we see an image that closely resembles this, we find it familiar and, as we shall see, this familiarity may increase interpersonal attraction.

EXERCISE 3.1

Averageness Effect in Faces ... Fish and Cars

Halberstadt and Rhodes (2003) suggested that the preference for averageness does not stop at faces. They showed that participants preferred the composite images of line-drawn fish and cars to their original independent images. Below, rate the attractiveness of the faces, fish, and cars and try to guess which ones are made up of the most images.[1]

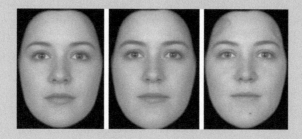

Figure 3.2   Composite photographs of faces

Source: Little et al. (2011)

Figure 3.3   Original and composite drawings of fish

Source: Halberstadt and Rhodes (2003)

Figure 3.4   Original and composite drawings of cars

Source: Halberstadt and Rhodes (2003)

Did you prefer the most average image? Why may this be?

---

[1]The first images are composed of the most images.

Psychological Attractiveness

While the previous section focused on facial attractiveness and its impact on liking, we are, of course, not *that* shallow. Thankfully (for my ugly mug), we like and are attracted to people for a whole host of reasons. In this section, we will see how birds of a feather flock together, personalities really do count, and just hanging around can lead to increased interpersonal attraction.

Familiarity

As alluded to in the averageness effect, we generally like things that are familiar. New, unfamiliar, unknown things, on the other hand, can cause uncertainty and apprehension because they could pose a threat and should, therefore, be treated with caution. However, by being repeatedly exposed to a new stimulus (and assuming there are no adverse effects), it becomes familiar, and we become more attracted to it because we realise our fears are unfounded and our apprehension therefore subsides.

Demonstrating this mere repeated exposure effect, Saegert et al. (1973) devised a study ostensibly investigating participants' evaluations of liquids ranging in pleasantness (e.g., soft drinks to vinegar). The participants went to various tasting stations in different rooms and happened to see other participants within the study. Once they had rated the liquids, the researchers asked them to rate how likeable the other participants were. Providing support for the mere exposure effect, the more times the participants had seen one another, the more they liked each other. Importantly, this was found for when they drank both pleasant *and* noxious liquids, suggesting that even when paired with unpleasant stimuli (e.g., drinking vinegar), familiarity can engender liking.

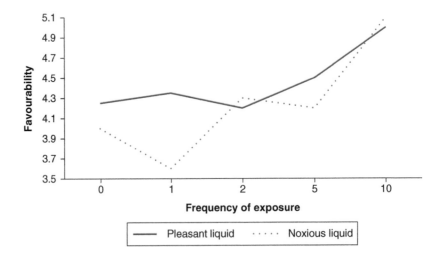

Figure 3.5 Favourability towards a person as a function of number of exposures and pleasantness of taste. Data from Saegert et al. (1973)

There are, of course, limits to the familiarity–attraction link. Familiarity does not breed liking for those with perceived unappealing qualities, nor if we are in overtly competitive contexts (Finkel et al., 2015). You can also have too much of a good thing and reach experiential saturation, in which exposure to the person surpasses the optimal level and boredom can set in – providing some support for the old adage that 'familiarity breeds contempt'.

Proximity

One, often overlooked, essential ingredient for interpersonal attraction is proximity – you need the opportunity to have contact with someone to become acquainted with them. Initially, this proximity was conceptualised as *physical* proximity, but, with technological advancements, proximity is now a more nuanced concept with people forming strong bonds without ever meeting in person. Nevertheless, physical closeness remains a very important factor in the development of most relationships. Such proximity can help increase liking via the mere exposure effect, as well as being a crude signal for potential similarities.

Leon Festinger (see Key Thinker box) highlighted the importance of proximity for the formation of relationships way back in 1950, noting that students were nearly twice as likely to become close friends with their next-door neighbours than those living a couple of doors down. Furthermore, compared to others who lived on the lower level, people who lived downstairs and near staircases were more likely to become friends with the people upstairs. Festinger and colleagues (1950) suggested that these passive contacts by the stairs increased the opportunity to interact with the upstairs neighbours and thus increased liking. As such, simply being near and being noticed seems to facilitate interpersonal attraction and friendships.

KEY THINKER

Leon Festinger

As the doctoral student of Kurt Lewin (the forefather of social psychology), it may not be surprising that Leon Festinger (1919–1989) became one of the most influential social psychologists. However, by his own admission, Festinger did not have such lofty aspirations early in his career: he did not even take a social psychological module throughout his studies! Despite these early reservations, Festinger made many important and long-lasting contributions to the discipline. After documenting the proximity effect (see above), he proposed the social comparison theory (1954), which suggests that individuals compare themselves to relatively similar others in order to accurately evaluate their own opinions and abilities. He further went on to develop cognitive dissonance theory (1957), arguably one of the most influential psychological

(Continued)

theories ever. In this, Festinger argued that when our attitudes and behaviours are incompatible with one another, we experience 'dissonance' – an uncomfortable, disconcerting state which motivates us to change either the attitude or the behaviour to restore balance and harmony in our thoughts and actions (see Chapter 6).

Festinger's legacy is further cemented by his ability to nurture, inspire, and mentor other great social psychologists, including the renowned Elaine Hatfield during her PhD studies at Stanford (see Key Thinker box). Hatfield describes Festinger as a brave and generous mentor who supported and enabled her to pursue her academic interests with great success. Combining these inspirational tales with his own outstanding theoretical and empirical contributions clearly shows that Festinger has had a tremendous, positive impact on social psychology *and* social psychologists.

Attitudinal Similarity

Just as familiarity does not ensure attraction, simply having proximity does not guarantee increased liking. Instead, these factors are best conceptualised as *facilitators* of attraction: being close to and getting to know someone helps us decide *whether* we like them, not that we *will* like them. They help us go beyond surface qualities (e.g., physical attractiveness) and assess individuals at a deeper level to evaluate how similar and compatible we are to one another.

Detailing the attraction of similarity, Newcomb (1961) recruited 17 transfer students to an intensive naturalistic longitudinal study investigating the 'acquaintance process'. Akin to a modern-day reality show, participants received free housing to live with complete strangers and have their thoughts, attitudes, and relationships analysed on a weekly basis. Initially, and in support of the importance of proximity, participants most liked the housemates living closest to them. However, as time went on and attitudes became more salient, especially through their weekly group meetings, participants began to favour housemates who held similar attitudes to themselves – as rated *before* they even entered the house. This suggests that interpersonal attraction is, at first, based on convenience, but given time, people tend to ditch those who hold dissimilar attitudes and prefer to form longer-lasting relationships with people who share similar attitudes and beliefs.

Reciprocity and Trust

Another factor that increases interpersonal attraction is whether the other individual likes us. In general, we all like to be liked and so we generally like people who like us, and dislike those who dislike us. Evidencing this reciprocity principle, Montoya and Insko (2008) told participants that they were going to complete an interdependent task with a partner. Before doing so, however, both partners completed and swapped their questionnaires to help get to know one another. After reading their 'partner's' questionnaire (which was actually completed by the researchers and was the same across conditions), the participants read their 'partner's'

thoughts about the upcoming experiment. Again, these 'thoughts' were written by the exper-
imenters and described either the *experiment* as fun and interesting (control-evaluation) or the
participant as fun and interesting (positive-evaluation). As shown in Figure 3.6, participants
who read favourable remarks about themselves (vs the experiment) perceived their partners
to like them more and reciprocated this liking by rating their partner as more likeable, as
wanting to engage with them more, and as being more trustworthy.

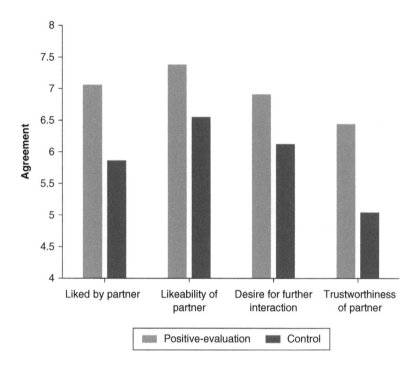

Figure 3.6 Reciprocal attraction after reading a positive evaluation of the self or the
experiment (control). Data from Montoya and Insko (2008)

In addition to these differences, Montoya and Insko (2008) showed that the reason why we
like those who like us is that we perceive those people to be trustworthy. That is, if someone
says they like us, we are likely to believe they have our best interests at heart, and we can rely
on them. In other words, we *trust* them – and since we trust them, we like them. In fact, trustworthiness is *essential* in interpersonal attraction and subsequent relationships. Cottrell et al.
(2007), for example, asked participants to rate the importance of traits in other people who
they were to have various relationships with (e.g., members of a study group, golf team, close
friend, employee). While most traits were deemed important for specific relationships (e.g.,
athleticism in a sport team member; intelligence in a study group member), one trait consistently stood out across all relationships: trustworthiness was paramount and, as the authors
state, showed its 'fundamental importance to human social interactions' (p. 227). Being able
to trust an individual is the absolute key to having a good relationship with them.

EXERCISE 3.2

Rate the Traits!

Cottrell et al. (2007) asked participants to rate the traits of their ideal partners in various relationships. Here we would like you to go a step further. Using a 9-point scale (1 = *not at all important* to 9 = *extremely important*), we would like you to rate how important each trait is for (i) your ideal teacher, (ii) your ideal best friend, and (iii) your ideal romantic partner. Are the traits you value similar across these relationships? Why? Why not?

The traits to rate are:

1. Trustworthy; 2. Cooperative; 3. Trusting; 4. Agreeable; 5. Outgoing; 6. Conscientious; 7. Emotionally stable; 8. Open-minded; 9. Intelligent; 10. Predictable; 11. Physically attractive; 12. Similar to me; 13. Healthy; 14. Assertive; 15. Funny; 16. Considerate; 17. Tolerant; 18. Respectful; 19. Nurturing; 20. Successful; 21. Ambitious; 22. Financially secure.

Next, if you have (or had) a teacher, best friend, or romantic partner, reflect on how much these people possess(ed) those traits. Is there a difference between the people you have had actual relationships with and the *ideal* people you have rated?

3.4.3 Friendships

As we have seen, there are numerous factors that explain why we may initially like people and gravitate towards them. But what happens after this initial attraction? What makes us promote some of our *acquaintances* to *friends*? How do these friendships blossom and what is so special about friends that enable us to have friendships that last through the decades, even entire lifetimes?

Self-Disclosure

An important aspect of friendships is the ability to confide in someone: to tell someone your hopes and fears; to share your successes, and even your embarrassments. However, it would be risky to share with just anyone, and so we tend to self-disclose to people whom we can trust most: our friends. But how do you get to that level of friendship?

Although there are variations and we may sometimes just 'click' with someone, becoming instant best friends, according to the social penetration model (Altman & Taylor, 1973), friendships typically develop in a well-paced process of reciprocal self-disclosure. At the start of the friendships, we initially share relatively sparse and superficial information about ourselves; for example, where we are from and what we are studying. At this stage, if we reveal too much too soon, the relationship may end abruptly due to over-sharing – after all, your nerdy obsession with the Spice Girls may put some people off. However, once we feel quite comfortable with our new friends, we start to disclose increasingly more about ourselves, including our guilty pleasures, which helps intensify the friendship. Importantly, our friends reciprocate our disclosures by revealing incrementally more information about themselves. Once we have solidified our friendships (and we know their secrets – and they know ours), self-disclosure levels off and is replaced with greater supportive communication which sustains the friendship. Nevertheless, if we or our friends start to withdraw and communicate less, de-penetration may occur, which can lead to the end of the friendship as we know it, which would be a shame as friendships are very beneficial.

Benefits of Friendships

Considerable research shows that friendships are good for us, improving both our mental and physical health. Remarkably, a meta-analysis revealed that having supportive and rewarding friendships has a stronger influence on mortality rates than many lifestyle behaviours, including smoking and physical activity (Holt-Lunstad & Smith, 2012). While this is impressive, the benefits of friendships do not stop there. Friendships do not just buffer us from stress and allow us to survive – they enable us to thrive. Friends certainly help us cope and even grow through adverse events, but they also prepare, inspire, and motivate us to accomplish our dreams and aspirations in the good times (Feeney & Collins, 2015). With such tremendous benefits, it is clear why we spend so much time and energy fostering those initial interpersonal attractions to life-long friendships.

3.4.4 Romantic Relationships

While friendships are clearly essential, it is romantic relationships that have historically captured the imaginations of poets, songwriters, and public alike. Due to their intensity, these unique interpersonal relationships were long assumed to be too mysterious and even miraculous to study scientifically. Fortunately, trailblazing psychologists in the 1950s began to methodically address the age-old question of 'what is love?'. While today such research is well established and respected, in the Guest Personal Journey, Professor Elaine Hatfield describes, first-hand, the obstacles she faced and the shocking backlash she received when pioneering social psychological research into romantic relationships.

GUEST PERSONAL JOURNEY

Elaine Hatfield

Source: © Elaine Hatfield

When I began my PhD at Stanford University in 1959, Psychology was preoccupied with mathematical modelling and rat runways. It seemed that to understand the complexity of *human* psychology – and to make any real contribution to the discipline – you needed to study *rat* behaviour. As interesting as the research was, my intellectual curiosity firmly lay with passionate love and sexual desire. After all, once we had put the rat mazes away for the night, these were the topics that captivated and consumed myself and my colleagues. Of course, I knew attempting to study such 'taboo' topics would be considered unscientific and too 'trivial'. Nevertheless, supported by my mentor, Leon Festinger, I was finally allowed to rigorously study love as part of my graduate work. It was a struggling start to a career journey that was never easy.

The next stumbling block came when I graduated. Despite Festinger telling me I was the 'best graduate student' he'd ever had (he probably told *everyone* that!), I was turned away from every institution. The reason? Because I was a woman. I finally managed to get a job at the University of Minnesota – arranging dances at the Student Activities Bureau! Hardly an academic position, but I persevered and managed to research dating relationships and volunteered to teach and supervise students. I must have done an adequate enough job as I was offered a position in the Psychology Department the next year.

Following a tremendous time at Minnesota, I moved to the University of Wisconsin in 1967 – this time to the Department of Sociology because the Psychology equivalent did not allow women on the faculty. Despite the sexism, I developed a research programme into love and sexual desire. But controversy soon found me. In 1975, Ellen Berscheid and I were awarded $84,000 from the National Science Foundation (NSF) to continue our research into passionate and companionate love. This prestigious award, however, was quickly followed by another: the 'Golden Fleece Award'. This was 'awarded' by a US Senator who targeted and ridiculed research he deemed 'unneeded' so as to 'save' the taxpayer money. It was a painful time. A tabloid, *The Chicago Tribune*, even ran a contest to see who was right: the Senator or me. I lost 87.5% to 12.5% and received bags full of critical mail. Worse still, the NSF withdrew the funding and suggested I refrain from submitting anything else for a while. I could do nothing else but agree.

But the tide does change and so it did for me in 1978. I kept doggedly at my work and wrote a prize-winning book, *A New Look at Love*, which emphasised the importance of social psychological research into love. From then, the path began to get easier albeit bumpy. Relationship research was no longer taboo, and the public and politicians began to realise relationships could – and should – be scientifically studied. Looking back, it was a rough journey at times, but it was certainly a good road to take – with thick-skin and wiliness.

KEY THINKER

Elaine Hatfield

As highlighted in the Guest Personal Journey above, Elaine Hatfield overcame societal taboos, blatant sexism, and even political backlash to become one of the most important social psychologists studying interpersonal relationships. In a career spanning over half a century, Hatfield was not only pivotal in establishing the field, with over 300 publications, she has made numerous important contributions.

Also publishing as Elaine Walster, Hatfield theorised about the importance of romantic partners being similarly attractive, with the matching hypothesis (Walster et al., 1966), was part of the research team that evidenced the 'what is beautiful is good' phenomenon (Dion et al., 1972), and proposed equity theory to explain the importance of cost–benefits analysis in romantic relationships (Walster et al., 1973). Hatfield was also one of the first to distinguish different types of romantic love – defining and differentiating passionate love and companionate love (Hatfield, 1982). Further still, she proposed the importance and processes of emotional contagion in romantic relationships – how we mimic and 'catch' each other's emotions in romances (Hatfield et al., 1993).

With such impressive contributions, it is no wonder Hatfield has been awarded lifetime achievement accolades from the Association for Psychological Science and the Society for the Scientific Study of Sex, to name but a few. Indeed, her work has been so influential that she has even inspired a hit record! *Would you...?* samples a research prompt from Clark and Hatfield's (1989) research: 'I noticed you around, I find you rather attractive, would you ... go to bed with me?' Not only were the research findings interesting, but the song reached the Top 10 in seven different countries.

Types of Love

Love is complex. And I mean, *really* complex. Even the way we use the word is confusing. We *love* pizza. We *love* our parents. We *love* our romantic partners. Yet we can all (hopefully!) agree that these proclamations of love are different from one another. In this section, we focus on the latter type: *romantic love* – the often-powerful emotions, thoughts, and acts associated with intimate relationships. This type of love is more than liking, and not just in a quantitative sense – love is *qualitatively* different from liking. Love is also not mere sexual attraction. That is, loving a romantic partner is not just really, really liking them,

> **Video:** *'Would you...?'* and the paper that inspired it https://www.youtube.com/watch?v=izBbP2kro-c

nor is it solely being physically attracted to them. But the differentiation does not stop there. Although romantic love does seem to be a universal emotion with key characteristics and components (Hatfield & Rapson, 1993), romantic love can be further classified into different typologies.

Passionate Love

> **Key concept – Passionate love:** The intense longing for a romantic partner that is typically present at the beginning of a relationship.

One of the most prominent types of romantic love, and possibly the most recognisable, is **passionate love** (Hatfield, 1982). This is the all-consuming type of love that typically occurs at the start of a romantic relationship when we are totally enamoured by our partner. It is when we cannot stop thinking about our loved one, how amazing they are, and how much we want to be with them. We forego food, friends, and even sleep because of the intensity. Intriguingly, the 'chemistry' felt in passionate love translates to actual physical chemistry in the brain: neuropsychologists have found that individuals in passionate love have increased levels of dopamine, the neurotransmitter responsible for pleasure. Similarly, fMRIs show that the brain region for reward and pleasure (the caudate nucleus) is activated when looking at pictures of romantic lovers but not when looking at friends (Fisher, 2004), suggesting that something unique happens to our brains when we fall in passionate love. It appears, then, Bonnie Tyler was nearly correct: passionate love causes a total eclipse of the ~~heart~~ brain.

The role of dopamine in passionate love may also explain why we sometimes fall for the 'wrong one'. In passionate love, dopamine leads to a sense of physiological arousal – the giddiness we feel when we are with our loved one. However, dopamine can also be released under stressful situations and, if we experience this stress-related arousal in front of an attractive person, this physiological arousal can be mistaken for romantic or sexual attraction (see Key study 3.3).

KEY STUDY 3.3

Attraction or Anxiety ... on a Bridge

Testing the excitation transfer process in which arousal is mistakenly attributed to an incorrect source, Dutton and Aron (1974) conducted a creative, albeit anxiety-inducing, study. Participants were approached on one of two bridges at a Canadian beauty spot and asked to write a story inspired by a photo shown to them. One bridge was three metres high and spanned a small stream. The other, shown in Figure 3.7, was a terrifying 70 metres high, which wobbled and swayed in the wind. Supporting the excitation transfer hypothesis, men who were approached by an attractive female researcher on the very high bridge used more sexual imagery in their stories than those on the lower bridge. These participants were also more likely to call the researcher for 'further details' once the study had been completed. It seems that the men on the higher bridge experienced greater arousal and misattributed the arousal as feelings towards the researcher rather than the actual source – the anxiety caused by the high bridge. So, the next time you fall for your paragliding instructor or ziplining guide, maybe take a moment to consider whether it is them you are attracted to or whether misattribution of arousal is at play.

Figure 3.7   The experiment took place on the Capilano Suspension Bridge in Vancouver, Canada

Source: Photo taken from: Markus Säynevirta, CC BY-SA 4.0, https://commons.wikimedia. org/w/index.php?curid=57619535

Companionate Love

> **Key concept – Companionate love:** The more subtle, enduring type of love which is characteristic of long-term romantic relationships and friendships. It is based on mutual respect, trust, and interdependence.

As exciting as passionate love is, the giddiness and intensity soon subside, and if the relationship continues, this passionate love is replaced by a more subtle, longer-lasting form of love: **companionate love**. This type of love is characterised by partners enjoying deeply entwined lives that are founded upon mutual liking and respect (Hatfield, 1982). Also found in close friendships, those experiencing companionate love become so entwined that they consider themselves as a single unit, going from 'you and me' to 'we'.

Triangular Theory of Love

While the basic distinction between passionate and companionate love is supported in the literature, such a simple differentiation cannot capture the variability of romantic love. Take, for example, people you know who are in relationships. There will be some who are in the giddy state of passionate love, others blissful in companionate love, yet others will be in empty marriages, and some solely interested in serial affairs. Acknowledging this variability, Sternberg (1986) suggests there are seven types of love,

> **Video:** Robert Sternberg describes his triangular theory of love https://www.youtube.com/watch?v=4a0FnoNU68g

which are categorised by the combination of three components: intimacy (closeness/strength of bond), passion (sexual excitement), and commitment (decision to maintain the relationship). Table 3.2 shows the combination of the components and the description of resultant loves.

Table 3.2 Components and typologies of love according to Sternberg's (1986) triangular theory of love

Label and description	Passion	Commitment	Intimacy
Nonlove: casual interactions without love	✗	✗	✗
Infatuation: fleeting, love at first sight feeling	✓	✗	✗
Empty love: decision to love without passion or emotional closeness	✗	✓	✗
Liking: close, non-romantic friendship that may not last	✗	✗	✓
Fatuous love: whirlwind romances that base commitment on passion without development of intimacy	✓	✓	✗
Romantic love: physically and emotionally drawn to one another but short-lasting, like a summer fling	✓	✗	✓

Label and description	Passion	Commitment	Intimacy
Companionate love: long-term, entwined deep friendship	✗	✓	✓
Consummate love: complete love; ideal to strive for and maintain	✓	✓	✓

Rewarding Relationships

Whatever the type of love, people generally search for rewarding relationships that will be satisfying. So, what is the secret recipe for relational success? Clearly, the answer is not simple, but drawing on social psychological research, we can identify some common aspects of satisfying relationships, including the perception of whether the relationships are fair, what sacrifices are given and why, and the importance of trust (again).

Rewards or Fairness?

According to social exchange theory (Homans, 1958), all social relationships are based on a simple cost: reward ratio in which we are motivated to maximise our profits and minimise our costs. Within relationships, this assumes we value and track the 'goods' we receive from our partners and weigh them against the 'goods' we provide. The 'goods' include both material (e.g., gifts, money) and non-material (e.g., love, care),

> **Key concept – Equity theory:** A theory that suggests that relationship satisfaction is dependent upon the perception of fairness, in terms of what the partners are putting into the relationship and what they are getting out of it.

and may be counted objectively (e.g., pounds and pence spent) and subjectively (e.g., feelings elicited). Once we have tallied up the costs and rewards, we continue with relationships that we perceive to be rewarding and terminate those that are too costly. Not a particularly romantic theory, but a very rational one.

But is love that straightforward? Do we tally up the hugs we give and receive? Do we aim to maximise our profits? **Equity theory** has a slightly different stance (Walster et al., 1973). According to this theory, we do indeed tally up the costs and rewards of our relationships, but we do so to make sure the relationship is fair. That is, we use these 'calculations' to ensure that we (and our partners) are getting out what we put into the relationship.

In explicating the theory, Hatfield and Traupmann (1981) showed that when individuals felt they reaped what they sowed and had an equitable relationship, they were highly satisfied and content with their relationship (Figure 3.8). Those who felt they put more into their relationship than they got out (the 'under-benefitted' partners) felt aggrieved, resentful, and were the least satisfied with their relationships. The 'over-benefitted' partners were also less satisfied with their relationships than the equitable partners. This seems to be at odds with social exchange theory because if the partners are getting *more* than they are putting into a relationship, they are maximising their profits and thus should be the happiest. However, the findings support equity theory: partners who feel they are getting more than they deserve perceive the unfairness, feel guilty, and are therefore less satisfied with their relationship.

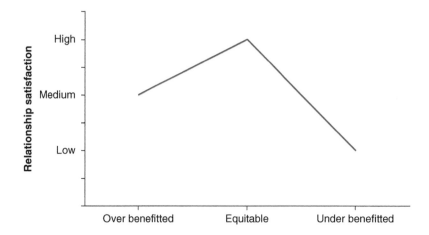

Figure 3.8 Relationship satisfaction as a function of perceived equity in relationships
Source: Hatfield and Traupmann (1981)

Sacrifices

We not only count what we put *into* relationships and what we get *out* of them, we also consider what we and our partner have *sacrificed* for the relationship. These sacrifices can range from relatively mundane everyday occurrences (e.g., watching your partner's favourite TV show instead of yours) to life-changing decisions (e.g., moving cities for your partner's new job) and can have huge impacts on relationship quality. According to Emily Impett (see Guest Personal Journey) and colleagues (2005), these impacts depend on the motivations behind the sacrifices. When partners sacrifice to prevent upsetting their partner or causing conflict in their relationship, this *avoidance* motive paradoxically increases relationship conflict and leads to poorer relationships. Conversely, when partners sacrifice to make their partner happy (an '*approach*' motive), people are happier with their life, partner, and relationship. One key reason for these positive impacts is that the approach motive increases trust in the partner and the relationship.

GUEST PERSONAL JOURNEY

Emily Impett

I always wish I had a sexy story to explain why I got into studying relationships as a career, but it all stemmed from rocking my undergraduate statistics course and the professor inviting me to join his research team studying sexual assault. I was hooked on research but realised quickly that I wanted to study sexuality from a positive perspective, and in the context of romantic relationships. For example, there was quite a negative view of sexual compliance at the time, but we wondered if, especially in the context of ongoing committed relationships, sexual compliance could have relational benefits. To answer questions like these, I use rich, ecologically valid methods (e.g., longitudinal, dyadic research) to understand when 'giving' to a partner – both inside and outside the bedroom – helps versus harms relationships (Impett et al., 2020).

Throughout my career, I have been fortunate to have worked with and been inspired by dream mentors (Drs Anne Peplau, Shelly Gable, Dacher Keltner, Oliver John) and many, many exceptional students. Our collaborations have led to meaningful insights, and I feel honoured to have been recognised with several research awards, including the Caryl Rusbult Early Career Award from the Relationships Researchers Interest Group.

Source: © Emily Impett

Trust and Trysts

As we have already noted, trustworthiness is crucial at all stages of relationships, from initial attraction to developing and maintaining friendships. As romantic relationships are particularly intimate and partners often invest heavily in terms of emotions and material goods (e.g., shared house, children), trust in these relationships is particularly important as there is a lot at stake. It will come as no surprise, then, to find that trust is also key to romantic satisfaction. Rempel et al. (1985), for example, found that married couples who perceived their partners to be dependable and had faith they would be responsive and caring in the future reported significantly greater happiness with their relationships than those who did not feel such trust.

A common threat to trust is infidelity – the violation of the assumption of sexual or emotional exclusivity. This cheating is such a threat to relationships that infidelity is the most common reason for divorce (Previti & Amato, 2003). Not only can such affairs obliterate the cornerstone of trust and end the relationship, research suggests that secret romances are just not worth the hassle. Being cheated on increases depression (Gordon et al., 2004) and being the cheater is associated with increased stress and reduced closeness to the existing partners (Lehmiller, 2009). So, while the excitement and mystery of a secret lover may seem appealing, research suggests that there are limited benefits to such betrayal.

To Stay or to Go? Enduring Relationships and Ending Relationships

Relationship satisfaction is typically an important factor for deciding whether a relationship can be sustained or whether it should end. However, satisfaction is only part of the equation. For instance, some people will leave seemingly perfect partnerships, while others persist in unhappy, and even toxic, relationships. Why is this the case? Addressing this question, Caryl Rusbult (see Key Thinker box) proposed the Investment Model (Rusbult, 1983).

KEY THINKER

Caryl Rusbult

When starting her career in the 1970s, Caryl Rusbult (1952–2010) noticed there was a great deal of research explaining interpersonal attraction and why people formed relationships, but little insight into why people *stayed* in those relationships (Finkenauer, 2010). It was simply assumed that partners remained committed to their relationships because they were satisfied. But as satisfaction fluctuates, Rusbult theorised that there must be other important factors at play. She proposed the *Investment Model* (see below), which identifies the importance of investment levels and quality of alternatives, as well as satisfaction, when choosing to remain in a relationship (Rusbult, 1983).

The theory was academically revolutionary and had huge practical implications. Previous theories could not begin to explain why people remained in dissatisfying and abusive relationships, which led to the assumption that there must be something 'wrong' with people who stayed with abusive partners – which was blatantly incorrect and extremely harmful. By emphasising the roles of investment and alternatives, Rusbult helped to switch the focus from blaming and therapising victims to addressing the underlying issues: how the lack of opportunities and an over-reliance on their partner trap victims of abuse. Such insight has been invaluable in informing strategies for empowering survivors of domestic abuse ever since.

In addition to making these immense contributions, Rusbult, by all accounts, was an incredible mentor. Her dedication to mentoring was so great that, after her untimely death at the age of 57, the Society for Personality and Social Psychology dedicated an annual award in her name to honour her achievements and her legacy to the discipline.

The Investment Model

According to the **Investment Model**, the decision to maintain a relationship – or relationship commitment – is predicted by three factors. *Satisfaction* is one factor: when partners are satisfied, they are more likely to be committed to the relationship since it is beneficial and rewarding. But even when relationships are unsatisfying, partners often persevere and endure. One reason is because of their *investment* in the relationship. This investment relates to the time and energy already put into the relationship, as well as the entanglement of family, mutual friends, shared hobbies, and material goods (e.g., housing). Undoing such investments can seem daunting and costly, so partners are more likely to stay committed when investments are high. Nevertheless, even when partners are unhappy and think it would be best to cut their investment losses, they may still be resolutely committed to their relationship. This brings us on to the third factor: *perceived quality of alternatives*. When considering whether to leave a relationship, partners are likely to weigh up their options: is staying with the current partner better than other options on offer, including having a different partner, being single, spending more time with friends, or taking up a new hobby? If the perceived alternatives are relatively low quality, commitment will be high; however, if a person perceives alternatives to their current relationship to be of high quality, their heads may be turned, and they may end the relationship to pursue the more appealing possibilities.

> **Key concept – Investment Model:** The model suggests that relationship commitment is dependent upon maintaining high levels of satisfaction, high levels of investment, and perceiving low quality alternatives.

Applying the Investment Model to abusive relationships, Rusbult and Martz (1995) analysed the relationships of 100 women who entered a refuge shelter fleeing from physically abusive male partners. In line with hypotheses, when women were more satisfied with their relationship, had fewer alternatives (in terms of education and income), and more investments (e.g., marriage, children), they were more likely to return to the abusers after leaving the shelter. Not only do the findings provide support for the Investment Model, they highlight the complexity of why abusive relationships continue. Notably, because the lack of alternatives and large investment size were stronger predictors of returning to the abuser than relationship satisfaction, it suggests that people experiencing abuse may remain in these relationships not because they want to stay, but because they are trapped and unable to leave.

Ending Relationships

If you have ever been in love, you are probably acutely aware that relationships falter and flounder. Some rebound while others end. According to Rusbult and colleagues (1982), the future of troubled relationships is dependent upon how the partners react to dissatisfaction, and these reactions vary along two dimensions: partners engage in either constructive or destructive behaviours and they are either active or passive. If a partner constructively wants to maintain the relationship, they will either actively *voice* their concerns (e.g., discussing problems) or passively show *loyalty* (e.g., giving things time to improve). If, however, they believe the relationship is over, they act destructively by either passively *neglecting* the relationship (e.g., ignoring the partner) or by actively *exiting* the relationship (e.g., formally ending the relationship).

Once partners decide to exit the relationship, Duck's (2007) relationship dissolution model suggests that partners progress through a four-stage process to detach from their long-term partner. In the initial *intrapsychic phase*, the individual considers the costs and benefits of the relationship and may discuss the problems with others. Next, the individual will talk with their partner in the *dyadic phase*, to discuss, negotiate, or argue about the situation and how best to proceed. When it is clear that the relationship is ending, the partners enter the *social phase*, in which they seek support from others to validate their decisions and will present themselves positively to try to save face. Finally, the *grave dressing phase* encompasses the functional aspects of the break-up where division of property and childcare arrangements are agreed. Social support is also important in this stage as individuals seek help and assurances from others to move on with their new lives.

Consequences of Ending Relationships

Considering that most of us do not end up marrying our nursery school sweethearts, it is somewhat inevitable that we will experience the end of a romantic relationship at some point in our lives. So how does it feel? Is it as heart-breaking as all the movies, poems, and songs suggest? Well, the research suggests it is a bit more complicated than that.

When discussing the consequences of ending relationships, the focus has generally been on the potential negative aspects, including heartbreak and despair. Partners often grieve for their former relationship, feel anger and/or guilt for their role in the separation, and sadness about what could, or should, have been. Adding to this, break-ups often include logistical and financial burdens which add to the significant stress and, together with the emotional trauma, may explain why divorce is related to poorer physical and mental health, and increased mortality (Sbarra et al., 2011).

While this makes for very grim reading, reactions to break-ups are much more nuanced than this simplistic view suggests. First, the negative consequences are dependent upon numerous characteristics, for example, those who initiate the break-up may feel more guilt (Baumeister et al., 1993) but are less likely to be depressed than the partner they left (Kitson & Holmes, 1992). Attachment style also plays a role, with securely attached and fearful-avoidant individuals reporting lower levels and shorter periods of sadness than dismissive-avoidant individuals (Sbarra & Emery, 2005).

Although the positives are often overlooked, break-ups can actually be extremely beneficial. Separation enables people to escape unfulfilling, negative, and even harmful relationships, promoting feelings of relief, empowerment, and excitement about future possibilities. Furthermore, even when left devastated with a broken heart and shattered dreams, all is not lost as individuals are likely to experience growth. Tashiro and Frazier (2003) found that after the end of a relationship, individuals reported greater self-confidence, improvements in communication strategies, better relationships with others, and more positive expectations about future relationships. As with other significant life events, break-ups can act as a catalyst for making big life changes, enabling individuals to grow beyond their previous level of psychological functioning. In sum, while relationship breakdowns can clearly be very stressful, maybe it is time to change the narrative away from the doom and gloom of break-ups and, acknowledging that most relationships are finite, view separation not just as an end but as a new opportunity to grow and better ourselves.

As we come to the end of this section, let's take a minute to reflect on what we have managed to cover. We have learnt about why we need relationships (need to belong), what types of relationships we form (attachment theory, friendships, romantic love types), who we select to be in relationships with and why (physical and psychological attraction, investment model), and the consequences of denying, developing, maintaining, and ending relationships (social exclusion, friendship benefits, rewarding relationships, relationship dissolution). That is a lot – but we're not done yet! In the following sections, we will build on this knowledge to think a little more in depth about emerging issues in interpersonal relationships research (Advances) and see how we put this knowledge to use in the real world (Applications), all the while discussing fascinating research that is central to this incredible and important discipline.

3.5 PART 2: ADVANCES

In this section, we focus a little more on some old debates and new developments. The examples show how no knowledge is set in stone and theory-driven research is the cornerstone of our exciting, interesting, and ever-evolving science.

3.5.1 Gender Differences in Attraction: Evolution or Biosocial Roles?

A discussion on attraction, and specifically sexual desire, would not be complete without the age-old debate of nature versus nurture. On the one hand, evolutionary psychologists explain attraction and sexual preferences as strategies that have developed over millennia to increase the likelihood of species survival. They suggest that women and men are innately driven to reproduce and will seek to mate with partners with good reproductive fitness (i.e., good genes that will help the survival of offspring). As noted in the 'Facial attractiveness' section, cues of genetic health, including facial symmetry, are valued and perceived as attractive because they suggest the potential mate can avoid or resist harmful pathogens and will share such important, life-saving genes with future offspring (Thornhill & Gangestad, 1999). Sexual strategies theory goes further and predicts notable differences in mate selection between women and men (Buss & Schmitt, 1993). As pregnancy and childbirth are time-consuming, risky, and costly for women, they are thought to want partners who can protect and provide for them and so are attracted to longer-term relationships with men who have resources and status. Men, meanwhile, suffer no such costs and can increase their chances of reproduction by having intercourse with as many fertile women as they possibly can, and so will be attracted to short-term mates who appear fertile (i.e., young and in good physical health).

The biosocial role theory (Eagly & Wood, 1999), on the other hand, proposes a more nuanced argument, suggesting that the evolutionary-based biological differences between women and men (e.g., pregnancy, muscle mass) have led the different sexes to perform specific roles in society, and it is those sex roles that explain mate preferences. For example, the biosocial role theory agrees that men in most societies typically prefer younger, attractive women, while women prefer resource-rich men, but these preferences are a consequence of the traditional gender roles found in societies at that time. That is, as women have typically been the primary caregivers, they have had fewer resources and little opportunity to gain any themselves, and so their roles have restricted them to seek men who had such resources, thus explaining the preference for high-status men. Men, on the other hand, have traditionally held all the resources and power and so viewed women as objects of exchange, valuing those who were most attractive. Crucially, however, as sex-based roles vary across cultures and time, this theory further suggests that when sex roles change and become more comparable (i.e., more equal in societies), the sex differences in mate preferences will decrease.

What Does the Research Say?

In his pioneering research, evolutionary psychologist David Buss (1989) found that on average and across 37 countries, men preferred women who were younger, and were more likely to rank good looks as more important than women did (e.g., cues to fertility). Women, meanwhile, preferred men who were older, and were more likely to rank good financial prospects as more important than men did (e.g., cues to resources). However, when the biosocial role theory proponents, Eagly and Wood (1999), re-analysed the data, they revealed that gender equality influenced the results: the more equal women and men were in society (as indicated by national-level data from the United Nations), their preferences were more similar to one another. This, they argue, shows that social roles are flexible and play a large part in mate preferences.

The debate, though, rages on. Following these landmark publications, many researchers have weighed in and attempted to explain sex differences and similarities in mate preferences. However, previous research has often been flawed by a lack of transparency, small sample sizes, together with inconsistent measures and analyses. To address this, Walter and colleagues (2020) collected data from over 14,000 people across a staggering 45 countries. They used the same measures throughout and employed Open Science best practices by pre-registering their methods and planned analyses. And what did they find? Across cultures, women rated good financial prospects as more important in potential mates than men did, while men rated physical attractiveness as more important in potential mates than women did. Women also rated good health, kindness, and intelligence more important in their mates than men did. So, there seem to be sex differences in mate preferences.

Next, the authors looked at whether these sex differences in mate preferences were similar across cultures *and* whether any differences could be explained by the two competing hypotheses derived from the evolutionary and biosocial roles perspectives: pathogen prevalence and gender equality. Generally, there were sex differences in mate preferences across all cultures, but these differences varied in size. For example, Sweden showed the smallest sex difference in ratings of good financial prospects and physical attractiveness, while Georgia showed the largest difference.

However, as to why there is cross-cultural variability in sex differences, that's difficult to know. Pathogen prevalence, measured by country-level data (e.g., the years of life lost to infectious and parasitic disease), was not related to any of the mate preferences, suggesting that pathogen avoidance may not explain cross-cultural differences. Gender equality, also measured by country-level data (e.g., gender inequality index), was not consistently related to mate preferences. However, one measure (the Global Gender Gap Index) was related to sex differences in ratings of good financial prospects – when there was more equality, the difference between men and women's ratings was significantly reduced. Furthermore, all measures of gender equality were related to the ages of the *actual* (rather than preferred) partners of participants: when there was more gender equality, women were less likely to mate with older men, and men were less likely to mate with younger women.

So, what does this all mean? It seems that men and women place different emphasis on the importance of physical attractiveness and good financial prospects in potential mates. But wait a minute, let's take a step back. The very same research also shows that women and men *most* value the same traits of health, kindness, and intelligence in mates, and there is little difference between these ratings. It is only lower down in the pecking order that these sex differences tend to emerge – and we still don't *really* know why these differences exist. Furthermore, the research asks about *preferences* rather than actual mate selection. Now, I don't know about you, but my preferences are not always met in reality, otherwise I would be married to Ryan Reynolds by now. So, building on these critiques, in the next exercise box, we'd like you to consider how social psychological research can build on these arguments and address questions about mate preferences that may become more important in the future.

EXERCISE 3.3

Critiquing Evolutionary and Biosocial Roles Perspectives

Cross-cultural research suggests that there are some differences in what men and women prefer in their mates: evolutionary theorists suggest that these differences can be explained by the different pressures that men and women experience during reproduction. Biosocial roles theorists, on the other hand, argue that the differences occur because of the norms and laws evident in society. Here, we would like you to think about these perspectives in detail, how they may be applied to explain different contexts and relationships, and how we can use social psychological methods to test the hypotheses from these two perspectives.

1. The research reported here focuses on men and women in heterosexual relationships. How can the theories explain preferences for people who are not attracted to heterosexual relationships, and for people who do not identify as either a man or a woman?
2. Evolutionary theory uses evolutionary pressures surrounding reproduction to explain gender differences. How can the theory explain relationships between people who do not want to have children, or relationships between those who are past child-bearing years?
3. As gender equality increases, longitudinal research can be employed to see whether societal changes in gender roles and norms influence individuals' mate preferences. Will men still prefer fertile women? Will women still prefer resource-rich men? What may evolutionary theorists hypothesise? What may biosocial role theorists hypothesise? What would *you* hypothesise?

3.5.2 The Stigma and Satisfaction of Single Life

As alluded to by this chapter, romantic relationships are undoubtedly important and a vital topic of research for social psychologists. Nevertheless, with 35% of people reporting being single in the UK (Office for National Statistics, 2020) and 31% in the US (Pew Research

Center, 2020), there is a growing need to study *singlehood* – the state of not being in a long-term relationship. Presently, there is a lack of research into the area, which is particularly troublesome because there remains a stigma surrounding being single and relatively little is known about the consequences of being single. In this section, we highlight the need for singlehood research by assessing attitudes towards being single and comparing the consequences of being coupled and uncoupled.

Singlehood Stigma

As shown in Figure 3.9, singlehood has been steadily on the rise for decades in countries such as the UK. However, while the demographics are clearly changing, attitudes and norms towards singlehood are slower to evolve. Documenting singlism – the stigmatisation of adults who are single – DePaulo and Morris (2006) provide compelling evidence of the negative stereotypes and discrimination single people face. In one study, undergraduate students were significantly more likely to describe singles as immature, self-centred, insecure, unhappy, lonely, and ugly. Married couples, meanwhile, were perceived to be more stable, honest, loving, and kind. These stereotypes, moreover, have tangible consequences. Single people are generally paid less than comparable coupled counterparts, receive fewer tax and pension benefits, and pay comparatively more for holidays and insurance. Single people also experience housing discrimination, with experiments showing rental agents preferring married and cohabiting applicants to comparable applicants who were described as platonic friends (DePaulo, 2011).

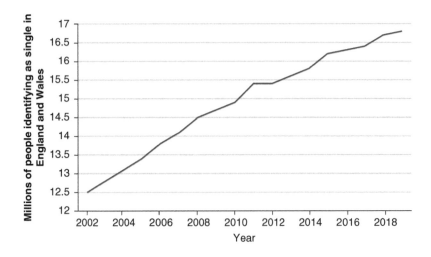

Figure 3.9 Increase of single people (never married or civil partnered) over the age of 16 in England and Wales. Data from Office for National Statistics (2020)

One possible reason for these negative perceptions and prejudice is a cultural lag between societal changes and associated norms (Byrne & Carr, 2005). In relatively recent generations, being single, particularly if you were single and having sex and children out of wedlock, was deeply shameful. Add to this the apparent necessity of being married to be financially secure (especially for women), being single was not particularly socially acceptable and possibly even burdensome for other family members. Societal norms, then, were used to strongly encourage marriage and to vehemently deter people from being single. Thus, when single persons violate these deeply entrenched beliefs, particularly if they explicitly challenge the belief system by leading happy and fulfilling lives, they are derided by those who endorse such prejudices (DePaulo, 2011).

Satisfaction of Singlehood

A more benevolent explanation for why coupling is generally encouraged over singlehood is the perception that people in relationships are happier and healthier. But is this the case? Research suggests that when there are differences between the happiness of singles and couples, they tend to be very small and, importantly, any differences are very much contingent upon the quality of the relationship. Exemplifying this, Lucas and colleagues (2003) tracked over 24,000 individuals for more than 15 years to assess how marital transitions influenced well-being. Individuals who remained single throughout the study were found to be less happy than people who got married and remained married. But this difference was very small (0.2 points on a 11-point scale) and hardly varied throughout the study, suggesting similar patterns of relatively high levels of happiness for both single and happily married people. Furthermore, single people generally reported higher levels of well-being across the 15 years than individuals who ended up getting divorced (i.e., even before the divorce). Singletons also avoided the heart-breaking lows of being widowed.

Further supporting the notion that single life is, in fact, satisfying, Hudson et al. (2020) compared life satisfaction among coupled and uncoupled individuals. They found that coupled participants, on the whole, reported moderately higher life satisfaction than uncoupled participants. There was, however, a major caveat to this finding. Coupled individuals only reported greater life satisfaction when their relationship was particularly high quality. Notably, single individuals not only reported greater life satisfaction than people in poor relationships, as would be expected; they also reported greater life satisfaction than people who were in relatively neutral relationships (i.e., scoring a 4.63 out of 7 when specifying whether their relationship was high quality). This suggests that being single is comparatively satisfying and good for your well-being, with only particularly healthy romances improving upon the single life.

The Secret to a Satisfying Single Life

While the majority of relationship research has examined the predictors of relationship satisfaction for couples, much less attention has been paid to identifying when and why single life is satisfying. There are, however, some clues. Single people avoid the pitfalls common to committed romantic relationships, including arguments, compromises, and jealousy, that can negatively impact on happiness. In addition, DePaulo and Morris (2006) suggest that, because singles do not choose to invest as much time in one individual, they are able to maintain a larger and more varied social network which may provide more diverse experiences as well as support. Relatedly, the extra time and resources means they are able to pursue their own passions without being tied down by the needs of others. So, bearing in mind that singlehood is increasing, yet relatively little is known about it, I reckon it is about time for a more nuanced study of relationships: one that better understands when and why romantic relationships are good for us, *and* when and why singlehood is good for us. What do you think?

3.5.3 Technological Advances and their Impacts on Relationships

Considering the world wide web was only released to the general public a mere 30 years ago, with Facebook arriving around 15 years later, it is safe to say that relatively recent developments in technology have revolutionised the way we live our lives, particularly our social lives. With an estimated 2.6 billion people on Facebook and around 50 million people on Tinder, the way in which we seek and maintain our friendships and romances has dramatically changed. Yet the impact that these media have on our relationships is still being examined. In this section, we provide an overview of how technological advances have improved our friendships and our romances, while delving into its darker sides by providing a critical account of how such technology can be used to harm our most intimate relationships. Then, later in the Applications section, we take a more in-depth look at how social psychological theories can inform the big business of internet dating.

Friend or Foe?

Figure 3.10 shows the percentage of young adults who use social media in a variety of countries across the world. This near ubiquitous usage clearly shows there is something powerfully attractive about using social media. Indeed, despite (problematic) social media usage being associated with depression and loneliness (Hunt et al., 2018), there are many benefits to platforms such as Facebook and Instagram. In terms of friendships, these platforms offer a highly convenient way in which to keep in touch with many friends both near and far. Being able to easily maintain relationships via these platforms has been shown to increase both closeness and satisfaction with friendships, particularly when friends use the platforms to send caring, personal messages rather than using the platforms to globally share information (e.g., post updates for all to see) or for friend surveillance (e.g., looking at friends' updates but not commenting on them; McEwan, 2013).

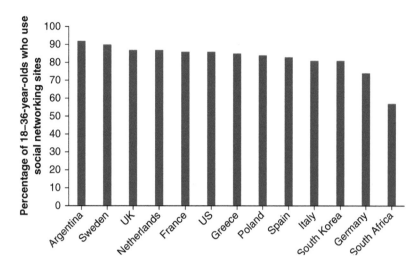

Figure 3.10 Percentage of 18–36-year-olds in a variety of countries who use social networking sites. Data from Pew Research Center (2018)

While technological advancements enable us to develop and maintain more friendships more easily than would be possible if we were to rely on face-to-face interactions, these advancements also provide a new landscape for old problems. Overt social rejection, for example, may be experienced online in the form of cyberbullying – online acts of aggression that are intended to cause harm or distress, including posting hurtful and threatening comments, spreading rumours, and distributing images without consent. This type of bullying is worryingly prevalent, with some estimating that 40% of people will be victims and experience its negative consequences, including emotional, physical, and educational impacts, for both victim and perpetrator (Kowalski & Limber, 2013).

In addition to these more explicit acts, the feeling of social ostracism can be facilitated by technological advances. Imagine for a moment that you are sitting with a friend enjoying a deep conversation when they receive a text message. Instead of carrying on their conversation with you, they pick up their phone and start replying. How do you feel? Probably not great. Indeed, research into phubbing – the act of ignoring a companion in order to pay attention to one's

> **Video:** Explaining phubbing https://www.youtube.com/watch?v=XCIDH1ZuY20

phone or other device – shows that when our friends choose their device over us, we are less satisfied with our interaction, trust our friends less, and feel less close to them (Chotpitayasunondh & Douglas, 2018). So, the next time you go out with your mates, maybe consider the effects of phubbing on friendship, and put your phone on silent.

Sweetheart or Stalker?

Thanks to the internet and the proliferation of dating websites, looking for love has seemingly never been so easy. Online dating provides convenient access to thousands, sometimes millions, of potential partners, who can be selected through the many filters and communication channels prior to meeting (Finkel et al., 2012). Although this relationshopping strategy may seem unromantic, choosing a partner through the internet relies on the same principles as offline dating, namely intimacy, trust, and communication (Anderson & Emmers-Sommer, 2006). Furthermore, a representative, nationwide study in the US, involving over 19,000 participants, revealed that not only does online dating provide more opportunities and save time and energy when deciding who to date, it generally has better outcomes than offline dating. That is, partners who met online were more satisfied with their marriages and less likely to divorce than partners who met offline (Cacioppo et al., 2013).

Clearly, technology has revolutionised the romantic landscape, but not all the advances have been positive. Using Facebook, for example, has been argued to increase and perpetuate relationship jealousy (Muise et al., 2009). Furthermore, interpersonal violence is being transformed by technological advances. Smartphones, watches, and home appliances, including tracking software, cameras, and heating/lighting controls, are now being used by abusers to control, stalk, and torment their targets. Although there is growing recognition of this type of abuse, public awareness and legal responses to it often lag behind, thereby making individuals vulnerable to attack by perpetrators who are often partners or ex-partners (Messing et al., 2020). It's really important, then, that we, as social psychologists, continue to research both the positive and negative impacts that technology can have on our lives. But further than that, we need to use this knowledge to help increase the benefits of technology and to reduce the risks associated with it. Such a thought brings us nicely onto the next section, Applications, where we show how social psychological knowledge can be used to improve people's lives in the real world.

3.6 PART 3: APPLICATIONS

So far, we have looked at a wide range of fascinating theories and research about – I hope you'll agree – all sorts of interesting and important topics. But what is the point of knowledge if we don't *use* it? In this section, we'll talk about how social psychological science has been applied to tackling inequality, reducing loneliness, and making money – basically showing how social psychology can be used to make the world a better place.

3.6.1 Striving for Equality

Looking through the discussion on attraction and romantic relationships, you may have spotted a notable omission. The research predominantly assumes and/or explicitly focuses on heterosexual romantic relationships and rarely acknowledges the presence of the many different sexual orientations and gender identities. In this section, we focus on why past research has often overlooked these LGBTQ+ relationships, discuss the similarities and differences between heterosexual and LGBTQ+ romances, and explain how interpersonal research can help to break down barriers and promote more accepting and inclusive societies.

Changing Perspectives on LGBTQ+ Relationships

Although same-sex love has been recorded for more than millennia (Kirkpatrick et al., 2000) and psychologists have recognised the diversity of human sexual attraction and behaviour for decades (Kinsey et al., 1948), many of the first social psychological theories on intimate relationships just focused on (assumed) heterosexual individuals. This is probably because homosexuality was illegal in most countries at the time. As such, studying the wide range of romantic and sexual attraction was difficult because it was illegal – and because few people were ready to 'out' themselves in the name of research.

As culture, context, and laws have changed, social psychology has come a long way in researching diverse forms of romantic love. Indeed, there are now many journals dedicated to LGBTQ+ research, including the *Journal of Homosexuality*, *Journal of Bisexuality*, and *Journal of Lesbian Studies*. These journals highlight a range of topics that are particularly relevant to LGBTQ+ individuals and relationships, including experiencing unique discrimination and legal challenges surrounding same-sex marriage, parenting, and gender recognition, to name but a few (Salvati & Koc, 2022).

Nevertheless, the discipline needs to continue to explore LGBTQ+ relationships because **heteronormative ideology** remains a significant issue in society (van der Toorn et al., 2020). This is the belief that there is a gender binary in which humans can be categorised as only women or men, and that heterosexuality (between women and men) is the default and *preferred* expression of sexual orientation. This belief leads to those who identify as having a different sexual orientation (e.g., gay, lesbian, bisexual, pansexual) and/or identify as different gender identities (e.g., trans and gender non-conforming people) experiencing discrimination, which adds considerable stress on the people and their potential romantic relationships. By acknowledging and specifically studying the variety of human sexualities and gender identities, social psychology is well placed to challenge these often deep-seated beliefs, providing a voice for people who are marginalised, and helping to promote more satisfying relationships for everyone.

> **Key concept – Heteronormativity:**
> The belief that heterosexuality is the default and preferred expression of sexual orientation. It often accompanies the belief that there is a gender binary consisting of only women and men.

Similar but Different

Research studies into LGBTQ+ relationships have typically investigated same-sex relationships, namely gay and lesbian. This research has shown many similarities between these relationships and heterosexual relationships. People value the same qualities in their partners (e.g., affection, similarity, shared interests), meet via similar ways, and engage in similar dates (Peplau & Fingerhut, 2007). Longitudinal data also shows that gay and lesbian couples report more equitable relationships, with similar – or higher – levels of intimacy and relationship satisfaction when compared to comparable heterosexual counterparts (Kurdek, 2004).

Despite the overwhelming similarities, LGBTQ+ relationships are distinct from heterosexual relationships due to their marginalised status in society: they receive less social support than heterosexual individuals, and their sexual orientations may even be targeted in hate crimes (Peplau & Fingerhut, 2007), resulting in some individuals hiding their sexuality or even being ashamed of who they are (Paterson et al., 2019a). This internalised homonegativity has significant negative effects on all aspects of life, including romantic relationships. Gay men and lesbian women who report higher levels of internalised homonegativity are less likely to be in relationships and, when they are in relationships, report more conflict, less satisfaction and less sexual intimacy, and have shorter relationships (see Frost & Meyer, 2009 for a review).

Shaping Laws and Lives

We now know a lot more about diverse relationships than we once did, but how, I hear you ask, does that research *actually* influence people's lives? Well, when it comes to LGBTQ+ relationships, social psychologists have had a huge impact. Take, for example, the work of Gregory Herek, who spent his entire career researching the prevalence and impacts of prejudice towards LGBTQ+ relationships (e.g., Herek, 2006). Herek wasn't content in just showing that LGBTQ+ relationships are *impacted by* prejudice, he used his research to *tackle* the prejudice. For example, when California banned same-sex marriage in 2008, Herek was called to Court as an expert witness and testified on the stand for seven hours! In that time, he used his expertise and research to help the plaintiffs convince the Court to overturn its ruling, thereby paving the way for same-sex couples to have the same legal rights as heterosexual couples in California.

These rights, it turns out, have considerable effects on people's lives. To show these positive impacts, Ogolsky and colleagues (2019) examined LGBTQ+ people's well-being across a year and, crucially, both before and after the US made same-sex marriage legal. Using a variety of statistical controls to help identify how the Supreme Court's ruling (and not other variables) affected participants' well-being, they found that people who felt greater stress about being LGBTQ+ at the start of the study reported an increase in life satisfaction and a decrease in psychological distress after the Court's ruling. This suggests that laws and policies – informed by social psychological research – can have a tangible, long-term, positive impact on LGBTQ+ relationships. Furthermore, considering same-sex relationships remain illegal, even punishable by death, in some countries, it is imperative that research into LGBTQ+ relationships continues to support equality and positively affect laws, lives, and love in the real world.

PERSONAL JOURNEY

Researching LGBTQ+ Love and Hate

One of the main reasons I love social psychology is because it can have a real impact on people's lives. For example, I worked on the *Sussex Hate Crime Project* (Paterson et al., 2018), which drew upon a range of social psychological theories, including social identity theory (Chapter 10), to examine the impacts of hate crime with the aim of informing policy and practice. Now, you may be wondering why would someone who is interested in love get a job researching hate? There are a couple of reasons. First, academic jobs are hard to come by, so beggars can't be choosers. Second, as well as being fascinated by love, I am intrigued by the opposite end of the spectrum – why do people hate and, more specifically, why do people hate others' loving relationships?

During the project, we worked closely with the LGBTQ+ community in England, a country that legalised same-sex marriage in 2014 and has strong anti-hate crime laws. Despite this legislation, we found hatred towards LGBTQ+ relationships to be staggeringly prevalent – 70% of our participants had been victims within the past three years (Paterson et al., 2018) – and extremely harmful – victims were fearful, angry, and even ashamed (Paterson et al., 2019a). Clearly, something needed to be done to tackle such injustices. So, working with the Crown Prosecution Service, we showed that hate crimes have a disproportionate impact not just on the individuals involved in the crime, but also on the individuals' entire identity group (e.g., LGBTQ+ community), thus showing that hate crimes are particularly harmful to society (Paterson et al., 2018). This information helped underpin the introduction of Community Impact Statements for hate crimes. Similar to victim impact statements, these statements are collected by the police to better understand the community-level impacts of the crime and are read to the Court so that the sentencing acknowledges the far-reaching harms of hate crimes, often leading to a longer sentence for the perpetrator. Such changes in this nationwide policy have a clear impact on people's lives and really highlight how social psychological research can be applied to fight injustice.

3.6.2 Combatting Loneliness

As you have probably gathered by now, humans are very much social beings and require connections with others to survive and feel fulfilled. Because of this need to belong, we spend a considerable amount of our lives creating, developing, and maintaining relationships with a wide variety of people. However, despite our best efforts, we are not always able to meet this need and end up feeling *lonely* – the unpleasant experience that occurs when we think our network of social relations is deficient in some important way, in terms of either the number of relationships we have and/or the quality of those relationships. These feelings arise due to many reasons, including experiencing social ostracism and rejection, as well as going through common life transitions such as moving house, changing jobs, and retiring (Haslam et al., 2016).

The Importance of Social Connectedness

Central to all these reasons of loneliness is feeling a lack of social connectedness, thus Haslam and colleagues (2016) argue that to alleviate loneliness, we need to tackle the crux of the issue – repairing social disconnectedness. As *Social Cure* proponents, Haslam and colleagues draw upon the social identity approach (see Chapter 10) and propose to utilise the power of social groups to increase social connectedness, decrease loneliness, and consequently, improve health. As discussed in Chapter 10, belonging to a social group brings about many benefits, including relevant factors for tackling loneliness: social groups increase social contact, provide social support, and can provide a stable identity and reassurance in the face of change. Thus, interventions that promote these group processes are likely to reduce feelings of loneliness.

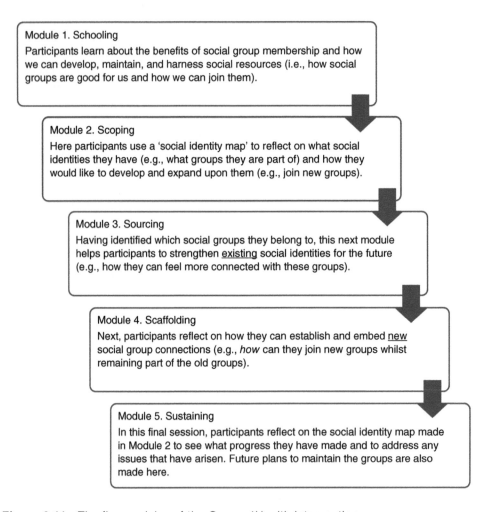

Figure 3.11 The five modules of the Groups4Health intervention

Source: Haslam et al. (2016)

Groups4health Intervention

Underpinned by social identity theory, Haslam and colleagues (2016) developed a five-step programme called *Groups4Health*, which is designed to increase individuals' knowledge and skills at maintaining their group memberships and related group identities. Figure 3.11 provides an overview of the content of the intervention. Modules are 60–75 minutes long, modules 1–4 are held weekly, and module 5 is held at least one month after module 4.

Haslam et al. (2016) tested the intervention with young adults who were suffering from loneliness and/or reported sub-clinical levels of psychological distress. Figure 3.12 shows that participants who engaged in the intervention reported a significant increase in the sense of connectedness and reduced loneliness, together with improvements in depression, stress, and self-esteem. Furthermore, these improvements remained at the six-month follow-up.

As the results for the *Groups4Health* intervention indicate, promoting social groups and identities can be an efficient and effective way to reduce loneliness and buffer against loneliness-related harms. Furthermore, these manualised, theory-driven social cure interventions are particularly notable not just because of the results, but because they have the potential to be used in a variety of contexts and with a wide variety of people, including breast cancer survivors, new mothers, care home residents, sports teams, people in drug and alcohol rehabilitation, and students (see Steffens et al., 2021, for a review).

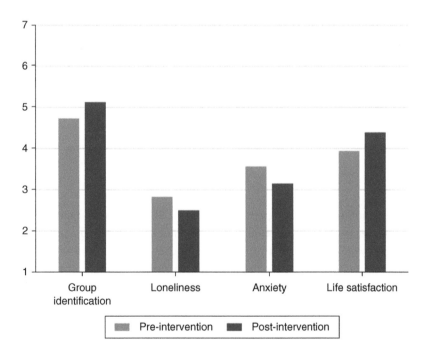

Figure 3.12   Self-reports of group identification, loneliness, anxiety, and life satisfaction before and after completing the Groups4Health intervention. Data from Haslam et al. (2016)

In addition to the more targeted intervention programmes, loneliness can be reduced by applying social psychological principles in a much broader sense. Australia, for example, introduced Neighbour Day in 2019 to raise awareness of the importance of connecting with the community. Fong et al. (2021) assessed this nationwide event and found that hosting a Neighbour Day event reduced loneliness and improved well-being even after six months. They also revealed that these improvements were made because the events helped to promote a neighbourhood identity, thereby showing the importance of group memberships and identities in combating isolation and loneliness.

Considering loneliness is not a pleasant experience and many, if not all, of us will feel it at some point in our lives, these types of interventions are of the utmost importance. It is imperative, then, as social psychologists, that we put this knowledge to use. Doing so has the potential to inform and develop simple and effective programmes that can be used to tackle loneliness and improve the lives and health of potentially millions of people at a population level. How awesome is that?

3.6.3 Translating Relationship Theories into Booming Business Ideas

As we have seen throughout this chapter, interpersonal relationships are a fundamental part of our lives. High-quality affiliations, friendships, and romantic relationships provide us with safety and security, as well as countless psychological and physiological benefits. Due to this importance, we devote an immense amount of time to finding, developing, and sustaining our close relationships. In pursuit of these happy, fulfilling, and lasting relationships, people often turn to professionals who harness social psychological knowledge to help guide the way to more satisfying relationships. In this section, we will review how professionals have utilised insights from the discipline to create billion-pound businesses focused on helping individuals to create and maintain their close connections.

Matchmaking and Money Making

Matchmaking is nothing new. Long before the advent of the internet, families and friends would often, either formally or informally, suggest and even arrange romantic pairings and marriages. There were even revered professionals, including astrologers and advisers, who would determine the love lives of entire communities. While individuals may still rely on these more personalised connections, more of us are turning to the internet to find our 'matches'. There are innumerable websites worldwide catering for nearly every imaginable taste, orientation, and relationship, all offering to pair us with the right partner(s). And most do so for a very healthy profit. *The Match Group*, for example, which owns online dating companies, including *Match.com* and *Tinder*, is reportedly worth US$45 billion, while *Bumble*'s estimated value was US$7 billion in 2021 (Gurdus, 2021). To say the matchmaking business is big and booming would be an understatement.

So, how does this relate to social psychology? Well, these companies embody several social psychological theories and methods when it comes to interpersonal attraction and relationship formation. *eHarmony*, for example, claims to use scientific methods to match partners based on the similarity-attraction principle (e.g., Newcomb, 1961; see also page 114 above). Upon joining the site, customers are requested to complete a battery of questionnaires and, using the similarity principle (and a patented algorithm), *eHarmony* proposes potential similar (rather than dissimilar) partners for the customers to review. The company also markets themselves on engaging psychological research methods to estimate what predicts long-term marital satisfaction to scientifically evidence its success.

More recent additions to the online dating sphere also exemplify social psychological principles. Instead of focusing on the principle of similarity, however, these newer companies tend to rely on proximity (see page 113), as well as highlighting the importance of facial attractiveness (see page 109). Companies, including *Tinder, Grindr*, and *HER*, to name but a few, are referred to as location-based, real-time dating apps that use the GPS of customers' devices to narrow down the pool of potential partners to a specified radius. By focusing on only those who are nearest, the apps highlight the importance of proximity in initial attraction (Festinger et al., 1950; and see page 101). A further key feature of these apps is the prominence of the picture (typically of the face), relative to all the other information (Figure 3.13). As these apps are clearly successful, this supports social psychological theories, suggesting that facial attractiveness is a very quick and clear predictor of initial attraction (Langlois et al., 2000; and see page 109).

Figure 3.13 An example of a profile on a dating app which prominently displays the image relative to the written caption

Source: © Kaspars Grinvalds via Shutterstock

Clearly, romantic relationships are not the only important relationships in our lives and so businesses have also been quick to use social psychologically inspired strategies to help individuals create a whole host of friendships. *Bumble BFF*, for example, aims to create meaningful relationships for people looking to expand their friendships and social connections in general. Other sites help to connect people who share similar roles, beliefs, and interests, including apps for new parents, music lovers, sport fans, and much more besides – a strategy that may be useful to combat loneliness (see page 139). Similar to the romantic relationship apps, these friendship apps often emphasise the importance of proximity and similarity in developing friendships. Thus, it seems that drawing upon social psychological theories, research, and methodologies has a very tangible real-world application: theories can be utilised to enable individuals to find love and friendship, while also being hugely profitable.

3.6.4 Future Applications

As we have seen in this chapter, recent applications of interpersonal relationships research have profoundly impacted people's lives by changing laws (i.e., marriage equality), reducing loneliness (e.g., *Groups4Health*), and creating multi-million-pound businesses (e.g., dating apps). But we will not stop there. As interpersonal relationships are integral to our lives, there will always be a strong demand for evidence-based insights that help us to find and form happy and healthy relationships.

The strive for equality, for example, is far from over: LGBTQ+ relationships continue to encounter prejudice and discrimination, and even remain illegal in some countries around the world. Using insights from interpersonal relationships research, we can continue to break down these ill-informed prejudices, support LGBTQ+ people, and challenge unjust laws. Relatedly, research can also broaden the scope to include other types of romantic relationships that are discriminated against. For example, couples who are from different racial backgrounds, different religions, and different nationalities also face prejudice towards their loving relationships (e.g., Paterson et al., 2019b), as do people not in relationships (see singlism, page 131). By understanding how these people experience and overcome relationship-based prejudice, we can develop interventions to reduce prejudice, increase resilience, and help a whole range of people live happier lives.

Furthermore, by using cutting-edge methodologies and technologies, interpersonal relationships research can make other vital improvements to our lives. As discussed above, location-based real-time apps are already being used by millions to find the love of their life (or night) and create meaningful social groups that can prevent loneliness. So, what about other technologies? Could, for instance, virtual reality have the same beneficial effects as real-life interactions? And what about the dark side of such technologies? It is clear from page 134 that research is needed to better understand how technology is being misused to stalk and harass, and so research exploring this could be used to help victims and inform new laws at restricting such abuses of power.

And these potential future applications are just the tip of the iceberg! As we continue to develop and test comprehensive theories, using a wide range of methodologies, adhering to Open Science practices, and working with important collaborators, we have the power to develop a wide range of applications that can transform people's lives.

3.7 SUMMARY

In this chapter, we have emphasised the importance of affiliations and interpersonal relationships. From birth, we have an innate need to belong and form attachments with caregivers that are likely to influence our subsequent relationships. This need for affiliation is so powerful that if we feel ostracised, even by those we despise, we suffer physically and psychologically.

In explaining whom we choose to affiliate with, we have looked at interpersonal attraction, which includes physical features such as facial symmetry and the concept of averageness, as well as psychological components, including familiarity, proximity, and attitudinal similarity. Self-disclosure enables this initial attraction to develop into friendships, which are extremely beneficial for both our mental and physical health.

Although similar to friendships, romantic relationships are qualitatively different and have been categorised into many different typologies, including intense, passionate love and enduring, companionate love. These romantic relationships seem to be most satisfying when they are characterised by equity and trust. According to the Investment Model, this relationship satisfaction is one component, along with investment size and perceived alternatives, which, together, predict relationship commitment. When partners are not committed, relationships may break down, the consequences of which can be negative (e.g., depression and despair) and positive (e.g., relief and empowerment).

We have also seen that future research is well placed to better understand: (i) the contribution of evolution and biosocial roles in explaining gender differences in attraction, (ii) the growing importance of singlehood, and (iii) the impacts of technology on relationships. Furthermore, the research has real-world applications which can help promote equality, inform interventions to reduce loneliness, and provide careers and profits for individuals and businesses alike.

3.8 REVISION

1   Drawing upon attachment theory, describe how our relationships with our primary caregivers are thought to shape our initial attachment styles during childhood, and how they may (or may not) influence our later, adult attachment styles and relationships.

2   Consider the physical and psychological components of interpersonal attraction. Explain which factors you believe are most important in (i) the initial formation of friendships, and (ii) the development and maintenance of long-lasting friendships.

3   Take a moment to reflect upon your own friendships. Do the theories and research described in this chapter match your own experiences? Think about how you met, how your friendship developed, and the benefits of your friendship.

4   Imagine you work at a charity that helps survivors of domestic abuse. A client of yours has suffered physical and psychological abuse perpetrated by their spouse for a decade.

The client does not want to return to the family home with their children, but feels they have no option because they are financially dependent on their spouse. Using the Investment Model, explain why the client may remain in the relationship, and propose some policies and practices that can improve situations like this and end domestic abuse.

5   When relationships break up, individuals feel a variety of emotions. According to the research, who is most likely to feel (i) guilt, (ii) depression, (iii) relief, and (iv) empowerment?

6   As an increasing number of people are choosing to remain single, use research to explain some of the advantages and disadvantages of singlehood.

7   Suppose you've just started at university (lucky you!) and your tutor has suggested you join some new social groups. Using insights from *Groups4Health*, in what ways may the new groups benefit you?

3.9 FURTHER READING

Foundations

Kulik, J. A., Mahler, H. I. M., & Moore, P. J. (1996). Social comparison and affiliation under threat: Effects on recovery from major surgery. *Journal of Personality and Social Psychology*, *71*(5), 967.

This experiment shows how affiliation and social comparison can aid in recovery after by-pass surgery, thereby highlighting the practical, important applications of the theories.

Ainsworth, M. S. (1989). Attachments beyond infancy. *American Psychologist*, *44*(4), 709.

In this summary, Mary Ainsworth provides an overview of how the attachments we form with our caregivers influence our affective bonds throughout our life. It is an insightful and encompassing review of attachment theory by its leading figure.

Montoya, R. M., Horton, R. S., & Kirchner, J. (2008). Is actual similarity necessary for attraction? A meta-analysis of actual and perceived similarity. *Journal of Social and Personal Relationships*, *25*(6), 889–922.

This meta-analysis provides an overview of of the importance of similarity in interpersonal attraction.

Feeney, B. C., & Collins, N. L. (2015). A new look at social support: A theoretical perspective on thriving through relationships. *Personality and Social Psychology Review*, *19*(2), 113–147.

This paper presents a new theoretical approach to understanding when and how close relationships help individuals thrive. In doing so, it helps shift the focus away from how social support helps us in times of need to recognising how friendships are also invaluable in encouraging us to grow and thrive.

Advanced

Buss, D. M., & Schmitt, D. P. (1993). Sexual strategies theory: An evolutionary perspective on human mating. *Psychological Review, 100*(2), 204–232.

This is the seminal proposal of how evolution theory can explain gender differences in human mating strategies.

Eagly, A. H., & Wood, W. (1999). The origins of sex differences in human behavior: Evolved dispositions versus social roles. *American Psychologist, 54*(6), 408–423.

Reanalysing the often-cited Buss (1989) data on sex differences in mating, this paper contrasts the evolutionary and biosocial roles perspectives to conclude that the social structural accounts are better able to explain the gender differences found.

DePaulo, B. M. (2011). *Singlism: What it is, why it matters, and how to stop it.* Charleston, SC: DoubleDoor Books.

This book uses social psychological insights to do as its title suggests: it explains what singlism is, why it is important, and how prejudice towards single people can be prevented.

Anderson, M., Vogels, E. A., & Turner, E. (2020, February). *The virtues and downsides of online dating.* Washington, DC: Pew Research Center.

Drawing on data from 4,860 participants, this Pew Research report from the US details the positives and negatives of online dating, reflecting the social psychological theory and research on the topic.

Applications

van der Toorn, J., Pliskin, R., & Morgenroth, T. (2020). Not quite over the rainbow: The unrelenting and insidious nature of heteronormative ideology. *Current Opinion in Behavioral Sciences, 34*, 160–165.

An insightful commentary on heteronormative ideology and suggestions of how to confront and overcome it.

Paterson, J. L., Walters, M. A., Brown, R., & Fearn, H. (2018, January). *The Sussex Hate Crime Project: Final report.* Brighton: University of Sussex. Available at: www.sussex.ac.uk/webteam/gateway/file.php?name=sussex-hate-crimeproject-report.pdf&site=430.

A shameless plug of my work on the Sussex Hate Crime Project, which examines the impacts of hating people for whom they love.

Social Identity and Groups Network (SIGN). (n.d.). https://sign.centre.uq.edu.au/

The Social Identity and Groups Network (SIGN) at The University of Queensland engages in a wide variety of applied social psychological interventions, including Groups4Health.

3.10 REFERENCES

Ainsworth, M. D. S., Bell, S. M., & Stayton, D. J. (1971). Individual differences in strange situation behaviour of one-year olds. In H. R. Schaffer (Ed.), *The origins of human social relations* (pp. 17–58). London: Academic Press.

Ainsworth, M. S. (1989). Attachments beyond infancy. *American Psychologist, 44*(4), 709.

Altman, I. & Taylor, D. (1973). *Social penetration: The development of interpersonal relationships.* New York: Holt.

Anderson, T. L., & Emmers-Sommer, T. M. (2006). Predictors of relationship satisfaction in online romantic relationships. *Communication Studies, 57*(2), 153–172.

Bartholomew, K., & Horowitz, L. M. (1991). Attachment styles among young adults: A test of a four-category model. *Journal of Personality and Social Psychology, 61*(2), 226.

Baumeister, R. F., & Leary, M. R. (1995). The need to belong: Desire for interpersonal attachments as a fundamental human motivation. *Psychological Bulletin, 117,* 497–529.

Baumeister, R. F., Wotman, S. R., & Stillwell, A. M. (1993). Unrequited love: On heartbreak, anger, guilt, scriptlessness, and humiliation. *Journal of Personality and Social Psychology, 64*(3), 377–394.

Bowlby, J. (1969). *Attachment and loss. Vol. 1: Attachment.* London: Hogarth Press.

Brumbaugh, C. C., & Fraley, R. C. (2006). Transference and attachment: How do attachment patterns get carried forward from one relationship to the next? *Personality and Social Psychology Bulletin, 32*(4), 552–560.

Buss, D. M. (1989). Sex differences in human mate preferences: Evolutionary hypotheses tested in 37 cultures. *Behavioral and Brain Sciences, 12*(1), 1–14.

Buss, D. M., & Schmitt, D. P. (1993). Sexual strategies theory: An evolutionary perspective on human mating. *Psychological Review, 100*(2), 204–232.

Byrne, A., & Carr, D. (2005). Caught in the cultural lag: The stigma of singlehood. *Psychological Inquiry, 16*(2/3), 84–91.

Cacioppo, J. T., Cacioppo, S., Gonzaga, G. C., Ogburn, E. L., & VanderWeele, T. J. (2013). Marital satisfaction and break-ups differ across on-line and off-line meeting venues. *Proceedings of the National Academy of Sciences, 110*(25), 10135–10140.

Chopik, W. J., Edelstein, R. S., & Fraley, R. C. (2013). From the cradle to the grave: Age differences in attachment from early adulthood to old age. *Journal of Personality, 81*(2), 171–183.

Chotpitayasunondh, V., & Douglas, K. M. (2018). The effects of 'phubbing' on social interaction. *Journal of Applied Social Psychology, 48*(6), 304–316.

Clark, R. D., & Hatfield, E. (1989). Gender differences in receptivity to sexual offers. *Journal of Psychology & Human Sexuality, 2*(1), 39–55.

Cottrell, C. A., Neuberg, S. L., & Li, N. P. (2007). What do people desire in others? A sociofunctional perspective on the importance of different valued characteristics. *Journal of Personality and Social Psychology, 92*(2), 208–231.

DePaulo, B. M. (2011). *Singlism: What it is, why it matters, and how to stop it.* Charleston, SC: DoubleDoor Books.

DePaulo, B. M., & Morris, W. L. (2006). The unrecognized stereotyping and discrimination against singles. *Current Directions in Psychological Science, 15*(5), 251–254.

Dion, K. K. (1972). Physical attractiveness and evaluation of children's transgressions. *Journal of Personality and Social Psychology, 24*(2), 207.

Dion, K. K., Berscheid, E., & Walster, E. (1972). What is beautiful is good. *Journal of Personality and Social Psychology, 24*(3), 285.

Downs, A. C., & Lyons, P. M. (1991). Natural observations of the links between attractiveness and initial legal judgments. *Personality and Social Psychology Bulletin, 17*(5), 541–547.

Duck, S. (2007). *Human relationships*. London: Sage.

Dutton, D. G., & Aron, A. P. (1974). Some evidence for heightened sexual attraction under conditions of high anxiety. *Journal of Personality and Social Psychology, 30*(4), 510–517.

Eagly, A. H., & Wood, W. (1999). The origins of sex differences in human behavior: Evolved dispositions versus social roles. *American Psychologist, 54*(6), 408–423.

Eisenberger, N. I., Lieberman, M. D., & Williams, K. D. (2003). Does rejection hurt? An fMRI study of social exclusion. *Science, 302*(5643), 290–292.

Feeney, B. C., & Collins, N. L. (2015). A new look at social support: A theoretical perspective on thriving through relationships. *Personality and Social Psychology Review, 19*(2), 113–147.

Feingold, A. (1992). Good-looking people are not what we think. *Psychological Bulletin, 111*(2), 304.

Festinger, L. (1954). A theory of social comparison processes. *Human Relations, 7*, 117–140.

Festinger, L. (1957). *A theory of cognitive dissonance*. Stanford, CA: Stanford University Press.

Festinger, L., Schachter, S., & Back, K. (1950). *Social pressures in informal groups: A study of human factors in housing*. New York: Harper.

Finkel, E. J., Eastwick, P. W., Karney, B. R., Reis, H. T., & Sprecher, S. (2012). Online dating: A critical analysis from the perspective of psychological science. *Psychological Science in the Public Interest, 13*(1), 3–66.

Finkel, E. J., Norton, M. I., Reis, H. T., Ariely, D., Caprariello, P. A., Eastwick, P. W., Frost, J. H., & Maniaci, M. R. (2015). When does familiarity promote versus undermine interpersonal attraction? A proposed integrative model from erstwhile adversaries. *Perspectives on Psychological Science, 10*(1), 3–19.

Finkenauer, C. (2010). Although it helps, love is not all you need: How Caryl Rusbult made me discover what relationships are all about. *Personal Relationships, 17*(2), 161–163.

Fisher, H. (2004). *Why we love: The nature and chemistry of romantic love*. New York: Holt.

Fong, P., Cruwys, T., Robinson, S. L., Haslam, S. A., Haslam, C., Mance, P. L., & Fisher, C. L. (2021). Evidence that loneliness can be reduced by a whole-of-community intervention to increase neighbourhood identification. *Social Science & Medicine, 277*, 113909.

Fraley, R. C. (2019). Attachment in adulthood: Recent developments, emerging debates, and future directions. *Annual Review of Psychology, 70*, 401–422.

Frieze, I. H., Olson, J. E., & Russell, J. (1991). Attractiveness and income for men and women in management. *Journal of Applied Social Psychology, 21*(13), 1039–1057.

Frost, D. M., & Meyer, I. H. (2009). Internalized homophobia and relationship quality among lesbians, gay men, and bisexuals. *Journal of Counseling Psychology, 56*(1), 97–109.

Gonsalkorale, K., & Williams, K. D. (2007). The KKK won't let me play: Ostracism even by a despised outgroup hurts. *European Journal of Social Psychology, 37*(6), 1176–1186.

Gordon, K. C., Baucom, D. H., & Snyder, D. K. (2004). An integrative intervention for promoting recovery from extramarital affairs. *Journal of Marital and Family Therapy, 30*(2), 213–231.

Gurdus, L. (2021). *Bumble vs Match Group: Two traders check out dating stocks ahead of Bumble's IPO.* Retrieved 11 May 2021 from www.cnbc.com/2021/02/11/bumble-ipo-vs-match-group-traders-check-out-dating-stocks.html

Halberstadt, J., & Rhodes, G. (2003). It's not just average faces that are attractive: Computer-manipulated averageness makes birds, fish, and automobiles attractive. *Psychonomic Bulletin & Review, 10*(1), 149–156.

Harlow, H. F., Dodsworth, R. O., & Harlow, M. K. (1965). Total social isolation in monkeys. *Proceedings of the National Academy of Sciences of the United States of America, 54*(1), 90.

Haslam, C., Cruwys, T., Haslam, S. A., Dingle, G., & Chang, M. X.-L. (2016). Groups4Health: Evidence that a social-identity intervention that builds and strengthens social group membership improves mental health. *Journal of Affective Disorders, 194*, 188–195.

Hatfield, E. (1982). Passionate love, companionate love, and intimacy. In M. Fisher & G. Stricker (Eds.), *Intimacy* (pp. 267–292). New York: Plenum.

Hatfield, E., Cacioppo, J. T., & Rapson, R. L. (1993). Emotional contagion. *Current Directions in Psychological Science, 2*(3), 96–100.

Hatfield, E., & Rapson, R. L. (1993). Historical and cross-cultural perspectives on passionate love and sexual desire. *Annual Review of Sex Research, 4*(1), 67–97.

Hatfield, E., & Traupmann, J. (1981). Intimate relationships: A perspective from equity theory. *Personal Relationships, 1*, 165–178.

Herek, G. M. (2006). Legal recognition of same-sex relationships in the United States: A social science perspective. *American Psychologist, 61*(6), 607.

Holt-Lunstad, J., & Smith, T. B. (2012). Social relationships and mortality. *Social and Personality Psychology Compass, 6*(1), 41–53.

Homans, G. C. (1958). Social behavior as exchange. *American Journal of Sociology, 63*(6), 597–606.

Hudson, N. W., Lucas, R. E., & Donnellan, M. B. (2020). The highs and lows of love: Romantic relationship quality moderates whether spending time with one's partner predicts gains or losses in well-being. *Personality and Social Psychology Bulletin, 46*(4), 572–589.

Hunt, M. G., Marx, R., Lipson, C., & Young, J. (2018). No more FOMO: Limiting social media decreases loneliness and depression. *Journal of Social and Clinical Psychology, 37*(10), 751–768.

Impett, E. A., Gable, S. L., & Peplau, L. A. (2005). Giving up and giving in: The costs and benefits of daily sacrifice in intimate relationships. *Journal of Personality and Social Psychology, 89*(3), 327.

Impett, E. A., Kim, J., & Muise, A. (2020). A communal approach to sexual need responsiveness in romantic relationships. *European Review of Social Psychology, 31*, 287–318.

Johnson, D. L., Wiebe, J. S., Gold, S. M., Andreasen, N. C., Hichwa, R. D., Watkins, G. L., & Boles Ponto, L. L. (1999). Cerebral blood flow and personality: A positron emission tomography study. *American Journal of Psychiatry*, 156(2), 252–257.

Judge, T. A., Hurst, C., & Simon, L. S. (2009). Does it pay to be smart, attractive, or confident (or all three)? Relationships among general mental ability, physical attractiveness, core self-evaluations, and income. *Journal of Applied Psychology*, 94(3), 742.

Kinsey, A. C., Pomeroy, W., & Martin, C. (1948). *Sexual behavior in the human male*. Philadelphia, PA: W. B. Saunders.

Kirkpatrick, L. A., & Hazan, C. (1994). Attachment styles and close relationships: A four-year prospective study. *Personal Relationships*, 1(2), 123–142.

Kirkpatrick, R. C., Blackwood, E., Dickemann, J. M., Jones, D., Muscarella, F., Vasey, P. L., & Williams, W. L. (2000). The evolution of human homosexual behavior. *Current Anthropology*, 41(3), 385–413.

Kitson, G. C., & Holmes, W. M. (1992). *Portrait of divorce: Adjustment to marital breakdown*. New York: Guilford Press.

Kowalski, R. M., & Limber, S. P. (2013). Psychological, physical, and academic correlates of cyberbullying and traditional bullying. *Journal of Adolescent Health*, 53(1), S13–S20.

Kulik, J. A., Mahler, H. I. M., & Moore, P. J. (1996). Social comparison and affiliation under threat: Effects on recovery from major surgery. *Journal of Personality and Social Psychology*, 71(5), 967.

Kurdek, L. A. (2004). Are gay and lesbian cohabiting couples really different from heterosexual married couples? *Journal of Marriage and Family*, 66(4), 880–900.

Landy, D., & Sigall, H. (1974). Beauty is talent: Task evaluation as a function of the performer's physical attractiveness. *Journal of Personality and Social Psychology*, 29(3), 299.

Langlois, J. H., Kalakanis, L., Rubenstein, A. J., Larson, A., Hallam, M., & Smoot, M. (2000). Maxims or myths of beauty? A meta-analytic and theoretical review. *Psychological Bulletin*, 126(3), 390.

Langlois, J. H., & Roggman, L. A. (1990). Attractive faces are only average. *Psychological Science*, 1(2), 115–121.

Lehmiller, J. J. (2009). Secret romantic relationships: Consequences for personal and relational well-being. *Personality and Social Psychology Bulletin*, 35(11), 1452–1466.

Lemay Jr, E. P., Clark, M. S., & Greenberg, A. (2010). What is beautiful is good because what is beautiful is desired: Physical attractiveness stereotyping as projection of interpersonal goals. *Personality and Social Psychology Bulletin*, 36(3), 339–353.

Little, A. C., Jones, B. C., & DeBruine, L. M. (2011). Facial attractiveness: Evolutionary based research. *Philosophical Transactions of the Royal Society B: Biological Sciences*, 366(1571), 1638–1659.

Lucas, R. E., Clark, A. E., Georgellis, Y., & Diener, E. (2003). Reexamining adaptation and the set point model of happiness: Reactions to changes in marital status. *Journal of Personality and Social Psychology*, 84(3), 527–539.

McEwan, B. (2013). Sharing, caring, and surveilling: An actor–partner interdependence model examination of Facebook relational maintenance strategies. *Cyberpsychology, Behavior, and Social Networking*, 16(12), 863–869.

Messing, J., Bagwell-Gray, M., Brown, M. L., Kappas, A., & Durfee, A. (2020). Intersections of stalking and technology-based abuse: Emerging definitions, conceptualization, and measurement. *Journal of Family Violence, 35*, 693–704.

Mondloch, C. J., Lewis, T. L., Budreau, D. R., Maurer, D., Dannemiller, J. L., Stephens, B. R., & Kleiner-Gathercoal, K. A. (1999). Face perception during early infancy. *Psychological Science, 10*(5), 419–422.

Montoya, R. M., & Insko, C. A. (2008). Toward a more complete understanding of the reciprocity of liking effect. *European Journal of Social Psychology, 38*(3), 477–498.

Muise, A., Christofides, E., & Desmarais, S. (2009). More information than you ever wanted: Does Facebook bring out the green-eyed monster of jealousy? *CyberPsychology and Behavior, 12*(4), 441–444.

Newcomb, T. M. (1961). *The acquaintance process.* New York: Holt, Rinehart & Winston.

Nezlek, J. B., Wesselmann, E. D., Wheeler, L., & Williams, K. D. (2012). Ostracism in everyday life. *Group Dynamics: Theory, Research, and Practice, 16*(2), 91.

Office for National Statistics. (2020). *Population estimates by marital status and living arrangements, England and Wales.* Retrieved from www.ons.gov.uk/peoplepopulationandcommunity/populationandmigration/populationestimates/datasets/populationestimatesbymaritalstatusandlivingarrangements

Ogolsky, B. G., Monk, J. K., Rice, T. M., & Oswald, R. F. (2019). Personal well-being across the transition to marriage equality: A longitudinal analysis. *Journal of Family Psychology, 33*(4), 422.

Paterson, J. L., Brown, R., & Walters, M. A. (2019a). The short and longer term impacts of hate crimes experienced directly, indirectly and through the media. *Personality and Social Psychology Bulletin, 45*(7), 994–1010.

Paterson, J. L., Turner, R. N., & Hodson, G. (2019b). Receptivity to dating and marriage across the religious divide in Northern Ireland: The role of intergroup contact. *Journal of Applied Social Psychology, 49*, 575–584.

Paterson, J. L., Walters, M. A., Brown, R., & Fearn, H. (2018). *The Sussex Hate Crime Project: Final report.* Brighton: University of Sussex. Available at: www.sussex.ac.uk/webteam/gateway/file.php?name=sussex-hate-crimeproject-report.pdf&site=430.

Penton-Voak, I. S., Jacobson, A., & Trivers, R. (2004). Populational differences in attractiveness judgements of male and female faces: Comparing British and Jamaican samples. *Evolution and Human Behavior, 25*(6), 355–370.

Peplau, L. A., & Fingerhut, A. W. (2007). The close relationships of lesbians and gay men. *Annual Review of Psychology, 58*, 405–424.

Pew Research Center. (2018). *Social media use continues to rise in developing countries but plateaus across developed ones.* Washington, DC: Pew Research Center. Available at: https://medienorge.uib.no/files/Eksterne_pub/Pew-Research-Center_Global-Tech-Social-Media-Use_2018.06.19.pdf

Pew Research Center. (2020). *A profile of single Americans.* Washington, DC: Pew Research Center. Available at: www.pewresearch.org/social-trends/2020/08/20/a-profile-of-single-americans/

Previti, D., & Amato, P. R. (2003). Why stay married? Rewards, barriers, and marital stability. *Journal of Marriage and Family*, *65*(3), 561–573.

Rempel, J. K., Holmes, J. G., & Zanna, M. P. (1985). Trust in close relationships. *Journal of Personality and Social Psychology*, *49*(1), 95–112.

Rusbult, C. E. (1983). A longitudinal test of the investment model: The development (and deterioration) of satisfaction and commitment in heterosexual involvements. *Journal of Personality and Social Psychology*, *45*(1), 101–117.

Rusbult, C. E., & Martz, J. M. (1995). Remaining in an abusive relationship: An investment model analysis of nonvoluntary dependence. *Personality and Social Psychology Bulletin*, *21*(6), 558–571.

Rusbult, C. E., Zembrodt, I. M., & Gunn, L. K. (1982). Exit, voice, loyalty, and neglect: Responses to dissatisfaction in romantic involvements. *Journal of Personality and Social Psychology*, *43*(6), 1230–1242.

Saegert, S., Swap, W., & Zajonc, R. B. (1973). Exposure, context, and interpersonal attraction. *Journal of Personality and Social Psychology*, *25*(2), 234.

Salvati, M., & Koc, Y. (2022). Advancing research into the social psychology of sexual orientations and gender identities: Current research and future directions. *European Journal of Social Psychology*, *52*(2), 225–232.

Sbarra, D. A., & Emery, R. E. (2005). The emotional sequelae of nonmarital relationship dissolution: Analysis of change and intraindividual variability over time. *Personal Relationships*, *12*(2), 213–232.

Sbarra, D. A., Law, R. W., & Portley, R. M. (2011). Divorce and death: A meta-analysis and research agenda for clinical, social, and health psychology. *Perspectives on Psychological Science*, *6*(5), 454–474.

Schachter, S. (1959). *The psychology of affiliation: Experimental studies of the sources of gregariousness*. Stanford, CA: Stanford University Press.

Snyder, M., Tanke, E. D., & Berscheid, E. (1977). Social perception and interpersonal behavior: On the self-fulfilling nature of social stereotypes. *Journal of Personality and Social Psychology*, *35*(9), 656.

Spitz, R. A. (1945). Hospitalism: An inquiry into the genesis of psychiatric conditions in early childhood. *The Psychoanalytic Study of the Child*, *1*(1), 53–74.

Steffens, N. K., LaRue, C. J., Haslam, C., Walter, Z. C., Cruwys, T., Munt, K. A., ... & Tarrant, M. (2021). Social identification-building interventions to improve health: A systematic review and meta-analysis. *Health Psychology Review*, *15*(1), 85–112.

Sternberg, R. J. (1986). A triangular theory of love. *Psychological Review*, *93*(2), 119–135.

Tashiro, T., & Frazier, P. (2003). 'I'll never be in a relationship like that again': Personal growth following romantic relationship breakups. *Personal Relationships*, *10*(1), 113–128.

Taylor, P., Rietzschel, J., Danquah, A., & Berry, K. (2015). Changes in attachment representations during psychological therapy. *Psychotherapy Research*, *25*(2), 222-238.

Thornhill, R., & Gangestad, S. W. (1999). Facial attractiveness. *Trends in Cognitive Sciences*, *3*(12), 452–460.

van der Toorn, J., Pliskin, R., & Morgenroth, T. (2020). Not quite over the rainbow: The unrelenting and insidious nature of heteronormative ideology. *Current Opinion in Behavioral Sciences*, *34*, 160–165.

Walster, E., Aronson, V., Abrahams, D., & Rottman, L. (1966). Importance of physical attractiveness in dating behavior. *Journal of Personality and Social Psychology*, *4*(5), 508–516.

Walster, E., Berscheid, E., & Walster, G. W. (1973). New directions in equity research. *Journal of Personality and Social Psychology*, *25*(2), 151–176.

Walter, K. V., Conroy-Beam, D., Buss, D. M., Asao, K., Sorokowska, A., Sorokowski, P., … & Zupančič, M. (2020). Sex differences in mate preferences across 45 countries: A large-scale replication. *Psychological Science*, *31*(4), 408–423.

Williams, K. D., Cheung, C. K., & Choi, W. (2000). Cyberostracism: Effects of being ignored over the internet. *Journal of Personality and Social Psychology*, *79*(5), 748.

Wirth, J. H., Sacco, D. F., Hugenberg, K., & Williams, K. D. (2010). Eye gaze as relational evaluation: Averted eye gaze leads to feelings of ostracism and relational devaluation. *Personality and Social Psychology Bulletin*, *36*(7), 869–882.

Zebrowitz, L. A., Wang, R., Bronstad, P. M., Eisenberg, D., Undurraga, E., Reyes-García, V., & Godoy, R. (2012). First impressions from faces among US and culturally isolated Tsimane' people in the Bolivian rainforest. *Journal of Cross-Cultural Psychology*, *43*(1), 119–134.

4
SOCIAL EMOTIONS
SMADAR COHEN-CHEN

Contents

4.1 AUTHOR'S PERSONAL JOURNEY

My interest in social emotions, and particularly the role of emotions in conflicts, began because I myself was born into the violent and extreme Israeli–Palestinian conflict. Throughout my childhood, periods of escalation and cycles of violence were followed by periods of de-escalation and relative quiet. Conflict was not a far-away concept, but a very bitter reality. When I was seven, my school had to shut for months because of the Gulf War. I spent many hours with my parents in a bomb shelter with gas masks on, waiting for the radio to give us the all-clear to come out. Throughout my teenage years, buses and cafés were blown up on a daily basis, leaving in their wake destruction and devastation. My entire school year's constant preoccupation with the upcoming mandatory military service was as prevalent as teens in other countries may be concerned with university applications or their future. If we came out on the other side we could think about higher education. The military brought with it new, more intense encounters of the conflict. I once had to ring my parents and tell them I could not come home because the base I was in was surrounded by snipers and no one could leave. A bus I missed going home one day exploded, killing a much-loved commander of mine. She had taught me a few weeks earlier in a course I took on teaching and instructing. A close childhood friend was killed in an ambush. But there were also times of hope, such as the Oslo Accords in 1993 and the possibility for a lasting peace between Israelis and Palestinians. There were encounters with Palestinians through peace organisations and non-governmental organisations (NGOs), which shone light on the pain and suffering experienced on their side, eliciting dialogue, empathy, and kindness. These experiences sparked my interest in understanding the ways that people who have grown up as enemies can be brought together and potentially overcome such deeply entrenched conflicts.

During my time at university, I realised that emotional experiences were highly prevalent in the conflict's narrative; the stories that people tell themselves, their children, and the other side are dominated by emotions. Stories shaped by hatred paint the other side as demonic, evil, and unchanging. A narrative shaped by hope paints the future as more positive, but also accepts that the present is negative, and needs changing. I noticed that the prevalent emotions of hatred and hope, but also guilt, empathy, anger, and contempt were colouring the narrative of the conflict, directing attention to different aspects or facts. I therefore joined the Psychology of Intergroup Conflict and Reconciliation (PICR) Lab in Israel, led by Eran Halperin, and subsequently started a PhD examining the role of hope in promoting peace and conflict resolution, with Eran Halperin and Richard Crisp as my supervisors. I examined the role of hope in promoting attitudes and behaviours conducive to peace and conflict resolution. Next, I developed simple and applicable interventions to induce hope for peace in contexts of intergroup conflict.

Overall, the fascination that social emotions hold for me continues to grow as I delve deeper into their role in both exacerbating and resolving conflict. While initially my research interests were motivated by my personal experiences, now that I have been involved with research on emotions and conflict for some time, it is research that upholds my personal perceptions of conflict – that there is always hope for change if people maintain that hope and use it to act for change.

4.2 INTRODUCTION

We all have emotions. We feel happy, sad, proud, angry, guilty, and hopeful. Some of us may be more inclined to experience a particular emotion, while others may experience entirely different emotions more strongly and frequently. But one thing is certain, a huge part of the human experience involves emotions. One of the things that people often believe (and repeat) is that rational individuals cannot, and should not, let their emotions control them. We are encouraged to make decisions, process information, and handle ourselves while ignoring and disregarding our emotions. But emotions are critical precisely *because* they guide behaviour. They help people to process information and form goals. We feel angry when we have been wronged, and are propelled to change our situation. We feel guilty when we have wronged others, and this motivates us to make amends. We feel hopeful when we see a possibility to improve our situation, and this drives us to attain a goal that is important to us. Like so many other things, underestimating the power of emotions often leads people to ignore them, and this ignorance can lead to problematic behaviours driven precisely by emotions. 'Those who fail to learn from history are doomed to repeat it' (Winston Churchill). Philosophers and leaders have used this phrase to indicate that humans have certain inclinations, and that reflecting on those inclinations, understanding them in depth, and harnessing them for good is important in making *conscious* decisions.

In this chapter we will define emotions (and other emotional phenomena) and understand how they are formed. We will consider their important role in making sense of social situations and guiding attitudes and behaviours in social contexts, particularly in the context of conflict. We will then delve more deeply and discuss different strategies to regulate and transform emotions, both directly and indirectly. The aim of the chapter is for you to learn about the nature of emotions, their structure and purpose, and the relationships between emotions and other key constructs, such as attitudes and actions. Most importantly, understanding emotions in depth and utilising that knowledge in interpreting social situations and contexts will help you to develop a mastery of emotions, and those who can master their emotions can prevent their emotions from mastering them.

4.3 LEARNING OBJECTIVES

By the end of this chapter, you will be able to:

- Define emotions and the process of emotion elicitation, including the relationship between events, emotions, and behavioural outcomes in social contexts;
- Describe how key frameworks explaining emotions have changed over time and what the current theories explaining emotions are;
- Differentiate between different emotional phenomena, both on individual and group levels;
- Understand what aggression is, why it occurs, how it is learned, and what happens when it is embedded in the form of intergroup conflicts;

- Identify the role emotions play in conflict processes and their resolution;
- Be able to critically analyse different strategies to regulate emotions, their strengths and weaknesses, and the ways this affects social contexts and interactions;
- Apply and consolidate theories of emotions and emotion regulation research to real world situations.

4.4 PART 1: FOUNDATIONS

4.4.1 Definition of Emotions

Emotions are prevalent in almost every aspect of human life. This includes our attitudes towards ourselves, relationships with significant others, in the workplace, as well as perceptions and behaviours on a group level. We all experience emotions multiple times – even hundreds of times – during the day, but we rarely think about what emotions actually are, why they exist, and what function they serve in our day-to-day lives. Understanding emotions is important because awareness can help us to predict what events will elicit which emotions, and how these emotions will shape human responses to these events. More importantly, these understandings lend themselves to developing ways in which emotions can be changed and transformed to affect negative social phenomena, such as prejudice, oppression, aggression, and conflict, or positive social phenomena, such as interpersonal helping or political participation.

> **Key concept – Emotion:** Flexible responses elicited when an individual appraises a situation, an event, or information as offering important challenges or opportunities.

So what *are* emotions?

Scherer (1984) defined emotion as a series of flexible and changing responses to an event perceived by a person as relevant to their concerns. A number of important observations derive from this definition. First, a person experiences emotions towards, or in light of, a stimulus (event, person, information, etc.) that they consider important and relevant. Second, the emotional response is predicted by the extent to which the stimulus poses a threat to or an opportunity for goals and interests. Third, emotions are associated with action tendencies, or the creation of intentions or plans for action. Lastly, emotions are experienced as a distinctive type of mental state, which is at times accompanied or followed by changes in the body, thoughts, and actions. Although the different components of emotions and their structure are debated, these aspects are generally agreed upon by emotion scholars.

Here is an example of how an emotional response might play out. Two people buy exactly the same piece of clothing in a store and take it home. However, the piece of clothing is ripped, which both people find out only when they get home later that evening. Person A shrugs; they will replace the item on the way to work tomorrow morning. It does not matter. But Person B has an important event that evening, to which they intended to wear this item of clothing.

Now they have nothing to wear to the event. They experience anger towards the retailer for selling them the faulty product. They complain, rant, try to get compensation, and want to punish those responsible. So what is the difference between the two responses? It could be that they are simply very different people; indeed, personality has been found to affect how people interpret social information (Tong, 2010). But research has shown that the difference between the two responses may well be rooted in the fact that – for one of these people – the fault in the clothing posed an obstacle to an important and relevant goal, which led them to *interpret* the situation in a different way and therefore respond differently from the other person. Notably, one's interpretation of those goals can also be influenced by personality traits, and therefore both context and personality come into play to some extent simultaneously.

Of course, this is a mundane example and is likely not life-changing or critical. But even such everyday events can lead to strong emotional reactions and intense behaviours or actions, based on the context in question. Thus, when we move to more crucial circumstances, ones that involve long-term implications, close relationships, and even life-and-death situations, emotions become more intense, pivotal, and extreme. For example, in the aftermath of the September 11, 2001 terror attacks, Americans whose emotional experience was dominated by anger supported aggressive military responses, while those who were mostly sad expressed reservations about a military attack (Sadler et al., 2005). Since emotions seem to play an important role in social and political spheres, it is important to look back on the developments in scholarly thought regarding emotions over the years.

4.4.2 Historical Overview of Emotion Theory

One of the first theories regarding emotions was *evolutionary theory*, put forth by Charles Darwin (1904). According to this theory, emotions have an evolutionary purpose and have adaptive functions to help the species (either human or other) to survive and thrive. Darwin observed physical manifestations of emotions (such as anger, fear, joy, disgust) across species and discussed their expressions and functions (Plutchik, 1970). Fear makes us sensitive to threat and triggers physical responses, such as elevated heartbeat and a rush of adrenaline, that will help us to survive (run away or fight the threat). Disgust helps us to spot things (like bad food or other substances) that could harm our bodies and drives our bodies to reject them for our own survival. Joy enables us to revel in (and therefore strive to maintain) functional and safe environments. This perception of emotions as important to our survival has been maintained throughout emotion theory, although the definition of 'functional' has been widened to include much more than just surviving in nature (social life, well-being, etc.).

The first examination of emotions using a testable theory was the James–Lange theory (Cannon, 1927). Independently proposed by both William James and Carl Lange, this theory perceived emotions as a physiological occurrence, and used bodily reactions to explain why they arose. According to this theory, bodily responses to a stimulus or event are reflexive, and the emotion is based on (1) awareness of the response, and (2) how one interprets the physiological response. In other words, the emotion is not the response to an event but an awareness and categorisation of a physical and instinctive reaction to an event.

Next came the Cannon–Bard theory (Cannon, 1927), which had the same key components of emotion-elicitation as the James–Lange Theory, but differed in terms of how they were configured. According to Cannon–Bard theory, the physiological and the emotional components occur simultaneously following an event or stimulus.

Based on these two approaches, Schachter and Singer (1962) developed the two factor theory, which introduced the importance of context in the interpretation of physiological responses. According to this theory, a stimulus will create a physiological response, followed by cognitive labelling of the reaction and an association with an emotion. Only then will the emotion itself be experienced.

KEY STUDY 4.1

Two Factor Theory of Emotion

Schachter and Singer (1962) conducted an experiment in which physiological arousal was induced among some participants using an injection of epinephrine, while others received a placebo of saline. Some participants were then informed of the side effects (raised heartbeat, tension), while others were not. Then, participants were joined by a confederate (presented as another participant) who expressed either euphoria (a high-arousal pleasant emotion) by playing and enjoying themselves in the room, or anger (a high-arousal unpleasant emotion), moving around angrily and venting. Results showed that in the physiological arousal condition, when no explanation was provided (participants did not know about the side effects), the arousal was attributed to an emotional response (either euphoria or anger), based on the emotional expressions of the confederate. In other words, the same physical manifestations were interpreted differently based on the *context* (created by another person).

According to two factor theory, our body responds first (heightened heartbeat), followed by our mind (Am I walking alone in the dark? Or am I interacting with an attractive potential partner?), and only then do we 'tag' the emotion as fear or romantic attraction. An interesting application of this theory is incidental moods/emotions (Bodenhausen et al., 1994), according to which people's judgement of a situation is affected by their emotions, even if the emotions have nothing to do with the situation itself (thus, incidental). People will ask themselves how they are feeling regarding certain information or an event, but they have a hard time differentiating the target of their emotions.

In one series of studies (Bodenhausen et al., 1994), researchers increased incidental happiness (e.g., by asking participants to recall and write down a happy event or to listen to music that made them happy). They were then given information regarding negative behaviour (violence or cheating) that another student was accused of and asked to make judgements regarding their guilt. The accused was either identified as a member of a group stereotypically associated with the alleged offence (stereotype condition) or not (no stereotype condition). Interestingly, happy participants were more likely to rely on stereotypes when making this social judgement (i.e., they were more likely to judge the accused student to be guilty in the stereotype condition). This is because happy people are not motivated to engage in cognitive effort (e.g., second guessing information, or questioning their own thought processes). However, when they were told in advance that they would be accountable for their decisions, happy people no longer reverted to stereotypical thinking in their decisions. Another related study (Schnall et al., 2008) showed that unrelated feelings of disgust (induced by 'fart spray' – who said this is not educational?) while making moral social decisions led people to make more severe moral social judgements (e.g., disagreeing with the marriage of first cousins). The feelings of disgust were, in this case, physiological and not relevant to the decisions, but they affected people's social judgements anyway.

All three of the aforementioned approaches to emotions focused on the physical manifestations of emotions, but over time, the interpretative elements came to the fore and complexities in the understanding of emotions were introduced in the literature. A theory that moved away from the physiological aspects and focused on the cognitive and behavioural aspects was suggested by Arnold (1960), who stated that emotions are generated when a stimulus is appraised by the individual as good or bad in the moment, and that this leads to either approach or avoidance towards that object. This led to further theorising, resulting in today's most widely utilised framework to understanding emotion, **appraisal theories of emotion** (e.g., Ellsworth & Scherer, 2003; Frijda, 1986; Lazarus, 1994).

One early natural experiment (Folkman & Lazarus, 1985) examined these assumptions by measuring university students' appraisals and associated emotions prior to taking an exam, after the exam, and before marks were released. Results showed that appraisal patterns (e.g., challenge, threat) predicted emotions and that appraisals were dependent on changing context and circumstances as well as individual factors. Another experiment (Siemer et al., 2007) brought participants into the lab and gave them negative feedback (standardised) followed by measures of appraisals and emotions. Although participants responded with a variety of appraisals, the appraisal *patterns* predicted emotional responses (e.g., appraisals of an injustice lead to anger and appraisals of threat lead to fear). In other words, people may respond and interpret events differently, but specific appraisals lead to and predict the same specific emotions in everybody.

> **Key concept – Appraisal theories of emotion:** Emotional processes are rooted in appraisals of meaningful events, leading to emotional goals (goals typically associated with particular emotions) and subsequently action tendencies. Importantly, appraisal theories of emotions suggest that each emotion has a unique 'story', stemming from its distinctive appraisal, emotional goals, and action tendencies. However, this theory takes into account individual differences (such as traits or ideology) when forming the appraisal about the event in question.

4.4.3 Emotional Phenomena

Up until now we have discussed emotions, and particularly discrete emotions which are activated by a specific event and are focused on a specific target. There are, however, additional emotional experiences that should be addressed. Moods (Beedie et al., 2005) are general, stable, and ambiguous affective states (the 'feeling' part of the emotion) which are not necessarily elicited from an event (as emotions are), but persist 'in the background' over time. Moods differ from emotions in two aspects. First, unlike emotions that are specific to a target, moods are not focused on any one thing or person in particular. Second, moods are a type of affective baseline unrelated to a specific event. This is different from emotions, which are induced based on an appraisal of a certain event. For example, sometimes we wake up feeling rather low, perhaps for no reason at all. This may change throughout the day, but can also last for a long time, as may be the case for someone suffering from chronic depression, for example.

Emotional sentiments (Frijda, 1986; Lazarus, 1994) are temporally stable, long-term, emotional dispositions towards a person, group, or symbol that are unrelated to any specific action or statement of that object. Sentiments differ from emotions because they are not specific to an event, but are specific to a target. Said differently, both sentiments and emotions have a specific target, but emotions are elicited by an *event* and sentiments are more baseline, dispositional, or background inclinations which persist over time (Frijda, 1986; Lazarus, 1994). Check out Table 4.1 to understand the differences and similarities between discrete emotions, sentiments, and moods.

Table 4.1 Similarities and differences in emotional phenomena

Type	Trigger	Time frame	Target	Example
Discrete emotion	Event	Short term	Specific (person/group/event/symbol)	Hope for peace in a specific conflict that increases or is elicited due to a specific event (a leader gives a speech outlining their plan for peace talks).
Sentiment	None	Long term	Specific (person/group/event/symbol)	An enduring hope for peace in a specific conflict that is unrelated to any event.
Mood	None	Long term	Non-specific (general feeling)	Optimism – a general feeling that things in general will and do turn out alright.

4.4.4 Social Emotional Phenomena

In social or intergroup contexts, the importance of group identity becomes very important. Social identity theory (Tajfel & Turner, 1979) postulates that people prefer (and will work pretty hard) to hold a positive self-image, and draw upon the group to which they belong as a source of positive self-esteem. People are inclined to view their ingroup in a positive light compared to other groups because that reflects positively on them as part of that group (see Chapters 5, 8, and 10). These perceptions lead people to favour their ingroup in terms of positive evaluation, resource allocation, and prosocial or helpful behaviour.

In order to understand how personal emotional experiences are related to social and group-based contexts, we must combine the importance of groups to people's self-image (Tajfel & Turner, 1979) and the different elements of appraisal theories of emotions, which emphasise the relevance and importance of events to the self in forming appraisals (Frijda, 1986). Smith and Mackie (2016) highlighted the importance of social context and their meanings in the formation of emotions and emotional appraisals. An event relevant to the individual can, in other words, be derived from their identity and group membership. This event leads to an appraisal regarding the self in a group context (ingroup/outgroup), which elicits an emotional response, and subsequently a relevant attitude or behavioural tendency.

When discussing social emotions, an additional layer is added to the emotional experience, particularly emotions elicited in group contexts like conflict or collective action, defined as action undertaken by people on behalf of their ingroup to achieve group goals (van Zomeren et al., 2008). These contexts elicit additional emotional phenomena: **group-based emotions** (Iyer & Leach, 2008; Smith et al., 2007) and **collective emotions** (Stephan & Stephan, 2000).

> **Key concept – Group-based emotions:** Emotions felt by a person as a result of perceived belongingness to a certain group. Group-based emotions are experienced 'in the name' of the group, although the experience itself is on the individual level.

In both the case of group-based and collective emotions, however, Bar-Tal and colleagues (2007) note that the emotion is elicited as a reaction to an event even though the individual is not necessarily personally involved in the event itself. An example of this is the Olympics. Imagine you are sitting at home and watching the Olympic Games. Your country's representative is participating, and you start to feel nervous. The tension mounts as you stretch out on the sofa and suddenly your country's athlete wins! You are nowhere near the Olympics, you could not be more sedentary, but you feel a wave of pride and happiness. These emotions are *group-based*, since the only relationship you have with the person who just won is that they represent your country; you are part of the same group. Now, as you are feeling a wave of pride, so are thousands (or millions) of other people from your country. None of them knows that athlete, none of them has participated in the Olympics, and none of them has any part in the victory. But the pride shared by all these people is the collective emotion of pride.

> **Key concept – Collective emotions:** Emotions shared by a large number of people in a group. When a large number, or indeed a majority of people in a group experience a similar emotional response towards the same target within the same context, this is considered a collective emotion.

> **Key concept – Emotions as social information (EASI) theory:** Emotional expressions exert interpersonal and intergroup effects by triggering emotional reactions and/or inferential (cognitive) processes in targets or observers, depending on (1) the target's information processing, and (2) the perceived appropriateness of the emotional expression.

Lastly, an important social aspect of emotions is emotional expressions as a type of social language. We have seen that emotions influence the attitudes and behaviours of those who experience them, but there is a whole field of research which examines how emotions influence those who *observe* them in others. Following appraisal theory of emotions, this line of work suggests that people's emotions themselves contain information about their feelings and intentions, which those interacting with them can use to glean important social information. Research on '**emotions as social information**' (**EASI**) (van Kleef, 2009) has shown that emotions provide information to observers indicating their feelings, thoughts, motivations, and intentions (van Kleef, 2009). In social environments, emotions are a way to convey interests, attitudes, and perceptions regarding events, people, and relationships. These expressions may be conveyed both consciously or unconsciously (Gross & Thompson, 2007).

According to this approach, some social contexts are conducive to emotional contagion, a reciprocal emotional experience in which one might 'catch' other people's emotions. However, its is true only for non-competitive relationships or contexts. This makes sense when we think about someone whom we are close to (a partner, friend, or family member), but with whom we are not competing. In this case, their happiness may feel contagious, and we will start to feel happy as well. On the other hand, when they are sad, we may start to experience a similar experience in response. Emotional contagion has been found to be one of the psychological mechanisms by which leaders influence followers (Bono & Ilies, 2006). Another response to emotional expressions that is based on reciprocity may involve complementary emotional responses in those observing the emotions (Keltner & Haidt, 1999). For instance, expressions of sadness and distress may lead observers to experience empathy or compassion towards the expresser, and anger may lead observers to experience fear (Dimberg & Öhman, 1996). These emotions may induce behavioural tendencies functional to the (non-competitive) social relationship.

Unlike a non-competitive context, observing emotions in competitive contexts has been shown to elicit very different responses compared to observing the very same emotions in a non-competitive context. The fact that emotional expressions inform observers about how expressers appraise a situation (Manstead & Fischer, 2001) may induce a different emotional reaction when those interests and appraisals are perceived as directly opposed to one's own. For example, in a competitive negotiation context, expressions of anger (compared to happiness) were found to lead to more concession-making by observers than when information processing was limited (van Kleef et al., 2004). Two important insights are gleaned from this work. First, observers were forced to consider the opponent's emotions in a situation where they could not get more 'concrete' information. Second, expressions of anger signalled information about the person's intentions (that they were not going to make any more concessions or felt they had been wronged). Another line of work (Cohen-Chen et al., 2022) examined the effect of indifference expressions in interpersonal conflict. This line of research examined how emotional expressions of indifference in a workplace conflict affected both negative emotions (towards the expresser) and expectations of collaboration (by the expresser), subsequently influencing levels of cooperation. Results showed that indifference expressions induced the most negative outcomes (even compared to contempt expressions!) in terms of emotional responses, expectations of expresser collaboration, and cooperation.

Taken together, all this research is important because it enables us to understand the complex role of emotions, especially when we aim to understand them in a social context and use this knowledge to change attitudes, foster prosocial behaviour, reduce aggression, and promote conflict resolution. So how can we characterise emotions to further understand their pivotal role in social relations and contexts?

4.4.5 Characterising Emotions

There are many ways to think about and categorise emotions. For example, one of the first emotion theorists, Paul Ekman, categorised emotions as primary versus secondary.

KEY THINKER

Paul Ekman

Paul Ekman is one of the most influential psychologists of the 21st century, and has been named as one of *TIME Magazine*'s 100 most influential people in the world. Ekman examined emotions and emotional expressions as a universal social language and developed a framework and tools to interpret and understand micro facial expressions. This further led to a coding system to detect emotional reactions and lie detection using facial expressions. Following his book *Telling Lies* (1985), Ekman was approached by many law enforcement organisations and developed training programmes based on his research. Ekman himself inspired the TV series *Lie To Me* (2009), on which he was also a scientific advisor, and served as the scientific advisor for the 2015 film *Inside Out*.

According to Ekman (1999), there are six *primary* or basic emotions (fear, disgust, surprise, anger, happiness, and sadness), which are fundamental and to some extent instinctive. These emotions have an evolutionary function, playing a role in our survival. Incidentally, they are also experienced by animals for the very same reasons. For example, fear is an emotion elicited in the face of immediate threat. It has physical manifestations, such as rapid breathing and heartbeat, a surge in adrenaline, and hyperfocus – all things that will help us to identify and deal with the threat speedily (by either fighting it or fleeing from it). *Secondary* emotions, on the other hand, are emotions that are more complex, and often combine two or more of the basic emotions. These emotions are unique to humans, and they involve more cognitive processing (such as thinking about an alternative reality or thinking far into the future or the past) rather than instinct. Examples include guilt, hope, nostalgia, anxiety, and hatred.

The use of primary and secondary emotions can be applied to our understanding of dehumanisation, the perception or treatment of people as less than fully human (Haslam & Stratemeyer, 2016). Dehumanisation underlies some of the worst of crimes against humanity in history, legitimising and normalising atrocities such as the Holocaust, slavery, genocide, apartheid, and the Occupation in the Israeli–Palestinian context. Dehumanisation enables people to commit terrible acts without feeling they have violated any moral norms or values (Haslam & Loughnan, 2014), because they are not wholly human. Research on infra-humanisation (Leyens et al., 2000) discovered that people attribute primary, 'animalistic' emotions to outgroups, and secondary, 'evolved' or 'complex' emotions to their ingroup. Gaunt et al. (2002) gave participants a text seemingly written by another person about a tendency to experience emotions. They manipulated the group membership (ingroup versus outgroup), the type of expressed emotions (primary; pleasure versus secondary; tenderness) and choice (versus no choice) in writing about that emotion. Participants used the information about choice to discount the emotional information, but only in the outgroup condition. Said differently, people chose to actively resist attributing secondary emotions to outgroup members, because it humanises them (remember the importance of ingroup perceptions set forth by social identity theory; Tajfel & Turner, 1979, and see Chapter 8).

Another approach used to categorise emotions is the emotion circumplex model (Russell, 1980). This framework focuses on the way emotions are experienced by the individual, and maps all emotions along two dimensions: arousal (the degree of physiological activation) and valence (pleasantness vs unpleasantness) (Barrett, 2006). The combination of these two dimensions creates a unique experience for each emotion. For example, both serenity and enthusiasm map onto the same side of the valence dimension, because they are experienced as positive by the individual. However, they map onto opposite sides of the arousal dimension. While serenity involves low arousal (the body is relaxed), enthusiasm involves high arousal and physical activation. Similarly, anger and excitement are similar in terms of arousal, because they both have high activation, but they are opposite in terms of valence. Anger is experienced as unpleasant, whereas excitement is experienced as pleasant.

While these frameworks help us to understand emotions in terms of the individual, other scholars examine emotions from a social perspective, focusing on the functions that emotions have in contexts such as collective action, conflict, aggression, and prosocial behaviour. In other words, these researchers wanted to examine and categorise emotions in terms of their role in promoting or hindering certain behaviours. A well-established framework which takes this view is the constructivist approach to emotions (Averill, 1980). This approach does not examine how emotions feel to the individual, but rather focuses on the outcomes of emotions, and the extent to which these outcomes are constructive or destructive. These can include attitudes (the predisposed state of mind about something), perceptions (the way things are interpreted and understood), action tendencies (the urge to carry out an action linked to a specific emotion), and behaviours that emotions elicit in those experiencing them. This approach does not view emotions as existing in a vacuum, or as important in and of themselves, but as a stage in understanding how humans act, react, and interact with one another.

All of these frameworks are valid ways of categorising and researching emotions. Different scholars approach emotions from different perspectives because of their different goals. For example, scholars who are interested in interpersonal processes, such as well-being, decision-making, or work performance, will choose to think about emotions that are particularly relevant to those domains. Things like what elicits the emotion in a personal context, or what outcomes this emotion yields in terms of work performance or cognitive abilities, will guide researchers. On the other hand, research that focuses on intergroup relations will often categorise emotions in terms of their benefit (or detriment) to intergroup harmony and conflict resolution (i.e., the constructivist approach). Researchers in these fields aim to induce emotional experiences that diminish prejudice and intergroup aggression (such as contact; see Chapter 9) and foster conflict resolution attitudes, regardless of their individually based valence (pleasantness).

4.4.6 Aggression

When considering behaviours that are affected by emotions, it is important to understand a little more about **aggression**, a realm of human behaviour that is directly linked to a range of emotions.

> **Key concept – Aggression:** Aggression is an act (physical, verbal, or even social) intended to cause harm (to other people, things, animals, etc.).

Research on aggression in general aims to explain why humans are aggressive. As in many phenomena in psychology, two diverse approaches are used to explain aggression from two opposing perspectives. One type of approach focuses on individuals themselves as the cause of aggression. This includes *biological theories*, such as psychodynamic theory (Freud, 1961 [1930]), which suggests that aggression is caused by a build-up of tension that is released to restore balance between the two opposing instincts we all possess – the life instinct and the destructive instinct. The evolutionary approach posits that humans are wired to behave aggressively, and that this serves an evolutionary purpose, as it does among other species, to help humans survive (Kenrick & Simpson, 1997). According to this approach, physical strength and dominance over others are needed to compete for limited resources in order to survive and reproduce. The problem with these theories is that many aggressive acts cannot be explained by a simple willingness to pass on our genes to offspring. This is particularly true when we look at conflicts over symbolic and value-based issues, which don't have an evolutionary basis.

Other theories aim to explain differences *between* individuals in levels of aggression, such as gender differences (Eagly & Steffen, 1986). Over the years, scholars have shown that gender difference is due to physical differences between men and women, such as significantly different levels of testosterone, making men more aggressive (Berman et al., 1993). Other work points to gender socialisation practices that affect the type of aggressive behaviour. Women are socialised to be more nurturing and caring, and are taught, explicitly and indirectly, to behave more calmly. Unlike physiological differences, personality differences have been used to explain why some people are more aggressive than others. It seems that some personality traits, such as high irritability and low agreeableness (Gleason et al., 2004), are predictive of aggression.

Taken together, you may notice that all these theories are based on traits or characteristics which determine *who* will be aggressive. However, critics of these theories provide a more nuanced or complex explanation. According to the opposing line of thought, most people are not simply either aggressive or non-aggressive. People can spend a lifetime behaving non-aggressively, but suddenly behave aggressively in a specific instance, or towards a specific person. The question is – are these people then to be classed as aggressive or non-aggressive? On the other hand, hardened criminals may treat specific people in their lives with care and compassion, or may suddenly carry out a non-aggressive act.

In response to this criticism, *situation-centred theories* arose, suggesting that context is important when observing and predicting aggression. Some researchers have found that physical conditions in the environment are conducive to aggressive behaviour. This includes, for example, heat, which has been found to increase irritability and negative emotions towards others (Baron & Bell, 1976), leading to more aggression. Anderson (1989) found that heat is associated with violent (more than non-violent) crime. Kenrick and MacFarlane (1986) conducted a study associating heat and horn honks. Spanning different temperatures in the spring and summer, a confederate stalled their car (causing participants to miss the green light) at an intersection at different times, and aggression was measured by counting the times participants honked their horn. Results showed that as the temperature increased, so did the honking. Other such predictors of aggression are crowding (Ng et al., 2001), and noise (Donnerstein & Wilson, 1976), which similarly facilitate aggressive behaviour by sparking physiological arousal, discomfort, irritation, and stress.

Rather than physiological or physical aspects, other situation-centred work focused on the psychological factors that lead people to behave aggressively. Much research has shown that a feeling of disadvantage, deprivation, or injustice when comparing oneself (or one's group) to another individual (or group) leads to aggressive actions (van Zomeren et al., 2008). This is particularly prevalent when the individual or group believes that normative or legitimate means cannot change the situation (Tausch et al., 2011). Several studies focus specifically on this perception of malleability. One study (Cohen-Chen et al., 2014c), conducted during a social protest, instilled in participants a malleable belief about groups' nature in general (versus stable and unchanging). Next, participants were asked about their levels of efficacy (the belief that the group can create change; van Zomeren et al., 2008) and their intention to engage in normative collective action to create social change. Results showed that the belief in group malleability induced collective action intentions through group efficacy. Shuman and colleagues (2016) conducted research within the context of social protests as well, and found three distinct emotional paths predicting different types of action. The belief that the world is malleable predicted hope, while a belief that groups are malleable predicted anger, both further predicting intentions to engage in normative action. However, the belief that groups in general are stable and cannot change predicted hatred towards the outgroup, subsequently predicting aggressive and non-normative action for change.

Building on situation-centred theories, which regard situations as existing in a void, some theories explain aggression as deriving from circumstances that stem from culture and group norms (Cohen et al., 1996). According to this line of thought, different cultures and subcultures may endorse, encourage, or discourage aggressive behaviour based on their history, circumstances, values, and norms. The empirical investigation of culture as predicting aggression is extremely challenging. It raises questions such as how to define aggression and has a hard time teasing additional factors apart from culture itself. However, it brings up an interesting question regarding the way in which people may become aggressive or adopt aggressive behaviours, norms, and values (for more about culture and intergroup relations, see Chapter 10).

These theories revolve around *learning*, and specifically how our behaviour, including emotions, is influenced by our social environments. Skinner (1953) examined the ways in which people learn, and suggested that any change in behaviour is a direct result of stimuli in a person's surroundings. This theory, called operant conditioning, examines how positive and negative reinforcement (reward and punishment) in response to a positive or negative behaviour influences subsequent behaviour. When someone behaves in a certain way, positive reinforcement (e.g., reward, praise) will strengthen the link (they will continue to behave in this way), while negative reinforcement (e.g., punishment) will weaken the link (they will not do that again). For example, we may observe that a child has trouble sharing and is snatching from their peers. Negative reinforcement would be to tell them off or take away privileges whenever they snatch. Positive reinforcement would be to reward and praise them when they share or take turns.

Today, this approach can be found almost anywhere, including the justice system, education, workplace incentives, and many more. But Skinner was the first to test the idea on animals and humans and provide empirical evidence that it works. Skinner's work led to many more questions and theories. One of these was social learning theory, proposed by Bandura (1977), who established that people can also learn behaviour indirectly by observing others' behaviour (modelling), and then observing whether that behaviour was rewarded or punished.

KEY STUDY 4.2

Bobo Doll

Bandura and colleagues (1961) showed that observing aggressive behaviour in others significantly increased aggressive behaviour among children. Here, children were brought into the lab, where some of them were exposed to an adult behaving aggressively towards a toy called 'Bobo doll'. The aggression itself was distinctive, so

(Continued)

that it could be attributed to that particular role model. Next, all the children were exposed to an aggression-inducing stimulus: they were taken into a room with toys and told they were not allowed to play with them. Lastly, they were taken to a third room in which there was a mix of toys, including the 'Bobo doll', and their responses were recorded. Results showed that those who had watched an adult behaving aggressively towards Bobo Doll were significantly more aggressive in general, and used the distinctively aggressive behaviour they had observed in their adult role model, indicating that aggression is a learned and socialised behaviour. Later, Bandura (1965) conducted the same study again, but this time, the aggressive role model was rewarded (given sweets and praise), punished (scolded), or had no consequence (control). When entering the playroom, children who had observed no consequence or a reward for aggression behaved more aggressively than those who had seen the model being punished.

Perhaps the most relevant context in which aggression affects people's lives in a deep-seated and widespread way is through intergroup conflict. These contexts have been historically, and are currently, the backdrop of some of the most harrowing acts of aggression, such as the Rwandan genocide, the civil war in Syria, and the conflict between Russia and Ukraine, all of which include displacement of entire groups of people, dehumanisation, physical and sexual violence, and death. Therefore, it is crucial that we understand the relationship between emotions and aggression in contexts where these phenomena are the most destructive.

EXERCISE 4.1

Social Learning

Social learning is still regarded as one of the most important and relevant theories regarding aggression. Nowadays, it is particularly important to think about the effects of simply observing aggressive behaviour when we think about the amount and type of content observed by people on social media. Most of us use social media, and there is a growing concern about the kind of social interactions and aggressive behaviours found on social media, including bullying, threatening, insulting, 'doxing', inflammatory language, and much more.

Think about what happens when online aggression is rewarded (nothing happens to those who threaten people online, or they receive more attention and 'likes') and when it is punished (Donald Trump was taken off social media for his behaviour). Using the frameworks discussed in this chapter, analyse your observations. Lastly, reflect on how societies (or the social media companies) can use social learning theories to address unwanted online behaviour.

4.5 PART 2: ADVANCES

4.5.1 Intergroup Aggression and Conflict

Conflict arises when two or more parties (1) perceive their goals or interests to be directly contradictory to one another's, and (2) decide to act upon the contradiction to change the observed situation. Intergroup conflicts are an inherent part of human life and interaction. Throughout history, conflicts have served as a means of social and political development to right grave wrongs by changing agendas and social priorities. However, under certain conditions, conflicts can result in extremely negative consequences, such as violent clashes, horrific acts, and widespread suffering.

A major focus of social psychology research has been on the predictors, outcomes, and resolution of intergroup conflict (Kriesberg, 1993). This focus has been guided by the belief that understanding the psychological underpinnings of intergroup conflict can ultimately lead to the development of ways to ameliorate these detrimental and often devastating situations. Years of theoretical and empirical research have uncovered different approaches to understanding psychological bases of intergroup conflict.

One line of research involves individual and personality-based explanations and differences in attitudes towards other groups, such as The Authoritarian Personality proposed by Adorno and colleagues (1950); with later, related constructs including Right Wing Authoritarianism (Altemeyer, 1981) and Social Dominance Orientation (Sidanius & Pratto, 1999). These approaches examine intergroup attitudes in terms of individual traits and implicit ideologies, but do not examine the role of social context and interactions in the development of intergroup attitudes (see Chapter 10).

Another line of work draws on intergroup theories such as social categorisation (of the ingroup relative to other groups) and intergroup dynamics in order to explain group-based attitudes (Tajfel & Turner, 1979). Sherif and colleagues (Sherif & Sherif, 1953) demonstrated that competition between groups for resources can intensify intergroup bias. Specifically, competition between groups led to intergroup conflict, while the introduction of superordinate goals led to conflict resolution. Based on this work, realistic conflict theory emerged, in which intergroup conflict is said to arise due to the perception of resource scarcity (Levine & Campbell, 1972; see Chapter 10). Competitive interactions by groups to obtain their goals lead to preferring the ingroup and perceiving it as better than other groups, and threat perception induces ingroup solidarity and hostility towards the outgroup.

Although intergroup conflicts seem to be a relatively frequent and natural phenomenon, some conflicts persist over long periods of time and seem resistant to conflict resolution attempts (Coleman, 2011). These conflicts are known as intractable conflicts (Bar-Tal, 2007; Coleman, 2011; Kriesberg, 1993), and are of particular interest to academic researchers because of their unique characteristics and disastrous outcomes. In today's world, it has been estimated that about 5% of conflicts in the world become intractable (Coleman, 2011). The conflicts between Israel and Palestine, and in Kashmir, Sri Lanka, Chechnya, Northern Ireland, and Cyprus, constitute prototypical examples of intractable conflicts.

While these conflicts deal with very tangible and real issues (such as territory, security, and natural resources) that must be addressed in the resolution process, it has been established that these conflicts are accompanied by unique socio-psychological dynamics that influence their nature and longevity (Bar-Tal, 2007). In other words, intractable conflicts are not merely extreme forms of intergroup conflict; they are situations so extreme that although the people involved understand that peace is in their best interest, they seem unwilling or unable to take the necessary steps towards conflict resolution.

This phenomenon has been ascribed to a number of unique features that characterise intractable conflicts (Bar-Tal, 2007; Kriesberg, 1993). First, intractable conflicts are *protracted* and last at least one generation, creating a situation in which large parts of society have been born into a state of conflict, and are not acquainted with peaceful life conditions (Kriesberg, 1993). In addition to affecting the collective memory of the conflict, being unfamiliar with peace may make it hard for people in conflict to desire, and therefore act to promote, conflict resolution. For example, research conducted with colleagues showed that in Israel and Cyprus, younger generations are actually less hopeful for peace, and subsequently less inclined to be conciliatory, than the older generations (Hasler et al., 2023).

Second, intractable conflicts are *predominant* since they cause widespread destruction and devastation. Although many intergroup conflicts may involve various forms of violent actions between the groups, intractable conflicts involve an ongoing cycle of wide-scale and extreme violence (such as war, occupation, terrorism, and limited military engagement), which escalates and de-escalates over time (Kriesberg, 1993). People who live in these societies are all touched by the conflict, directly and indirectly. Most people will have friends or family members, colleagues or acquaintances, who died in or are deeply traumatised by the conflict. This leads to another unique characteristic of intractable conflicts: their scope and sheer intensity leads to *extensive investment* made by the parties involved. There are two types of investment made in the conflict (Kriesberg, 1993). First, physical investment (e.g., financial and military) results from the need to maintain a huge armed force at all times to address the ongoing threat. In contrast, psychological investment (e.g., collective/group-based psychological phenomena, beliefs, and attitudes) enables the group to withstand the difficult conflict situation (Bar-Tal, 2007).

Two further features include the conflict's *centrality* and *totality*. While all intergroup conflicts exist in people's awareness and may be present in the collective narrative, intractable conflicts are highly predominant and play a central role in individuals' lives and decisions, as well as those of society as a whole. The conflict-related events happen on a regular basis and in high levels of intensity (Bar-Tal, 2007). The conflict becomes so prevalent that it penetrates almost all spheres in societal, cultural, educational, and political life and institutions. In essence, it is impossible for those involved in the conflict to ignore the situation or stay neutral, since the conflict is forced upon them throughout their lives and in multiple domains (Bar-Tal, 2007). Thus, in addition to vast material investment, negative attitudes and emotions are experienced by individuals as well as by the group as a collective.

In addition to the above characteristics, intractable conflicts are unique in the perceptions and beliefs held by the people involved in them. Bar-Tal and Halperin (2011) discuss the way in which the context of ongoing conflict and the need to cope with the conflict over time leads to the emergence of conflict-supporting beliefs, which are held and shared by society members. These influence individual and group-based emotions, attitudes, and behaviours. Importantly, these attitudes and emotions are integrated and institutionalised into the group in a socialisation process. Over time, the ethos of conflict (Bar-Tal, 2007; Bar-Tal et al., 2009), a cluster of shared societal beliefs that lend meaning to societal life and provide a dominant orientation as a result of the society's continuing experiences, develops. These beliefs serve as a psychosocial infrastructure for the group (Bar-Tal, 2007). While the ethos of conflict protects the group's positive self-perception and enables its members to withstand the conflict, the same ethos also perpetuates the conflict and prevents the steps that need to be taken for conflict resolution (Bar-Tal, 2007).

Although all intergroup conflicts involve a competitive approach over material and symbolic issues, the parties involved in intractable conflicts adopt a zero-sum perception of the conflict. The fact that the conflict is highly multifaceted and complex, together with the continuous threats to security, lead to a perception of the issues in question not only as important, but as existential to the group's very survival. Under these circumstances, any concession is seen as an essential loss and is highly threatening, as any gain to the outgroup is perceived as a loss to the ingroup (Kriesberg, 1993). Such perceptions lead to an unwillingness to compromise with the other side under any condition, further feeding into the intractability of the conflict. And because both groups understand that winning is not a possibility, but equally will not compromise, intractable conflicts involve a perception that the *conflict is irresolvable*. Since both sides cannot win and are locked in a stalemate, both sides expect the conflict to continue forever, and adjust accordingly both materially and psychologically (Bar-Tal, 2007; Kriesberg, 1993). This specific perception is the main underlying appraisal of hopelessness, and explains why hope is so crucial in conflict (Cohen-Chen et al., 2014a, 2015).

4.5.2 The Role of Emotions in Promoting and Preventing Intergroup Conflict

Conflicts are inherently pervaded by emotions. This is because they involve issues that are important to people, and constitute situations that challenge human relations and conditions to the extreme. Many affective scientists categorise positive versus negative emotions based on how they feel to the individual (Barrett, 2006). Others, mainly those concerned with the behaviours elicited by emotions and how they affect social and group phenomena, take a constructivist view of emotions, focusing on the outcomes of each emotion. Here, emotions are categorised as positive or negative based on the extent to which they are functional to positive social relations or contexts. This distinction is not very pronounced in many day-to-day contexts. Positively valenced emotions are linked to prosocial behaviours, helping, and cognitive ability (Fredrickson, 2013). On the other hand, negatively valenced emotions have been found to induce intergroup prejudice (DeSteno et al., 2004) and aggression (Smith & Mackie, 2016) (for more, see Chapters 9 and 10).

Extending the work on incidental emotions that we discussed in the previous section, recent work has evidenced a nuanced picture in the relationship between emotions and prejudice. DeSteno et al. (2004) examined how incidental anger (but not sadness or neutrality, as they are not competitive or conflict-relevant emotions) induced automatic prejudice towards a randomly created outgroup (rather than a social outgroup that may spark existing prejudice). In another line of work, Dasgupta and colleagues (2009) induced different emotions (anger and disgust) and then measured bias towards different outgroups. They found that the incidental emotions increased prejudice only when the emotion was relevant and applicable to prior expectations of the group. However, if the emotion-specific threat was not applicable to the target group, evaluations remained unchanged by prejudice.

However, note that in all the cases discussed, there is still an alignment between the way the emotions feel (valence) and their social function.

EXERCISE 4.2

Categorisation of Emotions

Categorising emotions as positive or negative has important implications for emotion researchers, because it drives our focus on certain emotions rather than others. Categorise the following emotions into positive and negative clusters: fear, regret, pride, guilt, anger, sadness, empathy, hope, happiness, contentment, anxiety, disgust, contempt, envy, love.

Now reflect on your choices. How did you determine which emotions are 'positive' and which are 'negative'? Was this based on how they feel to you in terms of pleasantness? Or did you choose to categorise them based on the actions or behaviours they elicit? Would the emotions move around (from positive to negative) based on different contextual elements? Can you think of an example of this?

Things become more complex in contexts involving discrepancies between goals, interests, or values. This incongruence is particularly salient when examining emotions in social and intergroup conflicts. In such contexts, emotions that lead people to attitudes or behaviours that promote conflict resolution often do not involve positive or pleasant affect. On the other hand, emotions that lead people to aggressive attitudes or behaviours often feel good because they lead to a sense of power, self-justification, or belonging to a group. Work in the field of emotions in conflict and its resolution seeks to understand the emotions relevant to such contexts. Since conflict involves many extreme forms of aggression, a basic question is therefore what emotions promote aggression and what emotions promote conciliation and harmony?

A new framework for categorising emotions in conflict maps emotions along two separate dimensions, which have, in the past, been separately highlighted: valence (the extent to which emotions are experienced as pleasant or unpleasant) and function (the extent to which emotions lead to outcomes supporting or hindering conflict resolution) (Cohen-Chen et al., 2020; see Figure 4.1). In other words, while some scholars think of positive emotions as emotions that 'feel good' and negative emotions as those that 'feel bad', other schools of thought believe positive emotions lead to 'doing good' while negative emotions lead to 'doing bad'. This framework suggests that it is important to consider both dimensions simultaneously, because of the role emotions play in guiding and motivating actual behaviour. Importantly, various factors can lead to emotions 'moving' on both the valence and function dimensions, making emotions that are unpleasant feel good (if they provide a sense of belonging to the group), or changing their outcome to be beneficial to the group (Cohen-Chen et al., 2020).

Figure 4.1   Valence/Function Framework for categorising emotions in conflict

Source: Cohen-Chen et al. (2020)

Because the experience of conflict is negative to those involved in it, many negative emotions occur within this context. Three examples of emotions that promote aggressive attitudes and behaviour are anger, hatred, and pride. *Anger* is an emotion elicited by an appraisal of a situation, person, or group as behaving unfairly towards the experiencer. This perception of an injustice induces behaviours associated with action and risk-taking, increasing a sense of power and a willingness to change the situation and right the wrongs inflicted on the individual or the group. It can often result in aggressive attitudes or actions towards the perpetrator (Mackie et al., 2000), but it can, under certain conditions, promote conciliation. For example, one study induced anger towards the outgroup (vs control), and then asked people about their support for concession-making to resolve the conflict. Results showed that people who were angry took more positive risks in the form of making concessions for peace (Reifen Tagar et al., 2011). *Hatred*, an extremely negatively valenced emotion, is rooted in the perception of the outgroup as inherently evil and unchanging. Hatred triggers aspirations of annihilation of the outgroup as a whole (Halperin, 2008). Referring back to previously discussed work, hatred has been linked to dehumanisation and dehumanising beliefs in situations like the Armenian genocide in Turkey, the Holocaust, and the genocide of Tutsis in Rwanda (Staub, 2005).

Unlike anger, which is focused on the action, hatred is targeted at the very nature of a person or group. Although these two emotions often go hand in hand, this key difference between them has important implications and results in very different outcomes. For instance, anger in the absence of hatred was found to induce concessions in conflict (Halperin et al., 2011a), and while anger motivated a willingness to engage in normative, non-violent action, such as participating in demonstrations or signing a petition, hatred induced intentions for violent action, such as blocking roads, clashing with police, or throwing rocks (Shuman et al., 2016).

In line with the do good/feel good framework, not only negatively valenced (unpleasant) emotions can promote aggression. Although *pride* is experienced as an elevating, enjoyable emotion, stemming from the perceived positive achievements or nature of the ingroup, it is associated with increased aggression, prejudice against outgroup members, and hostility towards outgroup members via increased nationalism (de Figueiredo & Elkins, 2003).

Moving on to the Do Good dimension in Figure 4.1, a number of emotions have been found to prompt conciliatory attitudes, promoting efforts for conflict resolution. Examples include hope, guilt, and sadness. *Hope* is a positively valenced emotion elicited in light of imagining a positive and desired goal in the future (Cohen-Chen et al., 2017a; Leshem & Halperin, 2020). Hope is associated with many peace-supporting attitudes. For example, one study presented participants with a 'news website' in which they could choose to open different short articles related to the Israeli–Palestinian conflict and the peace process. Results showed that those who had long-term sentiments of hope for peace were more inclined to choose articles supporting conflict resolution, compared to those who were more fearful, who chose information on reconciliation (Cohen-Chen et al., 2014b). Another study found that the more hope for peace participants experienced, the more they supported providing humanitarian aid to the outgroup (Halperin & Gross, 2011). Experimental work has also examined the causal role of hope in conflict by inducing the experience of hope and then measuring conciliatory attitudes, such as a willingness to make concrete concessions that would lead to resolving the conflict (Cohen-Chen et al., 2019), and openness to engaging with the outgroup and learning their narrative of the conflict (Saguy & Halperin, 2014).

Guilt is experienced as negative and stems from an appraisal of the ingroup as responsible for unjust and negative acts towards the outgroup (Branscombe et al., 2004). Despite the negative experience associated with the emotion, guilt is associated with support for reparations or apologies for past wrong-doing. For example, guilt predicted non-Indigenous Australians' support of a formal apology to Indigenous Australians for past wrongdoings (McGarty et al., 2005). Another study showed that white Americans' guilt regarding the treatment of African Americans predicted support for affirmative action (Iyer et al., 2003).

Another emotion that may feel unpleasant but has been found to promote positive intergroup attitudes is *sadness*, which is associated with an appraisal of significant loss, a recurrent experience for those involved in conflict. Sadness has been found to reduce political polarisation and promote peace-supporting attitudes (Gur et al., 2021). For example, reflecting on a personal sad event reduced the effect of participants' political ideology on conflict-related attitudes (support for conciliatory or aggressive policies).

4.5.3 Emotion Regulation

Thus far we have learned that emotions are an important part of the human social experience, because they shape how we perceive and respond to events on every level. This raises an important question, and that is whether (and how) we can change emotions and subsequent attitudes and behaviours. This question has been extensively addressed in the field of **emotion regulation** (Gross, 1998; Gross & Thompson, 2007).

> **Key concept – Emotion regulation:** The processes that influence which emotions people have, when they have them, and how they experience and express these emotions. It includes efforts to change the intensity, valence, or type of experienced emotion, and may be targeted towards positive as well as negative emotions, assuming the form of upwards (increasing levels of arousal; degree of physiological activation) or downwards (decreasing levels of arousal) regulation.

The first, classic model of emotion regulation was created by James Gross (1998). Previous literature had examined emotions and attempted to understand their role in various contexts, using them as predictors of attitudes or behaviours. The question of how people (should and do) manage and (should and do) control their emotions, however, was relatively understudied. Gross used appraisal theories of emotion and offered five main self-driven and intentional strategies of emotion regulation that follow the process and sequence of the way emotions evolve: situation selection, situation modification, attention deployment, cognitive change, and response modulation. Each of these strategies maps on to the process and sequence of the way emotions evolve (see Figure 4.2).

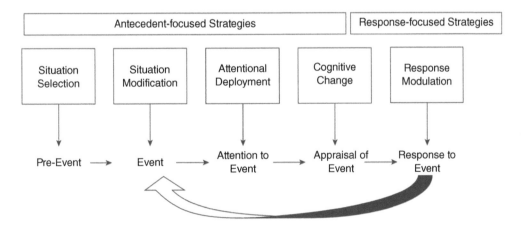

Figure 4.2 Strategies of emotion regulation mapped onto appraisal theory of emotion

Source: Adapted based on Gross & Thompson (2007)

The first two strategies occur around the emotion-eliciting event itself, which a person may choose to either avoid or engage in (situation selection). For example, a person can choose not to meet another person who may elicit anger, or they may choose not to read the news if they are bound to find it upsetting. The next strategy is to change the situation itself using various behaviours (situation modification). This may be walking home with a friend late at night in order to reduce fear. The third strategy focuses on the level of attention a person gives the event in question (attentional deployment), whether distracting themselves (taking a break and distracting oneself while dealing with something distressing) or concentrating fully. The fourth strategy occurs after the event has taken place, and focuses on changing the way the event is interpreted (cognitive change). The most widely established way to do this is cognitive reappraisal, in which the individual deliberately changes the way they think about the event in order to change their appraisal of the situation. It may include coming up with another interpretation for what happened, or a conscious decision to think about the event from an external and uninvolved perspective. If we get cut up while driving, for example, we may get angry at the inconsiderate and thoughtless driver. But we may choose to think that there may be an emergency that led them to drive that way, and when we think about what emergency this may be, our feeling of anger may change (perhaps to empathy or compassion) as our appraisal changes. This strategy has been widely researched in a plethora of contexts, including at both the individual and group levels (Goldenberg et al., 2017).

The first four strategies are *antecedent-focused strategies* because they focus on changing the emotion before it occurs. The fifth and last strategy is a *response-focused strategy* (response modulation) because it occurs when the emotion has already been elicited and the person is changing their response to the emotion. The most widely researched strategy is emotion suppression. Here, rather than expressing the emotion outwardly, the person chooses to suppress any external manifestations of the emotion. For example, participants are asked to look at pictures that elicit a wide range of emotions, such as fear, disgust, anger, and joy. They are then required to intentionally suppress any facial or physical expressions of these emotions, which has been found to change the emotional experience itself (Richards & Gross, 2000). However, this strategy has been found to be very cognitively and physically demanding. In one such experiment (Richards & Gross, 2000), participants were asked to engage with content (film, slide show) while either reappraising the content with an external, neutral perspective (reappraisal) or while suppressing the external expression of any emotion. Results showed that suppression (but not reappraisal) led to reduced memory.

There is a huge amount of research pointing to the effectiveness of emotion regulation in deliberately changing or transforming emotional responses, and the subsequent behavioural outcomes. Understanding the emotion-elicitation process has enabled scholars to develop numerous and diverse ways in which people can (with practice and intentional thought processes) change their own emotions. It is particularly true for cognitive reappraisal (compared to emotional suppression), which has been found to decrease negative emotional experiences and increase positive emotional experiences. Gross (1998) showed participants a disgusting film. Participants in the reappraisal condition were told to think about the film in such a way that they would feel nothing, while those in the suppression condition were told to behave such that someone watching them would not know they were feeling anything. In the control condition, they were not given any instructions. Results showed that both reappraisal and suppression reduced emotion-expressive behaviour, but that reappraisal actually decreased disgust, whereas suppression increased physiological activation, which can be detrimental to one's health.

KEY THINKER

James J. Gross

James Gross is a researcher who developed and led the field of emotion regulation. Gross completed his PhD in the University of California, Berkeley in 1993, and then started working at Stanford University, where he is currently the Ernest R. Hilgard Professor of Psychology. Gross has over 600 publications, and has been cited over 200,000 times. He is the founding co-president of the Society for Affective Science, and the Director of the Psychophysiology Lab at Stanford University. Gross has received a number of teaching and mentoring awards, in addition to awards commending his contributions to science and research.

EXERCISE 4.3

Emotion Regulation

Think about an event that made (or may make) you very angry. It can be watching the news, going to a family dinner with someone who upset(s) you, or being cut-up by a driver on the road. Try to imagine the event. When did it start? What exactly made you angry? How did you know you were angry? Now, try to apply each one of the five strategies of emotion regulation to this situation. How can you apply *situation selection*? *Situation modification*? *Attentional deployment*? *Cognitive change*? *Response modulation*? For each one, explain what you would do and how this would transform the emotional process. Which one do you think would work best for you and why?

4.6 PART 3: APPLICATIONS

In this section we will look at how all of the theories, frameworks, and concepts discussed in this chapter are applied to the development of interventions and messages used in the real world.

4.6.1 Methodological Issues

First, it is important to attend to some methodological issues and practices that come with shifting from a descriptive approach (understanding emotions) to an interventionist approach (aiming to change emotions and therefore attitudes; see Cohen-Chen & Halperin,

2023). First, although correlational and conceptual research is still used, intervention development mostly adopts experimental designs to establish causality. In other words, to be able to make a statement that an intervention can change an emotion, and in turn shift attitudes or behaviour, we must show directionality. Only then will we be able to justify its application in the real world.

This is often the difficult part in this field of research, because it necessitates thinking about how to create this change (and only this change!) while controlling for other elements, and then making sure that we influenced what we said we would, and nothing else. It is also the most interesting part of this field, because we develop unique manipulations in interesting and relevant contexts, and use creativity to establish our hypotheses.

Because we aim to combine scientific rigour (rather than just our interpretations) with real-world applications, and these applications are (hopefully) used to develop interventions, it is critical that we are able to replicate our findings. This means that, ideally, anyone can use the methods we used, under similar circumstances, and find the same results (or a good explanation for why they did not find them again). This is why more and more people in the field of social psychology, but particularly in fields such as emotional interventions, are engaging in Open Science Practices (Klein et al., 2018; Open Science Collaboration, 2015; for more on this see Chapter 1). Among the things that we do is document precisely where we collected our data (In the lab? On the train? At a protest?) and when (During a time of escalation or unrest? Before an election?). We describe who the participants are by collecting (only) relevant data about them, share the materials we used online (so others can critique them and use them to replicate our results), and use appropriate sample sizes (so we can ascertain they are not a fluke). Lastly, we report everything we administered and measured, and pre-register what we think we are going to find in advance. All of these steps are especially important in our field because we want to be sure we are conducting ethical, accurate, and applicable research.

4.6.2 Direct Interventions for Regulating Emotions in Conflicts

Specifically in intergroup contexts, emotion regulation interventions have been found to affect political attitudes. For instance, participants were asked to use cognitive reappraisal or emotional suppression while reading disturbing news articles about the outgroup, both of which reduced prejudice (compared to a control condition) (Westerlund et al., 2020). Israeli participants underwent cognitive reappraisal training, in which they were first instructed and then practised regulating their emotions in general. This training was found to reduce negative emotions towards Palestinians and increase support for conciliatory policies a week after the short session and then at five months later (Halperin et al., 2013). In another line of research, an online session in which Israeli participants received text-based instructions for cognitive reappraisal (vs control) reduced political intolerance towards minorities (Halperin et al., 2014b).

KEY THINKER

Maya Tamir

Maya Tamir is a professor of psychology at the Hebrew University of Jerusalem. Tamir has led the field of emotional preferences and motivated emotion regulation. Tamir completed her PhD in social psychology at the University of Illinois at Urbana-Champaign and held a post-doctoral fellowship at Stanford University. Tamir heads the Emotion and Self-Regulation Lab, has hundreds of publications, and has won numerous prestigious awards and grants. Her research has also featured in popular outlets such as *The New York Times*, *Psychology Today*, and *The Wall Street Journal*.

The power and importance of emotion regulation as a means to change attitudes and behaviours in intergroup relations raised an interesting and relevant question, addressed by Maya Tamir. While acknowledging that emotion regulation is an important tool for cognitive and emotional change, Tamir queried whether people necessarily (and always) *want* to regulate their emotions. An assumption that has persisted for a long time across the literature is that people always want to feel good. In other words, it was assumed that people have an innate preference for emotions that are pleasant rather than unpleasant. This makes intuitive sense, because in general we would always rather be happy than sad, and would prefer to feel proud than ashamed. But Tamir (Tamir & Ford, 2009) proposed the instrumental approach to emotion regulation, according to which people have different reasons for wanting to experience (or not experience) emotions, and these reasons guide their decisions in regulating their emotions. Tamir set out to examine these questions and found some fascinating results. The examination of these questions is encapsulated in research focused on **emotional preferences**.

> **Key concept – Emotional preferences:** These are the emotions and emotional states that people want to experience. General emotional preferences focus on which emotions people want to experience regardless of context, and are somewhat stable over time. Contextual or instrumental emotional preferences focus on what people are motivated to experience in particular contexts, and are based on the usefulness of emotions.

GUEST PERSONAL JOURNEY

Maya Tamir

I am not one of those people who always knew what they wanted to be when they grew up. Unlike my brothers, who knew they wanted to become doctors (like our father) since they could walk, I had no clue where I was headed. I just enjoyed

(Continued)

learning, and experiencing, and tasting new things. My mother, who taught literature and creative writing, introduced me to novels, poetry, paintings, sculptures, music, movies – and I was in awe. In awe of the emotions they elicited. From an early age, I was struck by how emotions bring colour to our lives. I was struck by how powerful emotions were, convincing people they can fly or drown. I wondered how these magnificent things work, how much power they have over us, and how much power do we have over them. These questions accompanied me always, but I never imagined I would address them as a profession. Instead, I gravitated toward wonderful people. Although I didn't originally intend to study psychology as an undergrad (I was a cinema studies major), I switched to psychology to study with my husband-to-be. Although I didn't originally intend to study psychology as a doctoral student (I was considering becoming an architect), I decided to study psychology after one conversation with my mentor-to-be. I found myself studying emotions – those magnificent things that imbue life with colour and flavour. Almost by accident, I learned that I could use scientific methods to address the very questions that had haunted me ever since I was a child. As a doctoral student, I studied how emotions influence how we think and behave (the power they have over us), and as a post-doctoral fellow, I started studying how and when we can influence our emotions (the power we have over them). Considering emotions with the same sense of awe and respect I had for them as a child, I wondered not only how we can influence emotions, but why we might want to influence them, and when it is advisable to do so. For several decades, I have had the luxury of studying motivation and emotion regulation. Throughout my career, I have continued to gravitate toward wonderful people – mentors, collaborators, students, and colleagues, who have made this journey particularly rewarding.

First, when considering which emotion they are motivated to experience, people think about the utility and function of emotions and not only the experience of the emotion as pleasant or unpleasant. Second, context is important when considering the utility or function of an emotion. For example, some people believe that feeling anxious about an exam makes them perform better (even if it may not feel very good at the time), which may make people prefer to feel anxious rather than enthusiastic. But this preference is specific to the context of an exam, and someone might not want, for example, to feel anxious before meeting up with good friends. Third, these perceptions of emotions and their utility in specific contexts can motivate people to regulate their emotions accordingly, in order to achieve the desired outcome. Those who believe that being anxious before an exam tend to increase their own anxiety in line with their beliefs and in order to achieve the goal of succeeding. Tamir and Ford (2009) found that although, in the short term, individuals are motivated to experience pleasant emotions and avoid unpleasant emotions, this changes if they think that the function of the emotion contributes or helps them in some way in the long term. For example, anger is considered a negative emotion because it involves negative valence. But what if you were in a situation in which you knew that getting angry would make you more assertive and that this would help you to fight against injustice, for example? In that case, you may be motivated to experience anger in order to achieve an important goal. Tamir and colleagues found that people who knew they were about to enter a confrontation (in the form of a video game) chose to listen to anger-provoking music in an earlier (seemingly unrelated) task (Tamir et al., 2008).

This is particularly true in intergroup conflict situations (see Chapter 10), in which additional layers of complexity, such as identity and intergroup perceptions, play important roles in emotional preferences. For example, a number of studies found that people in conflict were motivated to experience sadness as a way to enhance their feeling of togetherness with the ingroup (Porat et al., 2016a, 2016b). Sadness, although an unpleasant emotion, helped participants to feel connected to other people in their group, and this expectation led them to want to experience the loss and grief associated with memorial day. Relatedly, the motivation to experience emotions that may benefit the outgroup (such as empathy, which increases motivation to help) or may improve perceptions of the enemy is hard to induce (Tamir, 2016). People do not want to feel sorry for their perceived enemies, or see their group as needing to feel guilt for terrible acts.

Based on this line of thought, a number of scholars attempted to change people's motivation to experience certain emotions, rather than the emotion regulation *skills* required in order to do that. In other words, instead of teaching them how to regulate their emotions, researchers provided reasons for why an emotion should be experienced and regulated, either because it feels good (hedonic considerations), or because it serves some instrumental purpose by benefitting the person (it may make you smarter or kinder). Porat and colleagues provided participants with seemingly reliable information about anger in conflict (Porat et al., 2016b). In one condition (anger–harmful), participants were told that scientific findings showed that anger towards the outgroup is harmful because it clouds judgement and leads to impulsive behaviour. In the other condition (anger–useful), participants learned that anger towards the outgroup can be useful because it increases decisiveness. Results showed that participants in the anger–harmful (vs anger–useful) condition were less motivated to experience anger, which indeed led them to feel lower levels of anger towards Palestinians, and subsequently offer less support for political intolerance.

4.6.3 Indirect Interventions for Regulating Emotions in Conflicts

Another type of strategy addresses the issue of a lack of motivation to regulate emotions by creating indirect interventions for changing emotions. This approach is known as **indirect emotion regulation** (for a review, see Halperin et al., 2014a). Halperin suggested that although direct strategies for emotion regulation were effective when people want to change their attitudes and behaviours, the approach is

> **Key concept – Indirect emotion regulation:** A process of emotion regulation used to overcome the limitations of direct emotion regulation (such as the negative inverse reaction people involved in conflicts may have to direct attempts at changing their attitudes via emotional transformation). In this process, cognitive appraisals are altered indirectly, leading to attitude change by transforming discrete emotions.

not as relevant in extreme conflicts. This is because people (particularly those who hold very strong ideologies or beliefs) are not motivated to change their attitudes in conflicts.

KEY THINKER

Eran Halperin

Eran Halperin is a researcher who has pioneered the field of emotions and emotion regulation in political conflicts. Halperin wrote his PhD dissertation on the role of hatred in conflict, and after completing a post-doctoral period at Stanford University, he returned to Israel and founded a lab examining psychological barriers in conflict and conflict resolution, focusing particularly on emotions. I joined this lab, as one of the first three Master's students, and I continued to work there until I completed my PhD. Halperin has published in some of the best scientific journals in the world, including *Science, Nature*, and *Proceedings of the National Academy of Sciences of the United States of America* (*PNAS*), and is the originator and founder of *aChord Center*, a non-profit organisation that develops innovative, practical tools and interventions to improve intergroup relations using cutting-edge psychological research.

GUEST PERSONAL JOURNEY

Eran Halperin

I was born and raised in the context of the Israeli–Palestinian conflict – a long-term violent conflict. I grew up in a very liberal family, but also a family with a strong Zionist ethos, which clearly supported the army's actions. Part of that ethos also led me to join a special unit of the Israeli Defence Force, and at the age of 22 I was seriously injured in a militant encounter with Hezbollah fighters in the south of Lebanon. A long process of rehabilitation led me to think of my (then) current situation, the future of the country and conflict, and also about the things I want to do in life and achieve for my people. I realised that there must be something that we are missing in our attempt to stop the violence and that we should probably explore alternative ways to influence people's minds and hearts and to mobilise them to call for peace. I then decided to study political science and conflict resolution, but also psychology, which I saw as a potential gateway to people's hearts and minds. I started to form my perception of psychology as a way of changing the reality that had caused me to be so badly injured, and while studying psychology I realised the importance of emotions. I began to believe that emotions are probably the most important motivator of human behaviour, but also that they can be changed quite easily in various contexts, making them a prime intervention to achieve peace. This made me recognise that emotional change can be the vehicle to conflict transformation, which quite naturally led me to study and integrate emotion regulation work with conflict studies. Since then, I have focused my research on emotions and emotion regulation as a strategy, a tool for real-world change.

The process of indirect emotion regulation begins with uncovering the association between a conflict-related action tendency and the preceding discrete emotion. For example, researchers may be interested in how to reduce advocating for extreme violence against an outgroup. The literature on emotions suggests that such attitudes derive from the emotion of *hatred*, which is therefore the emotion one would seek to regulate. Next, core appraisal themes underlying the emotions (Scherer, 1984) are identified. Hatred is based on the appraisal of the outgroup as inherently and unchangeably evil (Halperin, 2008). Lastly, various interventions are employed to change those appraisals without necessarily mentioning the outgroup or the context of the conflict. In the case of hatred, interventionist research which sought to regulate hatred indirectly imparted the belief that groups in general are malleable (Dweck et al., 1995), without referring to the outgroup in question.

KEY STUDY 4.3

Implicit Theories as an Indirect Intervention for Conflict Resolution

In a ground-breaking set of studies, Halperin and colleagues let participants read a text (which was presented as scientific results in a study on human nature) about the changing (vs stable) nature of groups in general (Halperin et al., 2011b). Then, in a seemingly unrelated study, participants were asked to answer questions regarding hatred appraisals of the outgroup (such as 'the outgroup is inherently evil'), and lastly indicate their support for the conciliatory attitudes needed to achieve conflict resolution. This relatively simple, applicable, and indirect intervention, which did not refer to the conflict or the outgroup, successfully reduced intergroup hatred appraisals and increased support for concessions among Jewish-Israelis, Palestinians, and Palestinian citizens of Israel.

A similar intervention was developed to address intergroup *anxiety* (Halperin et al., 2012) in the conflict between Greek and Turkish Cypriots in Cyprus. The researchers aimed to increase willingness to make contact with outgroup members, which is negatively predicted by intergroup anxiety (Pettigrew & Tropp, 2008). Intergroup anxiety stems from an appraisal of the outgroup as unfamiliar and even demonised, which increases fears and worries from negative encounters with outgroup members. Participants read a text that portrayed aggressive groups as having a malleable nature (vs a fixed nature). Instilling the belief that groups are malleable and can change diminished the experience of intergroup anxiety and subsequently increased willingness to come into contact with the outgroup.

A related design addressed support for conciliatory policies, which is associated with the emotion of *hope*. Hopelessness is rooted in the appraisal of the conflict as irresolvable (Jarymowicz & Bar-Tal, 2006). Therefore, instilling the belief that various constructs related to the conflict (indirectly) are malleable and can change will subsequently open up the future possibility of peace, eliciting hope. Based on this rationale, a number of interventions instilled perceptions of general malleability. One line of my own research used seemingly reliable information in the form of a false news article, in which participants read about new research concluding that conflicts in general are malleable (vs stable) (Cohen-Chen et al., 2014a). Results showed that the malleable condition increased hope for peace in the Israeli–Palestinian conflict, and led to support for concession-making.

KEY STUDY 4.4

Perceptions of a Changing World Indirectly Change Hope

In a series of studies conducted in 2015, my colleagues and I administered malleability beliefs about the world in general (Cohen-Chen et al., 2015). In this study, we ran the experimental studies on the train in Israel. This was a unique and creative place to conduct research, as it offered a number of important advantages. First, the train in Israel offers the advantage of diversity. People on the train are diverse in terms of age, gender, religiosity, SES levels, and (most importantly) political orientation. Second (are you sitting down?), the study was conducted before smartphones were very popular, and this meant that people on the train were quite bored. They were mostly happy to fill in a short 10-minute questionnaire in return for a chocolate. Lastly, and perhaps most importantly in a field that is always grappling with ecological validity, this was a way of running an experiment in the field. This is important, because one of the things that myself and others aim to do is transform real-world attitudes using simple, indirect, and applicable interventions. Showing a significant shift in emotions and attitudes in an intractable conflict deriving from a short and general task on the train was both novel and relevant.

We wanted to test whether a general perception of the world as changing, fluctuating, and dynamic would enable people to experience hope in a specific conflict. We used the same intervention used previously, providing external information to participants, and indeed found that this increased hope and conciliatory attitudes. However, we then tested whether building on people's personal experiences and perceptions would work. Participants were asked to draw their first association when reading a malleable (vs stable) sentence about the world ('Our world is stable and unchanging'; 'Situations do not change over time'/'Our world is dynamic and changing'; 'Situations change over time'). Participants in the changing world condition drew things like changing seasons or people growing (see Figure 4.3 for an example), while those in the unchanging world condition drew things like repeated patterns or stable timelines.

Once again, the malleability condition, even though it did not mention or allude to the specific conflict (or any conflict for that matter), increased hope for peace in the Israeli–Palestinian conflict, and this led to more concession-making. Importantly, people who held different political ideologies were affected in the same way by the intervention.

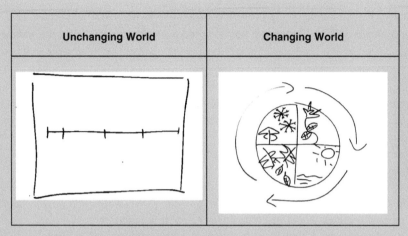

Figure 4.3 Example of (reproduced) drawings made by participants in the dynamic/static conditions

Source: Cohen-Chen et al. (2015, Study 4)

Relatedly, a set of workshops (presented as leadership-enhancing) taught participants that groups in general are malleable and can change. Results showed that this increased hope and concession-making even six months after the workshops (Goldenberg et al., 2018) compared to both a control condition and another well-established intervention for conflict resolution.

The last example involves the emotion of *guilt* (Branscombe et al., 2004), which induces support for reparations or apologies (Iyer et al., 2003; McGarty et al., 2005). Guilt is elicited by an appraisal of an unjust or immoral act perpetrated by an individual's ingroup towards an outgroup. However, the acceptance of ingroup responsibility is in stark contrast to the need group members have to preserve their group's positive image (Tajfel & Turner, 1979). A group of researchers (Čehajić et al., 2011) addressed this need by administering a self-affirmation intervention in which participants were asked to describe a personal success, how it made them feel, and what it reflected about them (for more about self and identity, see Chapter 2). The positive affirmation enabled group members to tolerate a threat to their group identity, take responsibility for ingroup wrongdoings, and offer reparations to the outgroup.

EXERCISE 4.4

Design a Study

Now it's your turn to be a behavioural scientist! You are going to design an intervention to regulate emotions in order to change a certain behaviour of your choosing. First, think about a context. Is it work? What type of organisation? What industry? Is it a

(Continued)

negotiation? What about? Is it a political context such as an NGO? Or perhaps a conflict? Maybe you want to stay at home, or focus on your university? Is it a behaviour you have noticed in a team assignment? Or something about your lecturers that you want to address?

Next, think about what emotions are prevalent in this context, and how they fit into the interpersonal or intergroup dynamics. Choose a particular behaviour you want to change, and link it to an emotion. Remember how emotions are defined, since this is key to regulating the emotion in question.

Now comes the fun part! Think creatively about how this emotion might be regulated. Will you choose direct or indirect strategies? What are the implications of each in this particular context? And what do you expect (hypothesise) will happen if you manage to change people's emotion in this case? What outcome do you think it will induce? And how would you measure it? Feel free to ignore cost or other administrative issues, and think as big and as outside the box as you wish!

4.6.4 Emotion-based Interventions

The last application focuses on interventions that may or may not affect the actual experience of emotions, but use emotional theories and emotional elements to change social attitudes. One such intervention uses emotional similarity to reduce dehumanisation (McDonald et al., 2017). Previously, we discussed research indicating that primary emotions (which are not uniquely human) are ascribed to outgroups, while secondary emotions (which are uniquely human) are ascribed to ingroup members. This work also suggests that this psychological mechanism enables unacceptable actions towards outgroups, because their humanity is reduced. McDonald et al. (2017) hypothesised that *sharing* an emotional reaction to the same event (regardless of whether it is a primary or secondary emotion) would increase humanisation of the outgroup and reconciliation attitudes. Israeli participants were asked to indicate their emotional reaction to an anger-inducing text. They were then told that Palestinian participants had the same reaction (vs not having the same reaction). Results showed that in the emotional similarity condition, participants humanised the outgroup more, and subsequently held more tolerant attitudes towards the outgroup.

Another line of research uses emotional expressions to address interpersonal and intergroup conflict. In the first part, we discussed the role of emotional expressions (particularly when information is scarce) in conveying social information. A growing line of work examines emotional expressions in the realm of intergroup contexts. Kamans and colleagues (2014) demonstrated that power-congruent emotional expressions served to legitimise the use of violence in intractable conflict. Violence was legitimised for the strong group when it expressed anger and for the weak group when expressing fear. In another line of work, Goldenberg et al. (2014) examined emotional burden – the effects of emotional expressions made by the ingroup on an ingroup member in conflict. Emotional reactions (e.g., guilt, anger) that were deemed appropriate, but were not shared with the ingroup, led to increased levels of group-based emotion, compensating for the collective's emotional response.

So how have emotional expressions been used to promote intergroup relations? A number of researchers have examined the role of expressions of hope in conflict. For example, Leshem and colleagues (2016) found that a hopeful message made by an outgroup member induced hope for peace and conciliatory attitudes. My colleagues and I (Cohen-Chen et al., 2017b) found that expressions of hope made by the outgroup as a whole (presented as results of a wide-scale survey) overrode messages of low support for a peace agreement and led to more positive perceptions of said agreement and its subsequent acceptance. In a later line of research, we found that expressions of hope made by an ingroup leader led to more hope and agreement acceptance in low-intensity conflicts, such as student protests over fees in the UK (Study 1), and an imaginary conflict (Study 2) (Cohen-Chen et al., 2019). However, in high-intensity conflict (the Israeli–Palestinian conflict), these were tempered by participants' political ideology. While, among Leftists, expressions of hope increased support for conflict resolution via experienced hope, it did not affect Rightists.

Solak and colleagues (2017) used an outgroup expression of disappointment in two intergroup contexts: the Israeli–Palestinian conflict (Israeli participants reading that Palestinians were disappointed in Israel vs fearful vs no expression), and racial relations in the USA (White American participants reading about Black Americans' disappointment vs fear vs no expression). In both cases, an expression of disappointment increased participant guilt and subsequently created more intentions to take part in collective action on behalf of the outgroup (Israelis were more motivated to protest against Israeli actions related to the 2014 Gaza war; White Americans were more motivated to act against institutional discrimination and police mistreatment). However, the effect was only found among participants who saw the intergroup situation as illegitimate in the first place.

4.7 SUMMARY

This chapter began (in Part 1: Foundations) with an introduction to emotions which included a definition and description of the evolution and development of emotions research. We examined how emotions differ from other emotional phenomena, and pointed to their importance in appraising, interpreting, and responding to social situations. In particular, we honed in on one particular social context, namely aggression, in which emotions play an important role. We looked at classic work on aggression and then explored the relationship between emotions and aggressive behaviour and attitudes. Notably, some emotions, such as anger and hatred, motivate aggressive intergroup behaviour, while other emotions, such as guilt and hope, drive conciliatory attitudes and actions.

In Part 2 (Advances), we tied aggression to the social phenomenon of conflict, and in particular intractable and extreme conflicts which are conducive to, and influenced by, heightened emotions. We presented a framework for categorising emotions in conflicts which considers both emotions' valence (pleasantness; feel good) and function (social outcome; do good) simultaneously. Using this framework, we discussed how different emotions 'behave' (i.e., how they feel and what action tendencies they elicit) in conflict and conflict resolution processes. We then moved on to learn about emotion regulation and the transformation of emotions in order to transform attitudes and actions.

In Part 3 (Applications), we moved beyond merely understanding emotions in conflict and using them to predict behaviour to a field that explores strategies to transform emotions, and subsequently intergroup outcomes. We defined and illustrated direct emotion regulation, but noted that emotional preferences can influence whether people are motivated to regulate their emotions and change their attitudes. We then considered and presented interventions using indirect emotion regulation, and finally, interventions that use emotional elements, such as emotional similarity and expressions.

4.8 REVISION

1   Use two different frameworks discussed in this chapter to categorise the following emotions: fear, anxiety, pride, guilt, boredom, regret, joy, sadness, hope, and nostalgia. See if you can create unlikely groups of emotions (e.g., guilt, regret, and nostalgia are all emotions that focus on past events).
2   Think about an emotion you have already experienced today, and describe it using appraisal theories of emotion. Think about what led to the emotion, how it felt, and what outcomes it led to.
3   What is the difference between group-based anger and collective anger, and where does this differentiation come into play during conflict?
4   A friend is preparing for an important job interview and is interested in your knowledge on emotions to help them do well in impressing the interviewers. See if you can come up with three 'tips' based on emotional knowledge to help your friend land this job. Now, the same friend is asking for advice on how to utilise emotions in a negotiation over salary. How do the 'tips' change based on the context? Remember the literature on emotional preferences and emotion regulation!
5   How can the literature on social learning and the literature on emotions be used to help children (and adults) in managing and understanding their emotions?
6   Prepare a short blog post (150 words) to explain social emotions to lay-people. What are emotions? Why are they important in understanding human (social) behaviour? Make it simple, short, and snappy so anyone can understand the role of emotions in their life!

4.9 FURTHER READING

Averill, J. R. (1980). A constructivist view of emotion. In R. Plutchik & H. Kellerman (Eds.), *Emotion: Theory, research and experience* (pp. 305–339). New York: Academic Press.

Cohen-Chen, S., Pliskin, R., & Goldenberg, A. (2020). Feel good or do good? A valence/function framework for understanding emotions. *Current Directions in Psychological Science, 29*, 388–393.

Ellsworth, P. C., & Scherer, K. R. (2003). *Appraisal processes in emotion.* Oxford: Oxford University Press.

Gross, J. J. (1998). The emerging field of emotion regulation: An integrative review. *Review of General Psychology*, *2*, 271–299.

Halperin, E. (2016). *Emotions in conflict: Inhibitors and facilitators of peace making.* New York: Routledge.

Halperin, E., Cohen-Chen, S., & Goldenberg, A. (2014). Indirect emotion regulation in intractable conflicts: A new approach to conflict resolution. *European Review of Social Psychology*, *25*, 1–31.

Mackie, D. M., Devos, T., & Smith, E. R. (2000). Intergroup emotions: Explaining offensive action tendencies in an intergroup context. *Journal of Personality and Social Psychology*, *79*, 602–616.

Van Kleef, G. A. (2009). How emotions regulate social life: The emotions as social information (EASI) model. *Current Directions in Psychological Science*, *18*(3), 184–188.

Useful websites include:

Paul Ekman Group: https://www.paulekman.com/
aChord Center: https://en.achord.huji.ac.il/

4.10 REFERENCES

Adorno, T. W., Frenkel-Brunswik, E., Levinson, D. J., & Sanford, R. N. (1950). *The authoritarian personality.* New York: Harper & Row.

Altemeyer, B. (1981). *Right-wing authoritarianism.* Winnipeg, MB: University of Manitoba Press.

Anderson, C. A. (1989). Temperature and aggression: ubiquitous effects of heat on occurrence of human violence. *Psychological Bulletin*, *106*(1), 74–96.

Arnold, M. B. (1960). *Emotion and personality.* New York: Columbia University Press.

Averill, J. R. (1980). A constructivist view of emotion. In R. Plutchik & H. Kellerman (Eds.), *Emotion: Theory, research and experience* (pp. 305–339). New York: Academic Press.

Bandura, A. (1965). Influence of models' reinforcement contingencies on the acquisition of imitative responses. *Journal of Personality and Social Psychology*, *1*(6), 589–595.

Bandura, A. (1977). Social learning theory. In A. Bandura & R. H. Walters, *Social learning theory* (Vol. 1). Englewood Cliffs, NJ: Prentice Hall.

Bandura, A., Ross, D., & Ross, S. A. (1961). Transmission of aggression through imitation of aggressive models. *The Journal of Abnormal and Social Psychology*, *63*(3), 575–582.

Baron, R. A., & Bell, P. A. (1976). Aggression and heat: The influence of ambient temperature, negative affect, and a cooling drink on physical aggression. *Journal of Personality and Social Psychology*, *33*(3), 245–255.

Barrett, L. F. (2006). Solving the emotion paradox: Categorization and the experience of emotion. *Personality and Social Psychology Review*, *10*(1), 20–46.

Bar-Tal, D. (2007). Sociopsychological foundations of intractable conflicts. *American Behavioral Scientist*, *50*, 1430–1453.

Bar-Tal, D., & Halperin, E. (2011). Socio-psychological barriers to conflict resolution. In D. Bar-Tal (Ed.), *Intergroup conflicts and their resolution: Social psychological perspective* (pp. 217–240). New York: Psychology Press.

Bar-Tal, D., Halperin, E., & de-Rivera, J. (2007). Collective emotions in conflict situations: Societal implications. *Journal of Social Issues, 63*, 441–460.

Bar-Tal, D., Raviv, A., Raviv, A., & Dgani-Hirsch, A. (2009). The influence of the ethos of conflict on Israeli Jews' interpretation of Jewish–Palestinian encounters. *Journal of Conflict Resolution, 53*, 94–118.

Beedie, C., Terry, P., & Lane, A. (2005). Distinctions between emotion and mood. *Cognition & Emotion, 19*(6), 847–878.

Berman, M., Gladue, B., & Taylor, S. (1993). The effects of hormones, Type A behavior pattern, and provocation on aggression in men. *Motivation and Emotion, 17*, 125–138.

Bodenhausen, G. V., Kramer, G. P., & Süsser, K. (1994). Happiness and stereotypic thinking in social judgment. *Journal of Personality and Social Psychology, 66*(4), 621–632.

Bono, J. E., & Ilies, R. (2006). Charisma, positive emotions and mood contagion. *The Leadership Quarterly, 17*(4), 317–334.

Branscombe, N. R., Slugoski, B., & Kappen, D. M. (2004). The measurement of collective guilt. In N. R. Branscombe & B. Doosje (Eds.), *Collective Guilt: International Perspectives* (pp. 16–34). Cambridge: Cambridge University Press.

Cannon, W. B. (1927). The James–Lange theory of emotions: A critical examination and an alternative theory. *The American Journal of Psychology, 39*(1/4), 106–124.

Čehajić, S., Effron, D., Halperin, E., Liberman, V., & Ross, L. (2011). Affirmation, acknowledgment of ingroup responsibility, group-based guilt, and support for reparative measures. *Journal of Personality and Social Psychology, 101*, 256–270.

Cohen, D., Nisbett, R. E., Bowdle, B. F., & Schwarz, N. (1996). Insult, aggression, and the southern culture of honor: An 'experimental ethnography'. *Journal of Personality and Social Psychology, 70*(5), 945–960.

Cohen-Chen, S., Brady, G. L., Massaro, S., & van Kleef, G. A. (2022). Meh, whatever: The effects of indifference expressions on cooperation in social conflict. *Journal of Personality and Social Psychology, 123*(6), 1336–1361.

Cohen-Chen, S., Crisp, R. J., & Halperin, E. (2015). Perceptions of a changing world induce hope and promote peace in intractable conflicts. *Personality and Social Psychology Bulletin, 41*(4), 498–512.

Cohen-Chen, S., Crisp, R. J., & Halperin, E. (2017a). A new appraisal-based framework underlying hope in conflict resolution. *Emotion Review, 9*, 208–214.

Cohen-Chen, S., Crisp, R. J., & Halperin, E. (2017b). Hope comes in many forms: Out-group expressions of hope override low support and promote reconciliation in conflicts. *Social Psychological and Personality Science, 8*(2), 153–161.

Cohen-Chen, S. & Halperin, E. (2023). Emotional processes in intractable conflicts: Integrating descriptive and interventionist approaches. In L. Huddy, D. O. Sears, J. S. Levy, & J. Jerit (Eds.), *Oxford Handbook of Political Psychology*. New York: Oxford University Press.

Cohen-Chen, S., Halperin, E., Crisp, R.J., & Gross, J.J. (2014a). Hope in the Middle East: Malleability beliefs, hope, and the willingness to compromise for peace. *Social Psychological and Personality Science, 5*, 67–75.

Cohen-Chen, S., Halperin, E., Porat, R., & Bar-Tal, D. (2014b). The differential effects of hope and fear on information processing in intractable conflict. *Journal of Social and Political Psychology*, *2*, 11–30.

Cohen-Chen, S., Halperin, E., Saguy, T., & van Zomeren, M. (2014c). Beliefs about the malleability of immoral groups facilitate collective action. *Social Psychological and Personality Science*, *5*, 203– 210.

Cohen-Chen, S., Pliskin, R., & Goldenberg, A. (2020). Feel good or do good? A valence/function framework for understanding emotions. *Current Directions in Psychological Science*, *29*, 388–393.

Cohen-Chen, S., Van Kleef, G. A., Crisp, R. J., & Halperin, E. (2019). Dealing in hope: Does observing hope expressions increase conciliatory attitudes in intergroup conflict? *Journal of Experimental Social Psychology*, *83*, 102–111.

Coleman, P. (2011). *The five percent*. New York: Public Affairs.

Darwin, C. 1904. *The expression of the emotions in man and animals*. London: Murray. (Original work published 1872.)

Dasgupta, N., DeSteno, D., Williams, L. A., & Hunsinger, M. (2009). Fanning the flames of prejudice: The influence of specific incidental emotions on implicit prejudice. *Emotion*, *9*(4), 585–591.

de Figueiredo Jr, R. J., & Elkins, Z. (2003). Are patriots bigots? An inquiry into the vices of in-group pride. *American Journal of Political Science*, *47*(1), 171–188.

DeSteno, D., Dasgupta, N., Bartlett, M. Y., & Cajdric, A. (2004). Prejudice from thin air: The effect of emotion on automatic intergroup attitudes. *Psychological Science*, *15*(5), 319–324.

Dimberg, U., & Öhman, A. (1996). Behold the wrath: Psychophysiological responses to facial stimuli. *Motivation and Emotion*, *20*, 149–182.

Donnerstein, E., & Wilson, D. W. (1976). Effects of noise and perceived control on ongoing and subsequent aggressive behavior. *Journal of Personality and Social Psychology*, *34*(5), 774-781.

Dweck, C. S., Chiu, C., & Hong, Y. (1995). Implicit theories and their role in judgments and reactions: A world from two perspectives. *Psychology Inquiry*, *6*, 267–285.

Eagly, A. H., & Steffen, V. J. (1986). Gender and aggressive behavior: A meta-analytic review of the social psychological literature. *Psychological Bulletin*, *100*(3), 309–330.

Ekman, P. (1985). *Telling lies: Clues to deceit in the marketplace, politics, and marriage*. New York: WW Norton & Company.

Ekman, P. (1999). Basic emotions. In T. Dalgleish & M. J. Powers (Eds.), *Handbook of cognition and emotion* (pp. 45–60). Chichester: John Wiley & Sons.

Ellsworth, P. C., & Scherer, K. R. (2003). *Appraisal processes in emotion*. Oxford: Oxford University Press.

Folkman, S., & Lazarus, R. S. (1985). If it changes it must be a process: Study of emotion and coping during three stages of a college examination. *Journal of Personality and Social Psychology*, *48*(1), 150–170.

Fredrickson, B. L. (2013). Positive emotions broaden and build. In P. Devine & A. Plant (Eds.), *Advances in experimental social psychology* (Vol. 47, pp. 1–53). New York: Academic Press.

Freud, S. (1961 [1930]). Civilization and its discontents. In J. Strachey (Ed. and Trans.), *The standard edition of the complete psychological works of Sigmund Freud* (Vol. 21, pp. 59–148). London: Hogarth Press. (Original work published in 1930.)

Frijda, N. H. (1986). *The emotions*. Cambridge: Cambridge University Press.

Gaunt, R., Leyens, J. P., & Demoulin, S. (2002). Intergroup relations and the attribution of emotions: Control over memory for secondary emotions associated with the ingroup and outgroup. *Journal of Experimental Social Psychology, 38*(5), 508–514.

Gleason, K. A., Jensen-Campbell, L. A., & South Richardson, D. (2004). Agreeableness as a predictor of aggression in adolescence. *Aggressive Behavior: Official Journal of the International Society for Research on Aggression, 30*(1), 43–61.

Goldenberg, A., Cohen-Chen, S., Goyer, J. P., Dweck, C. S., Gross, J. J., & Halperin, E. (2018). Testing the impact and durability of group malleability intervention in the context of the Israeli–Palestinian conflict. *Proceedings of the National Academy of Sciences, 115*(4), 696–701.

Goldenberg, A., Endevelt, K., Ran, S., Dweck, C. S., Gross, J. J., & Halperin, E. (2017). Making intergroup contact more fruitful: Enhancing cooperation between Palestinian and Jewish-Israeli adolescents by fostering beliefs about group malleability. *Social Psychological and Personality Science, 8*(1), 3–10.

Goldenberg, A., Saguy, T., & Halperin, E. (2014). How group-based emotions are shaped by collective emotions: Evidence for emotional transfer and emotional burden. *Journal of Personality and Social Psychology, 107*(4), 581–596.

Gross, J. J. (1998). The emerging field of emotion regulation: An integrative review. *Review of General Psychology, 2*, 271–299.

Gross, J. J., & Thompson, R. (2007). Emotion regulation: Conceptual foundations. In J. J. Gross (Ed.), *Handbook of emotion regulation* (pp. 3–24). New York: Guilford Press.

Gur, T., Ayal., S., & Halperin, E. (2021). A bright side of sadness: The depolarizing role of sadness in intergroup conflicts. *European Journal of Social Psychology, 51*(1), 68–83.

Halperin, E. (2008). Group-based hatred in intractable conflict in Israel. *Journal of Conflict Resolution, 52*, 713–736.

Halperin, E., Cohen-Chen, S., & Goldenberg, A. (2014a). Indirect emotion regulation in intractable conflicts: A new approach to conflict resolution. *European Review of Social Psychology, 25*, 1–31.

Halperin, E., Crisp, R. J., Husnu, S., Trzesniewski, K. H., Dweck, C. S., & Gross, J. J. (2012). Promoting intergroup contact by changing beliefs: Group malleability, intergroup anxiety, and contact motivation. *Emotion, 12*(6), 1192–1195.

Halperin, E., & Gross, J. (2011). Emotion regulation in violent conflict: Reappraisal, hope, and support for humanitarian aid to the opponent in wartime. *Cognition & Emotion, 25*(7), 1228–1236.

Halperin, E., Pliskin, R., Saguy, T., Liberman, V., & Gross, J. J. (2014b). Emotion regulation and the cultivation of political tolerance: Searching for a new track for intervention. *Journal of Conflict Resolution, 58*, 1110–1138.

Halperin, E., Porat, R., Tamir, M., & Gross, E. (2013). Can emotion regulation change political attitudes in intractable conflict? From the laboratory to the field. *Psychological Science, 24*, 106–111.

Halperin, E., Russell, A. G., Dweck, C. S., & Gross, J. J. (2011a). Anger, hatred, and the quest for peace: Anger can be constructive in the absence of hatred. *Journal of Conflict Resolution, 55*(2), 274–291.

Halperin, E., Russell, A. G., Trzesniewski, K. H., Gross, J. J., & Dweck, C. S. (2011b). Promoting the Middle East peace process by changing beliefs about group malleability. *Science, 333,* 1767–1769.

Haslam, N., & Loughnan, S. (2014). Dehumanization and infrahumanization. *Annual Review of Psychology, 65,* 399–423.

Haslam, N., & Stratemeyer, M. (2016). Recent research on dehumanization. *Current Opinion in Psychology, 11,* 25–29.

Hasler, B. S., Leshem, O. A., Hasson, Y., Landau, D. H., Krayem, Y., Blatansky, C., ... & Halperin, E. (2023). Young generations' hopelessness perpetuates long-term conflicts. *Scientific Reports, 13*(1), 4926.

Iyer, A., & Leach, C. W. (2008). Emotion in inter-group relations. *European Review of Social Psychology, 19,* 86–125.

Iyer, A., Leach, C. W., & Crosby, F. J. (2003). White guilt and racial compensation: The benefits and limits of self-focus. *Personality and Social Psychology Bulletin, 29*(1), 117–129.

Jarymowicz, M., & Bar-Tal, D. (2006). The dominance of fear over hope in the life of individuals and collectives. *European Journal of Social Psychology, 36,* 367–392.

Kamans, E., van Zomeren, M., Gordijn, E. H., & Postmes, T. (2014). Communicating the right emotion makes violence seem less wrong: Power-congruent emotions lead outsiders to legitimize violence of powerless and powerful groups in intractable conflict. *Group Processes & Intergroup Relations, 17*(3), 286–305.

Keltner, D., & Haidt, J. (1999). Social functions of emotions at four levels of analysis. *Cognition & Emotion, 13*(5), 505–521.

Kenrick, D. T., & MacFarlane, S. W. (1986). Ambient temperature and horn honking: A field study of the heat/aggression relationship. *Environment and behavior, 18*(2), 179–191.

Kenrick, D. T., & Simpson, J. A. (1997). Why social psychology and evolutionary psychology need one another. In J. A. Simpson & D. T. Kenrick (Eds.), *Evolutionary social psychology* (pp. 1–20). Mahwah, NJ: Lawrence Erlbaum Associates.

Klein, O., Hardwicke, T. E., Aust, F., Breuer, J., Danielsson, H., Mohr, A. H., ... & Frank, M. C. (2018). A practical guide for transparency in psychological science. *Collabra: Psychology, 4*(1).

Kriesberg, L. (1993). Intractable conflict. *Peace Review, 5,* 417–421.

Lazarus, R. S. (1994). Universal antecedents of the emotions. In P. Ekman & R. J. Davidson (Eds.), *The nature of emotion: Fundamental question* (pp. 163–171). New York: Oxford University Press.

Leshem, O. A., & Halperin, E. (2020). Lay theories of peace and their influence on policy preference during violent conflict. *Proceedings of the National Academy of Sciences, 117*(31), 18378–18384. https://psycnet.apa.org/doi/10.1073/pnas.2005928117

Leshem, O. A., Klar, Y., & Flores, T. E. (2016). Instilling hope for peace during intractable conflicts. *Social Psychological and Personality Science, 7*(4), 303–311.

Levine, R. A., & Campbell, D. T. (1972). Realistic group conflict theory. *Ethnocentrism: Theories of conflict, ethnic attitudes and group behavior* (pp. 29–43). New York: John Wiley & Sons.

Leyens, J. P., Paladino, P. M., Rodriguez-Torres, R., Vaes, J., Demoulin, S., Rodriguez-Perez, A., & Gaunt, R. (2000). The emotional side of prejudice: The attribution of secondary emotions to ingroups and outgroups. *Personality and Social Psychology Review, 4*(2), 186–197.

Mackie, D. M., Devos, T., & Smith, E. R. (2000). Intergroup emotions: Explaining offensive action tendencies in an intergroup context. *Journal of Personality and Social Psychology, 79*, 602–616.

Manstead, A. S., & Fischer, A. H. (2001). Social appraisal. In K. R. Scherer, A. Schorr, & T. Johnstone (Eds.), *Appraisal processes in emotion: Theory, research, application* (pp. 221–232). New York: Oxford University Press.

McDonald, M., Porat, R., Yarkoney, A., Reifen Tagar, M., Kimel, S., Saguy, T., & Halperin, E. (2017). Intergroup emotional similarity reduces dehumanization and promotes conciliatory attitudes in prolonged conflict. *Group Processes & Intergroup Relations, 20*(1), 125–136.

McGarty, C., Pedersen, A., Wayne Leach, C., Mansell, T., Waller, J., & Bliuc, A. M. (2005). Group-based guilt as a predictor of commitment to apology. *British Journal of Social Psychology, 44*(4), 659–680.

Ng, B., Kumar, S., Ranclaud, M., & Robinson, E. (2001). Ward crowding and incidents of violence on an acute psychiatric inpatient unit. *Psychiatric Services, 52*(4), 521–525.

Open Science Collaboration. (2015). Estimating the reproducibility of psychological science. *Science, 349*(6251), aac4716.

Pettigrew, T. F., & Tropp, L. R. (2008). How does intergroup contact reduce prejudice? Meta-analytic tests of three mediators. *European Journal of Social Psychology, 38*(6), 922–934.

Plutchik, R. (1970). Emotions, evolution, and adaptive processes. In M. Arnold (Ed.), *Feelings and emotions: the Loyola Symposium* (pp. 1–14). New York: Academic Press.

Porat, R., Halperin, E., Mannheim, I., & Tamir, M. (2016a). Together we cry: Social motives and preferences for group-based sadness. *Cognition & Emotion, 30*(1), 66–79.

Porat, R., Halperin, E., & Tamir, M. (2016b). What we want is what we get: Group-based emotional preferences and conflict resolution. *Journal of Personality and Social Psychology, 110*(2), 167–190.

Reifen Tagar, M., Halperin, E., & Frederico, C. (2011). The positive effect of negative emotions in protracted conflict: The case of anger. *Journal of Experimental Social Psychology, 47*(1), 157–163.

Richards, J. M., & Gross, J. J. (2000). Emotion regulation and memory: The cognitive costs of keeping one's cool. *Journal of Personality and Social Psychology, 79*(3), 410–424.

Russell, J. A. (1980). A circumplex model of affect. *Journal of Personality and Social Psychology, 39*(6), 1161–1178.

Sadler, M. S., Lineberger, M., Correll, J., & Park, B. (2005). Emotions, attributions, and policy endorsement in response to the September 11th terrorist attacks. *Basic and Applied Social Psychology, 27*(3), 249–258.

Saguy, T., & Halperin, E. (2014). Exposure to outgroup members criticizing their own group facilitates intergroup openness. *Personality and Social Psychology Bulletin, 40*, 791–802.

Schachter, S., & Singer, J. (1962). Cognitive, social, and physiological determinants of emotional state. *Psychological Review, 69*(5), 379-399.

Scherer, K. R. (1984). Emotion as a multicomponent process: A model and some cross-cultural data. *Review of Personality and Social Psychology, 5*, 37–63.

Schnall, S., Haidt, J., Clore, G. L., & Jordan, A. H. (2008). Disgust as embodied moral judgment. *Personality and Social Psychology Bulletin, 34*(8), 1096–1109.

Sherif, M., & Sherif, C. W. (1953). *Groups in harmony and tension.* New York: Harper and Brothers.

Shuman, E., Cohen-Chen, S., Hirsch-Hoefler, S., & Halperin, E. (2016). Explaining normative versus non-normative action: The role of implicit theories. *Political Psychology, 37*, 835–852.

Sidanius, J., & Pratto, F. (1999). *Social dominance.* New York: Cambridge University Press.

Siemer, M., Mauss, I., & Gross, J. J. (2007). Same situation–different emotions: How appraisals shape our emotions. *Emotion, 7*(3), 592–600.

Skinner, B. F. (1953). Some contributions of an experimental analysis of behavior to psychology as a whole. *American Psychologist, 8*(2), 69-78.

Smith, E. R., & Mackie, D. M. (2016). Group-level emotions. *Current Opinion in Psychology, 11*, 15–19.

Smith, E. R., Seger, C. R., & Mackie, D. M. (2007). Can emotions be truly group level? Evidence regarding four conceptual criteria. *Journal of Personality and Social Psychology, 93*, 431–446.

Solak, N., Reifen Tagar, M., Cohen-Chen, S., Saguy, T., & Halperin, E. (2017). Disappointment expression evokes collective guilt and collective action in intergroup conflict: The moderating role of legitimacy perceptions. *Cognition & Emotion, 31*(6), 1112–1126.

Staub, E. (2005). The origins and evolution of hate, with notes on prevention. In R. J. Sternberg (Ed.), *The psychology of hate* (pp. 51–66). American Psychological Association. https://doi.org/10.1037/10930-003

Stephan, W. G., & Stephan, C. W. (2000). An integrated threat theory of prejudice. In S. Oskamp (Ed.), *Reducing prejudice and discrimination* (pp. 225–246). Hillsdale, NJ: Erlbaum.

Tajfel, H., Billig, M., Bundy, R. P., & Flament, C. (1971). Social categorization and intergroup behaviour. *European Journal of Social Psychology, 1*, 149–178.

Tajfel, H., & Turner, J. C. (1979). An integrative theory of intergroup conflict. In W. G. Austin & S. Worchel (Eds.), *The social psychology of intergroup relations* (pp. 33–48). Monterey, CA: Brooks/Cole.

Tamir, M. (2016). Why do people regulate their emotions? A taxonomy of motives in emotion regulation. *Personality and Social Psychology Review, 20*(3), 199–222.

Tamir, M., & Ford, B. Q. (2009). Choosing to be afraid: Preferences for fear as a function of goal pursuit. *Emotion, 9*(4), 488-497.

Tamir, M., Mitchell, C., & Gross, J. J. (2008). Hedonic and instrumental motives in anger regulation. *Psychological Science, 19*(4), 324–328.

Tausch, N., Becker, J. C., Spears, R., Christ, O., Saab, R., Singh, P., & Siddiqui, R. N. (2011). Explaining radical group behavior: Developing emotion and efficacy routes to normative and nonnormative collective action. *Journal of Personality and Social Psychology, 101*(1), 129–148. https://doi.org/10.1037/a0022728

Tong, E. M. (2010). Personality influences in appraisal–emotion relationships: The role of neuroticism. *Journal of Personality, 78*(2), 393–417.

Van Kleef, G. A. (2009). How emotions regulate social life: The emotions as social information (EASI) model. *Current Directions in Psychological Science, 18*(3), 184–188.

Van Kleef, G. A., De Dreu, C. K., & Manstead, A. S. (2004). The interpersonal effects of anger and happiness in negotiations. *Journal of Personality and Social Psychology, 86*(1), 57–76.

van Zomeren, M., Postmes, T., & Spears, R. (2008). Toward an integrative social identity model of collective action: A quantitative research synthesis of three socio-psychological perspectives. *Psychological Bulletin, 134*(4), 504–535.

Westerlund, M., Santtila, P., & Antfolk, J. (2020). Regulating emotions under exposure to negative out-group-related news material results in increased acceptance of out-groups. *The Journal of Social Psychology, 160*(3), 357–372.

5
SOCIAL COGNITION
MARIO WEICK

Contents

5.1 AUTHOR'S PERSONAL JOURNEY

Source: © Mario Weick

I was born in mountainous Austria, but when I was a toddler my family moved to a small village in Southwest Germany in the Rhine delta. There was a tiny island nicknamed Corsica, which had little in common with Napoleon's famous birthplace. There were floods in the winter and swarms of mosquitoes in the summer. A nuclear power station towered over the area. It was my own version of *Schitt's Creek* (the TV series), except that my family was never rich. And just like in *Schitt's Creek*, it turned out to be OK – I met some wonderful people, joined sports clubs, and education was good and state-funded.

My father only completed primary school and my mother secondary school, but both supported me in my wish to go to university. I toiled with the idea of studying medicine, but my heart was not in it. One day it struck me to combine Psychology and Business. It felt fortuitous when I discovered that there was a field called Industrial and Organisational (I&O) Psychology, and the nearest university (Mannheim) was meant to be quite good in it. So off I went, commuting to Mannheim half of the week to pursue my supposedly full-time studies, and to Frankfurt the other half where I worked for a consultancy (that's another chapter). At Mannheim, I liked I&O Psychology, but I was more captivated by the beauty and precision of social psychology experiments.

Social psychology in Mannheim had an emphasis on social cognition, and I decided to gain further training in other branches of social psychology during a year abroad sponsored by the German Academic Exchange Service (the DAAD). My professors in Germany recommended the University of Kent in Canterbury, UK, to specialise in group processes and intergroup relations, so I enrolled in a one-year MSc programme there. Once in the UK, it didn't take long for me to pivot back to social cognition with a dissertation project on social power and knowledge activation and use. The topic of how power and social hierarchies more generally impact thoughts and actions has stuck with me all these years. It's a good example of how the social context impacts feelings, thoughts, and actions.

I very much enjoyed the research elements of the MSc programme, so what was meant to be a year abroad turned into an indefinite stint when I bumped into Dominic Abrams (one of the professors at Kent) in a corridor, and he encouraged me to apply for funding to pursue a PhD. Thankfully that worked out, but not without the help of Dominic and others, who took me under their wings, often paying it forward without any obvious benefits to themselves.

As a PhD student, I have fond memories of attending meetings by the European Social Cognition Network (ESCON) where early career researchers pushed the boundaries of the things you are going to read about in this chapter. After the PhD, I did two one-year postdocs, one working with a cognitive neuroscientist, and one that allowed me to spend some time at the University of California at Santa Barbara, working with Jim Blascovich. Jim is an inspiration. He spearheaded the use of psychophysiological measures to study motivation, and the use of virtual reality to study social influence processes. Those are great examples of our research methods toolbox, which, as you will see, is large and varied, and keeps things interesting.

Someone else I admire once said, 'great research has to be relevant'. I think one aspect that attracted me to social cognition all these years is that it feels so relevant and applicable. It's not a coincidence that many of the principles discussed in this chapter provide foundations for theories and applications of behaviour change.

Social cognition is a hub science that encourages you to dip your toes in different subjects and disciplines. Studying and researching social cognition has been a rewarding journey for me. I hope you too will discover something in this chapter that inspires you as you forge your own path.

5.2 INTRODUCTION

Social cognition is not just about how we perceive other people; it's far more than that. If you learn about social cognition, you learn about fundamental principles of how people make sense of the world and what drives their actions. Many of the non-fiction bestsellers in bookshops on the high street are on

> **Key concept – Cognition:** The mental processes and activities related to acquiring, processing, storing, and using information. It involves mental functions such as perception, attention, memory, language, problem-solving, and decision-making.

topics related to social cognition. I often tell my students that if it's interesting and relevant to most people, and there are elements of **cognition**, the books are either on social cognition or on mental ill health (also a popular topic). Of course, that's just a crude rule of thumb. Our chapter begins with a definition, so you will learn what social cognition is about.

Much of social cognition research centres on the idea of **construals** – mental representations that guide our perceptions, judgements, and actions. In Part 1: Foundations, you will learn about how construals are formed, and why they can lead us astray, into believ-

> **Key concept – Construal:** How people perceive and interpret information through inferences. It involves the formation of subjective mental representations.

ing that our often-biased perceptions are truthful and objective.

There is an emphasis on biases and errors in social cognition. That's not just because those are interesting, but also because they are useful to uncover fundamental principles of how the mind works. There are strong historic connections between the development of social cognition as a discipline, and research on heuristics and biases in judgement and decision-making. These connections will become clearer when we discuss different processing modes in the foundations section, as well as work on risk perception in the section on applications.

Social cognition researchers have been intrigued by the pervasiveness of automaticity in everyday life. I hope it intrigues you too. We will conclude the foundations section by looking at how automatic processes operate. Even though many processes are automatic, every so often we still manage to set goals and pursue longer-term objectives. In the advances section, we look more closely at how goals and self-regulation operate.

If you train a language-based artificial intelligence (AI) system long enough, would it eventually think like you? Who knows. What we do know from work on embodiment, discussed in the advances section, is that our senses and motor systems (muscle movements) are also building blocks of cognition, not just abstract language. We will also look at supernatural beliefs and superstitions, and you will learn how it is possible that people hold onto irrational beliefs.

Social cognition research is fun, but there are also many real-world applications, one of which is survey and questionnaire design. This is different from what you are taught in your typical statistics and research methods classes. If you are reading this, the chances are that you will be dealing with surveys or questionnaires at some point in your life. I encourage you to revisit the section on survey and questionnaire design when you do.

Social cognition research has also been applied to the field of consumer behaviour. Since most of our lives revolve around consumption in some way, this seems like a fitting topic to delve into further. As noted earlier, we will also discuss risk perception and behaviour, with a focus on natural disasters – sadly an increasingly pressing issue that affects us all. The chapter concludes with a summary and a revision section, as well as recommendations for further readings.

5.3 LEARNING OBJECTIVES

By the end of this chapter, you will know/understand:

- The components of the social information processing model, and the role of attention and prior knowledge in perception and construals;
- How biases can give people a sense that their views are truthful and objective;
- Different processing modes, and how they are linked to different perspectives on the social perceiver;
- Current perspectives on automaticity in everyday life, and the inner workings of goals and self-regulation;
- Embodiment and metaphoric mental representations;
- What gives rise to supernatural beliefs and superstitions;
- Social cognitive perspectives on survey and questionnaire design, including assimilation and contrast effects;
- Heuristics and biases when people reason about and respond to risks arising from natural disasters and other rare events;
- How social cognitive principles can be applied to consumer behaviour.

5.4 PART 1: FOUNDATIONS

In this section, we explore key concepts and themes that underpin the field of social cognition. Let's get straight to it.

5.4.1 Mapping Out the Subject Area

Social cognition is both a subject area as well as an approach to studying social behaviour. The preferred definition adopted in this chapter emphasises processes, focusing on *how* people make sense of the social world (e.g., Kunda, 1999). This process of sense-making or *construal* is critically important to the field of social cognition: the subjects of study are ideas and concepts that cannot be directly observed but require 'inferences'. Let's reflect on that a bit more. Say I am a scientist and want to know how people perceive the luminance of objects. I conduct an experiment asking participants to judge whether two squares shown on a computer screen have the same luminance. I can compare people's judgements with an objective measure of the luminance of the two squares. Now imagine instead of two squares I show pictures of two faces and ask participants to judge which person is more trustworthy. Trustworthiness is something that can't be directly observed, and there is no ruler or objective measure of trustworthiness. In other words, trustworthiness must be inferred from the faces. Going back to our definitions, judgements of trustworthiness, but not judgements of luminance, would fall under the umbrella of social cognition.

To be fair, most, if not all, psychological processes involve some elements of construals (including perceptions of luminance!), so the boundaries of social cognition as a subject area are sometimes not that clear-cut. Nevertheless, a focus on things that can't be directly observed and that require a significant level of inferences is characteristic of social cognition research. There are other features too. People are not just passive perceivers of the outside world. On the contrary, perception and action are inherently intertwined. Or as William James – one of the founding fathers of Psychology – put it, 'my thinking is first and foremost for the sake of my doing'. Going back to our hypothetical study, a social cognition researcher might not only ask which face is more trustworthy, but also whether people are more inclined to approach faces that appear to be trustworthy. The researcher might also be interested to see what the implications are of this trustworthiness–approach relationship for, say, social interactions or negotiations.

Another guiding principle is that mental processes serve adaptive actions. This means that mental processes don't just happen – they serve a purpose, such as understanding and predicting what is happening around us, or helping us fit into groups. Social cognition researchers have been at the forefront of trying to understand how motivation and goals intersect with cognition, and the role of feelings in this process.

Perhaps one reason why social cognition has such broad appeal is that our brains have evolved to process social stimuli (Adolphs, 2003). Human cognition is so attuned to processing social signals that we can all make judgements of, for example, whether someone looks friendly or trustworthy in a split second, and with a high level of agreement (Willis & Todorov, 2006). In fact, we are so attuned to processing social signals, we can't help but extract meaning from even the briefest glimpse of a person. And we don't stop there – we also ascribe human attributes to things such as (non-human) animals and inanimate objects. Exercise 5.1 encourages you to explore this more with a famous animation by Heider and Simmel (1944).

EXERCISE 5.1

Ascribing Human Minds to Inanimate Objects

If you enter 'Heider and Simmel 1944' into an internet search engine, you will quickly find a short video animation of two triangles and a circle moving around a rectangle. Take a look at the video. What's your interpretation of the scene? How likeable are the triangles and the circle? Notice how you are inclined to use human traits and stories to make sense of the situation. When you are done, you can compare your interpretation with others who have also watched the movie by reading an article written by Gottschall (2021).

> **Key concept – Bias:** The systematic deviation from objectivity or impartiality in judgement and decision-making.

Unfortunately, being experts in the processing of social signals does not imply being free of **bias** – far from it. Even with the best of intentions, our perceptions of, and responses to, the outside world are subject to many sources of influence, including stereotypes. A powerful demonstration of this derives from Eberhardt, Davies, Purdie-Vaughns, and Johnson (2006), who looked at murder convictions in the USA. The researchers found that defendants convicted of murder were more likely to receive the death penalty when the defendants looked stereotypically Black and the victims were White. A stereotypically Black appearance included having a broad nose, thick lips, and dark skin. This 'death penalty' for appearance persisted when the researchers controlled for a wide range of aggravating and mitigating circumstances. The study demonstrates the real-life relevance of social cognition research. It also illustrates why social cognition researchers often look at biases, such as those linked to skin colour, to gain a deeper understanding of how the mind works.

To wrap up, the International Social Cognition Network (ISCON) provides a contemporary definition, which goes like this:

> Social cognition is not a content area, but rather an approach to […] understand social psychological phenomena by investigating the cognitive processes that underlie them. The major concerns of the approach are the processes involved in the perception, judgement, and memory of social stimuli; the effects of social and affective factors on information processing; and the behavioural and interpersonal consequences of cognitive processes.

Put simply, how do we gain an understanding of ourselves and the social world we are living in? How are mental processes shaped by the context and our desires, goals, and subjective experiences? How do these factors determine our attitudes, judgements, and actions? These are the questions that lie at the heart of the discipline.

5.4.2 Overarching Themes

Let's begin our foray into social cognition with a discussion of a few core principles or over-arching themes. Most, if not all, research in social cognition draws on these principles in some way, so if you know about the principles, you already know a good deal about the subject area.

The Social Information Processing Model

At the most basic level, social cognition is concerned with the processes that link a stimulus event (e.g., a huge hairy spider popping up in front of you) and a response (e.g., you jump). As shown in Figure 5.1, the social information processing model assumes that the response follows on from the stimulus, and not vice versa. The model also assumes that perception and construal are two key steps that mediate the link between a stimulus and a response. Perhaps you recognise the stimulus–response connection as something that was key to Behaviourism, a tradition in Psychology that was popular towards the middle of the 20th century. Behaviourists wanted to distance themselves from earlier Psychoanalysis, so they treated everything that happened inside the head (i.e., in-between a stimulus event and a response) as a 'black box'. That approach had its merits, but Behaviourism wasn't well suited to explain how responses to the *same* stimulus *differ* depending on the context in which a stimulus is presented. A huge hairy spider is probably giving you more of a fright in your living room than in a zoo enclosure. Unlike Behaviourists, social cognition researchers love this situated aspect of cognition, which we will learn more about when we discuss automatic processes.

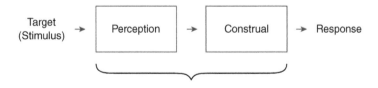

- Black box of behaviourism

- Attention and prior knowledge jointly impact perception and construal

Figure 5.1 The social information processing model. Adapted from Bless and Fiedler (2014) and Bodenhausen and Hugenberg (2009)

> **Key concept – Attention:** The cognitive process of selecting specific aspects of information from the environment while ignoring others.

> **Key concept – Perception:** The mental processing of sensory information from the environment.

Much of social cognition focuses on the roles of **attention** and prior knowledge (memory) in perception and construals. This is also reflected in our research methods, which often involve carefully crafted experiments to study attention and memory processes, similar to the methods found in cognitive psychology.

It's easy to see how inferences about others and the outside world can be coloured by the things we attend to as well as pre-existing ideas stored in memory. If you cast your mind back to the study by Eberhardt and colleagues, judges' assessments of the worthiness of capital punishment were evidently influenced by preconceptions linked to physical appearance. But what about **perception** – the processing of signals via our sensory systems? Let's take an example from a study by Drew, Võ, and Wolfe (2013) who asked 24 radiologists to perform a lung-nodule detection task; that is, a task to detect early signs of cancer in CT scans of patients' lungs. The researchers had a surprise up their sleeve: unbeknown to the radiologists, the researchers embedded a picture of a small gorilla in the scans. The gorilla had black and grey shades that blend well into the scans. At the same time, the gorilla was roughly the size of a matchbox, and it's obviously a foreign object that doesn't belong in a lung! Remarkably, out of the 24 radiologists, 20 did not notice the gorilla in plain sight, even though they were clearly looking at the scans. The study illustrates the role of attention in perception – without attention, we can miss seemingly obvious sensory inputs.

Interestingly, when I present the CT scans to students in my class, they are sometimes quite good at spotting the gorilla. Radiologists with their extensive knowledge of scanning images for nodules may find it more difficult to spot a gorilla than lay people who have no idea what to look for. Attention is guided by prior knowledge (memory), impacting both the perception and construal of stimuli. You may have heard about the cocktail-party effect, which is a related phenomenon that describes our capacity to filter out a single voice in a noisy setting. In a classic study on this effect, Moray (1959) found that people sharpen their hearing and start listening when noticing their own name in an auditory channel they were instructed to ignore (a task we are remarkably good at). Attention restricts the sheer volume of incoming information and it allows us to 'zoom in' on information that is relevant, with the most crucial information reserved for higher-order processes and conscious awareness. Thus, attention – shaped by prior knowledge – acts as a big filter that colours our perception of the social world.

Subjectivity and Naïve Realism

Subjectivity and naïve realism are important principles that run through most social cognition research. The starting point here is, quite simply, that perception and construals differ between people and situations. Crucially, people are often unaware of their 'subjectivity' – momentary representations of the (social) world are experienced as truthful and objective. This also implies that we believe others would and should see and appraise things the way we do. Ross and Ward (1996) coined this phenomenon **naïve realism**.

> **Key concept – Naïve realism:** The erroneous belief that one's mental representations of the world are objective and unbiased.

KEY STUDY 5.1

Confirmation Bias and Polarisation

Lord, Ross, and Lepper (1979) wanted to know what happens when people who hold strong opinions on complex social issues are exposed to conflicting evidence. Perhaps being exposed to mixed evidence would lead people to soften their stance? Lord and colleagues thought that a more tantalising and likely outcome is that, when faced with conflicting evidence, people would show a confirmation bias and become more polarised.

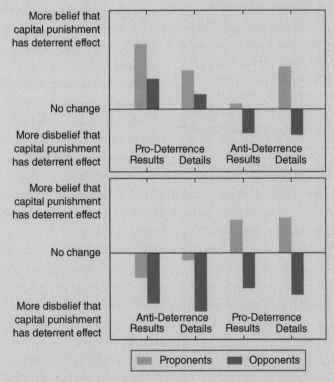

Figure 5.2 Changes in beliefs that capital punishment has deterring effects at different time points (1 to 4), starting with pro-deterrence information and then moving on to anti-deterrence information (top), or starting with anti-deterrence information and then moving on to pro-deterrence information (bottom). Darker bars represent opponents of capital punishment, and lighter bars represent proponents of capital punishment.

Source: Lord et al. (1979)

(Continued)

To test their predictions, Lord and colleagues recruited proponents and opponents of capital punishment. Participants then read two vignettes that described studies on the effectiveness of the death penalty as a deterrent. The information was counterbalanced carefully so that all participants were exposed to the same information, half of which supported and half of which opposed the deterring effects of the death penalty. Participants also learned about alleged criticism levelled at the vignette studies, and the study authors' rebuttals, so there was mixed and conflicting evidence.

As shown in Figure 5.2, the more participants were exposed to supporting and opposing evidence over the course of the study, the more the gap in beliefs towards the efficacy of capital punishment widened between proponents and opponents of the death penalty. Lord and colleagues' research is a timeless classic that can help explain why, in the advent of social media, there is a sense that people's opinions on complex social issues are more divided than ever.

> **Key concept – Implicit Association Test (IAT):** A test that measures the strength of a person's automatic associations between mental representations of objects or concepts. It is often used to assess implicit biases and attitudes that may not be evident through self-reporting.

To maintain an impression of truthfulness, people are strategic in the way they process information, both consciously and unconsciously. Hugenberg and Bodenhausen (2003) asked participants to rate the onset (Study 1) and offset (Study 2) of facial expressions of anger in computer-generated White and Black faces. Participants saw a series of pictures of a face, one by one. With each picture, the facial expressions became gradually more (Study 1) or less (Study 2) angry, starting and finishing with an expression of happiness, respectively. Notably, the researchers also employed an **Implicit Association Test (IAT)** (Greenwald, McGhee, & Schwartz, 1998) to see whether participants harboured any racial bias against Black (versus White) people. Participants were quicker to perceive anger in Black faces than in White faces transitioning from happiness to anger (Study 1), and slower to no longer perceiving anger in Black faces than in White faces transitioning from anger to happiness (Study 2). Importantly, this difference in the perceptions of the expressions of Black and White faces only emerged for participants who harboured **implicit prejudice** against Black people. This illustrates how prior knowledge (here: implicit prejudice) biases the encoding of information in a way that confirms people's existing views (here: prejudice of Black people being violent or aggressive).

> **Key concept – Implicit prejudice:** Unconscious negative attitudes towards specific groups, often uncovered using implicit measures such as the IAT.

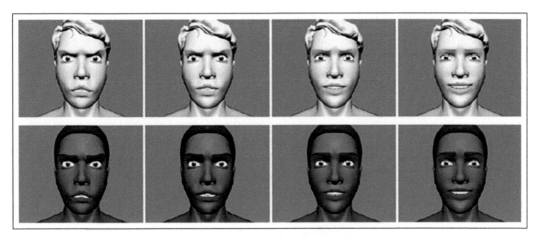

Figure 5.3 Computer-generated images showing White (top) and Black (bottom) faces becoming less (left to right) or more (right to left) angry. The study showed that people with high implicit racial prejudice more readily perceive anger in Black (vs White) faces

Source: © Hugenberg and Bodenhausen (2003)

A seminal study by Snyder and Cantor (1979) demonstrates a similar concept. However, instead of subjectivity in the encoding of external cues (i.e., biased perceptions of features of a target or stimulus), their study looked at subjectivity in memory retrieval. All participants read a description of a person, Jane, which portrayed her as behaving in an extraverted manner on some occasions and in an introverted manner on other occasions. Two days later some participants had to rate Jane's suitability for a stereotypically extravert job (real-estate agent), and some participants had to rate Jane's suitability for a stereotypically introvert job (librarian). Participants also had to recall facts about Jane. The results showed that participants' memories of Jane differed between conditions: participants tasked with assessing Jane's suitability for the extravert job recalled more information consistent with an extravert person, and participants tasked with assessing Jane's suitability for the introvert job recalled more information consistent with an introvert person. Ratings of suitability mirrored the observed differences in recall. The study illustrates how we can arrive at different conclusions based on the same information, while thinking that our judgements are truthful and objective.

It's a rare feat that researchers develop a popular concept or idea that becomes even more relevant and important over time, but to me Ross and Ward's work seems more pertinent in this day and age than ever, where naïve realism seems inescapable through our exposure to online media. Indeed, very much in line with Lord and colleagues' (1979) classic study on confirmation bias, recent work has shown that being exposed to divergent views on social media amplifies political polarisation (Bail et al., 2018).

KEY THINKER

Lee Ross

I never met Lee Ross, but I wish I had. Lee obtained a PhD from Columbia University and then had a long and prolific career at Stanford University. Lee is known, among many things, for the 'fundamental attribution error', which describes our tendency to overlook the influence of situations on behaviour. Apparently, his famous 1977 paper was Lee's attempt at summing up his intellectual contributions, in an effort to secure his tenure at Stanford (he succeeded). Lee is also known for his work on the false consensus effect – the tendency to overestimate the extent to which others share our beliefs and attitudes, bias blindspots (we think others are more biased than us), polarisation, and the 'hostile media effect', which describes people's tendency to accuse the media of bias when media reports don't align with people's political leanings. On the more applied side, Lee also worked on conflict resolution, and – perhaps not unrelatedly – climate change. Lee was the son of factory workers. He passed away in 2021.

Bottom-Up versus Top-Down Processing

Scrutinising faces is an example of a bottom-up process, and retrieving information from memory is an example of a top-down process. In other words, **top-down processes** draw on internal knowledge structures: categories, scripts, or schemas that generalise across people or situations. In contrast, **bottom-up processes** draw on external cues: the specific stimuli at hand, with all their idiosyncratic features.

Cues that are novel, surprising, or otherwise noticeably discrepant from their surroundings tend to be processed in a bottom-up fashion, attracting attention and further scrutiny when compared to cues that are familiar, unsurprising, or consistent with their surroundings. An illustration of a bottom-up process derives from Hansen and Hansen (1988), who showed that threatening faces (displaying anger) pop out of a collage of happy or neutral faces, presumably reflecting a greater salience of threat cues.

> **Key concept – Top-down and bottom-up processing:** Top-down processing uses existing knowledge and expectations to interpret information, while bottom-up processing starts with sensory input and builds understanding from specific details.

Novelty and surprise can derive from the discrepancy between one's prior knowledge and a given stimulus at hand. For example, on most university campuses it would be unusual, and hence inconsistent with one's prior knowledge, to see a student walking across campus in a wetsuit, carrying a surfboard. The student would probably attract some attention and closer scrutiny ('Who is this? What are they up to?'). However, in some places, such as the University of Santa Barbara where students are blessed with their own beach on campus, this is a familiar sight that aligns with students' prior knowledge and doesn't raise any eyebrows.

Categorisation is an important organising principle for prior knowledge. People, objects, or other mental contents are grouped in categories that share defining features. Such groupings are based on the level of overlap with proto-

> **Key concept – Categorisation:** The cognitive process of organising and grouping objects, ideas, or experiences into categories based on shared features.

types that are representative of the category. Once a stimulus is deemed to be similar to a prototype and allocated to a category, features of the category become mentally attached to the stimulus. Stereotypes are the prototypes of social categories that represent groups of people. Stereotypes define the features that we assign to people once they are assigned to a category.

Categories reduce the complexity of mental processes and serve as useful heuristics, freeing up mental space for other tasks. They also allow us to fill in the blanks when incoming infor-mation is imprecise or imperfect (as is

> **Key concept – Illusory correlation:** The perception of a connection between two variables when none or a weaker relationship exists.

usually the case), thereby giving meaning and reducing uncertainty (e.g., Hogg, 2000). However, categorisation can also have less desirable consequences, one of which is that differences between categories tend to be accentuated. This process of accentuating dif-ferences between categories can bias social perception in different ways. For example, studies have shown that so-called '**illusory correlations**' can lead us to attribute more negative characteristics to smaller groups, and more positive characteristics to larger groups, even when there are objectively no differences in the proportion of positive and negative characteristics between the two groups (Hamilton & Gifford, 1976). In a clever series of studies, Sherman and colleagues (2009) demonstrated that simply learning about features or characteristics of groups sequentially leads to the formation of distinct group stereotypes. By extension, group boundaries can lead us to view outgroup mem-bers negatively, provided that we preferentially use positive characteristics to define our own ingroup prototype (as is usually the case). Thus, categorisation can lead to preju-dice, which is a term used to denote positive and negative stereotypes of groups (Dovidio, Glick, & Hewstone, 2010).

GUEST PERSONAL JOURNEY

Jeffrey Sherman

When I was deciding what to study and what to do with my life, I knew one thing for sure: I was absolutely not going into psychology. My father and older sister both have PhDs in social psychology. My father was a professor at Indiana University and my sister went into market research. My mother has a PhD in clinical psychology. I was determined to stay far away and establish my independence in a different field.

In college, I started as a political science major before switching to philosophy. That was going just fine until I took a social psychology class from Phil Tetlock, which ruined everything. I was immediately hooked. Social psychologists were studying many questions related to my interests in philosophy of the mind, with one key advantage – they had data! My philosophy courses were training me to think systematically and construct sound arguments, which was great. But, at the end of the day, those arguments were all you had. Social psychologists had data! Your theory could be brilliant and elegant, but without empirical support it would eventually be abandoned. The final arbiter wasn't how clever you were (though that always helps); it was the data, which I loved. It seems I was destined for the family business.

I was fortunate to have great mentoring throughout my studies, first from Oliver John at the University of California (UC), Berkeley, and then from Dave Hamilton, Diane Mackie, and Stan Klein at UC Santa Barbara, where I received my PhD in 1994. Subsequently, I took a faculty position at Northwestern University for 10 years before finally making it back to my beloved California at UC Davis, where I try to pay it all forward in mentoring my own students.

The bottom-up versus top-down framework is useful to explain how the same stimulus can lead to different responses depending on people's motivations, processing capacity, and so forth. This is encapsulated in the Continuum Model (Fiske & Neuberg, 1990), which assumes that, by default, impressions of others are made quickly and relatively effortlessly in a top-down fashion using category-based knowledge. However, if there is poor fit between a target and a social category, and perceivers have the capacity and motivation to attend to a social target, then knowledge can be supplemented, or indeed overridden, with individuating information in a more effortful bottom-up process. This transition from categorisation to individuation is also known as decategorisation. Not surprisingly, decategorisation reduces stereotype-based biases (Crisp, Hewstone, Rubin, 2001).

Accessibility

There are a number of factors that determine how we categorise others. After all,
our social world is complex and people
belong to more than one social category.
We have already touched on the similarity to a prototype as one factor. Another

> **Key concept – Accessibility:** The
> ease with which mental contents can be
> brought to mind and influence cognitive
> processes.

important factor is **accessibility**, which describes the amount of stimulation needed for
prior knowledge to shift from a latent state – available in the mind but currently inactive – to
an active one involved in current thought and action. Advertisement is, in essence, the business of increasing the accessibility of products and anything advertisers want us to associate
with those products. We will come back to this in a later section.

In 1991, Sedikides and Skowronski published an article with the title 'The law of cognitive structure activation', which centred on the accessibility principle. The title is
provocative because psychologists normally emphasise the tentative nature of our principles and theories. Sedikides and Skowronski's 'law' stipulates that 'when a stimulus is
ambiguous enough to be encodable as an instance of multiple cognitive structures, the
stimulus will be most likely encoded as an instance of that cognitive structure that is the
most activated in memory and is the most semantically similar to the stimulus' (p. 170).
In other words, the effects of accessible knowledge on construal are most pronounced
when there is a high overlap between what is accessible and the stimulus, when the stimulus is ambiguous, and when broad, categorical knowledge is activated.

Accessibility is determined by the
recency and frequency of use, and by
people's goals, needs, and expectations.
Priming can be used as a tool to
increase the accessibility of prior knowl-

> **Key concept – Priming:** Priming occurs
> when exposure to a stimulus influences a
> person's response to a related stimulus.

edge. Classic studies on priming exposed participants to traits that implied certain
characteristics (e.g., reckless versus adventurous), typically using some kind of disguise or
cover story. Participants then read an allegedly unrelated, ambiguous description of a person
whose behaviour could be interpreted in different ways (e.g., Higgins, Rholes, & Jones, 1977).
The studies found that participants' impressions were biased in line with the traits that had
been primed and thus made accessible.

There are a whole range of priming techniques, and we will come across some of them in
this chapter. Techniques include (a) semantic priming, which usually involves asking participants to read or search for semantic contents (words), (b) episodic priming, which often
involves asking participants to recall past events, (c) procedural priming, which involves exposing
participants to rules or procedures, and (d) evaluative priming, which involves exposing
participants to positive or negative cues. Researchers have developed techniques to administer
primes (e.g., words or images) above and below the threshold of conscious awareness.
Priming effects have come under scrutiny recently, and questions have been raised regarding
whether priming 'works'. We will look into this more, but for now suffice to say that

Sedikides and Skowronski's 'law' remains a fundamental principle of social cognition. You don't need to take my word for it, though. Check out Exercise 5.2 to see for yourself if priming works!

EXERCISE 5.2

What Led Zeppelin Can Teach us About Accessibility and Priming

You are probably familiar with the rock band Led Zeppelin. Either way, chances are you have heard one of their most famous songs, 'Stairway to Heaven'. As it turns out, the song provides a beautiful illustration of priming effects if you listen to the song backwards (!). Go to an internet search engine and enter 'Led Zeppelin – Stairway to Heaven backwards TED'. Hold on! Be *extra* careful to pick the TED talk by *Michael Shermer*. Don't watch any other video just yet. This would spoil the exercise and you only have one shot at doing it. At the time of writing, there is a short version (2:25 minutes) posted on YouTube (www.youtube.com/watch?v=wYG2oZXSvdE). OK – you can go now and come back.

How was it? Did it convince you that priming works? Without the written lyrics, most people hear nothing or one word at most. However, with the written lyrics serving as prime and rendering the words temporarily accessible, the song played backwards is easy to understand. It's also a nice illustration of chronic accessibility if you read more about the full story behind Led Zeppelin and other rock music being played backwards. You can find out online about who 'discovered' those 'hidden messages', and then reflect on why they may have heard those words without seeing the written lyrics.

5.4.3 Naïve Scientists versus Cognitive Misers

Over the years, social cognition researchers adopted different perspectives to understand how people approach the task of social information processing (Fiske & Taylor, 2017). Those perspectives centre on the relative contributions of two modes of processing: controlled processes that are slow and resource-intensive on the one hand, and automatic processes that are fast and consume fewer cognitive resources on the other. We have already encountered the two modes earlier in our discussion of the Continuum Model (Fiske & Neuberg, 1990).

Research in the 1970s emphasised controlled processes and assumed that people would deliberately weigh up information to form a judgement, akin to a *naïve scientist* (Fiske & Taylor, 2017). This perspective formed the basis for attribution theories, which are concerned with how people explain the causes of behaviours and events. For example, Kelley's (1967) covariation model assumes that people carefully consider different inputs to decide whether an action or event should be attributed to a person (dispositional attribution) or the environment (situational attribution). For instance, to explain why a football team lost, one might consider the team's previous performance (consistency information), how other teams fared against the same opponent (consensus information), and situational factors that may have impacted performance

> **Key concept – Heuristics:** Mental shortcuts or rules of thumb that individuals use to simplify decision-making and problem-solving. They allow for quick judgements and decisions based on limited information.

such as the team's composition on the day (distinctiveness information). The perspective of people as more or less rational decision-makers still permeates the field of mainstream economics to this date.

The 1980s saw the emergence of a different perspective. Social cognition researchers in this era viewed people as *cognitive misers* who use **heuristics** and cognitive shortcuts to make rapid judgements (Taylor, 1981). The cognitive misers perspective recognises that processing resources are often constrained – we do not have unlimited time or cognitive resources to make sense of the social world. Heuristics and cognitive shortcuts are not perfect and can easily introduce biases. Nevertheless, they are efficient and allow us to make quick judgements and take actions that are 'good enough', especially when considering the sheer complexity of the task at hand.

We have already touched on social categories and stereotypes as heuristics that simplify information processing. There are many other heuristics and biases that social cognition researchers have studied. Other well-known heuristics include the availability heuristic, which entails using the ease of retrieving exemplars as a shortcut to judge the frequency or prevalence of an event (Tversky & Kahneman, 1973), or the anchoring heuristic, which describes the tendency for consecutive judgements to be biased towards a starting value (Wyer, 1976). Some of these heuristics are so pervasive that they also occur when people engage in careful deliberations.

Earlier work in the 1970s and early 1980s gave way to **dual-process models**, which assume that people can switch between an automatic processing mode (sometimes referred to as *System 1*) and a controlled processing mode (sometimes referred to as *System 2*) (for reviews, see Chaiken & Trope, 1999). The controlled mode (preferred by naïve scientists) is slow, conscious,

> **Key concept – Dual-process models:** Two systems or modes that determine how individuals process and respond to information: System 1, which is fast and intuitive, relies on automatic responses, and System 2, which is slower and analytical, requires conscious effort.

and supports flexible thinking and deliberation, giving rise to planning and problem solving. In contrast, the automatic mode (preferred by cognitive misers) is fast, unconscious, and supports efficient processing via learned associations, giving rise to instincts and intuitions. Fiske and Taylor used the term 'motivated tactician' to describe the perspective of the social thinker who can switch flexibly between different processing modes (see Fisk & Taylor, 2017).

Research in the tradition of the dual-process models focused on the conditions that lead people to favour one mode over the other, together with the consequences for social judgements and actions. In short, the controlled mode is favoured when people have time and mental capacity, when the issue at hand is deemed relevant or important, and when sufficient information is available to support deliberations. In contrast, the automatic mode is favoured when people are pressed for time, have limited capacity, when the issue at hand is not deemed relevant or important, or when there are gaps in the information at hand. For example, consistent with dual-process models, reduced executive control, which is often seen in elderly people (due to cognitive decline), makes it more likely for the elderly to stereotype others (von Hippel, Silver, & Lynch, 2000). Reduced processing capacity during mismatching circadian cycles (i.e., in the morning for 'night people' and in the evening for 'morning people') also facilitates the automatic application of stereotypes (Bodenhausen, 1990).

Dual-process models can be found in many areas of social psychology, including impression formation, attribution, and attitudes and attitude change. For example, as discussed in Chapter 6, researchers interested in persuasion have studied factors that promote attitude change in automatic and controlled modes. Dual-process models also gained traction in domains that were for a long time the preserve of rational thought. For example, Haidt (2001) put forward a social intuitionist model of moral judgements. He and others argued that decisions about morality are often done using intuitions that draw on emotions and automatic processes. Meanwhile, Kahnemann and Tversky applied dual-process models to probability judgements. They made the case that decisions involving uncertainty and risks draw on heuristics, whereby people substitute complex problems with a simpler one using intuitions (e.g., Kahneman, 2003). Kahneman and Tversky's participants were often highly educated and proficient in mathematics, which made their findings even more noteworthy.

> **Key concept – Automaticity:** Mental processes that operate quickly, efficiently, and with minimal conscious awareness or intentional control.

After the turn of the century, the focus of the field shifted again towards exploring the pervasiveness of **automaticity** in everyday life. This work gave rise to a perspective of people as 'activated actors' (Fiske & Taylor, 2017). The findings emerging from this work were puzzling because automaticity was found to be extremely pervasive. It led to the allied question of how higher-order (conscious) processes intersect with automatic processes to facilitate adaptive actions. We will return to this question, but let's first turn our attention to automatic processes.

5.4.4 Automaticity

How do we know whether a process is automatic? What distinguishes automatic from controlled processes? Answering this question is often not that easy because automaticity comes in many shades of grey. This prompted Bargh (1994) to put forward what he called the 'four horsemen of automaticity': four conditions that need to be satisfied for a process to be fully automatic. We will discuss each of the conditions because they provide windows into the inner workings of automaticity.

Defining Features of Automaticity

Awareness

Many forms of information acquisition are unconscious. This means we are not necessarily aware of the factors that feed into our judgements and actions. In a seminal paper, Nisbett and Wilson (1977) reviewed examples of this phenomenon, including shoppers who were unaware that they were being swayed by the placing of products in a supermarket, and recruiters who were unaware that their selection of candidates was influenced by whether a job candidate had spilled a coffee. Nisbett and Wilson drew largely on anecdotal evidence, but subsequent empirical studies support their conclusions. For example, there is good evidence that atmospheric variables, such as music or smell, influence consumer behaviour (Turley & Milliman, 2000).

Figure 5.4 Stores are carefully crafted to create enticing atmospheres
Source: © Clark Street Mercantile/Unsplash

Another powerful illustration of how we are not necessarily aware of the factors that feed into our judgements derives from work on **automatic trait inferences**, which looks at

> **Key concept – Automatic trait inferences:** The spontaneous and rapid judgements individuals make about someone's traits based on minimal information or brief encounters.

how people form impressions of people based on facial cues. In one study, impressions formed within as little as one second of seeing a face predicted the results of US congressional elections (Todorov, Mandisodza, Goren, & Hall, 2005). This effect is not down to know-ing the face of the successful candidates: even pre-school children playing a game that involves choosing a 'captain' to 'sail from Troy to Ithaca' tend to pick past winners of local elections (people who aren't famous and the children hadn't seen before) from pictures of election candidates (the children were given a bit more time to make a pick) (Antonakis & Dalgas, 2009). Most people are probably unaware of just how much their voting and other decisions can be swayed by superficial cues such as a person's facial appearance.

We can (hopefully) remember who we voted for, but in other circumstances we may be unaware of the consequences of automatic processes. For example, we may not realise that we value things simply because they are familiar to us (Zajonc, 1968), or that we are more likely to believe that 'The first animated film was shot in England' because a week ago we read that the 'The first animated film was shot in France' (Garcia-Marques, Silva, Reber, & Unkelbach, 2015). Often, we don't even realise we are making decisions in the first place. Consider how many micro-decisions it takes to get up and leave the house. Repeated decisions evolve into habits (Aarts & Dijksterhuis, 2000), so our (limited) mental energy can be devoted to other matters while brushing our teeth, putting our clothes on, switching the kettle on, and so forth.

GUEST PERSONAL JOURNEY

Teresa Garcia-Marques

Source: © Teresa Garcia-Marques

With a psychology degree from Lisbon University, I initiated my career in family therapy, with a systemic approach, focusing on drug addiction. Five years later, at the University of California Santa Barbara, I attended courses by David Hamilton, Diane Mackie, Chick McClintock, David Messick, G. Ashby, J. Levin, and others, marking a turning point in my life. I became deeply inspired by research in social cognition. The enthusiasm of fellow students, such as Steve Stroesser, Denise Driscol, Jeff Sherman, and Arlene Asuncion, not to mention my husband Leonel, played a crucial role in shaping my new path.

Following a Master's in probability and statistics, I embarked on my PhD journey with Diane Mackie, this time at Lisbon University. Intrigued by dualistic approaches, I delved into the differential activation of processes, building on Mackie's research on mood as a moderator. I explored cognitive regulation through familiarity, a positive feeling which could be confounded with mood.

While maintaining research collaborations with Diane and her students, I focused on a teaching career at Ispa-Instituto Universitário, the pioneer institution for psychology education in Portugal. My institutional commitment aimed at fostering the development of social cognition in Portugal, with a special emphasis on nurturing new researchers. The most inspiring aspect was the opportunity to interact with other key figures in social cognition, both through participation in Duke conferences and engagement in European Social Cognition Network gatherings. It's fascinating to have witnessed the evolution of prominent figures in the field since their early years as PhD students.

Intention

Intention describes the level of control over the instigation of a process. An intentional action is one that reflects someone's will. Wegner and Wheatley (1999) wondered whether our experiences of wilful actions are, in fact, only illusions created by conscious thoughts that coincide with an action. That's a tough research question! It required a clever study set up to control participants' thoughts and actions experimentally and independently from one another. Wegner and Wheatley did this in an ingenious way using a computer mouse repurposed as a Ouija board. Two players sat on opposite sides of a table placing their hands on a board in the middle (the repurposed computer mouse). By moving the board, the two players moved a cursor on a computer screen that showed various objects from a children's book (e.g., dinosaur, swan, car). Both players wore headphones, and participants were instructed to move the board with the other player until they started to hear music, which served as a cue to stop the cursor. After stopping the cursor, participants rated how much they intended to stop the cursor at the selected object (bearing in mind they did this together with the other player). Participants were told the other player was a participant. However, in reality participants played with a confederate, who was assisting the study researchers. Instead of hearing music, the confederate heard instructions when and where to stop the cursor. This was a way to influence or 'manipulate' how much control the 'real' participants had over the process of stopping the cursor. To make it less obvious, the confederate only took full control in a few critical trials, but otherwise played along as if the mouse was a real Ouija board. Participants not only heard the music over the headphones, but also words that sometimes matched the objects on the screen. The words appeared at different intervals before and after the forced stop, so Wegner and Wheatley were able to 'manipulate' whether participants' thoughts coincided with the stopping action.

Wegner and Wheatley discovered that participants rated their intentions to stop high (>50%) when the confederate forced a stop a short time (5 seconds or 1 second) after participants were reminded of the object via the headphones. When participants were reminded a longer time (30 seconds) before or after (1 second) the forced stop, they rated their intentions to stop as low (<50%). This led to the conclusion that (relevant) thoughts that cross people's minds shortly before an action can be misinterpreted as intentions to cause an action.

Provided that automatic processes can trigger *both* thoughts and actions, Wegner and Wheatley's study suggests that we may have less control over our actions than we perhaps would like to think. And there is good evidence that this is indeed the case: neurological correlates of decisions arise in the human brain as much as 10 seconds before we become aware of the decision (Soon, Braas, Heinze, & Haynes, 2008).

Efficiency

Efficiency describes the extent to which a process requires attentional resources. Controlled processes draw on our working memory, which is limited. This principle gave rise to Unconscious Thought Theory (UTT), which argues that unconscious thought can integrate more information into a coherent representation than conscious thought (Dijksterhuis & Nordgren, 2006). The theory is based on findings from studies in which participants were asked to choose between different options for things, such as four cars or four apartments, etc. (Dijksterhuis, 2004). Each option had different positive and negative attributes. The researchers wanted to see whether participants were able to identify the objectively best options, weighing up all pros and cons. Of note, participants had to make a choice straight after reading about all the attributes (immediate decision condition), after having had some time to think it through (conscious thought condition), or after completing an unrelated attention-consuming task (unconscious thought condition). Dijksterhuis reasoned that the unrelated task would interfere with conscious thoughts related to the earlier choice task, but not with unconscious thoughts that can still happen in the background, so to speak. Indeed, the results showed that participants in the unconscious thought condition performed best across a series of studies with different choice tasks. This led Dijksterhuis and Nordgren (2006) to argue that complex decisions are better made unconsciously.

UTT is intriguing because it suggests that we are better off doing something else than consciously dwelling over difficult decisions. However, the theory was criticised for being broad-brush. More recent studies also failed to replicate some findings. Nevertheless, it remains the case that automatic processes are very efficient when tasks can be resolved through learned associations.

Control

The control element of automaticity refers to the ability to counteract the impact of a stimulus. Automatic processes are difficult to control. I sometimes use the rubber hand illusion with students in class to illustrate this basic principle (Botvinick & Cohen, 1998). Watching a rubber hand being stroked while one's own (unseen) hand is synchronously stroked changes the sensed position of one's hand. This leads to the strong sense that the rubber hand is part of one's body. This sensory integration between vision and touch is automatic and hard to control. People consciously 'know' that the rubber hand is not theirs, but their senses tell them otherwise. It's a weird, jaw-dropping experience.

The notion that automatic processes are difficult to control has given rise to many implicit tests. A famous example is the Implicit Association Test (IAT) (Greenwald et al., 1998). The test uses reaction times to measure whether mental models or 'representations' of two categories (e.g., Black versus White people) have different positive and negative connotations. Over the years, researchers created many different versions of the IAT to measure automatic associations. Another family of tests, known as sequential priming tasks, also use reaction times to gauge semantic (words) or evaluative (good/bad) associations between concepts. These tests exploit the fact that it is difficult for people to control instant responses that can be captured with reaction times.

Current Perspectives

As Oscar Wilde put it, 'The truth is rarely pure and never simple'. Automatic processes don't just give rise to conscious thought – the reverse also holds: conscious thought can modify automatic associations. For example, being reminded of counterstereotypic (Blair, Ma, & Lenton, 2001) or admirable exemplars of a social group (Dasgupta & Greenwald, 2001) reduces implicit prejudice, much in the same way that thinking about Black criminals increases implicit racial prejudice (Correll, Park, Judd, & Wittenbrink, 2007). Rehearsal can also alter implicit associations (e.g., Kawakami, Dovidio, & van Kamp, 2005).

The notion that conscious thoughts influence and guide automatic processes can be traced back to William James (1899), who noted that 'Our acts of voluntary attention, brief and fitful as they are, are nevertheless critical, determining us, as they do, to higher or lower destinies' (p. 189). Bos, Dijksterhuis, and van Baaren (2008) expanded on James's idea of conscious thoughts that emerge at critical junctures. They surmised that conscious thoughts serve as an instigator, setting on course automatic processes that do the rest of the work until goals are achieved or there is a need for conscious thoughts to intervene again.

Bos and colleagues' ideas are consistent with research on implementation intentions (see also Chapter 11). Implementation intentions are explicit if–then plans that specify how people will perform an action (i.e., goal-directed behaviour) when encountering a specific situation in the future. This process is similar to the way habits operate and can be triggered by situations in an automatic fashion. One key difference is that the behaviour in question has not been repeated, as is the case for habits. In one study, Gollwitzer and Brandstätter (1997) asked students to complete a report over the Christmas holidays. Half of the participants were also instructed to form implementation intentions by specifying a time and place where they were going to work on the report, as well as visualising the situation. The other half of the participants were assigned to a control group and did not form implementation intentions. The results showed that the group of participants who had formed implementation intentions were twice as likely to complete the report than participants assigned to a control group (71% versus 32%). A large body of evidence supports the effectiveness of implementation intentions in facilitating future goal attainment. It's a nice example of the interplay between automatic and controlled processes.

Priming Automatic Behaviour

The behavioural consequences of priming have received considerable attention. Classic studies in this tradition found that presenting participants with primes (usually words) changed participants' subsequent behaviour, often measured in disguise to conceal the relationship between the prime and the behaviour. For example, well-known studies found that priming the concept of 'elderly' reduced participants' walking speed (Bargh, Chen, & Burrows, 1996), or priming the concept of 'hooligans' (versus 'professors') reduced participants' performance on a general knowledge test (Dijksterhuis & Van Knippenberg, 1998). However, researchers identified problems with the findings and several failed replications raised concerns about the robustness of the effects. This cast a shadow over the pervasiveness of automaticity in everyday behaviour.

> **Key concept – Subliminal and supraliminal:** Subliminal refers to stimuli operating below the threshold of conscious awareness, and supraliminal pertains to stimuli operating above the awareness threshold.

More recent concerted efforts to produce behavioural priming effects were successful though. In a series of studies, Payne, Brown-Iannuzzi, and Loersch (2016) demonstrated that priming impacts the decision to bet or pass in a gambling game when the decision is uncertain. These effects emerged for primes that were presented above (**supraliminal**) and below (**subliminal**) the threshold of conscious awareness, suggesting that priming can impact behaviour in an automatic fashion. A similar conclusion derived from a recent meta-analysis of the literature, which further suggested that behavioural priming is more robust when the prime–behaviour association is linked to people's values or goals (Weingarten, Chen, McAdams, Yi, Hepler, & Albarracín, 2016). This echoes Eitam and Higgins (2010), who argued that mental representations need to have motivational relevance to influence thoughts and actions.

In sum, the interplay between automatic and controlled processes is dynamic and fluid. Automatic processes are very prevalent but intertwined with conscious thoughts to engender adaptive action. In the next section, we build on this and look at the inner workings of goals and self-regulation.

5.5 PART 2: ADVANCES

We have covered lots of ground in the 'foundations' section. Armed with all that knowledge, you are now ready to deep-dive into some selected topics that illustrate nicely the sheer breadth of the field of social cognition.

5.5.1 Goals and Self-Regulation

Given the pervasiveness of automaticity in everyday life, how do we set and pursue goals and achieve long-term ambitions? **Goals** are desired states that one wishes to attain, and goal pursuit describes the process of reducing the discrepancy between a current state and the desired state. According to Goal Systems Theory (Kruglanski et al., 2002), people have mental representations of desired states and means to achieve those states, which are stored in the brain's neural

> **Key concept – Goals:** The mental representations of desired outcomes or objectives that one aims to achieve.

networks. Goals are linked to other goals in this neural structure, with facilitatory links to subgoals, and inhibitory links to competing goals. From this perspective, goals can be activated through priming. For example, an external cue (e.g., the big, eye-catching sign of a fast-food chain) or an internal cue (e.g., a rumbling empty stomach) can activate a goal-directed action that can be fully automatic (e.g., looking at the fast-food restaurant) or a mix between automatic and controlled processes (e.g., crossing the road and buying a burger).

Goals also influence the type of information that is activated when we encounter a stimulus. For example, goals can both suppress and facilitate the automatic activation of stereotypes (Kunda & Spencer, 2003). Furthermore, while goals share facilitatory links with associated means to achieve said goals, they share inhibitory links with other, competing goals (see Key study 5.2: Goal Shielding). In other words, goals are mentally represented and connected to other mental contents in ways that are conducive to successful goal pursuit.

KEY STUDY 5.2

Goal Shielding

Shah, Friedman, and Kruglanski (2002) reasoned that goals are mentally represented in our cognitive system. Their theory of goal shielding further posits that mental representations of goals are connected via inhibitory pathways, so the activation of a focal goal (i.e., a goal in your focus) lowers the activation of alternative goals that may get in the way of completing the focal goal. In essence, Shah and colleagues proposed that our cognitive systems are designed to support effective self-regulation, and the corresponding processes can operate in an automatic fashion through associative networks.

Shah and colleagues performed a series of studies to test their theory. In one of the studies, participants indicated, using one word, three activities they sought to pursue in the upcoming week, which served as their focal goals. Participants also indicated activities they did not intend on pursuing, which served as controls. Participants then performed a reaction time task. On each trial, a prime word appeared on the computer screen for 50 milliseconds, followed by a letter string to ensure that participants were not consciously aware of the prime words. The letter string was replaced with a target word that remained on the screen and participants had to decide as quickly as possible whether the word represented one of the activities they wanted to pursue.

The results showed that presenting a goal slowed participants' reaction time for alternative goals, consistent with the idea of automatic goal shielding (Figure 5.5). Shah

(Continued)

and colleagues also found evidence (not illustrated) that the inhibition of alternative goals is stronger the more people are committed to a focal goal. This work made an important contribution to our understanding of how goals interlink with our cognitive system in a way that facilitates effective goal pursuit.

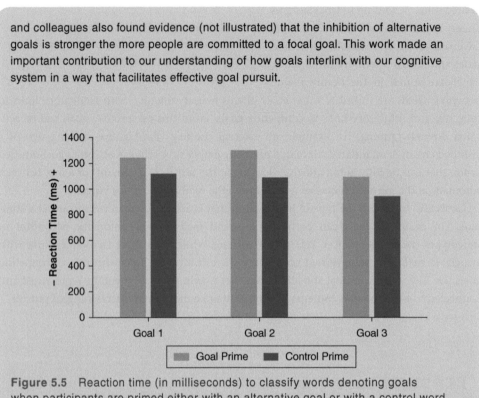

Figure 5.5 Reaction time (in milliseconds) to classify words denoting goals when participants are primed either with an alternative goal or with a control word

Source: Shah et al. (2002, Study 2)

Goals also have an affective-motivational component that signals that a state is desired and worth pursuing. Put differently, there is a difference between 'knowing' and 'wanting'. Custers and Aarts (2005) wanted to get to the bottom of how behavioural states, positive affect, and the motivation to pursue a goal are linked. Using sequential priming tasks, they showed that creating associations between positive affect and activities (e.g., going for a walk, moving house) increases 'wanting' and the effort invested to pursue a behaviour. These and related studies show that automatic processes are adaptable and can help to prepare and motivate behaviour towards desirable end states.

We have yet to fully uncover the many ways in which goals intersect with our cognitive systems. Interestingly, some of this work can be traced back to the 'new look' perspective of the 1950s, when researchers studied how goals may affect the perception of physical properties such as the sizes of coins. This perspective had a more recent revival – the 'new new look' if you will – with studies showing that perceptions of size and distance can change in a way that makes it easier to attain one's goals. For example, a water bottle may appear physically closer to people who are thirsty (Balcetis & Dunning, 2010). There has been a debate whether these effects can be attributed to genuine differences in lower-level perception. Regardless, work in the tradition of the 'new look' perspective attests to the dynamic interplay between goals and automatic processes.

So far we have focused on how automatic processes can be intertwined with motivation to facilitate goal attainment. However, goals can also trigger automatic processes that are counterproductive. Examples of this are automatic rebound effects following attempts to suppress thoughts. In a classic study of this phenomenon, Wegner, Schneider, Carter, and White (1987) found that setting oneself the goal not to think of a white bear actually made thoughts of white bears more rather than less likely. Rumination is another example of goals setting in motion automatic processes that do not facilitate moving from the current state to a desired end state.

We often must exert self-control to override or inhibit behavioural tendencies to refrain from acting on our impulses. Those impulses are themselves linked to goals; they have a strong incentive value and promise immediate gratification. This led Hofman, Friese, and Strack (2009) to propose a dual-systems model of **self-regulation**. The model has a

> **Key concept – Self-regulation:** The ways people control and manage thoughts, emotions, and behaviours to pursue less immediate objectives.

controlled, reflective route that is linked to self-regulation success, and an automatic, impulsive route linked to self-regulation failure. Executive control plays a critical role in determining the outcome of this yin and yang. With executive functions comes the ability to pursue goals in the face of distraction and engage in perspective taking. However, when executive functions are impaired, behaviour becomes more impulsive and we are more likely to give into temptations.

Figure 5.6 Sweets and other highly processed foods often have a strong incentive value. It's not easy to maintain a healthy diet in such an environment

Source: Greta Punch/Unsplash

However, painting the automatic system as the villain and the controlled system as the hero when it comes to self-regulation would be oversimplistic. According to justification-based accounts of self-regulation, reflective systems are also implicated in self-regulation failure (De Witt Huberts, Evers, & De Ridder 2014). Faced with a self-control dilemma, people often make excuses for discrepant behaviour. Sometimes excuses are quite elaborate and necessitate a fair bit of brainpower (OK, I eat the chocolate now, but I will ring my friend later to arrange for us to go to the gym tomorrow). By the same token, reflective processes can also be employed strategically to alter the environment to avoid self-control dilemmas altogether (Duckworth, Gendler, & Gross, 2016).

KEY THINKER

Ziva Kunda

Ziva Kunda gained a PhD from the University of Michigan and went on to hold positions at the Universities of Princeton and Waterloo (Canada). Ziva is well known for her work on 'hot cognition' – how motivation intersects with cognitive processes. For example, she asked the question: how and when are stereotypes activated and relied on to colour our judgements and actions, depending on the different goals that people have? Ziva authored a highly influential article titled 'The case for motivated reasoning', which has been cited more than 10,000 times (Kunda, 1990). In this article, she describes how motivation biases reasoning processes in a way that allows people to arrive at their desired conclusions. Ziva also wrote a fantastic textbook on social cognition filled with anecdotes (Kunda, 1999). The book was the core reading for an elective course on social psychology I took as an undergraduate student, which was taught by Sabine Sczesny. Sadly, Ziva passed away in 2004, well before her time.

5.5.2 Embodiment

In earlier sections of this chapter, I spoke about construals and mental representations as key aspects of social cognition research. The basic assumption is that thoughts and actions are guided by mental representations – a process that often operates outside our conscious awareness. This leads to the allied question: what is the nature of those representations? How do we store information in the brain? As we will see, answering these questions has implications for understanding the social perceiver.

Traditional perspectives on mental representations assume that cognitive operations are performed using abstract mental contents that have little or no relation to their original sensory modalities. From this perspective, cognition is often considered to be language-based, with the mind operating like a computer. Critics of this perspective question the emphasis on language, and they argue that it is unclear how cognition interfaces with sensory systems (the 'grounding problem'). The way our brains are structured also doesn't support the idea that mental representations are somehow separated from our sensory systems.

Unlike traditional perspectives, the **embodied cognition** perspective assumes that cognition is intertwined with perceptual states. From this perspective, mental representations are concrete (rather than abstract) and stored in different brain systems or modalities that are specialised for per-

> **Key concept – Embodied cognition:** The notion that cognitive processes are influenced by sensory and motor lexperiences, emphasising the role of the body in shaping how we think and process information.

ception and motor control. The same states used in online processing are also assumed to be used – at least partially – in offline processing (Barsalou, 1999). Say, for example, you encountered a menacing grizzly bear on a trail hike. If you live to tell the tale, then, from an embodiment perspective, thinking about your encounter would partially re-activate the same brain systems as those that fired up when the bear crossed your path, including systems that process sounds, smells, and your physical reactions. Thus, from an embodiment perspective, perception and action are important building blocks of memory and cognition. Perception here is broadly defined and includes both interoception capturing what's going on inside your body and exteroception capturing what's going on in the outside world.

Embodiment has a long tradition in social cognition research, dating back to early research on attitudes; for example, studies showing that head-nodding and head-shaking change evaluations and agreement to persuasive messages (e.g., Wells & Petty, 1980). Similarly, studies on the facial feedback hypothesis showed that participants rated cartoons less funny when they were instructed to hold pens in their mouths in a way that interfered with smiling muscles (Strack, Martin, & Stepper, 1988). Many studies also established a link between positive evaluations and approach movements, and negative evaluations and avoidance movements. For example, Cacioppo, Priester, and Berntson (1993) demonstrated that novel, neutral stimuli were evaluated more positively when they were encountered during approach, as compared to avoidance, movements. Meanwhile, Chen and Bargh (1999) showed that positive stimuli elicit approach movements, while negative stimuli elicit avoidance movements. These and other studies suggest that mental representations of what we like or dislike, and of what we approve or disapprove, are 'grounded' in motor systems.

Niedenthal, Winkielman, Mondillon, and Vermeulen (2009) extended these principles to emotional concepts. Their research looked at whether processing emotional contents elicits congruent motor responses. Participants in their studies read words associated with joy, disgust, or anger on a computer screen while activity in facial muscles was recorded using electromyography (EMG). The results showed that participants' judgements of whether objects evoked emotions were accompanied by activation in emotion-congruent facial muscles. For example, when participants rated emotion concepts linked to joy, muscles in the cheek and around the eyes were subtly activated. This suggests that mental representation of emotion concepts invoke sensory-motor states that accompany the actual experiences of emotions.

You have probably heard of Botox injections. Botox is a brand of botulinum toxin, which is a super-potent poison that paralyses muscles. If people undergo Botox treatment for frown lines, does this mean their mental representations of concepts that invoke frowning is impaired? This is exactly what Havas, Glenberg, Gutowski, Lucarelli, and Davidson (2010) found. In their study, participants who underwent Botox treatment were slower than a group of control participants to read sentences with contents that normally require the frowning muscle to express congruent emotions (anger, sadness). However, Botox treatment did not interfere with reading speeds for contents that require other facial muscles to express congruent emotions (happiness).

Head movements and facial expressions are not the only types of movement that facilitate mental representations of the outside world. Studies on gestures show a correspondence between actions implied in sentences and participants' own motor responses. For example, 'closing the drawer' is spontaneously accompanied by movements away from the body, and 'opening the drawer' with movement towards the body (Glenberg & Kaschak, 2002). Talking about hand gestures, studies have also shown that an extended middle finger increases perceptions of hostility (Chandler & Schwarz, 2009), and making a fist can increase a desire for revenge in some people (Strelan, Weick, & Vasiljevic, 2014).

Earlier I wrote about the connection between perception and action, quoting a phrase by William James that thinking is for doing. It's easy to see how the involvement of sensorimotor systems in memory and cognition can be useful to prepare us for action. From an embodiment perspective, seeing a door with a push plate activates areas in the brain that are also involved in pushing the door open. Ellis and Tucker (2000) demonstrated the existence of such 'object affordances' in a controlled experiment. They created an ingenious device that captured reaction times by either making a pinching movement with the thumb and index finger or a grabbing movement with the entire hand. The researchers then showed participants real, everyday objects and, on encountering an auditory prompt, participants had to make compatible or incompatible responses as fast as possible using their novel device. A 'compatible' response would be a pinching movement when seeing a 'coin' or a grabbing movement when seeing a 'frying pan'. An incompatible response would be a pinching movement when seeing a 'dust pan' or a grabbing movement when seeing a 'safety pin'. The results showed that response times were faster for compatible responses than for incompatible responses, pointing to the presence of motor simulations that facilitate the interaction with the objects.

Moving beyond dust pans and safety pins, there is also evidence that similar principles hold for perceptions of other people. For example, mirror neurons are brain cells that fire up when we perform an action and when we witness someone else perform the same action. Interestingly, we are more inclined to mirror people we affiliate with, but we tend to complement people who differ in power (Tiedens & Fragale, 2003; see also Weick, McCall, & Blascovich, 2017, described in Chapter 1). A complementary response would be displaying submissiveness if someone else is dominant or being dominant if someone else is submissive. This suggests that mental representations of others and their actions are embodied in a way that smooths social interactions.

Perhaps the most challenging task for social perceivers is to understand other people's inner experiences. Embodied cognition also facilitates that. For example, when we encounter someone who experiences disgust, happiness, or pain, neural structures are activated that also fire up when we have those experiences ourselves (Wicker, Keysers, Plailly, Royet, Gallese, & Rizzolatti, 2003). This not only helps us to understand other people's experiences and mental states, but also encourages us to respond in ways that are usually adaptive; for example, by avoiding things that are disgusting or by sympathising with others who are in pain.

Embodied perspectives are important to understand how metaphors operate and provide a tool for reasoning. Metaphors are very common; they often transcend cultural and language boundaries, and they are used frequently – up to six times per minute according to some estimates (Gibbs, 1994).

Metaphors convey the meaning of fairly intangible, abstract concepts by likening those concepts to something that can be directly perceived or experienced (e.g., a colour or a taste). Or as Salomon Asch, a pioneering social psychologist, put it very eloquently many years ago:

> When we describe the workings of emotion, ideas, or trends of character, we almost invariably use terms that also denote properties and processes observable in the world of nature. Terms such as warm, hard, straight refer to properties of things and of persons. We say that a man thinks straight; that he faces a hard decision; that his feelings have cooled. We call persons deep and shallow, bright and full, colorful and colorless, rigid and elastic. Indeed, for the description of persons we draw upon the entire range of sensory modalities … the language of social experience and action reveals the same characteristic. We are joined to people with ties and bonds; classes are high and low; groups exert pressure, maintain distance from other groups, and possess atmosphere. (Asch, 1958, pp. 86–87)

Consider the metaphor 'being stuck in a relationship': it is easy to understand, but the ideas conveyed aren't that simple. Metaphors can convey complex concepts by linking abstract target concepts to concrete source concepts. For example, the abstract target concept 'love' can be described with the concrete source concept of 'warmth' or 'closeness'; 'morality' can be linked to 'cleanliness' or 'dirt'; the 'past' lies 'behind' while the 'future' lies 'ahead', and so forth.

The fact that metaphors link abstract concepts and concrete source concepts is suggestive of an embodied process. However, we need more than linguistic linkages to show that metaphors are grounded in bodily experiences. Thankfully, there are many studies that have looked at mental representations of metaphors. Studies by Meier, Hauser, Robinson, Friesen, and Schjeldahl (2007) provide a nice example of this body of work. The researchers wanted to show that 'divinity' is represented in vertical space. In one of their studies, American participants saw words related to God (Almighty, Creator, Deity, and Lord) and the Devil (Antichrist, Demon, Lucifer, and Satan) either at the top or at the bottom of a computer screen. Participants had to press the Q key on the keyboard as fast as possible when words related to God, and the P key when words related to the Devil appeared on the screen. The results showed that participants were faster to identify God-related words at the top of the screen as compared to the bottom of the screen. Although in this particular study vertical positions did not impact reaction times for words related to the Devil, in subsequent studies the researchers did find evidence for vertical representations of the Devil (at the bottom).

Why are mental processes embodied? We have already touched on underlying brain structures that suggest mental representations are linked to sensory and motor systems. So, the embodiment of mental processes could be down to our evolutionary roots, reflecting the fact that we evolved from organisms whose neural architectures were geared towards perceptual and motor processes. However, it could also be linked to our development from infancy to adulthood, whereby earlier sensory and motor experiences provide the foundation for our understanding of more abstract and complex concepts. Evolutionary and developmental explanations aren't mutually exclusive, so it's tricky to get to the bottom of this question.

5.5.3 Supernatural Beliefs and Superstitions

Almost one in two Americans believe in ghosts, and nearly one in three Americans assert that they have witnessed a ghost (Spiegel, 2013). Americans are by no means alone in their ghostly convictions: more than one in two UK residents believe a house can be haunted by supernatural beings, or they are not sure (Dahlgreen, 2014). Across the United States, Canada, and Great Britain, 17% to 33% of people believe in astrology, and 15% to 29% believe that extra-terrestrial beings have visited earth (Lyons, 2005). Furthermore, 60% of British people and a staggering 85% of Hungarians believe in at least some conspiracy theories (Addley, 2018). We discussed earlier that one of the key guiding principles for social cognition researchers is that mental processes serve adaptive actions. In this section, we explore what underpins people's conviction in supernatural phenomena, and how this can be squared with the idea that mental processes are adaptive.

> **Key concept – Agency attribution:** The process of assigning causality or responsibility to an agent for a specific action or event. It involves perceptions of minds capable of intent and control.

If you hear an unusual sound at night, are you worried about an intruder? Thankfully, for most people, places of residence provide some protection from outside elements, but for a long time our ancestors did not have that privilege. For them, being on the lookout for patterns and being quick at discerning agency was beneficial in terms of detecting potential threats in their environments (e.g., intruders), outweighing the potential costs (e.g., getting up at night). From this perspective, beliefs in supernatural phenomena are a by-product of a cognitive system equipped with a 'hyperactive agency-detection device' (Barrett, 2000). This tendency to **attribute agency** can lead to the perception of intentional actions, even in situations where none exist.

Figure 5.7 An illustration of face pareidolia

Source: Ludovico Ceroseis/Unsplash

Pareidolia describes the human tendency to see images in random patterns (Figure 5.7). It's a common occurrence that can explain why one might see an image of aliens on Mars or the face of Jesus burnt into a tortilla. Often people see faces. Having a social brain that is attuned to the processing of social signals provides a proximate explanation for our readiness to detect faces and other social stimuli in meaningless noise. Natural selection favouring false-positive (detecting something meaningful when in reality there is just noise) over false-negative (the failure to detect something meaningful in noise) provides a compatible, more distal explanation.

Whitson and Galinsky (2008) manipulated participants' sense of control by giving them random performance feedback or asking them to recall a past situation in which they lacked control. The researchers found that inducing a low sense of control prompted participants to see illusory patterns in noisy images and in stock market data, form conspiracies, and develop superstitions. These and similar findings are consistent with the notion that perceiving illusory patterns can give people a sense of predictability and control over their environments.

People are motivated to find explanations for events or actions that are surprising or are causing uncertainty. Causal explanations that invoke minds and intentions are often preferred to explanations that assume actions or events are random or unintended. This basic principle extends to non-humans – we might assume that our electronic devices have a mind of their own or that worldly events were caused by all-powerful agents or God(s) (Waytz, Gray, Epley, & Wegner, 2010). This tendency to perceive agency is more pronounced when things go wrong – a gadget is not working or we witness human suffering.

Myths and folktales can also spread through cultural transmission, with individuals learning and adopting these beliefs from their social and cultural environment. Popular stories invoking spirits and other supernatural concepts often have 'minimally counterintuitive narratives' that mostly draw on intuitive concepts with only some counterintuitive elements (Norenzayan, Atran, Faulkner, & Schaller, 2006). The addition of some surprising elements creates a memory advantage that makes those stories more contagious. Many myths and urban legends also play on people's fears and disgust (touching toads, anyone?) while being considered plausible or carrying moral lessons, which makes them worth transmitting.

Tiger Woods is not only famous for his golf prowess, but also for wearing red shirts on finals. It may have started because golf tournaments were played on Sunday and Wood's mum is from Thailand where red is worn on Sundays, and perhaps it was a coincidence that Woods went to Stanford, where players also don red colours. Regardless of the origin, given Wood's stratospheric rise, one could be excused for drawing a connection between the red shirt and Wood's phenomenal success on the green. This would be an example of a superstitious belief arising from illusory correlations. Superstitions can be reinforced through **self-fulfilling prophecies**, whereby people act in ways that confirm their expectations (e.g., Damisch, Stoberock, & Mussweiler, 2010). The sight of Tiger Woods on a green in his red shirt must have been an intimidating sight for some of his opponents, and jittered nerves are not exactly conducive to the highest level of performance in a sport such as golf.

> **Key concept – Self-fulfilling prophecy:** When a belief or expectation influences a person's behaviour in a way that makes the belief come true.

Superstitious beliefs can also arise through motivated reasoning – not wearing his red shirt may have caused Woods some unease, so sticking to red seems perfectly reasonable for peace of mind! Intuitions can also very easily lead to illusions of causality. If X precedes Y, it's intuitive to conclude that X caused Y (Matute, Blanco, Yarritu, Díaz-Lago, Vadillo, & Barberia, 2015). As a child taking the school bus, it took me more years than I'm willing to admit to realise that pressing the button on the bus didn't actually open the door when the bus became stationary – it merely notified the driver that someone wanted to get out!

> **Key concept – Confirmation bias:** The tendency to favour information that confirms one's pre-existing beliefs or values while ignoring or discarding contradictory information.

Given Wood's success, it was easy for **confirmation bias** to take hold – red *was* his winning colour. Some superstitions are sneaky because they are linked to avoiding something that occurs rarely, if ever; for example, knocking on wood to avert something bad from happening. Superstitions focused on avoiding rare events are pretty hard to disprove.

In earlier parts of the chapter, we came across a study by Wegner and Wheatley (1999), which showed that conscious thoughts that coincide with an action can create experiences of wilful actions. This principle can be extended to outcomes or events that would imply having magic powers. For example, in one study, participants sticking pins in voodoo dolls felt responsible for someone else's headache when the person had been annoying (Pronin, Wegner, McCarthy, & Rodriguez, 2006). Attributions of magic powers are aided by vivid imaginations and a failure to appreciate alternative explanations.

When outcomes are yet to be known, people are often reluctant to tempt fate. 'Jinxing it' draws your attention to the negative outcome, thereby boosting the belief that such an event is likely to occur.

5.6 PART 3: APPLICATIONS

Earlier on I praised the relevance of social cognition research. In Part 3, we look into this more closely to see how social cognition research can be applied in the real world. The topics covered in this section are by no means exhaustive. If this work sparks your interest, you can carry on reading Chapter 11, which tells you how social cognition research (and allied fields) have informed the science of behaviour change.

5.6.1 Survey and Questionnaire Design

Social cognition research has a lot to say about the art and science of survey and questionnaire design. This perspective rarely finds its way into textbooks. This is a shame (and something we are going to rectify!), not least because the topic is relevant to so many people, not just those working in academia but those working in many other sectors too. When things go wrong with the design of surveys and questionnaires, it can be costly. At the time of writing these lines, there are rumours that the Bank of England is not happy that the Office for National Statistics (ONS) had to postpone publications of key labour force data because of issues with their surveys (Ford Rojas, 2023; see also Key Study 1.1 on 'An Election Poll Gone Wrong' described in Chapter 1).

The starting position for a social cognitive perspective on survey and questionnaire design is the realisation that what are often considered artefacts in survey design reflect actual psychological phenomena. In essence, if you fill in a survey, someone (a person or an anthropomorphised AI) is asking you questions. In normal circumstances, you want to provide an answer that is not totally random and is of some use. You would also assume that rules of normal conversation apply. So, for example, it would be fair to assume that the person who put together the questionnaire wouldn't ask you about something that is nonsensical (Schwarz, 1999). Considering this, perhaps it's not that surprising that 30% to 50% of respondents typically provide an answer to issues that are fictitious (Bishop et al., 1980).

At the same time, surveys aren't normal conversations. One key difference is that respondents are not engaged in an actual 'live' conversation and there are fewer cues to disambiguate what the researcher(s) had in mind. Consequently, respondents end up using cues in the survey to interpret the question and adjust or format their answer to fit with the response options (Schwarz, 1999).

Let's start by looking at some of the factors at play when people interpret survey questions. One factor that can be easily overlooked is that of answer scales, which provide cues about the distribution of the targeted behaviour or preferences. As shown in a study by Schwarz, Strack, Müller, and Chassein (1988), respondents can use response scales to disambiguate the survey question. They asked respondents how often they encountered situations in which they felt 'really annoyed', using either a low-frequency answer scale ranging from *less than once a year* to *more than once every three months*, or a high-frequency answer scale ranging from *less than twice a week* to *several times a day*. Participants also provided examples of their annoying experiences, which were rated by experts according to their level of annoyance. The ratings showed that participants in the low-frequency condition recalled qualitatively more annoying experiences than participants in the high-frequency condition. This suggests that the response alternatives changed participants' interpretation of the sort of experiences the researchers were after.

Other questions in the survey also provide a context or background for respondents to interpret questions. This is illustrated in a study by Strack, Schwarz, and Wänke (1991). They asked German university students about their attitudes towards an 'educational contribution' after either estimating the amount of money the Swedish government pays every student, or after estimating the average tuition fee in the USA. Participants were much more in favour of a contribution with a context implying government support for students than with a context implying privately funded tuition fees.

KEY THINKER

Norbert Schwarz

Source: © Norbert Schwarz

Norbert Schwarz obtained a PhD in Sociology at the University of Mannheim. He worked at the University of Heidelberg before becoming a director at ZUMA, a research centre at Mannheim. He later moved to the US, working at the University of Michigan and, more recently, at the University of Southern California. In his earlier work, Norbert explored how judgements are construed based on contextual cues. This work shed light on assimilation and contrast effects, and the role of accessibility in judgement and decision-making.

Norbert is also well known for his work on feelings-as-information, showing that people can use affective experiences (mood, emotion) as well as experiences associated with thought processes (e.g., ease of retrieval) as input to guide their decisions and actions. He has also contributed to the literature on embodiment, and is a well-known figure in consumer behaviour. Norbert left Mannheim before my time, but his work has had a lasting impact and influenced my own PhD research.

Respondents can use any aspect of a survey or questionnaire to infer what the researchers are after and provide a subjectively meaningful response. This includes the identity and perceived aims of the survey owners. For example, in a study by Norenzayan and Schwarz (1999), students provided explanations for mass murder cases using a questionnaire that identified the researchers as social scientists or as personality psychologists. Participants gave relatively more situational explanations in a survey run by social scientists than in one run by personality psychologists. Conversely, dispositional explanations outweighed situational explanations in the survey allegedly run by personality psychologists. The study shows that one can get different answers to the same survey question depending on 'who' is asking the question. 'Where' and 'when' can be equally important, and any associated variations may reflect meaningful differences in the way respondents construct the survey question.

Consider a situation where someone asks you a similar question twice. You may think the first time you didn't answer the question well, so the other person rephrased it. In a survey, interactions are more limited – you can't expect immediate feedback. However, if you see a similar question twice, you may still think that the person who put the questions together wants to know different things. After all, why else would they ask you twice? There is indeed evidence that respondents do mentally 'subtract' responses to previous answers in surveys and questionnaires. However, a generic question that follows several specific questions can also be interpreted as a prompt to 'sum up' one's responses. In this case, it is likely that the generic question is assimilated towards the specific questions, which serve as a prime and render related information more accessible (Schwarz, Strack, & Mai, 1991).

Subtraction is a by-product of conversational norms to provide new information that is not redundant (Schwarz, Groves, & Schuman, 1998). We have already come across priming effects, whereby construals of a target are assimilated towards a prime. A third process to consider is that of contrast effects. Contrasts are important to make predictions about the direction of priming effects, which is relevant for social cognition research more broadly, and questionnaires and survey design more specifically. Contrast effects occur when primes are not assimilated towards a target, but influence the construal of a comparison standard instead. This is illustrated by Schwarz and Bless (1992), who designed a questionnaire that prompted respondents to think about politicians embroiled in a political scandal. Subsequently, participants rated the trustworthiness of politicians in general, or the trustworthiness of other specific politicians who were not implicated in the political scandal. In line with an assimilation effect, reminding people of specific politicians embroiled in a scandal lowered ratings of trustworthiness for all politicians. However, it increased ratings of trustworthiness for other specific politicians. Both are examples of priming effects, but while, in the former case, the target (politicians in general) was assimilated towards the prime, in the latter case, the target (other specific politicians) was contrasted with the prime.

Any factor that influences categorisation can be consequential in determining when **assimilation and contrast effects** occur. This includes aspects such as how typical

> **Key concept – Assimilation and contrast effects:** An assimilation effect entails perceiving a new stimulus as similar to a reference point or category, while a contrast effect entails perceiving it as different.

the prime and the target are (i.e., representativeness), whether the prime and the target share a part/whole relationship, or whether the prime and target coincide in time and space. For example, reflecting on a happy or sad event may impact judgements of your life satisfaction differently, depending on whether the event happened recently (likely leading to assimilation) or in the distant past (likely leading to a contrast effect) (Bless & Schwarz, 2010).

People have relatively poor representations of frequent and mundane behaviours, quite possibly due to the prevalence of automaticity in everyday life, discussed earlier. Response scales in surveys provide a frame of reference, and consequently researchers seeking to measure frequent and/or mundane behaviour need to be extra cautious when choosing response options. Using landmarks (e.g., last Christmas) can be a useful strategy to increase the accuracy of self-reports.

5.6.2 Risk Perception and Behaviour

As noted earlier, social cognition research has a long tradition of examining the use of heuristics and cognitive shortcuts, which we tend to rely on to fill in gaps in the information at hand, and to make do with our limited cognitive resources. This bears relevance for perceptions of, and responses to, risks, which by definition imply a situation of uncertainty whether there is a potential for a loss. In this section, we focus on risks arising from natural disasters and other rare events, although we also touch on other risks.

When people make decisions involving uncertainties, those decisions are readily influenced by the **availability heuristic**. The heuristic is at work when decision-makers base their judgements on information that captures their attention easily. This makes sense: when exemplars come easily to mind, there is reason to assume that a target category (from which exemplars are drawn) is familiar and prevalent. However, in the context of rare events, the availability heuristic can lead to biases: when a recent disaster looms large, it is

> **Key concept – Availability heuristic:** A mental shortcut where people rely on easily accessible information when making decisions.

easy to overestimate the likelihood of a disaster happening again. This can explain why sales of flood insurance policies correlate with flood losses during the previous year, or why insurance premiums hike after major disasters (Browne & Hoyt, 2000).

KEY STUDY 5.3

Availability Heuristic

Tversky and Kahneman (1973) surmised that the ease with which thoughts come to mind can provide a heuristic to judge the frequency or probability of a class of events. For example, to figure out whether there are more first names starting with the letter A or the letter B, you can ask yourself whether it is easier to come up with a list of names starting with the letter A or B. Whichever list you find easier to generate is also going to be longer. So, strictly speaking, we do not know whether the ease of generating names influenced your decision, or whether it's the fact that you generated more names.

To tease those explanations apart, Schwarz, Bless, Strack, Klumpp, Rittenauer-Schatka, and Simons (1991) asked participants to list either a few (relatively easy) or many (relatively difficult) exemplars. For example, in one study, they asked participants to recall either a few or many examples of when they acted either assertively or unassertively in the past (Figure 5.8).

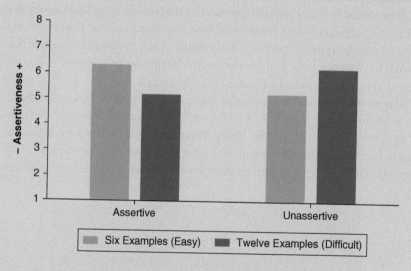

Figure 5.8 Ratings of assertiveness as a function of the number (six vs twelve) and type (assertive vs unassertive) of behaviours recalled. Assertiveness was assessed on a scale ranging from 1 to 10 with higher numbers denoting higher assertiveness

Source: Schwarz et al. (1991)

Participants who recalled a few examples of being assertive rated their own assertiveness higher than participants who recalled many examples of being assertive. The opposite was found for participants recalling examples of acting unassertively. If participants had judged their assertiveness purely based on thought contents or the

(Continued)

number of exemplars, then recalling more instances should have been more persuasive than recalling fewer instances. From these and other data, Schwarz and colleagues concluded that the ease of retrieving thoughts can indeed guide people's judgements, in line with Tversky and Kahneman's (1973) hypothesis. This was an important milestone that also laid the ground for research on cognitive experiences.

Availability is just one possible decision rule that people can apply to judge the likelihood of an event. The gambler's fallacy occurs when people falsely assume that a recent event is unlikely to repeat itself soon. Natural disasters are often prone to this type of bias (Cohen, Etner, & Jeleva, 2008). Whereas the availability heuristic leads to overestimates of recent losses repeating themselves, the gambler's fallacy leads to underestimates of such risks. The 'mean-reversion bias' describes a related decision rule, whereby people assume that, over time, a trend must return to 'normal', average levels. As we have seen with global warming, where records are broken year on year, the mean reversion bias is a poor decision rule in contexts where events are not random and the goalposts are moving.

A repeated theme in social cognition research is that information that captures our attention influences judgements and behaviours. One way that potential losses can capture our attention is through explicitly specified probabilities. When probabilities are specified – a job of risk analysts – people tend to overestimate the likelihood of rare events occurring, and they tend to give risks associated with rare events too much weight in decision-making. This is even more so the case for rare events and major disasters that elicit fear and dread. People have an aversion to the possibility of a loss, which can lead to irrational decisions in the context of very rare events (Sunstein, 2007). There are several reasons for biases that occur in the context of low-probability events, but what they have in common is that our minds are ill-equipped to form representations of events purely based on numeric probabilities.

Figure 5.9 We can be easily prone to biases when we try to make decisions related to floods and other natural disasters

Source: Kelly Sikkema/Unsplash

In many circumstances people make decisions involving risks without the benefit of a formal risk analysis. Or there may be a formal risk analysis that is sitting somewhere in a drawer. In a context where decisions are made from personal experience, events with small probabilities are often overlooked and given too little weight in decision-making (Hertwig & Erev, 2009). Even after an earlier attack on the World Trade Center in 1993, terrorism was covered as an unnamed peril in commercial insurance policies – an oversight that proved very costly for the insurance industry after 9/11 (Kunreuther & Pauly, 2006).

> **Key concept – Egocentric bias:** The tendency for individuals to rely too heavily on their own perspective, beliefs, or experiences when interpreting events or situations.

> **Key concept – Hindsight bias:** The tendency to believe that events were predictable or expected after they have already happened.

Although people have the ability to learn from others' experiences, the mind is **egocentrically biased** and prefers to base expectations on personal experience. This also has ramifications for dealing with rare risks, as people may disregard occasional losses incurred by others (Meyer, 2006). Since uncertainty is aversive, people often overestimate how predictable events really are. This **hindsight bias** can lead people to misjudge their own ability to predict and manage risks, especially when losses are incurred by others.

People's past experiences give rise to mental models and expectations that guide their actions. Professionals tasked with mitigating risks can capitalise on the fact that violations of expectations attract attention. For example, when street planners removed all markers and traffic signs in London's Kensington High Street, casualties fell by 43%. The lack of markers and traffic signs presumably led people to be more cautious and more prepared for unexpected events (Weick, Hopthrow, Abrams, & Taylor-Gooby, 2012).

Loss aversion describes the phenomenon that the pain associated with a potential loss looms larger than the amount of pleasure experienced from an equivalent gain (Tversky & Kahneman, 1991). Because

> **Key concept – Loss aversion:** A bias whereby people prefer avoiding losses more than acquiring equivalent gains.

people are attuned to threats and despise losses, they sometimes take bets with high stakes in the hope of avoiding a certain loss. Major financial scandals involving traders such as Jérôme Kerviel of Société Générale provide examples of people taking huge bets to recoup previous losses.

The 'sunk cost bias' is also linked to loss aversion. Sunk costs arise when people continue to invest in a suboptimal project or strategy in the hope of averting a large loss. Evidently, sunk costs increase over time, making it even more difficult to abandon a sub-optimal strategy. Failing IT or infrastructure projects are often prime examples of this.

5.6.3 Consumer Behaviour

Consumption and social behaviour are inherently intertwined, whether we interact with others via apps that make money through advertisement, or we purchase products to support our 'lifestyles' or express our identities. Similarly, others judge us by the clothes we wear, the shops we visit, and the products we own (think Mac versus PCs, or Tesla cars). Applications of social psychology to our understanding of consumer behaviour are vast and it would be impossible to cover all aspects within this section of the chapter. Instead, the focus will lie more narrowly on selected topics linked to social cognition.

> **Key concept – Anchoring:** Anchoring occurs when a person relies too much on the first piece of information encountered when making decisions, influencing subsequent judgements or estimates.

Shops often use reference pricing (offers) to entice shoppers to buy their products. In fact, reference prices are so popular, regulators often have to step in to make sure they are not misused. Reference pricing provides a relevant **anchor**, which is not only useful to judge the price, but also encourages prospective buyers to engage in mental hypothesis testing that a product is of higher quality than the reduced price may suggest (cf. Mussweiler & Strack, 1999).

In the earlier section on survey and questionnaire design, we came across assimilation and contrast effects that can also be applied to the evaluation of consumer products. Hoyer and Brown (1990) demonstrated that people's choices of peanut butter were much more dependent on the association with a popular brand than with the actual objective taste of the product. Their classic study provides an example of an assimilation effect. Brand extensions, whereby a company uses an established brand name on a new product, are similarly intended to produce assimilation effects. In a study on brand extensions by Aaker and Keller (1990), participants evaluated ®Häagen-Dazs candy bars favourably, but disliked a ®Häagen-Dazs cottage cheese. Whereas the candy bar was assimilated to the popular ice cream, the cottage cheese was perceived as a discontinuation and elicited a contrast effect. The fact that brand extensions can backfire will be familiar to the popular denim brand Levi's, which extended successfully into the market of Khaki trousers under the Levi's Dockers brand, but failed in their attempt to extend into the suit tailoring business (Aaker, 1990).

van Horen and Pieters (2012) looked at consumers' perceptions of products that copy the name, logo, and/or package design of well-known brands. Their studies showed that copycats are evaluated more positively, the greater their similarity to a well-known brand. However, this assimilation effect only occurred when the well-known product was absent. When the copycat and the well-known brand appeared side by side, consumers preferred less similar copycats over more similar copycats, pointing to a contrast effect. The German discounter Aldi is known for featuring own-brand products that share some similarity with branded products. This seems to be a good strategy as long as own-branded products do not appear alongside leading brands in the aisles.

Products are designed to persuade people to buy them through pleasant aesthetics, positive associations created by the imagery, and marketing claims. Just as respondents to surveys expect not to be asked about things that are nonsensical, consumers would not expect producers to present information on products that is completely irrelevant. One implication of this is that producers can highlight pretty much any ingredient as being present or absent in their product – consumers will be inclined to assume that that is supposed to be a good thing worth shouting about (Wänke & Reutner, 2010). Thinking about it, I wouldn't mind some cheese made with enzymes right now (note: all cheese is made with enzymes).

GUEST PERSONAL JOURNEY

Michaela Wänke

When I was in high school my Latin teacher, from time to time, as a treat, taught about psychology rather than Latin. It was mainly about Freud and did not have much to do with what I later learned about psychology, but for a 15-year-old it was fascinating and made me think about studying psychology. About the same time, I read Vance Packard's *The Hidden Persuaders*, a book about how advertising influences consumers (often subconsciously). This strengthened my decision to study psychology, with the goal to research consumer behaviour. Once enrolled, I soon found out that consumer psychology was not part of the curriculum but instead I discovered social cognition.

Source: © Michaele Wanke

After graduation, being torn between a career in industry or doing research, I first tried the 'real world' and worked in market research for some years before my passion for fundamental research won and I went back to university for a PhD. Since then, my research has combined my interest in social cognition and consumer psychology. I held a chair in social psychology at the University of Basel for ten years before accepting the newly established chair in consumer and economic psychology at the University of Mannheim, where I developed the first curriculum in consumer psychology in Germany.

I was lucky to have had inspiring and generous teachers in Norbert Schwarz, Sharon Shavitt, and Bob Wyer, as well as smart and stimulating peers and colleagues who have made work fun, most importantly, Herbert Bless, and more gifted and successful students and postdocs than I can list here. Over the years, it is from them that I have learned the most.

James Vicary was a market researcher who rose to fame in the 1950s for conducting a 'study' on subliminal advertising. He claimed that split-second advertisements for Coca-Cola and popcorn boosted sales in a cinema, even though moviegoers had no idea they were being influenced. The study was debunked five years later and turned out to be a fake (e.g., BBC, 2015). However, the idea that we can be influenced by cues presented below the threshold of conscious awareness remained a striking proposition. Fast forward half a century, and Karremans, Stroebe, and Claus (2006) showed that priming a brand (Lipton Ice Tea) subliminally influences product choices and intention to drink the primed brand. However, consistent with our earlier discussion of behavioural priming, this effect only emerged for participants who were thirsty.

Legal and ethical considerations aside, people don't like the idea of being influenced subliminally. An American anti-abortion group was not happy when the rumour spread that the word 'sex' flashed up in Walt Disney's film *The Lion King* (Nichols, 1995). Similarly, Bush's presidential campaign team was left red-faced when the news broke that the word 'rats' flashed up for a microsecond in a broadcast lambasting Democrats (Berke, 2000). Luckily for marketeers, there are other subtle influence techniques that are more palatable to consumers.

For example, brand names can capitalise on sound symbolism. The ice cream *Frosh* 'sounds' smoother, richer, and creamier than the ice cream *Frish* (Yorkston & Menon, 2004). Pushing the boundaries of this further, work on phonetic embodiment suggests that mouth and tongue movements can also impact brand perceptions, with consumers preferring brand names that require front-to-back movement, simulating food intake (e.g., BODIKA), over brand names that require back-to-front movement, simulating expulsion (e.g., KODIBA) (see Topolinski, Zürn, & Schneider, 2015). The previous section on embodiment explains why such an effect is perhaps less fanciful than it may sound.

> **Key concept – Implicit egotism:** The tendency to prefer things associated with oneself, such as names or initials, without necessarily being aware of this influence.

Imagine being single and not averse to the idea of having a romantic partner. You meet an attractive person in a bar. Things are going well and then you find out they share the same birthday as you. Wow! It often feels special, perhaps fateful, to meet people with the same birthday, or the same name, or the same … anything! We like things that are related to the self. This is a basis for the endowment effect, which describes our tendency to value items more when we own them compared to when they don't belong to us. **Implicit egotism** can be found in our preferences for brand names: we prefer names that start with the same letters as our names (Brendl, Chattopadhyay, Pelham, & Carvallo, 2005). The flipside of consumption is production; even how we choose to be productive (i.e., our jobs) appears to be influenced by our names (think Denis the dentist, Robert the roofer) (see Pelham, Mirenberg, & Jones, 2002). In Exercise 5.3, we look at an example of how implicit egotism can impact dating dynamics.

EXERCISE 5.3

When Implicit Egotism Backfires

There is currently a clip circulating on social media of a man lamenting how difficult it is to be single in his 30s. He recalls a recent encounter where, upon entering a busy coffee shop, he notices a woman behind him wearing a shirt of his favourite band. He compliments the woman on her music taste. The woman jumps ahead of him and orders a vanilla latte with an extra shot. Lo and behold, this also happens to be the man's go-to beverage! The man proceeds to order the same drink and then walks over to ask the woman about her favourite song by the band. She tells him in no uncertain terms to get lost, supposedly loud enough for everyone in the coffee shop to take notice. Ouch.

Considering what you have read about 'implicit egotism', why do you think this rejection was perhaps extra hurtful? Do you think the outcome may have been different if the man (rather than the woman) had been wearing a T-shirt of the band and had ordered the vanilla latte first? Given the actual order of events and choice of attire, do you think having those common tastes worked in the man's favour or against him?

Consider all the information presented in a single supermarket aisle – all the products, brand names, content labels, marketing claims, prices, offers, and God knows what else. You can be excused if your head starts to spin. We simply don't have the brain power to process it all. Even with computers in our pockets (aka smartphones), we are not going to input all the data to run some models to find the best option for a sandwich. Instead, we can ask ourselves how we feel about a product. Research has shown that experiences can sway product purchases. This includes affective experiences (diffuse mood states, concrete emotions), but also experiences related to bodily states (as anyone who ever went food shopping hungry knows) and thought processes (certainty, ease of processing). Chapter 11 looks at how negative emotions (dread, fear) can be leveraged to discourage the consumption of cigarettes and other products.

5.7 SUMMARY

This marks the end of our foray into social cognition. Our journey started with a discussion of overarching themes, which are essentially guiding principles that provide a firm foundation to understand the concepts and findings you have come across in this chapter and will hopefully come across in the future. We discussed how social cognition is perhaps best defined as an approach to understand social psychological phenomena by looking at cognitive processes, most notably perception and construals, which are themselves dependent on attention and prior knowledge. We discussed how people can maintain the belief that their views are truthful and objective when biases are widespread and fundamental to our thought processes. This can be seen in how we apply different processing modes (top-down vs bottom-up; automatic vs controlled) that are also linked to different perspectives on the social perceiver. We spent some time discussing features of automatic processes (awareness, intention, control, and efficiency) as well as current perspectives on the interplay between automatic and controlled thought processes. In the advances section, we saw how goals and motivation are intertwined with automatic and controlled processes, and how this dual process can also help us to understand self-regulation.

We also discussed the nature of mental representations and how they are grounded in sensorimotor systems, also when we reason about abstract concepts using metaphors. Perceiving agency and drawing inferences from patterns are core to social cognition, but the same processes can also foster supernatural beliefs and superstitions. I began this chapter by praising the relevance and applicability of social cognition research, which I hope has become clearer as we discussed applications to survey and questionnaire design, perceptions of risks arising from natural disasters and other rare events, and consumer behaviour.

5.8 REVISION

1   Explain the social information processing model. How does it propose that individuals process and interpret social information? What is the role of attention and prior knowledge in shaping the interpretation of social cues?

2 Explore the psychological mechanisms underlying naïve realism. What cognitive processes contribute to individuals' belief that their own perspectives are truthful and objective?

3 Define and explain the concept of accessibility in social psychology. How does the accessibility of information influence cognitive processes and decision-making in social situations? Discuss the role of priming in accessibility.

4 Define dual-process models in social cognition. Compare and contrast the two main modes. How do motivation, cognitive resources, and task demands impact the engagement of more deliberative and controlled thinking?

5 Examine the implications of the Four Horsemen of Automaticity in understanding social judgements and behaviour.

6 How do goals influence automatic processing, and what are the consequences for social behaviour?

7 Examine the impact of embodied cognition on social behaviour. How do bodily experiences and sensations influence social attitudes, decision-making, and interpersonal interactions? How do metaphors influence the way individuals conceptualise and understand abstract social concepts?

8 Evaluate the psychological functions of supernatural beliefs. How do cognitive processes, such as pattern recognition and control beliefs, contribute to the formation and persistence of superstitious behaviours?

9 How do social cognitive processes influence the way people interpret and respond to survey questions?

10 How do cognitive shortcuts and psychological biases contribute to the way individuals evaluate and respond to risks? What is the relationship between emotions and risk perception?

11 How can concepts in social cognition be applied to consumer behaviour?

5.9 FURTHER READING

Foundations

Bodenhausen, G. V., & Hugenberg, K. (2009). Attention, perception, and social cognition. In F. Strack & J. Förster (Eds.), *Social cognition: The basis of human interaction* (pp. 1–22). Philadelphia, PA: Psychology Press.

This is an excellent book chapter focused on the social information processing model.

Macrae, C. N., & Bodenhausen, G. V. (2000). Social cognition: Thinking categorically about others. *Annual Review of Psychology, 51*, 93–120. https://doi.org/10.1146/annurev. psych.51.1.93

This review paper discusses many of the basic principles covered in this chapter.

Advances

Duckworth, A. L., Gendler, T. S., & Gross, J. J. (2016). Situational strategies for self-control. *Perspectives on Psychological Science, 11*, 35–55. https://doi.org/10.1177/1745691615623247

This paper reviews different perspectives on self-regulation, and also develops some novel ideas on how controlled processes contribute to self-regulation.

Meier, B. P., Schnall, S., Schwarz, N., & Bargh, J. A. (2012). Embodiment in social psychology. *Topics in Cognitive Science, 4*, 705–716. https://doi.org/10.1111/j.1756-8765.2012.01212.x

This paper provides an excellent overview of the literature on embodiment in social psychology.

Applications

Schwarz, N. (1999). Self-reports: How the questions shape the answers. *American Psychologist, 54*, 93–105. https://doi.org/10.1037/0003-066X.54.2.93

This is a landmark article that reviews work on the social cognition of survey and questionnaire design.

Vasiljevic, M., Weick, M., Taylor-Gooby, P., Abrams, D., & Hopthrow, T. (2013). *Reasoning about extreme events: A review of behavioural biases in relation to catastrophe risks.* Lighthill Risk Network Report. Available from: https://dro.dur.ac.uk/26255/

This report provides an overview of various biases that occur in people's perceptions of, and responses to, natural disasters.

5.10 REFERENCES

Aaker, D. A. (1990). Brand extension: The good, the bad, and the ugly. *MIT Sloan Management Review*, July 15. https://sloanreview.mit.edu/article/brand-extensions-the-good-the-bad-and-the-ugly/

Aaker, D. A., & Keller, K. L. (1990). Consumer evaluations of brand extensions. *Journal of Marketing, 54*, 27–41. https://doi.org/10.1177/002224299005400102

Aarts, H., & Dijksterhuis, A. (2000). Habits as knowledge structures: Automaticity in goal-directed behavior. *Journal of Personality and Social Psychology, 78*, 53–63. https://doi.org/10.1037/0022-3514.78.1.53

Addley, E. (2018). Study shows 60% of Britons believe in conspiracy theories. *The Guardian*, November 23. www.theguardian.com/society/2018/nov/23/study-shows-60-of-britons-believe-in-conspiracy-theories

Adolphs, R. (2003). Cognitive neuroscience of human social behavior. *Nature Neuroscience, 4*, 165–178. https://doi.org/10.1038/nrn1056

Antonakis, J., & Dalgas, O. (2009). Predicting elections: Child's play! *Science, 323,* 1183–1183. https://doi.org/10.1126/science.1167748

Asch, S. E. (1958). The metaphor: A psychological inquiry. In R. Tagiuri & L. Petrullo (Eds.), *Person perception and interpersonal behavior* (pp. 86–94). Stanford, CA: Stanford University Press.

Bail, C. A., Argyle, L. P., Brown, T. W., Bumpus, J. P., Chen, H., Fallin Hunzaker, M. B., Lee, J., Mann, M., Merhout, F., & Volfovsky, A. (2018). Exposure to opposing views on social media can increase political polarization. *Proceedings of the National Academy of Sciences, 115,* 9216–9221. https://doi.org/10.1073/pnas.1804840115

Balcetis, E., & Dunning, D. (2010). Wishful seeing: More desired objects are seen as closer. *Psychological Science, 21,* 147–152. https://doi.org/10.1177/0956797609356283

Bargh, J. A. (1994). The four horsemen of automaticity: Awareness, intention, efficiency, and control in social cognition. In R. S. Wyer & T. K. Srull (Eds.), *Handbook of social cognition* (2nd ed., pp. 1–40). Hillsdale, NJ: Lawrence Erlbaum Associates.

Bargh, J. A., Chen, M., & Burrows, L. (1996). Automaticity of social behavior: Direct effects of trait construct and stereotype activation on action. *Journal of Personality and Social Psychology, 71,* 230–244. https://doi.org/10.1037/0022-3514.71.2.230

Barrett, J. L. (2000). Exploring the natural foundations of religion. *Trends in Cognitive Sciences, 4,* 29–34. https://doi.org/10.1016/S1364-6613(99)01419-9

Barsalou, L. W. (1999). Perceptual symbol systems. *Behavioral and Brain Sciences, 22,* 577–660. https://doi.org/10.1017/S0140525X99002149

BBC. (2015). Does subliminal advertising actually work? *BBC News,* January 20. www.bbc.co.uk/news/magazine-30878843

Berke, R. L. (2000). The 2000 campaign: The ad campaign, Democrats see, and smell, rats in G.O.P. ad. *The New York Times,* September 12. www.nytimes.com/2000/09/12/us/the-2000-campaign-the-ad-campaign-democrats-see-and-smell-rats-in-gop-ad.html

Bishop, G. F., Oldendick, R. W., Tuchfarber, A. J., & Bennett, S. E. (1980). Pseudo-opinions on public affairs. *Public Opinion Quarterly, 44,* 425–436. https://doi.org/10.1086/268584

Blair, I. V., Ma, J. E., & Lenton, A. P. (2001). Imagining stereotypes away: The moderation of implicit stereotypes through mental imagery. *Journal of Personality and Social Psychology, 81,* 828–841. https://doi.org/10.1037/0022-3514.81.5.828

Bless, H., & Fiedler, K. (2014). *Social cognition: How individuals construct social reality.* New York: Psychology Press.

Bless, H., & Schwarz, N. (2010). Mental construal and the emergence of assimilation and contrast effects: The inclusion/exclusion model. In M. P. Zanna (Ed.), *Advances in experimental social psychology* (Vol. *42,* pp. 319–373). San Diego, CA: Elsevier Academic Press.

Bodenhausen, G. V. (1990). Stereotypes as judgmental heuristics: Evidence of circadian variations in discrimination. *Psychological Science, 1,* 319–322. https://doi.org/10.1111/j.1467-9280.1990.tb00226.x

Bodenhausen, G. V., & Hugenberg, K. (2009). Attention, perception, and social cognition. In F. Strack & J. Förster (Eds.), *Social cognition: The basis of human interaction* (pp. 1–22). Philadelphia, PA: Psychology Press.

Bos, M. W., Dijksterhuis, A., & van Baaren, R. B. (2008). On the goal-dependency of unconscious thought. *Journal of Experimental Social Psychology*, *44*, 1114–1120. https://doi.org/10.1016/j.jesp.2008.01.001

Botvinick, M., & Cohen, J. (1998). Rubber hands 'feel' touch that eyes see. *Nature*, *391*, 756. https://doi.org/10.1038/35784

Brendl, C. M., Chattopadhyay, A., Pelham, B. W., & Carvallo, M. (2005). Name letter branding: Valence transfers when product specific needs are active. *Journal of Consumer Research*, *32*, 405–415. https://doi.org/10.1086/497552

Browne, M. J., & Hoyt, R. E. (2000). The demand for flood insurance: Empirical evidence. *Journal of Risk and Uncertainty*, *20*, 291–306. https://doi.org/10.1023/A:1007823631497

Cacioppo, J. T., Priester, J. R., & Berntson, G. G. (1993). Rudimentary determinants of attitudes: II. Arm flexion and extension have differential effects on attitudes. *Journal of Personality and Social Psychology*, *65*, 5–17. https://doi.org/10.1037/0022-3514.65.1.5

Chaiken, S., & Trope, Y. (Eds.). (1999). *Dual-process theories in social psychology*. New York: Guilford Press.

Chandler, J., & Schwarz, N. (2009). How extending your middle finger affects your perception of others: Learned movements influence concept accessibility. *Journal of Experimental Social Psychology*, *45*, 123–128. https://doi.org/10.1016/j.jesp.2008.06.012

Chen, M., & Bargh, J. A. (1999). Consequences of automatic evaluation: Immediate behavioral predispositions to approach or avoid the stimulus. *Personality and Social Psychology Bulletin*, *25*, 215–224. https://doi.org/10.1177/0146167299025002007

Cohen, M., Etner, J., & Jeleva, M. (2008). Dynamic decision making when risk perception depends on past experience. *Theory and Decision*, *64*, 173–192. https://doi.org/10.1007/s11238-007-9061-3

Correll, J., Park, B., Judd, C. M., & Wittenbrink, B. (2007). The influence of stereotypes on decisions to shoot. *European Journal of Social Psychology*, *37*, 1102–1117. https://doi.org/10.1002/ejsp.450

Crisp, R. J., Hewstone, M., & Rubin, M. (2001). Does multiple categorization reduce intergroup bias? *Personality and Social Psychology Bulletin*, *27*, 76–89. https://doi.org/10.1177/0146167201271007

Custers, R., & Aarts, H. (2005). Positive affect as implicit motivator: On the nonconscious operation of behavioral goals. *Journal of Personality and Social Psychology*, *89*, 129–142. https://doi.org/10.1037/0022-3514.89.2.129

Dahlgreen, W. (2014). 'Ghosts exist', say 1 in 3 Brits. *YouGov*, October 31. https://yougov.co.uk/politics/articles/10857-ghosts-exist-say-1-3-brits

Damisch, L., Stoberock, B., & Mussweiler, T. (2010). Keep your fingers crossed! How superstition improves performance. *Psychological Science*, *21*, 1014–1020. https://doi.org/10.1177/0956797610372631

Dasgupta, N., & Greenwald, A. G. (2001). On the malleability of automatic attitudes: Combating automatic prejudice with images of admired and disliked individuals. *Journal of Personality and Social Psychology*, *81*, 800–814. https://doi.org/10.1037/0022-3514.81.5.800

De Witt Huberts, J. C., Evers, C., & De Ridder, D. T. (2014). 'Because I am worth it': A theoretical framework and empirical review of a justification-based account of self-regulation failure. *Personality and Social Psychology Review, 18*, 119–138. https://doi.org/10.1177/1088868313507533

Dijksterhuis, A. (2004). Think different: The merits of unconscious thought in preference development and decision making. *Journal of Personality and Social Psychology, 87*, 586–598. https://doi.org/10.1037/0022-3514.87.5.586

Dijksterhuis, A., & Nordgren, L. F. (2006). A theory of unconscious thought. *Perspectives on Psychological Science, 1*, 95–109. https://doi.org/10.1111/j.1745-6916.2006.00007.x

Dijksterhuis, A., & van Knippenberg, A. (1998). The relation between perception and behavior, or how to win a game of Trivial Pursuit. *Journal of Personality and Social Psychology, 74*, 865–877. https://doi.org/10.1037/0022-3514.74.4.865

Dovidio, J. F., Glick, P., & Hewstone, M. (Eds.). (2010). *The SAGE handbook of prejudice, stereotyping and discrimination*. London: Sage.

Drew, T., Võ, M. L. H., & Wolfe, J. M. (2013). The invisible gorilla strikes again: Sustained inattentional blindness in expert observers. *Psychological Science, 24*, 1848–1853. https://doi.org/10.1177/0956797613479386

Duckworth, A. L., Gendler, T. S., & Gross, J. J. (2016). Situational strategies for self-control. *Perspectives on Psychological Science, 11*, 35–55. https://doi.org/10.1177/1745691615623247

Eberhardt, J. L., Davies, P. G., Purdie-Vaughns, V. J., & Johnson, S. L. (2006). Looking deathworthy: Perceived stereotypicality of Black defendants predicts capital-sentencing outcomes. *Psychological Science, 17*, 383–386. https://doi.org/10.1111/j.1467-9280.2006.01716.x

Eitam, B., & Higgins, E. T. (2010). Motivation in mental accessibility: Relevance of a representation (ROAR) as a new framework. *Social and Personality Psychology Compass, 4*, 951–967. https://doi.org/10.1111/j.1751-9004.2010.00309.x

Ellis, R., & Tucker, M. (2000). Micro-affordance: The potentiation of components of action by seen objects. *British Journal of Psychology, 91*, 451–471. https://doi.org/10.1348/000712600161934

Fiske, S. T., & Neuberg, S. L. (1990). A continuum model of impression formation, from category-based to individuating processes: Influence of information and motivation on attention and interpretation. In M. P. Zanna (Ed.), *Advances in experimental social psychology* (Vol. *23*, pp. 1–74). San Diego, CA: Academic Press.

Fiske, S. T., & Taylor, S. E. (2017). *Social cognition* (3rd ed.). London: Sage.

Ford Rojas, J.-P. (2023). Bank of England boss says jobs data may be out by one million. *This is MONEY*, December 10. www.thisismoney.co.uk/money/markets/article-12844815/Bank-England-boss-says-jobs-data-one-million.html

Garcia-Marques, T., Silva, R. R., Reber, R., & Unkelbach, C. (2015). Hearing a statement now and believing the opposite later. *Journal of Experimental Social Psychology, 56*, 126–129. https://doi.org/10.1016/j.jesp.2014.09.015

Gibbs, R. W. (1994). *The poetics of mind: Figurative thought, language, and understanding*. Cambridge: Cambridge University Press.

Glenberg, A. M., & Kaschak, M. P. (2002). Grounding language in action. *Psychonomic Bulletin & Review, 9*, 558–565. https://doi.org/10.3758/BF03196313

Gollwitzer, P. M., & Brandstätter, V. (1997). Implementation intentions and effective goal pursuit. *Journal of Personality and Social Psychology, 73*, 186–199. https://doi.org/10.1037/0022-3514.73.1.186

Gottschall, J. (2021). Our storytelling nature. *The Psychologist*, November 30. www.bps.org.uk/psychologist/our-storytelling-nature

Greenwald, A. G., McGhee, D. E., & Schwartz, J. L. K. (1998). Measuring individual differences in implicit cognition: The implicit association test. *Journal of Personality and Social Psychology, 74*, 1464–1480. https://doi.org/10.1037/0022-3514.74.6.1464

Haidt, J. (2001). The emotional dog and its rational tail: A social intuitionist approach to moral judgment. *Psychological Review, 108*, 814–834. https://doi.org/10.1037/0033-295X.108.4.814

Hamilton, D. L., & Gifford, R. K. (1976). Illusory correlation in interpersonal perception: A cognitive basis of stereotypic judgments. *Journal of Experimental Social Psychology, 12*, 392–407. https://doi.org/10.1016/S0022-1031(76)80006-6

Hansen, C., & Hansen, R. (1988). Finding the face in the crowd: An anger superiority effect. *Journal of Personality and Social Psychology, 54*, 917–924. https://doi.org/10.1037/0022-3514.54.6.917

Havas, D. A., Glenberg, A. M., Gutowski, K. A., Lucarelli, M. J., & Davidson, R. J. (2010). Cosmetic use of botulinum toxin-A affects processing of emotional language. *Psychological Science, 21*, 895–900. https://doi.org/10.1177/0956797610374742

Heider, F., & Simmel, M. (1944). An experimental study of apparent behavior. *The American Journal of Psychology, 57*, 243–259. https://www.jstor.org/stable/1416950

Hertwig, R., & Erev, I. (2009). The description–experience gap in risky choice. *Trends in Cognitive Sciences, 13*, 517–523. https://doi.org/10.1016/j.tics.2009.09.004

Higgins, E. T., Rholes, W. S., & Jones, C. R. (1977). Category accessibility and impression formation. *Journal of Experimental Social Psychology, 13*, 141–154. https://doi.org/10.1016/S0022-1031(77)80007-3

Hofmann, W., Friese, M., & Strack, F. (2009). Impulse and self-control from a dual-systems perspective. *Perspectives on Psychological Science, 4*, 162–176. https://doi.org/10.1111/j.1745-6924.2009.01116.x

Hogg, M. A. (2000). Subjective uncertainty reduction through self-categorization: A motivational theory of social identity processes. *European Review of Social Psychology, 11*, 223–255. https://doi.org/10.1080/14792772043000040

Hoyer, W. D., & Brown, S. P. (1990). Effects of brand awareness on choice for a common, repeat-purchase product. *Journal of Consumer Research, 17*, 141–148. https://doi.org/10.1086/208544

Hugenberg, K., & Bodenhausen, G. V. (2003). Facing prejudice: Implicit prejudice and the perception of facial threat. *Psychological Science, 14*, 640–643. https://doi.org/10.1046/j.0956-7976.2003.psci_1478.x

James, W. (1899). *Talks to teachers on psychology; and to students on some of life's ideals.* New York: Holt and Company.

Kahneman, D. (2003). A perspective on judgment and choice: Mapping bounded rationality. *American Psychologist, 58*, 697–720. https://doi.org/10.1037/0003-066x.58.9.697

Karremans, J. C., Stroebe, W., & Claus, J. (2006). Beyond Vicary's fantasies: The impact of subliminal priming and brand choice. *Journal of Experimental Social Psychology, 42*, 792–798. https://doi.org/10.1016/j.jesp.2005.12.002

Kawakami, K., Dovidio, J. F., & van Kamp, S. (2005). Kicking the habit: Effects of nonstereotypic association training and correction processes on hiring decisions. *Journal of Experimental Social Psychology, 41*, 68–75. https://doi.org/10.1016/j.jesp.2004.05.004

Kelley, H. H. (1967). Attribution theory in social psychology. In D. Levine (Ed.), *Nebraska symposium on motivation* (Vol. *15*, pp. 192–238). Lincoln, NB: University of Nebraska Press.

Kruglanski, A. W., Shah, J. Y., Fishbach, A., Friedman, R., Chun, W. Y., & Sleeth-Keppler, D. (2002). A theory of goal systems. In M. P. Zanna (Ed.), *Advances in experimental social psychology* (Vol. *34*, pp. 331–378). San Diego, CA: Academic Press.

Kunda, Z. (1990). The case for motivated reasoning. *Psychological Bulletin, 108*, 480–498. https://doi.org/10.1037/0033-2909.108.3.480

Kunda, Z. (1999). *Social cognition: Making sense of people*. Cambridge, MA: The MIT Press.

Kunda, Z., & Spencer, S. J. (2003). When do stereotypes come to mind and when do they color judgment? A goal-based theoretical framework for stereotype activation and application. *Psychological Bulletin, 129*, 522–544. https://doi.org/10.1037/0033-2909.129.4.522

Kunreuther, H., & Pauly, M. V. (2006). Insurance decision-making and market behavior. *Foundations and Trends® in Microeconomics, 1*, 63–127. http://dx.doi.org/10.1561/0700000002

Lord, C. G., Ross, L., & Lepper, M. R. (1979). Biased assimilation and attitude polarization: The effects of prior theories on subsequently considered evidence. *Journal of Personality and Social Psychology, 37*, 2098–2109. https://doi.org/10.1037/0022-3514.37.11.2098

Lyons, L. (2005). Paranormal beliefs come (super)naturally to some. *Gallup*, November 1. https://news.gallup.com/poll/19558/paranormal-beliefs-come-supernaturally-some.aspx

Matute, H., Blanco, F., Yarritu, I., Díaz-Lago, M., Vadillo, M. A., & Barberia, I. (2015). Illusions of causality: How they bias our everyday thinking and how they could be reduced. *Frontiers in Psychology, 6*, 146427. https://doi.org/10.3389/fpsyg.2015.00888

Meier, B. P., Hauser, D. J., Robinson, M. D., Friesen, C. K., & Schjeldahl, K. (2007). What's 'up' with God? Vertical space as a representation of the divine. *Journal of Personality and Social Psychology, 93*, 699–710. https://doi.org/10.1037/0022-3514.93.5.699

Meyer, R. (2006). Why we under-prepare for hazards. In R. J. Daniels, D. F. Kettl, & H. Kunreuther (Eds.), *On risk and disaster: Lessons from Hurricane Katrina* (pp. 153–174). Philadelphia, PA: University of Pennsylvania Press.

Moray, N. (1959). Attention in dichotic listening: Affective cues and the influence of instructions. *Quarterly Journal of Experimental Psychology, 11*, 56–60. https://doi.org/10.1080/17470215908416289

Mussweiler, T., & Strack, F. (1999). Hypothesis-consistent testing and semantic priming in the anchoring paradigm: A selective accessibility model. *Journal of Experimental Social Psychology, 35*, 136–164. https://doi.org/10.1006/jesp.1998.1364

Nichols, P. M. (1995). Some see 'sex' in the clouds of 'Lion King'. *The New York Times*, September 2. www.nytimes.com/1995/09/02/movies/some-see-sex-in-the-clouds-of-lion-king.html

Niedenthal, P. M., Winkielman, P., Mondillon, L., & Vermeulen, N. (2009). Embodiment of emotion concepts. *Journal of Personality and Social Psychology*, *96*, 1120–1136. https://doi.org/10.1037/a0015574

Nisbett, R. E., & Wilson, T. D. (1977). Telling more than we can know: Verbal reports on mental processes. *Psychological Review*, *84*, 231–259. https://doi.org/10.1037/0033-295X.84.3.231

Norenzayan, A., Atran, S., Faulkner, J., & Schaller, M. (2006). Memory and mystery: The cultural selection of minimally counterintuitive narratives. *Cognitive Science*, *30*, 531–553. https://doi.org/10.1207/s15516709cog0000_68

Norenzayan, A., & Schwarz, N. (1999). Telling what they want to know: Participants tailor causal attributions to researchers' interests. *European Journal of Social Psychology*, *29*, 1011–1020. https://doi.org/10.1002/(SICI)1099-0992(199912)29:8%3C1011::AID-EJSP974%3E3.0.CO;2-A

Payne, B. K., Brown-Iannuzzi, J. L., & Loersch, C. (2016). Replicable effects of primes on human behavior. *Journal of Experimental Psychology: General*, *145*, 1269–1279. https://doi.org/10.1037/xge0000201

Pelham, B. W., Mirenberg, M. C., & Jones, J. K. (2002). Why Susie sells seashells by the seashore: Implicit egotism and major life decisions. *Journal of Personality and Social Psychology*, *82*, 469–487. https://doi.org/10.1037/0022-3514.82.4.469

Pronin, E., Wegner, D. M., McCarthy, K., & Rodriguez, S. (2006). Everyday magical powers: The role of apparent mental causation in the overestimation of personal influence. *Journal of Personality and Social Psychology*, *91*, 218–231. https://doi.org/10.1037/0022-3514.91.2.218

Ross, L., & Ward, A. (1996). Naïve realism in everyday life: Implications for social conflict and misunderstanding. In T. Brown, E. Reed, & E. Turiel (Eds.), *Values and knowledge* (pp. 103–135). Hillsdale, NJ: Lawrence Erlbaum Associates.

Ross, L. (1977). The intuitive psychologist and his shortcomings. In L. Berkowitz (Ed.), *Advances in experimental social psychology* (Vol. *10*, pp. 173–220). New York: Academic Press.

Schwarz, N. (1999). Self-reports: How the questions shape the answers. *American Psychologist*, *54*, 93–105. https://doi.org/10.1037/0003-066X.54.2.93

Schwarz, N., & Bless, H. (1992). Scandals and the public's trust in politicians: Assimilation and contrast effects. *Personality and Social Psychology Bulletin*, *18*, 574–579. https://doi.org/10.1177/0146167292185007

Schwarz, N., Bless, H., Strack, F., Klumpp, G., Rittenauer-Schatka, H., & Simons, A. (1991). Ease of retrieval as information: Another look at the availability heuristic. *Journal of Personality and Social Psychology*, *61*, 195–202. https://doi.org/10.1037/0022-3514.61.2.195

Schwarz, N., Groves, R. M., & Schuman, H. (1998). Survey methods. In D. T. Gilbert, S. T. Fiske, & G. Lindzey (Eds.), *The handbook of social psychology* (pp. 143–179). New York: Oxford University Press.

Schwarz, N., Strack, F., & Mai, H. P. (1991). Assimilation and contrast effects in part-whole question sequences: A conversational logic analysis. *Public Opinion Quarterly*, *55*, 3–23. https://doi.org/10.1086/269239

Schwarz, N., Strack, F., Müller, G., & Chassein, B. (1988). The range of response alternatives may determine the meaning of the question: Further evidence on informative functions of response alternatives. *Social Cognition*, *6*, 107–117. https://doi.org/10.1521/soco.1988.6.2.107

Sedikides, C., & Skowronski, J. J. (1991). The law of cognitive structure activation. *Psychological Inquiry*, *2*, 169–184. www.jstor.org/stable/1449259

Shah, J. Y., Friedman, R., & Kruglanski, A. W. (2002). Forgetting all else: On the antecedents and consequences of goal shielding. *Journal of Personality and Social Psychology*, *83*, 1261–1280. https://doi.org/10.1037/0022-3514.83.6.1261

Sherman, J. W., Kruschke, J. K., Sherman, S. J., Percy, E. J., Petrocelli, J. V., & Conrey, F. R. (2009). Attentional processes in stereotype formation: A common model for category accentuation and illusory correlation. *Journal of Personality and Social Psychology*, *96*, 305–323. https://doi.org/10.1037/a0013778

Snyder, M., & Cantor, N. (1979). Testing hypotheses about other people: The use of historical knowledge. *Journal of Experimental Social Psychology*, *15*, 330–342. https://doi.org/10.1016/0022-1031(79)90042-8

Soon, C. S., Brass, M., Heinze, H. J., & Haynes, J. D. (2008). Unconscious determinants of free decisions in the human brain. *Nature Neuroscience*, *11*, 543–545. https://doi.org/10.1038/nn.2112

Spiegel, L. (2013). Spooky number of Americans believe in ghosts. *The Huffington Post*, February 2. www.huffingtonpost.com/2013/02/02/real-ghosts-americans-poll_n_2049485.html

Strack, F., Martin, L. L., & Stepper, S. (1988). Inhibiting and facilitating conditions of the human smile: A nonobtrusive test of the facial feedback hypothesis. *Journal of Personality and Social Psychology*, *54*, 768–777. https://doi.org/10.1037/0022-3514.54.5.768

Strack, F., Schwarz, N., & Wänke, M. (1991). Semantic and pragmatic aspects of context effects in social and psychological research. *Social Cognition*, *9*, 111–125. https://doi.org/10.1521/soco.1991.9.1.111

Strelan, P., Weick, M., & Vasiljevic, M. (2014). Power and revenge. *British Journal of Social Psychology*, *53*, 521–540. https://doi.org/10.1111/bjso.12044

Sunstein, C. R. (2007). *Worst-case scenarios*. Cambridge, MA: Harvard University Press.

Taylor, S. E. (1981). The interface of cognitive and social psychology. In J. Harvey (Ed.), *Cognition, social behavior, and the environment* (pp. 198–2011). Hillsdale, NJ: Erlbaum.

Tiedens, L. Z., & Fragale, A. R. (2003). Power moves: Complementarity in dominant and submissive nonverbal behavior. *Journal of Personality and Social Psychology*, *84*, 558–568. https://doi.org/10.1037/0022-3514.84.3.558

Todorov, A., Mandisodza, A. N., Goren, A., & Hall, C. (2005). Inferences of competence from faces predict election outcomes. *Science*, *308*, 1623–1626. https://doi.org/10.1126/science.1110589

Topolinski, S., Zürn, M., & Schneider, I. K. (2015). What's in and what's out in branding? A novel articulation effect for brand names. *Frontiers in Psychology, 6*, 585. http://dx.doi.org/10.3389/fpsyg.2015.00585

Turley, L. W., & Milliman, R. E. (2000). Atmospheric effects on shopping behavior: A review of the experimental evidence. *Journal of Business Research, 49*, 193–211. https://doi.org/10.1016/S0148-2963(99)00010-7

Tversky, A., & Kahneman, D. (1973). Availability: A heuristic for judging frequency and probability. *Cognitive Psychology, 5*, 207–232. https://doi.org/10.1016/0010-0285(73)90033-9

Tversky, A., & Kahneman, D. (1991). Loss aversion in riskless choice: A reference-dependent model. *The Quarterly Journal of Economics, 106*, 1039–1061. https://doi.org/10.2307/2937956

van Horen, F., & Pieters, R. (2012). Consumer evaluation of copycat brands: The effect of imitation type. *International Journal of Research in Marketing, 29*, 246–255. https://doi.org/10.1016/j.ijresmar.2012.04.001

von Hippel, W., Silver, L. A., & Lynch, M. E. (2000). Stereotyping against your will: The role of inhibitory ability in stereotyping and prejudice among the elderly. *Personality and Social Psychology Bulletin, 26*, 523–532. https://doi.org/10.1177/0146167200267001

Wänke, M., & Reutner, L. (2010). Pragmatic persuasion or the persuasion paradox. In J. Forgas, W. Crano, & J. Cooper (Eds.), *The psychology of attitudes & attitude change* (pp. 183–198). New York: Psychology Press.

Waytz, A., Gray, K., Epley, N., & Wegner, D. M. (2010). Causes and consequences of mind perception. *Trends in Cognitive Sciences, 14*, 383–388. https://doi.org/10.1016/j.tics.2010.05.006

Wegner, D. M., Schneider, D. J., Carter, S. R., & White, T. L. (1987). Paradoxical effects of thought suppression. *Journal of Personality and Social Psychology, 53*, 5–13. https://doi.org/10.1037/0022-3514.53.1.5

Wegner, D. M., & Wheatley, T. (1999). Apparent mental causation: Sources of the experience of will. *American Psychologist, 54*, 480–492. https://doi.org/10.1037/0003-066X.54.7.480

Weick, M., Hopthrow, T., Abrams, D., & Taylor-Gooby, P. (2012). *Cognition: Minding risks.* Lloyd's Emerging Risks Report. Available from: https://dro.dur.ac.uk/26256/

Weick, M., McCall, C., & Blascovich, J. (2017). Power moves beyond complementarity: A staring look elicits avoidance in low power perceivers and approach in high power perceivers. *Personality and Social Psychology Bulletin, 43*, 1188–1201. https://doi.org/10.1177/0146167217708576

Weingarten, E., Chen, Q., McAdams, M., Yi, J., Hepler, J., & Albarracín, D. (2016). From primed concepts to action: A meta-analysis of the behavioral effects of incidentally presented words. *Psychological Bulletin, 142*, 472–497. https://doi.org/10.1037/bul0000030

Wells, G. L., & Petty, R. E. (1980). The effects of overt head movements on persuasion: Compatibility and incompatibility of responses. *Basic and Applied Social Psychology, 3*, 219–230. https://doi.org/10.1207/s15324834basp0103_2

Whitson, J. A., & Galinsky, A. D. (2008). Lacking control increases illusory pattern perception. *Science, 322*, 115–117. https://doi.org/10.1126/science.1159845

Wicker, B., Keysers, C., Plailly, J., Royet, J. P., Gallese, V., & Rizzolatti, G. (2003). Both of us disgusted in my insula: The common neural basis of seeing and feeling disgust. *Neuron*, *40*, 655–664. https://doi.org/10.1016/S0896-6273(03)00679-2

Willis, J., & Todorov, A. (2006). First impressions: Making up your mind after a 100-ms exposure to a face. *Psychological Science*, *17*, 592–598. https://doi.org/10.1111/j.1467-9280.2006.01750.x

Wyer Jr, R. S. (1976). An investigation of the relations among probability estimates. *Organizational Behavior and Human Performance*, *15*, 1–18. https://doi.org/10.1016/0030-5073(76)90026-X

Yorkston, E., & Menon, G. (2004). A sound idea: Phonetic effects of brand names on consumer judgments. *Journal of Consumer Research*, *31*, 43–51. https://doi.org/10.1086/383422

Zajonc, R. B. (1968). Attitudinal effects of mere exposure. *Journal of Personality and Social Psychology*, *9*, 1–27. https://doi.org/10.1037/h0025848

6

ATTITUDES AND PERSUASION

CHRISTOPHER R. JONES & LAMBROS LAZURAS

Contents

6.1 AUTHORS' PERSONAL JOURNEYS

Christopher R. Jones

Source: © Christoper R. Jones

I first studied Psychology at A-Level (1997–1999) and never looked back. The novelty of the subject attracted me. Little did I know it would become my career. I studied for my undergraduate degree in Psychology at the University of Birmingham (1999–2002), where I found social psychology and the topic of attitude formation to be of particular interest. My undergraduate dissertation (supervised by Professor Richard Crisp) focused on the mere exposure effect – a mode of attitude formation introduced later in this chapter – and whether exposure to music might affect people's attitudes towards it.

My interests in attitude formation continued into my Master's degree (2002–2003) and PhD (2003–2007) at the University of Sheffield, under the tutelage of Professor Dick Eiser (a key thinker you will read about in this chapter). It was during my PhD when I first met my co-author, Lambros, who was also supervised by Professor Eiser. My postgraduate studies focused on how attitudes form towards spatial location as a result of our positive or negative experiences with them. This built on the 'BeanFest' studies devised by Prof. Eiser and Prof. Russell Fazio at Ohio State University, which you will learn about in Part 2 of this chapter. Professor Fazio is another of the key thinkers in this chapter. After completing my PhD, I took on a four-year postdoctoral research associate post at the University of Sheffield (2007–2011). The project focused on understanding public attitudes towards climate change and energy choices. It was during this time, and during my first lecturing post at Sheffield (2011–2017), that my identity as a psychologist evolved as I applied my social psychological training to better understanding environmental issues.

In 2017, I moved to the University of Surrey as a senior lecturer in Social and Environmental Psychology, before joining the University of Portsmouth as an Associate Professor of Applied Psychology in 2022.

Lambros Lazuras

Just before finishing secondary school, I joined a rock band as a drummer, and for a few years I was sure that I would become a true rock star. But, as they say, life happened. After an unexpected and painful band break-up, I served in the Greek army, and then I was left wondering what to do with my life. I tried different jobs, from flipping burgers to working at a convenience store. When I turned 20, I accidentally stumbled upon an introductory Psychology textbook of a friend who was studying Psychology at the time. That was it. I was drawn to it like a moth to a flame. Within a week I had read four chapters and this is when I realised I wanted to become a psychologist.

Source: © Lambros Lazuras

I completed my undergraduate degree in Psychology at the University of Sheffield (at the international campus in Greece). The topic of my undergraduate dissertation was attitudes towards smoking among young people, and this eventually became my first published study. As soon as I completed my undergraduate degree, I was awarded a PhD scholarship at the same university, under the supervision of Professor Dick Eiser. It was during a supervision meeting that I met my friend and co-author, Chris. My PhD (2004–2007) and first postdoctoral position (2007–2010) focused on the interplay between social norms and attitudes towards smoking and were funded by Cancer Research UK. In 2008 I became interested in the study of performance enhancement drug use (doping) in sport, a topic that I still study today.

Before moving to Sheffield Hallam University in 2015, I completed a second postdoctoral post at the Department of Developmental and Social Psychology, at La Sapienza University of Rome, Italy. During my time in Rome, I developed an interest in understanding why people engage in risky driving, with a focus on the association between personality traits and attitudes. I'm currently a professor at the University of Lincoln and visiting professor of Psychology at the University of Trento, Italy. Who knows where life will take me next …

6.2 INTRODUCTION

'I love advanced statistics!' is not a phrase we hear from the many undergraduate students we teach – although some surprise us. Leaving the obvious importance of statistics to psychology aside, what does this simple expression imply? Perhaps that the student derives pleasure from significance testing and sees the personal benefits in understanding the principles of linear regression. We might also *infer* that the student has a good record of attendance in their statistics classes, and is keen on doing additional reading. Or maybe the statement is one simply designed to placate the demands of the statistics professor.

What we can be certain of is that this is an expression of 'attitude', which is the focus of this chapter. An attitude is a person's positive, negative, or ambivalent evaluation of an attitude object. An attitude object can be anything from a person, group, or event, to an issue, concept, or thing. For instance, the 'object' being evaluated above by the student is the topic of 'advanced statistics', but their love – or hate, liking, disliking, or ambivalence – could have easily been expressed towards something more or less specific than advanced statistics.

The study of attitudes has long been synonymous with social psychology, to the extent that, historically, social psychology has been considered the 'science of attitudes' (Moscovici, 1963, p. 231). While the historical path of attitude research has taken many twists and turns, today the concept of attitudes remains as 'distinctive and indispensable' to social psychology as it did when Gordon Allport first made this claim back in the 1930s (Allport, 1935, p. 798).

Within this chapter, you will learn about the nature of attitudes: their structure, purpose, and relationships with other key constructs, like values. It will teach you about the core principles of attitude formation and change (including an introduction to some key models of persuasion) and how attitudes are measured, and will consider the (sometimes questionable) links between attitudes and behaviours.

The chapter will then dive deeper to consider advances in our understanding of how valence asymmetries form in our learning of positive and negative attitudes and the impact that framing has on our attitudes and preferences. It will end by appraising three areas where attitude theories are being applied to understand contemporary, real-world issues: pro-environmental behaviour, technology acceptance, and doping in sport.

> **Key concept – Attitudes:** An attitude is a relatively enduring mental construct that represents a person's positive, negative, or ambivalent evaluation of an attitude object (e.g., a person, group, event, issue, concept, or thing).

This chapter might not make you love advanced statistics, but it will hopefully go some way to helping you love **attitudes**.

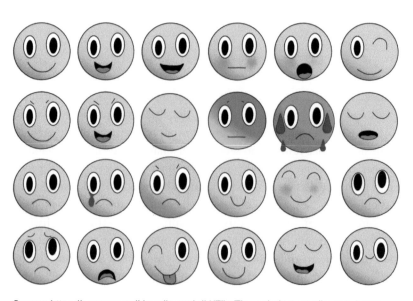

Source: https://commons.wikimedia.org/wiki/File:The_adoring_emojis_set_2.png

6.3 LEARNING OBJECTIVES

By the end of this chapter, you will know more about:

- The history of attitude research, what attitudes are, how they are defined, and how they function;
- The core principles of attitude formation and routes to persuasion and behaviour change;
- The attitude–behaviour relationship, including when and how attitudes influence behaviour, and how behaviours can affect attitudes;
- The means by which explicit and implicit attitudes are measured. You will develop an awareness of some of the key challenges to reliable and valid attitude assessment;
- The principles of attitude formation in situations where opportunities to learn about what is 'good' and 'bad' are contingent on our approach and avoidance behaviours;
- How the way in which information or decisions are 'framed' can affect our attitudes and behaviours;
- How attitude theory is currently being applied to better understand and resolve contemporary real-world issues, including pro-environmental behaviour, technology acceptance, and doping in sport.

6.4 PART 1: FOUNDATIONS

In this opening section, we aim to give you a foundational understanding of contemporary attitude theory. In addition to learning about the principles of attitude measurement, you will read about the structure and function of attitudes, some of the key routes by which attitudes form, how attitudes relate (and sometimes do not relate) to behaviours, and how attitudes might change in response to persuasive appeals.

6.4.1 The Structure and Function of Attitudes

There is not just one 'type' of attitude. Attitudes vary in their strength, accessibility, composition, and purpose. In this section, we explore the definition and dimensions of attitudes, consider the importance of attitude strength and accessibility to their ability to influence our thoughts and actions, and consider the distinct functions they can fulfil.

Definition and Dimensionality

An attitude is a knowledge structure that represents someone's positive, negative, or ambivalent evaluations of an 'attitude object'. The attitude object can be anything: a place, a sports team, your family, a piece of furniture, vaccination, and so on. Attitudes are based on up to three sources of information (Figure 6.1): our emotions and feelings relating to the attitude object (the **affect** or **A** component), the representations of our interactions with and action tendencies towards the attitude object (the **behaviour** or **B** component), and our beliefs about the attitude object (the **cognitive** or **C** component). So, if you had a positive attitude

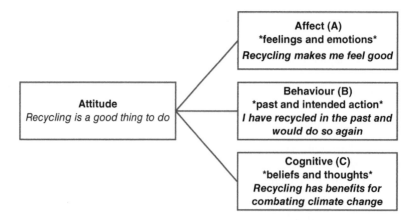

Figure 6.1 A visual representation of the ABC model of attitudes. This example depicts a person with a positive attitude towards recycling and how the affective (A), behaviour (B), and cognitive (C) inputs support this positive attitude. Note that the relationship between the attitude and these 'inputs' can be bidirectional. Affective, behavioural, and cognitive information can shape our attitudes, but our attitudes can also shape our feelings, actions, and thoughts relating to attitude objects

to this social psychology textbook (the attitude object), we might expect that you would *believe* there are benefits to owning it (correct!), that you will anticipate getting a *feeling* of satisfaction from reading it (naturally!), and that you wish to *behave* positively towards it, by reading it (we hope you do!).

Attitudes do not always have to be derived from all three sources of information. For example, some of the attitudes we hold can form in the absence of beliefs about the attitude object, essentially being based on 'gut feeling'. Also, the ABC inputs do not have to be aligned; it is possible to hold conflicting affective, cognitive, and behavioural information about an attitude object, which can give rise to ambivalence. For example, people who fear the dentist (affect) might still understand the benefits of attending (cognitive), and attend check-ups (behaviour).

How attitudes are represented in memory has long been debated by social psychologists. For example, a classic multidimensional model of attitudes known as the *tripartite model* (Hovland & Rosenberg, 1960) suggests that the ABC inputs *are* the attitude and that, being three qualitatively different bits of information, the ABC inputs should be assessed in different ways (e.g., asking people about their beliefs to assess the cognitive input, or observing people's overt actions to assess the behavioural input). Unidimensional conceptualisations of the attitude, however, view attitudes as distinct 'summary evaluations' of the information we hold about an attitude object, which can be measured on a common scale (Samra, 2014). Consistent with a unidimensional position, Russell Fazio (e.g., Fazio, 1990) – one of the key thinkers in this chapter – defines attitudes as object-evaluation associations (Figure 6.2); that is, the *association* that forms in memory between an 'attitude object' and the 'summary evaluation' of that attitude object. Fazio argues that the *strength* of this association is crucial in determining whether an attitude will affect our thoughts and actions.

While debate continues over the dimensionality of attitudes, unidimensional conceptual-isations have become increasingly dominant, reflecting trends in how we measure attitudes (Fabringar et al., 2018). Basically, our tendency to generate average or summative scores for attitudes on singular evaluative dimensions (e.g., good–bad, like–dislike) when assessing them tends to favour more unidimensional thinking (Samra, 2014).

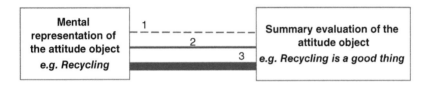

Figure 6.2 An interpretation of the 'object-evaluation' attitude concept. The attitude is the association between the mental representation of the attitude object and the summary evaluation of the object, derived from a fusion of the affective, cognitive, and behavioural inputs. The strength of the association determines the strength and accessibility of the attitude. Line 1 depicts a weak (inaccessible) attitude, Line 2 depicts a moderately strong (fairly accessible) attitude, and Line 3 depicts a very strong (highly accessible) attitude

Attitude Strength and Accessibility

Attitudes can vary on many different qualitative dimensions. For example, some attitudes are more affect-based ('hot'), while others are more belief-based ('cold'). Attitudes also vary in terms of strength. Whereas some attitudes are weak and easily changed, others are stronger and more enduring. Research has highlighted much about the attributes that affect attitude strength (Krosnick & Petty, 2014), some of which are outlined in Table 6.1.

While all these strength-related attributes have received research attention, one of the most critical to understanding how attitudes influence thoughts and behaviours is their *accessibility*. According to Fazio (2007), the strength of the association between an attitude object and its evaluation will determine the ease with which an attitude will become active in memory. It is only when an attitude is active and accessible that it can exert an impact on someone's perceptions, judgements, and behaviours.

Attitudes are believed to sit along a continuum of strength, with weak 'non-attitudes' at the lower end and strong attitudes at the upper end. Towards the upper end of the continuum, attitudes are

> **Key concept – Attitude accessibility:** The likelihood that attitudes will become active and influence our thoughts and behaviours is related to their accessibility in memory. Strong attitudes are highly accessible and are therefore likely to affect our thoughts and actions. Weaker attitudes are less accessible and therefore less influential.

Table 6.1 Some key attributes affecting attitude strength

Attribute	Definition
Certainty	The conviction with which someone holds the attitude
Extremity	The extent to which the attitude deviates from a neutral position
Personal relevance	The psychological significance or importance of the attitude to the individual
Evaluative consistency	The consistency between the evaluation of the attitude object and the beliefs and/or emotions associated with it
Knowledge	The amount of information held (or believed to be held) about an attitude object
Elaboration	The extent to which a person has thought carefully about the merits and demerits of an attitude object
Accessibility	The strength of the associative link between an attitude object and its evaluation in memory

thought to become automatically activated when the attitude object is directly or indirectly encountered (e.g., where it is observed or mentioned). They can therefore exert a strong impact on our thoughts and actions, even outside our conscious awareness. At the lower end of the continuum, people only have weak or no pre-existing evaluations of the attitude object and have to actively construct an attitude, if asked for their opinion. Consider the difference between the attitudes you hold for close friends and family (which are likely strong, enduring, and accessible) compared with those towards a stranger you have just passed on the street (which are likely to be weaker and constructed in the moment).

KEY THINKER

Russell H. Fazio

Source: © Russell H. Fazio

Russell H. Fazio is the Harold E. Burtt Professor of Social Psychology at Ohio State University in the United States, where he leads his Attitudes and Social Cognition Lab. Professor Fazio's research activity and thought leadership over the past half-century have contributed massively to our understanding of attitude theory, the principles of attitude formation and change, and the nature of the attitude–behaviour relationship. He has also advanced our means of accurately measuring attitudes.

Fazio and his colleagues have pioneered research into the 'associationist' concept of the attitude, and noted the related importance of **attitude accessibility** as a key factor influencing the strength of the relationship between attitudes and behaviour. His studies using the 'BeanFest' game (see Part 2 of this chapter) have shed light on the negative asymmetries that can arise in attitude formation where learning is reliant on our personal exploration or sampling of stimuli.

EXERCISE 6.1

Evaluating your personal 'need to evaluate'

People vary in terms of their 'need to evaluate' their lives and the things within it (i.e., their tendencies to form and use attitudes) (Jarvis & Petty, 1996). To calculate your own need to evaluate, complete the following measure. First, you will need to score yourself on a scale of 1 (extremely *uncharacteristic* of you) to 5 (extremely *characteristic* of you) for each of the 16 items.

1   I form opinions about everything
2   I prefer to avoid taking extreme positions (R)
3   It is very important to me to hold strong opinions
4   I want to know exactly what is good and bad about everything
5   I often prefer to remain neutral about complex issues (R)
6   If something does not affect me, I do not usually determine if it is good or bad (R)
7   I enjoy strongly liking or disliking new things
8   There are many things for which I do not have a preference (R)
9   It bothers me to remain neutral
10 I like to have strong opinions even when I am not personally involved
11 I have many more opinions than the average person
12 I would rather have a strong opinion than no opinion at all
13 I pay a lot of attention to whether things are good or bad
14 I only form strong opinions when I have to (R)
15 I like to decide that new things are really good or really bad
16 I am pretty much indifferent to many important issues (R)

Next, you need to 'reverse score' any items with an (R) next to them (i.e., a score of '1' becomes '5'; '2' becomes '4'; '3' remains '3'; '4' becomes '2', and '5' becomes '1'). Finally, add up your score for the 16 items. Your total should fall somewhere between 16 and 80. Based on Jarvis and Petty's (1996) studies, people scoring around 47 or lower are classified as having a 'low' need to evaluate, those scoring between 48 and 56 are 'moderate', and those scoring above about 57 are 'high'.

Attitude Function

The purpose, or function, of attitudes has long been a topic of interest. While various theories about the purpose of attitudes exist, Daniel Katz's (1960) functionalist theory is arguably the best known. Katz's theory, which has empirical support (Maio & Olson, 2000), posits that attitudes essentially satisfy four functions:

1   **Utilitarian**: Attitudes help to guide us towards reward ('good things') and away from punishment ('bad things'), aiding our survival (Figure 6.3). Consider, for instance, research into conformity and how we will often (publicly) express attitudes that concur with a perceived majority. This improves our chances of being accepted by the majority and avoiding rejection by them.

2 **Knowledge**: Attitudes provide us with information about how to structure and organise our social world by helping us to classify things as 'good' (e.g., liked, approachable) and 'bad' (e.g., disliked, to be avoided). For example, stereotypes are the attitudes we hold towards social groups that provide us with (sometimes questionable) information about those with whom we interact.

3 **Ego-defensive**: Attitudes can protect a positive sense of self against potentially threatening information. For example, we might form negative attitudes towards our 'friends' on social media who appear to be living the 'perfect life', in an attempt to justify the quality of our own life-choices.

4 **Value-expressive**: Attitudes can help us express the values that are important to us, a function that maps to people's inherent desire to verify their self-identity. For instance, we might form a positive attitude towards shopping for clothing in charity shops, as this helps us to express our pro-environmental values. Note, values differ from attitudes, as they are broader, more abstract principles that serve to generally guide our thoughts, attitudes, and behaviours (Rokeach, 1973). Attitudes, by contrast, are evaluative constructs tied to something specific (i.e., the attitude object).

Figure 6.3 One direction? Attitudes have a *utilitarian function* helping to direct us towards rewards and away from punishments, thereby helping to aid our survival

Source: Nick Youngson/www.nyphotographic.com, CC BY-SA 3.0

6.4.2 Attitude Formation

There are many routes to attitude formation. Attitudes can form via direct experience with an attitude object or indirectly (e.g., by what we are told by others); they can be actively 'created' or more passively 'absorbed' by what we see or hear (Kanekar, 1976). Below we outline some of the key affective, cognitive, and behavioural routes to attitude formation.

Affective Routes

The key affective (or 'feeling-based') routes to attitude formation include operant conditioning, classical/evaluative conditioning, and mere exposure.

Operant Conditioning

Operant (or instrumental) conditioning is a basic principle of learning. Learning via operant conditioning is grounded in the 'law of effect' (Thorndike, 1927). This states that the performance of actions which have pleasant outcomes (are rewarded or go unpunished) will tend to increase, while the performance of actions yielding unpleasant outcomes (which are punished or go unrewarded) will tend to decrease. Recall, B. F. Skinner's (1963) rats learning to press a lever to receive a rewarding food pellet, or Thorndike's (1932) cats learning to press a lever to escape confinement from a 'puzzle box' (Figure 6.4).

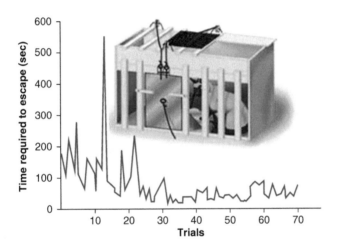

Figure 6.4 The law of effect. A figure shows the decreasing time it took for a cat to escape a puzzle box with repeated trials in Thorndike's studies. The cat learned that pressing a lever led to the reward of escaping the box, so it tended to repeat this action more quickly over time

Source: https://www.google.com/url?q=https://commons.wikimedia.org/wiki/File:Puzzle_box.jpg&sa=D&source=docs&ust=1720789738349740&usg=AOvVaw0XRDWoSHp-9HumPW5uqreD

There is good evidence that attitudes can form via operant conditioning. Insko (1965), for instance, investigated how verbal reinforcement of opinions expressed by students impacted on their attitudes. During a telephone interview, an interviewer used the word 'good' to reinforce participants' agreement or disagreement with a series of statements about the introduction of a university event ('Aloha Week'). A week later, participants were presented with a questionnaire about local issues featuring a question about 'Aloha Week'.

The verbal reinforcement from the interview had a sustained impact on participants' attitudes towards the event. Attitudes were more positive where the word 'good' had been used to reinforce statements endorsing the event.

Classical/evaluative Conditioning

Classical conditioning is also a form of associative learning, although no specific action is required on the part of the learner. The term 'classical conditioning' likely conjures up images of salivating dogs. In the 1890s, Pavlov famously paired the ring of a bell with the provision of food and measured the extent to which his subjects (dogs) would salivate. After a series of associative pairings, Pavlov observed that the dogs would salivate simply on hearing the bell, indicating that salivation had become a conditioned response to hearing the bell.

The principles of classical conditioning have been applied to the study of attitudes, in what is often referred to as 'evaluative conditioning' (Moran et al., 2023). Evaluative conditioning holds that pairing an attitude object with something positive or negative should lead to the attitude object becoming evaluated as positive or negative itself. This concept is often seen in advertising, where a new product (e.g., shampoo) is paired with positive imagery, music, or messaging in the hope that consumers will form positive attitudes towards the product and buy it (Moran et al., 2023) (Figure 6.5). Evaluative conditioning is somewhat different from other forms of classical conditioning. Whereas the effects of classical conditioning tend only to emerge with repeated pairings of the *conditioned stimulus* (CS) and *unconditioned stimulus* (UCS) (e.g., bell–food, bell–food, bell–food ...), the effects of evaluative conditioning on attitude formation can occur from just one CS–UCS pairing (De Houwer et al., 2001).

There is good evidence of evaluative (or classical) conditioning as a means of attitude formation (Moran et al., 2023), including studies demonstrating that it may occur outside people's conscious awareness. For example, Olson and Fazio (2001) had people participate in an apparent 'surveillance task' (Figure 6.6). Selections of images and words were presented to them on a computer screen and they were told to press a response key when they saw a specified target stimulus. Participants were unaware that embedded within the stream of words and images were some 'critical pairings'. These critical pairings occurred between two Pokémon characters and positive and negative stimuli. During the task, one Pokémon was consistently paired on screen with positive items and the other with negative items. In a subsequent evaluation task, participants evaluated both Pokémon characters. Despite participants having no explicit awareness of the critical pairings, they showed a clear preference for the Pokémon character that had been paired with the positive items.

Mere Exposure

It is not always necessary to have a conditioning stimulus for attitude formation to occur. The principle of 'mere exposure' holds that the simple repeated exposure of an individual to a stimulus can improve their attitude towards it. Basically, the more you encounter something, the more you tend to like it! Robert Zajonc (1968) (pronounced 'science')

Figure 6.5 Evaluative conditioner? For years, shampoo and conditioner product advertisers have associated their products with famous people and attractive models. Is this an attempt to condition consumers to buy their products?

Souce: https://www.google.com/url?q=https://commons.wikimedia.org/wiki/File:Yes,_Elizabeth_Taylor_uses_Lustre_Cr%25C3%25A8me_Shampoo,_1952.jpg&sa=D&source=docs&ust=1720789738344442&usg=AOvVaw2Toe_izqrshrDg1YfCLVw

pioneered research into this 'mere exposure effect'. You can learn about some of his early findings in Key study 6.1.

Research shows the mere exposure effect to be robust and reliable, with evidence of the effect found in studies using different stimuli (e.g., visual, auditory, gustatory), settings (e.g., laboratory, naturalistic), and response measures (e.g., ratings of liking, attractiveness). Studies have also revealed other interesting things about the effect, including that:

- a person does not have to be aware of having been exposed to the stimulus for the effect to occur. If anything, the strength of the effect is stronger under such conditions (Monahan et al., 2000);
- 'boredom' is a limiting factor for the effect. The strongest effects appear with relatively few exposures, after which point attitude enhancement can begin to tail off or even 'downturn' (i.e., attitudes begin to become less favourable) (Bornstein et al., 1990);

- the effect seems to be disrupted where the exposure stimuli are not deemed to be neutral in the first place. For example, in studies involving rock and roll music and abstract paintings, Brickman and colleagues (1972) found that where people initially disliked the exposure stimuli, repeated exposure led to a worsening of attitudes.

Along with operant and evaluative conditioning, mere exposure shows how attitudes can form from our affective responses to experiences with attitude objects. The mere exposure effect also confirms that 'preferences' do not necessarily need 'inferences' (Zajonc, 1980), or that attitudes do not always need to be tied to our beliefs about an attitude object. However, our beliefs and expectations about attitude objects do present another key route to attitude formation.

 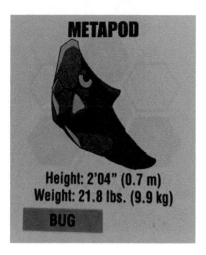

Figure 6.6 Pokémon used in Olson and Fazio's (2001) 'surveillance task' paradigm. Shellder and Metapod were selected for use in the study. One Pokémon was always paired with positive stimuli, while the other was paired with negative stimuli. A preference was shown for the character associated with the positive stimuli

Source: © Delia Martinez Alfonso

KEY STUDY 6.1

Attitudinal Effects of Mere Exposure

Zajonc's (1968) interest in the mere exposure effect was piqued by studies showing that people tend to assign better meanings to more frequently presented nonsense words (Johnson et al., 1960). Zajonc took these findings as indicative of mere exposure and designed experiments to find support for this as a means of attitude formation.

In the first of three experiments, Zajonc used 'Turkish' words (e.g., iktitaf, civadra) as the stimuli. These were not actually Turkish words but were 12 made-up words designed to be unfamiliar to participants. Each word was counterbalanced against six exposure frequencies (0, 1, 2, 5, 10, and 25 exposures). So, for each participant, two words received no exposure, two received one exposure, two received two exposures, two received five exposures, and so on. The counterbalancing ensured that exposure frequency and not the individual properties of a given word could account for any effects observed.

In each trial the participant was presented with a word, which the experimenter then read out loud. The participant then had to pronounce the word. At the end of this task participants were told that the words were Turkish adjectives and that they now should guess whether each word meant something good or bad. This was done on a 7-point good–bad scale, used as a proxy measure for 'liking'.

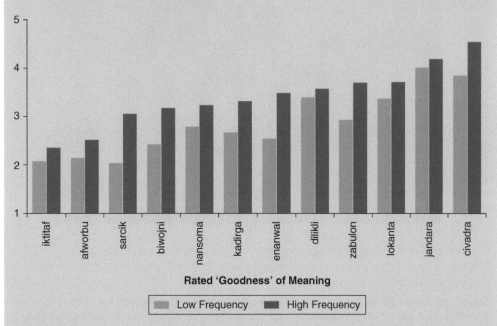

Figure 6.7 Average rated affective connotation of nonsense words exposed with low and high frequencies

Source: Zajonc (1968)

The results of Experiment 1 are presented in Figure 6.7. The bars summarise the 'goodness' ratings for each word provided by those seeing the word infrequently (0, 1, and 2 exposures) and those seeing the word more frequently (5, 10, and 25 exposures). Two patterns emerge: (1) some words were generally considered to have more positive meanings than others (e.g., 'civadra' was deemed more positive than 'iktitaf'); but also (2) exposure frequency affected participants' evaluations in the way Zajonc had hypothesised – the same word was deemed more positive where it had been exposed more frequently!

In two subsequent studies, Zajonc replicated these findings using 'Chinese' symbols as stimuli (Study 2) and college yearbook photos (Study 3). These experiments and other studies reported in Zajonc's monograph (1968) have provided the basis for considerable research into the mere exposure effect over the past 50 years, and even provided the inspiration for Chris's undergraduate dissertation.

Cognitive Routes

Consider you are shopping and that you pick out two black shirts of equivalent cost and quality. You only have enough money to buy one. You then notice that the label on one garment indicates that it has been made using sustainably sourced materials. Which shirt do you prefer? We hope you opt for the sustainably sourced one, bearing in mind the toll that the fashion industry has on the environment (Niinimäki et al., 2020) (Figure 6.8) . But how do you reach this decision?

Figure 6.8 Are you a conscientious consumer? What drives your clothes shopping decisions? Do you simply consider the financial cost or do you also look at the environmental cost of your purchases?

Source: https://www.google.com/url?q=https://openverse.org/image/025df98b-d71b-41fd-88bd-eb517bd-e7d4a?q%3Dperson%2520clothes%2520shopping&sa=D&source=docs&ust=1720789738332486&us-g=AOvVaw3dZlJY54lhHfpH6GcmC7nE

A key cognitive model of attitude, the expectancy-value model (Fishbein & Ajzen, 1975), posits that attitudes result from the cognitive arithmetic that we do in relation to our beliefs about an attitude object (in this case the shirt). According to this model, the 'belief' is defined as the subjectively determined probability (or expectancy) that an attitude object has a particular set of attributes (e.g., *'I expect there is a high probability that the shirt is sustainably sourced'*). Each of these attributes is then evaluated (assigned a value) by the individual (e.g., *'It is very important to me to be an ecologically conscious consumer'*). The person's attitude is then computed by combining all the accessible attribute–evaluation associations, while also factoring in the strength of these associations.

While proving that people actually compute attitudes this specific way is challenging (Hewstone & Young, 1988), the expectancy-value model of attitudes is popular and has underpinned psychological research in many areas, from consumer behaviour (Towler & Shepherd, 1992) to environmental preferences (Staats et al., 2003). It also underpins a key theory of how attitudes relate to behaviours, the Theory of Planned Behaviour (Ajzen, 1991), which you will learn about below.

The expectancy-value model can account for why people in possession of the same beliefs about an object can hold different attitudes towards it. This stems from differences in how people evaluate these beliefs. For example, Woo and Castore (1980) examined the attitudes of pro-nuclear and anti-nuclear citizen groups living close to the site of a proposed nuclear power station. The pro-nuclear and anti-nuclear groups, while holding the same number of positive and negative beliefs, differed in the relative value they placed on the positive (e.g., economic benefit) and negative (e.g., health and safety issues) outcomes, explaining their differences of opinion.

Behavioural Routes

Attitudes can also stem from the self-reflective inferences that we make of our own actions, and even from how we position and move our bodies (a process known as embodiment).

Self-reflecting on Behaviour

Returning to the shopping example above, you could ask why you have selected two black shirts to choose between? Perhaps confused by all the choices in the shop, you glance in the mirror, see you are currently wearing black and infer that you must particularly like the colour. The tendency for behaviour to shape attitudes appears to be particularly strong in ambiguous situations (e.g., where we lack appropriate contextual knowledge) and where our actions are (ostensibly) freely chosen and not (obviously) coerced in some way. According to self-perception theory (Bem, 1972), in such circumstances, we seek to make attributions for the causes of our behaviour. Where we conclude that the behaviour originated from ourselves (internal attribution) as opposed to some form of situational factor (external attribution), we infer that the behaviour is indicative of our attitudes.

Cognitive dissonance theory (Festinger, 1962) has also been used to explain attitude formation. This theory holds that we strive for consistency in our thoughts, attitudes, and actions. Any inconsistency causes unpleasant psychological tension that we are motivated to reduce. So, if we act in a way that is inconsistent with our attitudes, then we may seek to form or change our attitudes so that they align with our actions. In a key study on induced compliance, Festinger and Carlsmith (1959) had participants complete a series of tedious tasks. In the experimental condition, participants were told in advance that the task would be fun, while the control group were told nothing. After the task, members of the experimental group only were paid either $1 or $20 to introduce the task to a new participant and to tell them it would be fun (basically to lie). Participants were then asked to evaluate how enjoyable they had personally found the task. Who expressed the most positive attitudes? On average, the group who had been paid just $1!

This can be explained with reference to cognitive dissonance reduction. For the control group, and for the experimental group paid $20, there is little dissonance to resolve: the control group can truthfully say they found the task boring; the $20 group, while perhaps feeling bad about lying to another participant, have a handsome reward for doing so. The $1 group, however, receives only a small reward for lying, which is unlikely to reduce the uncomfortable dissonance they feel. However, if they choose to evaluate the boring tasks more positively, the dissonance is reduced, and they can feel happier about the whole situation!

Embodiment

There is growing evidence for the impact that our bodily movements and positioning can have on our attitudes (Briñol et al., 2012). For example, according to the facial feedback hypothesis, our attitudes can be affected by our facial expressions (e.g., smiling and pouting), even if something has not happened to make us feel positive or negative. Strack, Martin, and Stepper (1988) had people watch cartoons while holding a pen in their mouths. The pen was held either in (a) the teeth, activating the facial muscles associated with smiling, or (b) between the lips, activating a pouty expression. When asked to evaluate the cartoons, those in the 'smile' condition tended to evaluate the cartoons as funnier than those in the 'pout' condition (Figure 6.9).

The facial feedback hypothesis has received considerable attention due to its simple message: smile more, feel more positive. However, the reliability of the effect has been called into question, with some studies failing to replicate Strack et al.'s (1988) findings. Currently, the weight of evidence suggests that smiling can initiate feelings of happiness, but evidence for the simulation of these effects using the pen-in-mouth task is more inconclusive (Coles et al., 2022).

Figure 6.9 An illustration of embodiment. The pen on the left is held between the teeth, simulating a 'smiling' face. The pen on the right is held between the lips, simulating a pouting face

Image source: Wagenmakers et al. (2016), available at http://tinyurl.com/zm7p9l7. Reproduced under CC license https://creativecommons.org/licenses/by/2.0/

6.4.3 Attitudes and Behaviour

To this point, we have implied that there is a link between a person's attitudes and their behaviours. However, it is not always the case that people act in accordance with their attitudes. For example, most people living in the UK would tell you that caring for the planet is important to them – thereby expressing a strong pro-environmental attitude. However, whether these same people would forgo plane travel in the name of environmental conservation is a matter for debate (Kaklamanou et al., 2015). In fact, even climate change professors have been found to fly more than researchers in other fields (Whitmarsh et al., 2020). In this section, we will consider some of the key determinants of the attitude–behaviour relationship, and what leads people to behave in attitude-consistent or attitude-inconsistent ways.

When do Attitudes Predict Behaviour?

While there has been debate over the nature – or even the existence (e.g., LaPiere, 1934) – of the **attitude–behaviour** relationship, it is the case that attitudes often do impact our actions (Ajzen et al., 2018). Put succinctly, it is not a case of *whether* they do, but *when* they do. The nature of the attitude, how it is measured, how it is formed, a person's control beliefs, and situational characteristics are all important moderators of the relationship between a person's attitudes and their behaviours and can explain

> **Key concept – Attitude–behaviour gap:** Attitudes are one of many predictors of people's behaviour. Under some circumstances, attitudes are a strong predictor of people's behaviour, but in others the relationship is weaker or non-existent. This means that people will not always act in accordance with their attitudes, a phenomenon sometimes referred to as the attitude-behaviour gap.

why there is sometimes a lack of correspondence between them, i.e., an attitude-behaviour gap. See Table 6.2 for examples pertaining to each of these key factors.

Table 6.2   Key factors affecting the attitude–behaviour relationship

Factor	Example dimension	Details
Nature of attitude	Strength	People are more likely to act in accordance with their stronger attitudes, in part because they are more likely to be accessible from memory, more extreme, and/or held with greater certainty.
Measurement of attitude	Specificity	While a person's general attitudes can be a reasonable predictor of their general behavioural tendencies, more specific attitudes are a better predictor of specific actions. Vining and Ebreo (1992), in a study on community curbside recycling behaviour, found a stronger relationship between a person's specific attitudes towards recycling and their recycling behaviour, as compared with their more general environmental attitudes.
Formation of attitude	Direct or indirect experience	Attitudes formed on the basis of direct personal experience are often stronger, more accessible, and thus more predictive of behaviours than attitudes that are more indirectly acquired (e.g., via word of mouth). Spence and colleagues (2011) found that people with direct experience of flooding were more concerned with climate change (stronger attitude) than those who had not directly experienced flooding.
Behavioural control	Control beliefs	If people believe they have the ability and opportunity to act in accordance with their attitudes, this will increase the chance that they will do so. DeVellis and colleagues (1990) found that, particularly for people at high risk of cancer, control beliefs had a strong influence on their cancer screening intentions and actions.
Situational characteristics	Social context	Our beliefs about what is normative in a given context can shape whether attitude-consistent behaviour is or is not likely. People are more likely to act in a manner consistent with their attitudes when there is believed to be social support for it, particularly among those from salient or important groups to us (Smith & Louis, 2009).

Models of the Attitude–Behaviour Relationship

There are many models of the attitude–behaviour relationship, two of the main ones are the Theory of Planned Behaviour (TPB), and Motivation and Opportunity as Determinants (MODE) model.

Theory of Planned Behaviour

One of the most influential models of the attitude–behaviour relationship is the *Theory of Planned Behaviour*, which is an extension of a simpler model called the *Theory of Reasoned Action*. This model is based on the expectancy-value model of the attitude outlined above.

The Theory of Reasoned Action (TRA) (Fishbein & Ajzen, 1975) posits that a person's *attitudes* towards performing a behaviour, and their beliefs about what others think about their performing the behaviour (*subjective norms*) predict their behavioural *intentions*, which then predict their likelihood of performing the *behaviour*. For example, Chris is a Southampton FC fan and holds positive attitudes towards wearing their football shirt. However, Chris also lives in Portsmouth, whose football team (Portsmouth FC) are bitter rivals of Southampton FC. The subjective norms towards wearing the shirt locally are thus unfavourable. This will lower his intention to act in an attitude-consistent way and so he doesn't wear the shirt. When he is visiting his home town of Southampton, though, the subjective norms are more favourable, and so the shirt is worn.

The Theory of Planned Behaviour (TPB) (Ajzen, 1991) extends the TRA by including a construct called *perceived behavioural control* (PBC). This measures the perceived ease or difficulty with which someone believes they can perform a behaviour. The more able someone feels to act in a particular way, the more likely they are to intend to do so (see Table 6.2, control beliefs). The PBC construct acknowledges that people do not always believe that they have the resources and/or opportunity to act in an attitude-consistent way, which can reduce their intentions to do so. Whether or not a behaviour can be performed is also a product of someone's actual opportunity to do so. This is called *actual behavioural control*. In some situations, a person will literally not have the required skills, capability, and/or other

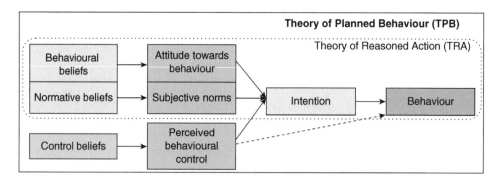

Figure 6.10 The Theory of Reasoned Action (TRA) and Theory of Planned Behaviour (TPB). The TPB augments the TRA through the addition of the perceived behavioural control (PBC) construct. To the extent that PBC is reflective of the actual control someone has over a behaviour, it can be used to predict behaviour directly (i.e., the dashed line)

KEY THINKER 6.2

Icek Ajzen

Icek Ajzen (pronounced 'Izen') is one of the most influential social psychologists of all time in terms of the cumulative impact of his research. He retired in 2012 and is now Professor Emeritus at the University of Massachusetts – Amherst in the United States, where he spent most of his professional career.

Professor Ajzen is most remembered for the work he completed with his long-term collaborator, Professor Martin Fishbein. Together, they devised the Theory of Reasoned Action (TRA), which is the forerunner to the Theory of Planned Behaviour (TPB). Ajzen's body of work has influenced fields as diverse as environmental psychology, health psychology, and marketing. He has

Source: © Icek Ajzen

led the way in advancing our understanding of attitude theory, the attitude–behaviour relationship, behaviour change, and **questionnaire design.**

resources required to act in a particular way, even if they intend to do so. For example, Chris might believe he has the ability to play professional football for Southampton FC, but in reality, he is not a good footballer (and is now in his 40s) and therefore lacks the required skills and resources to fulfil this particular ambition. PBC is often, though, a reasonable reflection of actual behavioural control. It is also typically easier

> **Key concept – Questionnaire design:** Designing a questionnaire based on relevant theory is important. Icek Ajzen provides recommendations about developing measures and attitudes and other components of the Theory of Planned Behaviour (TPB) using semantic differential scales (see https://people.umass.edu/aizen/pdf/tpb.measurement.pdf).

to assess than actual behavioural control and so is commonly relied upon in studies as a proxy measure for actual control. The TRA and TPB are both depicted in Figure 6.10.

The TPB is so popular that studies can be found in areas as diverse as health (Godin & Kok, 1996) and tourism (Ulker-Demirel & Ciftici, 2020). The TPB was also used to good effect in understanding responses to COVID-19. For example, Gibson and colleagues (2021) investigated how the TPB constructs related to intentions to socially distance at two time-points (three months apart) in a US sample. At both time-points, the TPB constructs were found to be good predictors of people's intentions to socially distance and their actual social distancing behaviour.

The TPB has several strengths. Its formulaic nature makes it simple to use and means that it is easy to compare and contrast the model's relevance to different target behaviours and groups. Its simple design also lends itself to the development, delivery, and assessment of behaviour change interventions even though it was never designed for this purpose (Ajzen,

2015). The TPB also has weaknesses. Sniehotta, Presseau, and Araújo-Soares (2014), for instance, question whether a model comprising just four constructs is suitably elaborate to explain *all* volitional behaviour, and point to how the explanatory power of the model is often improved via the addition of variables (e.g., past behaviour, values, moral norms). While Ajzen (1991) states that the TPB is open to such augmentation, Sniehotta et al. (2014) assert that the tendency to extend the TPB in this way is stifling the development of new, better theories that do not use the TPB framework as a basis.

Motivation and Opportunity as Determinants (MODE)

The motivation and opportunity as determinants (MODE) model was designed by Russell Fazio in 1990 to explain the processes by which attitudes affect behaviours (Fazio & Olson, 2014). The MODE model (Figure 6.11) distinguishes between the more spontaneous and more deliberative relationships that attitudes share with behaviours. The MODE model recognises that once activated from memory, attitudes can exert an impact on people's cognitions and behaviours: an influence that can even occur outside a person's conscious awareness. This is a strength of the MODE model compared with the TPB (Ajzen, 1991), as the TPB only really accounts for the role that attitudes play in predicting deliberated (i.e., reasoned) actions. The MODE model can also account for the fact that attitudes exert a conscious impact on people's behaviours (like in the TPB), but it specifies that this only happens when people are motivated to *and* have the opportunity (i.e., time and cognitive resources) to consider their attitudes before acting.

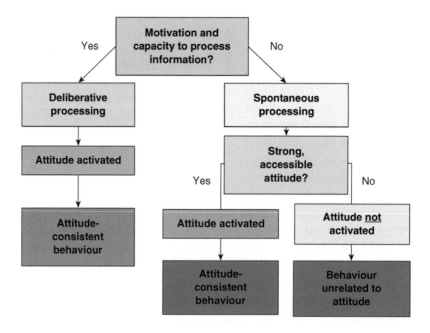

Figure 6.11 The Motivation and Opportunity as Determinants (MODE) model. The model shows how attitudes can influence behaviour through conscious deliberation and more spontaneously, depending on the strength and accessibility of the attitude. Image adapted from Fazio (1990)

Another strength of the MODE model is that it can explain how interactions between automatic and deliberative processes can affect the relationship between attitudes and behaviours. For instance, sometimes people are motivated to consciously override the influence of attitudes that might be spontaneously activated in a given situation, so as to be more socially desirable or appropriate. For example, this is exemplified in studies on prejudice and discrimination where people who are *motivated* to appear

> **Key concept – Implicit and explicit attitude measures:** Explicit measures of attitudes, like surveys, can be limited by their reliance on self-report and introspection. Implicit measures, like the IAT, will often use computerised tasks to assess how quickly people associate attitude objects with positive or negative attributes, thereby bypassing issues associated with self-report and introspection.

non-prejudiced will tend to correct for their spontaneously activated evaluations (implicit attitudes) on explicit measures of prejudice (Fazio & Olson, 2014). However, opportunity is crucial to overriding the influence of the spontaneously activated attitudes. Evidence shows that under time-pressure and/or where cognitive resources are limited (e.g., where a person is fatigued or under the influence of alcohol), there can be greater correspondence between responses to **implicit and explicit attitude measures** (e.g., Loersch et al., 2015). We discuss implicit attitude measures in more detail later in the Chapter.

6.4.4 Persuasion: Behaviour Change through Attitude Change

On August 20, 2018, a Swedish girl in Stockholm skipped school and instead spent her day outside the Swedish parliament. She sat on the street and held a placard with *'Skolstrejk for Climatet'* ('School Strike for Climate') written on it. This was the beginning of the 'Climate School Strikes' that swept the world in 2019. The girl was Greta Thunberg (Figure 6.12).

On April 30, 2020, amid the COVID-19 pandemic, then President of the United States of America, Donald Trump addressed the nation. President Trump had just been released from hospital following a COVID infection (Figure 6.13). He specifically addressed 'senior citizens' in his speech, saying how the drugs that doctors gave him were miraculous, and how during his presidency he managed to cut the red tape around

Figure 6.12 Greta Thunberg: Prominent environmental activist and persuasive role model for many young people during a Friday's for Future demonstration in Berlin, Germany

Source: https://www.google.com/url?q=https://openverse.org/image/025df98b-d71b-41fd-88bd-eb517bde7d4a?q%3Dperson%-2520clothes%2520shopping&sa=D&source=docs&ust=1720789738332486&usg=AOvVaw3dZIJY54IhHfpH6GcmC7

the approval of new drug treatments. He accused the previous administration of unnecessary bureaucracy and praised his own efforts to protect the nation from COVID-19.

Figure 6.13 Donald J. Trump: Highly influential but divisive former president of the USA shortly after his release from hospital following treatment for COVID-19

Source: https://www.google.com/url?q=https://commons.wikimedia.org/wiki/File:Donald_Trump_back_to_ White_House_after_treatment_in_WRNMMC_(2).jpg&sa=D&source=docs&ust=1720789738 323063&usg=AOvVaw3f2mdooCRuz5u0c-fg_lqp

In the 1950s, an advertisement was playing to American households, presenting the findings of a poll about the cigarettes that US doctors mostly preferred. Yes, you read this right! They did a poll among US doctors and found that they would prefer to smoke Camel cigarettes after a long and tiring day, and used this in their advertising.

These examples, while ostensibly unconnected, address a common theme: **persuasion**. Whether it's Thunberg's courageous example to alert young people to climate change, Trump's appeal to senior US citizens to garner their support for his re-election, or information about US doctors' smoking preferences, the ultimate goal is the same: to alter the audiences' attitudes, and subsequently, their behaviours towards the issue at hand.

> **Key concept – Persuasion:**
> Persuasion is an active attempt made by one social entity (e.g., a person or organisation) to change the attitudes, beliefs, or emotions of another person or persons.

Although attitude change is not *always* followed by behaviour change (see above about the attitude-behaviour gap), many persuasion theories are based on the idea that it is in some circumstances. In fact, persuasion theories address the elements of persuasive appeals, as well as the processes through which the persuasive message becomes encoded, stored, and acted upon by the recipient(s). We start our discussion of persuasion by discussing two leading theories, the Elaboration Likelihood Model (Petty & Cacioppo, 1986) and the Heuristic-Systematic Model (Chaiken, 1980).

Elaboration Likelihood Model

The Elaboration Likelihood Model (ELM) was developed by Richard Petty and John Cacioppo (1986). According to the ELM, cognitive processing of a persuasive message plays a key role in attitude change, and persuasive messages are always processed along a continuum of cognitive elaboration. When persuasive messages are considered with a great deal of cognitive effort, then high elaboration is likely. When, on the other hand, persuasive messages are processed more superficially and low cognitive effort is involved, then low elaboration is likely.

Cognitive elaboration reflects the extent to which a person thinks about and critiques the messages presented in a persuasive appeal. A transactional process is assumed to be at play here, so that situational factors influence a person's ability and motivation to engage with and process the persuasive message. For example, personally relevant messages are more likely to engage a person's attention, because we are naturally drawn to personally relevant information. The 'cocktail party effect' illustrates this point: our attention is (often unintentionally) drawn to personally relevant stimuli in our social environment (e.g., our name), even in the presence of distracting cues.

Attitude change can result from both high and low cognitive elaboration. However, the *quality* of attitude change is different when different modes of elaboration are involved. For instance, high elaboration is often associated with more stable attitudes and stronger attitude–behaviour associations. On the other hand, low elaboration likely results in weaker attitudes that can be easily swayed by counter-arguments or rival persuasive appeals. Accordingly, attitudes formed as a result of low elaboration might not always predict behaviour.

The ELM distinguishes between two 'routes' to persuasion: the central and the peripheral route. The *central route to persuasion* is characterised by high cognitive elaboration. Therefore, persuasive messages processed through the central route require high cognitive elaboration and more intense and careful processing. Attitude change will likely result because of the features and quality of the arguments presented in the message (see Figure 6.14). The *peripheral route to persuasion* involves low-level cognitive processing and attitude change is contingent on the presence of superficial persuasion cues, such as the attractiveness or perceived expertise of the communicator.

To illustrate, consider that a company wants to promote a new electric car. The marketing team comes up with two alternative advertisements. The first advertisement is aligned with the central route to persuasion and focuses on the car's technical specifications (e.g., range, 0–60 mph acceleration). The other advertisement relies on the peripheral route and focuses on the car's aesthetics and other peripheral cues (e.g., the use of lively music and physically attractive actors). The former advertisement requires consumers to think carefully, weigh up the pros and cons, and make an informed choice. The latter rests on the idea that lively music and attractive actors will elicit a positive emotional response, which may then increase consumers' preferences for the car. We cannot tell

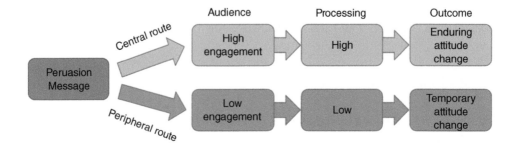

Figure 6.14 ELM: The central and peripheral routes to persuasion. Based on Petty and Cacioppo (1986)

which approach will lead to more car sales because this will largely depend on the engagement of the consumers with the advertisement and other factors (e.g., affordability of the car). This example does, however, illustrate how the ELM principles can be applied to marketing and consumer psychology.

The ELM further posits that attitude change is influenced by the function of a group of persuasion-related variables: the source of the message (who says it?), the content of the message (what is said?), the recipient of the persuasive message (to whom is it said?), and the context wherein persuasion takes place (where is it said?). The message recipients' motivation (e.g., personally relevant messages motivate more cognitive elaboration) and ability (e.g., distraction obscures cognitive elaboration) to think carefully will determine how these persuasion-related variables affect attitudes. For example, when motivation and ability to think are low, the perceived credibility of the source of the message or the emotional content of the message may serve as cues that guide attitude change. On the other hand, when motivation and ability to think are high, persuasion-related variables can influence the accessibility of message-relevant thoughts or be used as 'pieces of evidence' to validate the arguments contained in the persuasive message (Briñol & Petty, 2020).

Heuristic-Systematic Model

Around the same time Petty and Cacioppo (1986) developed the ELM, Shelley Chaiken (1980) proposed her own **dual-process model** of persuasion: the Heuristic-Systematic Model (HSM). Although different labels are used to describe persuasive processes in each model, both the ELM and the HSM share some common ground. Chaiken (1980) argued that persuasive messages are processed in either of two ways, systematically or heuristically. The *systematic processing mode* is very similar to the effortful central route to persuasion proposed by the ELM. Accordingly, the *heuristic processing mode* is very similar to the less effortful peripheral route to persuasion proposed by the ELM. When the heuristic processing mode is activated, people are also likely to use other heuristics or cognitive shortcuts (e.g., stereotypes) to make decisions. This may explain why, in many advertisements of personal hygiene products (e.g., toothpaste), the actors promoting the products are dressed as doctors in white coats, or why physically attractive celebrities play in TV commercials of beauty products.

Although the ELM and HSM describe very similar processes (*routes* or *modes* to persuasion), they have some notable differences. Unlike the ELM, the HSM describes three key hypotheses that explain the interaction between the systematic and the heuristic mode: attenuation, additivity, and bias. The *attenuation* hypothesis suggests that when features of the persuasive appeal (e.g., source of the message and message content) are incongruent, the systematic mode overrides the heuristic mode. For instance, when a credible source (e.g., a scientist) provides weak arguments about the benefits of vaccination (i.e., message content), then the effects of heuristic processing are attenuated and systematic processing alone can influence attitude change (Chaiken & Ledgerwood, 2011). The *additivity* effect takes place when both the heuristic and systematic processing modes can independently influence attitude change in the same direction. Lastly, according to the *bias* hypothesis, biased information-processing that originates in the heuristic mode can influence deliberate judgements made in the systematic mode (Todorov et al., 2002).

Let us consider the HSM in the context of social media influencers. Xiao, Wang, and Chan-Olmsted (2018) used the HSM to identify the factors that increase the persuasive appeal of YouTube influencers (Figure 6.15). Participants in their study completed a survey

> **Key concept – Dual-process model:** Dual-process models account for how cognitive processing can occur via different routes. Often these routes are separated into (1) more automatic, implicit, or unconscious processing, and (2) more explicit, controlled, effortful, or conscious processing.

Figure 6.15 Social media 'influencer' marketing has proliferated massively in recent years

Source: https://www.google.com/url?q=https://unsplash.com/
photos/a-woman-sitting-on-a-couch-with-a-cat-behind-her-TY1M2kMrYLg&sa=D&source=-
docs&ust=1720789738349345&usg=AOvVaw1YzxMcrNUXqf-20e7xlDKo

about the characteristics of the YouTube influencer, which reflected both heuristic (e.g., like-ability) and systematic processing cues (e.g., argument quality), before evaluating the credibility of the information provided by the influencer. The researchers found that the systematic processing cues (e.g., argument quality), but not heuristic cues (e.g., likeability), predicted the perceived credibility of the information provided by the influencer, lending support to the attenuation hypothesis of the HSM.

Individual Differences and Persuasion

The persuasion processes described in both the ELM and HSM are influenced by individual differences in the recipients of a message. Evidence suggests that people vary in their *need for cognition*, which is the tendency to engage in and enjoy effortful thinking as a way of organising information about the social environments, and that this can affect how they are influenced by persuasive appeals (Petty & Cacioppo, 1986). For instance, Haugtvedt, Petty, and Cacioppo (1992) demonstrated that people with a higher need for cognition engaged in more analytic thinking and scrutiny of information presented in commercial ads, as compared to people with a lower need for cognition. Moreover, simply labelling persuasive messages as more 'complex' is enough to motivate people with a higher need for cognition to process those messages in a more in-depth and analytic way (See, Petty, & Evans, 2009).

While some people are more likely to make choices based on analytic reasoning, others are more reliant on emotional criteria. Maio and Esses (2001) coined the term *need for affect* to describe the tendency to seek out (or avoid) situations that evoke emotions. While the need for cognition and the need for affect can be positively correlated, they tend to have a differential impact on persuasive outcomes. Research shows that persuasive appeals using cognitive-based messaging lead to greater attitude change among people high in need for cognition and low in need for affect. On the other hand, persuasive messages that are affect-laden (e.g., drinking a pleasant-tasting beverage) led to greater attitude change among people with higher need for affect and lower need for cognition (Haddock et al., 2008).

6.4.5 Attitude Measurement

> ... it is just as legitimate to say that we are measuring attitudes as it is to say that we are measuring tables or men. (Thurstone, 1928, p. 531)

Almost a century ago, Louis Leon Thurstone (1928), a pioneering American psychologist, argued that the simple principles used to assess the physical properties of structures (tables) or animate objects ('men', which in modern sexist-free language should read as 'humans') could be applied in the measurement of psychological entities, such as attitudes. Being a proponent of psychometric theory and methods, Thurstone recommended the following stepwise process for developing the so-called *Thurstone Attitude Scale*:

1   Clearly define the attitude object of interest (e.g., attitudes towards vaping).
2   Generate a large set of statements (between 80 and 100) to reflect diverse opinions towards vaping.
3   Ask a panel of judges (or participants) to classify the statements based on their evaluative properties along a continuum, say from 1 (= unfavourable) to 11 (= favourable), with a mid-point (e.g., scores between 5 and 6) indicating a neutral attitude towards vaping.
4   Administer the measure to another group of participants and ask them to indicate their degree of endorsement or rejection of each attitude statement.

Following this method, a researcher will be able to infer a person's overall attitude towards the attitude object by estimating how many positive or negative attitude statements were endorsed. So, in our example, a person endorsing 80% of the positively worded statements probably has a more positive attitude towards vaping than a person endorsing only 8% of the positive statements. Although pioneering, Thurstone's approach to attitude measurement was criticised as being overly cumbersome and time-consuming.

Rensis Likert and colleagues (1934) built on Thurstone's methodology by using a more pragmatic and simpler approach: after developing a set of statements about an attitude object (for simplicity, let's use vaping again), they presented participants with a fixed number of response options reflecting disagreement or agreement with each statement, along a continuum. This produced the popular 'Likert scale' that is used extensively today in questionnaire-based surveys. As with Thurstone's scale, the Likert scale presents two polar extremes (e.g., 1 = Strongly disagree, 5 = Strongly agree) passing through a 'Neutral' mid-point. While an ongoing matter of debate among statisticians, the Likert scale ostensibly presents response points that are differentiated by equal intervals, so that the difference between 'strongly disagree' and 'disagree' is equal in magnitude to the difference between 'agree' and 'strongly agree'.

Another popular method for measuring self-reported attitudes is the semantic differential scale developed by Osgood (1964). Unlike the Thurstone and Likert attitude scales, the semantic differential scale does not use attitude statement ratings. Rather, it requires participants to evaluate the attitude object across a continuum anchored by pairs of evaluatively polar adjectives (e.g., good – bad, pleasant – unpleasant, positive – negative). An example of evaluating attitudes towards vaping using Likert or semantic differential scales is shown in Figure 6.16.

Despite their differences, the aforementioned methods have one thing in common: they are developed to capture people's self-reported attitudes. However, self-report measures are inherently limited by response biases, particularly where surveys ask people about their attitudes towards sensitive or controversial topics (e.g., racial beliefs). There is a real possibility that survey responses in these instances may be influenced by socially desirable responding (i.e., people masking their 'true' feelings so as to appear more normative). To overcome this limitation, several 'unobtrusive' approaches to attitude measurement have been proposed.

For example, the Evaluative Space Model (Cacioppo et al., 2012) posits that neurophysiological processes underlie attitude evaluations, and attitudes can be captured by proxy measures of approach/avoidance tendencies, such as flexion (pulling something *towards* you) and extension (pushing something *away from* you) movements. Studies ranging from the

Likert Scale

	1 Strongly disagree	2 Disagree	3 Neither agree nor disagree	4 Agree	5 Strongly Agree
Vaping is a good thing		X			

Semantic Differential Scale

	For me, taking up vaping would be...				
	1	2	3	4	5
A bad idea		X			A good idea

Figure 6.16 Likert and semantic differential scales for measuring attitudes towards vaping

evaluation of unfamiliar Chinese ideographs (Cacioppo et al., 1993) to the assessment of racial attitudes (Kawakami et al., 2007) have confirmed that positive evaluations of attitude objects are associated with flexion (approach) movements, while negative evaluations are associated with extension (avoidance) movement tendencies.

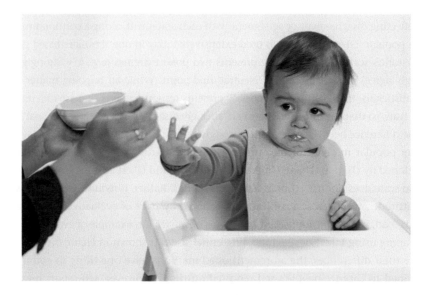

Figure 6.17 Here comes the train? Our approach and avoidance tendencies can be indicative of our attitudes.

The cognitive paradigm in attitude measurement was first conceived by Anthony Greenwald (Greenwald, McGhee, & Schwartz, 1998) and later developed by Mahzarin Banaji (see Key Thinker 6.3) and her colleagues (e.g., Greenwald, Banaji, & Nosek, 2015). The key tenet of this paradigm is that attitudes are mentally represented, and therefore can be activated and accessed without necessarily requiring introspection and self-report. In fact, one can assess the strength of associations between an attitude object (e.g., a racial group) and evaluative attributes (e.g., good or bad terms) outside conscious awareness – lending support to the idea that we can hold *implicit attitudes*.

The Implicit Association Test (IAT) is a computerised task that is widely used for the study of implicit attitudes (https://implicit.harvard.edu/implicit/takeatest.html). The original IAT involved the presentation of targets (e.g., flowers or insects) and positive or negative evaluative attributes (e.g., the words 'pleasant' or 'unpleasant'). The IAT measures how quickly people associate the targets with the evaluative attributes. The faster the response when the associations are presented, the stronger the underlying (implicit) attitude. So, people should be quicker to respond to more associated things (e.g., 'flowers' and 'pleasant') than less associated things (e.g., 'insects' and 'pleasant'). In the context of interracial relations, a negative implicit attitude towards an ethnic minority would be indicated by a faster association of minority group members with negative versus positive evaluative attributes. Unfortunately, there is quite a lot of evidence for this, although some researchers now question whether the IAT is measuring a person's own attitudes towards a subject, or whether it reflects societal attitudes that the person might not individually endorse (e.g., Olson & Fazio, 2004).

KEY THINKER 6.3

Mahzarin Banaji

Mahzarin Banaji is an American social psychologist of Indian origin. She is the Richard Clarke Cabot Professor of Social Ethics in the Department of Psychology at Harvard University in the United States. Professor Banaji's research has fundamentally changed our understanding of implicit (or unconscious) social cognition. This has included highlighting the nature and impacts of implicit attitudes, beliefs, and biases, particularly relating to group membership (e.g., race, gender, sexual orientation, religion, etc.).

Source: https://www.google.com/url?q=https://openverse.org/image/cf4a91cc-135c-4bd2-b87a-e8098965050c?q%3Dbaby%2520pushing%2520food%2520away&sa=D&source=docs&ust=1720789738336834&usg=AOvVaw21RuoIOtt1RhZHqdHGVhfb

Professor Banaji is also known for her work in developing the Implicit Association Test (IAT), an innovative means of assessing implicit prejudice and bias even among those who are outwardly egalitarian. Her work demonstrates that implicit attitudes are open to change and her findings have been applied to tackle prejudice and discrimination.

6.5 PART 2: ADVANCES

We have hopefully made clear by now that attitudes are truly an 'indispensable concept' to social psychology. In this next section, we will showcase two contemporary topic areas which relate to our own research. First, we will explore the asymmetries that exist in the attitudes we learn based on our own exploration of the physical and social world, before investigating the concept of framing and how it can affect people's attitudes.

6.5.1 Asymmetries in Attitude Learning via Experience

Much of what we learn, including our attitudes, comes from exploring our physical and social environments. We learn what (or who) is good and what (or who) is bad through direct, personal experience. Exploring the world is, though, inherently risky. While approaching new things can be rewarding, it can also result in unpleasant or hazardous consequences. It is this very risk that leads parents to advise their children not to eat 'yellow snow'!

The thing about learning from direct personal experience is that feedback is often contingent on us taking a risk. Only by approaching unfamiliar things can we learn whether they are good or bad. If we avoid them, we do not get this learning opportunity. In some cases, avoidance is the *correct* response – we dodge negative outcomes – but in other cases, avoidance is *incorrect* and leads us to miss out on something good (see Table 6.3). Crucially, our expectations about the likely outcomes of approach and avoidance responses often guide our behaviour (Fishbein & Azjen, 1975). Where we expect an approach response will yield a good outcome, we will be more likely to approach. Where we expect an approach response will yield a bad outcome, we will be more likely to withdraw.

Table 6.3   Attitude learning in experiential learning environments

Behaviour	Actual valence of attitude object	
	Good	Bad
Approach: e.g., eat, reach for, touch	**Correct** response: opportunity to confirm attitude and receipt of pleasant outcome	**Incorrect** response: but opportunity to correct 'false positive' attitude
Avoid: e.g., don't eat, reject, withdraw from	**Incorrect** response: missed opportunity and failure to correct 'false negative' attitude	**Correct** response: avoidance of potentially unpleasant, hazardous, or harmful outcome

Much of what we know about attitude formation in experiential learning environments stems from work using a simple computer game called *BeanFest* (Eiser & Fazio, 2013). In *BeanFest*, participants play the role of a forager, tasked with surviving in the game by choosing whether to 'eat' (approach) or 'not eat' (avoid) beans. In part one of the game, they are presented with unfamiliar beans that differ in shape and pattern (see Figure 6.18) and for each they must choose an approach or avoidance response. While some beans are 'good' (providing energy), others are 'bad' (sapping energy). Crucially, participants only receive feedback if beans are *actually* good or bad by approaching (eating) them.

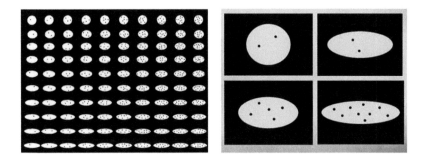

Figure 6.18 The positive and negative beans from *BeanFest*. The speckling and shape determine whether beans are 'good' or 'bad'. Participants must learn through trial and error which beans to 'approach' (eat) and which to 'avoid' (not eat). The left picture shows all 100 possible beans; the right picture is a close-up of four of the beans.

Source: Fazio, Eiser, and Shook (2004)

In part two of the game, participants complete a recall task. They are presented with beans from part one and asked if they were 'good' or 'bad'. They are also presented with new, unseen beans that they must label as 'good' or 'bad'. Through the 'recall' task, it is possible to assess the accuracy of participants' attitudes towards the beans and the extent to which they generalise these attitudes to new stimuli (i.e., the unseen beans).

BeanFest studies (Eiser & Fazio, 2013) reveal the emergence of three **negative asymmetries** in people's attitude learning and generalisation within the game. Specifically, people tend to:

1   learn better which beans to avoid than which beans to approach (see Figure 6.19);
2   be more accurate at recalling the valence of the 'bad' beans than the 'good' beans; and
3   be more likely to label unseen beans as 'bad' than 'good'.

The **negative *learning* asymmetries** (Asymmetries 1 and 2) emerge due to people forming more false-negative versus false-positive attitudes in the task (i.e., a 'learning bias'). When participants incorrectly approach a 'bad' bean, they have the opportunity to correct their false-positive attitude (i.e., they learn the bean is 'bad', not 'good'). Participants who avoid 'good' beans thinking they are 'bad', however, do not get corrective feedback and thus continue to incorrectly believe these beans to be 'bad' (i.e., the 'false-negative' attitudes remain). This ultimately results in more accurate learning of the negative beans than the positive beans. Support for this idea comes from variations of *BeanFest* where feedback on bean valence is no longer contingent on making approach responses. Within these variations, the negative *learning* asymmetries are virtually eliminated (Eiser & Fazio, 2013).

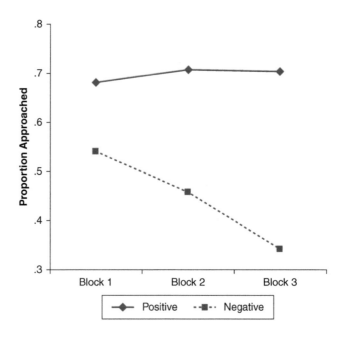

Figure 6.19 Evidence of a learning asymmetry forming in the *BeanFest* game. The figure depicts changes to the proportion of good and bad beans approached in the *BeanFest* game across three blocks of trials. While the approach of positive beans remains fairly consistent over time, the approach of negative beans falls rapidly, demonstrating participants' superior learning of the negative beans (i.e., a negative learning asymmetry).

Source: Fazio et al. (2004)

> **Key concept – Negative learning asymmetry:** In situations where learning is contingent on a person's willingness to explore, people tend to more accurately learn what is bad (negative) than what is good (positive). This is due to a greater propensity to correct false-positive beliefs (i.e., the belief that something is good when it is bad) than false-negative beliefs (i.e., the belief that something is bad when it is good).

The negative *generalisation* asymmetry (or 'weighting bias') (Asymmetry 3) is thought to be a product of a general 'negativity bias'. This is the tendency people have to give greater weight to negative information over positive information when making judgements (Rozin & Royzman, 2001). Due to this bias, people tend to more readily generalise from their negative experiences, as compared to their positive experiences. In *BeanFest*, this means that people are more likely to label unseen beans in part two of the game as 'bad' rather than 'good'.

Studies using *BeanFest* and similar paradigms (e.g., *Treasure Island* – Jones & Eiser, 2014; *StockFest* – Fiagbenu et al., 2021) have greatly advanced our understanding of how people form attitudes in settings where feedback is contingent on personal exploration. These studies have investigated topics as diverse as vulnerability to depression (Conklin et al., 2009) and biases in news selection (Soroka et al., 2021). Shook, Thomas, and Ford (2019) even examined the implications of disgust sensitivity for attitude learning in a study that used different flavoured jelly beans, including some that were actually 'dog food' flavoured!

EXERCISE 6.2

I Would Avoid Them if I Were You!

The *BeanFest* studies illustrate that our beliefs about the world can shape our exploratory behaviours and affect the attitudes we form. Importantly, these beliefs can be shaped by what we are told by others. Fazio and colleagues (2004) investigated how erroneous information about the beans in *BeanFest*, apparently from another participant, affected learning ('*I would avoid those beans if I were you*'). Participants were responsive to this information and would incorrectly avoid 'good' beans that the previous participant had labelled as 'bad'.

How might this relate to the real world?

Think of a time you have heard something about the world from another person and how this has affected your own attitudes and behaviour. Such advice is all around us, for example, in the consumer comments that guide our online purchase decisions. While some of this advice can be valuable (e.g., '*don't eat yellow snow*'), it can also be misleading. What if someone advises you to avoid a certain group of people because of negative connotations associated with their age, race, or religion? Following such advice might lead to the propagation and maintenance of prejudice due to the persistent avoidance of such groups (Deutsch & Fazio, 2008).

Perhaps you are guilty of propagating such rumours? If so, maybe it is time to think more critically about your attitudes!

Figure 6.20 I would avoid them if I were you! Do you think critically about the attitudes conveyed by others? Might you be guilty of propagating unjust stereotypes?

Source: https://www.google.com/url?q=https://pixy.org/2710911/&sa=D&source=-docs&ust=1720789738333250&usg=AOvVaw2ttGEWDAKsvfNvCMqu87-A

GUEST PERSONAL JOURNEY

J. Richard Eiser

Source: © J. Richard Eiser

My life as a psychologist started in 1963 when I went to Oxford to read Psychology and Philosophy. Social psychology occupied a relatively marginal position within the discipline, but one lecturer, Henri Tajfel, was an exception. With the Holocaust a raw memory and nuclear war a real fear, Tajfel showed that social psychology could tackle big issues *and* do so scientifically with experimental methods and theories based on fundamental cognitive processes. Enthused by tutorials with him, in 1966, I went to do a PhD in social psychology at the London School of Economics (LSE). My thesis applied Tajfel's work on perceptual accentuation to ratings of attitude statements. In 1968, while still writing up, I moved to Bristol as an assistant lecturer, where Tajfel was now professor. There I developed my work on accentuation theory and attitude research more generally. In 1973, I took a year's sabbatical at the University of Waterloo in Canada. This widened my perspective considerably and I made many friends among North American social psychologists. In 1975, I moved to the Institute of Psychiatry, London, to work primarily on smoking addiction. Why do many smokers not quit even knowing that smoking can kill? Nicotine addiction is part of the answer, but, joined by Stephen Sutton and Joop van der Pligt (a life-time collaborator until his untimely death in 2015), we showed that addiction itself depends on a self-attribution of inability to give up. We also looked at social influence in adolescent smoking. Then in 1979, I was appointed to a Chair at the University of Exeter to build a new group in social psychology (still strongly flourishing). After 20 years I moved to the University of Sheffield, where I remained until I retired.

Over this whole period, I enjoyed several interdisciplinary collaborations on applied topics. A project on community attitudes to nuclear power (with Joop, Russell Spears, Paul Webley, and Steve Reicher) took on a new dimension with the Chernobyl accident in 1986. This work broadened to include other energy technologies (e.g., wind), climate change, pollution, and environmental hazards such as earthquakes and volcanoes. Linking these topics was a focus (with Mathew White) on risk interpretation and trust. My work on attitude theory, especially with Russell Fazio, incorporated basic learning theory concepts to examine how attitudes are acquired through experience and resist change. I argued that attitudes are dynamical systems maintained by networks of associations at both intrapersonal cognitive and interpersonal and cultural levels.

Under autocracies, information control reinforces conformity and compliance. Whether suppressing or promoting change, attitudes really matter. Well, it's been a long journey. When I started, universities, by today's standards, were tiny, self-consciously elitist, and institutionally sexist. But tuition was free, and personal. Social psychology is no longer at the fringes of the discipline and we can be assertive about both its societal value and our identity as an empirical science. This depends not simply (or even primarily) on our methodologies, but also on the examination and incorporation of theoretical principles that have generality across topics, time, and place.

6.5.2 Framing Effects

Consider that you are out food shopping. You take your items to the counter and realise you don't have a bag with you. You have to decide now whether or not to run to the car to get your reusable bags. You note that there are disposable plastic bags for sale for a small charge (10p), which is framed as being either a *10p tax* on shoppers opting to use a disposable bag, or a *10p discount* for people who bring their own bags. Which of these messages resonates with you more? While both messages imply the same thing, evidence suggests that 'tax' framing would likely have a bigger impact on your decision.

For example, Homonoff (2018) found that framing a small surcharge on disposable bag use as a *tax* (a 'loss') decreased their use by 40%, while equivalent *bonus* framing (a 'gain') had no effect on behaviour. This difference is believed to stem from 'loss aversion': the fact that in decision-making we are more sensitive to (potential) losses than to equivalent size (potential) gains (Tversky & Kahneman, 1981).

Homonoff's (2018) findings are an example of *equivalency framing*. Equivalency framing occurs where logically equivalent choices are presented to people, but how they are presented – the *frame of communication* used – differs. For example, the framing can change from a focus on gains (e.g., bonuses) to a focus on losses (e.g., taxes). This is also exemplified in Tversky and Kahneman's (1981) seminal study (see Key study 6.2), and shows that even subtle changes in wording can have large effects on people's attitudes and actions, that is, **framing effects**.

Equivalency framing can be contrasted with *emphasis framing*, where the framing effects result from placing the onus on qualitatively different aspects of a given attitude object (e.g., issue, event, or thing)

> **Key concept – Framing effects:** The manner in which information or choices are presented can affect how people respond. For example, by focusing people's attention on different aspects of an attitude object, or by highlighting the 'gains' versus 'losses' associated with logically equivalent choices, it is possible to influence preferences. These 'framing effects' can occur in the presence or absence of attitude change.

(Chong & Druckman, 2007). Take the role of nuclear power in electricity generation. It is possible that you are worried about nuclear power due to memories of nuclear disasters like Chernobyl or Fukushima. However, nuclear power is also a low-carbon energy option and something which might help us address climate change. Bickerstaff and colleagues (2008) found that when framed in the context of climate change (i.e., where there was an *emphasis* on the low-carbon nature of nuclear power), people were more favourable to nuclear power, if somewhat reluctantly. Similarly, Jones and colleagues (2012) found that climate change framing had a positive impact on people's preferences for nuclear power within the UK, although this preference was driven indirectly by a desire to reduce reliance on fossil fuels.

These nuclear power examples also highlight an important conceptual difference between persuasion and framing. Whereas framing changes the relative importance given to the beliefs that underpin a person's existing attitudes, persuasion seeks to directly change these beliefs (Nelson et al., 1997). Thus, while framing *can* lead to attitude change, it is not necessary for framing effects to occur. Successful persuasion, however, requires attitude change (Chong & Druckman, 2007).

Framing has been shown to impact people's thoughts and actions towards many contemporary issues, such as COVID-19 vaccination (Borah et al., 2021) and climate change denial (Bain et al., 2016). Bain and colleagues (2016), for instance, suggest that by changing the frame of communication used when speaking to climate change sceptics, it is possible to motivate them to act more pro-environmentally. It is hypothesised that while traditional 'climate' messaging is unlikely to resonate with sceptics, emphasising the co-benefits that may come from efforts to mitigate climate change (e.g., new job prospects, improved social equality) may gain traction with this (alarmingly large) community.

In a cross-national study incorporating 6,196 people from 24 countries, Bain and colleagues (2016) showed that by emphasising the *social development* (i.e., the economic and scientific advancement) or *benevolence* (i.e., creating a moral, caring community) co-benefits that might come from efforts to tackle climate change, it was possible to motivate pro-environmental action even among their more sceptical participants. They concluded that by changing climate change messaging to emphasise the co-benefits of acting, it could be possible to achieve the scale of societal action required to combat this significant global threat. Crucially, the framing effects observed in Bain et al.'s (2016) study are not reliant on attitude change: the climate sceptics can remain sceptical! But by highlighting the co-benefits that would come with acting on the issue, you have resonated with things that the sceptics do value (e.g., a desire to live in a technologically advanced society), and thus they respond more favourably.

Consistent with the work of Bain and colleagues, there has been a recent growth in the tendency to yolk public messaging about the need to tackle climate change with messaging about the public health risks associated with the issue (Edmondson et al., 2022). As climate change can be a perceptively distant, abstract, and impersonal issue for many, emphasising the related but more immediate, personally relevant health risks (e.g., poor air quality, extreme heat) can be a means of promoting attitude and behaviour change (Herrmann et al., 2020).

KEY STUDY 6.2

The Framing of Decisions and the Psychology of Choice

In 1981, Amos Tversky and Daniel Kahneman published an article in *Science* noting how people's decision-making can be reversed by changing how choices are 'framed'. In one demonstration, a group of participants were asked to choose between two health programs designed to tackle the outbreak of an 'unusual Asian disease' that was expected to kill 600 people. 'Program A' guaranteed the **survival** of 200 people, while 'Program B' yielded one-third probability of saving all 600 people and a two-thirds probability of saving no one. Most participants were shown to be **risk averse**, favouring the guaranteed survival of 200 people ('Program A' = 72% of participants) over the gamble of saving all 600 lives ('Program B = 28%')

A second group was given the same problem but had to choose between 'Program C', guaranteeing the **death** of 400 people, or 'Program D' that gave a one-third chance that nobody would die and a two-thirds chance that all 600 people would die. Here, most participants were **risk taking**, favouring 'Program D' (78%), where everyone could die, over 'Program C' (22%), which guaranteed that some people would survive.

Crucially, the programs being evaluated by each group are essentially identical. 'Program A' and 'Program C' guarantee the survival of 200 people, but 'Program C' mentions the number of **deaths** rather than **survivors**. 'Program B' and 'Program D' both yield a one-third chance that everyone survives, but 'Program D' refers to the probabilities of **dying** rather than being **saved**.

These findings are summarised in Table 6.4 and illustrate a common pattern found in Tversky and Kahneman's work: people's choices tend to be risk averse when considering prospective gains (e.g., comparing Programs A and B that deal in *lives saved*) and choices tend to be risk seeking in situations of prospective loss (e.g., comparing Programs C and D that deal in *lives lost*). This is evidence of an *equivalency framing effect*, where different phrasing of otherwise logically identical choices can result in differences in people's stated or revealed attitudes.

Table 6.4 Summary of responses to Tversky and Kahneman's (1981) 'Asian Disease' paradigm

Programs	Framing: Survivors vs deaths	Guaranteed some people will survive (safer choice)	Good chance that everyone could die (riskier choice)	Overall cohort preference: Risk averse or risk seeking
Program A vs B	Survivors (gain frame)	A = 72%	B = 28%	Risk averse
Program C vs D	Deaths (loss frame)	C = 22%	D = 78%	Risk seeking

Note: Program A and C both guarantee the survival of 200 people; Program B and D both give = chance that everyone survives.

6.6 PART 3: APPLICATIONS

In this section, we introduce you to three areas where research on attitudes is being applied to understand contemporary issues: (a) the promotion of pro-environmental behaviour; (b) public acceptance of technologies; and (c) people's tendencies to engage in doping in amateur and professional sport.

6.6.1 Attitudes and Pro-environmental Behaviour

Pro-environmental behaviours (PEBs) can be defined as behaviours that harm the environment as little as possible, or that benefit the environment (e.g., recycling, conserving water, etc.) (Steg & Vlek, 2009). Attitudes are central to several key models used to explain environmental action. In this section, we will compare two of the most commonly used models: the Theory of Planned Behaviour (TPB) (Ajzen, 1991) and the Value-Belief-Norm model (VBN) (Stern, 2000).

Theory of Planned Behaviour (TPB)

As we saw earlier, the TPB asserts that people rationally weigh up their expectations about the personal costs and benefits associated with a particular behaviour before acting. The TPB has been used to model diverse PEBs, from energy and water conservation to 'green' consumerism.

In a review of 126 studies, Yuriev and colleagues (2020) confirm the value of the TPB as a model of PEBs, demonstrating that it typically accounts for around 46% of the variance in people's intentions, and around 37% in their actual actions. These figures are broadly consistent with the application of the TPB in other behavioural domains (e.g., health behaviours – Godin & Kok, 1996). Yuriev et al.'s (2020) review also reveals that in many instances where the TPB has been applied to PEBs, researchers have extended the basic model to include other predictors. The most common of these are *self-identity* (i.e., the extent to which acting in a particular way is important to one's self-concept), *moral/personal norms* (i.e., one's assessment of what is considered morally right or wrong), and *past behaviour*. The addition of these and other variables (e.g., environmental values, sense of community) tend to improve the explanatory power of the basic TPB by around 12% for intentions and 10–11% for behaviours.

Adding these variables to the TPB makes theoretical as well as statistical sense. Consider why you personally choose to act pro-environmentally. Perhaps it is the personal benefits derived from enjoying a litter-free environment, or maybe it is because you value protecting the environment for other people or wildlife. As PEBs stem from a mix of self-interested and self-transcendent motivations (Bamberg & Möser, 2007), it is unsurprising that the addition of variables like *moral norms* or *sense of community* add to the predictive power of the TPB in relation to PEBs.

Value-Belief-Norm (VBN) Model

In contrast to the ubiquitous TPB, the Value-Belief-Norm (VBN) model was designed with PEBs in mind (Stern, 2000). The VBN has its roots in a model of altruistic behaviour known as the Norm Activation Model (Schwartz, 1977). According to the Norm Activation Model, altruistic behaviours are predicted by personal (moral) norms, which are activated when someone is *aware of the consequences* of a particular action (or failure to act) and *ascribes responsibility* to themselves for acting. Consider, for instance, that you become aware of the environmental consequences of flying, and that you accept that your tendency to jet away on holiday is adding to the problem. This may activate your sense of moral duty to act differently (e.g., opting for a staycation).

The VBN extends the Norm Activation Model by linking it to a person's beliefs (or world-views) about nature, and their biospheric, altruistic, and egocentric values in a causal chain (see Figure 6.21). The more biospheric and altruistic (and less egocentric) a person's values, the more likely they are to have a pro-ecological worldview. This shapes a keener awareness of the consequence of human action (or inaction) for the environment and increases a person's sense of responsibility for acting, which ultimately activates a person's sense of moral obligation for acting and (hopefully) then results in PEB.

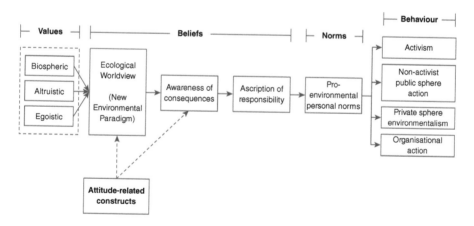

Figure 6.21 The Value-Belief-Norm model of environmental action. The model links values, beliefs, and personal norms in a causal chain to explain different PEBs. While not directly referenced, attitudes influence people's awareness of the consequences of their actions for the environment and their beliefs about the relationship that people share with the environment (NEP). Image based on Stern (2000)

While not explicitly named in the VBN, there are references to a person's attitudes in the 'awareness of consequences' and, in particular, the 'ecological worldview' constructs (see Key study 6.3 – Dunlap et al., 2000).

KEY STUDY 6.3

The New Environmental Paradigm (NEP) scale

The New Environmental Paradigm (NEP) scale (Dunlap et al., 2000) is an attitude measure that assesses people's beliefs about the relationships between humans and the natural environment (see also Dunlap, 2008). The assumption is that there are two broad belief systems that people hold about these relationships: (1) a Dominant Social Paradigm (DSP), where humans are believed to have mastery over nature, and (2) a New Environmental Paradigm (NEP), where humans are seen to be part of nature.

The revised NEP scale (see Table 6.5) contains eight items where agreement is associated with the endorsement of the NEP belief system and seven items where endorsement is consistent with the DSP belief system (reverse coded for analysis). Higher overall scores on the scale are equated with stronger pro-environmental attitudes (Dunlap et al., 2000). The NEP scale has been used to investigate environmental attitudes across

Table 6.5   15-item revised New Ecological Paradigm (NEP)

1	We are approaching the limit of the number of people the earth can support
2	Humans have the right to modify the natural environment to suit their needs
3	When humans interfere with nature it often produces disastrous consequences
4	Human ingenuity will ensure that we do NOT make the earth unliveable
5	Humans are severely abusing the environment
6	The earth has plenty of natural resources if we just learn how to develop them
7	Plants and animals have as much right as humans to exist
8	The balance of nature is strong enough to cope with the impacts of modern industrial nations
9	Despite our special abilities humans are still subject to the laws of nature
10	The so-called ecological crisis facing humankind has been greatly exaggerated
11	The earth is like a spaceship with very limited room and resources
12	Humans were meant to rule over the rest of nature
13	The balance of nature is very delicate and easily upset
14	Humans will eventually learn enough about how nature works to be able to control it
15	If things continue on their present course, we will soon experience a major ecological catastrophe

Note: Respondents answer on a 5-point scale (Strongly agree; mildly agree; neutral; mildly disagree; strongly disagree). Agreement with the eight odd numbered items and disagreement with the seven even numbered items is indicative of a pro-NEP response.

the world, although some have questioned its applicability outside of Western cultures (Hawcroft & Milfont, 2010).

Figure 6.23 Do you think the Earth is like a spaceship with very limited room and resources? If you do, then this might be evidence that you hold a positive environmental attitude

Source: https://commons.wikimedia.org/wiki/File:Earth-hands.jpg

Which is the Better Model of Pro-Environmental Behaviour?

Recognition of the relative strengths of the VBN and TPB has led to several attempts to combine them (e.g., Trihadmojo et al., 2020), but which of the two individual models is the better predictor of PEB? Kaiser and colleagues (2005) provided the first direct contrast of the two models as a predictor of conservation behaviours. Their analysis revealed that the TPB (with intention explaining 95% of the variance in behaviour) was a better model than the VBN (where personal norms explained 64%). Similarly, López-Mosquera and Sánchez (2012) found that the TPB was a better model for predicting people's willingness to pay for the conservation of a suburban park than the VBN. This does not mean that the VBN is a bad model, it is just better suited to explaining certain kinds of PEB, notably simpler actions or 'mundane environmentalism'. The TPB, however, is better at predicting more effortful or personally costly PEBs (Steg & Vlek, 2009).

Figure 6.22 To recycle or not to recycle, that is the question. Recycling is a key way in which we can reduce our environmental footprint. But what if it is unclear what bin to put things in? Could this act as a barrier to people acting on their positive environmental attitudes? Clear labelling can help people make the right decision

Source: https://commons.wikimedia.org/wiki/File:Recycling_station.jpg&sa=D&source=-docs&ust=1720789738325330&usg=AOvVaw3M7SygztVwVNoFFcAfHW5T

EXERCISE 6.3

Your Career: Environmental Psychology

Environmental psychology is a sub-discipline of psychology that studies the interrelationships between people and natural, built, and virtual environments. Environmental psychologists are interested in how humans influence their surroundings, and how a person's surroundings affect their thoughts, attitudes, and behaviours (Gifford, 2014). Research in environmental psychology tends to be problem-oriented, with psychologists working collaboratively with other disciplines to solve complex 'real-world' issues, such as helping to design spaces that reduce crime, aid navigation, or promote well-being, or delivering behaviour change interventions to mitigate environmental issues like climate change.

If environmental psychology sounds like an interesting career path, why not try a quick internet search to learn more about it and what career paths exist within the sector?

Figure 6.24 Carbon footprints and forensic fingerprints. Environmental psychologists do more than just study how the application of psychology can assist in addressing climate change. They also work in other settings, including how to design places to increase well-being and reduce criminal activity

Source: https://pixabay.com/vectors/fingerprint-touch-crime-criminal-150159/

6.6.2 Public Acceptance of Technology

The attitudes we hold towards technologies are a key determinant of our behaviours towards them, including whether we will purchase and use technologies at home, and whether we will petition for or protest against their introduction at national, regional, or local levels.

Diffusion of Innovation

Rogers' (1962) Diffusion of Innovation (DOI) theory seeks to explain how social innovations (e.g., new ideas) and physical innovations (e.g., new technologies) diffuse within a population. Evidence shows that people fall into one of five categories, depending on their willingness to adopt a given innovation (see Figure 6.25). First, you have a small group of *innovators*, characterised by the desire to be the first to try out the innovation, and who are accepting of the risks this implies. Next, you have a group of *early adopters*, who recognise the value of the innovation and are keen to embrace it early on. This is followed by the larger *early majority*, who like to be ahead of the curve in adopting an innovation, but want to see evidence of it working before they do. Then you have the *late majority*, who are more sceptical of the innovation and will only adopt it once it is proven. And finally, there are the *laggards*, who are more resistant to adopting the innovation.

The population segmentation afforded by DOI theory illustrates how people's attitudes towards innovation, including new technologies, can differ. It has implications for how we might seek to encourage the uptake of social or technological innovations. Enthusing innovators and early adopters should be fairly easy; however, strategies for persuading the late majority and the laggards will likely need more effort and a different approach.

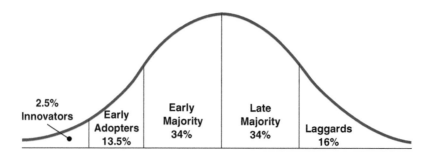

Figure 6.25 Rogers' Diffusion of Innovation Curve. People have different propensities to adopt innovation within a social system. People fall into one of five categories, from the keen innovators to the more resistant laggards

Source: Everett Rogers

What do we Mean by 'Acceptance'?

It is important to think critically about what we mean by the term 'technology acceptance'. First, there is a distinction between 'acceptability' and 'acceptance', with the former referring to a person's attitudes and the latter referring to their behaviours (Alexandre et al., 2018). A person who finds technology X acceptable (*positive attitude*) is more likely to accept or use it (*positive behaviour*). Second, there are questions as to what the term 'acceptance' implies about a person's behaviour. While often taken to mean 'support' – an *active* willingness to purchase, use, or host a technology – acceptance can also describe a more passive 'tolerance' of a technology. One can also delineate active forms of 'resistance' (e.g., protestation) from more passive 'connivance', which is opposition without action (Huijts et al., 2012).

Being precise with 'acceptance' terminology is important as people are responsive to even subtle differences in such terminology. For example, Batel and colleagues (2013) identified significant differences in the levels of 'support' and 'acceptance' that people expressed towards the proposed introduction of high voltage power lines in the UK and Norway. Public *support* for this technology was found to be lower than public *acceptance*, confirming that the terms were perceived differently, despite their surface-level parity.

Modelling Technology Acceptance

When it comes to consumer technologies (e.g., personal computers, smartphones), the more personally useful and relevant they are perceived to be, the more likely they are to be used. This is exemplified by the Technology Acceptance Model (TAM) (Davis, 1989). The TAM is a popular model of people's adoption and use of information and communication technologies based on the Theory of Reasoned Action (Ajzen & Fishbein, 1975). In the TAM, a person's intentions to use a technology are predicted by their attitude towards use of a technology. In turn, attitude is predicted by two constructs: (1) *perceived usefulness* – whether a person believes the technology will be useful in view of its intended purpose; and (2) *perceived ease of use* – the person's beliefs about how effortless and easy (or complicated and hard) it will be to use the technology.

The original TAM posits that the perceived usefulness and perceived ease of use of a technology are shaped by 'external variables'. These variables, summarised in Table 6.6, are outlined in an extension of the TAM, known as the TAM2 (Venkatesh & Davis, 2000) (see Figure 6.26). The TAM, TAM2, and related models have been used to understand the acceptance of an array of electronic technologies, including those relating to healthcare (Holden & Karsh, 2010), education (Granić & Marangunić, 2019), and energy consumption (Whittle et al., 2020).

Table 6.6   The variables with the TAM and TAM2

Model	Variable name	Definition of variable
TAM	Intentions to use	The extent to which a person intends to use the technology
	Attitude towards use	The extent to which a person believes that using a technology would be a good or bad thing
	Perceived usefulness	Whether a person feels that the technology will be useful to them
	Perceived ease of use	A person's beliefs about how effortless and easy (or complicated and hard) it would be to use the technology
TAM and TAM2	Subjective norm	Whether a person feels that other people important to them believe that they should use the technology or not
	Voluntariness	The extent to which people feel that adoption and use of the technology is voluntary rather than mandatory
	Image	The extent to which adoption and use of a technology is anticipated to enhance a person's social standing
	Experience	Experience using the technology. Experience can reduce the direct effect of subjective norms on use intentions
	Job relevance	The extent to which a technology is deemed to be applicable and important to a person's job
	Output quality	The extent to which a technology is seen to fulfil the job it is designed to do
	Result demonstrability	The degree to which the benefits of using a technology are apparent or visible to the user

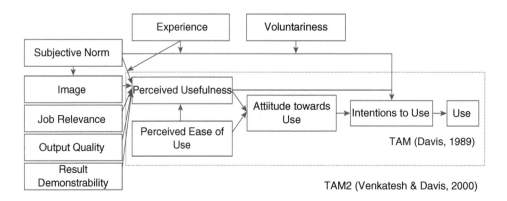

Figure 6.26 The Technology Acceptance Model (TAM) 1 and 2. In the TAM, perceived usefulness and perceived ease of use of a technology predict people's attitudes towards using the technology, which then affect their behavioural intentions and use of the technology. The TAM2 advances the model by specifying more of the key 'external factors' thought to shape the perceived usefulness of a technology. The TAM2 also tends to drop 'attitude' as a predictor of behavioural intentions

Sources: Davis (1989) and Venkatesh & Davis (2000).

Are Attitudes Actually Important to Technology Acceptance?

In studies using the TAM and related models, it has become normal to omit a direct assessment of people's attitudes (Yousafzai et al., 2007a, 2007b). This stems from a finding that, particularly in settings where people have the freedom to choose whether to use a technology, beliefs about the usefulness of the technology tend to be a stronger predictor of use intentions than a person's attitudes (Venkatesh et al., 2003). Attitudes are, though, important in some situations, particularly where use of the technology is imposed or deemed to be mandatory. In such circumstances, whether or not a person is favourable towards the technology can affect whether they support, resist, or even sabotage its introduction (Yousafzai et al., 2007a).

6.6.3 Doping Use in Competitive Sport

On different occasions between 1999 and 2012, the (now) infamous and retired professional cyclist Lance Armstrong publicly denied the use of prohibited substances or methods to boost his athletic performance (Figure 6.27). But in January 2013, the seven-times 'winner' of the Tour de France and role model for thousands of cycling aficionados across the globe, said during a live TV interview with Oprah Winfrey that he had repeatedly cheated through doping. His sporting success was largely attributed to his continuous use of doping substances and methods.

During his career he had used a wide range of drugs, from testosterone and growth hormone, to erythropoietin (EPO), and he had masterminded a large-scale blood doping programme (i.e., blood transfusions to artificially increase the number of red cells in the blood) for himself and his teammates. Doping is not uncommon in professional sport. From track-and-field to figure skating, sporting history is tainted with numerous doping scandals.

But what drives athletes to break the rules and use doping to pursue success in their sport? A large body of research on doping behaviour has used social psychological theories to explain why some athletes decide to dope. Unlike other forms of substance use (e.g., smoking, drinking), using doping substances is hardly a habitual and automatic behaviour, induced by cues in the environment. Rather, doping can be described as an intentional goal-directed behaviour. Athletes use doping substances because they want to achieve a higher goal, such as sporting success, fame, and financial rewards (Morente-Sánchez & Zabala, 2013). It is not surprising, therefore, that many studies in this area have used models of intentional action, such as the Theory of Planned Behaviour (Ntoumanis et al., 2014).

Figure 6.27 Lance Armstrong, seven-times 'winner' of the Tour de France and later discredited for admitting doping use

Source: https://commons.wikimedia.org/wiki/File:Lance_Armstrong_-_Tour_de_France_2003_-_Alpe_d%2527Huez_(cropped).jpg&sa=D&source=docs&ust=1720789738338494&usg=AOvVaw2FwzPhcSRPjLz5eDZGS_qY

Although doping is a complex behaviour that cannot be explained by the effects of a single risk factor alone, it is useful to focus on the role of attitudes. Attitudes towards doping have been consistently associated with self-reported doping intentions, susceptibility to dope, and the use of doping substances in different types and levels of sport (Blank et al., 2016). Some studies have measured doping attitudes using evaluative adjectives anchored on semantic differential scales (e.g., good–bad; ethical–unethical;

Lazuras et al., 2010), others using attitudinal statements to which athletes report their agreement or disagreement on Likert scales (e.g., 'doping is necessary to be competitive'; Petróczi & Aidman, 2009), and some studies have also developed implicit measures of doping attitudes using the methodology of the Implicit Association Test (Brand et al., 2011). So, if the decision to use doping substances is, at least partly, explained by athletes' attitudes towards doping, then it is theoretically plausible that by changing attitudes to doping, one can reduce the risk for doping use.

Horcajo and Luttrell (2016) examined whether doping attitudes formed under high cognitive elaboration, as opposed to low elaboration, are more strongly associated with concomitant doping intentions and are more resistant to change. They randomly assigned young football players in Spain into either a low- or high-elaboration condition, which further included persuasive messages for or against the legalisation of doping substances in sport (e.g., anabolic steroids, EPO). Messages in favour of doping legalisation highlighted the benefits of legalising doping in sport (e.g., countering the black markets that are involved in the trafficking of doping substances), whereas anti-legalisation messages emphasised the potential risks involved (e.g., health risks posed to athletes).

The researchers further manipulated *personal relevance* and *responsibility* to induce either high or low thinking (elaboration) of the persuasive message. In particular, in the high-elaboration condition, participants were told that a proposal to legalise doping substances was being examined by the international sport governing body for football (FIFA) and would have immediate effect (next season), thereby directly affecting the rules of football. They were also told that their views (self-reported attitudes and intentions) would be communicated to FIFA and affect its decision over doping legalisation, thus increasing the sense of personal responsibility. In the low-elaboration condition, on the other hand, participants were told that the proposal to legalise doping substances was examined by the World Anti-Doping Agency (WADA) and could be implemented in athletics and cycling a few years later.

After reading each message, participants were asked to report their attitudes and intentions towards doping legalisation (e.g., willingness to sign a petition supporting doping legalisation). Immediately after completing these measures, participants were presented with other messages that opposed the first one (so, if the initial message was in favour of doping legalisation, the second message was clearly against it). After reading this second message, participants were again asked to report their attitudes towards doping legalisation, as this would allow researchers to examine attitude consistency.

The results of the study showed that, independently of the level of cognitive elaboration, participants who initially received a message against the legalisation of doping reported significantly more negative attitudes towards legalisation, as compared to those who received an initial message that favoured it. Furthermore, in line with the ELM, legalisation attitudes that were formed under high (versus low) cognitive elaboration were more enduring. Athletes' intentions towards doping legalisation were more consistent with the initial message they received and their self-reported attitudes in the high-elaboration condition, as compared to the low-elaboration condition (Figure 6.28).

In a subsequent study, Horcajo and colleagues (2019) extended the findings of their 2016 study by examining the role of need for cognition in persuasion processes. In line with the expectations of the ELM, need for cognition moderated the relationship between

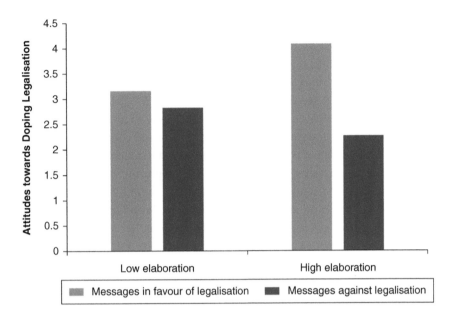

Figure 6.28 Attitudes towards doping legalisation under different levels of cognitive elaboration. Based on Horcajo and Luttrell (2016)

self-reported attitudes and intentions towards the legalisation of doping substances. Specifically, the attitude–intentions relationship was stronger among athletes with a higher (versus lower) need for cognition; thus, attesting to the importance of controlling for the effects of individual differences in need for cognition in persuasive communication research.

Taken together, these studies indicate how attitudes and classic theories of attitude change can usefully inform and guide research in different applied domains, such as doping use – a perennial problem that continues to plague competitive sport.

6.7 SUMMARY

Well, you have reached the end of this introduction to attitudes and persuasion. We hope you now *love* attitudes as much as we do. If you don't, then read the chapter a few more times and wait for the mere exposure effect to kick in.

The aim of this chapter was not only to provide you with a background to the attitude concept and the history behind the research into this most indispensable of social psychological topics, but also to showcase how research into attitudes continues at a pace, helping us to understand and resolve some of the big contemporary questions, including how to limit doping in competitive sport, how to increase the uptake of new technologies, and how we might promote action on big environmental issues, such as the climate crisis.

This chapter is just the tip of the iceberg when it comes to exploring what attitudes are and where, when, and how they impart their influence. We would encourage you to continue your expedition by having a go at answering some of the revision questions and by accessing some of the suggested further reading below.

6.8 REVISION

1 Think about an attitude object that is very important to you: How do you feel (*affect*) when you picture the object? What beliefs (*cognition*) do you hold about the object? And how have you behaved (*behaviour*) in relation to the object in the past (or how might you behave towards it in the future)? Now do the same but in relation to an attitude object that is less important to you. Compare and contrast the differences you note about the qualities of the attitudes you have just described.

2 Considering what you have learned about (a) the nature and determinants of people's attitudes and (b) the attitude–behaviour relationship, outline the key factors that are likely to affect whether or not someone will act in a pro-environmental way.

3 Reflecting on what you know about the different approaches for measuring attitudes, what are the advantages of using the Implicit Association Test?

4 Imagine that you are working for your local council on a project designed to reduce household energy consumption. The success of the project is reliant on local residents adopting a new technology that will help them to monitor their energy use. With reference to framing and persuasion, and what you have learned about technology acceptance, design a communication strategy to engage residents and promote the uptake of this technology.

6.9 FURTHER READING

Foundations

Albarracin, D., & Shavitt, S. (2018). Attitudes and attitude change. *Annual Review of Psychology, 69*, 299–327.

Greenwald, A. G., Poehlman, T. A., Uhlmann, E. L., & Banaji, M. R. (2009). Understanding and using the Implicit Association Test: III. Meta-analysis of predictive validity. *Journal of Personality and Social Psychology, 97*(1), 17–41.

Howe, L. C., & Krosnick, J. A. (2017). Attitude strength. *Annual Review of Psychology, 68*, 327–351.

Advanced

Eiser, J. R., & Fazio, R. H. (2013). Chapter 19: How approach and avoidance decisions influence attitude formation and change. In A. J. Elliot (Ed.), *Handbook of approach and avoidance motivation* (pp. 323–342). New York: Psychology Press.

Guenther, L., Jörges, S., Mahl, D., & Brüggemann, M. (2023). Framing as a bridging concept for climate change communication: A systematic review based on 25 years of literature. *Communication Research*, https://doi.org/10.1177/00936502221137165.

Applied

Elbe, A. M., & Barkoukis, V. (2017). The psychology of doping. *Current Opinion in Psychology*, *16*, 67–71.

Taherdoost, H. (2018). A review of technology acceptance and adoption models and theories. *Procedia Manufacturing*, *22*, 960–967.

Yuriev, A., Dahmen, M., Paillé, P., Boiral, O., & Guillaumie, L. (2020). Pro-environmental behaviors through the lens of the theory of planned behavior: A scoping review. *Resources, Conservation and Recycling*, *155*, 104660.

6.10 REFERENCES

Ajzen, I. (1991). The theory of planned behavior. *Organizational Behavior and Human Decision Processes*, *50*(2), 179–211.

Ajzen, I. (2015). The theory of planned behaviour is alive and well, and not ready to retire: A commentary on Sniehotta, Presseau, and Araújo-Soares. *Health Psychology Review*, *9*(2), 131–137.

Ajzen, I., Fishbein, M., Lohmann, S., & Albarracín, D. (2018). The influence of attitudes on behavior. In D. Albarracín & B. T. Johnson (Eds.), *The handbook of attitudes. Volume 1: Basic principles* (2nd ed., pp. 197–255). New York: Routledge.

Alexandre, B., Reynaud, E., Osiurak, F., & Navarro, J. (2018). Acceptance and acceptability criteria: A literature review. *Cognition, Technology & Work*, *20*, 165–177.

Allport, G. W. (1935). Attitudes. In C. Murchison (Ed.), *A handbook of social psychology* (pp. 798–844). Worcester, CA: Clark University Press.

Bain, P. G., Milfont, T. L., Kashima, Y., Bilewicz, M., Doron, G., Garðarsdóttir, R. B., ... & Saviolidis, N. M. (2016). Co-benefits of addressing climate change can motivate action around the world. *Nature Climate Change*, *6*(2), 154–157.

Bamberg, S., & Möser, G. (2007). Twenty years after Hines, Hungerford, and Tomera: A new meta-analysis of psycho-social determinants of pro-environmental behaviour. *Journal of Environmental Psychology*, *27*(1), 14–25.

Batel, S., Devine-Wright, P., & Tangeland, T. (2013). Social acceptance of low carbon energy and associated infrastructures: A critical discussion. *Energy Policy*, *58*, 1–5.

Bem, D. J. (1972). Self-perception theory. In L. Berkowitz (Ed.), *Advances in experimental social psychology* (Vol. 6, pp. 1–62). New York: Academic Press.

Bickerstaff, K., Lorenzoni, I., Pidgeon, N. F., Poortinga, W., & Simmons, P. (2008). Reframing nuclear power in the UK energy debate: Nuclear power, climate change mitigation and radioactive waste. *Public Understanding of Science*, *17*(2), 145-169.

Blank, C., Kopp, M., Niedermeier, M., Schnitzer, M., & Schobersberger, W. (2016). Predictors of doping intentions, susceptibility, and behaviour of elite athletes: a meta-analytic review. *SpringerPlus*, *5*, 1–14.

Borah, P., Hwang, J., & Hsu, Y. C. (2021). COVID-19 vaccination attitudes and intention: Message framing and the moderating role of perceived vaccine benefits. *Journal of Health Communication, 26*(8), 523–533.

Bornstein, R. F., Kale, A. R., & Cornell, K. R. (1990). Boredom as a limiting condition on the mere exposure effect. *Journal of Personality and Social Psychology, 58*(5), 791.

Brand, R., Melzer, M., & Hagemann, N. (2011). Towards an implicit association test (IAT) for measuring doping attitudes in sports: Data-based recommendations developed from two recently published tests. *Psychology of Sport and Exercise, 12*(3), 250–256.

Brickman, P., Redfield, J., Harrison, A. A., & Crandall, R. (1972). Drive and predisposition as factors in the attitudinal effects of mere exposure. *Journal of Experimental Social Psychology, 8*(1), 31–44.

Briñol, P., & Petty, R. E. (2020). Changing prejudiced attitudes, promoting egalitarianism, and enhancing diversity through fundamental processes of persuasion. *European Review of Social Psychology, 31*(1), 350–389.

Briñol, P., Petty, R. E., & Wagner, B. C. (2012). Embodied validation: Our bodies can change and also validate our thoughts. In P. Briñol & K. DeMarree (Eds.), *Social metacognition* (pp. 219–240). New York: Psychology Press.

Cacioppo, J. T., Berntson, G. G., Norris, C. J., & Gollan, J. K. (2011). The evaluative space model. In P. A. M. Van Lange, A. W. Kruglanski, & E. T. Higgins (Eds.), *Handbook of theories of social psychology* (pp. 50–72). Thousand Oaks, CA: Sage.

Cacioppo, J. T., Priester, J. R., & Berntson, G. G. (1993). Rudimentary determinants of attitudes: II. Arm flexion and extension have differential effects on attitudes. *Journal of Personality and Social Psychology, 65*(1), 5.

Chaiken, S. (1980). Heuristic versus systematic information processing and the use of source versus message cues in persuasion. *Journal of Personality and Social Psychology, 39*(5), 752–766.

Chaiken, S., & Ledgerwood, A. (2011). A theory of heuristic and systematic information processing. In P. A. M. van Lange, A. W. Kruglanski, & E. T. Higgins (Eds.), *Handbook of theories of social psychology*. Thousand Oaks, CA: Sage.

Chong, D., & Druckman, J. N. (2007). Framing theory. *Annual Review of Political Science, 10*(1), 103–126.

Coles, N. A., March, D. S., Marmolejo-Ramos, F., Larsen, J. T., Arinze, N. C., Ndukaihe, I. L., … & Liuzza, M. T. (2022). A multi-lab test of the facial feedback hypothesis by the many smiles collaboration. *Nature Human Behaviour, 6*(12), 1731–1742.

Conklin, L. R., Strunk, D. R., & Fazio, R. H. (2009). Attitude formation in depression: Evidence for deficits in forming positive attitudes. *Journal of Behavior Therapy and Experimental Psychiatry, 40*(1), 120–126.

Davis, F. D. (1989). Perceived usefulness, perceived ease of use and user acceptance of information technology. *MIS Quarterly, 13*(3), 319–339.

De Houwer, J., Thomas, S., & Baeyens, F. (2001). Association learning of likes and dislikes: A review of 25 years of research on human evaluative conditioning. *Psychological Bulletin, 127*(6), 853.

Deutsch, R., & Fazio, R. H. (2008). How subtyping shapes perception: Predictable exceptions to the rule reduce attention to stereotype-associated dimensions. *Journal of Experimental Social Psychology*, *44*(4), 1020–1034.

DeVellis, B. M., Blalock, S. J., & Sandler, R. S. (1990). Predicting participation in cancer screening: The role of perceived behavioral control 1. *Journal of Applied Social Psychology*, *20*(8), 639–660.

Dunlap, R. E. (2008). The New Environmental Paradigm Scale: From marginality to worldwide use. *The Journal of Environmental Education*, *40*(1), 3–18.

Dunlap, R. E., Van Liere, K. D., Mertig, A. G., & Jones, R. E. (2000). New trends in measuring environmental attitudes: Measuring endorsement of the New Ecological Paradigm: A revised NEP scale. *Journal of Social Issues*, *56*(3), 425–442.

Edmondson, D., Conroy, D., Romero-Canyas, R., Tanenbaum, M., & Czajkowski, S. (2022). Climate change, behavior change and health: A multidisciplinary, translational and multilevel perspective. *Translational Behavioral Medicine*, *12*(4), 503–515.

Eiser, J. R., & Fazio, R. H. (2013). Evaluation asymmetry. In J. R. Eiser & R. H. Fazio, *Handbook of approach and avoidance motivation* (2nd ed., pp. 323–340). New York: Psychology Press.

Fabringar, L. R., MacDonald, T. K., & Wegener, D. T. (2018). The origins and structure of attitudes. In D. Albarracín & B. T. Johnson (Eds.), *The handbook of attitudes. Volume 1: Basic principles* (2nd ed., pp. 109–157). New York: Routledge.

Fazio, R. H. (1990). Multiple processes by which attitudes guide behavior: The MODE model as an integrative framework. In M. P. Zanna (Ed.), *Advances in experimental social psychology* (Vol. 23, pp. 75–109). New York: Academic Press.

Fazio, R. H. (2007). Attitudes as object-evaluation associations of varying strength. *Social Cognition*, *25*(5), 603.

Fazio, R. H., Eiser, J. R., & Shook, N. J. (2004). Attitude formation through exploration: Valence asymmetries. *Journal of Personality and Social Psychology*, *87*(3), 293.

Fazio, R. H., & Olson, M. A. (2014). The mode model: Attitude–behavior processes as a function of motivation and opportunity. In J. W. Sherman, B. Gawronski, & Y. Trope (Eds.), *Dual process theories of the social mind*. New York: Guilford Press.

Festinger, L. (1962). *A theory of cognitive dissonance* (Vol. 2). Stanford, CA: Stanford University Press.

Festinger, L., & Carlsmith, J. M. (1959). Cognitive consequences of forced compliance. *The Journal of Abnormal and Social Psychology*, *58*(2), 203.

Fiagbenu, M. E., Proch, J., & Kessler, T. (2021). Of deadly beans and risky stocks: Political ideology and attitude formation via exploration depend on the nature of the attitude stimuli. *British Journal of Psychology*, *112*(1), 342–357.

Fishbein, M., & Ajzen, I. (1975). *Belief, attitude, intention and behavior: An introduction to theory and research*. Reading, MA: Addison-Wesley

Gibson, L. P., Magnan, R. E., Kramer, E. B., & Bryan, A. D. (2021). Theory of planned behavior analysis of social distancing during the COVID-19 pandemic: Focusing on the intention–behavior gap. *Annals of Behavioral Medicine*, *55*(8), 805–812.

Gifford, R. (2014). Environmental psychology matters. *Annual Review of Psychology, 65*(1), 541–579.

Godin, G., & Kok, G. (1996). The theory of planned behavior: A review of its applications to health-related behaviors. *American Journal of Health Promotion, 11*(2), 87–98.

Granić, A., & Marangunić, N. (2019). Technology acceptance model in educational context: A systematic literature review. *British Journal of Educational Technology, 50*(5), 2572–2593.

Greenwald, A. G., Banaji, M. R., & Nosek, B. A. (2015). Statistically small effects of the Implicit Association Test can have societally large effects. *Journal of Personality and Social Psychology, 108*(4), 553–561. https://doi.org/10.1037/pspa0000016

Greenwald, A. G., McGhee, D. E., & Schwartz, J. L. (1998). Measuring individual differences in implicit cognition: The Implicit Association Test. *Journal of Personality and Social Psychology, 74*(6), 1464.

Haddock, G., Maio, G. R., Arnold, K., & Huskinson, T. (2008). Should persuasion be affective or cognitive? The moderating effects of need for affect and need for cognition. *Personality and Social Psychology Bulletin, 34*(6), 769–778.

Haugtvedt, C. P., Petty, R. E., & Cacioppo, J. T. (1992). Need for cognition and advertising: Understanding the role of personality variables in consumer behavior. *Journal of Consumer Psychology, 1*(3), 239–260.

Hawcroft, L. J., & Milfont, T. L. (2010). The use (and abuse) of the new environmental paradigm scale over the last 30 years: A meta-analysis. *Journal of Environmental Psychology, 30*(2), 143–158.

Herrmann, A., Amelung, D., Fischer, H., & Sauerborn, R. (2020). Communicating the health co-benefits of climate change mitigation to households and policy makers. In D. C. Holmes & L. M. Richardson (Eds.), *Research handbook on communicating climate change* (pp. 279–289). Cheltenham: Edward Elgar Publishing.

Hewstone, M., & Young, L. (1988). Expectancy-value models of attitude: Measurement and combination of evaluations and beliefs 1. *Journal of Applied Social Psychology, 18*(11), 958–971.

Holden, R. J., & Karsh, B. T. (2010). The technology acceptance model: Its past and its future in health care. *Journal of Biomedical Informatics, 43*(1), 159–172.

Homonoff, T. A. (2018). Can small incentives have large effects? The impact of taxes versus bonuses on disposable bag use. *American Economic Journal: Economic Policy, 10*(4), 177–210.

Horcajo, J., & Luttrell, A. (2016). The effects of elaboration on the strength of doping-related attitudes: Resistance to change and behavioral intentions. *Journal of Sport and Exercise Psychology, 38*(3), 236–246.

Horcajo, J., Santos, D., Guyer, J. J., & Moreno, L. (2019). Changing attitudes and intentions related to doping: An analysis of individual differences in need for cognition. *Journal of Sport Sciences, 37*(24), 2835–2843.

Hovland, C. I., & Rosenberg, M. J. (1960). *Attitude organization and change: An analysis of consistency among attitude components* (Vol. 176). New Haven, CT: Yale University Press.

Huijts, N. M., Molin, E. J., & Steg, L. (2012). Psychological factors influencing sustainable energy technology acceptance: A review-based comprehensive framework. *Renewable and Sustainable Energy Reviews, 16*(1), 525–531.

Insko, C. A. (1965). Verbal reinforcement of attitude. *Journal of Personality and Social Psychology, 2*(4), 621.

Jarvis, W. B. G., & Petty, R. E. (1996). The need to evaluate. *Journal of Personality and Social Psychology, 70*(1), 172.

Johnson, R. C., Thomson, C. W., & Frincke, G. (1960). Word values, word frequency, and visual duration thresholds. *Psychological Review, 67*(5), 332.

Jones, C. R., & Eiser, J. R. (2014). Attitude formation through exploration: The 'Treasure Island' paradigm and the significance of risk predictability. *SAGE Open, 4*(3), 2158244014551927.

Jones, C. R., Eiser, J. R., & Gamble, T. R. (2012). Assessing the impact of framing on the comparative favourability of nuclear power as an electricity generating option in the UK. *Energy Policy, 41*, 451–465.

Kaiser, F. G., Hübner, G., & Bogner, F. X. (2005). Contrasting the theory of planned behavior with the value-belief-norm model in explaining conservation behavior 1. *Journal of Applied Social Psychology, 35*(10), 2150–2170.

Kaklamanou, D., Jones, C. R., Webb, T. L., & Walker, S. R. (2015). Using public transport can make up for flying abroad on holiday: Compensatory green beliefs and environmentally significant behavior. *Environment and Behavior, 47*(2), 184–204.

Kanekar, S. (1976). Observational learning of attitudes: A behavioral analysis. *European Journal of Social Psychology, 6*(1), 1–24.

Katz, D. (1960). The functional approach to the study of attitudes. *Public Opinion Quarterly, 24*(2), 163–204.

Kawakami, K., Phills, C. E., Steele, J. R., & Dovidio, J. F. (2007). (Close) distance makes the heart grow fonder: Improving implicit racial attitudes and interracial interactions through approach behaviors. *Journal of Personality and Social Psychology, 92*(6), 957.

Krosnick, J. A., & Petty, R. E. (2014). Attitude strength: An overview. *Attitude Strength: Antecedents and Consequences, 1*, 1–24.

LaPiere, R. T. (1934). Attitudes versus actions. *Social Forces, 13*, 230–237.

Lazuras, L., Barkoukis, V., Rodafinos, A., & Tzorbatzoudis, H. (2010). Predictors of doping intentions in elite-level athletes: A social cognition approach. *Journal of Sport and Exercise Psychology, 32*(5), 694–710.

Likert, R., Roslow, S., & Murphy, G. (1934). A simple and reliable method of scoring the Thurstone Attitude Scales. *The Journal of Social Psychology, 5*(2), 228–238.

Loersch, C., Bartholow, B. D., Manning, M., Calanchini, J., & Sherman, J. W. (2015). Intoxicated prejudice: The impact of alcohol consumption on implicitly and explicitly measured racial attitudes. *Group Processes & Intergroup Relations, 18*(2), 256–268.

López-Mosquera, N., & Sánchez, M. (2012). Theory of Planned Behavior and the Value-Belief-Norm Theory explaining willingness to pay for a suburban park. *Journal of Environmental Management, 113*, 251–262.

Maio, G. R., & Esses, V. M. (2001). The need for affect: Individual differences in the motivation to approach or avoid emotions. *Journal of Personality, 69*(4), 583–614.

Maio, G. R., & Olson, J. M. (2000). Emergent themes and potential approaches to attitude function: The function-structure model of attitudes. In G. R. Maio & J. M. Olson (Eds.), *Why we evaluate: Functions of attitudes* (pp. 417–442). Hillsdale, NJ: Lawrence Erlbaum Associates.

Monahan, J. L., Murphy, S. T., & Zajonc, R. B. (2000). Subliminal mere exposure: Specific, general, and diffuse effects. *Psychological Science, 11*(6), 462–466.

Moran, T., Nudler, Y., & Bar Anan, Y. (2023). Evaluative conditioning: Past, present, and future. *Annual Review of Psychology, 74*, 245–269. https://doi.org/10.1146/annurev-psych-032420-031815

Morente-Sánchez, J., & Zabala, M. (2013). Doping in sport: a review of elite athletes' attitudes, beliefs, and knowledge. *Sports Medicine, 43*, 395–411.

Moscovici, S. (1963). Attitudes and opinions. *Annual Review of Psychology, 14*(1), 231–260.

Nelson, T. E., Oxley, Z. M., & Clawson, R. A. (1997). Toward a psychology of framing effects. *Political Behavior, 19*(3), 221–246.

Niinimäki, K., Peters, G., Dahlbo, H., Perry, P., Rissanen, T., & Gwilt, A. (2020). The environmental price of fast fashion. *Nature Reviews Earth & Environment, 1*(4), 189–200.

Ntoumanis, N., Ng, J. Y., Barkoukis, V., & Backhouse, S. (2014). Personal and psychosocial predictors of doping use in physical activity settings: a meta-analysis. *Sports Medicine, 44*, 1603–1624.

Olson, M. A., & Fazio, R. H. (2001). Implicit attitude formation through classical conditioning. *Psychological Science, 12*(5), 413–417.

Olson, M. A., & Fazio, R. H. (2004). Reducing the influence of extrapersonal associations on the Implicit Association Test: Personalizing the IAT. *Journal of Personality and Social Psychology, 86*(5), 653–667. https://doi.org/10.1037/0022-3514.86.5.653

Osgood, C. E. (1964). Semantic differential technique in the comparative study of cultures. *American Anthropologist, 66*(3), 171–200.

Petróczi, A., & Aidman, E. (2009). Measuring explicit attitude toward doping: Review of the psychometric properties of the Performance Enhancement Attitude Scale. *Psychology of Sport and Exercise, 10*(3), 390–396.

Petty, R. E., & Cacioppo, J. T. (1986). The elaboration likelihood model of persuasion. In L. Berkowitz (Ed.), *Advances in experimental social psychology* (Vol. 19, pp. 123–205). New York: Acadmic Press. Reproduced in R. E. Petty & J. T. Cacioppo, *Communication and persuasion*. Springer Series in Social Psychology. New York: Springer. https://doi.org/10.1007/978-1-4612-4964-1_1

Rogers, E. M. (1962). *Diffusion of innovations* (1st ed.). New York: Free Press of Glencoe.

Rokeach, M. (1973). *The nature of human values*. New York: Free Press of Glencoe.

Rozin, P., & Royzman, E. B. (2001). Negativity bias, negativity dominance, and contagion. *Personality and Social Psychology Review, 5*(4), 296–320.

Samra, R. (2014). A new look at our old attitude problem. *Journal of Social Sciences, 10*(4), 143.

Schwartz, S. H. (1977). Normative influences on altruism. In L. Berkowitz (Ed.), *Advances in experimental social psychology* (Vol. 10). New York: Academic Press.

See, Y. H. M., Petty, R. E., & Evans, L. M. (2009). The impact of perceived message complexity and need for cognition on information processing and attitudes. *Journal of Research in Personality, 43*(5), 880–889.

Shook, N. J., Thomas, R., & Ford, C. G. (2019). Testing the relation between disgust and general avoidance behavior. *Personality and Individual Differences, 150*, 109457.

Skinner, B. F. (1963). Operant behavior. *American Psychologist, 18*(8), 503–515.

Smith, J. R., & Louis, W. R. (2009). Group norms and the attitude–behaviour relationship. *Social and Personality Psychology Compass, 3*(1), 19–35.

Sniehotta, F. F., Presseau, J., & Araújo-Soares, V. (2014). Time to retire the theory of planned behaviour. *Health Psychology Review, 8*(1), 1–7.

Soroka, S., Guggenheim, L., & Valentino, D. (2021). Valence-based biases in news selection. *Journal of Media Psychology: Theories, Methods, and Applications, 33*(3), 145.

Spence, A., Poortinga, W., Butler, C., & Pidgeon, N. F. (2011). Perceptions of climate change and willingness to save energy related to flood experience. *Nature Climate Change, 1*(1), 46–49.

Staats, H., Kieviet, A., & Hartig, T. (2003). Where to recover from attentional fatigue: An expectancy-value analysis of environmental preference. *Journal of Environmental Psychology, 23*(2), 147–157.

Steg, L., & Vlek, C. (2009). Encouraging pro-environmental behaviour: An integrative review and research agenda. *Journal of Environmental Psychology, 29*(3), 309–317.

Stern, P. C. (2000). New environmental theories: Toward a coherent theory of environmentally significant behavior. *Journal of Social Issues, 56*(3), 407–424.

Strack, F., Martin, L. L., & Stepper, S. (1988). Inhibiting and facilitating conditions of the human smile: A nonobtrusive test of the facial feedback hypothesis. *Journal of Personality and Social Psychology, 54*(5), 768.

Thorndike, E. L. (1927). The law of effect. *The American Journal of Psychology, 39*(1/4), 212–222.

Thorndike, E. L., & Columbia University, Institute of Educational Research, Division of Psychology. (1932). *The fundamentals of learning*. New York: Teachers College Bureau of Publications.

Thurstone, L. L. (1928). Attitudes can be measured. *American Journal of Sociology, 33*(4), 529–554.

Todorov, A., Chaiken, S., & Henderson, M. D. (2002). The heuristic-systematic model of social information processing. In J. P. Dillard & L. Shen (Eds.), *The persuasion handbook: Developments in theory and practice*. Thousand Oaks, CA: Sage.

Towler, G., & Shepherd, R. (1992). Application of Fishbein and Ajzen's expectancy-value model to understanding fat intake. *Appetite, 18*(1), 15–27.

Trihadmojo, B., Jones, C. R., Prasastyoga, B., Walton, C., & Sulaiman, A. (2020). Toward a nuanced and targeted forest and peat fires prevention policy: Insight from psychology. *Forest Policy and Economics, 120*, 102293.

Tversky, A., & Kahneman, D. (1981). The framing of decisions and the psychology of choice. *Science, 211*(4481), 453–458.

Ulker-Demirel, E., & Ciftci, G. (2020). A systematic literature review of the theory of planned behavior in tourism, leisure and hospitality management research. *Journal of Hospitality and Tourism Management, 43*, 209–219.

Venkatesh, V., & Davis, F. D. (2000). A theoretical extension of the technology acceptance model: Four longitudinal field studies. *Management Science, 46*(2), 186–204.

Venkatesh, V., Morris, M. G., Davis, G. B., & Davis, F. D. (2003). User acceptance of information technology: Toward a unified view. *MIS Quarterly, 27*(3), 425–478.

Vining, J., & Ebreo, A. (1992). Predicting recycling behavior from global and specific environmental attitudes and changes in recycling opportunities. *Journal of Applied Social Psychology, 22*(20), 1580–1607.

Wagenmakers, E. J., Beek, T., Dijkhoff, L., Gronau, Q. F., Acosta, A., Adams Jr, R. B., ... & Zwaan, R. A. (2016). Registered replication report: Strack, Martin, & Stepper (1988). *Perspectives on Psychological Science, 11*(6), 917–928.

Whitmarsh, L., Capstick, S., Moore, I., Köhler, J., & Le Quéré, C. (2020). Use of aviation by climate change researchers: Structural influences, personal attitudes, and information provision. *Global Environmental Change, 65*, 102184.

Whittle, C., Jones, C. R., & While, A. (2020). Empowering householders: Identifying predictors of intentions to use a home energy management system in the United Kingdom. *Energy Policy, 139*, 111343.

Woo, T. O., & Castore, C. H. (1980). Expectancy-value and selective exposure as determinants of attitudes toward a nuclear power plant. *Journal of Applied Social Psychology, 10*(3), 224–234.

Xiao, M., Wang, R., & Chan-Olmsted, S. (2018). Factors affecting YouTube influencer marketing credibility: A heuristic-systematic model. *Journal of Media Business Studies, 15*(3), 188–213.

Yousafzai, S. Y., Foxall, G. R., & Pallister, J. G. (2007a). Technology acceptance: A meta-analysis of the TAM: Part 1. *Journal of Modelling in Management, 2*(3), 251–280.

Yousafzai, S. Y., Foxall, G. R., & Pallister, J. G. (2007b). Technology acceptance: A meta-analysis of the TAM: Part 2. *Journal of Modelling in Management, 2*(3), 281–304.

Yuriev, A., Dahmen, M., Paillé, P., Boiral, O., & Guillaumie, L. (2020). Pro-environmental behaviors through the lens of the theory of planned behavior: A scoping review. *Resources, Conservation and Recycling, 155*, 104660.

Zajonc, R. B. (1968). Attitudinal effects of mere exposure. *Journal of Personality and Social Psychology, 9*(2, Pt 2), 1, 1–27.

Zajonc, R. B. (1980). Feeling and thinking: Preferences need no inferences. *American Psychologist, 35*, 151–175.

7
SOCIAL INFLUENCE
FANNY LALOT & JULIE VAN DE VYVER

Contents

7.1 AUTHORS' PERSONAL JOURNEYS

Julie Van de Vyver

I studied psychology as an undergraduate student at the University of Kent. Following graduation, I worked as a research assistant for Professors Dominic Abrams and Adam Rutland, on a project that examined intergroup and intragroup dynamics in children. I then conducted an MSc in Social and Applied Psychology, followed by a PhD in Social Psychology. During my graduate degrees, I tested social psychological mechanisms for promoting prosocial behaviour. I then worked as a lecturer for six years, teaching and researching the social psychology topics that fascinated me the most: prosocial behaviour, environmental behaviour, and inclusion. As a social psychologist, the thing that really drives me is using research to generate positive real-world change and impact; that is, to contribute positively to societies. I now work as a Behavioural Insights Consultant for a company called Magpie. In this role, I draw on my social psychology knowledge, and particularly social influence knowledge, and use academic insights to drive positive, meaningful, and real-world change.

Fanny Lalot

I was born in Geneva, Switzerland, where I first discovered social psychology during my undergraduate studies. I quickly became fascinated by the field, especially the sort of experiments that social psychologists devised to study the effect of the context on people's behaviour. The lab I worked in had a strong orientation towards social influence, and more specifically *minority* influence. In fact, the first study I ever helped conduct as an undergraduate research assistant was on minority influence. This theoretical framework would stick with me throughout my Master's studies, my PhD thesis, and beyond. After my PhD, I moved to the UK. As did Julie, I joined the Centre for the Study of Group Processes at the University of Kent. I worked there with Professor Dominic Abrams as a postdoctoral researcher for two and a half years. In 2021, I moved back to Switzerland and joined the Department of Social Psychology at the University of Basel, where I continue to work on, among other things, social influence, minority groups, and social norms. How does social change occur in society? What can we do to influence people's behaviour in a desired direction? What is it about the argumentative style of social minorities that makes them influential? These questions continue to fascinate me today.

We (Fanny and Julie) became acquainted indirectly, through our common collaborators in Kent. However, we have never actually met in person. Our collaboration, including the chapter you are reading, is the product of videocalls and many, many emails. Technology is definitely redefining how people work and meet!

7.2 INTRODUCTION

What's your favourite food? Who will you vote for in the next election? Would you speak up if you were in disagreement with your classmates during a group meeting? Although we tend to believe that these attitudes and behaviours reflect personal preferences, they are in fact largely shaped and influenced by the people around us. This of course means that *you* also have the power to influence others – probably more than you realise (Bohns, 2016). In this chapter, we break down the ways in which people influence people. The lessons from this chapter, grounded in theory and rigorous psychological research, can be directly applied to the real world, including, for example, marketing campaigns, charity appeals, the implementation of policy, and climate change communication. At the end of the chapter, we illustrate how research on social influence has been applied to three real-life domains: prosocial behaviour, sustainability, and the COVID-19 crisis.

Through reading this chapter, you will develop a deeper understanding of when and why people are influenced by others. You will discover which attributes of the person and the situation increase one's potential for influence, but also how people without any resources or social power can still obtain influence. You will familiarise yourself with the classic studies on social influence dating from the 1950s, 1960s, and 1970s, as well as the most recent developments and theoretical advancements in the field. Finally, you will learn how these academic insights can be applied to real-world events, both historic and contemporary.

7.3 LEARNING OBJECTIVES

By the end of this chapter, you will understand:

- Why social influence occurs (e.g., people want to be correct and to be included);
- The conditions that maximise social influence (the 'when' and 'where');
- The differences (and similarities) between majority and minority influence;
- The impact of authority and direct orders on behaviour;
- The power of social norms;
- The application of insights from social influence to real-world issues (prosocial behaviour, sustainability, COVID-19).

7.4 PART 1: FOUNDATIONS

7.4.1 What is Social Influence?

Let's open with an anecdote from Julie: 'As a lecturer, I observed an interesting phenomenon among my students each year. First-year university students take notepads and pens to class,

> **Key concept – Social influence:** Any change in an individual's thoughts, feelings, or behaviours caused by other people, who may be actually present or whose presence is imagined, expected, or only implied.

whereas second-year students take their laptops. As you might expect, first years quickly notice that their more experienced peers, whom they often look to for information, do things differently. And after only a week or two, all first years start turning up to class with laptops instead of their notepads and pens.' This is **social influence**.

Psychologists define social influence as 'any change which a person's relations with other people (individual, group, institution, or society) produce on their intellectual activities, emotions or actions' (*The Dictionary of Personality and Social Psychology*, 1986, p. 328). Put more simply, social influence is the effect that other people have on our conceptions, judgements, opinions, attitudes, and behaviour (Doise, 1980).

In this chapter, we consider different types of social influence: conformity, compliance, obedience, and minority influence. **Conformity** occurs when we adjust our attitudes and/or behaviour to be in line with an implied social norm. This adjustment is not always a

> **Key concept – Conformity:** The adjustment of one's opinions, judgements, or actions so that they become more consistent with the normative standards of a social group or situation. Conformity includes temporary outward acquiescence (compliance) and more enduring private acceptance (conversion).

conscious or mindful process. Compliance represents a change in a person's behaviour in response to a direct request. Obedience occurs when we adjust our attitudes and/or behaviour to be in line with an explicit order (not just a request), typically from powerful or authoritative figures. Finally, minority influence represents the process through which a social minority deprived of power and other psychosocial resources can still obtain some influence.

7.4.2 Why are we Influenced?

Before diving into the different forms of social influence it is worth wondering *why* people are influenced in the first place. Two perspectives are helpful here: the perspective of the *group*, and that of the *individual*.

To understand the group's perspective, ask yourself: why does a group exist? Groups are formed because they have an objective, a goal that could not be achieved by an individual alone. For example, a sports team might aim to win a tournament, a political party to win seats in a local election, and a student study group might aim for every member to pass their exams with success. Moving towards the group's goals requires some structure in the group as well as a sense of cohesion and uniformity: group members must agree on the group's structure and functioning, its goals, and the means to achieve these goals. This is what

Festinger (1950) called 'locomotion'. In sum, the group needs all members to align their attitudes and behaviours and it will try to influence those who might think and act differently from the rest.

In addition, some groups fulfil another function: they define *social reality*. Very few things can be defined as true or false outside any social contexts (e.g., physics or maths). Most others are subjective and depend on a social consensus: what makes someone 'beautiful', what qualifies as a good running performance, what political opinion is 'right' or 'wrong'? We depend on the group to learn the social reality of things. And for this as well, the group needs internal uniformity: a statement can only be considered valid if most group members agree on it. This is the second reason why groups will try to influence their members (Festinger, 1950).

> **Key concept – Normative influence:** The personal and interpersonal processes that cause individuals to feel, think, and act in ways that are consistent with social norms, standards, and conventions.

From the individual perspective, there are clear advantages of being part of a group. Humans have several fundamental psychological needs that can be satisfied through the group. Most notably, group affiliation can fulfil a crucial *need to belong* as well as *positive self-esteem* through social approval. Second, it can reduce *uncertainty* about the self and the world.

> **Key concept – Informational influence:** Those interpersonal processes that challenge the correctness of an individual's beliefs or the appropriateness of their behaviour, thereby promoting change.

Groups also confer access to many *resources* (some tangible, e.g., access to a club or financial help; and some symbolic, e.g., social status or reputation). On this basis, Deutsch and Gerard (1955) defined two types of social influence: **normative**, which refers to fulfilling the needs of affiliation, social approval, and rewards, and **informational**, which refers to the need to reduce uncertainty. Together, these needs explain why social influence occurs.

To summarise the functions of influence, let's look at an example supplied by Fanny: I love role-playing and board games and I like to think of myself as a gamer. Being part of a community of gamers (*need to belong*) contributes positively to my self-esteem (*need for positive self-esteem*). My D&D co-players and I form a very cohesive group and I know I can count on these people when I need them (*resources*). Yet this cohesion took some time to build. In our first sessions, different players wanted to do different things (one was a murder hobo, another only cared about his personal storyline) and the group could not agree on common goals. But with some help from the game master, we learnt that our interests could actually align quite well (*group uniformity*). From that point onwards, we were able to make more progress towards our objectives (*group locomotion*). I think this nicely illustrates why people join groups, but also what it entails, and the role of influence to create and maintain functioning groups.

7.4.3 Social Powers and Processes of Influence

Having identified why groups try to influence individuals, and why individuals readily accept this influence, it remains to discuss *how* influence occurs. Influence takes many forms, from innocent requests to more sophisticated methods for persuasion (such as implicitly making an action look desirable) and explicit orders. These have been summarised as a list of six bases of social power (French & Raven, 1959; Raven, 1965).

1 **Reward power**: the ability to give or promise rewards for compliance.
2 **Coercive power**: the ability to give or threaten punishment for non-compliance.
3 **Informational power**: the individual's belief that the group has more information than oneself.
4 **Expert power**: the individual's belief that the group has generally greater expertise and knowledge than oneself.
5 **Legitimate power**: the individual's belief that the group is authorised by a recognised power structure to command and make decisions.
6 **Referent power**: identification with, attraction to, or respect for the group.

EXERCISE 7.1

The Six Bases of Social Power

Think of the groups (or individuals) with whom you most often interact (family, friends, teachers, colleagues, etc.). Who do you particularly listen to and whose advice do you follow? Which of the six bases of social power do you associate with these groups or people? Does the power you recognise in them correspond with how much you think you are influenced by them?

While we present these powers as pertaining to the group, let's note that they can also be used to understand the potential for influence of individuals (such as leaders). For example, a study by Kelman (1958) illustrates several of these bases for social power (see Key study 7.1). Kelman proposed three processes of influence underpinned by different powers:

* **Compliance**: the individual reproduces the source's position because they want to achieve a favourable reaction from this source, irrespective of whether they believe in the content itself.
* **Identification**: the individual accepts influence because they want to form a positive, self-defining relationship to the source. Although the individual might agree with the content, this is secondary.

- **Internalisation**: the individual really integrates the content because they are intrinsically convinced the source's position is right. This process is most likely to lead to long-term influence.

KEY STUDY 7.1

In 1954, Kelman devised an experiment in a Black university in the USA, just before the abolition of segregation in the public schools, which was published as Kelman (1958). Students were exposed to an alleged radio programme in which a guest argued that it would be desirable to maintain some private all-Black institutions. This communicator (a Black man) was presented differently in three experimental conditions.

In the first condition, he was allegedly the president of the National Foundation for Black Universities (including the one in which the study was being conducted). During the interview, he made it clear that he would withdraw funding from any university in which the students took a different position on the issue (*high reward and coercive power*). In the second condition, the communicator was the president of the student council in another Black university. He made it clear that the position was not just his own, but also the consensus of a students' poll (*high referent power*). In the third condition, the communicator was a professor of history and a top expert in Black history. He made it clear that his position was based on research and the evidence of history (*high informational and expert power*).

After listening to the radio interview, participants filled out three questionnaires assessing their views on the topic. The first questionnaire was administered immediately, and students were requested to write down their name on the page, which would be forwarded to the communicator. The second questionnaire was administered immediately after the first but was meant to be anonymous and not to be seen by anyone outside the research team. The third questionnaire was administered a couple of weeks later, in a different place, and by a different experimenter, to be as separate as possible from the situation of influence.

The results showed that the different communicators obtained different forms of influence. The first communicator (whose power relied on resources and threats) only influenced responses in the first questionnaire where answers were non-anonymous (compliance). The second communicator (whose power relied on reference and identity) influenced responses as long as the communicator was salient (questionnaires 1 and 2) but not when its salience was removed (identification). Finally, the third communicator (whose power relied on information and expertise) influenced responses in all three questionnaires: his message was truly internalised by the participants (internalisation).

This study illustrates the different reasons why people are influenced, and already points to the fact that different contexts will lead to different patterns of influence, with some being more or less internalised and more or less long-lasting.

7.4.4 Social Influence Under Uncertainty

Here is another anecdote, this time from Julie: When I was six years old, my family moved from Belgium to the UK. My dad travelled a lot for work, so my mum had to quickly get used to many new cultural norms and, more practically, to driving on the left-hand side of the road. Whenever my mum got lost while driving (which happened fairly frequently without GPS), she would say that the best thing to do is to follow the driver in front. And that is what she did each time. She, quite literally, followed the nearest car. She used another person as a frame of reference. This is an illustration of *social influence under uncertainty*.

Dots Moving in the Dark: Sherif's Classic Study

In his classic social psychology study, Sherif (1935) tested the hypothesis: do people use other people as frames of reference when they are uncertain? Participants were invited to take part in a study on 'visual perception'. They were led to a room which was completely dark except for a small dot of light on the far wall. Sherif made use of a visual illusion called the autokinetic illusion, a phenomenon of visual perception whereby a stationary pinpoint of light in an otherwise darkened surrounding appears to move. This set-up was ideal for Sherif's study as it was an inherently subjective and uncertain task: the illusion enabled Sherif to study how people make sense of a stimulus in the absence of any physical or pre-established frame of reference. The experiment had three different conditions. The first condition was the *private* condition, where participants were given the following instructions:

> When the room is completely dark, I shall give you the signal READY, and then show you a point of light. After a short time, the light will start to move. As soon as you see it move, press the key. A few seconds later the light will disappear. Then tell me the distance it moved. Try to make your estimates as accurate as possible.

Participants were asked to make 100 judgements. They then returned to the lab on two consecutive days and repeated the exercise. Sherif found that participants established their own median and range of values during the course of the first session and maintained that median during the following sessions. Put differently, when left to their own devices, participants established their own frame of reference.

The second and third conditions were *group* conditions. In one condition, participants completed the first session as individuals, and then three subsequent sessions as members of two- or three-person groups. In another condition, participants completed the first three sessions as a group and the final session as individuals. The results show that in the group contexts, participants naturally converge to a common judgement: individual judgements gradually moved away from their own frame of reference to a group-based frame of reference (Figure 7.1, left). In addition, participants who started as a group maintained this common judgement even when later questioned alone (Figure 7.1, right). This demonstrates that even the basis of physical reality can have a social foundation, and that social norms naturally emerge under conditions of uncertainty.

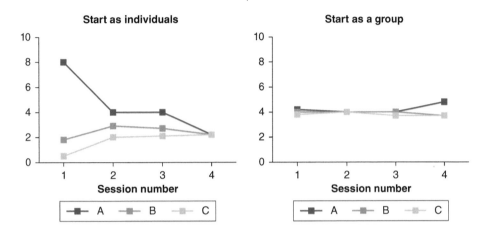

Figure 7.1   Results from Sherif (1935): Typical patterns of judgement for three participants (A, B, and C) who (left): start as individuals in Session 1, then come together as a group in Sessions 2–4, or (right): start as a group in Sessions 1–3, then make judgements as individuals in Session 4

Other researchers have replicated Sherif's results, relying on similar or inspired paradigms, mostly in the 1940s to 1970s (see Abrams & Levine, 2012). More recent studies have taken a slightly different approach. For example, Levine and colleagues (2000) studied the strategies that groups of three participants would develop to solve ambiguous, novel, lexical tasks. They observed that individual strategies quickly converge into a common group answer, in what the authors call the *development of a shared reality*. In other words, it does seem clear that people influence each other and develop new group-based frames of reference, and not just when it comes to dots moving in the dark.

7.4.5 Social Influence Under Certainty

Here is a question: In Figure 7.2, which line (A, B, or C) is the same length as the target line? What if I told you that all of your class peers said line A? Would you change your mind? What if you were asked to make these choices in a public class setting?

> **Video:**   Youtube – Asch's experiment presented by Philip Zimbardo https://www.youtube.com/watch?v=NyDDyT1IDhA

The correct answer is of course C. This is the paradigm that Solomon Asch (1955) used in his study on **social influence under certainty** (see Key study 7.2). In the

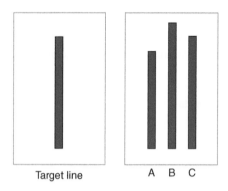

Target line   A   B   C

Figure 7.2 Material from Asch's study (1955)

study described above, Sherif showed that we use other people as frames of reference when we are uncertain. But what do we do when we are certain about the correct answer? What happens when our private opinion conflicts with the majority opinion? Do we conform?

KEY STUDY 7.2

Asch's Study of Line Length and Influence

In Asch's classic study (1955), participants were invited to take part in a study on 'visual perception', more specifically on the line length estimation. They were asked to sit around a table with six other people. While the participant thought that the six other people were fellow participants, they were not. They were in fact confederates (accomplices of the experimenter). The group of seven were first presented with a standard line, then with three comparison lines, labelled A, B, and C (see Figure 7.2). The task was for each person in turn to state which comparison line (A, B, or C) was the same length as the standard line. There were 18 trials in total, and participants always responded second to last.

For the first two trials, the confederates all chose the correct line. However, for 12 of the remaining 16 trials, the confederates unanimously chose the wrong line. What did participants do? Results showed that they conformed to the incorrect majority on 37% of the 'critical' trials. Moreover, 76% of participants conformed on at least one incorrect trial. Yet when participants made judgements alone, only 1% of participants made any errors, confirming that the task is unambiguous. So even when they are certain of the correct answer, participants will conform, at least some of the time, to the incorrect majority. They will amend their public attitudes, even though they are confident in the accuracy of their privately held attitudes.

Asch's findings have been replicated in a number of studies through the years, with some interesting additional results. For example, Berns and colleagues (2005) used fMRI to record participants' brain activity during the task. Not only did they replicate the original findings (41% of erroneous judgements), they also identified increased activity in the amygdala (showing accentuated emotions and anxiety) when the participant did *not* conform with the majority's erroneous response. This illustrates the cost of individual non-conformity.

In sum, Sherif's and Asch's studies illustrate two forms of influence arising under different conditions and for different reasons: the first identifies influence under uncertainty and the second identifies influence under certainty. Table 7.1 summarises the characteristics and findings of each study.

Table 7.1 Characteristics, mechanisms, and key findings of the seminal studies by Sherif (1935) and Asch (1955)

	Influence under uncertainty: Sherif (1935)	Influence under certainty: Asch (1955)
Task	Dot of light distance estimation	Line length estimation
Context	Uncertain/difficult/subjective	Certain/easy
Group members	Other participants	Confederates
Frame of reference	No physical or pre-established frame of reference	Physical frame of reference conflicts with majority
Key finding	Members naturally converged to common frame of reference when in a group	76% of participants conformed on at least one incorrect trial
Mechanism	Informational influence	Normative influence

In Sherif's light dot study, it makes sense to conform. Participants are uncertain, so they look to their peers for guidance – which should remind you of the mechanisms of *informational influence* described above. However, in Asch's line estimate study, participants are certain. There is no punishment for not conforming, no reward for conforming. Still, they do conform. Informational influence cannot explain conformism in such a task; other social aspects must be at stake here, leading participants to conformism through *normative influence*. A possibly relatable example of this for some of you might be when you are at a pub quiz, and your group is about to write down the wrong answer: you think you know the right answer but you don't speak up to correct the other group members. Maybe you go quiet, maybe you nod along. Why is it that, in these moments, many of us don't instantly correct our peers?

EXERCISE 7.2

Develop Your Critical Thinking

How can Asch's (1955) findings be applied to real-world issues? List at least three concrete, real-world examples (either societal, business-focused, or educational) where we might see evidence of such conformity.

Beyond Asch: Influence in Opinion and Moral Judgement Tasks

The line task in Asch's (1955) study was a trivial task. Yet other studies show that similar dynamics appear in more relevant, personally meaningful tasks. Kundu and Cummins (2013) tested whether people's *moral decision-making* is subject to the same conformity observed in Asch's line study. Morality, unlike visual perception tasks, forms an integral part of our identities and values. In addition, there is typically no correct or incorrect answer to opinion tasks or moral dilemmas: they are intrinsically more uncertain situations.

In the first condition ('private' condition), participants completed the study alone. In the second ('group' condition), they completed the study with three other ostensible participants (who were in fact confederates). Participants were asked to rate 12 moral dilemmas on a scale ranging from *highly impermissible* to *highly permissible* (see Table 7.2 for two examples). The moral dilemmas had been used in other published studies so the researchers knew which moral dilemmas most people find permissible and which they find impermissible. Similar to Asch's study, for the first dilemma, confederates provided 'typical' responses. However, for all remaining 11 dilemmas, confederates rated typically permissible dilemmas as impermissible and typically impermissible dilemmas as permissible. All confederates gave their answers before the participant.

The researchers found a strong conformity effect and broadly replicated Asch's findings. As you can see in Figure 7.3, participants' decisions in private completely reverse when they are faced with a majority who advocate the opposing moral viewpoint. In other words, moral judgements are also affected by the group – they are socially influenced.

Table 7.2 Typical moral dilemmas rated as highly permissible (top) and highly impermissible (bottom). Material sourced from Kundu and Cummins (2013)

Strong consensus – 'Permissible'	*Standard Trolley*: A runaway trolley is approaching a fork in the tracks. On the left track are five people. On the right track is one person. If you do nothing the trolley will go left, causing the deaths of five people. The only way to avoid this is to push a switch that will cause the trolley to go right, causing the death of the single person. Under the circumstances, is it morally permissible to push the switch?
Strong consensus – 'Not permissible'	*Sacrifice*: You, your spouse, and your four children are crossing a mountain range on your return journey to your homeland. You have inadvertently set up camp on a local clan's sacred burial ground. The leader of the clan says if you kill your oldest son with the clan leader's sword, he will let the rest of you live. l Under the circumstances, is it morally permissible to kill your oldest son?

In another study, Aramovich et al. (2012) examined whether people would conform to the majority opinion in the context of attitudes to torture. They were also interested in whether *moral convictions* buffer against social influence. The researchers measured attitudes

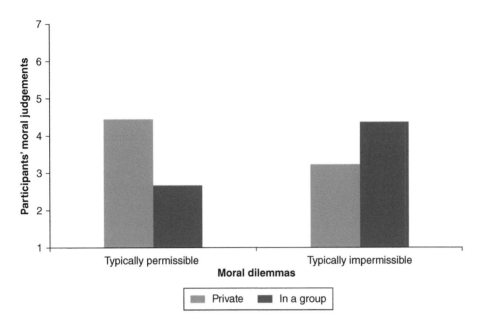

Figure 7.3 Results from Kundu and Cummins (2013): Participants' moral judgements in the moral dilemmas typically judged as permissible versus impermissible, depending on the condition (private versus group answers); 1 = highly impermissible, 7 = highly permissible

to torture and moral convictions at pre-test: this allowed them to see whether participants' attitudes changed following the experimental manipulation. Participants were university students, and all of them reported at pre-test that they were opposed to the use of torture. The experimental paradigm was also an adaptation of Asch's: each person in the group was asked to express their attitudes to torture, in turn. The participant was always the last to have their turn. The rest of the group, all confederates, consistently gave support for the use of torture.

The results revealed that conformity to the majority was common: 80% of participants reported less opposition to torture to their group than they reported privately at pre-test; 17% of participants reported the same degree of opposition; and 2% reported a greater level of opposition (counter-conformity). The data also showed that moral convictions buffer against social influence. Specifically, the strength of moral conviction about torture (measured at pre-test) negatively predicted the degree to which participants adjusted their attitudes.

In sum, the two studies by Kundu and Cummins (2013) and Aramovich et al. (2012) show that people do conform to the majority even in the context of moral judgements. However, strength of moral conviction can buffer against such social influence. This suggests that different people, different tasks, and different contexts can lead to various degrees of influence. We turn to these moderating factors in the next section.

7.4.6 When are we (Most) Influenced?

There are a number of factors that determine when we are most likely to be influenced. Some depend on the individual (i.e., some people are more open to influence than others) and some depend on the situation (i.e., contextual factors increase or decrease influence). In this section, we present some of the most important moderators of influence, starting with factors relevant for informational influence, then those relevant for normative influence, and finally those relevant for both.

Factors Affecting Informational Influence

You will remember that people are influenced by others when they are uncertain: adopting the shared point of view allows one to define what is correct and reduce uncertainty. In this view, it is not surprising that influence increases *when the task is more difficult* and more ambiguous. The increased uncertainty motivates people to turn to others and comply with their answers. For example, in an Asch-like paradigm, Klein (1972) had groups of four participants estimate which of two circles was the biggest. The circles were either visibly different in size (easy task) or very similar in size (difficult task). Participants were roughly five times more likely to adopt the answers from the group when the task was difficult than when it was easy.

Similar findings arise with tasks consisting of knowledge and logic questions (e.g., 'Avid means the same as or the opposite of: Eager, Vivid, Arid, Volatile?'). Participants conform more with the (erroneous) answer of the group for difficult questions (Coleman et al., 1958). Interestingly, there is no need for the group to be physically present. Participants filling an online quiz also adopted the response presented as the majority answer from 'others from [your community]' when questions were difficult (Rosander & Eriksson, 2012). If you are familiar with the popular TV show *Who Wants to Be a Millionaire*, this is the direct equivalent of the 'Ask the Audience' lifeline!

Relatedly, *self-confidence* decreases one's tendency to conform. People who are more self-confident experience less uncertainty when faced with an ambiguous task and feel a lesser need to rely on others' answers (Wijenayake et al., 2020). PS: the correct answer to the question above is Eager!

Factors Affecting Normative Influence

You will also remember that people accept others' influence as a way to fulfil their need of affiliation and social approbation. Such normative influence is stronger when the individual feels strongly attached or *identifies with the group*. For example, Terry et al. (1999) found that participants who said they identify more strongly with their group of friends modelled their own pro-environmental behaviour on that of their friends: if their friends engage in household recycling, they tend to do the same; if their friends do not, they do not either.

Conversely, normative influence decreases when the topic is personally relevant. People are happy to follow the group's views when they are not really invested in the topic since this provides them with easy opportunities to display their conformity. On the other hand, *personal involvement* acts as a shield to influence, motivating individuals to go against the group's judgement if they personally think differently. For example, and to remain in the realm of environmental behaviour, participants who consider energy conservation as a personally relevant topic display greater conservation behaviour regardless of the behaviour of their peers (i.e., even when their peers do not care about conservation) (Göckeritz et al., 2010).

Personality traits also play a role. Individuals high in *agreeableness* (warm, friendly, and helpful) try to avoid upsetting others, and as such avoid deviating from norms and easily comply with social expectations. In addition, individuals high in *conscientiousness* (methodical and persevering, with a high sense of duty and self-discipline) appreciate a clear group organisation and line of conduct, and as such easily conform to the group's demands. Bègue et al. (2015) found that participants were more likely to obey the experimenter's orders in a Milgram-like paradigm (see the section 'Obedience to Authority: The Psychology of Tyranny' below) when they were high in agreeableness and/or conscientiousness.

Finally, characteristics of the social interaction itself matter: expressing one's views *anonymously versus publicly* determines one's level of conformity with the group. This, however, is only true when the person is not really convinced by the group's position and is merely expressing a consensual view to avoid retaliation and exclusion from the group (remember Kelman's distinction between compliance, identification, and internalisation).

Factors Affecting both Informational and Normative Influence

A first factor that is important for influence in general (both informational and normative) is *group size*. If an individual is motivated to reduce uncertainty, then the views of a larger group are clearly more relevant: people interpret the larger consensus as an indication that the opinion must be correct. In addition, standing in disagreement with two or three others does not put the same pressure on the individual as disagreeing with 10 or 20. In the second case, the individual faces a much more obvious and visible situation of deviance, making them more likely to comply with the group's views.

Surprisingly, however, the effect of group size levels off pretty quickly. Research using the Asch paradigm finds a clear increase in conformity rates when the group size increases from one to two and three confederates, but then levels off when size increases further to four, eight, or sixteen confederates (Asch, 1955; see Figure 7.4). The perception of others as 'a group' seems to reach a psychological threshold when they reach the number of three, and growing above this number matters much less (Latané, 1981). This is an important lesson if you need to convince a parent, professor, boss, etc., to change their mind on something: you only have to find two other people to join you to be perceived as a coherent group and, maybe, exert some influence!

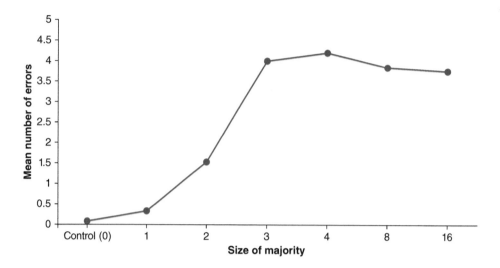

Figure 7.4 Results from Asch (1955): Mean number of erroneous answers participants give, depending on group size (from 0 to 16 confederates giving erroneous answers)

A second important factor that determines influence is the level of group *unanimity*. You will recall that in most of the studies presented so far, confederates gave unanimous (and erroneous) answers. What happens when their answers are not unanimous? Studies show that conformity drops considerably. In Asch's study (1956), participants had given the same erroneous response as the unanimous confederates 37% of the time. This figure dropped to 5% when one confederate broke the consensus and answered differently.

Interestingly, in objective, non-ambiguous tasks such as those in Asch's study, what matters most is that the consensus is broken. Conformity decreases when one confederate rallies to the participant's view and indicates the correct answer, but also when one confederate gives *another* erroneous answer that is different from that of the majority. *Breaking the consensus* restores the individual's impression that divergent answers are possible (the majority may actually be wrong, so following them will not serve informational needs anymore) and may be expressed.

It is a different story when it comes to opinion tasks. In cases where the group and the individual express their views on social subjects where there is no objectively correct answer but where opinions may define one's group membership, then conformity only decreases if a confederate rallies the participant's opinion, providing *social support*. Allen and Levine (1968) showed that participants refrained from endorsing the group's opinion and expressed their own divergent view only when a confederate expressed the same view as theirs, but not when the confederate diverged from the group in the opposite direction (i.e., holding more extreme views than the group, even further away from the participant).

Finally, let's mention the role of *culture*. People from more *interdependent* cultures consider other people's actions and opinions as more informative and rely on them more than people from more *independent* cultures. In a meta-analysis of 133 studies using the Asch paradigm across 17 countries, Bond and Smith (1996) found that conformity was greater in interdependent countries. They also identified regional differences linked to different interdependent norms within the same country, for example between different US States. Differences in normative influence arise at a more general level as well: people from more 'tight' cultures (which have stronger norms regarding how people should behave and have a lower tolerance for deviance, e.g., Pakistan, India, Malaysia) conform with norms to a greater extent, out of normative concerns and willingness to please the group. People from more 'loose' cultures (which have less strict norms and more tolerance for deviance, e.g., the Netherlands, New Zealand, Estonia), in contrast, conform less (Gelfand et al., 2011). Changes in the socio-political context affecting norms also lead to change in conformity through time. Bond and Smith (1996) found that compliance had declined in the US between the 1950s and late 1990s, which they related to a loosening of previously 'tight' norms and a greater tolerance of deviance.

7.4.7 Minority Influence

We have focused so far on processes of influence arising from the group or from those possessing various forms of power, in efforts to maintain the status quo. In other words, we have mostly talked about **majority influence**. Yet norms are not absolute or fixed in time. In the not-so-distant past in Western culture, gay marriage was impossible, women were not allowed to vote, and slightly before that chattel slavery was common – and that seemed normal for most people at the time. Over short periods of time, though, norms evolved. How did this happen? As Moscovici (1976) argued, many social movements around the globe started with a minority group who, although lacking power and other psychological resources, were firmly convinced that their actions and claims would eventually promote social change and innovation, and who succeeded. **Minority influence** is the term that describes this process (Butera et al., 2017).

> **Key concept – Majority influence:**
> Social pressure exerted by the greater part of a group on individual members and smaller factions within the group. Members usually respond to this pressure either by accepting the majority's position as their own (conversion) or by conforming publicly but retaining their own position privately (compliance).

> **Key concept – Minority influence:**
> Social pressure exerted on the majority of a group by a smaller faction of the group. Minorities who argue consistently prompt the group to reconsider even long-held or previously unquestioned assumptions and procedures.

Conversion Theory

Every time we are confronted by a person or a group whose opinion differs from our own, two main preoccupations emerge (remember the normative and informational processes of influence we described above): understanding *who* we disagree with, and *why* the disagreement has occurred. The first corresponds to a social preoccupation and speaks to the normative processes of influence: we should be more concerned to be disagreeing with (the majority of) a group that is important to us, since falling out with them could mean our exclusion from the group. On the other hand, there is no reason to worry much about disagreeing with a social minority that has no power over us. The second preoccupation is more epistemic and speaks to the informational processes of influence: Why does the source think differently, do they make good arguments – and might we be wrong? With conversion theory, Moscovici (1980) argued that while majorities keep people focused on the social preoccupation, minorities mostly trigger the epistemic preoccupation. In other words, minorities disturb the consensus and introduce a social conflict by proposing new alternative propositions. To solve the social conflict, people pay more careful attention to the propositions of the minority, resulting in a level of scrutiny and systematic thought that can produce genuine change in attitudes and opinions.

KEY THINKER

Serge Moscovici

Serge Moscovici (1925–2014) was a Romanian-born French social psychologist. He grew up in Romania where he initially trained as a mechanic. During World War II he was interned in a forced-labour camp, where he worked for a few years until the Soviet Red Army freed the camps in 1944. Moscovici then started to travel extensively, and taught himself French and philosophy. He was Jewish and suffered from antisemitic discrimination during his life in Romania. As the Cold War started, he helped Zionist dissidents cross the border illegally, for which he was involved in a trial and decided to leave Romania. He emigrated clandestinely to France in 1948. In Paris, he studied psychology at the Sorbonne and received a PhD in psychology in 1961. In the 1960s, he worked at Stanford University and at Yale in the US before returning to Paris. In his later life he became involved in politics and was one of the founders of the Green Party movement in France. Moscovici remains most known for two lines of research: the first on social representations (social representations theory) and the second on minority influence (conversion theory).

Moscovici's 'Blue-Green Paradigm'

The first studies to illustrate minority influence relied on the 'blue-green paradigm', a perceptual task where answers should be unambiguous (illustrating influence under certainty). The task was simple: groups of participants were shown blue slides that varied in luminosity and asked to say (out loud) the colour of the slide (Moscovici et al., 1969). Each group of six people was in fact composed of four genuine participants and two confederates who would play the role of the disagreeing minority.

In the first condition, both confederates systematically said that all slides were green (consistent condition). In a second condition (inconsistent condition), they answered 'green' for two-thirds of the trials and 'blue' for one-third (for each trial, however, the two confederates would give a similar answer). There was also a control condition where six genuine participants responded privately.

Two measures were taken. First, participants' (public and immediate) response to each slide served as a direct measure of influence. Compared to 0.25% of 'green' answers in the control condition (proving that the task was unambiguous) and 1.25% in the inconsistent minority condition, the consistent minority condition induced 8.42% of 'green' answers, revealing a weak but significant direct influence (in fact, it is quite remarkable that two individuals repeating clearly erroneous responses can have any influence on the remaining four!). The second measure, taken privately in a second step of the experiment, relied on a colour discrimination test: participants were presented with 16 coloured dots gradually changing from blue to green, and asked where they would put the threshold between 'blue' and 'green'. This measure was meant as an indirect measure of influence: if participants were truly influenced, their subjective perception of colour might have been impacted. Indeed, results showed that participants exposed to the consistent minority changed their threshold and perceived green earlier in the gradient than participants in the control group and those in the inconsistent minority condition.

To summarise, Moscovici showed that minorities could only obtain very modest direct influence, or none at all, but were able to obtain indirect influence, a different form of change suggesting a more profound integration of the minority's responses – what he called the conversion process. Other studies testing the influence of a majority of confederates (four confederates for two genuine participants) found the opposite pattern: when facing a majority, participants changed their immediate public responses and said 'green' more often (around 40%, which should remind you of Asch's results) but their colour perception in the second task was unaffected. The majority only obtained manifest influence or compliance, while the minority mostly obtained latent influence.

Minority Influence in Opinion Tasks

Minority influence is not limited to unambiguous stimuli. Other studies have found similar results for beliefs or opinions (i.e., influence under uncertainty). For example, Maass and Clark (1983) explored minority versus majority influence on people's opinions about gay rights. They gave participants a short text summarising an alleged group discussion between five students from their own university on gay rights. In the minority influence condition, one person presented arguments in favour of gay rights while the four others argued against it. In the majority influence condition, it was the opposite. Each side presented the same number of arguments (eight). Having read the summary, participants reported their own attitudes towards gay rights (note the year of the study: in the 1980s attitudes were much less tolerant than today, even among university students). Half of them had to report their attitudes publicly (their answers would be shared with a group of peers in anticipation of a group discussion session). The other half reported their attitudes privately (anonymous and confidential answers). In a control condition, participants did not read any text but simply reported their attitudes (publicly versus privately).

Results show that public attitudes follow closely the majority's position. When the majority was pro-gay, participants expressed more pro-gay attitudes; when it was anti-gay, participants expressed more anti-gay attitudes. Private attitudes, however, were influenced by the minority, and participants changed in the direction defended by the minority (see Figure 7.5). In sum, these results suggest that people integrate the minority's arguments better (probably because they are not preoccupied by the social consequences of disagreement and focus on the arguments themselves) but are wary of expressing this opinion publicly. Conversely, they merely reproduce the majority's position publicly with no integration of the arguments and thus no 'real' attitude change.

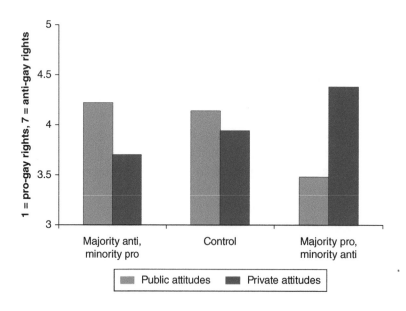

Figure 7.5 Results from Maass and Clark (1983): Participants' attitudes towards gay rights reported privately versus publicly, depending on the majority versus minority influence condition

Another study shows that attitude change obtained from minority influence is *sustained over the long term*. Tafani et al. (2003) had groups of participants discuss the issue of drug consumption, while a majority versus minority of confederates in the group introduced a divergent opinion. Again, two measures were taken: participants' immediate and public agreement with the majority (or minority) position, and their self-reported attitudes towards drug consumption, reported privately in a second step. On the first measure, the majority obtained significantly more (manifest) influence than the minority. On the second measure, however, the minority obtained significantly more (latent) influence than the majority.

When the Minority Becomes a Majority

Given that minorities actually have the potential to produce deep and long-term attitude change in those around them, an implication is that minority opinions can, over time, become majority opinions (as we highlighted at the beginning of this section). An intriguing question then arises: how does this success change the dynamics and relationships with the *minority-turned-majority group*? Research suggests that the transition is not easy to achieve. Original members of the group tend to disengage from the now-majority group, because they find it more dissimilar to the self and therefore less attractive (Prislin et al., 2000). They also express distancing and distrust of new members or 'converts' (Prislin & Christensen, 2002). Only after a long period of time will original members reinvest in the group, at which point they will need to learn to adapt their influence strategies, given the newly gained majority status of the group.

GUEST PERSONAL JOURNEY

Radmila Prislin

Ever since it helped to establish social psychology as an empirical science, scholarship on social influence has reflected the times of its development. Mine fits the picture. Having lived in a very dynamic world, I could not but take a dynamic view of social influence. I was born in Croatia, which then was part of Yugoslavia, where I received foundational education, including a college degree. This experience gifted me with a lasting bonus of inspired curiosity. It has been a driving force behind my life-long journey of turning challenges into opportunities. The journey took me to the University of Chicago on a Fulbright

Source: © Radmila Prislin

scholarship, back to the University of Zagreb, then to Texas A&M University, where I found myself when a war broke out in my country of origin. I remained in the United States, where I am now professor at San Diego State University.

(Continued)

Risking to romanticise challenges, which is not my intention, I will say that they may provide uniquely valuable growth opportunities. Professionally, they have informed my thinking about social influence in general, and minority influence in particular. When the goal of influence is social change, as it is for active minorities, it destabilises a group. To capitalise on the potential positives of social change, including change effected via minority influence, groups are well advised to recognise the accompanying destabilising forces and guard against them.

Interpersonally, my life journey has brought me into contact with some remarkable individuals whose extraordinary qualities never cease to inspire me. They come from such different walks of life that any attempt to fit them in the Procrustean bed of the common social categories would fail. From them I have learned that success, professional or otherwise, is bringing out the best in others by giving your best.

Summary

Social minorities can influence others even if they lack the power usually thought necessary for influence (Deutsch & Gerard, 1955). As a meta-analysis by Wood et al. (1994) concluded, this influence is latent rather than manifest: people avoid publicly associating themselves with minorities, but pay more attention to minority arguments and more often change their attitudes as a result.

Conversion theory implies that majority influence is always limited to mere compliance. The truth, however, is less extreme: majorities will typically elicit more compliance, but they can nonetheless also exert deeper influence and result in true, private attitude change. We come back to this in Part 2 with the presentation of the Source-Context-Elaboration Model (Martin & Hewstone, 2008).

7.4.8 Obedience to Authority: The Psychology of Tyranny

> **Key concept – Obedience:**
> Behaviour in compliance with a direct command, often one issued by a person in a position of authority.

So far, we have mostly focused on conformity. In this section, we discuss obedience. **Obedience** occurs when people follow an explicit order – typically from authoritative figures.

Milgram's Electric Shock Study

The most famous study of obedience is Milgram's electric shock study, conducted in 1961. Milgram wanted to understand the crimes of the Nazis and of those who obeyed them. He wondered whether their psychology was any different from that of the average person.

Against this possibility, Milgram hypothesised that under certain conditions people will comply with an immoral order and do things they did not think they would ever be capable of doing (Milgram, 1963).

KEY THINKER

Stanley Milgram

Stanley Milgram (1933–1984) was an American social psychologist. He was born to Jewish parents who had emigrated to the United States from Western Europe during World War I. Some of his relatives were sent to Nazi concentration camps during the Holocaust, and some survived and stayed with Milgram's family in New York for a time. This profoundly affected Milgram and initially motivated his obedience-to-authority research. He wanted to understand how German soldiers could have obeyed dramatic orders during the Nazi regime and committed atrocities. Milgram received a PhD in social psychology from Harvard in 1961. He worked as an assistant professor at Yale, then at Harvard, then finally at the City University of New York Graduate Centre, where he taught until his death in 1984. Milgram remains most famous for his obedience-to-authority studies.

Milgram invited male participants into his lab at Yale University. Participants were told that the goal of the study was to understand whether electric shocks would improve a learner's performance, and the experimenter emphasised the scientific importance of the study to the participants. The real goal of the study was of course something else entirely. Milgram wanted to see whether participants would be willing to follow the experimenter's instructions and deliver what appeared to be lethal shocks to a stranger.

Participants were ordered to administer increasingly more severe punishment to the learner. Punishment was administered using a shock generator which had 30 graded

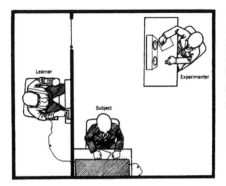 

Figure 7.6 Milgram's experiment: Room setting (left) and picture of the shock generator (right)

Source: Wikimedia Commons, reproduced under CC.03 License, https://commons.wikimedia.org/wiki/File:Milgram_Experiment.png

switches. The first switch, at 15 volts, was described as 'slight shock'; the penultimate level, at 375 volts, was described as 'danger: severe shock'; and the last level, at 450 volts, was described as an ominous 'XXX'. The learner was of course a confederate with scripted lines, which became more desperate as the experiment went on. At the start, the learner would say things like 'Ugh! Hey this really hurts'. At around 330 volts, the learner would demand to be let out, and from 345 volts onwards, the learner fell silent (see Figure 7.6 and Table 7.3).

The dependent variable was the maximum shock that the participants were willing to administer before they refused to continue. When participants showed reluctance, the experimenter would provide scripted prompts such as 'Please continue' and 'The experiment requires that you continue'. There were four pre-scripted prompts and the experiment would only end early if the participant refused to continue after the fourth prompt. Otherwise, it would continue until the maximum shock was administered.

Table 7.3 Paradigm from Milgram's study (1963): List of the switches and associated volts and labels displayed on the shock generator; scripted responses the confederate would give when the participant administered the corresponding shock

Switch	Volts	Labels	Scripted responses from the confederate
1	15	Slight shock	
2	30		
3	45		
4	60		
5	75	Moderate shock	Ugh!
6	90		Ugh!
7	105		Ugh! *(louder)*
8	120		Ugh! Hey, *this* really hurts.
9	135	Strong shock	Ugh!!
10	150		Ugh!!! Experimenter! That's all. Get me out of here, please. My heart's starting to bother me. I refuse to go on. Let me out.
11	165		Ugh! Let me out! *(shouting)*
12	180		Ugh! I can't stand the pain. Let me out of there! *(shouting)*
13	195	Very strong shock	Ugh! Let me out of here. Let me out of here. My heart's bothering me. Let me out of here! You have no right to keep me here! Let me out! Let me out of here! Let me out! Let me out of here! My heart's bothering me. Let me out! Let me out!
14	210		Ugh!! Experiment! Get me out of here. I've had enough. I *won't* be in the experiment any more.

Switch	Volts	Labels	Scripted responses from the confederate
15	225		Ugh!
16	240		Ugh!
17	255	Intense shock	Ugh! Get me *out* of here
18	270		*(Agonised scream)* Let me out of here. Let me out of here. Let me out of here. Let me out. Do you hear me? Let me out of here.
19	285		*(Agonised scream)*
20	300		*(Agonised scream)* I absolutely refuse to answer any more. Get me out of here. You can't hold me here. Get me out. Get me out of here.
21	315	Extreme intensity shock	*(Intensely agonised scream)* I *told you I refuse to answer*. I'm no longer part of this experiment.
22	330		*(Intense and prolonged scream)* Let me out of here. Let me out of here. My heart's bothering me. Let me out, I tell you. *(Hysterically)* Let me out of here. Let me out of here. You have no right to hold me here. Let me out! Let me out! Let me out! Let me out of here! Let me out! Let me out!
23	345		[Silence]
24	360		[Silence]
25	375	Danger severe shock	[Silence]
26	390		[Silence]
27	405		[Silence]
28	420		[Silence]
29	435		[Silence]
30	450	XXX	[Silence]

Note: Experiment prompts were as follows: (1) Please continue (or) Please go on; (2) The experiment requires that you continue; (3) It is absolutely essential that you continue; (4) You have no other choice, you must go on. Reproduced from Reicher et al. (2012).

Results are striking: over half of the participants (65%) went all the way to the maximum of 450 volts. Milgram did note that 'although obedient subjects continued to administer shocks, they often did so under extreme stress. Some expressed reluctance to administer shocks beyond the 300-volt level, and displayed fears similar to those who defied the experimenter; yet they obeyed' (Milgram, 1963, p. 376). Many variants of the original experiment were subsequently conducted, to further understand the boundary conditions of compliance. For example, bringing the victim closer reduced compliance, and so did the presence of a peer who rebelled or of a second experimenter who gave contradictory orders. The original experiment included only male participants, but a follow-up experiment found that female participants were just as likely to obey (Milgram, 1974).

Milgram's study had significant ethical implications. The experimental procedure put participants under extreme stress. Participants truly believed that they were administering real electric shocks. Moreover, as the researcher pressured participants to continue, it was not clear to participants that they were in fact allowed to leave. Finally, as participants were not told about the true purpose of the study, they could not provide fully informed consent. Studies like this would not be approved by ethics committees today. We psychologists now have a stringent code of ethics to follow with clear guidelines for research. For example, researchers must now explicitly inform participants that they can withdraw from a study at any time.

Implications

A crucial part of this study is the explanation of the results, and its implications. What does this mean for how we understand human behaviour, how we understand people's readiness to engage in tyranny? Milgram concluded that humans have a basic motivation to obey and conform, and inflicting harm on innocent people can occur as a consequence. He listed 13 features that he believed led to obedience in his study, including, for example, prestige of the scientist, the prestige and worth of the research, and the competing demands of two persons: the experimenter and the victim. Satisfaction for one comes at the exclusion of the other. Over time, Milgram focused increasingly on a quite specific explanation to do with the 'agentic self'. Milgram argued that, in the face of authority, people forget their own goals, and cede responsibility to those in authority. They become focused on completing their task well, rather than on what the task is (Milgram, 1974).

In recent years, fellow social psychologists have unpacked Milgram's research and have raised concerns around three key areas: (1) the integrity of Milgram's reports, (2) the validity of the explanation he offered, and (3) the broader relevance of his studies (see Haslam & Reicher, 2017). This more recent and comprehensive analysis of obedience research will be introduced in Part 2.

7.5 PART 2: ADVANCES

7.5.1 Obedience to Authority? Or Identification-based Followership?

Milgram's work on obedience is among the most famous in social psychology. His research led to a general belief that obedience occurs due to people's tendency to cede responsibility to those in authority, and therefore obey them. When applying this to the real world, it suggests that brutality occurs due to **passive conformity** to roles. However, there is now a significant body of work that contests these explanations and provides compelling evidence for an alternative explanation. Haslam and Reicher (2017) notably argue that engagement in brutality and tyranny is not passive. Instead, people who engage in brutality do so because they actively identify with their leader's cause and believe their actions to be virtuous. They state:

> Milgram's studies are not really about obedience to authority at all, but are better construed as studies of group-based leadership and followership in which parties are energised to do wrong not because they are ignorant, thoughtless, or blind, but because they believe what they are doing to be virtuous and even noble. (Haslam & Reicher, 2017, p. 61)

In this section we describe the more recent advances in the psychology of tyranny, and the important developments that have been made since Milgram's original research. In their 2017 review paper, Haslam and Reicher identified three key areas of concern related to Milgram's research, which we discuss here in turn.

The Integrity of Milgram's Reports

Gina Perry (2013) interviewed participants who had taken part in Milgram's research and examined post-experimental comments and audio recordings from the archives. These examinations revealed that many participants were actually suspicious about the authenticity of the shocks.

Russell and colleagues conducted archival analyses of Milgram's studies which revealed unreported ways in which Milgram carefully altered the study design in order to reduce opportunities for resistance on the part of the participants (Russell, 2014; Russell & Gregory, 2011). For example, Milgram deliberately designed the shock machine to make it a more imposing piece of scientific machinery, increased the number of switches from 12 to 30 so that the increments were smaller and therefore each step up felt less oppositional, and changed the labelling of the final point from 'lethal' to 'XXX', which made its meaning more ambiguous and less extreme – but he did not clearly document these choices.

The Validity of the Explanation He Offered

However, it is important to note that even if the perceived representation of Milgram's research was imperfect (integrity), this does not necessarily mean that the effects observed were not real (validity). Many studies have conceptually replicated the original Milgram study, and show that, under certain conditions, ordinary people are willing to engage in acts they would otherwise think unethical (e.g., Haslam et al., 2015). In terms of validity, the key issue concerns Milgram's explanation for the effects he observed. Did his results really demonstrate blind and passive obedience in the face of authority?

One way in which this question has been unpacked more recently is by taking a closer look at how the participants responded to the experimenter's prompts. The prompts were designed to encourage participants to continue, and they varied in content. They start with a polite request ('Please continue', Prompt 1), and then they become more forceful ('The experiment requires that you continue', Prompt 2; 'It is absolutely essential that you continue, Prompt 3), and then they turn into a direct order ('You have no choice, you must continue', Prompt 4). Interestingly, both in Milgram's own studies and in Burger's replication (Burger et al., 2011), Prompt 4 actually led to non-compliance, although the prompts were confounded with how far along participants were in the study, and Prompt 4 was the last Prompt that was given.

In an effort to understand the impact of giving a direct order (Prompt 4) on compliance, Haslam et al. (2014) manipulated prompts in a between-participant design. This means that some participants were only exposed to Prompt 1, others only to Prompt 2, etc. The study was an analogue paradigm of Milgram's study in which participants were instructed to use negative adjectives to describe increasingly pleasant groups. The results showed that participants who were given Prompt 4 broke off earlier than those given any of the other three prompts. Moreover, participants continued the longest when given Prompt 2, which appealed to the scientific objectives of the study. This research suggests that giving a direct order may actually be an ineffective way to induce compliance. However, participants are most likely to comply when they are invited to cooperate in a joint (in this case, scientific) enterprise. These findings go against the idea of blind obedience.

The Broader Relevance of Milgram's Studies to the Important Social Issues He Wanted his Research to Address

As we mentioned earlier, Milgram wanted to understand the crimes of the Nazis and of those who obeyed them. However, many researchers have since argued that pressure to obey was not key in understanding compliance during the Holocaust (Burger, 2014; Fenigstein, 2015; Haslam & Reicher, 2012). In other words, in the same vein as it is problematic to conclude blind obedience from Milgram's studies, so too it is problematic to understand tyranny in the world at large through this lens of blind obedience. Recent evidence points increasingly to this idea that compliance occurs as a consequence of *identification* with a leader's goals and a desire to play an active role in helping leaders to attain those goals (Haslam & Reicher, 2012).

When people define themselves by a given social identity (see Chapters 2, 8, and 10), they attach value and meaning to that group. As social identities form part of people's overall self and self-image, the group becomes a source of self-esteem (Tajfel & Turner, 1979). Importantly, social identity is a basis for social influence (Turner, 1991). When people define themselves as a group member, they try to understand what the group norms are, and how to act in line with those group norms and expectations. Important sources of such crucial social information include fellow ingroup members, but also ingroup leaders (Hogg, 2001). Research shows that leaders are more influential when they are representative or prototypical of the shared social identity (Haslam & Platow, 2001).

Haslam and Reicher (2012) argue that Milgram's findings should be interpreted using a social identity perspective. They propose that the compliance observed in Milgram's experiment was driven primarily by participants' identification with Milgram's scientific mission and from their sense that the experimenter represented this mission. The post-hoc analyses of Milgram's work (as discussed in the integrity section above) revealed that Milgram cultivated this shared social identity with the scientific mission, including by designing the shock generator as an imposing piece of scientific machinery and the way in which the study was introduced to participants. Additional empirical evidence for this idea comes from the research showing that the prompt that appealed to the experiment's scientific objectives was most effective, as we discussed above. It is also noteworthy that the social identity analysis is in line with Milgram's own early and private interpretation of the findings:

> [T]he subjects have come to the laboratory to form a relationship with the experimenter, a specifically submissive relationship in the interest of advancing science. They have not come to form a relationship with the subject, and it is this lack of relationship in the one direction and the real relationship in the other that produces the results. [...] Only a genuine relationship between the Victim and the Subject, based on identification [...] could reverse the results. (Cited in Haslam & Reicher, 2012, p. 69)

Reicher and colleagues (2012) gave participants (who were either expert social psychologists in Study 1, or naïve students in Study 2) Milgram's own descriptions of different versions of his experimental paradigm. Participants were asked the extent to which each different paradigm would lead them to (a) identify with the experimenter as a scientist and with the perspective of the scientific community that he represents, and (b) identify with the learner as a member of the general public and with the perspective of the general community that he represents. The researchers then examined whether social identity correlated with the level of obedience (or followership) observed within each of the experimental paradigms. The results showed that there was a strong and positive correlation between estimated identification with the experimenter and the level of followership observed. Moreover, there was a strong and negative correlation between estimated identification with the learner and followership. This provides empirical support for the idea that Milgram's studies are not necessarily evidence of obedience, but instead of social identity-based leadership, which induced active and committed followership.

Summary

In this section we have described the research led by Reicher and Haslam who, with colleagues, have systematically examined Milgram's work. They found considerable evidence to support the idea that brutality and tyranny is not passive. Instead, they show that people who engage in brutality do so because they actively identify with their leader's cause and believe their actions to be virtuous. This newer body of research described here continues to grow today. For example, researchers have begun to use virtual reality paradigms to further understand identification-based followership (Gonzalez-Franco et al., 2018). Moreover, researchers have also started to test the conditions under which identification-based followership is more or less likely to occur (e.g., Birney et al., 2023).

GUEST PERSONAL JOURNEY

Alexander Haslam

Source: © Alexander Haslam

I am Professor of Social and Organisational Psychology and Australian Laureate Fellow at the University of Queensland. My interest in psychology developed as an undergraduate at the University of St Andrews, where I studied between 1981 and 1985, having originally gone to Scotland to study a joint degree in English and Maths. I was introduced to social psychology by my honour's supervisor, Margaret Wetherell. After graduating and spending a year as a golf scholar at Emory University in Atlanta, it was at her suggestion that I applied for a Commonwealth Scholarship to work on a PhD with John Turner at Macquarie University in Sydney.

I completed my PhD on self-categorisation processes in stereotyping in 1991 and, after working unproductively at the University of Sydney for a year, I moved to work with John and colleagues at the Australian National University in Canberra. There, I wrote up my PhD research for my first book, *Stereotyping and Social Reality*. In Canberra I also started working on other projects related to research methods and organisational psychology, primarily because I had to teach introductory courses on these topics. However, I was struck by how user-unfriendly most of the texts in these fields were, and so decided to have a go at writing some myself.

In 2001, I moved back to the UK to take up a chair at the University of Exeter, where I stayed for 11 years. My collaborations there took me in a range of new and unexpected directions. I worked with Jolanda Jetten and Catherine Haslam on health-related topics. I worked with Michelle Ryan on research into the glass cliff and with Tom Postmes on studies of group dynamics. I worked with Steve Reicher on the BBC Prison Study and with Steve and Michael Platow on *The New Psychology of Leadership* (2011).

In 2012, I moved back to Australia to take up an Australian Laureate Fellowship at the University of Queensland. Here I worked with Steve Reicher and Kathryn Millard to apply the lessons of the BBC Prison Study to the study of obedience, work that culminated in the award-winning documentary *Shock Room*. At the same time, I worked on *The New Psychology of Health* with Cath Haslam, Jolanda Jetten, Tegan Cruwys, and Genevieve Dingle (2018). I also worked with Nik Steffens and Kim Peters on award-winning research into leadership development, and with Katrien Fransen and Filip Boen on *The New Psychology of Sport* (2020).

Over the course of my career I have received a range of awards from scientific bodies in Australia, the US, the UK, and Europe for this work, including prizes for social, political, organisational, and health psychology. In 2022, I was appointed a Member of the Order of Australia 'for significant service to higher education, particularly psychology, through research and mentoring.'

In another life I would have been a carpenter, a poet, or a very mediocre golfer. It seems unlikely, though, that these would have provided as much opportunity for collaboration and fun as a career in psychology. So, these are paths I am glad not to have taken.

> **Video:** Youtube – The psychology of tyranny – did Milgram get it wrong? TED talk by Alex Haslam **www.you tube.com/watch?v=HxXMKg8-7o0**

7.5.2 Majority and Minority Influence: The Source-Context-Elaboration Model

In our earlier description of minority influence, we described how, according to Moscovici's conversion theory, minorities obtain indirect but not direct influence, while the reverse is true of majorities. This, however, might be an oversimplification; after all, there are many rules and behaviours that we learn, accept, and adopt from a majority consensus. For example, we learn from others what type of food is appropriate to have at different moments of the day, and this is strongly determined by regional cultural norms (never try to order a cappuccino after 11 am in Italy!). Less trivially, most of us agree with and support the Universal Declaration of Human Rights, not just on paper, but truly.

Relatedly, mathematical models show that a source composed of a greater number of people exerts a stronger influence on a given target (Latané & Wolf, 1981). The objective consensus approach also posits that people apply a simple heuristic that the greater the number of people who find any idea correct (i.e., the greater the consensus), the more that idea will be considered correct (Cialdini, 1984). So, what influence do majorities really have? This is the question we aim to answer in this section.

Assumptions of the Source-Context-Elaboration Model

Martin and Hewstone (2008) developed the Source-Context-Elaboration Model (SCEM) to resolve this issue. The SCEM relies on the Elaboration Likelihood Model (ELM) of information processing (Petty & Cacioppo, 1986; see also Chapter 6 on attitudes and persuasion), which outlines two parallel cognitive routes to process information. First, the peripheral route is a 'lazy' processing that relies on external cues and heuristics and results in superficial influence only. Second, the central route is a more intense processing that implies paying attention to the core of the message. The central route results in deep influence (to the extent that the message proposes convincing arguments), but it is only activated if the person is both able and motivated to process the message.

During the 1980s, 1990s, and 2000s, several researchers proposed that minorities, or majorities, or both, could make it more likely for the central route to be activated. Martin and Hewstone reviewed years of such past findings in an effort to integrate them in a coherent whole. They proposed to organise these findings on the basis of the topic under investigation: either *against* the participants' self-interest, in *favour* of it, or *neutral*. In a nutshell, they argue that both majorities and minorities can trigger the central route for processing the influence message but this will depend on the personal relevance of the topic (Martin et al., 2007). In other words, the Source (majority versus minority) and the Context (personal relevance) together determine Elaboration Likelihood (that the central route is activated) – as summarised in the model's name (see Table 7.4). Martin and Hewstone (2008) hypothesised different effects of majority and minority sources at three levels of the elaboration continuum (determined, among other things, by personal relevance): low, intermediate, and high.

- At a *low* level of motivation (e.g., topic of low personal relevance), neither a majority nor a minority source would be able to trigger elaborative processing. Motivation to invest cognitive efforts in processing the message is just too low, so the peripheral route will be used. The source may serve as an external cue, resulting in superficial compliance when the source is a majority (as compared to a minority).
- At a *high* level of motivation (e.g., topic of high personal relevance), elaborative processing would occur regardless of the source status. The topic is relevant enough to ensure high motivation to process the message, so the central route will be used. This can result in latent influence for both minority and majority sources, assuming the arguments presented in the message are strong and convincing.
- The *intermediate* level of motivation is the level where the source status would be decisive. Here, a majority source would typically orient its targets towards low-effort processing, the easy option being to comply with the majority position without going to the trouble of considering its arguments in detail (peripheral route). This would lead to mere compliance with no real integration of the majority's arguments. In contrast, a minority source, because of the conflict it triggers, would orient towards effortful processing (central route), allowing for latent influence. In other words, conversion theory would apply specifically at this intermediate level of personal relevance and hence of intermediate motivation to process the message.

Table 7.4 Key comparisons concerning the Source-Context-Elaboration Model. Table reproduced from Martin and Hewstone (2008)

	Elaboration situation					
	Low		Intermediate		High	
	Source status					
	Majority	Minority	Majority	Minority	Majority	Minority
Process	Peripheral / heuristic	Peripheral	Peripheral / heuristic	Central	Central (sometimes plus heuristic)	Central
Message processing	= (none/low)		<		= (high)	
Focus of attention	Characteristics of majority	None	Characteristics of majority	Content of arguments	Content of arguments/ characteristics of majority	Content of arguments
Direct/public attitude change	High	Low	High	Low	High	High
Indirect/private attitude change	Low	Low	Low	High	High	High

Empirical Findings

Martin, Hewstone, and their colleagues conducted a series of studies to directly compare the impact of majority and minority sources at different levels of personal relevance. These studies typically compare messages presenting strong versus weak arguments, on the premise that the central route would result in greater influence following the strong message, whereas the peripheral route would show no difference between the strong and the weak messages (Martin & Hewstone, 2008; Martin et al., 2007).

In one study (Martin et al., 2007), participants were university students who were presented with a persuasion message defending the introduction of oral examination for one course (researchers knew from a pre-test that most students were opposed to such an exam). Participants were told that a group of 11 students had met to discuss the issue. Depending on the condition, they learnt that either nine (= majority source) or two (= minority source) of the 11 students were favourable to introducing the new exam. Participants then read the arguments allegedly given by those in favour. Arguments were manipulated, so that participants were presented with either weak or strong arguments. Finally, the importance of the topic was also manipulated: the exam was supposed to be introduced in the participants' own university (making it self-relevant and therefore more important), or only in another university (low importance), or this was not specifically stated (intermediate importance). The dependent measure was participants' own attitudes towards the introduction of the exam. Authors compared attitude change following strong versus weak arguments to infer whether participants had processed the message through the central route (in which case the strong message should lead to greater change) or through the peripheral route (in which case no difference should be observed). The results are summarised in Figure 7.7. Let us walk you through them.

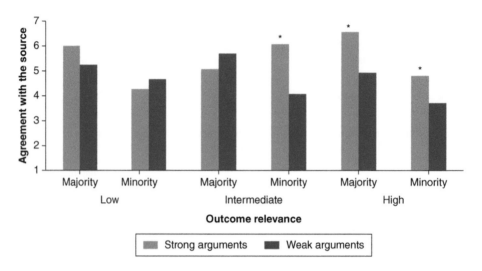

Figure 7.7 Results from Martin et al. (2007): Mean attitude scores as a function of source status, message quality, and outcome relevance

Note: *indicates significant differences between strong and weak arguments.

What do the results show? First, when the topic is not personally relevant (low importance), there is no difference between weak and strong arguments, suggesting that the peripheral route was activated. The majority obtains more influence than the minority on this direct measure of attitude change. When the topic is personally relevant (high importance), there is a clear difference between strong and weak arguments, with strong arguments leading to greater influence. This suggests that the central route was activated and, importantly, is true for both the majority and the minority source. Finally, at intermediate importance, we see that influence depends on the interaction of the source and the strength of the arguments. In the majority condition, there is no difference between weak and strong arguments, suggesting once again that the peripheral route was used. In the minority condition, however, strong arguments were more influential, suggesting that the central route was used.

We described here one study where motivation to process was determined by the personal relevance of the topic. It is worth noting that other elements can also impact motivation. For example, individuals with a higher need for cognition (i.e., one's tendency to engage in and enjoy activities that require thinking) are more likely to process persuasive messages via the central route regardless of the majority/minority source (Martin & Hewstone, 2017). Other studies also show that compared to majority influence, attitudes following minority influence were more resistant to counter-persuasion, more persistent over time, and more predictive of behaviour (Martin & Hewstone, 2008) – and this is explained by a greater number of message-congruent thoughts self-generated by the participant while reading the minority message (Martin & Hewstone, 2017).

Summary

In sum, the SCEM reconciles seemingly opposite views on majority and minority influence, most notably conversion theory (Moscovici, 1980) and the objective consensus approach. Importantly, to the extent that people hold only moderately strong attitudes on most topics (i.e., the intermediate level of elaboration is most likely to happen frequently), this suggests that Moscovici's conversion theory should make correct predictions most of the time. Only when motivation to process the message effortfully is particularly low or high would conversion theory not be appropriate.

7.6 PART 3: APPLICATIONS

In this section we illustrate how research on social influence has been applied to three specific real-life domains. We first discuss prosocial behaviour, before turning to sustainability and pro-environmental behaviour. We finally present social influence research that was conducted in the context of the COVID-19 pandemic.

7.6.1 Social Influence and Prosocial Behaviour

Prosocial behaviour can be understood as any behaviour that is intended to benefit another (Eisenberg, 1986). Zaki and Mitchell (2013, p. 466) argue that 'prosociality ranks among our species' most vital, defining features'. Indeed, research showed that most people were ready to sacrifice more money to reduce the number of electric shocks that would be given to a stranger, more so than to reduce the number of shocks they would receive themselves (Crockett et al., 2014). In other words, people prioritise other people's well-being over their own and are ready to pay a personal cost to do so. Nevertheless, they may make distinctions in whom they choose to help.

Prosociality and Group Membership

One source of distinction for helping behaviour is group membership. In one study, Levine and colleagues (2005) invited Manchester United FC fans into the lab. In the first part of the study, participants were asked to complete a Manchester United FC fan identification scale. The goal, unbeknown to the participant, was to ensure that their MU fan social identity was salient. Participants were then told that the second part of the study would take place in a different building and were given instructions to get there. On their way to the second building, participants witnessed a (staged) fall: a confederate, in running clothes, ran down a grass bank, slipped and fell over, holding onto his ankle and shouting in pain. He was either wearing a Manchester United FC t-shirt (ingroup), a Liverpool FC t-shirt (outgroup), or an unbranded t-shirt (neutral group). Three members of the research team (hidden in various places) independently recorded the behaviour of the participant. The results showed that participants were significantly more likely to help an ingroup member (12 out of 13 helped) than an outgroup member (4 out of 12 helped) or neutral group member (3 out of 10 helped). This provides clear evidence of intergroup bias in helping: people are significantly more likely to help ingroup members compared to outgroup members.

Social developmental research has also found evidence of intergroup bias in helping among children (see Over, 2018, for a review). For example, Abrams and colleagues (2015) found that children aged 5–9 years were less willing to help outgroup members compared to ingroup peers. Moreover, this bias was exacerbated under competitive contexts. So, what conditions are required for nurturing inclusive prosociality? Can we draw on the social influence literature to address this fundamentally crucial question?

In Part 2 of this chapter, in the section on Milgram, we demonstrated how social identity is a basis for social influence (Turner, 1991). When people define themselves as part of a group, they are motivated to understand and to follow the group norms. On this basis, Gaertner and colleagues (1993) developed a theory called the common ingroup identity model (see Chapters 2, 8, and 10). They propose that various social factors (e.g., status, societal norms, perceived interdependence) impact how people perceive group membership. Specifically, members of two groups can perceive that:

- they have completely separate group identities (intergroup categorisation);
- they are best represented as separate individuals rather than group members (a decategorisation process);
- they actually share a common group identity (recategorisation as one superordinate group).

Each of these perceptions has different implications for intergroup bias and, by extension, for prosociality. Gaertner and colleagues (1993) hypothesised that, compared to intergroup categorisation (which seems to be the default perception in many cases), recategorisation could reduce intergroup bias and increase inclusive prosociality. This was tested in a second football fan study (Levine et al., 2005). The procedure of this study was identical to that of the previous one, described above, except that this time, the identification scale was a *football* fan identification scale instead of a Manchester United FC one. In other words, the researchers were making the common group identity salient (recategorisation as one superordinate group). Results showed that this time participants were just as likely to help confederates wearing a Liverpool t-shirt (7 out of 10 helped) or a Manchester United t-shirt (8 out of 10 helped), as compared to those wearing a plain t-shirt (2 out of 9 helped). Both groups were now perceived as sharing a common interest for football, making them all members of a single superordinate group (from which the plain-t-shirt confederates were still excluded), equally deserving prosocial help.

EXERCISE 7.3

Check your understanding

What do the images below have in common?

Answer: They are all different examples of a superordinate identity.

Source: Adobe Stock

Prosociality Towards 'all of Humanity'

You may wonder whether it is possible for humans to show prosociality to all humans equally, beyond group memberships. McFarland and colleagues (2012) developed a psychometric scale to measure *identification with all of humanity* (e.g., 'To what degree do you think of all humans everywhere as "family"?'). Using this scale, they showed that people who report higher identification with all of humanity also report higher concern for global human rights and for humanitarian needs, choosing to learn more about humanitarian concerns, and showing a greater willingness to contribute to international humanitarian relief. Therefore, not only is it possible to hold a superordinate social identity to the level of humanity, but this level of identity is also predictive of inclusive prosociality.

Inclusive Group Norms

A key take-home message from this chapter is that we are influenced by others, notably through the norms conveyed by our social groups. In terms of prosocial behaviour specifically, studies with both children and adults consistently show that social norms substantially influence prosocial behaviour (see e.g., House, 2018, for a review).

A recent cross-cultural study of eight diverse societies, ranging from foragers to small-scale horticulturalists to large urban communities, examined the relationship between societal prosocial norms and actual prosocial behaviour, in both children and adults (House et al., 2020). The authors found that, in adults, cross-cultural variation in prosocial behaviour is predicted by what members of their society judge to be the correct social norm. Moreover, in middle childhood and early adolescence, children's prosocial behaviour increasingly resembles that of adults, and children's prosocial behaviour becomes increasingly aligned with their society's social norm.

Local norms also matter greatly. Nesdale and Lawson (2011) asked children aged 7–11 years how they felt about ingroup (e.g., children in their own team) and outgroup members

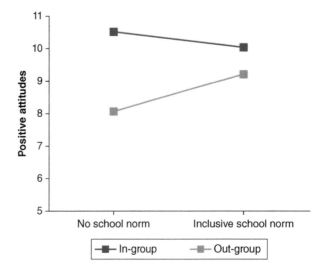

Figure 7.8 Results from Nesdale and Lawson (2011): Attitudes towards ingroup and outgroup members as a function of the school norm manipulation

(children in the other team), while also stressing an inclusive school norm versus not. In the inclusive school norm condition, the experimenter would say: 'Your principal and teacher have said to me that this school likes all the children to like kids in other groups and to be friendly toward them.' In the control condition, they said nothing in particular. When an inclusive school norm had been made salient, children's positive attitudes towards outgroup members increased compared to when there was no such school norm (see Figure 7.8).

Summary

In sum, prosocial behaviour is pervasive, yet also socially influenced. Humans have an incredible capacity for kindness, but also show significant intergroup biases in their prosocial decision-making. Nurturing superordinate social identities can help to overcome intergroup biases in helping. Furthermore, social norms are central to our understanding of human attitudes and behaviour, and prosocial behaviour is no exception. Thus, peers, families, colleagues, and institutions small or large can each play their part in nurturing prosociality by increasing the focus on inclusive social identities as well as on prosocial social norms.

Prosocial behaviour is a relatively new area within social psychology and many questions do remain. For example, there are many different types of prosocial behaviour (e.g., charitable giving, collective protest, helping in emergencies). It is likely that the processes for promoting different types of prosocial behaviours will vary. We are excited to see future researchers tackle research gaps like these.

7.6.2 Social Influence and Environmental Psychology

Concern for the environment has exponentially grown in the past 50 years since the very first international conference on environmentalism organised by the United Nations in 1972. Today, an increasing majority of nations and citizens are concerned about the environment. In fact, the author of conversion theory, Serge Moscovici (see the section on minority influence in Part 1 of this chapter), considered environmentalism the perfect example of successful minority influence. Yet, despite a global concern and positive attitudes towards the environment, the corresponding behaviours are often still lacking. This makes pro-environmental behaviour a very relevant target for social influence attempts. In this section, we present a few key experiments that have applied social influence theories to the study of environmental behaviour.

Pro-environmental Norms

The positive role of **norms** in general, and of environmental norms more specifically, has long been recognised. In a nutshell, people are more likely to adopt pro-environmental behaviour themselves if they perceive a pro-environmental norm, both **descriptive** (i.e., 'other people in my group act for the environment') and **injunctive** ('people in my group think I should act for the environment'). Chan and Bishop (2013), for example, found that a subjective injunctive norm ('most people who are important to me think I should recycle my household waste') predicted participants' self-reported recycling intentions and behaviour (for a review, see Yuriev et al., 2020).

> **Key concept – Descriptive norm:**
> Any of various consensual standards (social norms) that describe how most people typically act, feel, and think in a given situation.

> **Key concept – Injunctive norm:**
> Socially determined consensual standards (social norms) that describe how people should act, feel, and think in a given situation, irrespective of how people typically respond in the setting.

In a famous series of studies, Cialdini and his colleagues tested the impact of different normative messages on the behaviour of hotel guests. The objective was to convince hotel guests to reuse their towels in order to reduce the amount of laundry and contribute to an environmental conservation programme. The researchers investigated the behaviour of several thousands of guests across hotels in the USA. In a first study (Goldstein et al., 2008), they compared the effect of two printed signs positioned on the washroom towel tracks. The first message was a standard environmental message, asking guests to 'help save the environment … by reusing your towels during their stay'. The second message introduced the **descriptive norm**, stating: 'almost 75% of guests … help by using their towel more than once. Join your fellow guests in helping to save the environment'. While 35% of guests exposed to the standard environmental message reused their towel, 44% of those exposed to the normative message did so – a statistically significant increase – showing that participants were motivated to conform with the described majority norm.

In a follow-up study, a new message which described an even more specific norm related to the exact room the guests were staying in ('75% of the guests who stayed in this room … help by using their towel more than once') led to even stronger influence (49% compliance). This highlights the power not only of norms, but also of the specific context in which they are understood and their psychological closeness for the person – what Goldstein and colleagues (2008) dubbed 'provincial norms'.

KEY THINKER

Robert Cialdini

Robert Cialdini (1945–) is an American psychologist. He received a Bachelor of Science degree from the University of Wisconsin-Milwaukee in 1967 and a PhD in social psychology from the University of North Carolina in 1970. Over the years, he worked at Ohio State University, the University of California, the Annenberg School of Communications, and the

Graduate School of Business of Stanford University. He is currently a Professor Emeritus of Psychology and Marketing at Arizona State University. Cialdini's research focuses on social influence in real-life settings. He has always endeavoured to study real, directly observable behaviours, and as such he conducted many field experiments, including in used car dealerships, fund-raising organisations, telemarketing, hotels, and national parks. His focus theory of normative conduct was also a big influence on the field of normative influence. Cialdini has authored more than 100 articles and several books, including *Influence: The Psychology of Persuasion* (1984) and *Yes! 50 Scientifically Proven Ways to be Persuasive* (2008).

The effect of social norms is not limited to reusing towels. In a UK-based research programme, we (Fanny and colleagues) aimed to tackle engine idling at long-wait stops (Abrams et al., 2021). We designed three messages asking drivers to turn off their idling engine while waiting at a railway crossing in a city in the Southeast of England. The normative message read, 'Join other responsible drivers in Canterbury. Turn off your engine when the barriers are down' – thus, it was quite similar to the message used by Goldstein and colleagues (2008). Two other messages highlighted outcome efficacy ('[Through your action] you will improve air quality in the area') and private self-focus ('Think of your actions'). Each message was fixed to a pole and displayed for an entire week. Research assistants walked down the pavement when barriers were down and recorded how many stopping drivers had turned off their engine. Over a month, we observed more than 6,000 vehicles. Results showed that the percentage of engines being turned off increased from 27% (baseline rate, with no influence message) to 30% (private self-focus), 34% (outcome efficacy), and 39% (social norm), making the social norm message the most effective of all.

Pro-environmental Norm and Personal Behaviour: A possible 'Boomerang' Effect

The studies presented above suggest an overall positive impact of norms, which can be understood as a perception of what the majority of the group think or do. However, we have also seen that majority influence was sometimes limited to superficial compliance with no real integration of the content (see the section in Part 1 on minority influence). Similar findings have arisen when taking into account people's past behaviour, showing a possible **'boomerang' effect** of pro-environmental norms (Key study 7.3).

KEY STUDY 7.3

The 'Boomerang' Effect

Schultz and colleagues (2007) investigated the energy consumption of hundreds of California households, who agreed to share data from their energy metres. The researchers

(Continued)

read the metres at the start of the experiment (baseline measurement), then provided the inhabitants with *descriptive normative feedback*: they designed a message stating how much energy the household had consumed over the past week and indicating the average household consumption in their neighbourhood over the same period. In other words, inhabitants could compare their consumption to that of the neighbourhood average (= descriptive norm) and learn whether they were themselves better than the norm (in this case, consuming less energy, which is the desired behaviour), or worse (consuming more).

Then came the experimental manipulation: for half of the households, the information was accompanied by a hand-drawn emoticon (a smiling face if the household was consuming less than average, a sad face if it was consuming more). This manipulation was expected to *reactivate the injunctive pro-environmental norm*, reminding inhabitants that the normative, positively connoted behaviour was to save energy. The other half of households received the information with no emoticon. The researchers came back two weeks and five weeks later to read the households' electricity metres again. These were used to calculate a difference with baseline consumption rates. What did the results show?

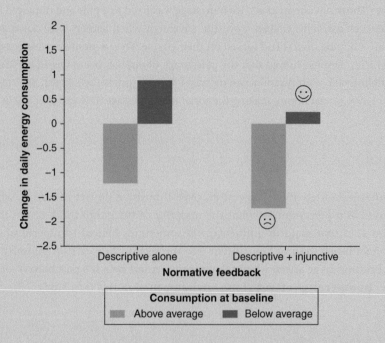

Figure 7.9 Results from Schultz et al. (2007): Change in daily energy consumption from baseline after two weeks, depending on baseline energy consumption (above vs below average) and feedback presented (reminder of injunctive norm with emoticons vs not)

Note: Similar results appeared on the long-term measure (five weeks), which are not displayed here.

First, households who received negative feedback (i.e., initially doing worse than average) significantly *decreased* their consumption, which shows straightforward normative influence and efforts to align with the behaviour of the relevant social group. Second, households who received positive feedback (i.e., initially doing better than average) reacted differently depending on the injunctive norm reminder. Households who had no reminder (no smiling emoticon) actually *increased* their consumption. The authors called this the 'destructive potential of social norms', showing how people might reduce their efforts if they feel they are already doing enough in comparison to the group norm. This is consistent with the idea of mere compliance advanced by Moscovici: if people feel that their initial behaviour is enough to prove their compliance to the majority norm, they then lose all motivation to continue further, and can 'slack off' (Lalot et al., 2018).

This 'boomerang' effect disappeared when households were reminded of the injunctive pro-environmental norm (with the smiling emoticon): they maintained their low rate of energy consumption (see Figure 7.9). Apparently, being reminded of the importance of the pro-environmental goal or value for the group eliminated the 'destructive potential' of positive feedback. This has important implications for the use of norms in social influence attempts and highlights that people will interpret and react to norms differently, depending notably on their own habits and past conducts.

EXERCISE 7.4

Develop Your Critical Thinking

Suppose the local railway company wants to encourage their customers to recycle their waste while on the train or at the station (notably their plastic bottles). They hire you, a consultant psychologist, to design the persuasive campaign. Drawing from your knowledge about social influence, what do you suggest?

Summary

Social influence is present in most life domains and pro-environmental behaviour is no exception. How much people act to preserve the environment was found to strongly depend on what they perceive other people to do and think. Of course, individual factors also come into play. If you remember, we described above (in the section on factors affecting normative influence) how personal involvement dampens normative influence: participants who considered energy conservation as a personally relevant topic displayed greater conservation behaviour even when their peers did not care about conservation (Göckeritz et al., 2010). In such a case, we might even hope that these personally motivated individuals could become an influential minority, eventually convincing the rest of their peers of the importance of conservation behaviour!

Environmental psychology is a rapidly growing field and more evidence is produced every year to help us to understand (and influence) environmental behaviour. Yet some open questions remain. For example, researchers currently debate how much self-reported behaviour and intentions (as measured in many studies) correspond to people's real behaviour, and how much they are affected by different reporting biases, such as a social desirability bias. There is a growing awareness that research needs to focus on consequential behaviour, and this is likely where the field will be moving next (Lange, 2022).

7.6.3 Social Influence in the COVID-19 Pandemic

In March 2020, the World Health Organisation (WHO) declared the outbreak of the novel coronavirus SARS-CoV-2 (COVID-19) as a global pandemic, marking the beginning of several years of global crisis. From the socio-psychological point of view, the COVID-19 pandemic has proved to be an extremely rich period in which to reflect on theories and models of human behaviour, notably in terms of social influence. We collectively experienced the rapid emergence of new norms (such as mask-wearing and social distancing) and were asked to comply with a number of government-imposed rules. In this section, we review how the different influence mechanisms described earlier applied in the context of the pandemic.

Complying with Government-enacted Restrictions

The first obvious object of study of social influence during the pandemic concerns *complying* with governmental restrictions. To contain the spread of the virus, governments enacted a number of rules and restrictions varying in intensity, from wearing face masks and keeping a distance from other people (1.5 or 2 metres), to forbidding meeting people from other households, even family and friends, to the most stringent forms of *lockdowns*, with schools and businesses being forced to close. People were also requested to quarantine if they were sick or had been in contact with a contagious person, and to regularly take COVID-19 tests. How well did people comply with the rules?

Evidence suggests that compliance was, mostly, very high. This emerges from both opinion polls (which, although anonymous, can be subject to desirability bias) and objective data. For example, large-scale international polls by YouGov showed that a majority of people said they were wearing a face mask in public places (between 60 and 90% of respondents across countries and months of 2020). A majority also said they were in favour of quarantining anyone who had been in contact with a contaminated patient and of cancelling large events (50–80% on average for both). Other studies relied on smartphone GPS data as an objective measure of people's movements during lockdowns. For example, one study in the UK showed that the daily number of trips dropped drastically during the first lockdown (March–May 2020): by 60% on weekdays and 85% on weekends (Jeffrey et al., 2020).

How do we explain such high rates of compliance? We described above how influence can serve both a normative and an informational function, and how the informational function becomes more important when **uncertainty** increases. It is hard to picture a more uncertain time than the year 2020: uncertainty about where the virus was coming from, the impact it would have, how the economy would cope, when a medical treatment would be available, etc. In such a situation, social influence theories predict that people will turn to sources of influence for guidance and answers to relieve their uncertainty (Kruglanski et al., 2021), and readily comply with the solution that leaders propose – which corresponds to what we observed, at least during the early days of the pandemic.

In some cases, however, complying or not complying with a specific regulation became more of an identity statement (i.e., corresponding to the normative function of influence). This was particularly salient in the USA, where President Trump expressed dissenting views about the pandemic, and notably about the usefulness of face masks (Lasco, 2020). This led to an intense politicisation of mask-wearing, with most Democrats strongly supporting mask-wearing and Trump-supporting Republicans opposing it. Face masks (or the absence thereof) therefore became a visible symbol of one's identification with the political group of Democrats versus Republicans (Lang et al., 2021). It illustrates how specific norms can emerge in subgroups of the population, with everyone conforming with the norm of the group most relevant for them.

> **Video:** Together Apart: Alex Haslam, Nik Steffens, Matthew Hornsey, and Frank Mols on social influence during COVID-19 https://www.youtube.com/watch?v=PODL0mnVclo

Using Social Power to Obtain Influence

A second question is to understand what forms of *leadership* are most effective in obtaining and sustaining citizens' compliance with social distancing measures. In other words, what bases of *social power* can be used to increase compliance?

First, country leaders and governments can make (and have made) use of their power of *reward* and *coercion*: social distancing measures were the law and people were fined for not respecting them. The introduction of vaccination passports (or 'covid passes'), which were mandatory to access indoor venues or restaurants or for travelling, also represented a use of reward power. Yet, we know that people dislike being told to do something, which may backfire and result in more disobedience than obedience (Steffens, 2020). Other routes to social influence may therefore prove to be more effective.

Indeed, research also shows that in times of crisis people express preference for strong leadership, that is, more directive and even authoritarian than in normal times (Hasel, 2013). This reflects the attribution of *informational* and *legitimate power* to the leader, who is perceived as the legitimate and trustworthy authority to determine new norms and ultimately help citizens cope with uncertainty. As such, leaders who communicated more clearly, gave straightforward directions, and demonstrated they were abiding by the rules they were enacting seemed to obtain greater influence on their citizens. Those clearly relying on the scientific evidence and working together with scientific advisors also fared better, presumably through an increased *expert power* (Van Bavel et al., 2020). In contrast, examples of politicians breaking the rules considerably decreased their perceived trustworthiness and legitimacy, and thereby affected the public's compliance. In the UK, for example, the 'Dominic Cummings scandal', where a member of the UK political elite travelled across the country while suffering from the virus, markedly decreased trust in the authorities (Davies et al., 2021), and so did, later on, 'Partygate'.

Finally, leaders can also use *referent power*, which is often conceptualised as their degree of charisma. Charismatic leaders communicate in a value-based, symbolic, and emotional manner, which increases people's identification with and respect for them. Antonakis (2021) found that charismatic governors in the USA had greater influence during the pandemic, as shown by a greater proportion of people staying at home following a speech given by a more charismatic leader (measured through mobile phone data).

In sum, there is evidence that all bases of social power can be and were used by leaders during the pandemic. Just as in Kelman's (1958) study (see the section in Part 1, Why are we influenced?), power is linked to compliance, identification, and internalisation processes, and can trigger differential influence in the short term versus the long term, and in public versus private situations.

Norms and Peer Influence

The third and final question we will treat here concerns not the 'vertical' influence (by leaders and governments) but rather the 'horizontal' influence between peers. Although compliance with social distancing measures was globally very high, people may have not perceived it this way. Indeed, people are very sensitive to counter-examples and can easily misinterpret a descriptive norm. If you are on your way to the supermarket and pass by a group of teenagers hanging out in the park, you might easily get the impression that 'young people are reckless' and 'no one respects the rules anymore', ignoring the fact that hundreds of people are presently in their homes respecting the distancing measures, making them precisely not visible to you.

Importantly, such misperceptions can lead to disengagement and reduced compliance. Some have warned against sustained news reports about singled out, infrequent, cases of non-compliant behaviour, highlighting the risk of unintended effects (Steffens, 2020). It was suggested instead to insist on the majority compliant behaviour, or, in case compliant behaviour was actually only being endorsed by a minority, to remind people of the *injunctive* norm instead (Van Bavel et al., 2020) – just as in Schultz and colleagues' (2007) study on energy consumption.

7.7 SUMMARY

This brings us to the end of this chapter. Reflecting on what you have read, you should now understand what social influence is and why it is such an important aspect of our everyday life. Keep in mind that influence involves two parties – the target and the source of influence – and that both have their own motivations to fulfil (the 'why' of influence). For the individual, fundamental needs to belong and to reduce uncertainty explain the motivation to accept and conform to the group's views. For the group, a degree of uniformity is necessary in order to advance towards the group's goals, explaining a motivation to push members towards conformity.

You should now be familiar with the conditions that maximise social influence (the 'when' and 'where' of influence) and understand that, although everyone is subject to social influence, different people and different contexts will lead to more or less influence. In addition, you should be able to distinguish between different forms of influence, from compliance to obedience to authority and private, long-lasting attitude change. You should know that majority and minority sources obtain influence through different processes (the 'how' of influence). You are also warned of the potential extreme consequences of obedience but should understand the boundary conditions for the phenomenon to appear and the different explanations for people's behaviour in obedience situations.

Finally, you have seen applications of insights from social influence to real-world issues and understand how influence can lead to both positive and negative outcomes, all depending on the perception of the target behaviour.

7.8 REVISION

Find the one correct answer to each of the multiple choice qestions below:

1   Deutsch and Gerard distinguish between normative influence and informational influence. With respect to their theory, which of the following statements is correct?

   a   The pattern of 'compliance' observed in Kelman's (1958) study is a manifestation of informational influence.

   b   Referent power (as defined by French and Raven, 1959) is particularly relevant for informational influence.

   c   Studies show that when people are expressing opinions in a group, the pressure to conform is reduced if another person in the group breaks the consensus to express a third opinion (different from the group and different from the target person).

   d   An individual who identifies more strongly with a group will also conform more easily with this group's views, which reflects normative influence.

2   Which of the following statements about Asch's (1956) and Sherif's (1935) studies is correct?

   a   Participants conform to a group norm only when there is no physical or pre-established frame of reference.

   b   Participants conform to a group norm regardless of whether there is a physical or pre-established frame of reference.

   c   Participants develop a group norm when there is no physical or pre-established frame of reference. And participants conform to a group norm some of the time when there is a physical or pre-established frame of reference.

   d   None of the above.

3   Which of the following statements about Milgram's work and the more recent developments led by Haslam and Reicher is correct?

   a   Milgram argued that brutality and tyranny occurs because people cede responsibility to authority, and therefore obey them. Haslam and Reicher argued that brutality and tyranny occur due to group-based leadership and followership.

   b   The conclusions by Milgram, and then by Haslam and Reicher, are broadly the same: people cede responsibility to authority, and therefore obey them.

   c   Milgram argued that brutality and tyranny occur due to group-based leadership and followership. Haslam and Reicher argued that brutality and tyranny occur because people cede responsibility to authority, and therefore obey them.

   d   None of the above.

4   Which of the following statements about minority influence is *not* correct?

   a   According to Moscovici's (1980) conversion theory, minorities can obtain influence because they introduce a social conflict by proposing new alternative propositions, leading targets to pay more attention to the minority's arguments.

   b   Because people always rely on a consensus heuristic, according to which the majority must be right, majorities always obtain more influence than minorities.

   c   Minorities typically obtain little influence on direct, public, and immediate measures, but greater influence on indirect, private, and delayed measures.

   d   The Source-Context-Elaboration Model (SCEM) (Martin & Hewstone, 2008) proposes that social influence depends on both the motivation of the target to process the message and the nature of the source (a majority versus minority source).

Answers: d, c, a, b.

7.9 FURTHER READING

Foundations

Normative Influence

Nolan, J. M., Schultz, P. W., Cialdini, R. B., Goldstein, N. J., & Griskevicius, V. (2008). Normative social influence is underdetected. *Personality and Social Psychology Bulletin, 34*(7), 913–923. https://doi.org/10.1177/0146167208316691

Influence Under Uncertainty

Sherif, M. (1935). A study of some social factors in perception. *Archives of Psychology*, *187*, 60.

Influence Under Certainty

Asch, S. E. (1951). Effects of group pressure upon the modification and distortion of judgments. In H. Guetzkow (Ed.), *Groups, leadership and men* (pp. 177–190). Lancaster: Carnegie Press.

Advances

Minority Influence

Butera, F., Falomir-Pichastor, J. M., Mugny, G., & Quiamzade, A. (2017). Minority influence. In S. G. Harkins, K. D. Williams, & J. Burger (Eds.), *The Oxford handbook of social influence* (pp. 317–337). Oxford: Oxford University Press. https://doi.org/10.1093/oxfor dhb/9780199859870.013.11

Obedience to Authority

Haslam, S. A., & Reicher, S. D. (2017). 50 years of 'obedience to authority': From blind conformity to engaged followership. *Annual Review of Law and Social Science*, *13*(1), 59–78. https://doi.org/10.1146/annurev-lawsocsci-110316-113710

Applications

Social Influence and Prosocial Behaviour

Levine, M., Prosser, A., Evans, D., & Reicher, S. (2005). Identity and emergency intervention: How social group membership and inclusiveness of group boundaries shape helping behavior. *Personality and Social Psychology Bulletin*, *31*(4), 443–453. https://doi. org/10.1177/014616 7204271651

Social Influence and Environmental Psychology

Keizer, K., & Schultz, P. W. (2018). Social norms and pro-environmental behaviour. In L. Steg & J. I. M. de Groot (Eds.), *Environmental psychology: An introduction* (pp. 179–188). Chichester: John Wiley & Sons. https://doi.org/10.1002/9781119241072.ch18

Social Influence During COVID-19

Krings, V. C., Steeden, B., Abrams, D., & Hogg, M. A. (2021). Social attitudes and behavior in the COVID-19 pandemic: Evidence and prospects from research on group processes and intergroup relations. *Group Processes & Intergroup Relations*, *24*(2), 201–209. https://doi.org/10.1177/1368430220986673

7.10 REFERENCES

Abrams, D., Lalot, F., Hopthrow, T., Templeton, A., Steeden, B., Özkeçeci, H., Imada, H., Warbis, S., Sandiford, D., Meleady, R., Fell, E., Abrams, Z., Abrams, A., Ngan, X. Q., Celina, S., Tanyeri, A., Gammon, M., Abrams, B., Fischer, L., Drysdale, S., Dewi, R., Leite, A., Mills, A., & Peckham, S. (2021). Cleaning up our acts: Psychological interventions to reduce engine idling and improve air quality. *Journal of Environmental Psychology*, *74*, 101587. https://doi.org/10.1016/j.jenvp.2021.101587

Abrams, D., & Levine, J. M. (2012). Norm formation: Revisiting Sherif's autokinetic illusion study. In J. R. Smith & S. A. Haslam (Eds.), *Social psychology: Revisiting the classic studies* (pp. 57–75). London: Sage.

Abrams, D., Van de Vyver, J., Pelletier, J., & Cameron, L. (2015). Children's prosocial behavioural intentions towards outgroup members. *British Journal of Developmental Psychology*, *33*(3), 277–294. https://doi.org/10.1111/bjdp.12085

Allen, V. L., & Levine, J. M. (1968). Social support, dissent and conformity. *Sociometry*, *31*(2), 138–149. https://doi.org/10.2307/2786454

Antonakis, J. (2021). Leadership to defeat COVID-19. *Group Processes & Intergroup Relations*, *24*(2), 210–215. https://doi.org/10.1177/1368430220981418

Aramovich, N. P., Lytle, B. L., & Skitka, L. J. (2012). Opposing torture: Moral conviction and resistance to majority influence. *Social Influence*, *7*(1), 21–34. https://doi.org/10.1080/15534510.2011.640199

Asch, S. E. (1955). Opinions and social pressure. *Scientific American*, *193*, 31–35. https://doi.org/10.1038/scientificamerican1155-31

Asch, S. E. (1956). Studies of independence and conformity: I. A minority of one against a unanimous majority. *Psychological Monographs: General and Applied*, *70*(9), 1–70. https://doi.org/10.1037/h0093718

Bègue, L., Beauvois, J.-L., Courbet, D., Oberlé, D., Lepage, J., & Duke, A. A. (2015). Personality predicts obedience in a Milgram paradigm. *Journal of Personality*, *83*(3), 299–306. https://doi.org/10.1111/jopy.12104

Birney, M. E., Reicher, S. D., Haslam, S. A., Steffens, N. K., & Neville, F. G. (2023). Engaged followership and toxic science: Exploring the effect of prototypicality on willingness to follow harmful experimental instructions. *British Journal of Social Psychology*, *62*(2), 866–882. https://10.1111/bjso.12603

Bohns, V. K. (2016). (Mis)understanding our influence over others: A review of the underestimation-of-compliance effect. *Current Directions in Psychological Science, 25*(2), 119–123. https://doi.org/10.1177/0963721415628011

Bond, R., & Smith, P. B. (1996). Culture and conformity: A meta-analysis of studies using Asch's (1952b, 1956) line judgment task. *Psychological Bulletin, 119*(1), 111–137. https://doi.org/10.1037/0033-2909.119.1.111

Burger, J. M. (2014). Situational features in Milgram's experiment that kept his participants shocking. *Journal of Social Issues, 70*(3), 489–500. https://doi.org/10.1111/josi.12073

Burger, J. M., Girgis, Z. M., & Manning, C. C. (2011). In their own words: Explaining obedience to authority through an examination of participants' comments. *Social Psychological and Personality Science, 2*(5), 460–466. https://doi.org/10.1177/1948550610397632

Butera, F., Falomir-Pichastor, J. M., Mugny, G., & Quiamzade, A. (2017). Minority influence. In S. G. Harkins, K. D. Williams, & J. Burger (Eds.), *The Oxford handbook of social influence* (pp. 317–337). Oxford: Oxford University Press. https://doi.org/10.1093/oxfordhb/9780199859870.013.11

Chan, L., & Bishop, B. (2013). A moral basis for recycling: Extending the theory of planned behaviour. *Journal of Environmental Psychology, 36*, 96–102. https://doi.org/10.1016/j.jenvp.2013.07.010

Cialdini, R. B. (1984). *Influence: How and why people agree to things.* New York: Morrow.

Coleman, J. F., Blake, R. R., & Mouton, J. S. (1958). Task difficulty and conformity pressures. *The Journal of Abnormal and Social Psychology, 57*(1), 120–122. https://doi.org/10.1037/h0041274

Crockett, M. J., Kurth-Nelson, Z., Siegel, J. Z., Dayan, P., & Dolan, R. J. (2014). Harm to others outweighs harm to self in moral decision making. *Proceedings of the National Academy of Sciences, 111*(48), 17320–17325. https://doi.org/10.1073/pnas.1408988111

Davies, B., Lalot, F., Peitz, L., Heering, M. S., Ozkececi, H., Babaian, J., Davies Hayon, K., Broadwood, J., & Abrams, D. (2021). Changes in political trust in Britain during the COVID-19 pandemic in 2020: Integrated public opinion evidence and implications. *Humanities and Social Sciences Communications, 8*(166). https://doi.org/10.1057/s41599-021-00850-6

Deutsch, M., & Gerard, H. B. (1955). A study of normative and informational social influences upon individual judgment. *The Journal of Abnormal and Social Psychology, 51*(3), 629–636. https://doi.org/10.1037/h0046408

Dictionary of Personality and Social Psychology (The). (1986). (R. Harré & R. Lamb, Eds.). Cambridge, MA: The MIT Press.

Doise, W. (1980). Levels of explanation in the *European Journal of Social Psychology. European Journal of Social Psychology, 10*(3), 213–231. https://doi.org/10.1002/ejsp.2420100302

Eisenberg, N. (1986). *Altruistic emotion, cognition, and behavior.* Hillsdale, NJ: Erlbaum.

Fenigstein, A. (2015). Milgram's shock experiments and the Nazi perpetrators: A contrarian perspective on the role of obedience pressures during the Holocaust. *Theory & Psychology, 25*(5), 581–598. https://doi.org/10.1177/0959354315601904

Festinger, L. (1950). Informal social communication. *Psychological Review, 57*(5), 271–282. https://doi.org/10.1037/h0056932

French, J. R. P. J., & Raven, B. H. (1959). The bases of social power. In D. Cartwright (Ed.), *Studies in social power* (pp. 150–167). Ann Arbor, MI: University of Michigan Press.

Gaertner, S. L., Dovidio, J. F., Anastasio, P. A., Bachman, B. A., & Rust, M. C. (1993). The common ingroup identity model: Recategorization and the reduction of intergroup bias. *European Review of Social Psychology, 4*(1), 1–26. https://doi.org/10.1080/14792779343000004

Gelfand, M. J., Raver, J. L., Nishii, L., Leslie, L. M., Lun, J., Lim, B. C., Duan, L., Almaliach, A., Ang, S., Arnadottir, J., Aycan, Z., Boehnke, K., Boski, P., Cabecinhas, R., Chan, D., Chhokar, J., D'Amato, A., Ferrer, M., Fischlmayr, I. C., Fischer, R., Fülöp, M., Georgas, J., Kashima Emiko, S., Kashima, Y., Kim, K., Lempereur, A., Marquez, P., Othman, R., Overlaet, B., Panagiotopoulou, P., Peltzer, K., Perez-Florizno Lorena, R., Ponomarenko, L., Realo, A., Schei, V., Schmitt, M., Smith Peter, B., Soomro, N., Szabo, E., Taveesin, N., Toyama, M., Van de Vliert, E., Vohra, N., Ward, C., & Yamaguchi, S. (2011). Differences between tight and loose cultures: A 33-nation study. *Science, 332*(6033), 1100–1104. https://doi.org/10.1126/science.1197754

Göckeritz, S., Schultz, P. W., Rendón, T., Cialdini, R. B., Goldstein, N. J., & Griskevicius, V. (2010). Descriptive normative beliefs and conservation behavior: The moderating roles of personal involvement and injunctive normative beliefs. *European Journal of Social Psychology, 40*(3), 514–523. https://doi.org/10.1002/ejsp.643

Goldstein, N. J., Cialdini, R. B., & Griskevicius, V. (2008). A room with a viewpoint: Using social norms to motivate environmental conservation in hotels. *Journal of Consumer Research, 35*(3), 472–482. https://doi.org/10.1086/586910

Gonzalez-Franco, M., Slater, M., Birney, M. E., Swapp, D., Haslam, S. A., & Reicher, S. D. (2018). Participant concerns for the Learner in a Virtual Reality replication of the Milgram obedience study. *PLoS One, 13*(12), e0209704.

Hasel, M. C. (2013). A question of context: The influence of trust on leadership effectiveness during crisis. *M@n@gement, 16*(3), 264–293. https://doi.org/10.3917/mana.163.0264

Haslam, S. A., & Platow, M. J. (2001). The link between leadership and followership: How affirming social identity translates vision into action. *Personality and Social Psychology Bulletin, 27*(11), 1469–1479. https://doi.org/10.1177/01461672012711008

Haslam, S. A., & Reicher, S. D. (2012). Contesting the 'nature' of conformity: What Milgram and Zimbardo's studies really show. *PLoS Biology, 10*(11), e1001426. https://doi.org/10.1371/journal.pbio.1001426

Haslam, S. A., & Reicher, S. D. (2017). 50 years of 'obedience to authority': From blind conformity to engaged followership. *Annual Review of Law and Social Science, 13*(1), 59–78. https://doi.org/10.1146/annurev-lawsocsci-110316-113710

Haslam, S. A., Reicher, S. D., & Birney, M. E. (2014). Nothing by mere authority: Evidence that in an experimental analogue of the Milgram paradigm participants are motivated not by orders but by appeals to science. *Journal of Social Issues, 70*(3), 473–488. https://doi.org/10.1111/josi.12072

Haslam, S. A., Reicher, S. D., & Millard, K. (2015). Shock treatment: Using immersive digital realism to restage and re-examine Milgram's 'obedience to authority' research. *PLos One*, *10*(3), e109015. https://doi.org/10.1371/journal.pone.0109015

Haslam, S.A., Reicher, S.D., & Platow, M.J. (2011). *The new psychology of leadership: Identity, influence and power*. London: Routledge.

Hogg, M. A. (2001). A social identity theory of leadership. *Personality and Social Psychology Review*, *5*(3), 184–200. https://doi.org/10.1207/S15327957PSPR0503_1

House, B. R. (2018). How do social norms influence prosocial development? *Current Opinion in Psychology*, *20*, 87–91. https://doi.org/10.1016/j.copsyc.2017.08.011

House, B. R., Kanngiesser, P., Barrett, H. C., Broesch, T., Cebioglu, S., Crittenden, A. N., Erut, A., Lew-Levy, S., Sebastian-Enesco, C., Smith, A. M., Yilmaz, S., & Silk, J. B. (2020). Universal norm psychology leads to societal diversity in prosocial behaviour and development. *Nature Human Behaviour*, *4*(1), 36–44. https://doi.org/10.1038/s41562-019-0734-z

Jeffrey, B., Walters, C. E., Ainslie, K. E. C., Eales, O., Ciavarella, C., Bhatia, S., Hayes, S., Baguelin, M., Boonyasiri, A., Brazeau, N. F., Cuomo-Dannenburg, G., FitzJohn, R. G., Gaythorpe, K., Green, W., Imai, N., Mellan, T. A., Mishra, S., Nouvellet, P., Unwin, H. J. T., Verity, R., Vollmer, M., Whittaker, C., Ferguson, N. M., Donnelly, C. A., & Riley, S. (2020). Anonymised and aggregated crowd level mobility data from mobile phones suggests that initial compliance with COVID-19 social distancing interventions was high and geographically consistent across the UK. *Wellcome Open Research*, *5*, 170. https://doi.org/10.12688/wellcomeopenres.15997.1

Kelman, H. C. (1958). Compliance, identification, and internalization: Three processes of attitude change. *Journal of Conflict Resolution*, *2*(1), 51–60. https://doi.org/10.1177/002200275800200106

Klein, R. L. (1972). Age, sex, and task difficulty as predictors of social conformity. *Journal of Gerontology*, *27*(2), 229–236. https://doi.org/10.1093/geronj/27.2.229

Kruglanski, A. W., Molinario, E., & Lemay, E. P. (2021). Coping with COVID-19-induced threats to self. *Group Processes & Intergroup Relations*, *24*(2), 284–289. https://doi.org/10.1177/1368430220982074

Kundu, P., & Cummins, D. D. (2013). Morality and conformity: The Asch paradigm applied to moral decisions. *Social Influence*, *8*(4), 268–279. https://doi.org/10.1080/15534510.2012.727767

Lalot, F., Falomir-Pichastor, J. M., & Quiamzade, A. (2018). Compensation and consistency effects in proenvironmental behaviour: The moderating role of majority and minority support for proenvironmental values. *Group Processes & Intergroup Relations*, *21*(3), 403–421. https://doi.org/10.1177/1368430217733117

Lang, J., Erickson, W. W., & Jing-Schmidt, Z. (2021). #MaskOn! #MaskOff! Digital polarization of mask-wearing in the United States during COVID-19. *PLoS One*, *16*(4), e0250817. https://doi.org/10.1371/journal.pone.0250817

Lange, F. (2022). Behavioral paradigms for studying pro-environmental behavior: A systematic review. *Behavior Research Methods*, *55*, 600–622. https://doi.org/10.3758/s13428-022-01825-4

Lasco, G. (2020). Medical populism and the COVID-19 pandemic. *Global Public Health*, *15*(10), 1417–1429. https://doi.org/10.1080/17441692.2020.1807581

Latané, B. (1981). The psychology of social impact. *American Psychologist, 36*(4), 343–356. https://doi.org/10.1037/0003-066X.36.4.343

Latané, B., & Wolf, S. (1981). The social impact of majorities and minorities. *Psychological Review, 88*(5), 438–453. https://doi.org/10.1037/0033-295X.88.5.438

Levine, J. M., Higgins, E. T., & Choi, H.-S. (2000). Development of strategic norms in groups. *Organizational Behavior and Human Decision Processes, 82*(1), 88–101. https://doi.org/10.1006/obhd.2000.2889

Levine, M., Prosser, A., Evans, D., & Reicher, S. (2005). Identity and emergency intervention: How social group membership and inclusiveness of group boundaries shape helping behavior. *Personality and Social Psychology Bulletin, 31*(4), 443–453. https://doi.org/10.1177/0146167204271651

Maass, A., & Clark, R. D. (1983). Internalization versus compliance: Differential processes underlying minority influence and conformity. *European Journal of Social Psychology, 13*(3), 197–215. https://doi.org/10.1002/ejsp.2420130302

Martin, R., & Hewstone, M. (2008). Majority versus minority influence, message processing and attitude change: The source-context-elaboration model. In M. P. Zanna (Ed.), *Advances in experimental social psychology* (Vol. 40, pp. 237–326). San Diego, CA: Academic Press. https://doi.org/10.1016/S0065-2601(07)00005-6

Martin, R., & Hewstone, M. (2017). Attitude persistence to persuasive messages as a function of numerical majority versus minority source status. In S. Papastamou, A. Gardikiotis, & G. Prodromitis (Eds.), *Majority and minority influence: Societal meaning and cognitive elaboration* (pp. 117–136). Abingdon: Routledge.

Martin, R., Hewstone, M., & Martin, P. Y. (2007). Systematic and heuristic processing of majority and minority-endorsed messages: The effects of varying outcome relevance and levels of orientation on attitude and message processing. *Personality and Social Psychology Bulletin, 33*(1), 43–56. https://doi.org/10.1177/0146167206294251

McFarland, S., Webb, M., & Brown, D. (2012). All humanity is my ingroup: A measure and studies of identification with all humanity. *Journal of Personality and Social Psychology, 103*(5), 830–853. https://doi.org/10.1037/a0028724

Milgram, S. (1963). Behavioral study of obedience. *The Journal of Abnormal and Social Psychology, 67*(4), 371–378. https://doi.org/10.1037/h0040525

Milgram, S. (1965). Some conditions of obedience and disobedience to authority. *Human Relations, 18*(1), 57–76. https://doi.org/10.1177/001872676501800105

Milgram, S. (1974). *Obedience to authority: An experimental view*. London: Tavistock Publications.

Moscovici, S. (1976). *Social influence and social change*. San Diego, CA: Academic Press.

Moscovici, S. (1980). Toward a theory of conversion behavior. In L. Berkowitz (Ed.), *Advances in experimental social psychology* (Vol. 13, pp. 209–239). San Diego, CA: Academic Press. https://doi.org/10.1016/S0065-2601(08)60133-1

Moscovici, S., Lage, E., & Naffrechoux, M. (1969). Influence of a consistent minority on the responses of a majority in a color perception task. *Sociometry, 32*(4), 365–380. https://doi.org/http://dx.doi.org/10.2307/2786541

Nesdale, D., & Lawson, M. J. (2011). Social groups and children's intergroup attitudes: Can school norms moderate the effects of social group norms? *Child Development, 82*(5), 1594–1606. https://doi.org/10.1111/j.1467-8624.2011.01637.x

Over, H. (2018). The influence of group membership on young children's prosocial behaviour. *Current Opinion in Psychology, 20*, 17–20. https://doi.org/10.1016/j.copsyc.2017.08.005

Perry, G. (2013). *Behind the shock machine: The untold story of the notorious Milgram psychology experiments*. New York: The New Press.

Petty, R. E., & Cacioppo, J. T. (1986). The Elaboration Likelihood Model of persuasion. In L. Berkowitz (Ed.), *Advances in experimental social psychology* (Vol. 19, pp. 123–205). San Diego, CA: Academic Press. https://doi.org/10.1016/S0065-2601(08)60214-2

Prislin, R., & Christensen, P. N. (2002). Group conversion versus group expansion as modes of change in majority and minority positions: All losses hurt but only some gains gratify. *Journal of Personality and Social Psychology, 83*(5), 1095–1102. https://doi.org/10.1037/0022-3514.83.5.1095

Prislin, R., Limbert, W. M., & Bauer, E. (2000). From majority to minority and vice versa: The asymmetrical effects of losing and gaining majority position within a group. *Journal of Personality and Social Psychology, 79*(3), 385–397. https://doi.org/10.1037/0022-3514.79.3.385

Raven, B. H. (1965). Social influence and power. In I. D. Steiner & M. Fishbein (Eds.), *Current studies in social psychology* (pp. 371–382). New York: Holt, Rinehart & Winston.

Reicher, S. D., Haslam, S. A., & Smith, J. R. (2012). Working toward the experimenter: Reconceptualizing obedience within the Milgram paradigm as identification-based followership. *Perspectives on Psychological Science, 7*(4), 315–324. https://doi.org/10.1177/1745691612448482

Rosander, M., & Eriksson, O. (2012). Conformity on the internet – the role of task difficulty and gender differences. *Computers in Human Behavior, 28*(5), 1587–1595. https://doi.org/10.1016/j.chb.2012.03.023

Russell, N. (2014). The emergence of Milgram's bureaucratic machine. *Journal of Social Issues, 70*(3), 409–423. https://doi.org/10.1111/josi.12068

Russell, N. J. C., & Gregory, R. J. (2011). Spinning an organizational 'web of obligation'? Moral choice in Stanley Milgram's 'obedience' experiments. *The American Review of Public Administration, 41*(5), 495–518. https://doi.org/10.1177/0275074010384129

Schultz, P. W., Nolan, J. M., Cialdini, R. B., Goldstein, N. J., & Griskevicius, V. (2007). The constructive, destructive, and reconstructive power of social norms. *Psychological Science, 18*(5), 429–434. https://doi.org/http://dx.doi.org/10.1111/j.1467-9280.2007.01917.x

Sherif, M. (1935). A study of some social factors in perception. *Archives of Psychology, 187*, 60. http://search.ebscohost.com/login.aspx?direct=true&db=psyh&AN=1936-01332-001&site=ehost-live

Steffens, N. K. (2020). Compliance and followership. In J. Jetten, S. D. Reicher, S. A. Haslam, & T. Cruwys (Eds.), *Together apart: The psychology of COVID-19* (pp. 41–45). London: Sage.

Tafani, E., Souchet, L., Codaccioni, C., & Mugny, G. (2003). Influences majoritaire et minoritaire sur la représentation sociale de la drogue. *Nouvelle Revue de Psychologie Sociale, 2*(3), 343–354. https://archive-ouverte.unige.ch/unige:15874

Tajfel, H., & Turner, J. C. (1979). An integrative theory of intergroup conflict. In W. G. Austin & S. Worchel (Eds.), *The social psychology of intergroup relations* (pp. 33–47). San Francisco, CA: Brooks/Cole.

Terry, D. J., Hogg, M. A., & White, K. M. (1999). The theory of planned behaviour: Self-identity, social identity and group norms. *British Journal of Social Psychology, 38*, 225–244. https://doi.org/https://doi.org/10.1348/014466699164149

Turner, J. C. (1991). *Social influence*. Buckingham: Open University Press.

Van Bavel, J. J., Baicker, K., Boggio, P. S., Capraro, V., Cichocka, A., Cikara, M., Crockett, M. J., Crum, A. J., Douglas, K. M., Druckman, J. N., Drury, J., Dube, O., Ellemers, N., Finkel, E. J., Fowler, J. H., Gelfand, M., Han, S., Haslam, S. A., Jetten, J., Kitayama, S., Mobbs, D., Napper, L. E., Packer, D. J., Pennycook, G., Peters, E., Petty, R. E., Rand, D. G., Reicher, S. D., Schnall, S., Shariff, A., Skitka, L. J., Smith, S. S., Sunstein, C. R., Tabri, N., Tucker, J. A., Linden, S. v. d., Lange, P. v., Weeden, K. A., Wohl, M. J. A., Zaki, J., Zion, S. R., & Willer, R. (2020). Using social and behavioural science to support COVID-19 pandemic response. *Nature Human Behaviour, 4*(5), 460–471. https://doi.org/10.1038/s41562-020-0884-z

Wijenayake, S., van Berkel, N., Kostakos, V., & Goncalves, J. (2020). Impact of contextual and personal determinants on online social conformity. *Computers in Human Behavior, 108*, 106302. https://doi.org/10.1016/j.chb.2020.106302

Wood, W., Lundgren, S., Ouellette, J. A., Busceme, S., & Blackstone, T. (1994). Minority influence: A meta-analytic review of social influence processes. *Psychological Bulletin, 115*(3), 323–345. https://doi.org/10.1037/0033-2909.115.3.323

Yuriev, A., Dahmen, M., Paillé, P., Boiral, O., & Guillaumie, L. (2020). Pro-environmental behaviors through the lens of the theory of planned behavior: A scoping review. *Resources, Conservation and Recycling, 155*, 104660. https://doi.org/10.1016/j.resconrec.2019.104660

Zaki, J., & Mitchell, J. P. (2013). Intuitive prosociality. *Current Directions in Psychological Science, 22*(6), 466–470. https://doi.org/10.1177/0963721413492764

8
GROUP PROCESSES
DAVID RAST, III & AMBER GAFFNEY

Contents

8.1 AUTHORS' PERSONAL JOURNEYS

David Rast, III

As a child, I moved around the midwestern and southern United States living in both urban and rural areas. I noticed early in life that people behaved differently depending on where I lived at the time. It was while living in a rural area of Arkansas as a child and teen in the 1990s that I also noticed that certain groups of people lived in enclaves and segregation was present. This piqued my interest, as I could not understand why people with different skin colors were discouraged from living among White people or interacting with White people. People who claimed to be members of the Ku Klux Klan would openly and publicly harass people for no reason beyond skin color. This was confusing, as my previous years were spent in Chicago, where I had not experienced anything like this.

From an early age I began wondering why people acted differently depending on their group memberships, why they spoke differently, and why people would want to include or exclude people based on their group memberships. Since then, I have not stopped thinking about these questions and how to better understand group dynamics to facilitate social change. This led me to pursue an undergraduate honors degree, where I studied social identity and social categorization under the supervision of cultural psychologist Heather Coon. Seeing my passion around social identity, Professor Coon encouraged me to pursue graduate studies with Professor Michael Hogg at Claremont Graduate University in Los Angeles. I completed my Master's and PhD under Professor Hogg's supervision and mentorship. It was during this time that Dr Amber Gaffney and I met as newly minted graduate students in Prof. Hogg's lab. Amber and I have been close friends and collaborators ever since in our never-ending journey to better understand group processes and intergroup relations.

Amber Gaffney

I think that I've always had an interest in niche groups. I grew up in very rural Northern California (off the grid, a 90-minute drive from school, an only child with lots of animals around), and always felt a little different because of how I was raised. Although a science teacher encouraged my love of astronomy, a guidance counselor informed me that physics has a lot of math and girls might not be that good at math (I wish I had had the tools at the time to respond to that comment!). I chose psychology and disliked it until I took stats, methods, social psychology, and the psychology of prejudice. In social psychology, particularly studying social identities, my interest in niche groups made so much sense, and also those outsider feelings surrounding the things that made me feel different made so much sense. I earned a BA in Psychology from California State Polytechnic University, Humboldt (I love Northern CA!) and completed my PhD at Claremont Graduate University, working under Professor Michael Hogg's supervision. True to form, I adopted niche identities, which my supervisor supported – during graduate school I was a professional cyclist. After my post-doc, I had the immense pleasure of coming back home to Humboldt and am now an Associate Professor. I feel fortunate to continuously pursue exciting new science with the goal of contributing to a knowledge base on groups and social change. In this chapter, we cover the basics of groups – their compositions, their formations, and their influence over individuals. Although groups in general are fascinating, some of us have a preference for studying how the 'weird' group members create change.

8.2 INTRODUCTION

Groups are everywhere in our lives. We live and work in groups, we coordinate and perform activities in groups, we socialize in groups, and we are born into certain groups. Groups differ in size, purpose, duration, mode of interaction (face-to-face, computer-mediated), structure, hierarchy, and leadership, just to name a few. Groups largely determine where we live, the language(s) we speak, the attitudes we hold, our cultural practices, our political beliefs, and so on. Groups define who we are and who we are not. In this chapter, we will define a group, then discuss aspects of group behavior (such as productivity, performance, norms, minority influence, and leadership), categories of groups, motives for joining groups, and group structure.

8.3 LEARNING OBJECTIVES

By the end of this chapter, you will be able to:

- Define a group;
- Explain why people join groups;
- Differentiate types of groups;
- Understand individual performance during group tasks;
- Differentiate leadership theories;
- Apply theoretical understanding of group processes to leadership rhetoric, extremism, and ostracism.

8.4 PART 1: FOUNDATIONS

The question 'what is a **group**?' is a deceptively simple question. For example, most people might agree that a sports team is a group, but what about people waiting at a bus stop, strangers in a doctor's office waiting room, individuals walking down the same sidewalk – are these groups as well? Most likely not. Not all clusters of people can be considered groups. These collections of people are better described as aggregates of individuals rather than groups.

Key concept – Group: Three or more individuals who are connected by and within social relationships.

From a social psychology perspective (e.g., Turner et al., 1987), we are interested in groups in terms of the psychological, social, and cognitive representation of the group. However, social psychologists differ in their definitions for a 'group'. Forsyth (2014) identified five characteristics of groups:

1 Collection of two or more individuals who interact with one another (note that our definition requires three or more group's members because group dynamics are more than simply an aggregate of dyadic relationships).
2 Groups have purpose and work towards a shared goal.
3 Members are interdependent on one another and influence each other.
4 Groups are organized, and have structure defining roles, status, and norms.
5 Groups are cohesive in the sense that members are united knowing they share the same group membership.

Forsyth's brief definition of a 'group' is 'two or more individuals who are connected by and within social relationships' (2014, p. 4). Each part of this definition incorporates his five group characteristics. 'Two or more individuals' provides a clear numeric value: small groups contain two or three members; large groups might include all of humanity. 'Who are connected' refers to group members who have social ties with one another, that is, members who interact, communicate, and are mutually dependent on each other. Finally, 'by and within social relationships' describes the idea that group membership is defined by a shared boundary of who is or is not part of the group, and that members are working towards a common goal. Going back to the early questions, people walking down a sidewalk, waiting at a bus stop, or sitting in a doctor's office likely do not meet Forsyth's definition of a group (they lack purpose and interdependence and have no roles, structure, or cohesiveness), whereas a sports team meets all five characteristics. Forsyth's definition, although brief, provides the bare requirements for a group (although Williams' (2010) definition of 'two or more people' likely wins the brevity award).

Whereas this definition provides a foundation to defining groups, we are left with many unanswered questions about groups, for example: Why join groups? Why do group members conform to norms? What is the role of leadership in groups? Moreover, other social psychologists take the position that a group must have three or more members (Hogg, 2006). It is only with three or more members that group processes come into play (e.g., ostracism, leadership, subgroup factions, schism). As a result, in this chapter, we use Hogg's definition: a group must have three or more members. Now that we can define a group, we must consider the different types of groups.

8.4.2 Types of Groups and Categories

There are many different types of groups. One property of groups, consistent with Forsyth's definition, is entitativity. **Entitativity** refers to the multi-dimensional aspects of groups that make them 'groupy' (Campbell, 1958). For instance, high entitativity groups have clear boundaries, defined social structure, shared fate, are highly cohesive, and are more homogeneous; while low entitativity groups have ambiguous boundaries and social structure, are less cohesive, and are more heterogeneous. The more entitative features a group displays, the more they appear to be a unit. Lickel and colleagues (2000) found qualitative differences, resulting in four different types of groups with increasing entitativity: loose collections (e.g., people at a bus stop), social categories (e.g., race, ethnicity), task groups (e.g., sport team members, jury members), and intimacy groups (e.g., family members, close friends). Lickel and colleagues' taxonomy provides a reasonable classification system from which to categorize a wide range of groups.

> **Key concept – Entitativity:** 'An individual's cognitive assessment of a social unit as a "group"' (Blanchard, Caudill, & Walker, 2020).

Another distinction can be made between groups: common-bond groups or common-identity groups (Prentice, Miller, & Lightdale, 1994). **Common-bond groups** refer to groups based on attachment among members, whereas **common-identity groups** refer to groups based on direct attachment to the group itself. A common-bond group, for example, might be a book club or friendship group, where you are more attached to the members, whereas being more attached to a group/organization, such as your political party or university, is consistent with a common-identity group. In common-bond groups, personal goals and interpersonal relationships are more salient and important. In common-identity groups, shared goals and attachment to the group (not other members) are more salient and important. In theory, one could be high or low in either common bond or common identity, but not high in both simultaneously. These group types can impact people's motivation to join or leave a group.

EXERCISE 8.1

Which is More 'Groupy'?

As a brief example of entitativity, take a moment to look at these two photos. Which is more of a group to you?

Source: Fons Heijnsbroek/Unsplash and AMISOM Public Information/Flickr

(Continued)

The picture on the right of the soccer team is more 'groupy' than the people waiting at the train station on the left. Considering the dimensions of entitativity described in this section, which group is more entitative and why?

KEY THINKER

Marilynn Brewer

Marilynn Brewer is Professor Emeritus of Psychology at Ohio State University. She has had a long and distinguished career in which she researched social cognition, self and identity, social identity, and intergroup relations. Her research and theorizing had major impacts across the study of these four areas. For instance, Marilynn's work shaped how researchers conceptualize personal identity, relational identity, and social identity; changed how prejudice is defined as not simply 'ingroup love or outgroup hate'; introduced ideas about social identity complexity; proposed novel motivations as to why people join groups (discussed below); reintroduced entitativity to group processes research; and even challenged the effectiveness of research methods being used (i.e., priming methods), to name a few of her many contributions. Marilynn previously served as President for several scientific societies, including the American Psychological Society and the Society for Personality and Social Psychology. She received numerous awards for her contributions to psychology, such as the Donald T. Campbell Award for Distinguished Research in Social Psychology (Brewer completed her PhD under Campbell) from the Society for Personality and Social Psychology, and the Distinguished Scientific Contribution award from the American Psychological Association. She was also an elected fellow of the American Academy of Arts and Sciences. Marilynn's research on these topics (and others!) will forever shape the study of psychology.

8.4.3 Why do People Join Groups?

Humans are social animals, and as such, we have an inherent need to belong to groups. The study of the social psychology of group behavior has been critical in understanding why people join groups and the effects of group membership on individuals and society as a whole. People join groups for a variety of reasons, including the need for identity, social support, status, interpersonal attraction, social comparison, group norms, common goals, protection, social influence, and psychological needs. These motivations can be broken into two categories: basic need fulfillment (e.g., food, security, reproduction) and the fulfillment of psychological needs. The latter consists of a basic drive for enhancement (we like to feel good about ourselves and our groups can help us to do this) and an epistemic motive wherein groups provide us with a significant amount of information that we can use to feel confident and certain in our worlds and the people around us. Understanding the motivations behind group behavior is important for understanding why individuals join groups and how group membership can influence behavior and attitudes. By understanding the social psychology of group behavior, we can better understand human behavior and social dynamics, and work towards creating more positive and cohesive group environments.

One of the primary reasons people join groups is to establish a sense of identity (see Turner et al., 1987). Group membership provides individuals with a sense of belonging and helps them to define who they are (see Chapter 2 on self and identity). Groups offer a framework for understanding oneself and a way to categorize oneself in relation to others. When people join groups that they feel represent their identity, they experience a sense of validation and self-esteem (Abrams & Hogg, 1988). For example, individuals who join social or political groups may feel a strong sense of identity and purpose from aligning with others who share similar beliefs and values. The part of the self-concept that people derive from important group memberships (Tajfel, 1978), provides people with attitudes, behaviors, and a sense of self based on the normative properties of the group. That is to say, people conform to the group the more strongly they identify with it (Hogg & Reid, 2006). There are thus two primary motives that drive group identification: an epistemic motive, which is fulfilled by the knowledge people gain about themselves by understanding both the features that group members have in common and those that distinguish them as a distinct entity from other groups; and an enhancement motive, which is fulfilled by making favorable comparison between one's own group and other groups. These will become apparent in the many benefits of group membership that we describe below.

> **Key concept – Social identity:** The part of one's self-concept based on one's perceived group membership combined with the emotional significance associated with that group membership (Tajfel & Turner, 1979).

EXERCISE 8.2

Social Identification

Part A. Picture yourself as a member of a group that is really important to you. Write down three things about yourself that make you feel confident and certain. Now, can you relate any of the things you wrote down to your important group? This is an example of a psychological prime. If you wrote down aspects of yourself that are consistent with the group you identified, you likely did so because that group is psychologically salient and you are using it as a reference point for knowledge about the self (self-concept).

(Continued)

Part B. Picture that same important group. Can you picture a group with which your group might compete? How do you feel if your group loses status or resources to that group? This is an example of how we use groups as a source of esteem, but sometimes, other groups can threaten our ability to feel favorably about our own group!

Groups also offer social support, which can be critical to an individual's well-being (see Chapter 3 on affiliation, friendship, and love; see also, Haslam et al., 2021). Social support can come in different forms, such as emotional support, informational support, and tangible support. Group members can provide each other with emotional support by offering sympathy, understanding, and empathy. Informational support may involve sharing information and advice on various topics, such as parenting, health, or work. Tangible support may include providing practical assistance, such as transportation or childcare. The social support that groups offer can help individuals cope with stress and other challenges in their lives.

Table 8.1   Examples of groups that have clear prosocial outcomes

Group type/identity	Outcome	Researcher(s)
Exercise Groups	Identification with an exercise group positively predicts self-efficacy in exercise, which in turn positively predicts exercise behaviors.	Grant, Hogg, & Crano (2005)
Exercise Specific Identity (e.g., 'crossfitter, cyclist, runner')	Having an exercise specific identity positively predicts self-efficacy with physical activity and frequency of exercise behaviors.	Brouwer (2017)
Study Groups	First year university students randomly assigned to feel uncertain, identified with an entitative 'study' or 'party' group – this shows the power of providing entitative positive groups!	Cruwys, Gaffney, & Skipper (2017)
Autistic Identity	Strength of identification as autistic positively predicts self-esteem and negatively predicts anxiety and depression amongst people with autism	Cooper, Smith, & Russell (2017)
Recovery Groups	Groups that replace 'addict identity' (e.g., 'user') with the recovery group identity (e.g., 'former user') have favorable cessation outcomes.	Buckingham (2017)

Group type/identity	Outcome	Researcher(s)
Recovery Groups	Membership in at least one recovery group positively predicts cessation and negatively predicts relapse.	Best et al. (2016)
Groups 4 Health	Increasing neighborhood identification lessens loneliness and increases social cohesion in disadvantaged communities.	Cruwys et al. (2022)

There is also an additive effect for multiple groups: there is a positive relationship between the number of groups to which one belongs and engaging in healthy behavior (Sani et al., 2015a) and reduced likelihood of depression (Sani et al., 2015b).

EXERCISE 8.3

Social Cure versus Social Curse

The positive effects of group membership on health and well-being, referred to as the 'social cure', are well documented (e.g., Wakefield et al., 2019). However, group membership can also be a 'social curse' (Kellezi & Reicher, 2012). Kellezi and Reicher argue that groups can be a burden, resulting in greater humiliation, stress, dehumanization, and shame. Groups may also possess oppressive leaders or political groups who maim, kill, and start wars against other groups. Take a moment to list three groups that have a positive impact on your day-to-day life or activities, and then list three groups that have a negative impact on your day-to-day life or activities. Write one sentence about why you joined each of these groups. Note how difficult it would be to leave both the negative and positive groups you belong to.

Group membership offers a sense of social status. Being a member of a particular group can confer prestige, power, and influence. People often seek out groups that they per-

Video: 'Groups4Health' www.you tube.com/watch?v=5kEAVcR2I50

ceive as having high status, such as elite academic institutions, exclusive clubs, or prestigious professional organizations. Nobel Prize-winning economist George Akerlof went so far as to argue that choosing which groups one joins 'may be the most important "economic" decision people make' (Akerlof & Kranton, 2000, p. 717). For instance, the university or college we attend may have a tremendous impact on how others perceive us or how we perceive ourselves, or on how much money we earn over a lifetime, or it may open or close doors to join other groups, etc. The status associated with group membership can increase an individual's self-esteem and sense of identity.

People may join groups because of interpersonal attraction (Hogg & Turner, 1985). This refers to the attraction that individuals feel towards others within the group. Interpersonal attraction can be influenced by various factors, such as physical appearance, similarity, and shared experiences. People are attracted to others who share their interests, values, and beliefs, which can lead to the formation of close friendships and social bonds (Byrne, 1971). The sense of belonging and connection that interpersonal attraction creates can be a powerful motivator for group membership.

KEY THINKER

Michael Hogg

Source: Michael Hogg

Mike is a Professor of Social Psychology and Director of the Social Identity Lab at Claremont Graduate University in Los Angeles. He was born in Calcutta, India, to British parents who worked in India. His family moved to Sri Lanka when he was two years old and eventually returned to England when he was about 14 years old. Mike attended the University of Birmingham for his undergraduate studies. He started as a physics major, but found it dull. Instead, he found himself interested in student protests and the social issues of the day. He switched majors to psychology, with an emphasis on social psychology. After completing his undergraduate degree in psychology in 1977, Mike spent a year traveling around central and south America. He returned to England to start his doctoral studies at Bristol University under the supervision of John Turner. At the time, Bristol University's Psychology Department was a powerhouse in social psychology, with faculty members such as John Turner, Henri Tajfel, Howard Giles, and many other very influential researchers. When starting at Bristol, Mike was part of Turner's first batch of PhD students, which is perhaps one of the most highly regarded social psychology PhD student cohorts ever. All of them went on to enormously successful careers, helping to develop self-categorization as part of their PhD dissertations (see Turner et al., 1987).

After Tajfel's untimely death, the faculty and PhD students (who graduated or were soon to graduate) at Bristol University Psychology Department slowly left. Mike remained at Bristol for three more years as an assistant professor, where he 'inherited' Tajfel's courses and Giles' office, and was soon joined by Dominic (Dom) Abrams. This led to the start of a lifelong collaboration with Dom, resulting in numerous articles, chapters, and books, as well as the founding of *Group Processes & Intergroup Relations*, the journal of a social psychology sub-discipline developed solely to publish research on group processes and intergroup relations.

In 1985, Mike moved to Australia, where he spent the next 21 years at Macquarie University, the University of Melbourne, but mainly at the University of Queensland.

In 2006, Mike relocated to Claremont Graduate University in Los Angeles, where he remains today. Due to his movements from Europe to Australia to the United States, along with his visiting and sabbatical appointments (e.g., Princeton University, University of California at Santa Barbara, University of Kent, Sapienza Università di Roma), where he trained dozens of students, Mike is widely credited with helping the social identity framework become the meta-theoretical approach it is today.

Mike's research on intergroup relations, group processes, influence and leadership, and self and identity is associated with the development of social identity theory, and has been widely published. As well as being founding Editor-in-Chief, with Dominic Abrams, of the journal *Group Processes & Intergroup Relations*, he is an Associate Editor of *The Leadership Quarterly*, and a former Associate Editor of the *Journal of Experimental Social Psychology*. He is an Honorary Professor at the University of Kent, a former Australian Research Council Professorial Fellow, and a past President of the Society of Experimental Social Psychology. He is a Fellow of the British Academy and a Fellow of the Academy of the Social Sciences in Australia, and the recipient of numerous distinguished achievement awards. He is a Fellow of the Association for Psychological Science, the Society for Personality and Social Psychology, the Society of Experimental Social Psychology, and the Society for the Psychological Study of Social Issues. He has been presented with eight 'best paper' awards (although the 'best' of those is obviously the one awarded to Rast, Hogg, and Gaffney!).

Joining a group can provide individuals with a way to make **social comparisons**. Social comparison is the process by which people evaluate their own abilities, opinions, and behavior in relation to others. By being part of a group, individuals can compare themselves to other members and gain a

> **Key concept – Social comparison:** Individuals determine their self- and social worth, and also their abilities to navigate their social worlds, by assessing their thoughts, attitudes, behaviors, abilities, and beliefs relative to other people.

sense of their own social standing. These types of social comparison allow group members to increase self-esteem, by comparing themselves to less skilled or less favored ingroup members or less favorable outgroups. This is particularly true when individuals feel a need to improve their own status or feel a sense of competition (e.g., Smith & Leach, 2004).

Social comparisons also help to fulfill the epistemic motive for group identification. Being similar to others allows people to understand their own abilities and opinions (Festinger, 1954), and comparing themselves with other group members, particularly those who are normative of the group, along with comparing the ingroup to an outgroup, provides people with necessary information about themselves in a social context (see Chapter 7 on social influence). Context is key and social comparison provides people with context. If a student earns a 'B' grade on a chemistry exam, they will want to know what a 'B' grade means in that class. To adequately assess their ability in the class, they wouldn't turn to the teaching assistant or the professor as a source of comparison, they would turn to other students. In this case, other students (similar others) provide context for how to interpret their ability in the chemistry class.

Groups often have established norms and values that members are expected to follow. Joining a group can provide individuals with a sense of structure and order, which can be reassuring. Group norms and values can help individuals feel like they belong and provide a sense of shared purpose. The shared beliefs and values that groups offer can provide individuals with a sense of meaning and identity, which provides them with confidence in their understanding of the world around them (see Chapter 2 on self and identity).

Group membership can be motivated by a shared sense of purpose or a common goal (Ellemers, de Gilder, & Haslam, 2004). Individuals may join groups to work together to achieve a particular objective, such as a political campaign, a community project, or a sports team. The shared sense of purpose can provide a sense of epistemic meaning and fulfillment. Moreover, the goal of such action is often to enhance the group's relative status. This is the case with political campaigns (let's get our candidate or party elected!) and sports teams (let's take the title this year!). Working towards a common goal with others can also foster a sense of cooperation and teamwork. This shared sense of purpose can also result in greater conformity to the group's norms and values. Indeed, the impact of the presence of others around us, whether real or imagined, can have a significant impact on our behavior, opinions, attitudes, and even our individual performance on different tasks or activities.

8.4.4 Social Inhibition and Social Facilitation

EXERCISE 8.4

Personal Application

Imagine a time when you performed a *routine* task on your own without anybody else around. How did you perform on this task? Did you complete the task faster than usual or more slowly? Was your heart rate higher or lower than normal? Did you feel anxious, nervous, or excited?

Now imagine a recent time when you performed a brand *new* activity while surrounded by others. What were your experiences while performing this task?

You probably performed better while completing the first routine task alone than the second novel task surrounded by others. You more than likely experienced increased heart rate and sweating, and also felt anxious and nervous in the latter task, but not in the former one. These are examples of social inhibition and social facilitation, which has been long studied in social psychology.

Perhaps one of the oldest questions in social psychology is why people's performance is impacted by the presence of others. That is, do you perform better or worse on a task in the presence of others? In 1898, Norman Triplett set out to answer this question in what many believe was the first social psychology experiment (see Key study 8.1). His finding was that an individual's performance can indeed be affected by the presence of others.

KEY STUDY 8.1

The First Social Psychology Experiment

In the late 19th century, Norman Triplett observed that a cyclist's time trial performance was better when he was cycling against another competitor than when he was cycling alone. In what many believe is the first social psychology experiment, he set out to examine why this might be (Triplett, 1898).

Figure 8.1   A peloton of cyclists
Source: Markus Spiske/Unsplash

   To study this idea in a lab context, he recruited 40 children aged 9–15 years old to participate in a study where they reeled in a fishing line alone or in pairs. Participants would enter the experiment area where two fishing reels were positioned. To complete the task, participants had to reel the fishing line in 150 complete rotations. Participants first reeled in the line alone in a practice trial, then they completed five more trials alternating between doing the task alone and competing against another person. Triplett found that children reeled in the f ishing line quicker when competing in pairs compared to doing it alone. This led Triplett to conclude that competing against another person or multiple people improves task performance.

Figure 8.2   A single cyclist

Source: Coen van de Broek/Unsplash

Key concept – Social facilitation: An increased level of individual effort or performance due to the real, imagined, or implied presence of others.

In 1924, Floyd Allport expanded on Triplett's observations, going beyond competition effects to arguing that the mere presence of others, real or imagined, could improve task performance. He coined the term **social facilitation**, which refers to the tendency for people to display improved performance due to the mere presence of others.

Social facilitation was one of the most heavily researched phenomena in the earlier days of social psychology. Not only did this research produce interesting results with humans (e.g., eating more, running faster), it also showed that social facilitation occurs in other species as well: cockroaches run faster, chickens eat more. But this research revealed a problematic result as well: sometimes performance diminishes in the presence of others – what is called **social inhibition**.

Key concept – Social inhibition: A decreased level of individual effort or performance due to the real, imagined, or implied presence of others.

When looking through the research, it became clear that task type was influencing the results on social facilitation and inhibition. Task performance improved for people who completed simple tasks in the presence of others, while performance worsened for those who completed complex tasks in the presence of others (see Harkins, 1987). Most of us can probably easily identify times when either of these outcomes has occurred. However, extant theory could not explain why the presence of others could produce two opposing effects due to task type. This resulted in three dominant perspectives to explain these effects: drive theory, evaluation apprehension, and distraction-conflict theory.

Zajonc (1965) published his classic paper on drive theory, in which he argued that physiological arousal determines whether the presence of others facilitates or inhibits performance. Drive theory has two basic propositions. First, people are physiologically aroused by the presence of others, whether it is real or imagined. From an evolutionary perspective, he argues that the presence of others produces an instinctual reaction (arousal) because the other people could be a threat to survival or a possible mate. Second, this physiological arousal improves performance for a dominant response (e.g., a well-practiced or easy task) but impairs performance on a non-dominant response (e.g., a complex or difficult task). Zajonc referred to these as correct dominant responses (easy task) or incorrect dominant responses (difficult task). Therefore, whether social facilitation or inhibition occurs is dependent on whether the correct or incorrect dominant response results from the physiological arousal. Thus, the match between correct/incorrect response and task type determines social facilitation or inhibition.

Let's look at a student example to see how a correct versus incorrect dominant response and physiological arousal can impact performance. Imagine a student has an important exam coming up in a week's time, and they feel anxious because they haven't studied much yet. According to drive theory, the correct dominant response would be when the student recognizes their internal drive to perform well in the exam and takes action to reduce the anxiety and meet the need for preparation. They create a study plan, organize their study materials, and allocate dedicated time each day to study for the exam. As they progress through the study plan, they feel more confident and less anxious, reaching a state of equilibrium as they feel better prepared for the upcoming exam. For an incorrect dominant response, instead of acknowledging the anxiety and the need to study, the student chooses to ignore their feelings and avoids studying altogether. They may engage in distractions, such as spending excessive time on social media, playing video games, or hanging out with friends. As a result, the student's anxiety may worsen, and they risk not being adequately prepared for the exam, which can lead to poor performance and increased stress. In this example, the correct dominant response involves recognizing the internal drive to perform well in the exam and taking action to meet the need for preparation. By addressing the drive through effective studying, the student reduces anxiety and increases their likelihood of better academic performance. Conversely, the drive theory dominant incorrect response involves neglecting the internal drive and avoiding preparation, leading to increased anxiety and potentially negative consequences in the form of poorer academic performance.

It is important to note that task difficulty is subjective. Although giving a lecture or a research talk is 'easy' for those of us who have completed this task in front of audiences for years, it is difficult for those who are new to public speaking. Moreover, take the example of one of the authors of this chapter. She took a guitar class as an undergraduate student. She practiced her final piece in her room by herself. She knew it inside out. When the time came to perform her final song in front of the instructor, she froze. Because she had not developed a dominant response conducive to playing guitar in front of an audience – she had never done this before – her dominant response was to freeze.

Although research largely supports drive theory (Geen & Gange, 1977), some have questioned whether the presence of others automatically elicits physiological arousal. Instead, others have argued that evaluation apprehension (Cottrell, 1972) is what causes physiological arousal (rather than instincts). Evaluation apprehension is the concern that one is being judged by others. That is, in the presence of others, we are concerned that the social rewards or punishments (e.g., peer approval versus rejection) are based on the judgments others make of us and our performance. Thus, we are apprehensive about the possible negative evaluation we might receive from others. For example, my pre-teen daughter is very concerned about being positively or negatively evaluated by her peers. Sometimes she strives to perform a novel task at a ridiculously high standard so that she is accepted by her peers, or so that they think positively about her. At other times, she purposefully performs a well-practiced task poorly, also to be accepted or perceived more favorably by her peers.

Research has generally supported the evaluation apprehension approach. For example, Cottrell and colleagues (1968) asked participants to pronounce nonsense words aloud (a simple task) while alone, in front of a two-person blindfolded audience, or in front of a two-person non-blindfolded audience. According to drive theory, the blindfolded and non-blindfolded audience would produce physiological arousal and performance would be similarly facilitated in both conditions. However, according to Cottrell and colleagues (1968), the blindfolded audience is merely present but inattentive to the participant's performance, while the non-blindfolded audience is present and attentive to the participant's performance. The results showed participants' performance to be socially inhibited when alone or performing in front of a blindfolded audience, but was facilitated when in front of a non-blindfolded audience. Said differently, participants pronounced more nonsense words correctly in front of a non-blindfolded audience than those who performed the task alone or in front of a blindfolded audience. This supports the evaluation apprehension hypothesis but not the drive theory hypothesis. Although this research contradicts drive theory, it has a major limitation: it cannot readily explain why cockroaches complete mazes faster when another cockroach is present or why chickens peck or eat more when around other chickens. Presumably these animals and insects are not worried about being evaluated by other members of their species.

The third explanation for social facilitation and inhibition is distraction-conflict theory (Baron, 1986), which attempts to explain social inhibition and facilitation in humans and non-humans. According to the distraction-conflict theory, people in our social environment can distract us. The presence of others produces attentional conflict between attending to the task at hand or the person/people present. The presence of others causes a distraction and impairs performance on complex tasks. However, the cognitive conflict of trying to attend to other people causes arousal, resulting in increased performance on easy or well-learned tasks. The distraction-conflict explanation extends beyond other people, as the distraction can be any stimulus in our environment.

At this point, we might conclude that distraction-conflict, evaluation apprehension, or drive theory each fail in explaining social facilitation or inhibition. However, these three explanations are not mutually exclusive and each has merit in explaining these effects. All these ideas seem to impact social facilitation and inhibition. Indeed, this notion is supported by a meta-analysis conducted by Bond and Titus (1983), which included over 24,000 participants across more than 240 social facilitation and inhibition experiments. They found that the mere presence of other people does increase physiological arousal and it does improve performance on easy tasks, while worsening performance on complex tasks. However, the mere presence of others only accounted for 0.3% to 3% of variance in human behavior across the 240+ experiments. That means there are still many possible reasons for improved or worsened performance while around others. And this indicates that there is more going on beyond these three explanations. It seems reasonable that moving from individuals and dyads to actual groups can help explain these processes. For instance, group performance is not just about one person's performance while in or around other people. Performance might be impacted by one's desire to be a part of the group, to avoid being ostracized or rejected by the group, or it might be impacted by the perceived behaviors or thoughts of other group members, and so on. Groups and their performance are also impacted by their leaders.

Determinants of Social Facilitation versus Social Inhibition

Numerous meta-analyses have been conducted examining the impact of different variables on whether social facilitation, social inhibition, or neither will occur (e.g., Bond & Titus,

1983; Karau & Williams, 1993). Below is a list of eight empirically supported factors for when social facilitation or social inhibition are likely to occur:

1 **Task complexity**: The complexity of the task being performed can influence whether social facilitation or inhibition occurs. Simple or well-practiced tasks tend to be facilitated, while complex or novel tasks may lead to inhibition.

2 **Audience familiarity**: Familiarity with the audience or co-actors can influence social facilitation and inhibition. People may be more comfortable performing in front of familiar individuals, which can lead to facilitation, while unfamiliar audiences may lead to inhibition.

3 **Evaluation apprehension**: The fear of being judged or evaluated by others can impact social facilitation and inhibition. When individuals are concerned about their performance being scrutinized, they may experience inhibition.

4 **Task type**: The nature of the task is important. Tasks that are individual and not easily influenced by others may not show strong social facilitation or inhibition effects compared to tasks that involve direct competition or cooperation.

5 **Skill level**: The skill level of the individual can be a moderator. For highly skilled individuals, the presence of others may enhance performance (facilitation), but for less skilled individuals, it may lead to decreased performance (inhibition).

6 **Personality traits**: Certain personality traits can influence social facilitation and inhibition. For example, extroverted individuals may thrive in the presence of others (facilitation), while introverted individuals may feel more inhibited.

7 **Group size**: The size of the group can impact social facilitation and inhibition. Larger groups may elicit stronger effects due to increased evaluation apprehension and social influence.

8 **Cultural factors**: Cultural norms and expectations regarding social behavior can play a role in social facilitation and inhibition effects.

A Special Case of Social Inhibition: Social Loafing

There are several phenomena outlined by psychologists that fall under the umbrella of social inhibition. For example, the bystander effect or bystander apathy, which is outlined in Chapter 10, is a special case of social inhibition in which the presence of others inhibits helping behavior. But in this section we will discuss **social loafing**, or the tendency to do less when the person is part of a team, which is is a special case of social inhibition.

> **Key concept – Social loafing:** The tendency for an individual to put in less effort when they are part of a team than when alone. That is, being a part of a team effort inhibits output or performance.

We've all been members of a team where we feel that someone isn't pulling their weight. Routinely, students complain to us that their teammates on a group project are not doing their share of the work. Here we need to stop to reflect. When have you 'social loafed' and why? One of the authors of this chapter (her initials are AMG) has to admit to herself that she sometimes socially loafed on committee assignments if the outcome lacks meaning and her input into the committee assignment also lacks meaning. Alas, we all do this. Why?

1 **Output equity**: We seek to protect our output effort. If we feel that other people are not doing enough, we do less so that we do not feel that they are taking advantage of this (Jackson & Harkins, 1985). However, if everyone does this, we get *pluralistic ignorance*.

2 **Evaluation apprehension**: Have you ever been the new person on a team or felt that you didn't have the skills or the knowledge to contribute to the team? If this is the case, you may have worked less hard because you did not want your teammates to negatively evaluate you (Harkins, 1987).

3 **Matching to the standard – no clear performance standard**: If we do not know what the standard for excellence is, we cannot achieve it. There needs to be a personal or collective goal clearly outlined. Without it, the task can seem meaningless, and from what we've seen from the author's anecdote above, this can produce social loafing (Harkins & Szymanski, 1987)!

There are a variety of factors that either increase or decrease social loafing. Said differently, there are a variety of factors that may increase or decrease individual effort or performance on team tasks. These are the things that impact whether or not people socially loaf or socially compensate, which is when a person increases their performance on behalf of the team (Zaccaro, 1984). They are listed in Table 8.2.

Table 8.2 Factors that either increase or decrease social loafing

Moderator	Personal output/effort
High individual accountability	+. If we know that our output is being monitored, we tend to increase effort.
Anonymity	−. Opposite from the previous, when our output/effort is anonymous, we decrease effort.
Perceived dispensable effort	−. If we feel that our own effort is not meaningful to the overall task, we decrease effort.
High domain importance	+. If the domain is important to us, we work hard, above and beyond those other factors.
High group identification	+. If we identify strongly with the team, we work hard for the team, thus our individual effort is high.

Social psychologists have demonstrated social loafing effects across numerous domains, both in laboratory experiments and in the field. The findings show that people clap less, cheer less hard, exert less effort in a tug-of-war, generate fewer ideas in brainstorming, perform worse in mazes, and tip less (in the US) when in the presence of others who are ostensibly working collectively, than when they are alone. Tipping is part of American culture, and in most states, people tip a minimum of 20% of the bill. Freeman and colleagues (1975) found that about 20% of people give tips when sitting alone, but 13% of people give tips when seated with five or six other people. Tipping is, in part, driven by group norms as well.

8.4.5 Group Norms

Group norms are shared expectations and guidelines for behavior that develop within a group (for extensive discussion of norms, see Chapter 7 on social influence). Norms can be explicit or implicit and develop over time through interaction among and communication between group members. Explicit norms are rules or guidelines for behavior within the group that are often written down (e.g., formal rules or policies), while implicit norms are unspoken expectations for behavior that are conveyed through social cues and interactions. An example of an implicit norm would be walking through a doorway. It would be strange to walk through a doorway backward when entering a room, or to see someone else do it. We walk forward through doorways when entering buildings or rooms. Norms can be shaped by a range of factors, such as culture, gender, age, and ethnicity.

Group norms can have a significant impact on individual behavior, attitudes, and beliefs. Individuals are often motivated to conform to group norms to maintain social harmony and to avoid social rejection (Asch, 1956; Packer, 2008). Norms can also provide a sense of identity and belonging, which can be motivating factors for individuals to conform. However, conformity to group norms can also lead to negative consequences such as **groupthink**, in which group members prioritize group consensus over individual critical thinking (Janis, 1972).

> **Key concept – Group norm:** Shared pattern of thoughts, feelings, and behaviors within groups that inform how people communicate, interact, and behave.

> **Key concept – Groupthink:** A dysfunctional group decision-making process whereby a group polarizes to an extreme position to reach a consensus without fully considering the consequences.

Groups are more susceptible to groupthink when they are very cohesive, lack diversity, conduct inadequate searches for relevant information, operate in conditions of high stress or uncertainty, and have directive leadership (Turner & Pratkanis, 1998). Groupthink has been used to explain countless decisions resulting in fiascos such as the Bay of Pigs, Watergate, the *Columbia* and *Challenger* space shuttle explosions, the 2003 US invasion of Iraq, and so on. Janis (1982) provided nine recommendations to avoid groupthink:

1   Assign a 'devil's advocate' who challenges all positions to the group.
2   Leaders should refrain from putting their own position forward to foster a more open dialogue.
3   Bring in outside experts to get their opinions.
4   Split the group into smaller subgroups to work on different solutions to the same problem.

5   There should be a norm allowing group members to be critical and challenge ideas.
6   Group members should discuss the group's ideas with people outside the group to get different and impartial perspectives.
7   Allow group members to provide anonymous comments and opinions.
8   Assign group members to specific roles within the group.
9   Leaders should hold a 'second chance' meeting before any decision is made so that group members can cast any remaining doubts.

Even when all nine of these recommendations are met, groupthink can still occur as people can still ignore the warnings signals prior to rendering poor decisions (e.g., Oceangate's *Titan* submarine implosion in 2023).

Deviance from group norms can lead to social sanctions such as ridicule, ostracism, or exclusion from the group (see section 8.5.2 on social control). However, deviance can also have positive consequences, such as the introduction of new ideas or the challenging of groupthink. In some cases, deviance can lead to the development of new norms within the group (see the discussion on minority influence in Chapter 7). The response to deviance may depend on the severity of the deviation and the attitudes of other group members. Leaders seem to be granted an exception to deviate from the group's norm to change the group, bring about innovation and creativity, and so forth (Abrams et al., 2018).

8.4.6 Leadership

> **Key concept – Leadership:** 'A process of social influence through which an individual enlists and mobilizes the aid of others in attainment of a collective goal' (Chemers, 2001, p. 376).

Leadership is fundamentally a group process. Without followers, there cannot be leaders; and wherever there are followers, there are leaders. Leaders are agents of influence who motivate social change, provide a distinct vision for the group, coordinate a group's efforts, define group norms, and promote a distinctive group identity. Leaders serve this purpose in groups big and small, homogeneous and diverse.

Because leadership is such a broad topic, there is no universally accepted definition; however, it is generally accepted that social influence is a core component of leadership. An inclusive definition of leadership is provided by Chemers (2001, p. 376): 'A process of social influence through which an individual enlists and mobilizes the aid of others in attainment of a collective goal.' Many of these definitions are closely related to a specific leadership approach or theory. Leadership approaches can be categorized into individual differences and personality theories (e.g., The Great Person approach), situational leadership models (e.g., contingency theory), relationship-based leadership models (e.g., leader–member exchange theory (LMX), transformational leadership), and group-based models (e.g., social identity theory of leadership, intergroup leadership theory).

EXERCISE 8.5

What is a Leader?

Defining leadership is a difficult task. There are countless definitions of leadership. It seems as though leadership is a concept fitting United States Supreme Court Justice Potter Stewart's famous 1964 quote: 'I know it when I see it.'

Take out a sheet of paper or open a note-taking application and spend 3–5 minutes thinking about and identifying the people who best personify effective leadership to you. After completing that list, think about and write down the qualities, traits, characteristics, etc., that make those individuals personify effective leadership. Maybe it's their appearance, intelligence, education, work experience. There are no wrong answers. Next, go through the list of qualities, traits, etc., and remove any that are not absolutely required to be an effective leader. You have completed the task once you believe the list contains only the barest of essential aspects for effective leadership.

This activity is continued at the end of this section.

Leader Personality and Behavior

The leader personality approach to leadership suggests that certain personality traits are associated with effective leadership. The idea for this approach is that leaders are born, not made. Certain people are born with traits and characteristics that make them predisposed to be leaders, while others are not. The earliest studies in this area, such as the 'Great Man' theory (gendered language is intended as the theory is a product of its time), focused on identifying traits that were believed to be inherent in effective leaders but without any guiding framework. It resulted in different research groups coming up with lots of lists of very different traits (Northouse, 2021). Later research refined the approach, particularly around the Big Five personality traits, identifying a range of personality traits associated with effective leadership, such as extraversion, conscientiousness, emotional intelligence, and openness to experience (Judge et al., 2002).

Critics of the leader personality approach argue that it oversimplifies the complex nature of leadership and ignores the impact of situational factors. They argue that personality traits may be less important in some contexts and that effective leadership may require different traits or behaviors depending on the situation. For example, a leader who is charismatic and confident may be effective in a crisis situation, but may not be as effective in a team-oriented environment where collaboration and empathy are valued.

The leader behavior approach to leadership emphasizes the importance of the behaviors and actions that leaders exhibit. This approach suggests that effective leaders engage in certain behaviors, such as providing feedback, setting clear goals, and demonstrating empathy, that enable them to motivate and inspire their followers. The behavioral approach also acknowledges the impact of situational factors, as effective leadership behaviors may vary depending on the context in which they are employed.

Some leadership scholars argue that both leader personality and leader behavior are important factors in determining leadership effectiveness. The trait approach suggests that certain personality traits are necessary but not sufficient for effective leadership, and that leadership skills and behaviors must also be developed and practiced. The behavioral approach, meanwhile, acknowledges the importance of personality traits in shaping leadership behavior, but also emphasizes the importance of situational factors in determining which behaviors are most effective in each context.

Effective leadership is a complex and multifaceted phenomenon that cannot be reduced to any single factor. While leader personality and leader behavior are both important components of effective leadership, it is essential to understand the interplay between personality traits, leadership behaviors, and situational factors to gain a more nuanced understanding of what it takes to be an effective leader in a variety of contexts. Indeed, a seminal meta-analysis by Judge and colleagues (2002) indicates modest relationships between personality traits and leader effectiveness. Thus, it emphasizes the importance of the context and the group in leadership.

Situational/Contingency Leadership Approaches

To address issues associated with the 'Great Man' theory, namely that leadership is innate but can be trained, leadership scholars created contingency approaches. These approaches generally incorporated what was learned from the 'Great Man' approaches but add the context as a variable to explain when different traits, skills, or behaviors are more effective for leaders. There are two dominant approaches in this area: contingency theory and path–goal theory.

Contingency theory (Fiedler, 1967) proposes that the effectiveness of a leader depends on the situation in which they find themselves. This theory suggests that there is not one leadership style that is universally effective. Instead, leaders must adjust their style to fit the situation they are in. The theory proposes two leadership styles: task-oriented and relationship-oriented. Task-oriented leaders focus on getting the job done, while relationship-oriented leaders focus on building strong relationships with their followers. Contingency theory is useful for managers who want to identify which leadership style is most effective in a situation. Contingency theory is generally supported empirically (Schriesheim et al., 1994); however, it is difficult to implement in practice.

One other major contingency-based leadership approach model was developed with better empirical support and ease of implementation in mind. Path–goal theory (House, 1971) is a leadership theory that proposes that the effectiveness of a leader depends on the extent to which the leader is able to clarify the path that followers must take to achieve their goals. The key proposition is that leaders must provide guidance and support to their followers to help them achieve their goals. The theory proposes four leadership styles: directive, supportive, participative, and achievement-oriented. For instance, if a leader must clarify goals and a task is novel, then directive leadership ought to be effective. But if a task is boring, then supportive leadership ought to be effective. Unfortunately, there is mixed empirical support for path–goal theory (Schriesheim & Neider, 1996).

These theories suggest that there is no one-size-fits-all approach to leadership. That is, there is not one leadership style that is universally effective, and leaders must adjust their style to fit the situation they are in. However, these approaches tend to be overly simplistic and difficult to implement. The trait approach and contingency approaches produced the groundwork for other leadership theories, such as charismatic leadership, which focuses on an interaction between the leader and the social environment to determine when a leader will be more or less effective. Extending from trait and contingency approaches, relationship-based leadership theories focus primarily on the interplay between the leader and the social context.

Relationship-based Leadership

There are three major relationship-based leadership models: leader–member exchange theory, transformational leadership, and charismatic leadership. Each of these models presents leadership as a psychological or social process between a follower and a leader. Leader–member exchange theory (LMX) (Graen & Uhl-Bien, 1995) is based on the premise that leaders develop different relationships with each of their followers, depending on their level of performance, commitment, and trustworthiness. Leaders form high-quality exchanges with their 'ingroup' members, who are those followers with whom they have strong and positive relationships. These members receive more support, communication, and opportunities for advancement than those in the 'outgroup,' who have weaker and more formal relationships with the leader. One of the key benefits of LMX theory is that it recognizes the importance of individualized support and feedback. By building positive relationships with their followers, leaders can better understand their strengths and weaknesses, provide tailored support, and motivate them to perform at their best. Additionally, LMX theory suggests that leaders should focus on developing high-quality exchanges with all their followers, not just a select few. This approach can improve overall job satisfaction, performance, and retention rates, according to meta-analytic evidence (Gerstner & Day, 1997).

Transformational leadership (Bass, 1985; Burns, 1978) is a leadership style that emphasizes inspiring and motivating followers to achieve their full potential. Transformational leaders use a variety of techniques, such as providing a clear vision, setting high standards, and offering individualized support, to create a positive and empowering work environment. They encourage creativity, innovation, and collaboration, and foster a sense of shared purpose and identity among their followers. Transformational leadership can improve employee motivation and commitment. By providing a clear vision and setting high standards, leaders can inspire their followers to take ownership of their work and strive for excellence. Transformational leaders often focus on the growth and development of their followers, which can lead to increased job satisfaction and career advancement opportunities. Gandhi and Martin Luther King Jr. are prime examples of transformational leaders.

Charismatic leadership (Conger & Kanungo, 1998; House, Spangler, & Woycke, 1991) relies on the personal charisma and charm of the leader to inspire and motivate followers. Charismatic leaders possess strong communication skills, a compelling vision, and a willingness to take risks. They are seen as exceptional individuals with extraordinary abilities, who are capable of inspiring and influencing others to achieve their goals. Highly charismatic leaders can create a sense of excitement and enthusiasm among followers. Charismatic leaders can inspire their followers to work towards a shared vision and achieve goals that they may have thought were unattainable (Fiske & Dépret, 1996). However, charismatic leadership can also have drawbacks, such as the potential for the leader to become overly focused on their own goals and ignore the needs and perspectives of their followers (Meindl, Ehrlich, & Dukerich, 1985). Leaders such as Barack Obama, Jack Welch, Steve Jobs, and even Donald Trump are considered charismatic.

Leader–member exchange theory, transformational leadership, and charismatic leadership are three important theories of leadership that highlight the importance of building positive relationships between leaders and followers. Each theory emphasizes different aspects of leadership, such as the importance of individualized support, the ability to inspire and motivate, and the power of personal charisma. By understanding these theories, leaders can develop the skills and strategies necessary to build positive relationships with their followers and create a positive and empowering work environment. However, these approaches still over-emphasize the individual leader while under-emphasizing followers.

Group-based Leadership

Although leadership is conceptualized as a group process consisting of leaders and followers, few leadership theories emphasize the group aspect of leadership. The two dominant perspectives in this area are the social identity theory of leadership (intragroup) and intergroup leadership theory (intergroup).

The social identity theory of leadership (Hogg, 2001; Hogg, van Knippenberg, & Rast, 2012a) posits that as group membership becomes more salient to one's self-concept, then leader effectiveness depends on whether the leader is perceived as being prototypical of the group (i.e., representative of the group). Prototypical group leaders are perceived as an embodiment of the group's attributes and features. Group members conform more to highly prototypical leaders, like them more, rate them as more trustworthy, evaluate them more positively, perceive them as being more charismatic, and so forth. From this perspective, leaders and followers share the same social identity, where leaders are seen as 'one of us'. The social identity approach to leadership has received robust empirical support (e.g., Barreto & Hogg, 2017; Steffens et al., 2021). However, this model of leadership only applies to an intragroup leadership context, where a leader is providing leadership to one group (e.g., Donald Trump providing leadership to MAGA followers), but does not apply to an intergroup context (e.g., Donald Trump providing leadership to Democrats and Republicans).

Leadership often takes place in an intergroup context, where leaders must bridge the divide between multiple groups to achieve harmony and collaboration or to reduce conflict. As noted previously, most leadership theories focus solely on the leader, in a vacuum, or they focus on dyadic leader–follower relations, without consideration for the wider intergroup dynamics challenging leaders.

Intergroup leadership theory (Hogg, van Knippenberg, & Rast, 2012b) addresses this problem directly by arguing that successful intergroup leaders promote a cohesive, superordinate identity without erasing or diluting subgroup identities. To do this, intergroup leaders must create, promote, and maintain an intergroup relational identity. An intergroup relational identity is defined as a social identity that incorporates one's ingroup relationships with one or more other outgroups. For instance, students, as a group, are not defined on their own; students are defined relative to teachers. It is the same with parents and children, nurses and doctors, liberals and conservatives, and so forth. Leaders can create or promote an intergroup relational identity through their rhetoric or behavior, such as interacting with both ingroup and outgroup members.

Intergroup leadership theory assumes that group memberships are important to people's self-concepts. Any attempt to threaten or weaken those memberships, such as creating a common ingroup identity, will backfire, thereby creating more intergroup conflict. Research on this model supports the basic propositions that facilitating and embodying an intergroup relational identity improves leader effectiveness, intergroup cooperation, and reduces intergroup conflict (see Hogg & Rast, 2022).

KEY THINKER

Ashleigh Shelby Rosette

Ashleigh Shelby Rosette is the James L. Vincent Distinguished Professor of Leadership of Management and Organizations, and Center of Leadership and Ethics scholar at the Fuqua School of Business at Duke University, US. Ashleigh is one of the foremost scholars on the intersection of leadership, gender, and race. Her research demonstrates how business leader stereotypes result in White leaders receiving more positive evaluations than non-White leaders. She has also shown that Black female (and White male) leaders are perceived and evaluated more positively when they are dominant and assertive, whereas White female (and Black male) leaders experience a backlash when behaving dominantly. Ashleigh has won excellence in teaching and research awards, and has been ranked as one of the 50 most influential business professors. Her research on leadership, race, and gender is particularly timely, insightful, and cutting-edge.

In addition, what is prototypical is context-specific and changes with time. Recall from earlier in this chapter that 'prototypical' refers to the most normative or group representative position within a group. In the US, George W. Bush was once prototypical of the Republican party, but Donald J. Trump helped to change that. He successfully positioned himself as a prototypical leader who was not just the *average* Republican, but 'better' than average, demonstrating idealistic

> **Video:** 'What Leaders Need to Know about Race in the U.S.' www.you tube.com/watch?v=e8NRAndvddk

qualities that allowed Republicans to polarize away from their political rivals, Democrats. In some contexts, the average group member is preferred, because they are prototypical, but in polarized climates, people often prefer a leader who moves their group away from their rivals. We will come back to these ideas in Parts 2 and 3 of this chapter.

EXERCISE 8.5

What is a Leader? (Continued)

Recall the previous activity where you listed leaders and their effective leadership qualities. Take out the final list of qualities, traits, etc., that are absolutely essential for leadership. Having read this section, do any revisions need to be made to your list?

Most likely, the answer is yes. What we have found when conducting this activity in classes is that people often have lots of great leaders in mind with lots of wonderful and terrible qualities, traits, characteristics, etc. However, by the end of the activity they have no items remaining on their list that are absolutely essential for effective leadership. This is because defining leadership is such a complicated task. The exercise also reflects how we colloquially think about leaders. Often, students miss the one and only essential aspect of effective leadership: influence. Leaders must be influential. Many of the traits or qualities you listed are probably only effective if or when they impact a leader's capacity to be influential. Leadership, regardless of theoretical or practical approach, is about influencing followers.

8.5 PART 2: ADVANCES

The domain of group processes is an exciting and growing area of research. In this section, we focus on three cutting-edge theoretical and research advances on group processes. In particular, we focus on the role of uncertainty in leadership, we examine the causes and effects of social control, and we address how group processes research can explain the rise of populist and extremist movements.

8.5.1 Leadership Under Uncertainty

Many leadership theories posit that leaders are more effective or certain types of leaders are more likely to emerge during times of uncertainty or crisis. In fact, the idea that social or economic crises render different leadership qualities salient dates back to at least Weber's seminal *Economy and Society* (Weber, 1922). Despite its theoretical importance, there has been limited research examining leadership during uncertainties or crises (for an overview, see Rast, 2015). Recently, however, researchers have begun addressing this oversight. Integrating the social identity theory of leadership and uncertainty-identity theory (Hogg, 2007), researchers began studying how feelings of uncertainty impact leader performance and evaluations. Uncertainty-identity theory argues that feelings of uncertainty, particularly those relating to one's self-concept or identity, are aversive and motivate uncertainty reduction. Because this uncertainty implicates the self, social identity processes are well suited at reducing uncertainty. Indeed, there is compelling evidence that identifying more strongly with groups, especially those that are important to oneself or those that are highly entitative, reduce uncertainty (Choi & Hogg, 2020).

Applied to leadership, uncertainty-identity theory argues that people will seek reliable and consensual information about their ingroup **prototype**. Given that group leaders are often highly prototypical of their group, these individuals are reliable and attractive sources of

> **Key concept – Prototype:** A context-dependent fuzzy set of attributes (e.g., attitudes, opinions, norms, behaviors) that characterize one group while distinguishing it from other groups.

group prototypical information. Thus, one could argue that feeling highly self-uncertain results in greater support for highly group-prototypical leaders compared to less prototypical leaders. This is precisely what Cicero and colleagues (2007, 2010) found. In a series of organizational surveys, they found leader prototypicality was positively associated with leader evaluations, and this effect was stronger under high rather than low proxies for uncertainty.

Of note, in these studies participants rated their current leader or manager and **self-uncertainty** was not directly assessed. Rast and colleagues (2012) conducted experiments

> **Key concept – Self-uncertainty:** Feelings of doubt or ambiguity about one's identity or self-concept.

where they manipulated a leader candidate's (instead of a current leader) prototypicality or measured self-uncertainty directly. They argued that, in this context, self-uncertainty would weaken support for prototypical leaders but strengthen support for non-prototypical leaders. That is, heightened uncertainty would elicit support for any ingroup leader when only one leadership option is available. They found that when uncertainty was low, prototypical leaders received more support than non-prototypical leaders. But, under high uncertainty, this prototypical leader preference disappeared. Furthermore, it disappeared due to an increase in support garnered by non-prototypical leaders, not by a reduction in support for prototypical leaders. This led Rast and colleagues (2012) to surmise that non-prototypical leaders could gain influence and support under high uncertainty, especially if there was no other ingroup leader available. These studies showed that uncertainty plays a role in leader preference and evaluation. It means that, in times of uncertainty, groups may look to different or anti-normative leaders to provide a new pathway forward for the group or to signal change. For instance, women and ethnic minorities are likely to be placed into leadership positions during times of uncertainty (e.g., Rast, 2015; see also Gaffney, Rast, & Hogg, 2018). Followers desire a leader who can reduce their uncertainty.

Rast, Hogg, and Giessner (2013) took these ideas a step further. Conducting surveys with organizational employees, they measured self-uncertainty, autocratic leadership style, leader prototypicality, and leader evaluations. Rast and colleagues (2013) demonstrated that increasing feelings of uncertainty were associated with greater support for autocratic leaders, while lower feelings of uncertainty were associated with greater support for non-autocratic leaders. Furthermore, this effect was mediated by leader prototypicality: non-autocratic leaders were perceived as more prototypical when uncertainty was low, which resulted in greater support, while autocratic leaders were perceived as more prototypical when uncertainty was high, resulting in greater support. Their study shows that uncertainty not only impacts leader preference but also impacts how leaders are perceived by their followers. Rast, Hogg, and Giessner (2016) conducted a similar study, but instead of autocratic leaders, they examined whether participants rated their current leader as being more or less change-oriented. They found increased uncertainty was positively associated with support for change-oriented leaders, but lower levels of uncertainty were associated with greater support for stasis-oriented leaders. Given that leadership is often defined as being change-oriented (e.g., Weber, 1947; Yukl, 1999), Rast, Hogg, and Giessner's (2016) study could be argued to show that uncertainty is a necessary but insufficient condition to elicit true leadership.

8.5.2 Social Control

Sometimes group members do not fit in with the group and/or they break important norms. When this happens, there are several informal (e.g., ostracism) and formal (e.g., imprisonment) mechanisms that groups use to address their 'fringy', 'weird', or 'deviant' group members. When ingroup members behave badly, embarrass the group, or break norms, groups typically seek to sanction, address, punish, or change the behavior. As a last resort, the rule breaker may be ejected from the group. Ejection is rare as groups typically seek to stay together. There are various forms of social control that groups enact to address member deviance.

Ostracism

Ostracism, the act of intentionally excluding someone from a group or social interaction, is an *exclusionary* response to ingroup deviance. It is exclusionary because the point is to explicitly 'other' and exclude the deviant. Ostracism can have profound effects on the victim's psychological and emotional well-being (Williams, 2007). Groups often have explicit or implicit norms that dictate who is accepted and who is excluded, and individuals usually feel pressure to conform to these norms to avoid social rejection. Indeed, it is often learned during childhood that people conform to the group's norms or face exclusion for deviating from the group's norms (Abrams & Rutland, 2010). Additionally, group members may exclude others as a way to assert their own status or power within the group (e.g., Jetten et al., 2013).

EXERCISE 8.6

Ostracism in the Movies

Now would be a good time for us to recommend that you watch the 2004 classic film, *Mean Girls* (2004). Regina George, a popular bully and leader of the 'Plastics' (a high school clique known for their popularity and poor treatment of others), finds herself in a situation in which the other 'Plastics' ostracize her for gaining weight and wearing sweat-pants. She can no longer sit at the 'Plastics' table and they stop talking to her.

This video can be watched via YouTube at: www.youtube.com/watch?v=W8_POt2KlfQ

If you were in Regina's place, how would you feel at the end of this clip? Can you think of a time where you might have ostracized somebody or been ostracized by others? How did you feel when ostracizing others or when being ostracized?

The consequences of ostracism can be severe, both for the victim and for the group as a whole (Cacioppo & Cacioppo, 2016; Williams, 2007; Zadro & Gonsalkorale, 2014). Ostracism can lead to feelings of loneliness, depression, and anxiety, as well as a decrease in self-esteem and self-efficacy. Indeed, being ostracized threatens the following fundamental human needs:

1   By threatening self-esteem, self-worth (depressed self-esteem is an indicator that one is not fitting in), and belonging, ostracism creates an *inclusionary need*. When this occurs, people:

    a   act prosocially towards their group in an effort to regain entry (e.g., by increasing their performance on collective tasks) (Williams & Sommer, 1997; for a related argument, see Hohman, Gaffney, & Hogg, 2017);

    b   comply with inaccurate responses from other group members, both in private and in public (Williams et al., 2000);

    c   become particularly obedient (e.g., Riva et al., 2014);

    d   show improved memory for social information as a sign of increased monitoring of their social environment (e.g., Gardner et al., 2005).

2   Ostracism also can threaten an individual's self-efficacy (if they don't think I am any good, I must not have any skills) and sense of power (the ostracism takes away feelings of autonomy and meaningful existence – why am I even here?). When this happens, people may respond *aggressively* in an attempt to restore feelings of personal power and gain attention (Ren, Wesselman, & Williams, 2018) by:

    a   engaging in bullying behaviors;

    b   enacting individual acts of terrorism.

Over time, ostracism can lead to social withdrawal and isolation, which can exacerbate the victim's feelings of rejection and despair (Wesselmann et al., 2021). Ostracism is not only felt psychologically, it also manifests itself as physical pain (Eisenberg, Liberman, & Williams, 2003). That is, social exclusion results in physical pain! The effect is so strong that we even feel the pain of being ostracized when witnessing another person being ostracized (Giesen & Echterhoff, 2018; Wesselman, Bagg, & Williams, 2009). Not only do we feel negative when ostracized and excluded by our ingroups, we also feel it when we are ostracized by outgroups that we hate (see Key study 8.2).

KEY STUDY 8.2

Being Ostracized by Despised Groups Still Hurts

Psychology, and particularly social psychology, has produced loads of shocking research findings that fly in the face of convenient wisdom, such as Milgram's obedience study (no pun intended) (Milgram, 1963), the Stanford Prison study (Haney, Banks, & Zimbardo, 1973), the Asch line study (Asch, 1956), or Bem's extrasensory perception studies (Bem, 1972). Up there on that list should be Gonsalkorale and Williams's (2007) study. While we know that being excluded or ostracized does not feel good, nobody would guess that being ostracized by an outgroup we hate would make us feel badly. In fact, some of us might even believe we would wear that outgroup's ostracism as a badge of honor.

Gonsalkorale and Williams (2007) disagree, however. They conducted an experiment with 98 beginner psychology students (not too dissimilar from yourselves!) at the University of New South Wales, Australia. Students were told that they were participating in a study on the personality traits of people who support diverse groups in Australia. Students were asked their preference for one of three different groups: the Australian Labor Party, the Liberal Party of Australia, or the Imperial Klan of Australia. The first two are the largest political parties in Australia. Participants had already confirmed that they were a member of one of the first two groups (Labor or Liberal party members). The Imperial Klan of Australia is an online white supremacist branch of the Ku Klux Klan. These groups were coded as ingroup, relevant outgroup, and hated outgroup, which was confirmed by participant evaluations of these groups – the Imperial Klan was despised by all participants. For instance, if a participant reported being a member of the Labor Party, then that was coded as an ingroup for them, while the Liberal Party was coded as a relevant outgroup, and the Imperial Klan was coded as a hated outgroup.

After evaluating these groups, participants played rounds of Cyberball, an online ball-tossing game (see Chapter 3 on affiliation, friendship, and love for more examples of Cyberball). In this game, participants toss a virtual ball around with other players, who are actually controlled by a computer. Participants can be thrown a ball a lot (over-included) or a little (under-included) relative to the other players. Participants played with two members of either their ingroup, relevant outgroup, or despised outgroup. After completing the games of Cyberball, participants responded to questions assessing their own levels of self-esteem, belongingness, control, meaningful existence, and finally how warmly they felt towards their ingroup, relevant outgroup, and hated outgroup.

Gonsalkorale and Williams found that participants reported lower levels of belonging, self-esteem, control, and meaningful existence when they were ostracized compared to higher ratings when they were included. When it came to their group ratings, participants rated their own group as equally positive whether they were excluded or included; however, they rated both outgroups better when they were included and worse when they were excluded. Taken as a whole, Gonsalkorale and Williams (2007) found that participants experienced ostracism just as adversely when excluded by a relevant outgroup as when ostracized by a group they despise, such as the Imperial Klan of Australia.

Given that the negative effects of ostracism are so pervasive and damaging, it is important that researchers determine how to best prevent or lessen the effects of being excluded. Although important across the lifespan, this area is still actively in development. Nevertheless, there are some research-supported interventions that can be used to prevent or mitigate the effects of ostracism (e.g., Williams, 2007; Williams & Nida, 2022). Mindfulness training, joining new social groups, and even prayer have been shown to help people to recover from the short-term effects of ostracism (Hales, Wesselmann, & Williams, 2016; Molet, Macquet, Lefebvre, & Williams, 2013; Williams & Nida, 2011). Other longer-term strategies have been proposed, mostly in the public education setting: implementing training of what is and is not ostracism, fostering inclusive groups, combining anti-bullying and anti-ostracism efforts, and creating ostracism awareness campaigns (Williams & Nida, 2022).

Ingroup Deviants

The bulk of ostracism research looks at the effects of social control (i.e., ostracism) on the target of ostracism. The subjective group dynamics model (e.g., Abrams et al., 2000; Pinto et al., 2010) examines why groups exert social control over non-normative or deviant group members (referred to as **ingroup anti-norm deviant, normative ingroup member, ingroup pro-norm deviant, and outgroup anti-norm deviant**), and which

> **Key concept – Ingroup anti-norm deviant:** An ingroup member who expresses an opinion or action that blurs the boundaries between the ingroup and the outgroup. For example, a 'slightly' pro-choice Republican is an example of an anti-norm deviant for the Republican Party. Ingroup anti-norm deviants tend to be derogated in comparison to outgroup anti-norm deviants, ingroup normative members, and ingroup pro-normative deviants. This is the *black sheep effect*.

members of a group receive the harshest punishment for their deviance. The subjective group dynamics model looks at two inclusive responses to ingroup deviants: derogation and persuasion.

> **Key concept – Normative ingroup member:** An ingroup member who expresses an opinion or action that is consistent with the modal position of the ingroup. For example, if the mean response on a 1–11 scale for California State Polytechnic University, Humboldt students' concerns over climate change is '8', then a Cal Poly Humboldt student with a score of '8' is normative.

> **Key concept – Ingroup pro-norm deviant:** An ingroup member who expresses an opinion that is more extreme than the normative position, in a direction that is polarized *away* from an outgroup's position. For example, if Cal Poly Humboldt's average climate change score is '8' on a 1–11 scale and University of Alberta's score is '3', a Cal Poly Humboldt student with a score of '11' is a pro-norm deviant. Ingroup pro-norm deviants tend to be upgraded in comparison to ingroup anti-norm deviants and outgroup anti-norm deviants.

> **Key concept – Outgroup anti-norm deviant:** An outgroup member who expresses an opinion that is similar to an ingroup anti-norm deviant. For example, a 'slightly' pro-choice Democrat who is more conservative than the normative Democrat's position on abortion is an outgroup anti-norm deviant for Republicans. These outgroup members tend to be upgraded in comparison to ingroup anti-norm deviants.

When ingroup members violate norms, people may derogate them and often attempt to persuade them to change their ways to be more normative. Whereas people tend not to have a problem with outgroup members who deviate from their own group norms (in fact, this either has no effect on evaluations of outgroup deviants or people sometimes even upgrade outgroup deviants), ingroup deviants who veer in the direction of an outgroup (an ingroup anti-norm deviant) blur the distinction between groups, and sometimes these so-called 'black sheep' threaten the integrity of the positive ingroup identity. These mechanisms are outlined by the subjective group dynamics model (e.g., Marques, Abrams, & Serôdio, 2001), and have implications for group polarization, ingroup support of extremist behavior, and leadership processes (discussed in 8.5.3, following).

Depending on their status within the group, some members may be able to deviate from norms to a greater extent than others. Examining deviations of generic prescriptive norms (norms that do not denote category differentiation *per se*, but violating them makes the ingroup look bad), Pinto and colleagues (2010) showed that new or marginal group members (members who had once held status in the group but had lost it) were less likely to be deemed black sheep than when full members violated the same norm (a full member is someone with tenure and status in the group). This occurs, presumably, because the full members are the focus of the group's attention and their violation makes the ingroup look particularly bad.

Leader status is important as well. As discussed earlier in this chapter, we often give leaders the ability to transgress and deviate from group norms (Abrams, Randsley de la Moura, & Travaglino, 2013). In the political context, this is particularly true of newly elected leaders, because their election legitimizes their leadership position (Gaffney et al., 2019; Syfers, Rast, & Gaffney, 2021).

8.5.3 Polarization, Extremism, and Populism

Over the past decade, not only have we seen the rise of multiple authoritarian or autocratic leaders during crises and uncertainty, but we have also witnessed the surge of populism, radicalized terrorist networks, and political radicalism around the globe. As discussed in the previous section, people identify more strongly with their groups when they feel more uncertain. Not everyone identifies with or joins extreme groups, which begs the question of why and when people identify with these groups. A recent meta-analysis of 35 studies showed that self-uncertainty is, in fact, related to more strongly identifying with one's ingroup (Choi & Hogg, 2020). This supports the basic uncertainty-identity theory proposition that people who feel self-uncertain identify more strongly with their existing groups or join new groups. This effect is stronger when groups are highly hierarchical, distinctive, rigidly structured, and have strong leadership – that is, highly entitative groups are better at reducing self-uncertainty (Hogg et al., 2007). These are the same features that many, if not all, extremist and zealous groups possess. It makes these groups attractive sources for uncertainty reduction.

Recent research has explored the conditions under which people are drawn to or seek out these polarized or extremist groups. For example, Gaffney and colleagues (2014) examined when people would support the Tea Party, an

> **Key concept – Group polarization:**
> When a group's initial position on a given opinion is enhanced following a group discussion.

extremist, right-wing US political group. They found that, when primed to feel more self-uncertain, people supported extreme messages from a Tea Party leader when that message was provided in the presence of liberals than in the presence of other conservatives. This is partially a **group polarization** effect: under heightened uncertainty, when hearing a message from a similar other, we seek to differentiate ourselves from dissimilar, disliked outgroups but not so much from similar, liked outgroups. We can readily observe this in the media's coverage of political rallies, such as when a liberal speaks to a group of liberals, moderates, or conservatives, and vice versa. Self-uncertainty has also been shown not only to increase identification with extremist groups, but also to increase support for radical and extreme protest actions and behaviors (Hogg, Meehan, & Farquharson, 2010). In a particularly chilling demonstration, Hogg and Adelman (2013) surveyed Palestinian Muslims and Israeli Jews. They found that self-uncertainty was associated with more support for suicide bombing and hostile, aggressive military action against the opposing group.

Although self-uncertainty can promote identification with and support for radicalized, extremist, or populist groups, coupling self-uncertainty with other undesirable group processes (e.g., ostracism, loneliness, relative deprivation) worsens this effect. Across a pair of experiments, Hales and Williams (2018) either ostracized or included participants using the Cyberball paradigm and then measured participants' self-uncertainty and interest in an extreme group. They found that ostracism not only induced self-uncertainty, it also increased interest in the extreme group. Hales and Williams concluded that uncertainty is a negative result of ostracism, which lends itself to maladaptive behaviors such as supporting/joining extreme groups.

In addition to joining or supporting extremist or populist groups, uncertainty also motivates some people to seek leadership positions. Guillén, Jacquart, and Hogg (2022) conducted four studies and found that people's own leadership attainment motivation was associated with increased uncertainty among leaders with 'the dark triad' of personality traits (i.e., personality traits associated with being self-servingly manipulative, having a grandiose sense of self-importance, and deficiencies regulating one's own emotions or feeling empathy towards others).

Optimal distinctiveness theory (ODT) (Brewer, 1991; Leonardelli, Pickett, & Brewer, 2010) explains why people are motivated to join groups (recall this discussion from the early part of this chapter). This model posits that human beings have two opposing needs regarding their self-concept and group memberships. First, people have a need for inclusion and assimilation. They want to belong and be included in social groups. Second is the need for differentiation from others, where people want to be separate from and unique compared to their groups. Whether people are pursuing assimilation or differentiation is determined by which motive is stronger, and thus activated, in that particular social context. When people are over-included, they will seek opportunities to differentiate themselves from their group. When people shift towards extreme individuality, they seek opportunities to assimilate with their group. People have to keep these competing needs in check. One way to do so is by joining and identifying with groups that have the capacity to satisfy both needs simultaneously: groups that satisfy one's need for inclusion *and* provide distinctiveness from other relevant groups. Versteegen (2023) investigated ODT as a motivation for people to join extremist groups (Key study 8.3).

KEY STUDY 8.3

Optimal Distinctiveness Theory in Extreme Groups

Recently, optimal distinctiveness was identified as a motivation for why people join and identify with populist groups and movements. Versteegen (2023) argued that members of populist groups might perceive themselves as ordinary people who are also excluded from society. Feeling ordinary ought to elicit a drive for differentiation, while feeling excluded should arouse a desire to assimilate. Versteegen posits that members of populist groups are experiencing these conflicting motives in such a way that they are shifting their social identities between their superordinate group (e.g., national identity, majority group) and their subgroups (e.g., marginalized political groups, minority groups). He further argues that populist and extremist groups offer reprieve from individuals' feelings of neglect and disrespect associated with the narrative that their majority group is in decline and being discriminated against.

To test these ideas, Versteegen recruited 30 participants who were active members of the German Populist Radical Right (PPR) and conducted semi-structured, mostly in person, interviews with them. When analyzing the interview responses, themes emerged around German heritage, history, and tradition, and German identity in contrast to relevant national, ethnic, religious, and sexual outgroups. Another theme was a lack of uniqueness, a desire for uniqueness, an inability to publicly express their own beliefs and values, and feeling disrespected and neglected due to their traditional values and beliefs. The responses to semi-structured interview questions supported Versteegen's main ideas: PPR members viewed themselves as ordinary Germans who felt excluded due to being part of the dominant majority groups of white, male, heterosexual, and conservative people. This lack of uniqueness and desire to express their beliefs and values motivated them to identify more strongly with the PPR, which gave them a small, yet protective, group in which to express themselves, feel validated and heard, and included. Overall, Versteegen's (2023) study provides support for ODT as a reasonable explanation for why people join extreme or populist groups.

The research described in this section shows how uncertainty can motivate people to join extremist groups, support populist messages, dehumanize outgroups, and even pursue radicalized and violent group agendas. It is only through investigating this dark side of uncertainty that we can begin to understand and combat the negative outcomes associated with self-uncertainty and better understand the benefits it produces as well. We will explore the latter in Part 3.

8.6 PART 3: APPLICATIONS

8.6.1 Identity Leadership and Insurrections

'And we fight. We fight like hell. And if you don't fight like hell, you're not going to have a country anymore.' (Donald J. Trump, January 6, 2021, 'Stop the Steal' rally)

Words have the capacity to change nations. When used by leaders, words have the power to transform the future as well. Using social identity language can have profound effects for leaders and their groups. Some have argued that effective leadership hinges on using social identity language such as 'we', 'us', 'they', and 'them' (e.g., Haslam, Reicher, & Platow, 2020; Seyarian & Bligh, 2008; see also Part 1 of this chapter). Donald J. Trump's 'Stop the Steal' speech on January 6, 2021 contains more than 700 instances of using six simple social identity words ('our', 'we', 'us', 'them', 'they', 'their') to connect with his followers, create a shared social identity, promote a shared collective goal, create a common enemy, and evoke collective action. This type of leadership, where the leader's and followers' self-conception as group members are addressed, is referred to as identity leadership (Haslam, Gaffney, Hogg, Rast, & Steffens, 2022).

Over the course of Trump's one-and-a-quarter-hour speech, he created a shared social identity with his followers. He used about 350 instances of 'us', 'we', and 'our' to connect with his followers. For example, he stated 'We created Space Force. We, we, we. Look at what we did' to create the sense that he and his followers are not only part of the same collective group, but also that he, along with his followers, shared in this accomplishment. This language reaffirms the idea that Trump and his followers are seen as 'us' or 'we' and changes followers' self-conception from personal to social identity. Trump positions himself as representing his followers, their interests, their well-being, and their future: 'Our exciting adventures and boldest endeavors have not yet begun. My fellow Americans, for our movement, for our children, and for our beloved country.' He is constructing the group, what they stand for, who they are, and he is ensuring it is aligned with their social identity.

Trump also uses social identity language to define the social context to create a meaningful shared experience. One that is defined by perception and attitudes, which can be transferred to subsequent behavior. For example, he stated 'We will not be intimidated into accepting the hoaxes and the lies that we've been forced to believe' and 'All of us here today do not want to see our election victory stolen by emboldened radical-left Democrats, which is what they're doing'. These statements create a meaningful shared perception that Trump and his followers are being lied to and their electoral college win was somehow stolen by the radical outgroup (Democrats). His narrative fits his followers' shared perception and makes it real for them. It is through these shared perceptual experiences that our social identity can become the impetus for behavior.

But, before translating these perceptions into action, Trump emboldens the 'us' versus 'them' division. He even creates two shared enemies for his followers: Democrats and Republicans who do not endorse Trump's view. For instance, Trump stated 'The Democrats are hopeless', 'They're weak Republicans, they're pathetic Republicans'. Further creating an 'us' versus 'them' mentality, he repeatedly stated 'they' are bad or evil people who are breaking the law: 'They should be regulated, investigated, and brought to justice under the fullest extent of the law. They're totally breaking the law.' And, while stating his followers are good and just, 'They want to come in again and rip off our country. Can't let it happen. As this enormous crowd shows, we have truth and justice on our side.' Trump has used social identity language to create shared meaning and create a relevant outgroup (or two) who are responsible for his followers' plight.

These different social identity rhetorical devices can then be used to motivate and underpin the ingroup's behavior. Trump communicates what his followers must do to prevent their electoral defeat: 'We got to get rid of them. We got to get rid', 'It was going to be great and now we're out here fighting', 'We must stop the steal and then we must ensure that such outrageous election fraud never happens again, can never be allowed to happen again', 'And we fight. We fight like hell. And if you don't fight like hell, you're not going to have a country anymore', 'we can't let this stuff happen. We won't have a country if it happens', and he ends with the final marching order: 'So let's walk down Pennsylvania Avenue.' What followed this speech was a breach and siege of the US Capitol building by 2,000 protestors, lasting seven hours, in which five people died and approximately 140 police officers were injured. Millions of dollars' worth of damage was caused, and Congress was compelled to recess until it could be recovered to confirm Biden's electoral win. It was not until Trump finally told the insurrectionists to 'go home in peace' that the siege ended.

This summary of the January 6, 2021 US Capitol insurrection provides a compelling (and scary) example of just how powerful social identities can be and how leaders can use them. However, although this example is negative, social identity (and identity leadership) can be used for good, inclusivity, and positivity as well (see Haslam & Reicher, 2016, for examples). Haslam and a team of 11 researchers, who were working either in teams or independently, came together to analyse the January 6 insurrection (Haslam et al., 2023). Their **dual-agency model of identity leadership** and engaged followership shows that Trump did not have to command his followers to storm the US Capitol. He lived with them in their rage and his followers had the creativity and agency to act on his behalf. Trump never uttered words such as 'Storm the Capitol' – he did not have to. The people who rioted did so of their own accord, believing it was the appropriate course of action to take on behalf of a collective identity that Trump pointed out was threatened. Therefore, the rioters were striving to enact the group's identity and goals as put forth by their leader (Trump) (Haslam et al., 2023). This is similar to Milgram's own observations in his obedience study – that his participants were not truly obeying, they were cooperating with the experimenter to achieve the experiment's goals (see the discussion of Milgram's obedience study in Chapter 7 on social influence).

> **Key concept – Dual-agency model of identity leadership:** A model of identity leadership, derived from the social identity perspective, that states that the leadership process is a co-production between leaders and followers. Leaders create, promote, and advance a sense of shared social identity while followers can accept and embrace that group identity and work towards advancing the leader's vision. It's a dual-agency model in the sense that both leaders and followers are creating and advancing the group's social identity and goals.

Although this section paints a bleak picture of identity leadership in the context of an insurrection, the power of identity leadership lies in the power to influence and mobilize groups. It can be used to achieve bad (e.g., the January 6 insurrection) or good (e.g., Martin Luther King Jr's *I Have a Dream* speech). When used for the social good, identity leadership can be used to resist authoritarian regimes, oppose repression, and bring diverse people together (e.g., Martin Luther King Jr or Gandhi).

8.6.2 Combating Extremism via Social Connections

Extremism is pervasive in our society and continues to grow rapidly. As an example, the Southern Poverty Law Center (2021, 2023), which tracks hate and anti-government groups in the United States, reported a rise from 838 hate groups in 2020 to 1,225 in 2022. To address this phenomenon, psychologists have started to examine the underlying motivations and causes for radicalization and joining extremist groups (e.g., Hogg, 2021; Horgan, 2008; Kruglanski et al., 2014). Two of the most common explanations for why people radicalize or join extremist groups are marginalization (Hales & Williams, 2018) and self-uncertainty (Hogg, Kruglanski, & Van den Bos, 2013). Both of these explanations implicate group memberships and feelings of social connectedness (or lack thereof) as a means to combat extremism.

Recall from Part 2 that ostracism is socially and physically painful, and can result in people feeling lonely, depressed, and anxious. Williams (2007) argues that people are motivated to restore social connections following ostracism. However, not only do people want to restore their belongness, they are also willing to lower their standard for which groups they will join. Building on an eating analogy that people are motivated to *socially snack* when they are excluded (Gardner, Pickett, & Knowles, 2005), Hales and Williams (2018, p. 76) state that 'just as people lower their thresholds for what they are willing to eat, they also lower their threshold for the types of groups they are interested in joining when they are ostracized'. They argue that ostracism evokes self-uncertainty, which in turn increases interest in extreme groups.

As we've seen throughout this chapter, uncertainty is aversive. People are motivated to reduce uncertainty, particularly uncertainty related to one's self-concept or identity. Uncertainty-identity theory (Hogg, 2007, 2021) has been adapted to explain and predict when and why people may join extreme groups. Extreme groups tend to be highly entitative: they are highly distinctive, intolerant of dissent, have clear and focused norms, are hierarchically organized, and often have strong, directive leadership (see Hogg, Adelman, & Blagg, 2010). When people feel highly uncertain, these extreme groups become attractive for these very reasons. Indeed, self-uncertainty has been shown to cause students to identify with extreme groups more strongly and to support their radical behaviors (Hogg, Meehan, & Farquahrson, 2010). Self-uncertainty was also more strongly associated with support for suicide bombing and swift military aggression (Hogg & Adelman, 2013), an increased desire to join or affiliate with gangs, and support for violent behavior (Goldman, Giles, & Hogg, 2014).

Although these studies demonstrate when and why people seek out extreme groups, we can also draw on this research to better understand how to reduce extremism and radicalization. For instance, we can create interventions aimed at reducing feelings of uncertainty and instability in people's social identities, as well as addressing the underlying causes of social identity threats. Individuals who experience uncertainty or instability in their identity may be more vulnerable to extremist ideologies and groups as a result of their desire for a clear and rigid sense of identity and purpose (Hogg, 2021). Therefore, providing support and resources to individuals who are experiencing identity-related stress or crises can help to reduce their susceptibility to extremist ideologies and groups. Support can take many forms, such as counseling services, mentoring, or financial assistance (e.g., see the 'social cure' discussion earlier in this chapter, and more extensively in Chapter 3 on affiliation, friendship, and love). Providing support and resources to individuals who are experiencing identity-related stress or crises can help them to develop a more stable and confident sense of identity, which can reduce their susceptibility to extremist ideologies and groups (Lüders, Jonas, Fritsche, & Agroskin, 2016; Williams, Hales, & Michels, 2019).

Finally, targeting an individual's social identity complexity (Roccas & Brewer, 2002) is another potential strategy to counter extremism and radicalization. Social identity complexity refers to the subjective representation of the self in relation to one's multiple ingroup memberships (see Chapter 2 on self and identity). These representations can be simple (e.g., two discrete, non-overlapping identities) or complex (two intersecting identities with significant overlap). For example, an African-American female who is a mother can have a simple social identity where she is either an African-American, a female, or a mother, but these identities are not related to one another and they do not impact each other. However, another person with these same social identities may represent her self-concept as a combination of two or more of these identities that do overlap and impact each other, such that she regularly thinks about herself as an African-American, female mother.

We've seen in previous sections the influence of social identities. If people feel uncertain and they have a simple social identity structure, they may feel as though they have only a single group with which they can identify. In the case of a radicalized extremist, this would be their extremist group. Feeling uncertain will make them identify even more strongly with the extreme group and insulate themselves further into their group. A more adaptive approach to remedy radicalization is to promote complex identity structures (Hogg, 2021). Promoting identification with multiple groups, especially non-extreme groups, provides alternative social identities to provide a clear self-concept. Salient group membership that one can turn to, particularly during heightened uncertainty, can help individuals to feel accepted and included rather than marginalized and thus susceptible to the appeal of strong and extreme groups.

Interventions informed by uncertainty-identity theory can be effective for reducing and countering extremism and radicalization. It is important to remember that there is no one-size-fits-all approach to reducing and countering extremism, and interventions must be tailored to specific contexts and individuals. By utilizing strategies informed by uncertainty-identity theory, we can take important steps towards creating a more peaceful and inclusive world. However, much research is still needed in order to understand this area.

8.6.3 Social Identity Continuity, Immigration, and Migration

Social identities are not just important for leadership and extremism, but also for human migration. Migration and immigration policies have become important issues around the world that are shaped by a range of social, economic, and political factors. Recently, **social identity continuity** has been proposed as a tool for improving immigration policy. Social identities are temporally situated such that group members have a shared representation of their group, its history, its present, and its future, which impacts how they perceive and interact with their social environments in the present.

> **Key concept – Social identity continuity:** The perception that one's ingroup identity is consistent and aligned across the past, present, and future (e.g., Sani et al., 2007).

Social identity continuity has been explored in numerous domains, ranging from suicide prevention (Chandler & Lalonde, 1998) and stroke recovery (Haslam et al., 2008) to organizational mergers (van Knippenberg, van Knippenberg, Monden, & de Lima, 2002) and leadership (Selvanathan, Crimston, & Jetten, 2022). This work tends to focus on how social identity continuity has positive outcomes while social identity discontinuity results in negative outcomes.

Threats to social identity continuity are associated with higher levels of uncertainty and collective angst and increased attempts to restore continuity (e.g., Wohl, Squires, & Caouette, 2012). Recently, Smeekes and Verkuyten (2015) applied social identity continuity to immigration policy and reform. For instance, they found that when people's national identity is threatened, they become more supportive of policies restricting immigration (Smeekes & Verkuyten, 2013). However, the authors also showed that social identity continuity predicted improved post-migration health and well-being among refugees (Smeekes et al., 2017).

In the context of migration and immigration policies, social identity continuity work suggests that policies should aim to support migrants and immigrants in maintaining a sense of continuity with their cultural heritage and social identity. By doing so, policies can help to promote psychological well-being and reduce the negative effects of acculturation stress. For instance, one approach is to support the preservation and celebration of cultural heritage through policies that promote cultural diversity and inclusivity. This can include funding for cultural festivals and events, the recognition and celebration of important cultural holidays, and language classes that support the maintenance of native languages.

As we've seen in other sections, social identity is an influential tool. Creating and promoting more important and meaningful social groups and connections is beneficial. As such, another approach is to provide support for the creation of social networks and communities that allow migrants and immigrants to maintain a sense of continuity with their cultural heritage. This can include support for community centers, social clubs, and religious organizations that serve as a hub for cultural and social activities.

There are several challenges and considerations that need to be considered when applying social identity continuity to migration and immigration policies. One challenge is that policies that promote cultural diversity and inclusivity may be met with resistance from members of the dominant culture. To overcome this challenge, it is important to engage in public education and awareness campaigns that help to promote the benefits of cultural diversity and inclusivity.

Another challenge is that policies promoting social and economic integration may be viewed as promoting assimilation (i.e., adopting the norms and values of the majority group), which can be seen as a threat to cultural heritage and identity. To address this challenge, it is important to ensure that policies are designed in collaboration with members of the immigrant and migrant community and are sensitive to their cultural needs and preferences.

8.7 SUMMARY

Groups are central to our everyday lives. They provide countless benefits for us and nearly everything in our lives is determined by groups, ranging from the languages that we speak, to the things we believe, to whether leadership is more or less effective. Not belonging to a group, or being ostracized from our group, can have significant negative effects on our personal well-being. We often overlook the importance of our groups, but they literally make us who we are.

Throughout this chapter we have covered how groups are defined, different types of groups, why people join groups, the benefits of being in a group, the consequences of being ostracized from groups, how people enhance or impair the performance of others, the impact and power of norms on behavior, and the role of leaders and their influence on group members. It is impossible to cover all aspects of group processes in a single chapter, but we've covered the foundational aspects of group processes to get you started on your journey into social psychology.

The study of group processes is ever-changing. Humans are naturally social beings who congregate in groups. As the world's population continues to grow and technological advances continue, there will undoubtedly be a future for you in researching group processes. For instance, how will X (formerly Twitter) and other micro-blogging sites influence groups over the next decade? What role will artificial intelligence (AI) play in groups, especially when it starts to replace humans in the workplace? And what impact will present-day political unrest have on the state of free speech and democracy in the future? These are only a few questions on the minds of today's researchers, but it is the next generation of psychologists who will need to answer them.

8.8 REVISION

Please select the correct or best answer to each of the multiple-choice questions below:

1   Which of the following statements accurately describes social facilitation?

   a   Social facilitation typically enhances performance on tasks that are simple or well practiced for the individual, but hinders performance on complex or novel tasks.
   b   Social facilitation primarily impacts introverts, leading to improved performance on complex tasks and decreased performance on simple tasks.
   c   Social facilitation has a consistent effect on all individuals, improving performance on complex tasks and showing no significant impact on simple tasks.
   d   Social facilitation mainly benefits extroverts, leading to improved performance on both simple and complex tasks compared to introverts.

2   Entitativity is:

   a   the measure of a group's cohesiveness and how well its members cooperate to achieve common goals;
   b   the tendency of individuals to categorize others based on superficial characteristics within a group setting;
   c   the degree to which a group is perceived as a distinct and unified entity, possessing its own identity;
   d   the process through which individuals in a group compete to establish their dominance and hierarchical position.

3 Which of the following statements about Triplett's (1898) study is correct?

    a   Children participants reeled the fishing line faster when in the presence of their parents.

    b   Children participants reeled the fishing line faster when in the presence of another child.

    c   Children participants reeled the fishing line faster when in the presence of their romantic partner.

    d   Children participants reeled the fishing line faster when in the presence of their teacher.

4 What is the most powerful word a leader can use?

    a   Fight!

    b   Me!

    c   I!

    d   Us!

5 The social cure, a concept in social psychology, refers to:

    a   The process of using social interactions and support to improve an individual's physical health.

    b   The phenomenon where being in a social setting increases the likelihood of succumbing to peer pressure.

    c   The tendency of individuals to seek social validation through excessive use of social media platforms.

    d   The idea that social connectedness and belongingness can positively impact an individual's well-being and alleviate psychological distress.

Answers: a, c, b, d, d.

8.9 FURTHER READING

Foundations

Brewer M. B. (1991). The social self: On being the same and different at the same time. *Personality and Social Psychology Bulletin, 17*, 475–482.

A seminal paper introducing the idea of 'optimal distinctiveness' as an innate human motivation to join groups.

Stürmer S., & Simon B. (2004). Collective action: Towards a dual-pathway model. *European Review of Social Psychology, 15*, 59–99.

A paper that proposes a model of articulating when people will engage in social action or not, based on internal and external motivations. It provides ample examples of application for different social movements.

Turner, J. C., Hogg, M. A., Oakes, P. J., Reicher, S. D., & Wetherell, M. S. (1987). *Rediscovering the social group: A self-categorization theory*. Oxford: Blackwell.

This book provides research and evidence demonstrating the psychological, social, and motivational processes for the social identity theory of the group (i.e., self-categorization theory).

Advances

Haslam S. A., & Reicher S. D. (2012). When prisoners take over the prison: A social psychology of resistance. *Personality and Social Psychology Review*, *16*, 154–179.

A modern-day replication of the Stanford Prison Study with a group-based (rather than individual-based) explanation of the results.

Hogg M. A., van Knippenberg D., & Rast D. E. III (2012). The social identity theory of leadership: Theoretical origins, research findings, and conceptual developments. *European Review of Social Psychology*, *23*, 258–304.

The most up-to-date overview and extension of the social identity theory of leadership, which, arguably, is the only true group-based leadership theory.

Applications

Reicher S. D., & Stott C. (2011). *Mad mobs and Englishmen? Myths and realities of the 2011 riots*. London: Constable and Robinson.

Accessible and easy-to-read social psychological re-interpretation of collective action and crowd behavior.

Swann W. B., Gómez Á., Seyle D. C., Morales J. F., & Huici C. (2009). Identity fusion: The interplay of personal and social identities in extreme group behavior. *Journal of Personality and Social Psychology*, *96*, 995–1011.

Well-cited research demonstrating how social identity can impact people's willingness to engage in extreme group behavior (both good and bad!). Several practical ideas for interventions and applications are described within.

8.10 REFERENCES

Abrams, D., & Hogg, M. A. (1988). Comments on the motivational status of self-esteem in social identity and intergroup discrimination. *European Journal of Social Psychology*, *18*, 317–334. doi:10.1002/ejsp.2420180403

Abrams, D., Marques, J. M., Bown, N., & Henson, M. (2000). Pro-norm and anti-norm deviance within and between groups. *Journal of Personality and Social Psychology*, *78*, 906–912. doi:10.1037/0022-3514.78.5.906

Abrams, D., Randsley de Moura, G., & Travaglino, G. A. (2013). A double standard when group members behave badly: Transgression credit to ingroup leaders. *Journal of Personality and Social Psychology*, *105*, 799–815. doi:10.1037/a0033600

Abrams, D., & Rutland, A. (2010). Children's understanding of deviance and group dynamics: The development of subjective group dynamics. In J. Jetten & M. J. Hornsey (Eds.), *Rebels in groups: Dissent, deviance, difference and defiance* (pp. 135–157). Hoboken, NJ: Wiley Blackwell.

Abrams, D., Travaglino, G. A., Marques, J. M., Pinto, I., & Levine, J. M. (2018). Deviance credit: Tolerance of deviant ingroup leaders is mediated by their accrual of prototypicality and conferral of their right to be supported. *Journal of Social Issues, 74*, 36–55.

Akerlof, G. A., & Kranton, R. E. (2000). Economics and identity. *Quarterly Journal of Economics, 115*, 715–753.

Allport, F. H. (1924). *Social psychology*. Cambridge, MA: Riverside Press.

Asch, S. E. (1956). Studies of independence and conformity: A minority of one against a unanimous majority. *Psychological Monographs: General and Applied, 70*, 1–70.

Baron, R.S. (1986) Distraction-conflict theory: Progress and problems. *Advances in Experimental Social Psychology, 19*, 1-39. doi:10.1016/S0065-2601(08)60211-7

Barreto, N. B., & Hogg, M. A. (2017). Evaluation of and support for group prototypical leaders: A meta-analysis of twenty years of empirical research. *Social Influence, 12*(1), 41–55.doi:10.1080/15534510.2017.1316771

Bass, B. M. (1985). *Leadership and performance beyond expectations*. New York: Free Press.

Bem, D. J. (1972). Self-perception theory. In L. Berkowitz (Ed.), *Advances in experimental social psychology* (Vol. 6, pp. 1–62). New York: Academic Press.

Best, D., Irving, J., Collinson, B., Andersson, C., & Edwards, M. (2016). Recovery networks and community connections: Identifying connection needs and community linkage opportunities in early recovery populations. *Alcoholism Treatment Quarterly, 35*(1), 2–15. doi:10.1080/07347324.2016.1256718

Blanchard, A. L., Caudill, L. E., & Walker, L. S. (2020). Developing an entitativity measure and distinguishing it from antecedents and outcomes within online and face-to-face groups. *Group Processes & Intergroup Relations, 23*, 91–108. doi:10.1177/1368430217743577

Bond, C. F., & Titus, L. J. (1983). Social facilitation: A meta-analysis of 241 studies. *Psychological Bulletin, 94*(2), 265–292. doi:10.1037/0033-2909.94.2.265

Brewer, M. B. (1991). The social self: On being the same and different at the same time. *Personality and Social Psychology Bulletin, 17*(5), 475–482.

Brouwer, A. M. (2017). *Motivation for sustaining health behavior change: The self-as-doer identity* (1st ed.). New York: Routledge. https://doi.org/10.4324/9781315178653

Buckingham, S. A. (2017). The associative reflective model of social identification (ARMS): With a particular emphasis upon addiction, behavioural change and social identity. In S. A. Buckingham & D. Best (Eds.), *Addiction, behavioral change and social identity: The path to resilience and recovery* (pp. 99–115). New York: Routledge.

Burns, J. M. (1978). *Leadership*. New York: Harper & Row.

Byrne, D. (1971). *The attraction paradigm*. New York: Academic Press.

Cacioppo, S., & Cacioppo, J. T. (2016). Research in social neuroscience: How perceived social isolation, ostracism, and romantic rejection affect our brain. In P. Riva & J. Eck (Eds.), *Social exclusion*. Cham, Switzerland: Springer International. doi:10.1007/978-3-319-33033-4_4

Campbell, D. T. (1958). Common fate, similarity, and other indices of the status of aggregates of persons as social entities. *Behavioral Science, 3*, 14–25. doi:10.1002/bs.3830030103

Chandler, M. J., & Lalonde, C. (1998). Cultural continuity as a hedge against suicide in Canada's First Nations. *Transcultural Psychiatry, 35*(2), 191–219. doi:10.1177/136346159803500202

Chemers, M. M. (2001). Leadership effectiveness: An integrative review. In M. A. Hogg & R. S. Tindale (Eds.), *Blackwell handbook of social psychology: Group processes* (pp. 376–399). Oxford: Blackwell.

Choi, E. U., & Hogg, M. A. (2020). Self-uncertainty and group identification: A meta-analysis. *Group Processes & Intergroup Relations, 23*(4), 483–485.

Cicero, L., Pierro, A., & Van Knippenberg, D. (2007). Leader group prototypicality and job satisfaction: The moderating role of job stress and team identification. *Group Dynamics: Theory, Research, and Practice, 11*, 165.

Cicero, L., Pierro, A., & Van Knippenberg, D. (2010). Leadership and uncertainty: How role ambiguity affects the relationship between leader group prototypicality and leadership effectiveness. *British Journal of management, 21*, 411-421.

Conger, J. A., & Kanungo, R. N. (1998). *Charismatic leadership in organizations.* Thousand Oaks, CA: Sage.

Cooper, K., Smith, L. G. E., & Russell, A. (2017). Social identity, self-esteem, and mental health in autism. *European Journal of Social Psychology, 47*(7), 844–854. https://doi.org/10.1002/ejsp.2297

Cottrell, N. B. (1972). Social facilitation. In C. G. McClintock (Ed.), *Experimental social psychology* (pp. 185–236). New York: Holt, Rinehart, & Winston.

Cottrell, N. B., Wack, D. L., Sekerak, G. J., & Rittle, R. H. (1968). Social facilitation of dominant responses by the presence of an audience and the mere presence of others. *Journal of Personality and Social Psychology, 9*(3), 245–250.doi:10.1037/h0025902

Cruwys, T., Gaffney, A. M., & Skipper, Y. (2017). Uncertainty in transition: The influence of group cohesion on learning. In K. I. Mavor, M. J. Platow, & B. Bizumic (Eds.), *Self and social identity in educational contexts* (pp. 193–208). London: Routledge. https://doi.org/10.4324/9781315746913-ch11

Cruwys, T., Haslam, C., Rathbone, J. A., Williams, E., Haslam, S. A., & Walter, Z. C. (2022). Groups 4 Health versus cognitive–behavioural therapy for depression and loneliness in young people: Randomised phase 3 non-inferiority trial with 12-month follow-up. *The British Journal of Psychiatry, 220*, 140–147. doi:10.1192/bjp.2021.128

Eisenberger, N. I., Lieberman, M. D., & Williams, K. D. (2003). Does rejection hurt? An fMRI study of social exclusion. *Science, 302*, 290–292.

Ellemers, N., de Gilder, D., & Haslam, S. A. (2004). Motivating individuals and groups at work: A social identity perspective on leadership and group performance. *The Academy of Management Review, 29*, 459–478. doi:10.2307/20159054

Festinger, L. (1954). A theory of social comparison processes. *Human Relations, 7*, 117–140. doi:10.1177/001872675400700202

Fiedler, F. (1967). *A theory of leadership effectiveness.* New York: McGraw-Hill.

Fiske, S. T., & Dépret, E. (1996). Control, interdependence and power: Understanding social cognition in its social context. *European Review of Social Psychology, 7*(1), 31–61. doi: 10.1080/14792779443000094

Forsyth, D. R. (2014). *Group dynamics* (6th ed.). Belmont, CA: Cengage.

Freeman, S., Walker, M. R., Bordon, R., & Latané, B. (1975). Diffusion of responsibility and restaurant tipping: Cheaper by the bunch. *Personality and Social Psychology Bulletin, 1*, 584–700.

Gaffney, A. M., Rast III, D. E., & Hogg, M. A. (2018). Uncertainty and influence: The advantages (and disadvantages) of being atypical. *Journal of Social Issues, 74*, 20–35.

Gaffney, A. M., Rast III, D. E., Hackett, J. D., & Hogg, M. A. (2014). Further to the right: Uncertainty, political polarization and the American 'Tea Party' movement. *Social Influence, 9*(4), 272–288. doi:10.1080/15534510.2013.842495

Gaffney, A. M., Sherburne, B., Hackett, J. D., Rast III, D. E., & Hohman, Z. P. (2019). The transformative and informative nature of elections: Representation, schism, and exit. *The British Journal of Social Psychology, 58*, 88–104. doi:10.1111/bjso.12279

Gardner, W. L., Pickett, C. L., Jefferis, V., & Knowles, M. (2005). On the outside looking in: Loneliness and social monitoring. *Personality and Social Psychology Bulletin, 31*(11), 1549–1560.

Gardner, W. L., Pickett, C. L., & Knowles, M. L. (2005). Social 'snacking' and social 'shielding': The satisfaction of belonging needs through the use of social symbols and the social self. In K. D. Williams, J. Forgas, & W. Hippel (Eds.), *The social outcast: Ostracism, social exclusion, rejection, and bullying*. New York: Psychology Press.

Geen, R. G., & Gange, J. J. (1977). Drive theory of social facilitation: Twelve years of theory and research. *Psychological Bulletin, 84*, 1267–1288. doi:10.1037/0033-2909.84.6.1267

Gerstner, C. R., & Day, D. V. (1997). Meta-analytic review of leader–member exchange theory: Correlates and construct issues. *Journal of Applied Psychology, 82*(6), 827–844. doi:10.1037/0021-9010.82.6.827

Giesen, A., & Echterhoff, G. (2018). Do I really feel your pain? Comparing the effects of observed and personal ostracism. *Personality and Social Psychology Bulletin, 44*, 550–561.

Goldman, L., Giles, H., & Hogg, M. A. (2014). Going to extremes: Social identity and communication processes associated with gang membership. *Group Processes & Intergroup Relations, 17*, 813–832.

Gonsalkorale, K., & Williams, K. D. (2007). The KKK won't let me play: Ostracism even by a despised outgroup hurts. *European Journal of Social Psychology, 37*(6), 1176–1186.

Graen, G. B., & Uhl-Bien, M. (1995). Relationship-based approach to leadership: Development of leader–member exchange (LMX) theory of leadership over 25 years: Applying a multi-level multi-domain perspective. *The Leadership Quarterly, 6*(2), 219–247. doi:10.1016/1048-9843(95)90036-5

Grant, F., Hogg, M. A., & Crano, W. D. (2015). Yes, we can: Physical activity and group identification among healthy adults. *Journal of Applied Social Psychology, 45*, 383–390. https://doi.org/10.1111/jasp.12305

Guillén, L., Jacquart, P., & Hogg, M. A. (2022). To lead, or to follow? How self-uncertainty and the dark triad of personality influence leadership motivation. *Personality and Social Psychology Bulletin, 49*(7). doi:10.1177/01461672221086771

Hales, A. H., Wesselmann, E. D., & Williams, K. D. (2016). Prayer, self-affirmation, and distraction improve recovery from short-term ostracism. *Journal of Experimental Social Psychology, 64*, 8–20. doi:10.1016/j.jesp.2016.01.002

Hales, A. H., & Williams, K. D. (2018). Marginalized individuals and extremism: The role of ostracism in openness to extreme groups. *Journal of Social Issues, 74*(1), 75–92. doi:10.1111/josi.12257

Haney, C., Banks, W. C., & Zimbardo, P. G. (1973). Study of prisoners and guards in a simulated prison. *Naval Research Reviews, 9*(1–17). Washington, DC: Office of Naval Research.

Harkins, S. G. (1987). Social loafing and social facilitation. *Journal of Experimental Social Psychology, 23*, 1–18. doi:10.1016/0022-1031(87)90022-9

Harkins, S. G., & Szymanski, K. (1987). Social loafing and social facilitation: New wine in old bottles. In C. Hendrick (Ed.), *Review of personality and social psychology: Group processes and intergroup relations* (Vol. 9, pp. 167–188). Newbury Park, CA: Sage.

Haslam, C., Haslam, S. A., Jetten, J., Cruwys, T., & Steffens, N. K. (2021). Life change, social identity, and health. *Annual Review of Psychology, 72*, 635–661. doi:10.1146/annurev-psych-060120-111721

Haslam, C., Holme, A., Haslam, S. A., Iyer, A., Jetten, J., & Williams, W. H. (2008). Maintaining group memberships: Social identity continuity predicts well-being after stroke. *Neuropsychological Rehabilitation, 18*(5–6), 671–691. doi:10.1080/09602010701643449v/pmc/articles/PMC3502509/

Haslam, S. A., Gaffney, A. G., Hogg, M. A., Rast III, D. E., & Steffens, N. K. (2022). Reconciling identity leadership and leader identity: A dual-identity framework. *The Leadership Quarterly, 33*. doi: 10.1016/j.leaqua.2022.101620

Haslam, S. A., & Reicher, S. D. (2016). Rethinking the psychology of leadership: From personal identity to social identity. *Daedelus, Journal of the American Academy of Arts and Sciences, 145*, 21–34.

Haslam, S. A., Reicher, S. D., & Platow, M. J. (2020). *The new psychology of leadership: Identity, influence and power* (2nd ed.). London: Routledge. doi:10.4324/9781351108232

Haslam, S. A., Reicher, S. D., Selvanathan, H. P., Gaffney, A. M., Steffens, N. K., Packer, D., Van Bavel, J. J., Ntontis, E., Neville, F., Vestergren, S., Jurstakova, K., & Platow, M. J. (2023). Examining the role of Donald Trump and his supporters in the 2021 assault on the US Capitol: A dual-agency model of identity leadership and engaged followership. *Leadership Quarterly, 34*(2), [101622]. doi:10.1016/j.leaqua.2022.101622

Hogg, M. A. (2001). A social identity theory of leadership. *Personality and Social Psychology Review, 5*, 184–200.

Hogg, M. A. (2006). Social identity theory. In P. J. Burke (Ed.), *Contemporary social psychological theories* (pp. 111–136). Redwood City, CA: Stanford University Press.

Hogg, M. A. (2007). Uncertainty-identity theory. In M. P. Zanna (Ed.), *Advances in experimental social psychology* (Vol. 39, pp. 69–126). San Diego, CA: Academic Press.

Hogg, M. A. (2010). Influence and leadership. In S. T. Fiske, D. T. Gilbert, & G. Lindzey (Eds.), *Handbook of social psychology* (5th ed., Vol. 2, pp. 1166–1207). New York: Wiley.

Hogg, M. A. (2021). Uncertain self in a changing world: A foundation for radicalisation, populism, and autocratic leadership. *European Review of Social Psychology, 32,* 235–268.

Hogg, M. A., & Adelman, J. (2013). Uncertainty-identity theory: Extreme groups, radical behavior, and authoritarian leadership. *Journal of Social Issues, 69*(3), 436–454. doi:10.1111/josi.12023

Hogg, M. A., Adelman, J. R., & Blagg, R. D. (2010). Religion in the face of uncertainty: An uncertainty-identity theory account of religiousness. *Personality and Social Psychology Review, 14,* 72–83.

Hogg, M. A., Kruglanski, A. W., & Van den Bos, K. (2013). *Uncertainty and the roots of extremism* [Special issue]. *Journal of Social Issues, 69*(3), 407–418.

Hogg, M. A., Meehan, C., & Farquharson, J. (2010). The solace of radicalism: Self-uncertainty and group identification in the face of threat. *Journal of Experimental Social Psychology, 46*(6), 1061–1066. doi:10.1016/j.jesp.2010.05.005

Hogg, M. A., & Rast, D. E. (2022). Intergroup leadership: The challenge of successfully leading fractured groups and societies. *Current Directions in Psychological Science, 31,* 564–571. doi:10.1177/09637214221121598

Hogg, M. A., & Reid, S. A. (2006). Social identity, self-categorization, and the communication of group norms. *Communication Theory, 16,* 7–30. doi:10.1111/j.1468-2885.2006.00003.x

Hogg, M. A., Sherman, D. K., Dierselhuis, J., Maitner, A. T., & Moffitt, G. (2007). Uncertainty, entitativity, and group identification. *Journal of Experimental Social Psychology, 43*(1), 135–142.

Hogg, M. A., & Turner, J. C. (1985). Interpersonal attraction, social identification and psychological group formation. *European Journal of Social Psychology, 15,* 51–66.

Hogg, M. A., van Knippenberg, D., & Rast III, D. E. (2012a). The social identity theory of leadership: A decade of research and conceptual development. *European Review of Social Psychology, 23,* 258–304. doi:10.1080/10463283.2012.741134

Hogg, M. A., van Knippenberg, D., & Rast III, D. E. (2012b). Intergroup leadership in organizations: Leading across group and organizational boundaries. *Academy of Management Review, 37,* 232–255. doi:10.5465/amr.2010.0221

Hohman, Z. P., Gaffney, A. M., & Hogg, M. A. (2017). Who am I if I am not like my group? Self-uncertainty and feeling peripheral in a group. *Journal of Experimental Social Psychology, 72,* 125–132. doi:10.1016/j.jesp.2017.05.002

Horgan, J. (2008). From profiles to pathways and roots to routes: Perspectives from psychology on radicalization into terrorism. *The ANNALS of the American Academy of Political and Social Science, 618,* 80–94.

House, R. J. (1971). A path–goal theory of leadership effectiveness. *Administrative Science Quarterly, 16,* 321–338.

House, R. J. (1977). A 1976 theory of charismatic leadership. In J. G. Hunt & L. Larson (Eds.), *Leadership: The cutting edge* (pp. 189–207). Carbondale, IL: Southern Illinois University Press.

House, R. J., Spangler, W. D., & Woycke, J. (1991). Personality and charisma in the U.S. presidency: A psychological theory of leader effectiveness. *Administrative Science Quarterly, 36*(3), 364–396. doi:10.2307/2393201

Jackson, J., & Harkins, S. G. (1985). Equity in effort: An explanation of the social loafing effect. *Journal of Personality and Social Psychology, 49,* 1199–1206.

Janis, I. L. (1972). *Victims of groupthink: A psychological study of foreign-policy decisions and fiascoes.* Boston, MA: Houghton Mifflin.

Janis, I. L. (1982). *Groupthink: Psychological studies of policy decisions and fiascos.* Boston, MA: Houghton Mifflin.

Jetten, J., Iyer, A., Branscombe, N. R., & Zhang, A. (2013). How the disadvantaged appraise group-based exclusion: The path from legitimacy to illegitimacy. *European Review of Social Psychology, 24,* 194–224. doi:10.1080/10463283.2013.840977

Judge, T. A., Bono, J. E., Ilies, R., & Gerhardt, M. W. (2002). Personality and leadership: A qualitative and quantitative review. *Journal of Applied Psychology, 87,* 765–780.

Karau, S. J., & Williams, K. D. (1993). Social loafing: A meta-analytic review and theoretical integration. *Journal of Personality and Social Psychology, 65,* 681–706. doi:10.1037/0022-3514.65.4.681

Kellezi, B., & Reicher, S. (2012). Social cure or social curse? The psychological impact of extreme events during the Kosovo conflict. In J. Jetten, C. Haslam, & S. A. Haslam (Eds.), *The social cure: Identity, health and well-being* (pp. 217–233). New York: Psychology Press.

Kruglanski, A. W., Gelfand, M. J., Bélanger, J. J., Sheveland, A., Hetiarachchi, M., & Gunaratna, R. (2014). The psychology of radicalization and deradicalization: How significance quest impacts violent extremism. *Political Psychology, 35,* 69–93.

Leonardelli, G. J., Pickett, C. L., & Brewer, M. B. (2010). Optimal distinctiveness theory: A framework for social identity, social cognition, and intergroup relations. In M. P. Zanna (Ed.), *Advances in experimental social psychology* (Vol. 43, pp. 63–113). San Diego, CA: Academic Press.

Lickel, B., Hamilton, D. L., Wieczorkowska, G., Lewis, A., Sherman, S. J., & Uhles, A. N. (2000). Varieties of groups and the perception of group entitativity. *Journal of Personality and Social Psychology, 78(2),* 223–246. doi:10.1037/0022-3514.78.2.223

Lüders, A., Jonas, E., Fritsche, I., & Agroskin, D. (2016). Between the lines of us and them: Identity threat, anxious uncertainty, and reactive in-group affirmation: How can antisocial outcomes be prevented? In S. McKeown, R. Haji, & N. Ferguson (Eds.), *Understanding peace and conflict through social identity theory: Contemporary global perspectives* (pp. 33–53). Cham, Switzerland: Springer International.

Marques, J., Abrams, D., & Serôdio, R. G. (2001). Being better by being right: Subjective group dynamics and derogation of in-group deviants when generic norms are undermined. *Journal of Personality and Social Psychology, 81,* 436–447. doi:10.1037/0022-3514.81.3.436

Meindl, J. R., Ehrlich, S. B., & Dukerich, J. M. (1985). The romance of leadership. *Administrative Science Quarterly, 30,* 78–102.

Milgram, S. (1963). Behavioral study of obedience. *The Journal of Abnormal and Social Psychology, 67(4),* 371–378. doi:10.1037/h0040525

Molet, M., Macquet, B., Lefebvre, O., & Williams, K. D. (2013). A focused attention intervention for coping with ostracism. *Consciousness and Cognition, 22,* 1262–1270.

Northouse, P. G. (2021). *Leadership: Theory and practice* (9th ed.). Thousand Oaks, CA: Sage.

Packer, D. J. (2008). On being both with us and against us: A normative conflict model of dissent in social groups. *Personality and Social Psychology Review, 12,* 50–72. doi:10.1177/1088868307309606

Pinto, I. R., Marques, J. M., Levine, J. M., & Abrams, D. (2010). Membership status and subjective group dynamics: Who triggers the black sheep effect? *Journal of Personality and Social Psychology, 99,* 107–119. doi:10.1037/a0018187

Prentice, D. A., Miller, D. T., & Lightdale, J. R. (1994). Asymmetries in attachments to groups and to their members: Distinguishing between common-identity and common-bond groups. *Personality and Social Psychology Bulletin, 20*(5), 484–493. doi:10.1177/0146167294205005

Rast III, D. E. (2015). Leadership in times of uncertainty: Recent findings, debates, and potential future research directions. *Social and Personality Psychology Compass, 9,* 133–145. doi:10.1111/spc3.12163

Rast III, D. E., Gaffney, A. M., Hogg, M. A., & Crisp, R. J. (2012). Leadership under uncertainty: When leaders who are non-prototypical group members can gain support. *Journal of Experimental Social Psychology, 48,* 646-653.

Rast III, D. E., Hogg, M. A., & Giessner, S. R. (2013). Self-uncertainty and support for autocratic leadership. *Self and Identity, 12*(6), 635–649. doi:10.1080/15298868.2012.718864

Rast III, D. E., Hogg, M. A., & Giessner, S. R. (2016). Who trusts charismatic leaders who champion change? The role of group identification, membership centrality, and self-uncertainty. *Group Dynamics: Theory, Research, and Practice, 20,* 259–275. doi:10.1037/gdn0000053

Ren, D., Wesselmann, E. D., & Williams, K. D. (2018). Hurt people hurt people: Ostracism and aggression. *Current Opinion in Psychology, 19,* 34–38.

Riva, P., Williams, K. D., Torstrick, A. M., & Montali, L. (2014). Orders to shoot (a camera): Effects of ostracism on obedience. *The Journal of Social Psychology, 154*(3), 208–216. doi:10.1080/00224545.2014.883354

Roccas, S., & Brewer, M. B. (2002). Social identity complexity. *Personality and Social Psychology Review, 6*(2), 88–106.

Sani, F., Bowe, M., Herrera, M., Manna, C., Cossa, T., Miao, X., & Zhou, Y. (2007). Perceived collective continuity: Seeing groups as entities that move through time. *European Journal of Social Psychology, 37*(6), 1118–1134.

Sani, F., Madhok, V., Norbury, M., Dugard, P., & Wakefield, J. R. (2015a). Greater number of group identifications is associated with healthier behaviour: Evidence from a Scottish community sample. *British Journal of Health Psychology, 20*(3), 466–481. doi:10.1111/bjhp.12119

Sani, F., Madhok, V., Norbury, M., Dugard, P., & Wakefield, J. R. (2015b). Greater number of group identifications is associated with lower odds of being depressed: Evidence from a Scottish community sample. *Social Psychiatry and Psychiatric Epidemiology, 50*(9), 1389–1397. doi:10.1007/s00127-015-1076-4

Schriesheim, C. A., & Neider, L. L. (1996). Path–goal leadership theory: The long and winding road. *The Leadership Quarterly, 7*(3), 317–321. doi:10.1016/S1048-9843(96)90023-5

Schriesheim, C. A., Tepper, B. J., & Tetrault, L. A. (1994). Least preferred co-worker score, situational control, and leadership effectiveness: A meta-analysis of contingency model performance predictions. *Journal of Applied Psychology, 79*(4), 561–573. doi:10.1037/0021-9010.79.4.561

Selvanathan, H. P., Crimston, C. R., & Jetten, J. (2022). How being rooted in the past can shape the future: The role of social identity continuity in the wish for a strong leader. *The Leadership Quarterly, 33.* doi:10.1016/j.leaqua.2022.101608

Seyranian, V., & Bligh, M. C. (2008). Presidential charismatic leadership: Exploring the rhetoric of social change. *The Leadership Quarterly, 19*(1), 54–76. doi:10.1016/j.leaqua.2007.12.005

Smeekes, A., & Verkuyten, M. (2013). Collective self-continuity, group identification and in-group defense. *Journal of Experimental Social Psychology, 49,* 984–994.

Smeekes, A., & Verkuyten, M. (2015). The presence of the past: Identity continuity and group dynamics. *European Review of Social Psychology, 26*(1), 162–202, doi: 10.1080/10463283.2015.1112653

Smeekes, A., Verkuyten, M., Çelebi, E., Acartürk, C., & Onkun, S. (2017). Social identity continuity and mental health among Syrian refugees in Turkey. *Social Psychiatry and Psychiatric Epidemiology, 52*(10), 1317–1324. doi:10.1007/s00127-017-1424-7

Smith, H. J., & Leach, C. W. (2004). Group membership and everyday social comparison experiences. *European Journal of Social Psychology, 34,* 297–308.

Southern Poverty Law Center. (2021). *The year in hate and extremism 2020.* Mongomery, AL: Southern Poverty Law Center.

Southern Poverty Law Center. (2023). *The year in hate and extremism 2022.* Mongomery, AL: Southern Poverty Law Center.

Steffens, N. K., Munt, K. A., van Knippenberg, D., Platow, M. J., & Haslam, S. A. (2021). Advancing the social identity theory of leadership: A meta-analytic review of leader group prototypicality. *Organizational Psychology Review, 11*(1), 35–72. doi:10.1177/2041386620962569

Syfers, L., Rast III, D. E., & Gaffney, A. M. (2021). Leading change by protecting group identity in the 2019 Canadian general election. *Analyses of Social Issues and Public Policy, 21,* 415–438. doi:10.1111/asap.12255

Tajfel, H. (Ed.). (1978). *Differentiation between social groups: Studies in the social psychology of intergroup relations.* London: Academic Press.

Tajfel, H., & Turner, J. C. (1979). An integrative theory of intergroup conflict. In W. G. Austin & S. Worchel (Eds.), *The social psychology of intergroup relations* (pp. 33–47). Monterey, CA: Brooks/Cole.

Triplett, N. (1898). The dynamogenic factors in peacemaking and competition. *American Journal of Psychology, 9,* 507–533.

Turner, J. C., Hogg, M. A., Oakes, P. J., Reicher, S. D., & Wetherell, M. S. (1987). *Rediscovering the social group: A self-categorization theory.* Oxford: Blackwell.

Turner, M. E., & Pratkanis, A. R. (1998). Twenty-five years of groupthink theory and research: Lessons from the evaluation of a theory. *Organizational Behavior and Human Decision Processes*, *73*, 105–115. doi:10.1006/obhd.1998.2756

van Knippenberg, D., van Knippenberg, B., Monden, L., & de Lima, F. (2002). Organizational identification after a merger: A social identity perspective. *British Journal of Social Psychology*, *41*, 233–252. doi:10.1348/014466602760060228

Versteegen, P. L. (2023). The excluded ordinary? A theory of populist radical right supporters' position in society. *European Journal of Social Psychology*, *53*(7), 1327–1341. https://doi.org/10.1002/ejsp.2977

Wakefield, J. R., Bowe, M., Kellezi, B., McNamara, N., & Stevenson, C. (2019). When groups help and when groups harm: Origins, developments, and future directions of the "Social Cure" perspective of group dynamics. *Social and Personality Psychology Compass*, *13*, e12440. doi:10.1111/spc3.12440

Weber, M. (1922). *Economy and society*. Berkeley, CA: University of California Press.

Weber, M. (1947). *The theory of social and economic organization* (Trans. A. M. Henderson & T. Parsons). New York: Oxford University Press.

Wesselmann, E. D., Bagg, D., & Williams, K. D. (2009). 'I feel your pain': The effects of observing ostracism on the ostracism detection system. *Journal of Experimental Social Psychology*, *45*, 1308–1311.

Wesselmann, E. D., Williams, K. D., Ren, D., & Hales, A. H. (2021). Ostracism and solitude. In R. J. Coplan, J. C. Bowker, & L. J., Nelson (Eds.), *The handbook of solitude: Psychological perspectives on social isolation, social withdrawal, and being alone* (2nd ed., pp. 209–223). Oxford: Wiley Blackwell.

Williams K. D. (2007). Ostracism. *Annual Review of Psychology*, *58*, 425–452. doi:10.1146/annurev.psych.58.110405.085641

Williams, K. D. (2010). Dyads can be groups (and often are). *Small Group Research*, *41*, 268–274. doi: 10.1177/1046496409358619

Williams, K. D., Cheung, C. K. T., & Choi, W. (2000). Cyberostracism: Effects of being ignored over the Internet. *Journal of Personality and Social Psychology*, *79*(5), 748–762. doi:10.1037/0022-3514.79.5.748

Williams, K. D., Hales, A. H., & Michels, C. (2019). Social ostracism as a factor motivating interest in extreme groups. In S. C. Rudert, R. Greifeneder, & K. D. Williams (Eds.), *Current directions in ostracism, social exclusion and rejection research* (pp. 18–31). Abingdon: Routledge. https://psycnet.apa.org/doi/10.4324/9781351255912-2

Williams, K. D., & Nida, S. A. (2011). Ostracism: Consequences and coping. *Current Directions in Psychological Science*, *20*, 71–75.

Williams, K. D., & Nida, S. A. (2022). Ostracism and social exclusion: Implications for separation, social isolation, and loss. *Current Opinion in Psychology*, *47*, 101353.

Williams, K. D., & Sommer, K. L. (1997). Social ostracism by coworkers: Does rejection lead to loafing or compensation? *Personality and Social Psychology Bulletin*, *23*, 693–706. doi: 10.1177/0146167297237003

Wohl, M. J. A., Squires, E. C., & Caouette, J. (2012). We were, we are, will we be? The social psychology of collective angst. *Social and Personality Psychology Compass, 6,* 379–391. doi:10.1111/j.1751-9004.2012.00437.x

Yukl, G. (1999). An evaluation of conceptual weaknesses in transformational and charismatic leadership theories. *The Leadership Quarterly, 10,* 285–305.

Zaccaro, S. J. (1984). Social loafing: The role of task attractiveness. *Personality and Social Psychology Bulletin, 10,* 99–106.

Zadro, L., & Gonsalkorale, K. (2014). Sources of ostracism: The nature and consequences of excluding and ignoring others. *Current Directions in Psychological Science, 23,* 93–97. doi:10.1177/0963721413520321

Zajonc, R. B. (1965). Social facilitation. *Science, 149,* 269–274.

9
PREJUDICE
SHELLEY MCKEOWN, AMANDA WILLIAMS, & SHAZZA ALI

Contents

9.1 AUTHORS' PERSONAL JOURNEYS

Shelley McKeown

I was born in and grew up in Northern Ireland, a society marred by the legacy of historical and ongoing tensions between two dominant ethno-religious groups: Catholics and Protestants. I didn't set out to be a social psychologist, but I found myself inspired by the excellent training in social psychology that I was lucky to experience as a first-generation student at the University of Ulster, first through an undergraduate degree in social psychology, and second through learning from and working with the late, great Professor Ed Cairns for my PhD. I am now a Professor of Social Psychology at the University of Oxford, and my research focuses on how group identities and contextual factors contribute to the perpetuation of prejudice and how this knowledge can contribute to interventions that reduce group-based prejudice and intergroup conflict.

Amanda Williams

I was born and raised in Ontario, Canada, which is where I studied. Canada is known for embracing its large multicultural population. Immigration and resulting population diversity have long been considered as being among Canada's strengths. But outside the major cities, as in the suburb where I grew up, racial minorities were underrepresented. On the infrequent occasions when I came face to face with racialized individuals, it was always a brief and superficial interaction. It wasn't until I went to university that I had the opportunity for more meaningful interactions with individuals and groups of people from different racial/ethnic backgrounds. Because of my experiences, I'm interested in better understanding perceivers' individual-level factors that lead to prejudice and the consequences of prejudice on both perceivers and targets.

Shazza Ali

I was born and raised in London, UK, a 'superdiverse' city that brings together an eclectic mix of people and cultures. The diverse makeup of the city, coupled with my mixed heritage, meant that I grew up meeting and appreciating people from all walks of life. My interest in psychology was sparked while working in an inner-city London primary school, where I became interested in supporting young people in becoming the best versions of themselves. However, first- and second-hand experiences highlighted how social group memberships, such as race, ethnicity, gender, and religion, greatly influence our experiences – how we see ourselves and how others see us. With this in mind, I decided to study psychology and completed my BSc, MSc, and PhD at the Centre for the Study of Group Processes at the University of Kent. I recently started a lectureship in social psychology in the School of Education at the University of Bristol.

Despite our different starting points, we take a complementary approach to studying the causes and consequences of prejudice in different contexts. We see the potential benefits that social psychology can offer society and people's daily lives. As social psychologists and social scientists, we are often encouraged to leave our experiences at the door when it comes to conducting our research. And yet, many of us are inspired to do what we do because of our desire to understand our experiences and improve society. It is important to recognise the biases we bring into our work. Some people think researching prejudice is boring and not 'real science', but we argue that given the consequences and pervasiveness of prejudicial attitudes and behaviours for individuals, groups, and society at large, we need the study of prejudice more than ever. Coming together, we do not argue about which is more important in the perpetuation of prejudice, but instead appreciate that combining individual- and group-level perspectives will provide a more complete and richer understanding of prejudice, its consequences, and how best to develop and evaluate interventions to reduce prejudice.

9.2 CHAPTER OUTLINE

Following a brief introduction to the topic and the chapter learning objectives, this chapter consists of three main parts. The first, *Foundations*, defines prejudice and considers individual to group-level explanations for it. It also considers the perspective of those who experience prejudice and how prejudice can be reduced. The second, *Advances*, focuses on new advances in the study of prejudice, specifically on the development of prejudice across the lifespan and how prejudicial attitudes and behaviours can be measured. The third, *Applications*, takes the theoretical underpinning of what we know about prejudice and prejudice reduction and applies it to the real world. Specifically, it focuses on how social psychological understanding of prejudice has been applied in diversity initiatives, such as implicit bias training, and through intergroup contact interventions. The chapter ends with a summary, ideas for revision, and suggestions for further reading.

9.3 INTRODUCTION

You only need to turn on the news or check your social media feed to see that prejudice is all around us – in the interactions we have with others, in the ways groups are represented in the media, and in the discriminatory behaviours we see in our everyday lives. But what is prejudice? Broadly speaking, prejudice refers to a 'a hostile attitude or feeling toward a person solely because he or she belongs to a group to which one has assigned objectionable qualities' (Allport, 1954, p. 7). What this means is that you may experience negative behaviour from others because of the assumptions and stereotypes that they hold about the groups you belong to, such as your race, ethnicity, religion, sexuality, gender identity, or even what sports team you support. At this point, it is important to note that prejudice can be both blatant, such as aggressive behaviours, or subtle, such as holding stereotypes about particular groups (see Chapter 10 for a detailed discussion of intergroup relations). This distinction matters because it informs not only how we measure prejudice, as detailed in Part 2, but also how we might intervene to reduce different forms of prejudice.

Understanding more about prejudice matters because regardless of whether prejudice is based on your racial, gender, or other identities, experiencing prejudice can have negative consequences for each of us as individuals. For example, if you are treated badly because of the ethnic group you belong to, it may lower your self-esteem, cause you to perform worse at school, or impact the type of job you are willing to apply for or even get. And this has knock-on effects for society; for example, some groups are more represented in certain professions than others. In Part 1, we explain several different forms of prejudice, how they manifest, and the many consequences they can have. However, it is not all doom and gloom – there is some good news. Theory and research have demonstrated that we can reduce the prejudice that individuals hold towards particular groups. And further, there is some evidence that this can improve relations between groups within society more broadly. It is this potential of prejudice-reduction approaches that we discuss in Part 1, and then we focus on how these approaches have been applied in practice in Part 2.

In sum, prejudice matters because it affects individuals, groups, and society. We need to know more about not only how prejudice develops across the lifespan, but also how it manifests and what we can do to support more positive and cohesive societies.

9.4 LEARNING OBJECTIVES

In this chapter, you will learn about prejudice and its antecedents, associated behaviour, consequences, and what we can do about it. You will be introduced to definitions of prejudice and be made aware of its various forms, become familiar with different explanations for prejudice and its development, critique approaches to prejudice reduction, and learn how to apply psychological theory to practice and intervention design. Part 1 of this chapter will focus specifically on forms and explanations of prejudice, and consider both target and perpetrator perspectives as well as approaches to reducing prejudice. Part 2 will then consider advances in prejudice research, reflecting on a developmental perspective to prejudice development and how prejudice can be measured. Part 3 will round off the chapter by focusing on applications.

By the end of this chapter, you will be able to:

- Describe and distinguish between different forms of prejudice;
- Explain prejudice development drawing on different theoretical perspectives;
- Critique approaches to prejudice reduction;
- Evaluate the measurement of prejudice and behaviour;
- Apply theoretical understandings of prejudice to design and evaluate prejudice reduction interventions.

9.5 PART 1: FOUNDATIONS

This section defines prejudice and considers individual- to group-level explanations for it. It also considers the perspective of those who experience prejudice and how prejudice can be reduced.

9.5.1 What is Prejudice?

People differ on an unlimited number of characteristics. Some of these characteristics are directly observable, such as height, age, or skin colour. Other characteristics are not observable, such as religion, national identity, or choice of hobby (although it is possible to show one's belonging to a group through behaviour and appearance). To simplify our social world, humans tend to think of people as belonging to groups based on their shared characteristics – these are called social groups. For example, all people who attend Mass may be grouped together as the social group 'Catholics'. All people with a light peach skin tone may be categorised as 'Caucasian' or 'White'. A single person can belong to numerous social groups at one time. For example, it is possible to be both Catholic and White. And, as we will see when we discuss essentialism in section 9.6.1, group membership is fluid: it is possible to both join and leave the social groups that we identify with and/or belong to.

Human beings have a fundamental need to belong. We seek to form stable, meaningful relationships with other people (Baumeister & Leary, 1995). To meet this need, we readily form attachments to other people. Social groups – groups that have shared common characteristics – are one dimension we use as the basis of forming relationships. Because of shared common characteristics, the groups to which people belong become affiliated with the self. For example, Amanda grew up in Canada and holds many cultural values that reflect this upbringing. While living in the UK, she felt very attached to this Canadian identity. She would often form friendships with other Canadians who had the same cultural upbringing. You, dear reader, have likely had similar experiences when you first attended university – particularly if you moved away from your home town. When far away from the familiar, it is likely that if you met someone from your home town, you would have considered them a friend! Or at least you would have had a conversation with them, likely about things you both miss from your home town. The shared characteristics – the same home town – served as a point of connection and feeling of familiarity. While this shared cultural understanding can have the benefit of encouraging social connections, it also runs the risk of **ethnocentrism**, whereby groups to which an individual belongs (ingroup) are considered to be superior to groups to which an individual does not belong (outgroups). Ingroups are seen as the default comparison point for outgroups. This occurs for any type of social group, even when groups are formed along

> **Key concept – Ethnocentrism:**
> Ethnocentrism can be understood as cultural narrowness; in other words, seeing the world through the eyes of one's own culture.

> **Key concept – Prejudice:** A preconceived negative belief or attitude about a person or people based solely on their social group membership(s). Prejudice is an attitude that can be expressed either openly (blatant prejudice) or slyly (subtle prejudice).

> **Key concept – Discrimination:** Occurs when others are treated poorly because of their group memberships (e.g., not hiring an individual for a job because of their racial or sexual identity). Discrimination is behaviour or actions that can be manifested either openly (e.g., slurs) or subtly (e.g., microaggressions).

arbitrary dimensions (Hammond & Axelrod, 2006). These arbitrary groups are known within prejudice research as 'minimal groups', and we will return to them below.

But what does preferring one's ingroup mean for how we think about and treat outgroup members? Does the perceived superiority of the ingroup or 'ingroup love' result in holding **prejudice** towards the outgroup or 'outgroup hate'? Sometimes, depending on social norms, ingroup love does correspond to outgroup hate. But more often – especially in Western societies – ingroup love leads to preference for ingroup members, but not to the derogation of outgroup members. Although ingroup love does not always lead to outgroup hate (Allport, 1954; Brewer, 1999), preference for ingroup members can be manifested in such a way that outgroups experience differential treatment. **Discrimination** occurs when an individual's behaviour or actions result in another person being treated poorly because of their group memberships.

Ingroup love may explain a dilemma that exists in Western societies. In the absence of deliberate derogation of outgroup members, and despite legislation and social norms that promote equal opportunities for all, social group disparities persist. These disparities can be seen from 'cradle to grave', meaning they are evident across all aspects of life – within health-care, income and socioeconomic status, education, employment, criminal justice, and so on. Given legislation and social norms that promote equity, it is likely that these disparities are not because of outgroup hate. Instead, disparities exist and persist because of ingroup love, corresponding feelings of familiarity with ingroup members, and centring the ingroup. We expand on these ideas when discussing different forms of prejudice below.

EXERCISE 9.1

Manifestations of Prejudice in the Real World

This exercise is designed to get you thinking about how explanations of prejudice can be used to understand examples of real-world prejudice (attitudes) and resulting discrimination (behaviour). Let's consider different sexual groups. Has there been a time when you have experienced prejudice or discrimination in your own life because of your sexuality, or where you have observed prejudice or discrimination towards others because of their sexuality? Reflecting on what you have learned about explanations for prejudice, where do you think the prejudices and resulting discrimination you have experienced or observed stemmed from? Were they a function of personality and individual differences, social and cognitive processes, or a combination of all of these? Draw on theoretical perspectives discussed in this chapter to come to a conclusion.

GUEST PERSONAL JOURNEY

Jaysan Charlesford

In 1980s London, the odds that a child three generations from Windrush, in single-parent social housing, would become a lecturer in psychology were slim, but luckily I'd won a penis in the great lottery of life. Some amazing (overwhelmingly, female) teachers nurtured me through A-levels. I got as far from London as my grades would allow. At uni, I lurched from night shifts into 9 a.m. lectures, silently wrestling demons of self-doubt and otherness; academia was not an institution I could see myself in. A 2:1, into a chaotic Master's year, then parenthood flipped my world. I paused my studies, got married, reconnected with God, and found balance. Under the mentorship of a wonderful (female) supervisor, I completed my PhD. Sheer passion and doggedness took me to viva, where I was met by two field-experts who looked me square in the eye and grilled me as an equal and potential-future-peer. With new-found self-belief, I jumped into two postdocs (both supervised by fantastic women) and my first lectureship swiftly followed. Presently (coincidentally[!]), I explore the social psychology of intergroup relations and equality-in-practice, yet my fervent wish is to nurture a crop of PhD students who will go forth and improve this broken world.

9.5.2 Forms of Prejudice

The previous section outlined that social group disparities (such as the gender wage gap, the under-employment of racialized individuals, etc.) persist in societies that seemingly value diversity and equity. This paradox is partly related to the different forms that prejudice can take. Western societies strive to be egalitarian, where all people are considered equal and deserving of equal rights and opportunities. In such contexts, **blatant prejudice** and the corresponding overt and conscious expression of bias are less likely to occur (e.g., Pearson et al., 2009; Pettigrew & Meertens, 1995). For example, in the UK, the Equality Act 2010 prohibits the discrimination of employees based on nine protected characteristics: age, disability, gender reassignment, marriage and civil partnership, pregnancy and maternity, race, religion or belief, sex, and sexual orientation (UK Government, 2010). Therefore, in the UK, we are unlikely to see companies explicitly justify firing someone based on these protected characteristics; it is, for example, illegal to fire a person who has just given birth.

> **Key concept – Blatant prejudice:** The most obvious form of prejudice that we see in our everyday lives. At extreme levels, it is displayed directly and openly, when ill-intentioned individuals act aggressively towards outgroup members.

> **Key concept – Subtle prejudice:** An automatic and often unintentional response based on biases that are acquired from cultural narratives and personal experiences.

Instead of being driven by blatant prejudice, social group disparities are more likely to be caused by **subtle prejudice** (Pettigrew & Meertens, 1995). Subtle prejudice is the often-unintentional expression of negative beliefs and behaviours towards outgroup members. Subtle prejudice can be expressed even when a person supports principles of equality and seeks to be non-prejudiced. Subtle prejudice is often indirect and explained away or rationalised (Pearson et al., 2009). But even when the expression of bias is subtle, the consequence is not.

Using the workplace, we can explore one example of how subtle prejudice can impact people's lives. As a result of the COVID pandemic, between October and December 2020 the UK unemployment rate increased overall. For people from White backgrounds the unemployment rate increased by 1.4%, from 3.1% in 2019 to 4.5% during the same period in 2020. But for people from a minority ethnic background, the unemployment rate doubled as compared to White people; it increased by 3.7%, jumping from 5.8% in 2019 to 9.5% during the same period in 2020 (Francis-Devine & Powell, 2022). This is an example of racial disparity in unemployment rates. Subtle prejudice is one explanation for why unemployment rose at a greater rate for minority ethnic individuals. Employment decisions, such as who to fire, can be based on subjective criteria. This includes feelings of who belongs or 'fits' with the company (Elvira & Zatzick, 2002). Subtle prejudice stemming from ingroup preference, where individuals feel more comfortable around ingroup members, may lead managers and other stakeholders (who are predominantly White individuals) to feel outgroup members 'fit' less well within their organisation. But the disparate firing of minority ethnic individuals was explained away using the economic turmoil caused by COVID-19 and the necessity of firing less critical employees to keep the organisation running – a seemingly rational explanation.

Expressions of Prejudice

Although there are two main forms of prejudice, these can be expressed in many ways. How blatant prejudice is expressed is relatively straightforward. It is the open, obvious, and unashamed communication of negative attitudes directed to outgroups and outgroup members. In contrast, the expression of subtle prejudice is complex, nuanced, and variable. Below we will outline some of the more common ways subtle prejudice is expressed, including implicit bias, micro-aggressions, and dehumanisation.

Implicit Bias

When processing the world around us, we have instinctive reactions. For example, seeing something negative, such as a car accident, is likely to make our stomach drop. Seeing something positive, such as a favourite food, is likely to bring a smile to one's face. These 'gut' feelings are referred to as implicit reactions. Implicit reactions also occur in response to people. Implicit reactions to social groups are known as implicit bias. Stated another way, implicit biases are beliefs and attitudes that are activated by the mere presence of an attitude object (Greenwald & Banaji, 1995). You have likely heard about implicit bias – it is commonly referred to as 'unconscious bias', 'unconscious prejudice', 'unconscious attitudes', or the like. The tag of 'unconscious' attempts to indicate that people are unaware that they have instinctive reactions towards members of social groups. But avoid this term! It is incorrect. People can be aware (or conscious) that they hold implicit bias towards others (Gawronski et al., 2006). Regardless of whether implicit bias operates consciously or unconsciously, it is considered a subtle prejudice because these beliefs are unintentionally and automatically activated, and often (but not always) operate outside introspection (i.e., they are 'gut reactions'), can fly under the radar of detection when influencing behaviour, and are difficult to suppress.

For this automatic activation or gut reaction to occur, the object and attitude or evaluation must be linked (associated) in memory (Devine, 1989) (see Key study 9.1). Through a combination of personal experience (such as one's familiarity with outgroups, one's level of ingroup preference) and environmental cues (such as how different groups are represented in the media, structural hierarchies; Payne et al., 2017), particular social categories are likely to become associated with positive (i.e., women as nurturing and thus positive) or negative (i.e., Black men as aggressive and thus negative) evaluations and affect. An individual may personally endorse these associations, or they may not. Regardless, information reflecting personal experience and environmental cues intersect to form a filter that is often (unintentionally) used to process incoming information in bias-consistent ways. This can happen despite one's best intentions to be egalitarian. Implicit bias illustrates how the environments in which we live can shape our beliefs about – and subsequently our behaviour towards – other people.

KEY STUDY 9.1

Connecting Stereotypes and Prejudice

How is it that even people who reject racial prejudice and stereotyping still show discriminatory behaviour? Patricia Devine (1989) made one of the initial attempts to answer this question, which is still plaguing researchers today. Across three studies,

(Continued)

Devine's results revealed that undergraduate research participants were able to generate (Study 1 and 3) and identify (Study 2) the components of the cultural stereotype of Black people, and exposure to the cultural stereotype automatically influenced their perceptions of ambiguous behaviours performed by a race-unspecified target (Study 2). The pattern of results did not differ for participants identified to be high or low in explicit racial prejudice (Study 1–3), even when given the opportunity to reflect on personal (explicit) beliefs (Study 3). Together, these findings revealed that even individuals who consciously rejected racism exhibited automatically activated biases that influenced their perceptions and judgements of others. The work by Devine demonstrated the pervasive nature of implicit biases, including the complex interplay between explicit and implicit prejudice. Devine's (1989) paper is an essential read for students who are interested in learning more about automatic processing, social cognition, and intergroup relations.

Microaggressions

Another expressor of prejudice can be found in the display of microaggressions. But what are microaggressions? Individuals who belong to dominant social groups (some examples relevant to the UK context would be wealthy, White, male, heterosexual, cisgender, etc.) are more likely to hold dominant positions of authority and power in society (e.g., politicians, teachers, police officers, university professors, business owners, and so on). This clustering is thought to reflect the relative advantage that comes along with dominant social group membership. Commonly described as 'death by a thousand cuts', **microaggressions** are subtle indignities that individuals from historically disadvantaged groups face daily. Although microaggressions encompass a range of behaviours (see Sue et al., 2007a), what is common among these brief, everyday exchanges is that they send disparaging messages to individuals from historically disadvantaged groups *because* of their group membership (Sue et al., 2007b).

> **Key concept – Microaggressions:** Small actions (typically unintentional) that individuals in dominant positions engage in that discriminate against individuals from historically marginalized and disadvantaged groups.

The concept of microaggressions was first developed to explain everyday experiences of racial discrimination, but has subsequently been extended to illustrate how culture can inform subtle prejudice directed towards individuals from any marginalised group, including women, LGBT+ people, and people with a disability, excess weight, following a particular religion, etc. Although qualitative research is most frequently conducted on this topic, quantitative surveys have been developed where researchers use questionnaires to assess how often individuals experience microaggressions (see Nadal, 2011, for an example). Microaggressions are so ingrained within culture that the microaggressor is often unaware of their prejudiced actions. Even being a subject matter expert in prejudice does not provide immunity against performing microaggressions. Let me (Amanda) explain.

> One day, I was walking up a very long, steep hill (Park St, Bristol, for those of you in the know) on my way to work. I was carrying a shoulder bag that was very heavy (wallet, laptop, water, books, etc in it). I was approaching the top of the hill when I saw a Black man walking down on the same side as my shoulder bag. As the man passed me, I moved my bag to the other shoulder. If asked in that moment, I would have justified my behaviour on an unrelated dimension – my bag was heavy! But why did I pick that moment to move my bag to the other shoulder? Upon reflection I see that this was a microaggression – a subtle behaviour that sent an (unintended) message to all around me: I baselessly assumed that the man was somehow 'criminal' and would steal from me. (Sue et al., 2007b)

This is but one example. There is an endless list of what microaggressions look like. But all microaggressions have shared features: they are subtle behaviours that are hard for microaggressors to detect and for targets to object to. Overall, this makes microaggressions difficult to

Table 9.1 Explaining microaggressions. Adapted from: www.themicropedia.org

Example behaviour	Why it is considered a microaggression
'You're so resilient' 'You're so brave'	When stated in response to an individual sharing experience of discrimination, this is typically meant as a compliment. But such statements suggest that there is something inherently difficult or abnormal about a particular identity. Instead of helping to identify root causes, such statements lead to centring resilience and bravery when sharing narratives of oppression.
'Where are you really from?'	This statement assumes that minority ethnic individuals were not born in the host country and must be immigrants. It reinforces the idea that whiteness is synonymous with being British and anyone who is not White is an outsider.
Correcting someone's grammar	This type of behaviour is shaming, and is often used on social media to make people think an individual is uneducated or to discredit the content posted. It reinforces perceptions linked to education, speech, intelligence, and worth.
Interrupting only women in a meeting	This reflects the belief that men (or other dominant groups) are more powerful in society and thus can interrupt women, especially in work settings. It also plays into gendered expectations of women being quiet and not assertive. Over time such behaviour can make it difficult for women to speak up, as they might be uncomfortable or unwilling to interject.
'But you look so normal'	This phrase is often used when a characteristic (including but not limited to disability) is invisible. It perpetuates the notion that the characteristic is abnormal. It also implies that people with particular characteristics need to present in similar ways.

prevent. The best way to prevent microaggressions from occurring is to point them out and raise awareness of such behaviour and consequences.

The power of microaggressions lies in their subtle and ambiguous nature, particularly when they are intended as a compliment. This subtleness enables the microaggressor to excuse their behaviour as inconsequential and explain away the harm with seemingly unbiased and valid reasons (Gartner et al., 2020). The examples provided in Table 9.1 illustrate how microaggressions are woven into the fabric of society as pervasive, everyday experiences.

Although most of the research conducted on microaggressions has documented experiences in a North American context, the UK is not immune. In a small sample of students attending universities in Northern England, all individuals who identified as a racial minority reported experiencing at least one racial microaggression in the previous six months (Williams et al., 2016). The cumulative pattern of microaggressions reinforces structural hierarchies and sends messages about what is considered to be 'normal' or 'typical' behaviour for social group members (McTernan, 2018). Over time, experiencing microaggressions can negatively impact mental health (Nadal et al., 2010) and self-esteem (Nadal et al., 2014).

Dehumanisation

The final form of expressions of prejudice discussed in this chapter is dehumanisation, which is related to thoughts about the 'humanness' of people. Specifically, when people are dehumanised, they are denied unique and fundamental human characteristics (e.g., they are seen as lacking agency, depth, warmth and emotionality, and are likened to animals or inanimate objects (Haslam & Loughnan, 2014).

The denial of humanness can be overt and implicated in violent atrocities or can be more subtle, yet still evident in everyday behaviours. Early research used dehumanisation theories to explain why people committed violent atrocities against others during inter-ethnic conflicts. For example, in World War II, Jews were portrayed as rats (Bytwerk, 1998), and in the 1994 Rwandan genocide, Tutsi people were commonly called cockroaches (Ndahiro, 2014). Thus, likening members of these ethnic groups to animals and not human individuals, coupled with explicit calls to harm or kill them, played a huge part in their genocide. However, it would be misleading to think that blatant dehumanisation is a thing of the past or something that occurs solely within the context of conflict. Blatant dehumanisation can be observed in hate speech for both historical (e.g., in war propaganda) and current events. For example, in 2018, UK Foreign Secretary Boris Johnson said that Muslim women wearing burkas looked like letterboxes (Johnson, 2018), and in 2018, when speaking about immigrants, US President Donald Trump stated 'You wouldn't believe how bad these people are. These aren't people. These are animals' (USA Today News, 2018).

KEY THINKER

Nour Kteily

Recent research highlights the continuing prevalence and relevance of blatant forms of dehumanisation. In decades past, psychologists primarily focused on relatively subtle forms of dehumanisation, like downplaying an outgroup's ability to experience more complex secondary emotions or traits, or holding an implicit association between outgroups and non-human entities. Underlying this important research was an assumption that individuals today are unlikely to explicitly hold and overtly express views of other groups as 'lower' animals. Yet, a paper by Kteily and colleagues (2015), which introduced the 'Ascent of Human' measure of blatant dehumanisation (see section 9.6.2 on measuring prejudice and predicting behaviour), showed that, in fact, individuals do hold and report views of certain outgroups as 'less evolved' and more like quadrupedal apes. For example, Americans viewed Arabs as significantly less human than the ingroup; ethnic Hungarians expressed substantial dehumanisation of the Roma population; and Israelis and Palestinians viewed one another as closer to animals than humans. Blatant dehumanisation also appears to be consequential, predicting hostile policies (e.g., anti-immigration attitudes, support for violent aggression) and behaviour (e.g., donation behaviour) beyond more subtle forms of dehumanisation and beyond mere prejudice (Kteily & Bruneau, 2017). Dehumanisation can also promote vicious cycles of conflict: those who feel dehumanised by another group (i.e., meta-dehumanisation) often reciprocate in kind, reinforcing mutual hostility (Kteily et al., 2016; Kteily & Landry 2022).

The list of groups that can be dehumanised is almost endless, and includes refugees as well as people from racial, ethnic, national, religious, and minority groups, those with certain university or political party affiliations, meat eaters, businessmen, doctors, women, employees, older people, LGBT+ people, obese people, people with poor mental health, and those with low socio-economic status, to list a few. With such a wide range of groups experiencing dehumanisation, it is important to understand the conditions under which it emerges. Research suggests that dehumanisation is likely to occur when groups are in conflict, of low status, and are interdependent within the ingroup (Leyens et al., 2001). Although the process of dehumanisation is debated, there is no denying that it is widespread and can have detrimental effects on the targets.

Above, we have reviewed a few forms that blatant and subtle prejudice can take. These examples illustrate that these subtle biases permeate societies, preserve societal inequalities, contribute to disparities between dominant and marginalised groups, and, as such, have severe consequences for those on the receiving end. The forms of prejudice range from violent atrocities to subtle everyday behaviours, that can be personally endorsed – or not! – by the perpetrator. Overall, more blatant forms of prejudice may be easier to address (Solorzano et al., 2000) because they lack ambiguity. The more subtle forms of prejudice typically fly under the radar for the perpetrators (but not the targets) and thus there is the additional challenge of making the invisible visible in addition to confronting the cause of prejudice, whether it be personal beliefs or structural inequalities. Therefore, there is an increased call for open and honest dialogue examining how biases can be perpetuated via cultural conditions and acted on by those in positions of relative advantage.

EXERCISE 9.2

Modern-Day Dehumanisation

This exercise is designed to get you thinking about modern-day dehumanisation and support for discriminatory practices and/or hostile policies in the media. Have a look online at reports of conflicts or disadvantage faced by people in different parts of the world and make a note of any differences that you notice (e.g., in the description of the group or the relief efforts). Think about what may be driving any differences that you find.

For example, in early 2022, many international news channels reported on Russia's invasion of Ukraine. However, there were noticeable differences in how Ukrainians were described in comparison to victims of war from other parts of the world. Many Western reports conveyed explicit ingroup bias as they focused on the location of Ukraine (forming part of Europe), the appearance of Ukrainians, and how shocking it was to see people from these social groups suffering in this way. Some reports made comparisons to other conflicts and, in the process, dehumanised victims from other parts of the world and rendered their negative experiences as somehow normal and expected (Al Jazeera, 2022; Arab News, 2022). Not only were there differences in reports of the conflict, there were also stark differences in the relief efforts that followed. That is, many European countries created specific initiatives to help accommodate Ukrainian refugees, and although efforts like these are praiseworthy, it became apparent that refugees fleeing from other conflicts had not received the same hospitality.

9.5.3 Explaining Prejudice

Up until this point, we have provided definitions of prejudice and discussed some of the various forms that prejudice can take. Now, we are going to move on to consider explanations for why prejudice occurs. First, we will consider evolutionary explanations for prejudice before moving on to individual-level explanations, such as personality, and then social and cognitive explanations. Here, we ask the question whether prejudice is a result of individual personalities, the social group, the social situation, or a mixture of all of these.

Evolutionary Perspectives

Humans are social beings and have an inherent desire to belong to groups; however, people are often excluded from groups, based on a range of criteria (see Chapter 8: Group Processes). The evolutionary perspective suggests that in order to ensure survival and successful reproduction, our ancestors would have had to discriminate between things in their environments (e.g., food-stuffs, animals, individuals) and avoid those that could have negative consequences (e.g., plants containing deadly toxins, dangerous animals, individuals that posed a threat to their welfare; Schaller & Neuberg, 2012). So, the psychological mechanisms that helped them to accurately identify and minimise threats would have been evolutionarily adaptive (Neuberg et al., 2011).

When early humans encountered other humans, they would primarily categorise them based on physical attributes (such as skin colour, physique) and avoid those who evoked fear (e.g., those with whom they were unfamiliar or unsure about) or who showed signs of ill-health, under the premise that this would help to decrease their vulnerability to interpersonal harm or infectious diseases. However, it's important to note that our psychological processes are not always perfect, and when it comes to threat detection, we have the tendency to over-generalise (e.g., to perceive non-threatening stimuli as threatening). While this may be rooted in maximising survival and minimising potential harm (especially for our ancestors), it also increases processing errors, resulting in prejudices which are often expressed against individuals (and groups) who pose no actual threat (Schaller & Neuberg, 2012).

Evolutionary change is relatively slow and lags far behind cultural change. As such, evolutionary processes continue to influence our emotions, cognitions, and behaviours in contemporary environments, and many have problematic consequences. Although our ancestors' prejudiced responses may have been adaptive in the past, they don't serve the same function in today's global societies, where people from diverse backgrounds live inter-dependently and in proximity. Yet, people from many different social or cultural groups are often implicitly assumed (based on superficial features alone) to pose some sort of potential threat and are subsequently pre-judged and stigmatised.

The evolutionary perspective offers one explanation for the origins of some of the prejudices that we see today. However, some researchers argue that we should avoid describing prejudice as 'hardwired' or 'in our nature', since we can challenge our own processes, and there are many other factors that contribute to how, when, and why prejudice may occur.

Personality and Individual Differences

There are several different theories that focus on how prejudice might be a function of individual differences. Let's think about a few of these in more depth.

The Authoritarian Personality

When observing prejudice, people often want to know whether prejudice is a result of individual personality, and this question has attracted quite a lot of research. One of the most influential classical individual-level psychological theories to explain prejudice and resulting conflict is Adorno and colleagues' (1950) authoritarian personality theory. This theory grew out of attempts to explain antisemitism and is largely based on Freudian ideas. Individuals who have an authoritarian personality are thought to hold conventional beliefs, have a high respect for and obedience towards authority figures, and be intolerant towards those who hold non-conventional beliefs, which can result in prejudice towards other groups.

Adorno and colleagues (1950) believed that an authoritarian personality could be measured using the Fascist scale (F-scale), and found that scoring highly on authoritarianism, as measured by the F-scale, was strongly associated with prejudice. An example scale item is:

> Obedience and respect for authority are the most important virtues children should learn.

However, in later developments, Altemeyer (1981) questioned the utility of Adorno and colleagues' F-scale and argued that authoritarianism could be better measured by a pattern of personality that he called **right-wing authoritarianism** (RWA). Altemeyer then developed one of the most used measures of RWA of all time, the RWA scale. An example item of this scale is:

> Our country desperately needs a mighty leader who will do what has to be done to destroy the radical new ways and sinfulness that are ruining us.

This scale has, however, been critiqued for treating RWA as a unitary concept when, in fact, RWA should perhaps be considered more as a multi-dimensional construct – in other words, comprising different aspects. For example, Duckitt and colleagues (2010) drew on Altemeyer's original theorising to reconceptualise RWA as comprising three components that represent social/ideological attitudes rather than personality. These are: authoritarianism, conservatism, and traditionalism. Contemporary research finds support for this multi-dimensional approach, with each of these factors being found to be distinct from one another and to predict prejudice across a range of samples (Duckitt & Bizmuic, 2013).

> **Key concept – Right-wing authoritarian:** A person who holds high respect for and tends to conform to authority figures and is intolerant towards those who are thought to hold unconventional beliefs.

Social Dominance Theory

Another reason why individuals might hold prejudicial attitudes is because of their desire to maintain hierarchies within society, something known as holding high levels of social dominance orientation. Put forward by Sidanius (1993), social dominance theory tries to explain why individuals, and in turn societies, seek to maintain group-based dominance, where one group holds considerable power and privileges over other groups. It distinguishes between two forms of legitimising myths: hierarchy-enhancing (or hierarchy-legitimising) myths, which help to maintain or increase group-based inequality, and hierarchy-attenuating myths, which help to decrease group-based inequality and promote egalitarian relations among social groups. Examples of hierarchy-legitimising myths include ethnic prejudice, sexism, and political-economic conservatism (capitalism), whereas examples of hierarchy-attenuating myths include feminism, human rights, and meritocracy (Pratto et al., 1994).

To measure individual preferences for group-based inequalities, support for group hierarchies, and a preference for the ingroup to dominate over other groups in society, Pratto and colleagues (1994) developed the **social dominance orientation** (SDO) scale. Evidence shows that individuals who score high on SDO demonstrate high levels of prejudice (Pratto et al., 1994) and negative attitudes towards ethnic minorities (Hiel & Mervielde, 2005). An example item from this scale is:

Some groups of people are just more worthy than others.

Like RWA, however, some commentators suggest that SDO might be better considered as including two components: SDO-dominance (a preference for group status dominance) and SDO-egalitarianism (a preference for unequal rights between groups). Example items include:

Some groups of people must be kept in their place (SDO-D).

Group equality should not be our primary goal (SDO-E).

In their study, Ho and colleagues (2012) found that SDO-D and SDO-E were two separate constructs when tested among seven samples in the US and in Israel and Palestine, and found that each differently predicted indicators of prejudice.

SDO is considered by many social psychologists to be a modern measure of prejudice and is increasingly measured alongside RWA. It is argued that using the two together represents a dual-process model, with each predicting distinct components of prejudice and in different ways (Duckitt, 2001). For example, it is thought that SDO measures ideologies associated with maintaining ingroup superiority and dominance, while RWA measures ideologies associated with threat-driven goals to establish and maintain social order and security (Duckitt 2001; Duckitt & Sibley, 2007).

> **Key concept – Social dominance orientation:** The individual tendency to support and wish to maintain group-based social hierarchies. Social dominance orientation (SDO) can be broken down into SDO-dominance, which is a preference for group status dominance, and SDO-egalitarianism, which is a preference for unequal rights between groups.

Social and Cognitive Processes

Now that we have considered both evolutionary and personality antecedents of prejudice, do you think there may be other factors that go beyond the individual that can explain prejudice? Let's now think about some of the social and cognitive processes that may play a role.

When we look at the world around us, we find ourselves dividing people into social categories that represent the groups they do or do not belong to (e.g., businessman, student, wealthy, etc.). When we categorise people in this way, we form impressions of them, i.e., what we think people may be like. This process of impression formation involves a complex series of mental processes, starting with attaching specific qualities to the target based on their group membership (and possibly informed by what's going on around them; see Fiske & Neuberg, 1990). The beliefs that we have about particular groups and how we expect their members to behave are often understood as **stereotypes**.

> **Key concept – Stereotypes and stereotyping:** Stereotypes are the qualities that are perceived to be associated with particular groups or categories of people(e.g., 'Irish people drink a lot'). Stereotyping is the process of forming and applying stereotypes during impression formation, when you observe someone and form an impression of them based on socially constructed knowledge or schemas.

The knowledge we use to create these impressions of others, and the associated stereotypes, are based on information stored in our long-term memory. For example, if we see a doctor, we will likely draw on our knowledge of what doctors do (e.g., help people), our experience with doctors in the past, what the media says about doctors, and how doctors are generally viewed in society, to make an impression that anyone who is a doctor is probably a good person. In addition, any information that we receive that confirms the stereotypes that we hold (e.g., seeing a doctor treating a patient confirms the stereotype that doctors are good) is also more likely to be stored within our long-term memory than information that counters that stereotype (e.g., seeing a doctor drink and drive doesn't fit with the 'doctors are good' stereotype) (e.g., Cohen, 1981; Rothbart et al., 1979).

> **Key concept – Illusory correlation:** The belief that two objects are associated with each other, even when there is little or no actual association between them (e.g., that wearing a lucky pair of socks means you will do better in your exams because you once did well when wearing those socks before).

Not all stereotypes are positive. In fact, we often pay more attention to negative stereotypes than positive ones (Spiers et al., 2017), which can be problematic as negative behaviours are often perceived as being more characteristic of minority groups relative to majority groups (Hamilton & Gifford, 1976). For instance, in North America, the term 'Black on Black crime' is often used to describe a situation when a Black person is killed or injured by another Black person, but you probably haven't heard of the terms 'White on White crime' or 'Asian on Asian crime'. Think about it: when a White person commits a crime against another White person, it's usually just reported as a crime and race isn't mentioned, and so using terms like 'Black on Black crime' give the impression that intra-racial violence is specific to the Black community and perpetuates the common stereotype that Black people are inherently more violent. However, reports in the USA have shown that both Black and White people tend to commit violent acts against members of their own race to a similar extent (see Bureau of Justice, 2019). Thus, the use of the term 'Black on Black crime' and the perpetuating stereotype that Black people are more violent are examples of an **illusory correlation**.

As outlined above, stereotypes can guide beliefs and behaviours that others demonstrate toward members of social groups. In addition, members of social groups can also (inadvertently) apply these beliefs to themselves. Stereotype threat occurs when a negative stereotype about a group is made salient, which leads members of those groups to perform in a manner that confirms the stereotype (e.g., that women are bad at maths). Those affected don't have to believe the stereotype; just knowing that it exists is enough to impact performance. Stereotype threat has been observed in African Americans in relation to intelligence, in older people in relation to memory, and in women in relation to maths (see Key study 9.2).

KEY STUDY 9.2

Effects of Stereotype Threat

Martens and colleagues (2006) undertook a study to investigate the effects of stereotype threat. They found that women who were led to believe that they were negatively stereotyped in the domain of maths and reasoning ability (i.e., they were told that women often find these tasks difficult) performed worse on a subsequent test than those who were not threatened in this way. This is known as a standard *stereotype threat effect*. However, women who were given the opportunity to self-affirm (i.e., by thinking about personal values that were important to them) did not underperform. Thus, having the opportunity to re-affirm oneself as competent and able may help to buffer the negative effect of stereotype threat.

Although we are aware of some of the stereotypes that we hold, they are often automatically activated when we see someone. This activation can have implications for us in terms of how we try to manage our use of stereotypes. For example, sometimes we want to suppress our thoughts and avoid thinking about a stereotype that we hold. This is known as stereotype suppression. However, trying to suppress stereotypes can have the opposite effect, whereby we end up thinking about the stereotype even more, which is known as stereotype rebound. This is because when we actively try to suppress a stereotype, we have to monitor our thoughts and, in the process, we actually increase the accessibility of the stereotypes. Macrae and colleagues (1994) found that when students were asked to actively suppress stereotypes about a particular group, and then think about the average day in the life of an individual belonging to that group, they had more stereotypical thoughts and displayed more discriminatory behaviours than students who hadn't been asked to previously suppress stereotypes. However, it is important to note that stereotype rebound may depend on people's underlying attitudes about stereotypes in general (Monteith et al., 1998).

One of the problems with stereotypes is that they can influence how we feel about and act towards group members, regardless of whether the stereotypes hold true or not. They can encourage (implicit) biases and discriminatory behaviour as well as influence how we interpret situations – that is, we are more likely to interpret neutral or ambiguous situations in a stereotypical way (Karmali et al., 2019).

Social Identity

Inherent in categorisation and stereotyping is the nature of group belonging and its impact in helping us to explain prejudice. Arguably the most renowned theory to explain group membership effects on prejudice is social identity theory. Developed by Tajfel and Turner (1979), social identity theory aims to explain the relationship between personal (individual) and social (group membership) identity to specify and predict the circumstances under which individuals think of themselves as individuals or as group members, and the consequences this has on intergroup behaviour (Hogg, 2016). Social identity theory developed out of attempts to understand the results of a series of studies conducted by Henri Tajfel called the minimal group experiments (see Chapter 10 on intergroup relations for more detail of these experiments and their methods). It is believed that individuals strive for a positive self-concept, one source of which can be from the social groups we belong to. In other words, if our group is positively evaluated, then we also see ourselves as positively valued. We are motivated to increase the status of our social groups because if your group does better, we also look better as individual members of that group.

According to Tajfel and Turner (1979), there are three main cognitive processes that underlie the basic tenants of a social identity approach to understanding prejudice: (1) categorisation, where we categorise ourselves into the groups we feel we belong to; (2) identification, where we then identify with groups; and (3) social comparison, whereby we compare our group with other groups, which can help us to boost our self-esteem if we are compared relatively favourably (see Martiny & Rubin, 2016, for an overview of social identity's self-esteem hypothesis).

When we make comparisons between groups, evidence shows that we tend to see intergroup differences as greater than intragroup differences. In other words, differences *between* groups (intergroup) are seen as bigger than differences *within* (intra) groups. Individuals are said to be motivated to maintain a positive group-level social identity and this may cause them to focus on the less favourable characteristics of outgroups or to downplay the importance of positive outgroup characteristics. It can lead to negative relations between groups. Motivation to ensure a positive social identity is thought to underlie outgroup derogation and, in turn, intergroup conflict, but demonstrating favouritism towards your group doesn't always mean demonstrating outgroup hate (Brewer, 2001).

Imagine, for example, that you are attending a rugby match as an Ireland supporter. You are wearing your rugby shirt, you are at your home stadium, and so your rugby supporter identity is salient. Around you are New Zealand rugby supporters. You observe them and you quickly categorise them as being the other group and that you do not identify with them (as an Ireland rugby supporter). During the game you note that Ireland is playing particularly well – the All Blacks keep dropping the ball. Your team looks good, and you feel good as a consequence. Ireland wins the match and you go home feeling happy. The good feeling wasn't a result of you being derogatory towards another group – unless, of course, you happened to chant taunts at the New Zealand supporters on your way out of the stadium and this made you feel even happier.

Social identity theory is particularly interesting because it has been applied to understand a wide range of attitudes and behaviours across a range of social and political contexts, including intergroup conflict (Brewer, 2001). For example, it has been used to understand conflicts in settings such as Northern Ireland, Israel and Palestine, and Cyprus, as well as group relations in settings such as Canada, Australia, and South Africa. It has also been applied to topical issues such as health, climate change, and tyranny (see McKeown et al., 2016).

9.5.4 Reducing Prejudice

Now that we have reviewed the various definitions and explanations of prejudice, we turn to understanding how we might reduce prejudice by examining our beliefs about social groups (ideology) and our interactions with people from different social groups (intergroup contact).

Diversity Ideologies

Broadly, an ideology is a set of ideals and beliefs that a person may hold about an individual or about a group of people. Ideologies can be held for any type of social group, but here we focus on diversity ideologies. These are people's beliefs and practices regarding how to best navigate racial diversity and interactions with racial outgroup members.

> **Key concept – Colourblind ideology:** An ideology that minimises the attention given to differences and instead stresses how people are similar.

As you will see, how we think about racial diversity has implications for racial prejudice. There are numerous diversity ideologies, including colourblind, multicultural, **polycultural** and **intercultural ideology**. In this Chapter we focus on the two that have been most frequently researched: colourblindness and multiculturalism.

Colourblindness

Western societies are dominated by norms of social equality. In such settings, **colourblind ideology** is a popular approach to racial difference and diversity. 'Colourblindness' is the widespread belief that all individuals are created equal and should receive the same treatment

> **Key concept – Multicultural ideology:** An ideology that emphasises and explicitly draws attention to the unique cultural contribution of different racial and ethnic groups in a way that preserves distinct cultural heritages.

> **Key concept – Polycultural ideology:** An ideology that stresses the interconnectedness of racial and ethnic groups. Identities are not assimilated into one another; instead, the boundaries between groups are blurred to allow people to feel more connected to each other.

regardless of their race, ethnicity, and/or culture. From the perspective of this colourblind worldview, the differences between social groups create tension and division. Social harmony is achieved by ignoring racial differences and instead adopting a singular, common identity across social groups. Children's story books that stress between-group similarity (i.e., despite looking different, we are all the same underneath our skin) or within-group differences (i.e., each and everyone of us is a special and unique individual) are examples of how colourblind ideology can be manifested (Rosenthal & Levy, 2010).

Although colourblindness may be rooted in good intentions and the general belief that all people should be treated equally, ignoring race won't make it go away. Colourblind ideology has been theoretically linked to promoting prejudice. It is thought that ignoring differences sends a message that racial injustice and its corresponding impact on ethnic minority groups are not important (Rosenthal & Levy, 2010). It also provides an opening for advantaged groups to explain racial disparities with non-racial factors (Plaut et al., 2015). At an organisational or societal level, if policies require that everyone be treated in the same way, then differential outcomes for racialised individuals are considered to be caused by some other factor unrelated to race.

The research examining the relation between colourblindness and prejudice is mixed. On the one hand, colourblind minority members have been shown to demonstrate less positive behaviour in intergroup interactions (Apfelbaum et al., 2012). On the other hand, the relationship has gone in the opposite direction, where colourblindness is linked with reducing racial bias. For example, those adopting a colourblind ideology have been found to express lower ingroup bias and ethnocentrism. Whether colourblindness is effective as a prejudice-reducing ideology remains to be seen. Generally, there is increasing agreement that colourblindness is not the most effective ideology for reducing prejudice. Research findings suggest that another ideology – multiculturalism – has been more consistent in reducing prejudice. We turn to this ideology next.

Multiculturalism

Instead of being colourblind and minimising racial differences, individuals and policy adopting a **multicultural ideology** acknowledge, embrace, and celebrate difference. Raising attention to and respect for group differences is thought to affirm group identities and promote the acceptance of outgroup members. An example would be Black History Month or other awareness-raising and/or educational initiatives. Such strategies explicitly draw attention to the unique characteristics associated with racial and ethnic groups and seek to enhance how these differences bring value to society.

Taking this multicultural approach to diversity appears to be more effective in reducing prejudice as compared to adopting a colourblind approach (Whitley & Webster, 2019).

Valuing diversity can also lead to behaviour change. For example, children who were read a story that placed value on racial diversity were more likely to identify acts of racial discrimination (Apfelbaum et al., 2010) and more likely to sit next to racially diverse peers in the school lunchroom (McKeown et al., 2017). Thus, placing value in racial diversity may reduce concerns about talking about race, resulting in less stressful and more successful interactions (Vorauer et al., 2009).

> **Key concept – Intercultural ideology:** An ideology that is achieved through intergroup dialogue that stimulates identity flexibility, which allows for the formation of new mixed identities where individuals develop a sense of belonging together.

GUEST PERSONAL JOURNEY

Aneeta Rattan

I grew up in Tampa, Florida, USA with parents of South Asian Indian origin from Punjab, India, and Nairobi, Kenya. Living in a largely White community at the time, with family stories and histories infused with the complicated dynamics of intergroup relations, I was attuned to issues of diversity, equity, and inclusion early. Halfway through my undergraduate degree at Columbia University, I lucked into taking a psychology course with Dr Carol S. Dweck, which completely transformed my interests and career goals. Carol would ultimately be my PhD advisor at Stanford University. I declared a new major, started learning basic research skills, and decided to pursue a PhD in social psychology. While my research develops core theory in the study of mindsets and diversity, my interest in applying research to the real world led me to join the faculty at London Business School, where I am an Associate Professor. On one side of my work, I identify organisational and leadership messages that foster greater belonging among members of underrepresented groups (e.g., racial minorities, women, LGBTQ+ individuals). In another programme of work, I study how the growth mindset (i.e., people's beliefs that their basic abilities can develop and 'grow') can be leveraged by both individuals and organisations to confront acutely difficult diversity moments, for example when someone openly communicates a stereotype or bias.

Critiques of Diversity Ideologies

Three main shortcomings of diversity ideologies have been identified. The primary argument is that there is no consideration of the role that structural inequalities have in creating and maintaining inequalities. For example, under colourblind ideology, different lived experiences are ignored and instead similarities are emphasised, which fails to acknowledge how system oppression contributes to the persistence of inequality.

The focus or intent of diversity ideologies is considered another limitation (Mayorga-Gallo, 2019). Diversity ideologies, particularly multiculturalism, are primarily focused on improving representation. This is because fair representation is seen as the solution for racial inequity. For example, within a policing context, a recruiting drive for new officers would be considered successful if there were more applicants belonging to historically disadvantaged groups as compared to previous recruiting attempts. Although increased representation is arguably good, the actual barriers to equity are not addressed. If the only concern is increased representation, aspects of the organisation that make individuals from historically disadvantaged groups less likely to want to become (and stay) police officers will not be addressed. Within diversity ideologies, there is no focus on the systemic changes necessary to remove barriers and oppression. It is enough that people from diverse backgrounds show up; whether individuals feel integrated or included is not of concern.

Given these flaws, we might begin to wonder who benefits most from diversity ideologies. The value of diversity is often expressed in terms of the benefits that racialised people bring into White spaces, such as increased innovation and creativity into workplace settings, and more interesting food, entertainment, and cultural options into neighbourhoods (Smith & Mayorga-Gallo, 2017). Differences in lived experiences are ascribed to 'culture' instead of structural inequities. White individuals are seen as the beneficiaries to diversity ideologies; they are seen as having an open mind and being accepting of other people while at the same time maintaining all the social and legal benefits within the current social system. Further, racialised individuals carry the responsibility for both integrating into White spaces 'appropriately' in adherence to normative expectations and carrying the burden of diversity work (e.g., including but not limited to educating and absolving others, committee work, recruiting similar others) (Mayorga-Gallo, 2019).

In summary, there are limitations to diversity ideologies as a be-all-end-all solution to racism. If the goal of an intervention is to diversify representation within a particular space, then multicultural ideology will likely be successful. But if the goal of the intervention is to challenge underlying systems of oppression, diversity ideology will not be enough. Instead, there is a need to push toward action-focused interventions that challenge underlying systems of oppression (Smith & Mayorga-Gallo, 2017). In the next section we focus on intergroup contact as one such intervention.

Intergroup Contact

In his 1954 book *The Nature of Prejudice*, Gordon Allport presented what has become known as the contact hypothesis, which puts forward the idea that it is possible to reduce prejudice towards outgroup members by encouraging groups who don't like each other to interact with one another, known as **intergroup contact**. Allport argued that intergroup contact works best under certain conditions. First, there should be equal status between the groups involved in the interactions. While this can be difficult to achieve where conflict is often a result of gross inequalities, Pettigrew (1998) later formulated that equal status within the contact situation is particularly important. Imagine a school classroom where

all children (regardless of their racial or religious identities) are treated equally within
that context. Second, contact should
involve working in cooperation towards a
common goal. Again, imagine a school
classroom where young people are working
across religious divides on a school project.
Third, there should be social or institutional support for contact, evidenced
through normative practices that support
equality. If we return to our classroom
example, a supportive school environment may be one in which the school conditions
promote integration between groups through their ethos and the normative practices of
teachers within the school.

> **Key concept – Intergroup contact:**
> The face-to-face interactions between
> people from different social groups
> (e.g., individuals from different racial
> groups working on a school project
> together in the classroom). Good
> quality and frequent intergroup
> contact have been found to be
> associated with prejudice reduction.

Although the contact hypothesis has been criticised for what has been argued to be
an almost endless list of contact conditions, contemporary researchers view Allport's
conditions as facilitating, rather than essential, in reducing prejudice (see Pettigrew &
Tropp, 2006).

For the most part, research shows that contact works in reducing prejudice. In their
2006 meta-analysis, Pettigrew and Tropp (2006) reported that of 515 studies, over 94%
found a positive relationship between intergroup contact and prejudice reduction. And
since the contact hypothesis' inception, there has been a substantial body of research
examining how, when, and why contact reduces prejudice. Researchers have demonstrated
that positive contact enables individuals to challenge stereotypes associated with outgroup
members, that through having positive contact individuals can feel less anxious about
interacting with outgroup members and feel less threatened by them (Aberson, 2015).
There is also evidence to show that positive interactions are associated with higher levels
of empathy towards outgroup members and with outcomes such as trust and forgiveness
in contexts such as Northern Ireland (Hewstone et al., 2008). It is through these processes
that contact can then be associated with more positive attitudes and reduced prejudice
towards outgroups.

Intergroup contact can take many forms, from the fleeting and informal 'hellos' in person or online to someone you walk past to the deepest of friendships. And yet, not all
contact is or needs to be in the form of direct face-to-face interactions. Contemporary
research has explored a wide range of ways in which individuals can reap the benefits of
intergroup contact without directly engaging in contact; for example, by imagining interactions with members of other groups (known as imagined contact), by having a friend tell
you about an outgroup friend they have (known as extended contact), or by reading about
them in story books (known as vicarious contact). This is particularly important given that,
for many, there is no or little opportunity for face-to-face contact in the first place; here,
consider highly segregated societies such as Israel and Palestine or Northern Ireland. We
discuss more about the different types of intergroup contact and associated interventions
in Part 3 of this chapter.

GUEST PERSONAL JOURNEY

Linda Tropp

The topics I study are very closely related to my origins: I was born and raised in Gary, Indiana, an industrial steel city in the Midwest of the United States. Like in many Midwestern cities, many Black Americans relocated to Gary during the 'Great Migration' from the Southern US (1910s–1970s), and I grew up in Gary during a time of major demographic and economic shifts – where many White families moved out as growing numbers of Black families moved in ('White flight'). This meant that I grew up as a White minority in a city where the population was 80–85% Black by the time I started high school, and in the midst of some very turbulent times, including tense relations between racial groups and a period of severe decline due to the closing of steel mills and the disappearance of manufacturing jobs that had once bolstered the local economy. I believe these early experiences have contributed to my long-standing interest in studying intergroup relations, and especially how people from distinct groups often perceive and interpret the same situations quite differently, depending on their relative positions and experiences within the larger social structure.

Critiques of Intergroup Contact

Despite the promises of contact, there are some important criticisms to consider. One critique is that when given the opportunity, individuals do not necessarily engage in interactions. Think about the social spaces you inhabit. Do people tend to sit with those who are similar to themselves? The answer is probably yes. Using observational mapping approaches, researchers have found this to happen across a range of different social spaces. For example, Campbell, Kruskal, and Wallace (1966) used observations in school classrooms in the USA to map the racial and gender seating patterns of school children over the period of a semester. To do this, they had observers in the classrooms mark on a pre-drawn map of the classroom layout the seating arrangement, and the race and gender of each person on each seat in the classroom. The authors used these maps to conduct advanced statistical analysis which revealed that school children remained racially segregated in their seating choice throughout the school year, despite being in a mixed-race environment, suggesting a lack of intergroup contact within such racially mixed spaces.

In recent decades, work in this area has expanded to examine a greater variety of settings with a range of research techniques. This includes, for example research on beaches (Dixon & Durrheim, 2003) and universities (Koen & Durrheim, 2010) in South Africa, in schools (McKeown et al., 2015) and community groups in Northern Ireland (McKeown et al., 2012) and in secondary (Al Ramiah et al., 2015) and primary (McKeown et al., 2017) schools in England. Results from these studies show that even in shared spaces, individuals remain clustered in racially or religiously similar groups while going about their everyday behaviour. And this arguably has implications for prejudice, since we know that contact is a good way to reduce prejudice.

Contact theory has also come under fire for focusing heavily on the positive effects of interactions and for failing to fully examine the ways in which contact might work or not for different groups, particularly when comparing minority and majority groups (Tropp & Pettigrew, 2005). This is problematic given that contact can sometimes go 'wrong', reinforcing stereotypes and, in turn, resulting in more negative outgroup attitudes. Contemporary research, therefore, has started to consider the effects of both positive and negative contact on group relations, with some evidence demonstrating that positive contact experiences can buffer negative contact experiences (Paolini et al., 2014).

Researchers have also focused on the potential detrimental effects of intergroup contact. Evidence suggests that even when contact does reduce prejudice, it may undermine collective action efforts (Saguy et al., 2009). In other words, if a disadvantaged group in society gets to like an advantaged group, then they are less likely to support policies that fight against the inequality that they experience. However, evidence for such ironic effects is little and variable, with a recent meta-analysis demonstrating that the ironic effects of positive contact on collective action for disadvantaged individuals disappear when the relationship between negative contact and collective action is considered (Reimer & Sengupta, 2022).

Despite these contemporary critiques, the contact hypothesis has attracted substantial empirical support and offers exciting avenues for intervention to promote better community relations. See Part 3 for more information on applications.

9.6 PART 2: ADVANCES

This section of the chapter focuses on new advances in the study of prejudice, specifically on the development of prejudice across the lifespan and how prejudicial attitudes and behaviours can be measured.

9.6.1 Development of Prejudice Across the Lifespan

Earlier in the chapter we noted that prejudice can emerge from our need to form social bonds and an innate preference for ingroups relative to outgroups. We outlined how more subtle forms of prejudice can operate in the absence of personal endorsement or even awareness. These subtle forms of prejudice are better thought of as stemming from cues about the associations between groups and attributes learned through the social environment, rather than as something that is developed by individuals themselves. Given the multitude of dimensions along which humans differ, however, how do we learn which characteristics to use for grouping people? And once we have people in groups, how do we acquire group-level beliefs? These two questions have been the focus of recent work examining the development of prejudice in childhood.

Scholars (and parents!) have not agreed on a single theory to explain where prejudice comes from. Some theorists think that prejudice develops in similar ways for both children and adults. Other theorists think that it is important to consider how child development and brain maturation impacts prejudice. And still other theorists think that the environment and culture impacts how prejudice forms. Like all things in social psychology, it is likely a blend between individual and situational factors that can best explain how prejudice develops across the lifespan. Indeed, more recent theories for explaining prejudice focus on how children think (cognitive psychology) about people (social psychology) as they age (developmental psychology). These newer approaches assume that prejudice is something that is developed versus something people are born with, and that it is more efficient to stop prejudice from developing rather than to eradicate the beliefs after they are formed (Bigler & Patterson, 2017). As such, it is critical to understand how children come to endorse such beliefs so we can stop prejudice before it begins.

One theory that is increasingly used as a framework for examining the development of implicit and explicit prejudice and stereotyping is Developmental Intergroup Theory (DIT) (Bigler & Liben, 2007). According to this theory, children begin to notice different groups/ categories based on the cues in their environment. Specifically, some groups are more likely to become psychologically salient because they are perceptually discriminant and marked by distinct features, are disproportionately represented in smaller groups, are explicitly labelled by adults and identified for attention, and implicitly used to group people to make categories noticeable, unique, and distinct. Let's take the example of gender. Men and women have perceptually distinct features and are disproportionately represented across different domains, and adults often explicitly use gender to identify people when talking with children. Consequently, gender becomes a psychologically salient category to children early in development, one that is consistently and spontaneously used by preschool-aged children (Shutts, Banaji, & Spelke, 2010).

Once a category becomes psychologically salient, children start to use this feature to organise their social world, meaning that they are more likely to categorise others along this dimension. Once categories are consistently used to organise the social world, children begin to acquire information about these categories (attributes) from cues in the environment. For example, children may be exposed to explicit messages that directly teach the attributes associated with groups (e.g., toys labelled as being appropriate for either boys or girls, or that big boys don't cry). Information from the environment can also be communicated through implicit messages. These mainly take the form of illusory correlations where children pick up on patterns of associations within the environment that are not necessarily explained to them (e.g., more televised footage of women crying and men yelling indicates, therefore, that women are emotional and men are angry).

In addition to information coming in from the environment, internally driven processes, such as psychological essentialism and ingroup favouritism, are also used to infer beliefs about a particular social category. As we explain further below, **essentialism** is a concept borrowed from developmental psychology. It captures the idea that certain categories, such as 'cats' or 'teachers', have an underlying reality that cannot be directly observed but is shared by all category members. These shared features make up the 'essence' of category membership (Gelman, 2004). When applied to prejudice development, it is believed that children high in essentialism will be more likely to see social categories as important and membership in a category as rigid (e.g., believing that the difference between men and women is biologically based and you can't change between them). When essentialism is combined with ingroup favouritism, it is thought to result in biased attention towards, and memory for, positive information about ingroups and negative information about outgroups.

By looking at how external messages from the environment intersect with internal processes as they change across development, DIT outlines how children might learn to organise other people by particular categories and use environmental cues to form beliefs about these groups.

More detailed explanations of where prejudice comes from present expanded opportunities for interventions. In the case of DIT, interrupting how children group people together, which is also called social categorisation (see Chapter 10 for a detailed explanation), should theoretically stop prejudice from forming. Although research is beginning to examine this idea, the reality of how social categorisation unfolds outside controlled laboratory experiments is complex: sometimes people are not categorised as belonging to a particular social group, sometimes they are spontaneously and implicitly categorised, sometimes one category will be more salient (intrinsically or because of the environment) and 'trump' another category, and sometimes people are categorised along more than one dimension simultaneously.

That said, other aspects of DIT can be used to explain when people are grouped into categories – or not. For example, essentialism can be used to understand how children think about categories. Children with high essentialist beliefs are more likely to consider social groups as being fundamentally distinct and different from each other. Surface characteristics, such as hair length or skin tone, are thought to reflect deep-seated underlying differences (i.e., they reflect the 'essence' of the category). Children high in essentialist beliefs are more likely to use categories to group people together and thus acquire prejudice. Under these conditions, when prejudice does form, it may also be difficult to change because these are rigid beliefs about the 'essence' underlying social categories (see Pauker et al., 2017, for a review).

Another prejudice intervention that aligns with DIT is to challenge the beliefs children may hold about social categories in and of themselves. More recent research has done this by presenting counter-stereotypical information about social categories. This includes things like using environmental cues to make non-contentious social categories (i.e., emotion) more salient than contentious social categories (i.e., race) within experiments (Lipman et al., 2021), encouraging children to challenge more traditional beliefs and reflect on whether social categories embody social (instead of biological) differences (Rhodes et al., 2018). Such interventions are encouraging. Not only are they successful in reducing prejudice among children (and adults too!), but they are easy for adults to put into practice when working with children in everyday settings.

As can be seen across the different topics covered in this chapter so far, early theorising about prejudice as reflecting individual factors, such as personality or personally held beliefs, has been replaced by the appreciation that individuals exist in complex cultural systems which influence their beliefs and behaviours – wittingly or not. This more holistic approach to studying prejudice has also been extended to prejudice development and is now being used to inform interventions geared towards stopping the formation of prejudice in childhood.

9.6.2 Measuring Prejudice and Predicting Behaviour

Earlier in the chapter we identified prejudice as being either blatant (explicit) or subtle (implicit). Regardless of the form, researching prejudice involves measuring attitudes, and attitudes are not directly observable. This presents researchers with the challenge of trying to define the unobservable construct *prejudice* into something that is measurable, a process called operationalisation. The distinction between different types of prejudice is helpful in creating definitions of how prejudice can be understood (or operationalised) so that it can be measured.

To assess blatant prejudice, participants are typically administered a direct measure, such as a questionnaire, a process known as 'self-reporting'. Here, participants are asked to indicate the extent to which they agree with statements (e.g., 'Over the past few years, Black people have gained more economically than they deserve') on a Likert scale, where responses range from 1 = strongly disagree to 7 = strongly agree (Modern Racism Scale; McConahay, 1986). Responses are averaged and used to infer the extent to which an individual is prejudiced. The problem, however, is that individuals are not always honest when responding to questions about socially sensitive issues. So, researchers have developed different measures to capture prejudiced attitudes and behaviours.

More recently developed measures may instead ask participants to respond to questions that indirectly capture prejudice, such as by measuring dehumanisation (Haslam & Loughnan, 2014). Questions are designed to elicit responses indicating the perceived humanness of different social groups. One such measure is the Ascent of Humans scale (Kteily et al., 2015), which presents participants with an image depicting human evolutionary progress, ranging from our ape-like human ancestors (a score of 0) to advanced modern humans (a score of 100), and asks them to rate where different groups rest on the scale (Figure 9.1).

Figure 9.1 Ascent of Man dehumanisation measure

Source: Kteily et al. (2015)

In addition to the examples already discussed in the Key Thinker box by Nour Kteily, in the UK, research using scales like these have found that Muslim people are seen as less evolved than British people (Kteily et al., 2015), obese people are less evolved than those who are not obese (Kersbergen & Robinson, 2019), and people lower in social class (e.g., 'chavs') are seen as less evolved than people higher in social class (e.g., 'not chavs') (Loughnan et al., 2014).

There are, however, two main issues with measures of explicit prejudice or connected concepts. First, given the influence of social norms that value equality in Western societies, it is impossible to determine whether anti-racist responses on these types of explicit questionnaires reflect an actual lack of personal endorsements of prejudice or increased social desirability, where participants do not wish to be seen as racist. And relatedly, what people say does not always match what people do (see Chapter 11 on behavioural change). Although indirect explicit measures are more likely to capture true attitudes than are direct measures, they are not without problems.

To address concerns with socially desirable responding and to assess more subtle forms of prejudice, researchers are increasingly using implicit measurement techniques. A direct implicit measure might show a person an ambiguous picture and ask them to describe it. The descriptions would then be coded for prejudice-consistent responses. Indirect implicit measures are the more common way to measure subtle bias. The Implicit Association Test (IAT) (Greenwald et al., 1998) is most frequently used to measure implicit bias (e.g., Nosek et al., 2011). The IAT is a computer-based task that captures the speed with which people are able to match concepts. By doing so, the IAT measures the strength of associations between these concepts.

Let's take an example of a researcher measuring implicit weight bias, as indicated by more positive attitudes towards thin people as compared to obese people. On one set of critical trials, research participants would view a header where the words 'Obese' and 'Pleasant' would appear in the top-left corner of the screen and 'Thin' and 'Unpleasant' would appear in the top-right corner. A single picture would be presented in the middle of the screen and the participant would use one of two computer keys to categorise it. If the picture was of an obese person or a pleasant object, the research participant completing the IAT would be instructed to use a key on the left of the keyboard to match the image to the header (usually the 'E' key). If the picture was of a thin person or an unpleasant object, the research participant completing the IAT would be instructed to use a key on the right of the keyboard to match the image (usually the 'I' key). In the second set of critical trials, the social category labels have switched sides. Now research participants would be presented with 'Thin' and 'Pleasant' in the top-left corner, and 'Obese' and 'Unpleasant' in the top-right corner of the screen. They would be instructed to hit 'E' in response to thin or pleasant images and 'I' in response to obese or unpleasant images.

EXERCISE 9.3

Measuring Implicit Attitudes

This exercise is designed to help you understand more about how implicit prejudice can be measured. Take at least two different versions of the Implicit Association Test (IAT). They can be accessed on Harvard University's Project Implicit website

(Continued)

(https://implicit.harvard.edu/implicit/user/uk/uk.static/takeatest.html). When you have taken the tests, reflect on the following questions:

- What were you asked to do?
- What did your results show?
- Are you confident about these results? If yes, why, and if no, why not?
- Do you think the Implicit Associations Test really measures implicit prejudice? If yes, why, and if no, why not?

The IAT is scored by comparing the speed with which research participants correctly categorise the pictures across the two sets of critical trials. According to the theorising, if the participant holds implicit biases that favour thin over obese people, they will be more accurate and faster to categorise pictures on the 'Thin/Pleasant + Obese/Unpleasant' trials. Correspondingly, participants will be less accurate and slower to categorise pictures on the 'Obese/Pleasant + Thin/Unpleasant' trials. A difference score (called a D-score) is created by subtracting the average response speed to 'Thin/Pleasant + Obese/Unpleasant' from 'Obese/Pleasant + Thin/Unpleasant' trials. Positive scores are interpreted as indicating stronger implicit bias that favours thin over obese people. Negative scores are interpreted as indicating stronger implicit bias that favours obese over thin people.

Although most frequently used, the IAT is not without limitations and controversy (e.g., Nosek et al., 2011). Some of these concerns focus on the lack of understanding of what it is the IAT actually measures. Because of the structure of the measure, it is assumed that positivity towards one category (i.e., thin) corresponds to negativity towards the contrasting category (i.e., obese), and vice versa. But, as outlined above, (in)group love does not necessarily correspond to (out)group hate. As such, the distinct attitudes that drive D-scores are unknowable (Williams & Steele, 2019). There is also debate on whether implicit bias reflects personally endorsed beliefs (e.g., Connor & Evers, 2020) or cultural representations (e.g., Payne et al., 2017). Taking this to our example, do D-scores capture how the participant feels about thin and obese people? Or do D-scores represent how thin and obese people are represented within cultural contexts (i.e., positive portrayal in the media) and are they less effective as a predictor of behaviour? The reality – as most psychological constructs – is likely that the IAT captures the interplay between individuals and their environments (e.g., Rivers et al., 2017).

But a bigger question is whether these different types of measures are useful predictors of behaviour. Social psychology is ultimately concerned with better understanding why people do the things they do. But given the volume of scholarly work in the area of prejudice, relatively few studies have focused on whether explicit and implicit measures are trustworthy predictors of behaviour. Within a controlled lab-based setting, a predictive link between attitudes and behaviour has been observed. Mapping onto theorising regarding a dual system of attitudes (Devine, 1989), where explicit attitudes correspond to overt, intentional behaviour and implicit attitudes correspond to covert, unintended behaviour, early research demonstrated that in an interracial interaction with a Black partner, White participants' explicit questionnaire scores predicted their verbal responses whereas their reaction-time measure scores predicted their non-verbal behaviour (Dovidio et al., 2002). Overall, a meta-analysis reviewing 217 research papers involving over 36,000 participants demonstrated an association between implicit measures and intergroup behaviour (Kurdi et al., 2019). Further, implicit measures have been found to predict behaviour above and beyond explicit measures (Greenwald et al., 2009).

KEY STUDY 9.3

The Influence of Bias on Behaviour

Thanks in no small part to Devine (1989), researchers have gained a better understanding of the automatic and controlled components of prejudice, and how these impact perceptions and judgements. But what influence do explicit and implicit bias have on *behaviour*?

This was the question that Dovidio et al. (2002) set out to answer in their single-study paper, published in the *Journal of Personality and Social Psychology*. The results indicate that for White undergraduate participants, explicit attitudes were more strongly related to verbal behaviour and positive perception of the self during an interracial interaction. By contrast, implicit attitudes were more strongly related to non-verbal behaviour and perceptions of the partner during an interracial interaction. This pattern of findings is consistent with the idea that explicit prejudice can be consciously controlled and modified through social norms and personal beliefs, while implicit prejudice operates at an automatic level and is more resistant to change. Theoretically, this paper demonstrated the distinct streams of processing on intergroup behaviour, highlighting the importance of addressing both streams to effectively reduce prejudice and discrimination. The paper was also methodologically innovative, setting the framework for coding behaviour during lab-based interaction studies.

Contemporary research has started using new technologies to better understand the potential connections (or not) between explicit prejudice, implicit prejudice, and behaviour. For example, Palazzi and colleagues (2016) examined body movements alongside heart rate, emotional arousal, and implicit and explicit attitudes in their observations of intragroup (White–White) and intergroup (White–Black) interactions in a laboratory setting. In their study, participants wore a device that captured their heart rate and emotional arousal while they interacted either with a peer from their own (White) or another racial group (Black). Interestingly, it was found that participants who scored higher on implicit prejudice were more likely to maintain distance from outgroup than ingroup members. No associations, however, were found between the implicit and explicit measures and the heart rate or emotional response measures.

To summarise, given that prejudice often takes covert rather than overt forms, and that implicit attitudes have been shown to predict behaviour above and beyond explicit attitudes, measures that seek to capture subtle prejudice are more likely to provide insights into people's behaviour in everyday settings. But there is uncertainty as to which behaviours are consistently predicted by which measures. As such, more research is needed in this area.

9.7 PART 3: APPLICATIONS

Unsurprisingly, the research related to understanding prejudice is most often applied to attempts to reduce prejudice. In this section we take the opportunity to emphasise that interventions – regardless of the topic – must address the root cause of the problem and not just the symptoms, in order to be successful. In line with this mantra, we take implicit bias training as our starting point. Although incredibly popular, we argue that this approach will be ineffective in the long term. We then move on to present theories and interventions that focus on altering situational contexts, and are therefore better placed to address the root causes of prejudice in applied settings.

9.7.1 Diversity Initiatives

In this section we will discuss two types of diversity initiatives: implicit bias training and diversity initiatives in the workplace.

Implicit Bias Training

Implicit bias training is designed to expose subtle biases by making people aware of them. The assumption is that increased awareness will result in less prejudice and more positive behaviour towards individuals from historically underrepresented groups. It's likely that you, dear reader, have undergone implicit bias training as part of employment or university induction. This approach is everywhere. But implicit bias training is flawed in at least one fundamental way. Let us explain.

Earlier in this chapter contextual and environmental cues were identified as root causes of implicit bias, at least in part. But implicit bias training does not address these root causes. Instead, it seeks to bring awareness to beliefs that might otherwise fly under the radar. Implicit bias training does not challenge barriers to equity that exist within the culture of the workplace or within larger systems within a society. Reflecting this, the success of implicit bias training programmes, when they are effective at all, are short lived; bias returns to baseline after a few days or weeks (Forscher et al., 2017; Lai et al., 2014). Such interventions have temporary influences because implicit associations 'snap' back into what exists in the dominant context or culture. Without addressing the cause of implicit bias by challenging cultural and societal stereotypes, these interventions have limited potential in altering behaviour over sustained periods of time (Payne et al., 2017). There are many alternatives to implicit bias training (e.g., Cox et al., 2022; FitzGerald et al., 2019). In the next section, we outline two such approaches: shifting social norms through diversity initiatives and reducing prejudice through contact-based interventions in schools.

Diversity Initiatives in the Workplace

Interventions are needed that shift norms concerning acceptable behaviour and/or strategies for effectively managing diversity. In this section, we draw on research related to ideologies – beliefs about how to navigate important differences – and on diversity practices aimed at improving experiences in diverse workplaces.

As mentioned in section 9.5.4 on ideologies to reduce prejudice, there are two general approaches to thinking about diversity: a colourblind approach and a multicultural approach. When adopting a colourblind approach, demographic differences such as race, ethnicity, religion, and age are minimised. The idea is that de-emphasising demographic differences (e.g., in schools or workplaces) should ensure that decision-making is based on abilities, and that everyone is treated equitably and meritocratically. At first glance, adopting a colourblind approach seems like a simple way to alleviate potential tensions to do with obvious demographic differences. For example, if individuals and institutions do not see race, then there shouldn't be any racial bias, especially as some studies on interracial interactions have shown that when White people mention race when it is not relevant, it can increase Black people's feelings of distrust (Dovidio et al., 2002; Tropp et al., 2006) and concerns about being judged based on their racial group membership (Branscombe et al.,1999).

However, talking about race is not always a bad thing and sometimes disregarding race can be counterproductive. In fact, another series of studies exploring interracial interactions found that White people who avoided talking about race (so as to seem less racist) were actually perceived as being less friendly by Black observers than those who openly mentioned race (Apfelbaum et al., 2008). Thus, one of the issues with the colourblind approach is that it may discourage people from talking about race, even in situations where it is important or even necessary to do so, a phenomenon that has been described as strategic colourblindness.

Simply put, colourblindness doesn't equate to inclusivity, and sometimes it is important to consider demographics such as gender, age, physical ability, and religion. For example, when choosing venues and organising catering for events with diverse attendees, it is beneficial to ensure that the space is accessible and that specific dietary requirements are catered for. On the other hand, sometimes personal characteristics are not relevant to the context and should not be the main point of discussion, such as when hiring someone with the best skill set for the job. Relatedly, adopting a colourblind approach in contexts where racial or gender bias is rife, such as in recruitment practices (Moss-Racusin et al., 2012), can be useful. One way to address these biases is with anonymous recruitment methods, whereby the name, age, and gender of applicants are concealed, which should diminish potential (implicit) biases that are elicited by these demographic cues. Decision-making in these processes that prevent rushing and fatigue, and instead encourage controlled and systematic processing of information, are also likely to be effective in offsetting the influence of implicit prejudice (Payne et al., 2017).

Whereas the colourblind approach implies that members of minority groups should adopt the practices, values, and behaviours of the majority group, encouraging **cultural assimilation** in those settings, multicultural approaches are based on the premise that learning about different groups will promote better knowledge, understanding, and appreciation. Indeed, culturally diverse teams can increase performance and innovation (e.g., Filbeck et al., 2017; Phillips et al., 2006). Nevertheless, issues often still exist. As such, organisations are increasingly concerned about how to successfully foster diversity and reap the benefits. Often, workplaces make changes to recruitment and resource practices to attract and employ people from diverse backgrounds (e.g., non-discriminatory recruitment practices, diversity statements, and targeted recruitment) and enrol employees in diversity training programmes (see the subsection on implicit bias in section 9.5.2). However, the actual working environment may not feel welcoming or be inclusive to diverse team members because underlying structures or systems that contribute to inequality are not addressed.

> **Key concept – Cultural assimilation:** The process in which a minority group or culture adopts the behaviours, values, rituals, and beliefs of their host nation's majority group.

Therefore, additional diversity practices are needed. Some of these include human resource practices such as supporting employee resource groups or diversity networking groups, which are specifically designed to be safe spaces in which target members can network and support one another. An example of this is *Elevate*, an award-winning creative leadership programme for Black, Asian, and minority ethnic women who work in universities in the UK (Elevate, 2021). Employers can also adopt accountability practices by actively assessing career gaps between group members, and adopting ways to reduce them, as well as setting diversity goals within the organisation and regularly monitoring performance in relation to them (Leslie, 2019). Another important initiative is that of grievance systems, which are systems put in place so that individuals can report any instances of discrimination or other events that inhibit progress towards diversity goals (e.g., accessibility issues). In turn, organisations should take action to address any issues that are raised. An example of how to address explicit prejudice in the workplace is outlined in Key Study 9.4.

KEY STUDY 9.4

Diversity in the Workplace – Addressing Explicit Prejudice

Rattan and colleagues (Rattan & Dweck, 2010, 2018; Rattan & Georgeac, 2017) have explored issues relating to diversity in the workplace, specifically on explicit prejudice and how to address it. An example of explicit bias is a man saying to a woman that women are too emotional to be good managers. The studies show that how the victim chooses to behave in response to the remark may depend on whether they think that the perpetrator's views are subject to change or not, that is whether they assume a fixed mindset or a growth mindset. To illustrate the difference between these mindsets, think about the saying 'a leopard never changes its spots' – it refers to a fixed mindset. However, the belief that people are malleable and can develop over time reflects a growth mindset. Rattan, Dweck, and Georgeac's research has shown that when exposed to prejudiced views, women and minorities who have a growth mindset are more likely to speak out about the occurrence and confront the perpetrator of prejudice. Those with a growth mindset also hold more positive expectations of the perpetrator – that is, they are more likely to redeem them and to believe that they can change, and less likely to withdraw from future interactions with them.

9.7.2 Intergroup Contact Interventions in Schools

Earlier in this chapter you were introduced to the prejudice reduction promises of intergroup contact. In this section, we focus on how intergroup contact theory can be applied to promote community relations in school classrooms. First, why should we care about intergroup contact in schools? Well, for many young people, school may be the first place where they come into close contact with individuals from different ethnic or racial groups, an important phenomenon given the prejudice-reducing qualities of intergroup contact (Pettigrew & Tropp, 2006). Evidence shows, for example, that more intergroup contact can lead to less preference for same-ethnic friendship groups among students in school classrooms (Jugert et al., 2011). And importantly, such intergroup friendships in schools have been found to be associated with benefits that go beyond prejudice reduction. For example, with lower feelings of vulnerability, there is less peer rejection, there are fewer internalising symptoms, and there is higher academic engagement among students in school classrooms (Graham et al., 2014; Kawabata & Crick, 2015).

In addition to the benefits of intergroup contact and friendships when they are left to form naturally within ethnically or racially diverse school settings, there have been lots of studies that have used interventions within school settings to further promote intergroup contact. Typical interventions in schools involve cooperative learning approaches or school linking programmes.

An example of cooperative learning is the 'jigsaw classroom' (Aronson, 1978), in which students within a classroom are required to split into smaller groups, with each group member being required to become an expert in a given topic and then share this knowledge with other group members. Evidence shows that use of the jigsaw classroom is associated with prejudice reduction among students (Aronson & Thibodeau, 2006), primarily due to the cooperation involved, which is a key condition of intergroup contact theory, according to Allport (1954).

An example of school linking programmes is where students from different schools (usually ethnically, religiously, or racially separate schools) are paired with other schools to engage in educational or social activities together. A recent initiative that highlights this approach is Shared Education, which focuses on offering collaborative opportunities for students from different schools and backgrounds to learn together through sharing classrooms and resources. Shared Education is adopted in a range of contexts and has been found to have beneficial effects for students. For example, in their research on Shared Education in Northern Ireland, Reimer and colleagues (2021) found that students who take part in shared education classes reported more intergroup contact outside class as well as more positive attitudes towards outgroup members compared to students who did not take part in shared classes.

Even in the absence of the opportunities for direct contact between different groups, schools can provide a place where young people can interact with other groups in an indirect way or learn about difference (e.g., through curriculum subjects such as religious or civic education or through engaging with materials in the classroom that include representation of people from different groups, such as in books or videos). Interventions such as these, which do not involve face-to-face interactions between members of two different groups, are referred to as indirect contact interventions. Examples of indirect contact interventions include: (1) extended contact (Wright et al., 1997), which is the knowledge that ingroups have friendships with outgroup members; (2) imagined contact (Turner et al., 2007), which is mental simulation of an interaction with an outgroup member; and (3) vicarious contact (Dovidio et al., 2011), which involves observing an interaction between ingroup and outgroup members via media such as film, TV, and books. Let's take each of these in turn.

Extended contact interventions in schools typically involve story reading. For example, Cameron and Rutland (2006) explored whether reading story books that highlighted friendships between disabled and non-disabled children would be associated with more positive attitudes towards people with disabilities among children. They found support for extended contact being associated with prejudice reduction. In another study by Cameron and colleagues (2006), they found that students who read a story book that emphasised friendships between English children and refugee children was associated with British children demonstrating more positive attitudes towards refugees, compared to a control condition of students who did not read a story book.

In contrast to extended contact, where students read about interactions, imagined contact interventions ask students to use their imagination to think about an interaction with an outgroup member. Even this imagined form of contact has been found to have positive effects among children in school contexts. For example, Cameron and colleagues (2011) found that asking students to imagine an interaction with disabled peers was associated with more positive attitudes towards disabled people, as well as higher feelings of warmth and competence towards disabled people, compared to a control condition of children who did not imagine an interaction. Similar findings have been observed by Stathi and colleagues (2014), who found that White children who imagined interactions with Asian children in the UK context demonstrated more positive attitudes, were more likely to see White people and Asian people as similar, and were more interested in interacting with Asian children in the future, compared to a control condition of White children who did not imagine interactions with Asian children.

Vicarious contact is somewhat less researched in school settings, compared to extended and imagined contact. An interesting example of a vicarious contact intervention in schools was carried out by Vezzali and colleagues (2019) in schools in Italy. The authors worked with students to create videos of direct contact occurring between Italian and immigrant students, and then asked other students who were not involved in making the videos to watch the video. They found that students who watched the videos reported more positive attitudes and fewer stereotypes towards outgroup members and more willingness to interact with outgroup members in the future, compared to a control condition of students who did not watch any videos.

Taken together, there is substantial evidence that intergroup contact interventions in schools (both direct and indirect) can have a wide range of benefits for students, promoting more positive attitudes, facilitating the development of friendships, and impacting student engagement and well-being.

KEY THINKER

Loris Vezzali

To achieve theoretical advancement and provide relevance to research in the field, Vezzali and colleagues have worked on different forms of intergroup contact, aiming to understand their potential and limits in real-world studies and interventions. They found that direct, face-to-face contact is an effective form of contact that can reduce prejudice at the implicit level and motivate individuals to engage in actions to restore social equality (Vezzali et al., 2021). Vezzali and colleagues' research has also focused on indirect, non-face-to-face contact forms, such as extended contact, vicarious contact, media contact, imagined contact. For all of them, they found that long-term effects were generally as strong as those of direct contact (Vezzali et al., 2022). Their effects extend to the reduction of dangerous forms of bias, such as dehumanisation and group-based bullying (Vezzali et al., 2020). They can easily be applied in field contexts like schools, where they are generally appreciated by children and adolescents, providing there is the necessary motivation and engagement needed to take advantage of them.

EXERCISE 9.4

Applying Theory to Practice: Designing a Prejudice-Reduction Intervention

This exercise is designed to get you thinking about how to apply theory to practice in the real world. Imagine that you are a teacher in a secondary school (ages 11–18) that has young people from a wide range of ethnic backgrounds. You are responsible for a class of 13–14-year-olds and you want to promote a shared understanding and reduce prejudice among the students in your class.

Step 1: Design an Intervention

Using what you have learned from this chapter on intergroup contact theory, diversity ideologies, and the development of prejudice, design a two-hour short intervention that aims to promote relations in your classroom. Plan out the activities you would undertake and what you would discuss.

Step 2: Evaluate the Intervention

Once you have designed the intervention, plan how you will evaluate whether it works. For example, will you use a survey to examine student attitudes before and after the intervention, or will you have some students take part in the intervention and some not, and then compare the attitudes of the two groups? What types of questions will you ask in your survey, and why?

9.8 SUMMARY

Well, dear reader, we have reached the end. Our intention in writing this chapter was to provide foundational knowledge and to highlight the controversies and potential avenues for future investigation. We sincerely hope that this romp through the prejudice literature was as exhilarating for you as it was for us.

We began by defining prejudice and the different manifestations of prejudice, ranging from traditional (explicit) to modern (subtle) operationalisations. We outlined where prejudice might come from, meandering through individual-focused (personality, personally held beliefs) and intergroup-focused (social cognition, group relations) explanations. We then identified emergent areas of research, including developmental explanations for prejudice formation, how diversity can be used as a tool to encourage prejudice reduction (ideologies), and future directions for measurement. To encourage knowledge transfer from academia to the real world, we ended the chapter by bridging into prejudice reduction in applied settings.

If you take but one thought with you as you go, take this one: Prejudice is intertwined with social environments. This is true both theoretically (definitions and measurement approaches) and practically (development and reduction). Since social environments are dynamic and ever-changing, so too is prejudice. What this means for a scholar and future researcher like yourself is that while much is known about prejudice, there is always more to learn. Taking a bird's-eye view of the field, we can identify two gaps in particular. The first is using new technology and methods to better understand the components of prejudice and their influence on intergroup relations. The second is using emergent and well-established information from the academic realm to make evidence-based decisions in applied settings. The application of theory and research beyond the pages of journal articles will serve to improve the lived experiences of all members of society.

9.9 REVISION

Please select the correct or best answer to each of the multiple-choice questions below:

1   Imagine that a young child views their own national identity very positively. Which of the following is *not* a good descriptor of the phenomenon?

    a   Ethnocentricism
    b   Ingroup preference
    c   Prejudice
    d   Essentialism

2   Which of the following is most likely to be successful as an intervention to reduce workplace discrimination and harassment?

    a   Providing opportunities for senior management to select working groups
    b   Providing opportunities for all employees to work with a wide range of colleagues
    c   Implicit bias training for senior management and other key decision-makers
    d   Implicit bias training for all employees

3   Which of the following lists contain items related to *only* implicit forms of prejudice?

    a   Verbal behaviour; Implicit Association Test; questionnaire
    b   Questionnaire; non-verbal behaviour; heartrate response
    c   Verbal behaviour; non-verbal behaviour; Implicit Association Test
    d   None of the above

4   Which of the following is the best way to approach others in order to reduce your own prejudice?

    a   Ignore differences
    b   Celebrate similarities
    c   Acknowledge differences
    d   Learn from others about differences

5   _____ refers to the explicit endorsements of beliefs about outgroups.

   a   Microaggressions
   b   Implicit attitudes
   c   Dehumanisation
   d   Infrahumanisation

6   A covert measure is based on the assumption that one would respond faster to concepts closely associated rather than those weakly associated. The measure is known as

   a   Bogus pipeline
   b   Implicit Association Test (IAT)
   c   Thematic Association Test (TAT)
   d   Projective tests

Answers: c, a, d, d, c.

9.10 FURTHER READING

Basic

Brewer, M. B. (1999). The psychology of prejudice: Ingroup love and outgroup hate? *Journal of Social Issues, 55*(3), 429–444.

Fiske, S. T. (2002). What we know now about bias and intergroup conflict, the problem of the century. *Current Directions in Psychological Science, 11*(4), 123–128.

Haslam, N., & Loughnan, S. (2014). Dehumanization and infrahumanization. *Annual Review of Psychology, 65*, 399–423.

Rosenthal, L., & Levy, S. R. (2010). The colorblind, multicultural, and polycultural ideological approaches to improving intergroup attitudes and relations. *Social Issues and Policy Review, 4*(1), 215–246.

Advanced

Apfelbaum, E. P., Sommers, S. R., & Norton, M. I. (2008). Seeing race and seeming racist? Evaluating strategic colorblindness in social interaction. *Journal of Personality and Social Psychology, 95*(4), 918.

Brewer, M. B. (2001). Ingroup identification and intergroup conflict. *Social Identity, Intergroup Conflict, and Conflict Reduction, 3*, 17–41.

Hewstone, M., Rubin, M., & Willis, H. (2002). Intergroup bias. *Annual Review of Psychology, 53*(1), 575–604.

McKeown, S., Haji, R., & Ferguson, N. (Eds.). (2016). *Understanding peace and conflict through social identity theory.* Contemporary Global Perspectives. Cham, Switzerland: Springer International.

Pauker, K., Apfelbaum, E. P., Dweck, C. S., & Eberhardt, J. L. (2022). Believing that prejudice can change increases children's interest in interracial interactions. *Developmental Science*, *25*(4), e13233.

Applied

Cocco, V. M., Bisagno, E., Visintin, E. P., Cadamuro, A., Di Bernardo, G. A., Trifiletti, E., Molinari, L., & Vezzali, L. (2021). Fighting stigma-based bullying in primary school children: An experimental intervention using vicarious intergroup contact and social norms. *Social Development*, *31*(3), 782–796.

Leslie, L. M. (2019). Diversity initiative effectiveness: A typological theory of unintended consequences. *Academy of Management Review*, *44*(3), 538–563.

Reimer, N. K., Hughes, J., Blaylock, D., Donnelly, C., Wölfer, R., & Hewstone, M. (2021). Shared education as a contact-based intervention to improve intergroup relations among adolescents in postconflict Northern Ireland. *Developmental Psychology*, *58*(1), 193–208.

Vezzali, L., Stathi, S., Giovannini, D., Capozza, D., & Visintin, E. P. (2015). 'And the best essay is …': Extended contact and cross-group friendships at school. *British Journal of Social Psychology*, *54*, 601–615.

9.11 REFERENCES

Aberson, C. L. (2015). Positive intergroup contact, negative intergroup contact, and threat as predictors of cognitive and affective dimensions of prejudice. *Group Processes & Intergroup Relations*, *18*(6), 743–760.

Adorno, T. , Frenkel-Brunswik, E., Levinson, D.J., & Sanford, N. R. (1950). *The authoritarian personality*. New York: Harper.

Al Jazeera (2022). 'Double standards': Western coverage of Ukraine war criticised. *Al Jazeera*, 27 February. News|Russia-Ukraine war. www.aljazeera.com/news/2022/2/27/western-media-coverage-ukraine-russia-invasion-criticism

Al Ramiah, A., Schmid, K., Hewstone, M., & Floe, C. (2015). Why are all the White (Asian) kids sitting together in the cafeteria? Resegregation and the role of intergroup attributions and norms. *British Journal of Social Psychology*, *54*(1), 100–124.

Allport, G. W. (1954). *The nature of prejudice*. Reading, MA: Addison-Wesley.

Altemeyer, B. (1981). *Right Wing Authoritarianism*. Winnipeg, MB: University of Manitoba Press.

Apfelbaum, E. P., Norton, M. I., & Sommers, S. R. (2012). Racial color blindness: Emergence, practice, and implications. *Current Directions in Psychological Science*, *21*(3), 205–209.

Apfelbaum, E. P., Pauker, K., Sommers, S. R., & Ambady, N. (2010). In blind pursuit of racial equality? *Psychological Science*, *21*(11), 1587–1592.

Apfelbaum, E. P., Sommers, S. R., & Norton, M. I. (2008). Seeing race and seeming racist? Evaluating strategic colorblindness in social interaction. *Journal of personality and Social Psychology, 95*(4), 918.

Arab News (2022). Journalists' racist comments towards Arabs and Afghans spark online uproar. *Arab News*, 28 February. www.arabnews.com/node/2033121/media

Aronson, E. (1978). *The jigsaw classroom.* Beverley Hills, CA: Sage.

Aronson, E., & Thibodeau, R. (2006). The jigsaw classroom: A cooperative strategy for reducing prejudice. In J. Lynch, C. Modgil, & S. Modgil (Eds.), *Cultural diversity and the schools. Vol. 2: Prejudice, polemic or progress* (2nd ed., pp. 231–255). London: Routledge.

Baumeister, R. F., & Leary, M. R. (1995). The need to belong: Desire for interpersonal attachments as a fundamental human motivation. *Psychological Bulletin, 117*, 497–529.

Bigler, R. S., & Liben, L. S. (2007). Developmental intergroup theory: Explaining and reducing children's social stereotyping and prejudice. *Current Directions in Psychological Science, 16*(3), 162–166.

Bigler, R. S., & Patterson, M. M. (2017). Social stereotyping and prejudice in children: Insights from novel group studies. In A. Rutland, D. Nesdale, & C. S. Brown (Eds.), *The Wiley handbook of group processes in children and adolescents* (pp. 184–202). Hoboken, NJ: Wiley.

Branscombe, N. R., Ellemers, N., Spears, R., & Doosje, B. (1999). The context and content of social identity threat. In N. Ellemers, R. Spears, & B. Doosje (Eds.), *Social identity: Context, commitment, content* (pp. 35–58). Oxford: Blackwell Science.

Brewer, M. B. (1999). The psychology of prejudice: Ingroup love and outgroup hate? *Journal of Social Issues, 55*(3), 429–444.

Brewer, M. B. (2001). Ingroup identification and intergroup conflict: When does ingroup love become outgroup hate? In R. D. Ashmore, L. Jussim, & D. Wilder (Eds.), *Social identity, intergroup conflict, and conflict reduction* (pp. 17–41). Oxford: Oxford University Press.

Bureau of Justice (2019) Criminal victimization, 2018. *US Department of Justice.* https://bjs.ojp.gov/content/pub/pdf/cv18.pdf

Bytwerk, R. (1998). *German Propaganda Archive. Calvin University 1876.* https://research.calvin.edu/german-propaganda-archive/sturmer.htm

Cameron, L., & Rutland, A. (2006). Extended contact through story reading in school: Reducing children's prejudice toward the disabled. *Journal of Social Issues, 62*(3), 469–488.

Cameron, L., Rutland, A., Brown, R., & Douch, R. (2006). Changing children's intergroup attitudes toward refugees: Testing different models of extended contact. *Child Development, 77*(5), 1208–1219.

Cameron, L., Rutland, A., Turner, R., Holman Nicolas, R., & Powell, C. (2011). Changing attitudes with a little imagination? Imagined contact effects on young children's intergroup bias. *Anales de Psicología, 27*(2), 708–717. http://revistas.um.es/analesps/article/view/135311

Campbell, D. T., Kruskal, W. H., & Wallace, W. P. (1966). Seating aggregation as an index of attitude. *Sociometry, 29*(1), 1–15.

Cohen, C. E. (1981). Person categories and social perception: Testing some boundaries of the processing effect of prior knowledge. *Journal of Personality and Social Psychology, 40*(3), 441–452.

Connor, P., & Evers, E. R. (2020). The bias of individuals (in crowds): Why implicit bias is probably a noisily measured individual-level construct. *Perspectives on Psychological Science, 15*(6), 1329–1345.

Cox, W. T., Devine, P. G., Cox, W., & Devine, P. (2022). Changing implicit bias vs empowering people to address the personal dilemma of unintentional bias. In J. A. Krosnick, T. H. Stark, & A. L. Scott (Eds.), *The Cambridge handbook of implicit bias and racism*. Cambridge: Cambridge University Press.

Devine, P. G. (1989). Stereotypes and prejudice: Their automatic and controlled components. *Journal of Personality and Social Psychology, 56*(1), 5.

Dovidio, J. F., Eller, A., & Hewstone, M. (2011). Improving intergroup relations through direct, extended and other forms of indirect contact. *Group Processes & Intergroup Relations, 14*(2), 147–160.

Dovidio, J. F., Gaertner, S. E., Kawakami, K., & Hodson, G. (2002). Why can't we just get along? Interpersonal biases and interracial distrust. *Cultural Diversity and Ethnic Minority Psychology, 8*(2), 88–102.

Dovidio, J. F., Kawakami, K., & Gaertner, S. L. (2002). Implicit and explicit prejudice and interracial interaction. *Journal of Personality and Social Psychology, 82*(1), 62–68.

Duckitt, J. (2001). A dual process cognitive-motivational theory of ideology and prejudice. In M. Zanna (Ed.), *Advances in experimental social psychology* (Vol. 33, pp. 41–113). San Diego, CA: Academic Press.

Duckitt, J., & Bizumic, B. (2013). Multidimensionality of right-wing authoritarian attitudes: Authoritarianism-conservatism-traditionalism. *Political Psychology, 34*(6), 841–862.

Duckitt, J., Bizumic, B., Krauss, S. W., & Heled, E. (2010). A tripartite approach to right-wing authoritarianism: The authoritarianism-conservatism-traditionalism model. *Political Psychology, 31*(5), 685–715.

Duckitt, J., & Sibley, C. G. (2007). Right wing authoritarianism, social dominance orientation and the dimensions of generalized prejudice. *European Journal of Personality: Published for the European Association of Personality Psychology, 21*(2), 113–130.

Elevate. (2021). Elevate takes off! *The Ubele Initiative*, 28 January. www.ubele.org/news/elevate-takes-off

Elvira, M. M., & Zatzick, C. D. (2002). Who's displaced first? The role of race in layoff decisions. *Industrial Relations: A Journal of Economy and Society, 41*(2), 329–361.

Filbeck, G., Foster, B., Preece, D., & Zhao, X. (2017). Does diversity improve profits and shareholder returns? Evidence from top rated companies for diversity by DiversityInc. *Advances in accounting, 37*, 94–102.

Fiske, S. T., & Neuberg, S. L. (1990). A continuum of impression formation, from category-based to individuating processes: Influences of information and motivation on attention and interpretation. In M. P. Zanna (Ed.), *Advances in experimental social psychology* (Vol. 23, pp. 1–74). San Diego, CA: Academic Press.

FitzGerald, C., Martin, A., Berner, D., & Hurst, S. (2019). Interventions designed to reduce implicit prejudices and implicit stereotypes in real world contexts: A systematic review. *BMC Psychology, 7*(1), 1–12.

Forscher, P. S., Mitamura, C., Dix, E. L., Cox, W. T. L., & Devine, P. G. (2017). Breaking the prejudice habit: Mechanisms, timecourse, and longevity. *Journal of Experimental Social Psychology*, *72*, 133–146.

Francis-Devine, B. & Powell, A. (2022). Unemployment by ethnic background (Research Briefing 6385). London: House of Commons Library. SN06385.pdf (parliament.uk)

Gartner, R. E., Sterzing, P. R., Fisher, C. M., Woodford, M. R., Kinney, M. K., & Victor, B. G. (2020). A scoping review of measures assessing gender microaggressions against women. *Psychology of Women Quarterly*, *44*(3), 283–306.

Gawronski, B., Hofmann, W., & Wilbur, C. J. (2006). Are 'implicit' attitudes unconscious? *Consciousness and Cognition*, *15*(3), 485–499.

Gelman, S. A. (2004). Psychological essentialism in children. *Trends in Cognitive Sciences*, *8*(9), 404–409.

Graham, S., Harris, K. R., & McKeown, D. (2014). The writing of students with learning disabilities, meta-analysis of self-regulated strategy development writing intervention studies, and future directions: Redux. In H. L. Swanson, K. R. Harris, & S. Graham (Eds.), *Handbook of learning disabilities* (pp. 405–438). New York: Guilford Press.

Greenwald, A. G., & Banaji, M. R. (1995). Implicit social cognition: Attitudes, self-esteem, and stereotypes. *Psychological Review*, *102*(1), 4.

Greenwald, A. G., McGhee, D. E., & Schwartz, J. L. (1998). Measuring individual differences in implicit cognition: The Implicit Association Test. *Journal of Personality and Social Psychology*, *74*(6), 1464.

Greenwald, A. G., Poehlman, T. A., Uhlmann, E., & Banaji, M. R. (2009). Understanding and using the Implicit Association Test: III. Meta-analysis of predictive validity. *Journal of Personality and Social Psychology*, *97*, 17–41

Hamilton, D. L., & Gifford, R. K. (1976). Illusory correlation in interpersonal perception: A cognitive basis of stereotypic judgments. *Journal of Experimental Social Psychology*, *12*, 392–407.

Hammond, R. A., & Axelrod, R. (2006). The evolution of ethnocentrism. *Journal of Conflict Resolution*, *50*(6), 926–936.

Haslam N., & Loughnan S. (2014). Dehumanization and infrahumanization. *Annual Review of Psychology*, *65*, 399–423.

Hewstone, M., Kenworthy, J. B., Cairns, E., Tausch, N., Hughes, J., Tam, T., . . . & Pinder, C. (2008). Stepping stones to reconciliation in Northern Ireland: Intergroup contact, forgiveness, and trust. In A. Nadler, T. E. Malloy, & J. D. Fisher (Eds.), *The social psychology of intergroup reconciliation* (pp. 199–226). Oxford: Oxford University Press.

Hiel, A. V., & Mervielde, I. (2005). Authoritarianism and social dominance orientation: Relationships with various forms of racism. *Journal of Applied Social Psychology*, *35*(11), 2323–2344.

Ho, A. K., Sidanius, J., Pratto, F., Levin, S., Thomsen, L., Kteily, N., & Sheehy-Skeffington, J. (2012). Social dominance orientation: Revisiting the structure and function of a variable predicting social and political attitudes. *Personality and Social Psychology Bulletin*, *38*(5), 583–606.

Hogg, M. A. (2016). Social identity theory. In S. McKeown, R. Haji, & N. Ferguson (Eds.), *Understanding peace and conflict through social identity theory.* Peace Psychology Book Series. Cham, Switzerland: Springer International.

Johnson, B. (2018). Denmark has got it wrong. Yes, the burka is oppressive and ridiculous – but that's still no reason to ban it. *The Telegraph*, 5 August. www.telegraph.co.uk/ news/2018/08/05/denmark-has-got-wrong-yes-burka-oppressive-ridiculous-still/

Jugert, P., Noack, P., & Rutland, A. (2011). Friendship preferences among German and Turkish preadolescents. *Child Development, 82*(3), 812–829.

Karmali, F., Kawakami, K., Vaccarino, E., Williams, A., Phills, C., & Friesen, J. P. (2019). I don't see race (or conflict): Strategic descriptions of ambiguous negative intergroup contexts. *Journal of Social Issues, 75*(4), 1002–1034.

Kawabata, Y., & Crick, N. R. (2015). Direct and interactive links between cross-ethnic friendships and peer rejection, internalizing symptoms, and academic engagement among ethnically diverse children. *Cultural Diversity and Ethnic Minority Psychology, 21*(2), 191–200.

Kersbergen, I., & Robinson, E. (2019). Blatant dehumanization of people with obesity. *Obesity, 27*(6), 1005–1012.

Kteily, N. S., & Bruneau, E. (2017). Darker demons of our nature: The need to (re)focus attention on blatant forms of dehumanization. *Current Directions in Psychological Science, 26*(6), 487–494.

Kteily, N., Bruneau, E., Waytz, A., & Cotterill, S. (2015). The ascent of man: Theoretical and empirical evidence for blatant dehumanization. *Journal of Personality and Social Psychology, 109*, 901–931.

Kteily N. S., Hodson, G., & Bruneau, E. (2016). 'They see us as less than human': Meta-dehumanization predicts intergroup conflict via reciprocal dehumanization. *Journal of Personality and Social Psychology, 110*(3), 343–370.

Kteily, N. S., & Landry, A. (2022). Dehumanization: Emerging trends, insights, and challenges. *Trends in Cognitive Sciences, 26*(3), 222–240.

Kurdi, B., Seitchik, A. E., Axt, J. R., Carroll, T. J., Karapetyan, A., Kaushik, N., ... & Banaji, M. R. (2019). Relationship between the Implicit Association Test and intergroup behavior: A meta-analysis. *American Psychologist, 74*(5), 569.

Lai, C. K., Marini, M., Lehr, S. A., Cerruti, C., Shin, J.-E. L., Joy-Gaba, J. A., . . . & Nosek, B. A. (2014). Reducing implicit racial preferences: I. A comparative investigation of 17 interventions. *Journal of Experimental Psychology: General, 143*(4), 1765–1785.

Leslie, L. M. (2019). Diversity initiative effectiveness: A typological theory of unintended consequences. *Academy of Management Review, 44*(3), 538–563.

Leyens, J. P., Rodriguez-Perez, A., Rodriguez-Torres, R., Gaunt, R., Paladino, M. P., Vaes, J., & Demoulin, S. (2001). Psychological essentialism and the differential attribution of uniquely human emotions to ingroups and outgroups. *European Journal of Social Psychology, 31*(4), 395–411.

Lipman, C., Williams, A., Kawakami, K., & Steele, J. R. (2021). Children's spontaneous associations with targets who differ by race and emotional expression. *Developmental Psychology, 57*(7), 1094.

Loughnan, S., Haslam, N., Sutton, R., & Spencer, B. (2014) Dehumanization and social class: Animality in the stereotypes of 'white trash,' 'chavs,' and 'bogans'. *Social Psychology, 45*(1).

Macrae, C. N., Bodenhausen, G. V., Milne, A. B., & Jetten, J. (1994). Out of mind but back in sight: Stereotypes on the rebound. *Journal of Personality and Social Psychology, 67*(5), 808–817.

Martens, A., Johns, M., Greenberg, J., & Schimel, J. (2006). Combating stereotype threat: The effect of self-affirmation on women's intellectual performance. *Journal of Experimental Social Psychology, 42*(2), 236–243.

Martiny, S. E., & Rubin, M. (2016). Towards a clearer understanding of social identity theory's self-esteem hypothesis. In S. McKeown, R. Haji, & N. Ferguson (Eds.), *Understanding peace and conflict through social identity theory: Contemporary global perspectives* (pp. 19–32). Cham, Switzerland: Springer International.

Mayorga-Gallo, S. (2019). The white-centering logic of diversity ideology. *American Behavioral Scientist, 63*(13), 1789–1809.

McConahay, J. B. (1986). Modern racism, ambivalence, and the Modern Racism Scale. In J. F. Dovidio & S. L. Gaertner (Eds.), *Prejudice, discrimination, and racism* (pp. 91–125). New York: Academic Press.

McKeown, S., Cairns, E., Stringer, M., & Rae, G. (2012). Micro-ecological behaviour and intergroup contact. *Journal of Social Psychology, 152*, 340–358.

McKeown, S., Haji, R., & Ferguson, N. (Eds.). (2016). *Understanding peace and conflict through social identity theory*. Contemporary Global Perspectives. Cham, Switzerland: Springer International.

McKeown, S., Stringer, M., & Cairns, E. (2015). Classroom segregation: Where do students sit and what does it mean for intergroup relations? *British Educational Research Journal, 42*, 40–55.

McKeown, S., Williams, A., & Pauker, K. (2017). Stories that move them: Changing children's behaviour toward diverse peers. *Journal of Community and Applied Social Psychology, 21*, 381–387.

McTernan, E. (2018). Microaggressions, equality, and social practices. *Journal of Political Philosophy, 26*(3), 261–281.

Monteith, M. J., Spicer, C. V., & Tooman, G. D. (1998). Consequences of stereotype suppression: Stereotypes on AND not on the rebound. *Journal of Experimental Social Psychology, 34*(4), 355–377.

Moss-Racusin, C. A., Dovidio, J. F., Brescoll, V. L., Graham, M. J., & Handelsman, J. (2012). Science faculty's subtle gender biases favor male students. *Proceedings of the National Academy of Sciences, 109*(41), 16474–16479.

Nadal, K. L. (2011). The Racial and Ethnic Microaggressions Scale (REMS): Construction, reliability, and validity. *Journal of Counseling Psychology, 58*(4), 470–480.

Nadal, K. L., Rivera, D. P., & Corpus, M. J. (2010). Sexual orientation and transgender microaggressions: Implications for mental health and counseling. In D. W. Sue (Ed.), *Microaggressions and marginality: Manifestation, dynamics, and impact* (pp. 217–240). Hoboken, NJ: John Wiley & Sons.

Nadal, K. L., Wong, Y., Griffin, K. E., Davidoff, K., & Sriken, J. (2014). The adverse impact of racial microaggressions on college students' self-esteem. *Journal of College Student Development, 55*(5), 461–474.

Ndahiro, K. (2014). Dehumanisation: How Tutsis were reduced to cockroaches, snakes to be killed. *The New Times*, 13 March. www.newtimes.co.rw/article/104771/National/dehumanisation-how-tutsis-were-reduced-to-cockroaches-snakes-to-be-killed

Neuberg, S. L., Kenrick, D. T., & Schaller, M. (2011). Human threat management systems: Self-protection and disease avoidance. *Neuroscience & Biobehavioral Reviews, 35*(4), 1042–1051.

Nosek, B. A., Hawkins, C. B., & Frazier, R. S. (2011). Implicit social cognition: From measures to mechanisms. *Trends in Cognitive Sciences, 15*(4), 152–159.

Palazzi, A., Calderara, S., Bicocchi, N., Vezzali, L., di Bernardo, G. A., Zambonelli, F., & Cucchiara, R. (2016, September). Spotting prejudice with nonverbal behaviours. In *Proceedings of the 2016 ACM International Joint Conference on Pervasive and Ubiquitous Computing* (pp. 853–862). New York: ACM.

Paolini, S., Harwood, J., Rubin, M., Husnu, S., Joyce, N., & Hewstone, M. (2014). Positive and extensive intergroup contact in the past buffers against the disproportionate impact of negative contact in the present. *European Journal of Social Psychology, 44*(6), 548–562.

Pauker, K., Williams, A., & Steele, J. R. (2017). The development of racial categorization in childhood. In A. Rutland, D. Nesdale, & C. S. Brown (Eds.), *The Wiley handbook of group processes in children and adolescents* (pp. 221–239). Hoboken, NJ: Wiley.

Payne, B. K., Vuletich, H. A., & Lundberg, K. B. (2017). The bias of crowds: How implicit bias bridges personal and systemic prejudice. *Psychological Inquiry, 28*(4), 233–248.

Pearson, A. R., Dovidio, J. F., & Gaertner, S. L. (2009). The nature of contemporary prejudice: Insights from aversive racism. *Social and Personality Psychology Compass, 3*(3), 314–338.

Pettigrew, T. F. (1998). Intergroup contact theory. *Annual Review of Psychology, 49*(1), 65–85.

Pettigrew, T. F., & Meertens, R. W. (1995). Subtle and blatant prejudice in Western Europe. *European Journal of Social Psychology, 25*(1), 57–75.

Pettigrew, T. F., & Tropp, L. R. (2006). A meta-analytic test of intergroup contact theory. *Journal of Personality and Social Psychology, 90*(5), 751–783.

Phillips, K. W., Northcraft, G. B., & Neale, M. A. (2006). Surface-level diversity and decision-making in groups: When does deep-level similarity help? *Group Processes & Intergroup Relations, 9*(4), 467–482.

Plaut, V. C., Cheryan, S., & Stevens, F. G. (2015). New frontiers in diversity research: Conceptions of diversity and their theoretical and practical implications. In M. Mikulincer, P. R. Shaver, E. Borgida, & J. A. Bargh (Eds.), *APA handbook of personality and social psychology: Vol. 1. Attitudes and social cognition* (pp. 593–619). Washington, DC: American Psychological Association.

Pratto, F., Sidanius, J., Stallworth, L. M., & Malle, B. F. (1994). Social dominance orientation: A personality variable predicting social and political attitudes. *Journal of Personality and Social Psychology, 67*(4), 741–763.

Rattan, A., & Dweck, C. S. (2010). Who confronts prejudice? The role of implicit theories in the motivation to confront prejudice. *Psychological Science, 21*(7), 952–959.

Rattan, A., & Dweck, C. S. (2018). What happens after prejudice in the workplace? How minorities' mindsets affect their outlook on future social relations. *Journal of Applied Psychology, 103*, 676–687.

Rattan, A., & Georgeac, O. (2017). Understanding intergroup relations through the lens of implicit theories (mindsets) of malleability. *Social Personality Psychology Compass, 11*(4), e12305.

Reimer, N. K., Hughes, J., Blaylock, D., Donnelly, C., Wölfer, R., & Hewstone, M. (2021). Shared education as a contact-based intervention to improve intergroup relations among adolescents in postconflict Northern Ireland. *Developmental Psychology, 58*(1), 193–208.

Reimer, N. K., & Sengupta, N. K. (2022). Meta-analysis of the 'ironic' effects of intergroup contact. *Journal of Personality and Social Psychology, 124*(2), 362–380.

Rhodes, M., Leslie, S. J., Saunders, K., Dunham, Y., & Cimpian, A. (2018). How does social essentialism affect the development of inter-group relations? *Developmental Science, 21*(1), e12509.

Rivers, A. M., Rees, H. R., Calanchini, J., & Sherman, J. W. (2017). Implicit bias reflects the personal and social. *Psychological Inquiry, 28*(4), 301–305.

Rosenthal, L., & Levy, S. R. (2010). The colorblind, multicultural, and polycultural ideological approaches to improving intergroup attitudes and relations. *Social Issues and Policy Review, 4*(1), 215–246.

Rothbart, M., Evans, M., & Fulero, S. (1979). Recall for confirming events: Memory processes and the maintenance of social stereotypes. *Journal of Experimental Social Psychology, 15*, 343–355.

Saguy, T., Tausch, N., Dovidio, J. F., & Pratto, F. (2009). The irony of harmony: Intergroup contact can produce false expectations for equality. *Psychological Science, 20*(1), 114–121.

Schaller, M., & Neuberg, S. L. (2012). Danger, disease, and the nature of prejudice(s). In M. P. Zanna & J. M. Olson (Eds.), *Advances in experimental social psychology* (Vol. 46, pp. 1–54). San Diego, CA: Academic Press.

Shutts, K., Banaji, M. R., & Spelke, E. S. (2010). Social categories guide young children's preferences for novel objects. *Developmental Science, 13*(4), 599–610.

Sidanius, J. (1993). 7. The psychology of group conflict and the dynamics of oppression: A social dominance perspective. In S. Iyengar & W. J. McGuire (Eds.), *Explorations in political psychology* (pp. 183–220). Durham, NC: Duke University Press.

Smith, C. W., & Mayorga-Gallo, S. (2017). The new principle-policy gap: How diversity ideology subverts diversity initiatives. *Sociological Perspectives, 60*(5), 889–911.

Solorzano, D., Ceja, M., & Yosso, T. (2000). Critical race theory, racial microaggressions, and campus racial climate: The experiences of African American college students. *Journal of Negro Education, 69*(1–2), 60–73.

Spiers, H. J., Love, B. C., Le Pelley, M. E., Gibb, C. E., & Murphy, R. A. (2017). Anterior temporal lobe tracks the formation of prejudice. *Journal of Cognitive Neuroscience, 29*(3), 530–544.

Stathi, S., Cameron, L., Hartley, B., & Bradford, S. (2014). Imagined contact as a prejudice-reduction intervention in schools: The underlying role of similarity and attitudes. *Journal of Applied Social Psychology*, *44*(8), 536–546.

Sue, D. W., Bucceri, J., Lin, A. I., Nadal, K. L., & Torino, G. C. (2007a). Racial microaggressions and the Asian American experience. *Cultural Diversity and Ethnic Minority Psychology*, *13*(1), 72.

Sue, D. W., Capodilupo, C. M., Torino, G. C., Bucceri, J. M., Holder, A., Nadal, K. L., & Esquilin, M. (2007b). Racial microaggressions in everyday life: Implications for clinical practice. *American Psychologist*, *62*(4), 271.

Tajfel, H., & Turner, J. C. (1979). An integrative theory of intergroup conflict. In W. G. Austin & S. Worchel (Eds.), *The social psychology of intergroup relations* (pp. 33–47). Monterey, CA: Brooks/Cole.

Tropp, L. R., & Pettigrew, T. F. (2005). Relationships between intergroup contact and prejudice among minority and majority status groups. *Psychological Science*, *16*(12), 951–957.

Tropp, L. R., Stout, A. M., Boatswain, C., Wright, S. C., & Pettigrew, T. F. (2006). Trust and acceptance in response to references to group membership: Minority and majority perspectives on cross-group interactions. *Journal of Applied Social Psychology*, *36*(3), 769–794.

Turner, R. N., Crisp, R. J., & Lambert, E. (2007). Imagining intergroup contact can improve intergroup attitudes. *Group Processes & Intergroup Relations*, *10*(4), 427–441.

UK Government. (2010). *Equality Act 2010*. www.legislation.gov.uk/ukpga/2010/15/contentsEquality Act2010(legislation.gov.uk)

USA Today News. (2018). Trump rails against Calif. for its sanctuary policies [video]. *USA Today News*, 16 May. https://eu.usatoday.com/story/news/politics/2018/05/16/trump-immigrants-animals-mexico-democrats-sanctuary-cities/617252002/

Vezzali, L., Birtel, M. D., Di Bernardo, G. A., Stathi, S., Crisp, R. J., & Cadamuro, A. (2020). Don't hurt my outgroup friend: Imagined contact promotes intentions to counteract bullying. *Group Processes & Intergroup Relations*, *23*, 643–663.

Vezzali, L., Di Bernardo, G. A., Stathi, S., Visintin, E. P., & Hewstone, M. (2019). Using intercultural videos of direct contact to implement vicarious contact: A school-based intervention that improves intergroup attitudes. *Group Processes & Intergroup Relations*, *22*(7), 1059–1076.

Vezzali, L., McKeown, S., MacCauley, P., Stathi, S., Di Bernardo, G. A., Cadamuro, A., . . . & Trifiletti, E. (2021). May the odds be ever in your favor: The Hunger Games and the fight for a more equal society. (Negative) media vicarious contact and collective action. *Journal of Applied Social Psychology*, *51*(2), 121–137.

Vezzali, L., Trifiletti, E., Wölfer, R., Di Bernardo, G. A., Stathi, S., Cocco, V. M., . . . & Hewstone, M. (2022). Sequential models of intergroup contact and social categorization: An experimental field test of integrated models. *Group Processes & Intergroup Relations*, *26*(6).

Vorauer, J. D., Gagnon, A., & Sasaki, S. J. (2009). Salient intergroup ideology and intergroup interaction. *Psychological Science*, *20*(7), 838–845.

Whitley Jr, B. E., & Webster, G. D. (2019). The relationships of intergroup ideologies to ethnic prejudice: A meta-analysis. *Personality and Social Psychology Review*, *23*(3), 207–237.

Williams, A., Oliver, C., Aumer, K., & Meyers, C. (2016). Racial microaggressions and perceptions of internet memes. *Computers in Human Behavior, 63*, 424–432.

Williams, A., & Steele, J. R. (2019). Examining children's implicit racial attitudes using exemplar and category-based measures. *Child Development, 90*(3), e322–e338.

Wright, S. C., Aron, A., McLaughlin-Volpe, T., & Ropp, S. A. (1997). The extended contact effect: Knowledge of cross-group friendships and prejudice. *Journal of Personality and Social Psychology, 73*(1), 73–90.

10
INTERGROUP AND INTERCULTURAL RELATIONS
MICHÈLE DENISE BIRTEL

Contents

10.1 AUTHOR'S PERSONAL JOURNEY

Source: © Michele D. Birtel

I grew up and was educated in Germany and lived my entire adult professional life in the UK. I now have dual nationality: German-British. Interestingly, my German friends tell me 'You're so British', whereas my British friends tell me 'You're so German'. Personally, I perceive my social identity as European.

Living in different parts of Germany (e.g., Munich, Mannheim, Dortmund, near Speyer) and the UK (e.g., London, Oxford, Manchester, Canterbury) has come with exciting new experiences, allowing me to interact with many people different from me. I have had many opportunities to learn about other cultures and enhance my personal and professional growth. My many moves also came with many challenges, such as adapting to a new part of Germany and a new school when I was 10 years old, and to a new culture in the UK when I was 26. I experienced loneliness and homesickness. Other challenges were speaking a foreign language, impostor syndrome, finding my feet in the academic professional world after my PhD, and Brexit. I overcame challenges by reminding myself of my goals, taking setbacks as a motivation to learn more, and surrounding myself with kind and supportive friends, colleagues, and collaborators. My greatest advice is to connect with like-minded people. Social support is incredibly important and it makes you realise that there are others with similar challenges and the same curiosity about diversity.

Being exposed to different places and people has always fascinated me, and therefore inspired my research in areas reviewed in this chapter. My research has taken different directions along the way, from a purely social psychological angle using experimental methods, to incorporating a health angle and a more diverse array of methods, including cross-sectional, longitudinal, and qualitative studies. This is a result of working at different universities, so seeing different ways to undertake research. Particularly, moving rather directly from a PhD straight to a lectureship, without having had a post doc period to build a secure collaborative network, with additional teaching and administrative roles added to my workload and being the only social psychology researcher, was a daunting experience. So I explored a new angle: applying social psychological theories to the domain of mental health. I am grateful for these experiences as they showed me new, interesting paths. My advice is that even though some paths seem harder, persistence and self-reflection will help you find the important lessons rather than feeling disheartened. From adversity can come strength. Exploring different paths can also help highlight different perspectives and enable you to learn more about what you want.

Success for me is when I feel that my research has the potential to make a difference in people's lives. I particularly enjoyed involving school children in my research on studying intergroup relations in segregated areas. I am also proud of having worked with students on mental health and substance-use disorders, such as cross-cultural differences in psychosis and depression, as well as social support and internalised stigma in individuals in treatment for substance use. I discuss some of this work later in the chapter.

10.2 INTRODUCTION

In today's world, more than ever before, you will encounter people from different social and cultural backgrounds, for example in your neighbourhood, education setting, workplace, leisure time, social media, or the news. You will meet people who are similar to or different from you in terms of ethnicity, religion, gender identity, sexuality, mental health, or disability.

Prejudice and discrimination are pervasive despite the efforts of scientists, practitioners, and policy-makers at conflict resolution, prevention, and social change. Many recent real-world examples, such as the murder of George Floyd, a Black man, in Minneapolis (USA) by a White police officer in 2020 (Figure 10.1), the riots in Northern Ireland between loyalists and unionists, the murder of Sarah Everard by a police officer in London in 2021, or the sexual abuse of women by men in positions of power (e.g., Harvey Weinstein in 2017), show how persistent intergroup conflict and the negative treatment of certain groups are.

Social movements are aimed at breaking the silence, creating awareness, and empowering its members to take action to achieve social change for disadvantaged groups. Examples are 'Black Lives Matter' to combat White supremacy and racially motivated violence against Black people, 'Me Too' to target sexual harassment and abuse of women, and the Time to Change campaign to reduce stigma against people with mental health problems.

Figure 10.1 George Floyd memorial near the place where he was killed while in the custody of the police in Minneapolis

Source: © Chad Evans 2020. Reproduced under CC-BY-2.0 license

This chapter aims to stimulate and encourage your own independent and critical thinking about intergroup and intercultural relations, and how to achieve social change for a more equal society.

The first part of the chapter will equip you with the major classical and contemporary theories and empirical evidence in intergroup relations. You will learn about how we are influenced by our groups, how the groups we belong to relate to other groups, and how categorising people into 'us' versus 'them' can create intergroup conflict. You will see why existential angst and intergroup stress can contribute to prejudice and health inequalities. You will take a closer look at the role of social identity for emotions and threat as well as intergroup interactions. You will examine how social identity contributes to collective action to achieve social change and explain why crowd behaviour is meaningful.

The second part will dive deeper into understanding intergroup relations from a cultural perspective, shed more light on an example of intergroup relations relating to mental health, and critically discuss a way to reduce conflict when contact is difficult using mental simulation. You will learn how culture influences relations between groups, for example the role of different self-concepts, acculturation processes of migrants, and cross-cultural differences in perceptions of mental health.

The third part will present applications to three real-world problems: managing social and cultural diversity, a nationwide campaign to reduce mental health stigma, and targeting hate crime as an extreme form of prejudice. Crucially, you will learn about how to deal with today's diversity in education and the workplace as well as how to reduce prejudice and stigma, using the example of the 'Time to Change' campaign.

10.3 LEARNING OBJECTIVES

In this chapter, we will be answering the following questions:

- Why and how does social categorisation lead to prejudice?
- What role does social identity play in people's lives?
- How do intergroup processes lead to health inequities?
- How does culture influence relations between groups?
- Why are diversity, mental health stigma and hate crime global societal challenges?
- What are theoretical and practical approaches to tackling prejudice and stigma?

By the end of this chapter, you will be able to:

- Provide a critical evaluation of the major theories and empirical evidence relevant to intergroup and intercultural relations, such as theories relating to realistic conflict, social identity, intergroup emotions, stereotype content, intergroup threat, terror management, intergroup stress, intergroup contact, collective action, crowd behaviour, individualism and collectivism, acculturation, and mental health stigma;
- Compare and contrast the different models in intergroup and intercultural relations and their predictions;

- Critically reflect on the strengths and limitations of classic and contemporary research in intergroup and intercultural relations;
- Apply the major theories and empirical evidence to contemporary societal issues relevant to intergroup and intercultural relations, such as diversity in schools and work teams, mental health, and hate crime;
- Synthesise the knowledge and understanding gained during the chapter to take it forward for future scientific research and application in the real world.

10.4 PART 1: FOUNDATIONS

Chapter 9 focused on explaining the causes of prejudice by looking at factors within a person (*intrapersonal level*) and identified relevant individual differences as well as cognitive processes. To fully understand prejudice, we need to consider the individual in their context (*person-by-situation* interactions) and examine relations between members of different groups (*intergroup level*). In this chapter, we will discuss how seeing oneself as part of some groups but not others (e.g., in terms of ethnic background or gender) can lead to prejudice (e.g., racism, sexism). Such an intergroup perspective on prejudice has evolved since a 'crisis of confidence' in social psychology in the 1960s and 1970s, which involved concerns about psychological theories being too individualist and reductionist (see Chapter 1), focusing on explaining the causes of social behaviour through individual experiences and differences (see Chapter 9) rather than considering the bigger picture, that is, the social context of the human experience (Hogg & Williams, 2000). New theories and methodologies emerged from the discussions and with them the new approach to intergroup relations.

10.4.1 Social Categorisation

Prejudice forms and persists because we perceive our world in social categories, dividing people into groups we belong to (ingroups) and groups we do not belong to (outgroups). For example, we might identify with a certain national-

> **Key concept – Social categorisation:**
> A process by which people categorise themselves and others into ingroups and outgroups based on shared attributes.

ity and gender, with being a student at a particular university or an employee within a certain occupation. This process of dividing people into ingroups and outgroups is called **social categorisation** (Allport, 1954).

Intergroup relations are the relations between different social groups. A person can feel, think, and act as an individual and form interpersonal relations with other individuals. A person can also feel, think, and act based on the groups they identify with. This is what we call intergroup behaviour.

10.4.2 Realistic Conflict

When perceiving the world in terms of the social groups it contains, conflict arises when these groups have a conflict of interest, such as competition for scarce resources that are valued by both groups.

Realistic Conflict Theory

> **Key concept – Ethnocentrism:** The belief that one's own culture or ingroup is superior to other cultures or outgroups, and that all cultures and groups should be measured by the standard of one's own culture or group.

Realistic conflict theory, formulated by Sherif and colleagues (1961), is an inter-group explanation of prejudice and proposes that intergroup conflict and prejudice arise when ingroup and out-group goals are mutually exclusive, in which either the ingroup or the out-group can gain the limited resources (zero-sum conflict). Such competition for resources can be a real threat and cause intergroup conflict, and thereby increase **ethnocentrism** (LeVine & Campbell, 1972).

Robbers Cave Experiment

Sherif developed his realistic conflict theory following a series of three field experiments (1949, 1953, 1954) in the Robbers Cave State Park in Oklahoma. In the main study that involved all study stages, 22 boys aged 11 years stayed in a summer camp for three weeks and went through three stages. In *Stage 1* (group formation), the boys were divided into two groups which stayed in separate areas of the 200-acre wooded area without the knowledge of the other group's exist-ence. They engaged in activities together (e.g., swimming, boating, hiking, camping out) that were aimed at developing bonds. At the end of the week, they reported liking their group mem-bers and each group came up with their own name (the 'Rattlers' and the 'Eagles'), which they put onto t-shirts and flags. In *Stage 2* (intergroup conflict), the two groups learned about the existence of the other group and were brought together for several competitions (e.g., tug-of-war, baseball, treasure hunt) in which the winner received rewards. In this stage, hostility developed which involved the burning of group flags, raids of one another's cabins, and name-calling. In *Stage 3* (conflict reduc-tion), different strategies at reconciliation were tested. First, the researchers estab-lished positive, non-competitive contact, such as watching a movie, having a meal, or shooting firecrackers together. These activities were enjoyable for individuals; however, this mere contact between

> **Key concept – Superordinate goals:** Goals that require interdependence between the ingroup and outgroup to be achieved. This means these are goals that are valuable for both groups but can only be achieved by cooperating.

groups did not work to reduce hostility; for example, the meal together ended in a food leftover and rubbish fight. Only the introduction of **superordinate goals** – such as staging the breakdown of the truck that brought the food to the camp, a problem that could only be solved by both groups working together – promoted more positive intergroup relations.

By showing that it is possible to go through all stages of intergroup formation, conflict, and resolution within three weeks without signs of a certain prejudiced personality, Sherif's research provided a different perspective on explaining prejudice during the aforementioned 'crisis of confidence', namely one that focuses on a broader picture of individuals as members of their groups as well as the relations between these groups in the broader social context.

Additionally, the Robbers Cave studies highlighted that mere intergroup contact is not enough to reduce conflict again. The attempts at bringing opposing group members together for enjoyable activities were not sufficient to reduce conflict. The contact required the introduction of superordinate goals and working cooperatively towards them. These conditions are in line with Allport's (1954) four optimal conditions of intergroup contact (see Chapter 9).

KEY THINKER

Muzafer Sherif

Muzafer Sherif (1906–1988) was a Turkish-American social psychologist. He was born in Turkey and educated at the Universities of Istanbul (Turkey) as well as Harvard and Colombia (USA). After World War II, which he spent in Turkey, he returned to the US and worked at Yale before he became a professor at the University of Oklahoma and later at Pennsylvania State University. He is best known for his work in three lines of research: social judgement theory and attitude change, social influence, and social conflict. His pioneering research using the autokinetic effect demonstrated the power of groups in norm formation and group conformity to social norms. The Robbers Cave studies are considered the most successful field experiment on how intergroup conflict arises, changes, and can be resolved. From these experiments, he developed his famous realistic conflict theory, which inspired further theories on intergroup relations.

10.4.3 Social Identity

Minimal Group Paradigm

Realistic conflict theory provides an explanation for prejudice as a conflict of interest and competition over limited resources. However, competition is not a

> **Key concept – Minimal group paradigm:** Experimental design to test the minimal conditions necessary for intergroup bias. Participants are categorised into social groups based on arbitrary criteria.

necessary condition for intergroup hostility to develop. Conflict can already develop on the basis of the mere categorisation of people into ingroups and outgroups without real resources being at stake and without meaningful pre-existing social categories. In a series of experiments employing the **minimal group paradigm**, Tajfel and colleagues (1971) tested the minimal conditions necessary for intergroup bias.

Boys aged 14–15 years were invited to the laboratory and divided into groups of eight that were given two tasks. In the first task (social categorisation), boys were allocated into two separate groups. In Experiment 1, they were asked to estimate the number of dots presented briefly on a screen across 40 trials. On this basis, they were informed that they were either an 'overestimator' or 'underestimator' of dots. In Experiment 2, they had to state their preference for paintings by Klee or Kandinsky. In fact, in both experiments, boys were randomly assigned to one of the two groups. Their placement in a group was not based on their actual performance in the dots task or their preference for paintings. After they were randomly allocated to one of the two groups, they undertook a second task (reward allocation), in which they were presented with reward matrices and asked to allocate points to participants which they were told could, in turn, be exchanged for money. They only knew the code and group membership of the other person. The idea of dividing the points between an ingroup and an outgroup member was to rule out self-interest, because allocations to the entire group would mean that the participant would have personally benefited from allocations to their ingroup.

Tajfel and colleagues' (1971) idea was to test which allocation strategies participants used to assign points between ingroup and outgroup members. They found that participants showed ingroup favouritism and a preference for the maximum differentiation strategy. This maximises outcomes for the ingroup in relation to the outgroup but reduces the absolute outcome for the ingroup. A preference for this strategy indicated that it was more important for the ingroup to maximise the difference in outcome compared to the outgroup, rather than to maximise the rewards for the ingroup. Results of the minimal group paradigm showed that intergroup discrimination even develops in the absence of conflict and that prejudice reflects group interest.

The conditions of social categorisation were minimal because the participants had no past or current interaction (within or between groups), they were randomly divided into groups using arbitrary criteria, they had no knowledge about group members (anonymity), there was no competition for limited resources, and there were no personal gains to rule out self-interest. Interestingly, this still created ingroups and outgroups based on arbitrary social categories.

However, self-interest may still be involved as people have expectations of ingroup reciprocity. This is the idea that ingroup members should reward each other, which reflects positive interdependence (goals can be achieved through cooperation) within the ingroup and negative interdependence with the outgroup.

KEY THINKER

Henri Tajfel

Henri Tajfel (1919–1982) was a Polish social psychologist. He was born in Poland to a Jewish family and served in the French army in World War II, concealing his Polish-Jewish heritage to escape the concentration camps until he was made a prisoner of war by the Germans. After the war, he helped to resettle Jewish refugee children. Then he moved to the UK and graduated from psychology at Birkbeck College, University of London, in 1954 at the age of 35 as a mature student. During his academic career, he worked at the Universities of Durham and Oxford before taking up a Chair at the University of Bristol. His family and most of his friends were killed in the Nazi Holocaust, which profoundly influenced his work. He is best known for his pioneering work on social identity theory, which he developed at Bristol with John Turner from his studies using the minimal group paradigm. This famous theory had an enormous influence on various areas of psychology, such as intergroup relations, group dynamics, and organisational psychology. Social identity theory also inspired the advancement of social psychology in Europe by providing a new focus to explain prejudice, taking into account social processes in addition to prejudiced personalities. In 1966, he was among the founders of the European Association of Experimental Social Psychology, which is a major scientific organisation in social psychology to date.

As we have seen in Chapter 9, prejudice can take the form of ingroup favouritism and ingroup love or outgroup derogation and outgroup hate. Using the minimal group paradigm, researchers have found a positive–negative asymmetry in social discrimination (Mummendey & Otten, 1998); that is, participants show ingroup favouritism when allocating positive outcomes (e.g., money), but not when allocating negative outcomes (e.g., punishments). However, in the real world, for example in intractable conflicts such as the Israeli–Palestinian conflict, people show outgroup derogation, ranging from dehumanisation to physical violence. The social identity approach, which we will discuss next, provides an explanation for ingroup favouritism in minimal social groups. The intergroup emotions theory, which we will discuss in section 10.4.4, provides an explanation for more extreme forms of prejudice involving outgroup derogation.

Social Identity Theory

The minimal group studies demonstrate the significance of mere social categorisation for the formation and persistence of prejudice. People can display negative intergroup behaviour

Key concept – Social identity: Part of people's self-concept, that is, the sense of who they are that is based on their memberships of groups that are significant to them.

Key concept – Group identification: The sense of belonging to a particular group.

even in the absence of self-interest or group interest when competing for limited resources. These insights have inspired the idea that we possess not only a personal identity, but also a **social identity** that influences our perception of, and interactions in, our social world (Tajfel & Turner, 1979).

Such social identities, which are independent of realistic conflict, are the key focus of the social identity approach, which encompasses *social identity theory* (Tajfel et al., 1971) and *self-categorisation theory* (Turner et al., 1987). Core to the social identity approach are three major components: (1) we organise the world into social groups, a process called social categorisation; (2) we compare our groups with other groups we are not part of (social comparison); and (3) we want our **social identity** to be positive, which forms the basis for positive self-esteem and certainty.

Social identity theory postulates that when we identify with groups, we categorise ourselves and others into 'us' versus 'them' and perceive our world in terms of ingroups and outgroups. Our interactions then take place at an intergroup level, and as ingroup members we are influenced by our group's norms. When the different groups are salient, we have the tendency to enhance similarities within our group ('we ingroup members are all the same') and differences between the groups ('we ingroup members are different from the outgroup members'). The stronger we identify with our group – **group identification** – the more we perceive ourselves as attached to the group and perceive the group as being important.

Similar to our motivation to attain and maintain a positive self, we also strive for a positive social identity. Drawing on Festinger's (1954) social comparison theory (see Chapter 2), Tajfel and Turner (1979) argued that we not only compare ourselves to other individuals, we also compare our ingroups to outgroups. Other groups serve as a point of reference. Through this social comparison process, we achieve a *positive distinctiveness* between our ingroup and outgroups and in doing so form a positive social identity. An example is when we think about fans of rival sports teams. When the media reports positively about the sports team that fans identify with, compared to their rival team, it can increase positive distinctiveness and a positive social identity as a fan of this sports team. The idea that favouring the groups we belong to over groups we do not belong to has been argued not only to fulfil the need for a positive self-concept (i.e., the overall perception of oneself), but also to enhance self-esteem (i.e., the affective evaluation of one's value) (Abrams & Hogg, 1990) and reduce uncertainty (Hogg, 2000).

The self-esteem hypothesis postulates that the strategy of positive differentiation between ingroup and outgroup leads to greater self-esteem through a positive social identity. By emphasising our links to a successful group, we can boost our self-esteem when this group performs well – an effect labelled *basking in reflected glory (BIRGing)* (Cialdini et al.,

1976). For example, when the sports team we identify with wins a match, it can boost our own self-esteem as an ingroup member (Figure 10.2). Two predictions can be derived from social identity theory, namely that lower self-esteem can lead people to display greater prejudice (H1) and that displaying greater prejudice can enhance people's self-esteem (H2) (Abrams & Hogg, 1990). Greater support has been found for hypothesis 2 than for hypothesis 1. However, researchers have criticised that many studies included measures of individual self-esteem which would not be sensitive enough to test the self-esteem hypothesis and could explain why convincing evidence is missing (Martiny & Rubin, 2016). They argued that measures of collective self-esteem reflect the assumptions of social identity more accurately than measures of individual self-esteem. This is because collective self-esteem refers to the specific social identity currently being evaluated, rather than an overall evaluation of one's personal self-esteem over time.

Figure 10.2 Fans of the Netherlands national football team wearing football shirts and other accessories in their team's orange colour

Source: https://pxhere.com/en/photo/693467

Another explanation for the positive differentiation between ingroup and outgroups is the need we have to reduce uncertainty in our world – uncertainty reduction theory (Hogg, 2000). Uncertainty can be reduced by gathering information and understanding about where our place in the world is and what its meaning is. Identifying with groups and specifying the relationship between groups helps to create more certainty for us because we can better predict how we should act and how others will act.

Self-Categorisation Theory

Self-categorisation theory (Turner et al., 1987) expands the cognitive element of social identity theory. It distinguishes between a personal and a social identity. Personal identity refers to an individual's idiosyncratic traits and relationships, whereas social identity refers to an individual's membership of social categories and the consequences of these memberships on the individual's feelings, thoughts, and behaviours. Self-categorisation theory proposes that a shift in our self-concept takes place during the process of social categorisation. When a certain social identity is salient, by categorising the social world into groups, the process of depersonalisation starts. This is a cognitive process of defining the self more in terms of shared similarities with members of the ingroup (and differences with members of the outgroup) and less in terms of the unique attributes of the individual. In other words, we perceive ourselves less as individuals and more as prototypical representatives of our ingroup. Intergroup behaviour rather than interpersonal behaviour comes into the foreground. Each group has a prototype that is represented in people's minds. A prototype maximises the similarities between members of the ingroup and the differences between members of the outgroup. In other words, it refers to the general idea of what the ideal group member might look like, for example, what the prototypical Bayern Munich fan would look like. The more we identify with a group, the more we identify with and conform to this prototype of the group.

Each group develops norms for its members that lay out what kind of intergroup behaviour is appropriate in certain situations, within the group as well as in relation to outgroups. For example, norms can prescribe what to wear to a Bayern Munich football match, which songs to sing, and how to interact with the rival team (e.g., no physical violence). In a specific situation, social identities can be more or less salient, and some more salient than others. This determines where one sits on the continuum of depersonalisation, whether we see ourselves as individuals or more as members of a group. For example, singing out loud may be an excellent idea when driving in the car, but not so much when sitting in the lecture theatre, which activates the social identity of belonging to the group of students. When group identities become salient and self-categorisation leads to depersonalisation, we tend to conform to the norms of the group and its prototype (see section 10.4.7 for its role in explaining crowd behaviour).

Key concept – Black sheep effect: Tendency to judge likeable ingroup members more positively than likeable outgroup members (e.g., for norm-compliant behaviour) and to judge unlikeable ingroup members more negatively than unlikeable outgroup members (e.g., for norm-violating behaviour).

However, if ingroup members deviate from the ingroup norms, it has larger consequences than an outgroup member displaying the same behaviour. Such ingroup deviants are judged more harshly as they threaten the ingroup's social identity (known as the **black sheep effect**) (Marques & Yzerbyt, 1988).

For example, if Bayern Munich fans hold the norm that there should be no violence towards the rival team, but a Bayern Munich fan punches another football fan, then they would be judged more harshly than the rival team fan displaying the same violence. This is because being peaceful when losing a match may be an important part of what it means to be a Bayern Munich fan, and fans who violate this norm threaten the social identity of Bayern Munich fans.

Social Identity and Low-Status Groups

Not all groups are perceived as equally valuable by society. Social identity theory also makes assumptions as to how differences in intergroup status and power positions (low/high), the perceived nature of the ingroup–outgroup boundaries (secure/insecure status relationships), the strength of the ingroup identification, and beliefs about the existing social system impact group members' social identity and strategies to attain and maintain a positive social identity. Groups with lower status also strive to achieve a positive social identity but are faced with constraints. To decide on a strategy, lower status groups will evaluate the perceived permeability of the group boundaries and the perceived security of the status relations (stability, legitimacy). To achieve a positive social identity as a lower status group, various strategies have been proposed by Tajfel and Turner (1979), as set out in Figure 10.3 (see also section 10.4.7 for collective action).

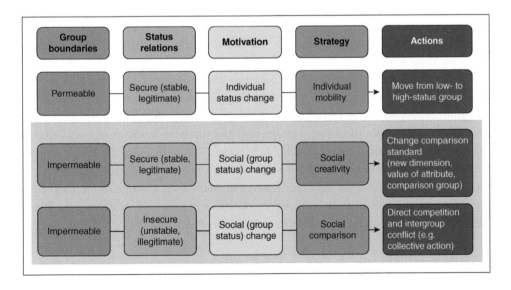

Figure 10.3 Social identity theory: Strategies of low-status groups. Based on information in Tajfel and Turner (1979)

10.4.4 Intergroup Emotions

While social categorisation and social identity theory explain ingroup favouritism, they do not explain more extreme forms of prejudice that are characteristic of intractable conflicts, namely outgroup derogation such as aggression and retaliation. We know from interpersonal relations that emotions can be powerful in motivating certain behaviours. An intergroup emotions approach to prejudice, such as intergroup emotions theory and stereotype content model, can not only explain more extreme forms of intergroup bias, including hate (see also 10.6.3 for an application to hate crime), but also distinguish between and predict different types of prejudice, such as racism or sexism.

Intergroup Emotions Theory

> **Key concept – Group emotions:** Emotions that are experienced as an ingroup member rather than as an individual.

Intergroup emotions theory (Mackie & Smith, 2002) is grounded in the social identity approach and appraisal theories of emotions. Its fundamental idea is that emotions can be felt not only at an individual and interpersonal level, but also at an intergroup level. When people perceive themselves as members of a social group with which they identify, they can experience the emotions associated with that group membership (**group emotions**), and thus the emotions that are related to other ingroup members or other social groups (intergroup emotions).

When ingroup members encounter a situation in which their social identity is activated, appraisals about whether this situation is helping or harming the ingroup's goals (primary appraisal) and whether the group has sufficient resources to cope with the situation (secondary appraisal) trigger specific intergroup emotions, which are then linked with certain intergroup behaviours. For example, intergroup anger has been associated with the desire to harm an outgroup, intergroup fear with outgroup avoidance, and collective guilt with the desire to compensate the outgroup. A feedback loop (reappraisal) examines whether a certain intergroup behaviour can be carried out successfully. Unsuccessful or failed responses to the outgroup will exacerbate the intergroup emotion and motivate future intergroup behaviour aimed at dissipating the emotion (Smith & Mackie, 2015). For example, Russia attacking buildings and civilians in Ukraine elicits anger among Ukrainians (intergroup emotion), and through this a desire to fight back and remove Russians from Ukraine (intergroup behaviour). Reappraising the situation as being unsuccessful at removing Russians from Ukraine exacerbats the anger and motivates further actions (feedback loop).

Stereotype Content Model

The stereotype content model (Fiske et al., 2002) proposes four types of emotional prejudice. Societal structures (e.g., group status) predict the content of stereotypes on two dimensions (competence, warmth) that are attributed to a group. *Competence* is influenced by the relative status of the group in society, with higher status predicting higher competence. *Warmth* is influenced by perceived competition with the ingroup, with greater perceived competition predicting lower warmth. Based on this appraisal, groups elicit specific intergroup emotions (contempt, pity, envy, pride), and such emotional prejudice is the basis for discrimination (Fiske, 2018) (see Table 10.1).

In the most stigmatised quadrant – low competence and low warmth – we find groups with low status, such as homeless people or immigrants, who compete with members of the host society for resources. This appraisal along the two dimensions elicits feelings of contempt, disgust, and anger, also called '*contemptuous prejudice*'. Groups that are perceived as low in competence but high in warmth (i.e., '*paternalistic prejudice*') elicit feelings of pity and sympathy, such as older adults or women. An example of this type of prejudice is benevolent sexism towards women. Appraisals of low warmth but high competence elicit feelings of envy or jealousy ('*envious prejudice*'), for example bankers. In the high competence and high warmth group (i.e., '*admiration*'), we find our ingroup as well as groups that are perceived as allies who elicit feelings of pride.

The stereotype content model was originally tested in the US context and has since been validated across cultures (Cuddy et al., 2009). The two dimensions of warmth and competence were also reliably found in seven European nations and three East Asian nations. As in the US context, high-status groups were perceived as high in competence, and competitive groups were perceived as low in warmth.

Table 10.1 Stereotype content model. Based on information in Fiske et al. (2002) and Fiske (2018)

Warmth (friendliness, trustworthiness)	Competence (capability, assertiveness)	
	Low	High
High	Paternalistic prejudice Low status, not competitive Pity, sympathy E.g., older adults, disabled people, women (benevolent sexism)	Admiration High status, not competitive Pride, admiration E.g., ingroup members, close allies
Low	Contemptuous prejudice Low status, competitive Contempt, disgust, anger, resentment E.g., immigrants, homeless people, people with drug addiction	Envious prejudice High status, competitive Envy, jealousy E.g., Jews, feminists, rich people

Warmth also plays a role in misunderstanding and masking prejudice in the form of sexism. Ambivalent sexism theory (Glick & Fiske, 1996) distinguishes between hostile sexism (i.e., the belief that women are inferior to men and that men deserve greater status and power) and benevolent sexism (i.e., dominating, patronising behaviours that appear flattering but undermine women). Benevolent sexism is used to legitimise gender inequality and prevent women from challenging it. Hopkins-Doyle and colleagues (2019) demonstrated that the warmth associated with benevolent sexism plays a role in concealing sexism as such. A series of seven studies (observational, correlational, experimental) demonstrated that women perceive benevolent sexism as less sexist, and protest against it less because they perceive benevolent sexist men as warmer. They also perceive benevolent sexist men as more supportive of gender equality. This poses issues for social equality (see also section 10.4.7 for the ironic consequences of positive intergroup contact on social change).

10.4.5 Intergroup Threat

So far, we have seen that emotions related to group membership can drive intergroup behaviour (intergroup emotions approach) and that various factors can threaten the ingroup, such as competition for limited resources (realistic conflict theory), lower status (i.e., groups that are stigmatised by society such as minority ethnic groups), and an unfavourable comparison with the outgroup, leading to a negative social identity (social identity theory). There are different types of threat to the ingroup. **Intergroup threat theory** (Stephan et al., 2009) distinguishes between two types of threat – realistic and symbolic threat – and refers to perceptions of threat, rather than objective threat. Realistic threat refers not only to competition for limited resources, but also to power and the general safety and welfare of the ingroup. Symbolic threat refers to threats to the ingroup's values and beliefs as well as a general worldview, such as people's negative reactions towards increased immigration and the worldwide refugee crisis. Intergroup threat has a range of negative implications for intergroup relations, and a meta-analysis found that intergroup threat is associated with greater prejudice (Riek et al., 2006).

> **Key concept – Intergroup threat:**
> A threat that is experienced by an individual perceiving themselves as an ingroup member and seeing the outgroup as being in the position to cause harm to the ingroup.

In situations of threat, the ingroup shows intergroup bias, such as ingroup favouritism (i.e., a more positive evaluation of the ingroup compared to the outgroup on valuable dimensions) or even outgroup derogation (i.e., discrimination in terms of allocating limited resources). Another response to intergroup threat is collective narcissism. Collective narcissism is an extension of individual narcissism onto the intergroup level and involves a grandiose view of the ingroup that requires constant external validation (Golec de Zavala et al., 2009). Studies show that it correlates positively with perceived outgroup threat to the ingroup's image, prejudice, and conspiracy theories relating to the outgroup.

Experiencing a threat to one's social identity is a form of intergroup stress that can negatively impact stigmatised group members' health and well-being (see sections 10.4.7 and

10.5.2). Furthermore, another type of threat, the threat to our cultural worldview, is associated with existential angst and can increase prejudice, which we consider next.

10.4.6 Terror Management

A theory that considers both ideas of protecting self-esteem (see section 10.4.3 for social identity and self-esteem) and using strategies to deal with threats is terror management theory (TMT) (Greenberg et al., 1986). As human beings, we have the cognitive ability to reflect on our own death, and being reminded of our own mortality (**mortality salience**) evokes the fear of our own death.

> **Key concept – Mortality salience:**
> Awareness that one's death is inevitable.

According to TMT, we can cope with this existential angst by adopting and conforming to *cultural worldviews*, which increases our *self-esteem* through the belief of being a valuable contributor to a meaningful world. A cultural worldview is a set of important beliefs about the nature of reality; it is shared by others and provides meaning, stability, and safety. We are motivated to protect our worldview and meet its associated standards. This protects us against death-related concerns as we obtain an illusion of immortality and ensure that the worldview continues to exist even when we have died.

Furthermore, when mortality is salient, people will prefer those who are supporting their worldview over those who are challenging their worldview (worldview defence) and ingroup bias can arise. In order to serve as an anxiety buffer, people need continuous reassurance that their worldview is valid and shared by others, and those who do not share the faith in one's worldview are threatening. According to TMT, prejudice is not a result of social categorisation, but rather a coping mechanism to deal with mortality salience and death-related threat (Greenberg et al., 2016). For example, Arndt and colleagues (2009) showed that American Christian medical students' cardiac risk assessment of a Muslim patient is affected by mortality salience, which increased prejudice towards the patient. In the mortality salience condition, they completed the Fear of Death scale with 15 questions relating to their anxiety about their own death to increase mortality salience. In the control condition, they completed questions regarding their anxiety about their future. To manipulate the religion of the patient, a fictitious physician record was created, and the information differed regarding the name (Muslim versus Christian name), race, and religion between conditions. Medical students in the mortality salience condition estimated the likelihood that the patient with chest pain had coronary artery disease or was at risk of myocardial infarction as lower for the Muslim than the Christian patient. There was no difference in estimates of cardiac risk between the patients in the control condition (see Figure 10.4). Arndt and colleagues' findings suggest that mortality salience can lead to biased and prejudicial medical judgements and decisions. This can be particularly relevant in healthcare settings when the physician is confronted with medical issues that activate death-related thoughts (e.g., cancer).

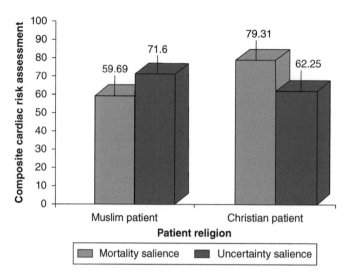

Figure 10.4 Composite cardiac risk values as a function of salience and patient religion. Adapted from Arndt et al. (2009)

The **Open Science** movement, a movement that emerged from concerns about the lack of replicability across scientific fields (known as the 'replication crisis', see Chapter 1) and that is aimed at increasing the transparency and accessibility of scientific knowledge, has failed to replicate a classic TMT finding – the mortality salience effect. A group of researchers from 17 labs (Klein et al., 2022) conducted a replication of a study by Greenberg under high power (1,550 participants). The original study included 59 psychology students from a US introduction to psychology class. The Many Labs project found little evidence that priming mortality salience (e.g., by asking participants to think about their own death) can increase worldview defence (e.g., a more positive evaluation of the writer of a pro-American essay than of the writer of an anti-American essay) compared to a control condition. It remains open whether the original findings were a false positive or whether necessary conditions to replicate the original findings are not fully understood or available.

10.4.7 Intergroup Interactions

Having discussed intergroup theories that explain prejudice in the first half of this part of the chapter, such intergroup processes can be particularly impactful when groups of different status come together. We will now consider how these theories explain intergroup interactions between advantaged and disadvantaged groups in terms of intergroup stress and health, collective action efforts to achieve social change, and explanations of crowd behaviour.

Intergroup Stress and Health

Majority and minority group members have different interpersonal concerns when interacting with each other, which can cause intergroup stress. Majority group members are concerned about appearing prejudiced, and so they may feel uncomfortable and anxious in an intergroup interaction (**intergroup anxiety**; Stephan & Stephan, 1985), or even experience intergroup threat. Minority group members, in contrast, are concerned about being the target of prejudice and discrimination, and about confirming the negative stereotypes the majority holds of them. Anxiety regarding negative consequences of intergroup interactions in the form of rejection, embarrassment, or discrimination inhibits interest in the outgroup and can lead to hostility.

Trawalter and colleagues (2009) applied Lazarus and Folkman's (1984) **transactional model of stress and coping** to the intergroup context. In general, a threat is experienced when an individual appraises a situation as stressful and their coping strategies as insufficient, so there is risk of failure. A challenge is experienced when an individual appraises a situation as stressful and their coping strategies as sufficient, so there is an opportunity for growth. In intergroup relations, both majority and minority group members often appraise interracial interactions as a threat rather than as a challenge due to the awareness of potential prejudice and conflict. Intergroup stress is then evident in affective, cognitive, behavioural, and physiological stress reactions.

Blascovich and colleagues (2001), for example, found anxiety and threat responses to an interaction with a physically stigmatised partner on subjective, physiological, and behavioural measures. Having had positive intergroup contact experiences in the past, however, can buffer people from these negative outcomes, for example it can reduce the physiological threat response during contact with a Black person, and even facilitate physiological recovery following a stressful interracial contact (Page-Gould et al., 2010).

As well as being a source of stress, intergroup interactions can lead to pervasive health inequalities. In their model, Major and colleagues (2013) describe how health inequalities can be explained by characteristics of intergroup relations (e.g., social categorisation, social hierarchies between low- and high-status groups, warmth/competence stereotype content) that lead to intergroup processes (e.g., ingroup bias and discrimination, stereotype threat, or mistrust), producing health inequalities in three areas. First, experiences of discrimination enhance the life stress of minority groups, which then affects their health and well-being negatively. Second, to cope with being the target of prejudice, people may choose unhealthy behavioural strategies such as smoking, alcohol abuse, or comfort eating. Third, healthcare interaction can be seen as a micro intergroup context to which both patient and healthcare professional bring their intergroup biases. Such biases can affect the quality of healthcare, for example due to miscommunication or lower quality of treatment (for a detailed review, see Major et al., 2013).

EXERCISE 10.1

Taking a Perspective

Imagine that you are a member of an advantaged group meeting a member of a disadvantaged group (e.g., ethnicity, sexual orientation, age, mental health, etc.) or you are a member of a disadvantaged group meeting a member of an advantaged group. How do you feel? How do you behave? What makes this situation challenging? Apply the theories of intergroup relations in your answer. This exercise will develop your skills to take the perspective of another person and to apply theories to real-world problems.

Social Identity and Intergroup Contact

To understand when intergroup interactions may work best to avoid stress and what role social categorisation and social identity play during contact, different models of contact have been proposed (see Chapter 9 for a detailed account of intergroup contact theory). Each model has a different perspective on whether the ingroup–outgroup categories should be salient in an intergroup interaction or not, for example by highlighting the nationality of the interaction partner.

The **decategorisation model** (Brewer & Miller, 1984) proposes that interactions should take place at an *interpersonal* level (low salience of intergroup boundaries). This way interaction partners pay less attention to stereotypical information based on each other's categories and more attention to idiosyncratic information.

The **mutual intergroup differentiation model** (Hewstone & Brown, 1986) proposes that interactions should take place on an *intergroup* level (high category salience). This way each group can maintain their social identity. In interactions, each group has a complementary role, and each group enhances their distinctive positive qualities. The strengths of each group should be recognised and valued.

The **common ingroup identity model** (Gaertner et al., 1989) proposes that interactions should take place on an *intragroup* level by recategorising the former ingroup and outgroup into a common, superordinate identity. This is a cognitive transformation of 'us versus them' into an inclusive social group 'we'. For example, while there may be students from many different nationalities in the classroom, one identity everyone has in common is that they are university students.

A further development of this model is the **dual identity model** (Gaertner & Dovidio, 2000). Instead of shifting focus from an original identity to a new common identity, which can be threatening, both the original subordinate identities (e.g., different nationalities) and the new common superordinate identity (e.g., university student) remain salient simultaneously. This way interactions take place at a level on which the common ingroup identity allows the discovery of a shared identity, while still mutually recognising the subordinate identities.

However, people do not always engage spontaneously in positive interactions and often interactions can be negative. Also, contact can only reduce prejudice when social groups have the opportunity to engage in interactions. Unfortunately, because prejudice goes hand in hand with segregation, there are many situations in which establishing meaningful interactions between communities may be difficult. Examples are the segregation of Latino and White communities in the United States, Catholic and Protestant communities in Northern Ireland, the Green Line in Cyprus and the West Bank in Israel. In section 10.5.3 we will consider a prejudice-intervention based on a mental simulation that does not require direct contact.

Social Identity and Collective Action

Not only is intergroup contact not always possible, attempts at prejudice reduction through positive intergroup contact can actually lead to ironic effects, reducing the awareness of inequalities and, with this, actions towards social change. In two studies,

Saguy and colleagues (2009) tested whether intergroup contact results in more positive outgroup attitudes but reduces attention to inequality and increases expectations for equality among disadvantaged group members. Study 1 varied the power of the group (IV1) – whether participants were randomly allocated to the advantaged or disadvantaged group – and the type of contact (IV2) – whether participants engaged in commonality-focused contact or differences-focused contact. Power was operationalised by giving participants either 10 research credits to distribute to both groups (high power) or 10 marbles (low power). Contact type was manipulated by asking participants to discuss things they have in common with the other group or things that are different. Participants from the disadvantaged group in the commonality-focused contact condition reported more positive outgroup attitudes and less attention to intergroup inequality and, because of this, greater expectations of outgroup fairness (more credits). However, the advantaged group discriminated against the disadvantaged group in both contact conditions, despite reporting more positive outgroup attitudes. Commonality-focused contact did not result in greater intergroup equality, but it led to unrealistic optimism among the disadvantaged group members (see Figure 10.5).

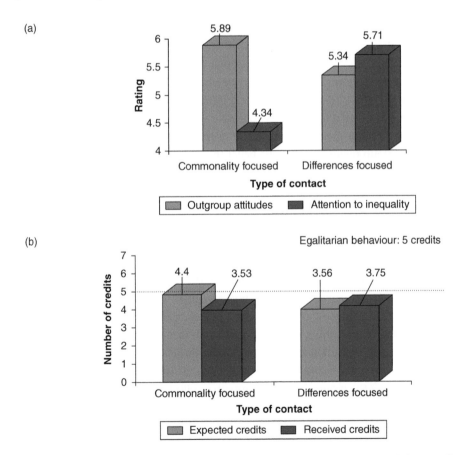

Figure 10.5 Outgroup attitudes and attention to intergroup inequality (a) as well as expected versus received credits, with five credits indicating equality (b). Adapted from Saguy et al. (2009)

In Study 2, participants were from an actual disadvantaged group (Israeli Arabs), and their intergroup contact with Jews was measured. Results showed that positive intergroup contact was associated with lower support for social change, because it enhanced perceptions of Jews as fair.

In addition to these ironic effects of positive contact, while the high-status group may support equality in principle, they can be reluctant to support changes of the social system that require giving up privileges to ensure such equality (known as the principle implementation gap; Dixon et al., 2007). Results from a survey in South Africa (Dixon et al., 2007) suggest that while White South African participants generally supported the principle of equality in areas of education, employment, or land ownership, they opposed certain practices designed to implement equality, such as educational quotas or affirmative action.

The prejudice-reduction model based on intergroup contact (Chapter 9) has been criticised for focusing on the majority group and on only improving attitudes, but not on social equality for the minority group. Dixon and colleagues (2012) proposed a collective action model that focuses on the minority group and on collective action to achieve social change. The main goal of this model is not the reduction but the instigation of intergroup conflict, not as a threat but to challenge inequality.

To explain efforts at collective action, the concept of social identity has been integrated with other psychological perspectives, such as in the integrative social identity model of collective action (SIMCA) (van Zomeren et al., 2008). The SIMCA proposes three key predictors of what mobilises minority group members to engage in collective action: (1) perceived injustice towards the group, (2) perceived group efficacy, and (3) social identity. Minority group members are motivated to engage in collective action (1) when they perceive a group-based inequality following social comparison with the outgroup that arouses group-based anger, (2) when ingroup members share the belief that they have the power to change their group's situation through action, and (3) when ingroup members identify highly with the group and status relations are perceived as illegitimate and unstable.

Tausch and colleagues (2011) tested the two SIMCA routes to collective action in three studies with German students, Indian Muslims, and British Muslims. They predicted that *normative* collective action (i.e., actions that conform to the rules of society, e.g., protests, fly-ers) is driven by different intergroup emotions and different levels of efficacy than *non-normative* collective action (i.e., actions that violate the rules, e.g., throwing stones, terror-ism). *Anger* predicted normative collective action. Anger is a constructive emotion where reconciliation is the ultimate goal. Actions based on anger are aimed at correcting wrongdoing and improving the relationship. *Contempt* predicted non-normative collective action. Contempt is a destructive emotion that can develop as a result of anger and a feeling of lack of control when reconciliation is no longer possible. Actions based on contempt are aimed at distancing oneself from the group. Similarly, normative collective action was driven by a high sense of efficacy (i.e., the group's belief that their actions can change the perceived injustice). Non-normative collective action was driven by a sense of low efficacy. When groups feel they do not have the power to reach the appropriate agents for change, they engage in non-normative collective action to achieve social change in a different way (e.g., influencing the public, creating a movement for change) (see also Guest Personal Journey: Nicole Tausch).

GUEST PERSONAL JOURNEY

Nicole Tausch

My personal and academic journey was shaped by sudden historical events that propelled me from a working-class family in a small East German village, via a PhD at Oxford University, to a permanent academic position at the University of St Andrews. Born in 1976, I came of age during the political and social turmoil that followed the fall of the Berlin wall. I experienced the rapid transformation and almost complete disappearance of the state I grew up in, with all the uncertainties – due to mass unemployment, vanishing security structures, and demographic changes – this generated for my parents' generation. For me and many of my generation, however, 'die Wende' created a strong desire to seize new

Source: Nicole Tausch

opportunities. Although I was taught Russian at school, I was always an anglophile, so as soon as I finished school, I spent one year as an au pair in New York, to learn English and broaden my horizons. This was followed by several years of studying psychology (as the first person in my family to go to university) at Martin-Luther University in Halle/Saale, Cardiff University, and the University of Oxford. I learned to navigate unfamiliar social worlds, as an East German in a new (and Western-dominated) political, economic, and educational system, as a foreigner in the US and Britain, and as a working-class academic at an elite university. This generated an interest in social psychology, in particular in how our social identities inform our worldviews, the structural factors that shape intergroup relations, and the psychological forces that drive protest and social change. My current goal is to develop a better understanding of the socio-political polarisation and the success of populist movements we are witnessing around the world. I believe that my East German background enables me to empathise with those who feel disadvantaged, disrespected, and unheard by national politics, and my hope is to contribute to the development of platforms that foster a truly mutual exchange to find fair solutions to the complex social problems ahead of us.

Social Identity and Crowd Behaviour

Intergroup processes take place not only between two existing groups, but also between groups that newly form out of a crowd, such as people protesting to achieve social change (a form of collective action). The social identity approach has provided a new explanation for the intriguing phenomenon of crowd behaviour, for example how people with and without institutional power behave during crowd events.

Early theories perceived crowd behaviour as what happens when individuals in large groups lose their sense of personal identity and responsibility due to the anonymity of the group (deindividuation). People were seen as unable to resist the emotions of the crowd, which were spread among its members (contagion), with their actions perceived as irrational, impulsive, and destructive. Other theories focused on explaining crowd behaviour through a cost–benefit analysis of the crowd members or on norms that emerge through interpersonal interaction between the crowd members.

The **social identity model of deindividuation effects** (SIDE) (Reicher et al., 1995) was established in response to criticism towards the traditional model of deindividuation and proposes that self-categorisation plays a role in explaining crowd behaviour. The anonymity of the context shifts a person's focus from other individuals to the group. Depersonalisation and immersion into the group enhance a person's social identity. People's identity shifts from a personal to a shared social identity, which is the basis for newly established group norms. Crowd behaviour is a result of increasing the salience of a social identity and consequently conforming to group norms that are salient. For example, if a group of White people supports racism, then deindividuation will increase the salience of this social identity and its associated norms, and with this racist behaviour towards Black people. If a group of men rejects sexism towards women, then deindividuation will lead to behaviour that challenges sexism towards women. Instead of considering human behaviour in crowd situations as an impulsive and irrational emotional reaction due to deindividuation (i.e., the loss of one's identity), the SIDE suggests that crowd behaviour can be socially meaningful.

The **elaborated social identity model** (ESIM) (Drury & Reicher, 2009; see also Guest Personal Journey: John Drury) further developed this new explanation for crowd behaviour. The model explains crowd behaviour in terms of a change in people's social identity and a change of social relations between the ingroup (e.g., participants of a protest) and the outgroup (e.g., the police during a protest). Crowd behaviour develops as a function of intergroup dynamics. Crowd members act in terms of their social identity, whereby these actions become the new context for actions of the other group. Through the interaction, an intergroup context is established in which ingroup and outgroup may develop different understandings of their identity and actions of each group. While the ingroup (protesters) may view themselves as peaceful and legitimate, the outgroup (police) may perceive protesters as a threat to public order. The police may view themselves as defending the public order; the protesters, on the other hand, may perceive the police's actions as unnecessarily harsh. This sheds light on why some crowd situations can turn violent unintentionally. If there is an asymmetry of power relations and the outgroup has legitimate power to enact their understanding (e.g., intervention), crowd members are confronted with a new and unexpected social position. This dynamic can lead to a self-fulfilling prophecy of peaceful protesters becoming violent because they are being treated as a threat. Qualitative studies on crowd events (e.g., environmental protest) provide support for the ESIM. The feeling of a common fate and a mutual ingroup empowers people to continue to oppose the authorities and participate in social movements to achieve social change.

GUEST PERSONAL JOURNEY

John Drury

I left school at 16. I was so disillusioned by formal education that I didn't read a book for years. I went back to formal education when I was 24 because I wanted to be a psychotherapist. However, when I was on my BA Social Psychology course at the University of Sussex, I realised that I wanted to stay in academia. I had always been fascinated by riots and protest crowds. But I didn't realise that these could be the subject of scholarly investigation until I started at Sussex. Reading Steve Reicher's study of the 1980 St Pauls riot, I wanted to do something similar. I was inspired not only by the topic, but by the approach of

Source: John Drury

Reicher and other researchers, who argued against the profoundly ideological approaches of the early crowd psychologists as well as against individualism in social psychology more generally. The social identity approach seemed to have considerable utility, and we thought we could apply it to other neglected crowd phenomena, not just riots and protests. Therefore, after my PhD, I started to investigate the topic of crowd behaviour in mass emergencies. This proved just as difficult to research as riots and protests – how can you gather data from such unpredictable and distressing events? We had to use a variety of methods, including interviews with survivors, archive data, and virtual reality experiments. After my colleagues Steve Reicher and Chris Cocking and I had studied a number of differ-ent mass emergency events, we started getting interest from non-academics – people in the live events industry, emergency planners, and the emergency services. I realised that to make our findings accessible for these non-academic audiences we had to think beyond the usual academic format of journal articles. We started producing accessible reports and presentations. Over the years, this work with professionals outside academia has been particularly rewarding. In the live events industry, for example, many professionals are eager to use the research on crowd behaviour to improve their practices, and equally I have learned much through engaging with these non-academics.

10.5 PART 2: ADVANCES

Now we take a closer look at advanced issues in intergroup relations. We will illustrate the importance of considering groups in their cultural context to understand relations between cultures and, as an example of a devalued social identity, how culture influences mental health stigma. We will also take a closer look at how the mental simulation of contact can address the issues we discussed in section 10.4.7 on the lack of opportunities for positive, stress-free intergroup interactions.

10.5.1 Intercultural Relations

In today's multicultural world, it is common to spend some time abroad for further studies, work placements, or a gap year. Encountering a different culture, whether from the migrant- or host-culture perspective, often involves coming across different explicit and implicit rules and behaviours. For example, as a foreigner in the UK, you may be greeted with 'How are you?', and while you are inhaling to tell your colleague all about your misery from your breakup with your partner, that colleague is already miles down the corridor in the kitchen making coffee. Excuse me! What happened?

> **Key concept – Culture:** A collective system of beliefs, values, social norms, expectations, and practices that are shared with members of a society that are transmitted across generations and that distinguish the members from another society.

Culture is a multifaceted and complex concept and goes beyond sociodemographic variables such as ethnicity, religion, or language. Culture influences people's feelings, thoughts, and behaviours (Hofstede, 2011).

Researchers have come up with different ways to measure culture at both the individual level (self-construals) and the nation-level (individualism-collectivism).

Independent and Interdependent Self-Construals

How we see ourselves and what we know about ourselves is an active construal process that takes information from multiple sources within the person and in interaction with others and the social world (self-construal). How we feel about ourselves (affect, self-esteem), what we think about ourselves (cognition, self-concept), and how we behave (behaviour) are influenced by the groups we belong to, as we have seen in section 10.4.3, depending on the social identity that is salient.

Cultures differ in their self-concept. Markus and Kitayama (1991) distinguish between two forms of self-construal: an independent and an interdependent self-construal. People who hold an independent view of the self, as is common in Western cultures (e.g., Western Europe, North America), define themselves in terms of individual traits (e.g., funny, honest) and personal goals, see themselves as separate from others and unique, are competitive, and emphasise autonomy. People who hold an interdependent view of the self, as is common in non-Western cultures (e.g., Southern Europe, Afric, Latin America, Asia, and Indigenous peoples), define themselves in terms of their relationships with other people (e.g., sister, friend), attach importance to harmonious interpersonal and group-based relations, are cooperative, and emphasise conforming to the expectations and social norms of ingroup members. The type of self-concept determines what is culturally sanctioned (i.e., whether one achieves personal goals or whether one disrupts social harmony) and this is important for the expression of emotions. While the expression of anger has been linked with poorer health in Western cultures, in non-Western cultures it can buffer against poor health. Kitayama and colleagues (2015) demonstrated cultural differences in the link between the expression of anger and ill-health among Americans and Japanese (see Key study 10.1).

KEY STUDY 10.1

Cultural Differences in the Link Between Expression of Anger and Ill-Health

Research predominantly from Western cultures shows that the expression of anger is associated with poorer physical health, such as inflammation, cardiovascular morbidity, and mortality. Kitayama and colleagues (2015) examined cultural differences in the link between expression of anger and biological health risk in Americans and Japanese. Anger expression has two functions that depend on contextual variables, such as culture. In Western cultures with an independent self-concept, the expression of anger is acceptable and reflects frustration when a person feels that pursuing their goals and desires is blocked, in particular when they are of low social status. In non-Western cultures with an interdependent self-concept, the expression of anger is not acceptable as it disrupts social harmony, and is only acceptable as a function of displaying power and dominance by people with high social status. Furthermore, trait anger is associated with poorer self-reported health in European Americans, and better self-reported health in ethnic-minority groups. It was hypothesised that the relationship between anger expression and biological health risk (BHR) is moderated by culture, with anger expression to be associated with increased BHR in Americans and decreased BHR in Japanese.

Method

Americans ($N = 1,054$; 578 women, 476 men; mean age = 58.04) and Japanese ($N = 382$; 214 women, 168 men; mean age = 55.47) took part in a survey and provided biological data. Anger expression was measured using the eight-item Anger-Out subscale of the State-Trait Anger Expression Inventory. BHR was

(Continued)

measured using pro-inflammatory markers (interleukin-6 and C-reactive protein) and indices of cardiovascular malfunction (systolic blood pressure and ratio of total to high-density lipoprotein cholesterol).

Results

Results supported the predictions, even when controlling for age, gender, health status (chronic conditions, waist-to-hip-ratio), health behaviours (smoking, alcohol consumption), social status, and reported experience of negative emotions. Greater expression of anger was associated with increased BHR for Americans and with decreased BHR for the Japanese (see Figure 10.6). Other facets of anger, such as trait anger, anger suppression, and anger control, were found not to be important.

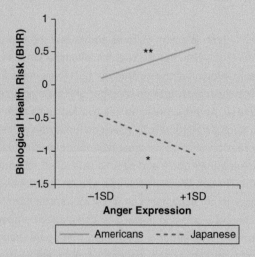

Figure 10.6 Biological health risk as a function of anger expression as a function of culture, for Americans and Japanese

Source: Kitayama et al. (2015).

Conclusion

The findings point towards the importance of considering culture in the link between anger and health. In the American cohort, expressing anger indicates how much people are dealing with negative life events, and in the Japanese cohort expressing anger indicates their power and entitlement.

KEY THINKER

Shinobu Kitayama

Shinobu Kitayama (born 1957) is a Japanese social psychologist. He was born in Japan and educated at the Universities of Kyoto (Japan) and Michigan (US). Previously, he was an academic at the Universities of Kyoto and Oregon, and he is currently a Robert B. Zajonc Collegiate Professor of Psychology at the University of Michigan. He is best known for his work significantly advancing cultural psychology, in particular the role of culture in the self. Together with Hazel Rose Markus, he argued that an independent self is characteristic for Western cultures and an interdependent self for East Asian cultures. He also is a pioneer in the use of neuroscience measures (e.g., fMRI, EEG) to examine the interaction between brain and culture.

Singelis (1994) developed a 24-item scale to measure whether people are higher on the independent or the interdependent self-construal (see Figure 10.7).

Individualism and Collectivism

We can also measure culture on a nation level, capturing the shared meaning within a nation. Individualism-collectivism is one of Hofstede and colleagues' (2010) dimensions of culture that characterises differences between nations. It captures whether society emphasises individual autonomy (individualism) or connections with other group members (collectivism). Albeit capturing similar ideas, the independent/interdependent self-construal is an individual differences variable, whereas the individualism/collectivism dimension is a cultural variable at the level of the society. In individualistic cultures, the self-concept is autonomous of other groups and relationships can be dropped when the costs are perceived to be higher than the benefits, personal goals have priority, and attitudes are the best predictor of behaviour. In collectivist cultures, people define themselves in relation to groups, and relationships are very important, group goals have priority, and social norms are the best predictor of behaviour. Triandis (1995) distinguishes between two types of cultural patterns within individualism/collectivism. Vertical individualism/collectivism is a cultural pattern in which there are status differences and inequality. Horizontal individualism/collectivism refers to equality between individuals and ingroup members.

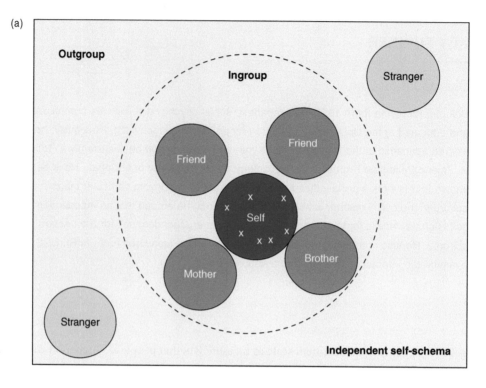

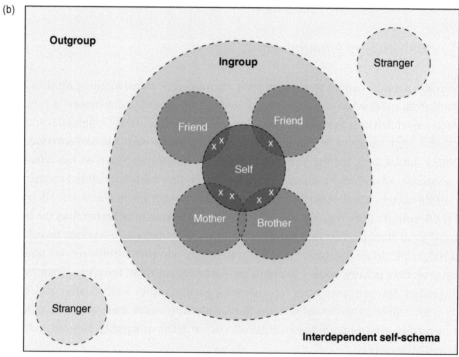

Figure 10.7 Independent and interdependent self-construal. Based on Markus and Kitayama (2010)

EXERCISE 10.2

Are You an Individualist or a Collectivist?

Complete the 16-item scale to measure the four dimensions of individualism and collectivism by Triandis and Gelfand (1998). For each statement indicate the extent of your agreement/disagreement on a 9-point scale, ranging from 1 = *never or definitely no* to 9 = *always or definitely yes*. Then sum up the answers for each subscale, which will give you a score between 4 and 36. Reflect on your result. What factors, individual and/or societal, do you think contribute to your score?

Horizontal individualism

1   I'd rather depend on myself than others.
2   I rely on myself most of the time, I rarely rely on others.
3   I often do my own thing.
4   My personal identity, independent of others, is very important to me.

Vertical individualism

1   It is important for me to do my job better than the others.
2   Winning is everything.
3   Competition is the law of nature.
4   When another person does better than I do, I get tense and aroused.

Horizontal collectivism

1   If a co-worker gets a prize, I feel proud.
2   The well-being of my coworkers is important to me.
3   To me, pleasure is spending time with others.
4   I feel good when I cooperate with others.

Vertical collectivism

1   Parents and children must stay together as much as possible.
2   It is my duty to take care of my family, even when I have to sacrifice what I want.
3   Family members should stick together, no matter what sacrifices are required.
4   It is important to me that I respect the decisions made by my groups.

Acculturation

It has become increasingly common for people from collectivist cultures (e.g., Asia, Africa) to move to individualistic cultures (e.g., Europe, North America), in the direction of wealth. When people from different cultures come into contact (e.g., through migration), such contact results in changes in one or both cultures. Both the acculturating individuals (e.g., South Asians in the UK) and the host society (e.g., White British in the UK) bring different psychological and cultural qualities (e.g., values, norms), and the compatibility of these qualities determines the relationship between both cultural groups. Such a relationship is also influenced by whether the contact is respectful or hostile, and whether there is a power difference between the groups, such as the host culture being in an advantaged position (Sam & Berry, 2010).

This process of psychological and sociocultural change has been referred to as acculturation (Berry, 1997). The consequence of acculturation is adaptation, which can be psychological (e.g., life satisfaction, well-being, self-esteem) as well as sociocultural (e.g., learning a new language, social competence, school adjustment). Acculturation can be considered a major life stress event that can lead to acculturative stress (e.g., depression and anxiety) in both cultural groups, that is, the one that is coming to a new culture and the one that is meeting people from a different culture (e.g., when being faced with discrimination).

Berry's (1997) acculturation model outlines four strategies for solving potential conflicts between people's original cultural identity and the identity of the new host culture (see Figure 10.8). People need to decide whether (a) retaining or losing their original culture and (b) adapting to the new host culture is valuable or not to them. Two of the four proposed strategies involve identifying with only one culture, either the host culture (*assimilation* to the host culture) or their original culture (*separation* from the host culture). The third strategy is to reject both the original and the host culture (*marginalisation*). The fourth strategy is *integration* of both the original and host culture. It means being an active participant in the host culture while at the same time also sustaining the values and behaviours of one's original culture.

Integration is the most adaptive strategy with the best psychological and sociocultural outcomes (Sam & Berry, 2010). However, whether this strategy is adopted depends on various factors, such as the attitudes of the host society towards immigrants. In a large international cross-sectional study with over 5,000 first- and second-generation immigrant adolescents from 13 countries, as well as over 2,500 nationals, Berry and colleagues (2006) found that immigrants in settler societies that welcome immigration (e.g., Canada, Australia) were more likely to adopt the integration strategy than in non-settler societies (e.g., UK, France). Furthermore, experiencing discrimination predicted a lower preference for the integration strategy as well as poorer psychological and sociocultural adaptation.

In addition, when the integration strategy is adopted, bicultural individuals differ in how well they have integrated both cultures and perceive their new social identity. Bicultural individuals are those who see themselves as part of both cultures. However, some find it easier to integrate both cultures into a meaningful new dual identity while others may struggle to integrate incompatible social identities (Benet-Martínez & Haritatos, 2005).

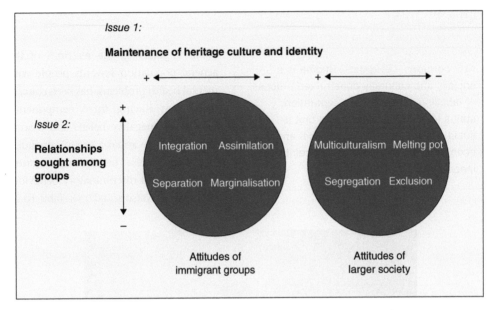

Figure 10.8 Acculturation strategies. Based on Sam and Berry (2010)

10.5.2 Mental Health Stigma

Minority groups can have poorer well-being, for example due to immigration being a major life event and experiencing discrimination, which enhances life stress. Those who are experiencing a mental health problem are often stigmatised by society, particularly in certain cultures. Mental health stigma is an other example of social categorisation (see section 10.4.1), which leads to a social identity that is devalued by society and, as a result, to discrimination. **Stigma** is often defined as a discrediting attribute of a person that devalues their identity, reducing the individual from a whole person to a tainted or discounted one. However, stigma is not a characteristic within a person but rather a more complex phenomenon within the social context. It can be considered a socially and culturally constructed process in which people identify and label human differences. These labels are linked to negative stereotypes and categorise individuals into 'us' versus 'them'. As a result of emphasising differences, labelled individuals experience devaluation in form of status loss and discrimination (e.g., overt exclusion, microaggressions). Social, political and economic power difference enables these processes of labelling, stereotyping, separation, status loss and discrimination – perpetuating social inequalities (Link & Phelan, 2013).

Stigma can have pervasive consequences in various areas of life: structural inequalities (e.g., education, employment, housing, the criminal justice system), poverty, homelessness, poorer relationships and reduced social support, poorer mental and physical health (e.g., reduced life expectancy), lack of seeking help, and poorer treatment due to stigma from health professionals (Schulze & Angermeyer, 2003).

Public Stigma

> **Key concept – Stigma:** Stigma is a socially and culturally constructed process of labelling, stereotyping, separation, status loss and discrimination that is sustained through social, political and economic power dynamics and reinforces inequalities.

Public stigma, i.e., the reactions of the general population towards people with mental health problems, has been conceptualised as having three components: stereotypes (negative beliefs and inaccurate knowledge about a group), prejudice (endording these beliefs and negative emotions), and discriminatory behaviour (Corrigan & Watson, 2002; see Table 10.2).

Figure 10.9 A sad person
Source: https://pixabay.com/photos/girl-sad-portrait-depression-alone-6059889/

Not all mental health problems are perceived in the same way. For example, in the UK, people with schizophrenia and substance use disorders are among the most severely stigmatised and are perceived as being a danger to other people and unpredictable, whereas people with depression are mainly perceived as being hard to talk to. Not only people directly affected by a mental health problem, but also people associated with them (e.g., family, friends), can experience stigmatising reactions such as social exclusion or negative treatment, namely stigma by association (Larson & Corrigan, 2008).

One source of stigma can be the beliefs the general population and health professionals hold about the causes of mental health problems. Explanations of what may cause mental health problems can be divided into biological, psychosocial, and spiritual causes (Schulze & Angermeyer, 2003). Endorsing biological causes of mental health problems rather than psychosocial ones is associated with perceptions of greater abnormality and stigma and lower empathy in clinicians (Larkings & Brown, 2018).

Health professionals have been rated as even more stigmatising than the general population. Such stigma provides a barrier to accessing healthcare and it can prevent help-seeking and lead to a poorer quality of healthcare. For example, general ward nurses reported reduced quality contact with people with mental health problems than the general population in the UK. They also reported greater stigma, such as more negative attitudes, greater dehumanisation, lower empathy, and lower contact intentions (Birtel & Oldfield, 2022).

KEY THINKER

Patrick Corrigan

Patrick Corrigan is an American psychologist, licensed clinical psychologist and Distinguished Professor of Psychology at the Illinois Institute of Technology. Prior to that, he was a Professor of Psychiatry at the University of Chicago. He is the principal investigator of the National Consortium on Stigma and Empowerment (NCSE) funded by the National Institute of Mental Health. He is best known for his work on the impact of mental health stigma and ways to overcome it, as well as social determinants of health among people with health conditions and disabilities. In 2016, he launched the new journal *Stigma and Health*, published by the American Psychological Association. He has lived experience with mental health problems, which informs his research on stigma. See: www.psychologytoday.com/us/blog/the-stigma-effect/201901/i-am-person-mental-illness

Internalised Stigma and Identity-Threat

Modified labelling theory (Link et al., 1989) suggests that through socialization people develop beliefs about mental health problems. These lay theories about mental illness encompass expectations whether people with mental health problems will be rejected and devalued. The process of receiving a diagnosis and entering treatment makes these beliefs personally relevant. When social labels are internalised, this fosters expectations of rejection and can lead to negative behavioural responses to avoid rejection (such as social withdrawal), creating a self-fulfilling prophecy of actual rejection and further negative outcomes (e.g., for self-esteem, social support, health).

When negative perceptions of the general population or health professionals (public stigma) are internalised by people with a mental health problem, this means that the person becomes aware of the stigmatising attitudes of others, agrees with them, and applies them. For example, a person with schizophrenia who internalises that they are a danger to others and should be avoided may withdraw from society. Other consequences of such self-stigma are feelings of shame, blame, low self-esteem, and failure to seek help (Rüsch et al., 2005; see Table 10.2). Therefore, stigma can be considered as a 'second illness', reducing people's quality of life further (Gronholm et al., 2017; Major et al., 2013).

According to the stigma-induced identity threat model (Major & O'Brien, 2005), possessing a social identity that is devalued by society, such as belonging to a group of people with mental health problems, increases the risk of being exposed to situations that are perceived as threatening one's social identity (e.g., being ostracised). In such situations, people experience identity threat when a stigma-relevant stressor is appraised as potentially harmful to their social identity and exceeding their coping resources. Responses to identity threat involve involuntary stress responses (e.g., anxiety) and voluntary coping responses (e.g., increasing or reducing identification with the stigmatised group). These responses affect outcomes such as self-esteem and health.

Table 10.2 Components of public stigma and self-stigma. Adapted from Rüsch et al. (2005)

	Public stigma	Self-stigma
Stereotype	Negative belief about a group (e.g., 'people with schizophrenia are dangerous')	Negative belief about the self (e.g., 'I am weak and incompetent')
Prejudice	Agreement with belief and/or negative emotional reaction towards a group (e.g., anger, fear)	Agreement with belief and/or negative emotional reaction (e.g., low self-esteem, low self-efficacy)
Discrimination	Behavioural manifestation of prejudice (e.g., social exclusion, withholding help)	Behavioural response to prejudice (e.g., self-isolation, no help-seeking)

Cultural Differences in Stigma

While people from all cultures can experience mental health problems, cultures differ in their explanations about the causes of mental health problems and how people perceive individuals with mental health problems. In Western cultures, the distinction between physical and mental disorders is stricter. In Asian cultures, there is a tendency to experience psychological symptoms as somatic symptoms, and to focus on medical help for physical health symptoms instead of psychological help (Lauber & Rössler, 2007).

Mental health stigma seems to be greater in Eastern than in Western cultures (see also Guest Personal Journey: Aisha Mirza). It is important to consider the role of the social and cultural context as Western concepts cannot be easily applied to non-Western cultures (Krendl & Pescosolido, 2020). Research found cross-cultural differences in what people believe causes mental health problems. For example, South Asians in the UK reported higher beliefs in supernatural and moral causes of psychosis and depression, whereas White British endorsed greater biological causes (Birtel & Mitchell, 2023; Mirza et al., 2019). While Western cultures rather seem to emphasise biological (e.g., antidepressants, antipsychotic medication) or psychosocial approaches to treatment, in Asian countries greater emphasis is placed on religious, supernatural, and magical approaches (Lauber & Rössler, 2007).

In cultures characterised by interdependent self-construals and with higher emphasis on family and relationships, such as Asian cultures, mental health stigma is likely to have greater social consequences, affecting the whole family (Lauber & Rössler, 2007). For example, South Asians in the UK reported greater stigma by association and, as a result, a greater desire for social distance from people with depression than White British (Birtel & Mitchell, 2023). This is particularly concerning, because social support from close others is an important factor in help-seeking, treatment, and recovery. For example, in individuals with substance use, greater perceived social support was associated with lower internalised stigma and shame, and thus with lower depression and anxiety, higher quality of sleep, and greater self-esteem (Birtel et al., 2017). Family members are a major source of social support because stigma often inhibits help-seeking, and access to mental healthcare is becoming increasingly difficult due to funding cuts. Reducing stigma (see also section 10.6.2) poses challenges such as lack of contact.

GUEST PERSONAL JOURNEY

Aisha Mirza

I classify as a British Asian, Pakistani to be more specific. I grew up in a conservative Pakistani family and was trying to hide the Asian part of me, impossible given my brown skin colouring! I often tried to magnify the British part of me by trying to do all the things to 'fit in'. However, like many others I was often excluded, discriminated against, and treated with little respect, which sent me on a journey of discovery into my history, accepting my identity and claiming my vibrant South Asian heritage. Becoming a clinical psychologist, working at the Mersey Care NHS Foundation Trust, was not a smooth journey. The career path is competitive and was predominantly middle-class, White British. As a profession, it has not always been an inclusive

Source: © Aisha Mizra

space for me or others from a minority background. I always felt I was not good enough or I had to be grateful for my place. My interest in mental health came from my own South Asian community that I grew up in, as mental health, a Western concept, is stigmatised, often shameful, and a taboo topic. I was always aware of families that had family members who were described as 'simple', or didn't like being out in public, or the narratives were that the person was inflicted by jinn's or other supernatural maladies, but they were never mentally unwell. One of the fundamental principles has been about equality, fairness, and inclusivity in all the work I do.

At present, seven years post qualification from my Clinical Psychology Doctorate, I am undertaking my Qualification in Clinical Neuropsychology (QiCN). My journey into understanding brain function and behaviour continues, and I have a specialist interest in forensic neuropsychology. Forensic populations have a lot of stigma attached to them, despite mental illness and trauma being highly prevalent in this group. The COVID-19 pandemic has highlighted health inequalities that are deeply rooted in systemic and institutional inequalities. Therefore, as a clinician, it is important for me to work to break down barriers, break the stigma that surrounds mental health, and strive for equality. The journey continues.

10.5.3 Mental Simulation of Contact

In contexts characterised by segregation, in which people do not have the opportunity for contact or actively avoid contact, approaches based on the power of mental imagery may reduce intergroup conflict, such as imagined contact. Imagined contact means mentally simulating a positive social interaction with an outgroup member (Crisp & Turner, 2009) and is a further implementation of intergroup contact theory.

A large body of research has demonstrated the benefits of mental imagery in various areas, such as attitudes towards blood donation or safety laws, intentions towards time spent studying or health behaviours like dieting or exercising, and behaviour in terms of remaining in psychotherapy (Crisp et al., 2011). A mental experience of a particular social context can have the same effect as an actual experience of that context (Blair et al., 2001). Functional neuroimaging studies have shown that similar neural mechanisms are activated during performing, perceiving, and imagining behaviour, and that simulations employ the same neurological mechanisms involved in memory, emotion, and motor control (Kosslyn et al., 2001).

The typical instruction used in studies on imagined contact is 'We would like you to take a minute to imagine yourself meeting [an outgroup] stranger for the first time. Imagine that the interaction is positive, relaxed, and comfortable'. To reinforce the instruction, participants describe in a few sentences the scenario they imagined. Then participants receive measures of intergroup experiences, which are assessed against a control group (e.g., thinking of an outdoor scene or contact with an ingroup member).

A meta-analysis of imagined contact studies (Miles & Crisp, 2014) showed that imagined contact can improve intergroup relations for both children and adults, in terms of promoting positive attitudes and emotions, intentions for future contact, and positive behaviour in areas characterised by a high intensity of conflict and across a range of target groups.

Imagined contact can be combined with other approaches involving mental imagery. For example, Birtel and Crisp (2012) applied principles of exposure therapy to the mental simulation of outgroup contact. During exposure therapy, the patient is confronted with the fear-evoking stimulus within a safe environment, for example through imaginal exposure, which involves imagining a certain person, object or situation, or *in vivo* exposure, which involves direct exposure, such as touching a spider or giving a speech in front of a large audience. The aim is, first, to activate the fear memory (step 1) to modify it in the second step with corrective, positive information (Foa & Kozk, 1986). Applying these principles to intergroup relations, the stigmatised group can be conceived as a type of phobic stimulus and intergroup anxiety as a non-pathological fear structure. The memory can be activated by imagining negative contact with the outgroup first (step 1), before imagining positive contact (step 2), and can reduce negative feelings towards the outgroup. In Birtel and Crisp's (2012) study, negative imaginal exposure prior to positive imaginal exposure was more effective in reducing prejudice towards three target groups (adults with schizophrenia, gay men, and British Muslims) than a repeated positive or single positive imaginal exposure. Intergroup anxiety and positive feelings towards the outgroup mediated the relationship between imaginal exposure and contact intentions.

Critics of the imagined contact approach (e.g., Bigler & Hughes, 2010; Lee & Jussim, 2010) have proposed limitations such as alternative explanations for the imagined contact effect, low sample size, and the power of previous studies, the evidence being limited to short-term effects or doubtful applicability to real-world conflicts. Researchers addressed the criticism in various ways. A variety of control conditions were tested, including neutral contact, no contact, non-relevant positive interactions, and outgroup priming. Studies ruled out informational load, stereotype priming, positive affective priming, non-relevant social interactions, and demand characteristics as alternative explanations for the imagined contact effect (Miles & Crisp, 2014). Furthermore, high-quality imagined contact even emerges spontaneously without being part of an experimental manipulation or an intervention. Participants can actively choose to engage in imagined contact over negative contact. It can also reduce prejudice in conflict-ridden settings, such as Cyprus, over a period of several months.

Schuhl and colleagues (2019) addressed the issue of publication bias in science, that is, the tendency that significant and novel studies have a greater chance to be published than non-significant studies or replications of published studies. Such scientific practices promote bad science, for example, discarding data with non-significant results, cherry-picking results, and reformulating a priori hypotheses so they match the results (HARKing). They conducted a conceptual replication of an existing imagined contact study and pre-registered their study materials, hypotheses, and data analysis plan on the Open Science Framework. Their findings suggest that a single imagined contact session has the power to reduce prejudice over a longer period of time.

Mental simulation can be incorporated into interventions in education (e.g., reducing bystander effects against bullying in schools; Vezzali et al., 2020) and the workplace (e.g., reducing workplace bias towards people with disabilities; Carvalho-Freitas & Stathi, 2017). Education and the workplace are contexts characterised by increasing levels of social and cultural diversity. In the next section, we will consider the challenges of diversity.

10.6 PART 3: APPLICATIONS

The social psychological work on intergroup relations in this chapter can inform a range of real-world issues. We have seen that culture influences intergroup processes. Now we want to consider how we can manage the benefits and challenges of cultural and social diversity. We have discussed mental health stigma as an example of a devalued social identity and its consequences for health and well-being as well as the mental simulation of contact as a prejudice-intervention. Next we consider a campaign based on intergroup contact theory to reduce mental health stigma. Lastly, we look at hate crime as an example of an extreme form of prejudice.

10.6.1 Managing Diversity

Our world is characterised by increasing levels of geographical mobility, coupled with wars and humanitarian crises that create ever more refugees. As a result, identities in societies are changing to become a complex combination of diverse social, cultural, ethnic, and religious groups. The question of whether diversity is good or bad has been the subject of an ongoing and often heated debate among scientists, politicians, and the public. Indeed, both the former German Chancellor Angela Merkel and the former British Prime Minister David Cameron contended that 'multiculturalism has failed'. Furthermore, the tenure of Donald Trump as US President as well as the UK's exit from the European Union (Brexit) have highlighted the public's scepticism towards immigrants and diverse societies.

Figure 10.10 An interracial group of friends

Source: Linpaul Rodney/Unsplash

Diversity Change

Among scientists, there is no consensus about whether diversity is good or bad. Some scientists argue that diversity has a range of benefits for intergroup relations (Crisp & Turner, 2011; Plaut, 2010), while others argue that diversity is associated with lower levels of trust and tolerance within societies, at least in the short term (Putnam, 2007). Research shows that first being exposed to and interacting with members of different social groups can result in a 'diversity shock'. Such cross-group interactions can be qualitatively worse than same-group interactions (MacInnis & Page-Gould, 2015). For example, Birtel and colleagues (2020) conducted a longitudinal study with White and Asian British children in segregated primary schools who moved to a new mixed secondary school, and examined how such a change in ethno-religious diversity affected their intergroup experiences (see Key study 10.2).

KEY STUDY 10.2

Change in School Ethnic Diversity and Intergroup Relations

Cross-race interactions can be qualitatively worse than same-race interactions. However, people adapt to social diversity over time after initial negative effects. Birtel and colleagues (2020) examined the impact of a change in school diversity on school children's intergroup experiences. It tested whether (1) children in segregated versus mixed schools differ in their intergroup experiences (diversity), (2) majority and minority group members differ in their intergroup experiences (group membership), and (3) the transition from segregated to mixed school improves intergroup relations (diversity change).

Method

School children ($N = 551$; 283 girls, 264 boys, 251 White British, 300 Asian British, mean age = 11.32) from 14 primary schools in an ethnically segregated town in Northern England (Oldham: 78% White, 17% Asian) were tracked transitioning from segregated primary to mixed versus segregated secondary school (six schools) four months later.

Results

To analyse the data, a multivariate, multilevel model was estimated, using a range of outcome measures capturing intergroup experiences. The cross-sectional results at Time 1 suggested a role of diversity: both White and Asian British children reported more positive intergroup relations in the mixed compared to the segregated school (e.g., greater contact quantity and quality, future contact intentions, intergroup trust, intergroup empathy, and social norms for outgroup contact). At Time 2, after levels of diversity changed, ethnicity-specific differences were found. Asian British children's intergroup experiences improved when moving from segregated to mixed school (greater contact, future contact intentions, and intergroup empathy), but not White British children's experiences.

Conclusion

The findings are important for understanding the early stages of diversity exposure and the impact of changing diversity levels on majority and minority groups.

Over time, when ingroup and outgroup members have the chance to take up the opportunities for intergroup contact that diversity offers, such initial scepticism can settle down as people get to know each other better, and diversity, through positive intergroup contact, reduces prejudice. For example, Ramos and colleagues (2019) conducted one of the largest studies on diversity to test how changes in religious diversity affect people's perceived quality of life over time. They combined worldwide representative data from the World Values Survey, the European Social Survey, and the Latino-barómetro, which gave them a data set of more than 100 countries across 20 years. Religious diversity was measured at the country level using the Herfindahl index, and intergroup contact, trust, and quality of life were measured at the individual level. Quality of life consisted of an index of life satisfaction, happiness, and self-reported health. In the short term (over two years), greater diversity change was associated with lower trust in others and thereby with lower perceived quality of life. In the long term (over 12 years), positive intergroup contact compensated for the negative effect of religious diversity change on perceived quality of life due to intergroup contact enhancing trust. In particular, diversity plays a role in education and the workplace, contexts that are characterised by increasing levels of diversity and in which we spend a large proportion of our lives.

Diversity in Work Teams

During our leisure time, we can choose who to have contact with and be friends with, and whether these are people from diverse backgrounds or not. In education or at work, people cannot choose their colleagues and are expected to collaborate with people from different social and cultural backgrounds. This can have benefits, but can also pose challenges.

Work teams can be diverse in various ways. Diversity can be categorised as surface-level diversity (educational background and demographics such as age, gender, race) and deep-level diversity (knowledge, experience, attitudes, social status). Some of these are job-oriented and some are relations-oriented (Yadav & Lenka, 2020). Diversity can have outcomes at an individual level (satisfaction, turnover, individual creativity), team level (conflict, group performance, team creativity), and organisation level (productivity, competitiveness) (Hundschell et al., 2022).

At the individual level, previous research has shown that multicultural experiences are associated with greater creativity in individuals, in particular experiences such as living or working abroad, being bilingual, having a bicultural identity, and having multicultural relationships (Maddux et al., 2021). Individuals bring these experiences to the work teams they are a part of.

At the team level, results of studies examining diversity have been inconsistent. Some show positive outcomes within work teams and some show negative outcomes in relation to performance and cohesion (Hundschell et al., 2022). The **categorisation-elaboration model** (CEM) (van Knippenberg et al., 2004) integrates two major perspectives to explain the contradicting findings (see Figure 10.11). The information/decision-making perspective is used to explain the positive effects of diversity on performance outcomes, while theories of intergroup relations, such as social identity theory and self-categorisation theory, are used to explain the negative effects of diversity. Cultural diversity in teams can have positive effects through cognitive processes such as the knowledge and perspectives diverse team members bring. It enhances elaboration of task-relevant diverse information, and thus can promote creativity. Diversity can have negative effects in teams through social and intergroup processes such as prejudice, negative expectations, group conflict, and low cohesion, and these effects can hinder creativity. The CEM proposes that both processes, information/decision-making processes and social categorisation processes, play a role simultaneously, and that mediators (e.g., conflict, group identification) and moderators (e.g., diversity beliefs, diversity climate) explain how to overcome the negative effects of diversity.

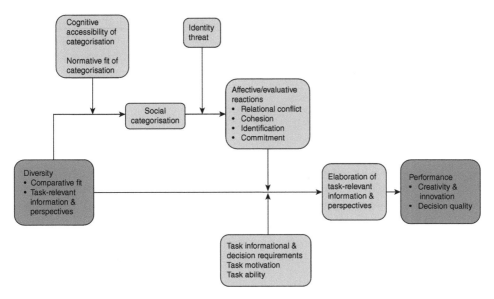

Figure 10.11 The categorisation-elaboration model (CEM). Adapted from van Knippenberg et al. (2004)

For example, creating a climate that encourages employees to explore and integrate differences plays a moderating role in the relationship between team cultural diversity and creativity in multicultural work teams. In a study using time-lagged data from 57 multicultural work teams with 384 employees and their leaders, Li and colleagues (2015) found that team-level cultural diversity was associated with higher team-level creativity, through greater information exchange in the team. This relationship was stronger for teams with a stronger team climate for inclusion. Team creativity was measured by asking the team leader to rate the extent to which their team is creative compared to other work teams.

At an organisational level, the composition of the leadership team and its values and actions (e.g., recruitment, training, promotion) play an important role in establishing a pro-diversity organisational culture. Factors that determine whether diversity is managed effectively in organisations are work group (climate, leadership), organisation (diversity management, management beliefs), and society (culture, legislation) (Guillaume et al., 2014).

10.6.2 Reducing Mental Health Stigma: The Time to Change Campaign

We discussed earlier that stigma towards people with mental health problems can have severe consequences for the individual and their close others. Research has examined different anti-stigma campaigns targeted at the public, based on education (promoting accurate knowledge and reducing myths), protest (asking the public and the media to stop believing and spreading false representations about mental health), and intergroup contact (e.g., face to face, through the media, mental simulation). Evaluations of the different types of interventions suggest that contact seems to be more effective than education, while protest is found to be problematic as stigma suppression can lead to rebound effects. Multifaceted interventions have been encouraged (Corrigan et al., 2001). Anti-stigma interventions targeting specific groups, such as healthcare professionals or police officers, have also been tested (Gronholm et al., 2017).

The Campaign

The Time to Change (TTC) campaign was an evidence-driven social movement run by the charities Mind and Rethink Mental Illness. It ran across England between 2007 and 2021 and aimed to facilitate the reduction of public prejudice, stereotypes, and discrimination towards people with mental health problems in education settings, workplaces, and communities, and to empower service users to engage in action to challenge stigma. Other countries also introduced successful anti-stigma programmes, such as 'Beyondblue' in Australia, 'Hjärnkoll' in Sweden, and 'Open Minds' in Canada (Gronholm et al., 2017).

FACETS OF THE TIME TO CHANGE CAMPAIGN

What they Did

- Educated young people aged 11–18 years, parents and teachers, and trained employees
- Encouraged open conversations about mental health
- Shared stories of lived experiences by young people, employees, and community members
- Incorporated mental health into the schools' well-being agenda
- Encouraged organisations to publicly commit
- Helped to develop action plans in organisations
- Devised anti-stigma activities and local community activities
- Communicated based on behaviour change models in social media marketing campaigns and in the media

How it Tackled Stigma

- It raised awareness
- It increased understanding of mental health and reduced misbeliefs
- It normalised mental health
- It increased confidence in disclosure
- It promoted fair treatment and support
- It empowered people to tackle stigma
- It improved social contact

The TTC used scientific evidence to design the interventions in schools, workplaces, and the community. The campaign was extended globally in areas such as India, Nigeria, Ghana, Kenya, and Uganda.

The TTC aimed at empowering people to tackle stigma based on two behaviour change models: the eight-step change management model (Kotter, 1996) and the EAST framework (Behavioural Insights Team, 2012). It also included a social contact element in various parts, based on intergroup contact theory (Allport, 1954), in which people with lived experiences of mental health problems interacted with those who did not have such experiences. Social contact (e.g., face to face or virtual via social media) turned out to be a key factor in promoting positive attitudes and behaviours towards people with mental health problems.

EXERCISE 10.3

Time to Talk!

Go to YouTube and search for videos of the Time to Change campaign. What do you think of the campaign? How did they apply psychological theory when designing their campaign? The link below is a TV advert of the Time to Change campaign to encourage communication and normalisation of mental health problems. The video captures Dave, who has been off work because of a mental health problem. When he returns to work, his colleagues ask him how he is feeling. What could have gone 'wrong'? See www.youtube. com/watch?v=hdPZ7rwOwMc

Impact Evaluation

The impact of the campaign was evaluated on core stigma outcomes (attitudes, discrimination, empowerment) over time between 2008 and 2019 to determine the impact on the public and service users. Overall, *public attitudes* improved by 12.7% (5.4 million people) across the 11 years. Similarly, public willingness to have contact with people with mental health problems (e.g., privately and at work) improved by 12% between 2009 and 2019 (Time to Change, 2020).

In another evaluation, Henderson and colleagues (2017) examined the relationship between awareness of the social marketing of the TTC campaign and disclosure and help-seeking between 2012 and 2016. Public awareness of the TTC campaign was associated with greater comfort disclosing a mental illness to a close person or an employer, and intentions to seek professional help from a physician. There is also evidence in 2016 that newspaper coverage is reporting more anti-stigmatising articles and fewer stigmatising articles, and anti-stigmatising articles were more common for all diagnoses (e.g., depression, anxiety disorder, eating disorder, obsessive compulsive disorder) apart from schizophrenia (Anderson et al., 2020).

More recently, people with mental health problems reported fewer *experiences of discrimination* in the Big Mental Health Survey, undertaken by the Mind charity. For example, in 2019, respondents (*N* = 7,204) reported a decrease in discrimination in friendships/relationships (5%), social life (5%), and family (3%), but an increase in employment discrimination (4%) (Time to Change, 2020). Corker and colleagues (2016) examined in a cross-sectional study (*N* = 6,470) whether service users experienced less discrimination during the TTC between 2008 and 2014. Overall, fewer service users reported discrimination based on their mental illness in one or more areas of life. In particular, in 2014 compared to the previous year, they experienced less discrimination in the areas of family, dating, social life, mental health staff, police, public transport, and being shunned. However, there was no evidence that social capital (i.e., resources within social networks) had increased. Of the champions with lived experience (*N* = 796), 72% reported greater *empowerment* in the form of challenging stigma in 2019. The TTC is an example of how evidence-based interventions can reduce stigma. It provides further evidence that intergroup contact can be effective in applied settings, such as mental health. Since then, the new Lancet Commission on Ending Stigma and Discrimination in Mental Health was launched on 10 October 2022 on World Mental Health Day (Thornicroft et al., 2022). Over 50 experts worldwide collaborated on a report summarising the impact of stigma and stigma-reduction interventions. It includes contributions from people with lived experience of mental health conditions. People from stigmatised groups not only experience negative attitudes from the public, but can also become victims of hate crimes.

10.6.3 Hate Crime

Hate crimes are an extreme manifestation of societal prejudice. Hate is different from other related emotions (e.g., anger, contempt, disgust) through specific appraisal patterns (stable, dispositional attribution of malicious intentions to a person or group, accompanied by feelings of danger and powerlessness), action tendencies and motivational goals (desire to harm and destroy) (Fischer et al., 2018). As an emotion, it takes longer to evolve but also longer to dissolve. Similarly to interpersonal hatred, intergroup hatred is an intergroup emotion that has the aim of eliminating the outgroup. Intergroup hatred is related to the motivational goal of taking revenge and to the action tendency to attack. Hate spreads easily for three reasons: it is shared among ingroup members, feelings of collective victimhood evolve, and it increases despite having no personal contact between the ingroup and the hated outgroup. Hate can lead to the dehumanisation of outgroups.

In society, intergroup hate spreads through hate crimes. A hate crime is a criminal offence that is motivated by hostility or prejudice because of the victim's belonging to a specific group, for example, of different race, religion, sexual orientation, disability, transgender. Hate crimes can involve physical assault, verbal abuse, or incitement to hatred (e.g., via social media).

McDevitt and colleagues (2002) analysed 169 crime reports from the Boston Police Department categorising hate crime perpetrators into four types depending on their motivation. Thrill seekers commit hate crimes because they dislike the outgroup or are bored and seek excitement. Alcohol and peer pressure may contribute to such a hate crime, for example a group of teenage men who attack a member of the LGBT community. The defensive perpetrator is motivated to protect their ingroup territory from the outgroup. They may perceive realistic intergroup threat, anger, and shame, for example verbal abuse against a single person such as a new immigrant in the neighbourhood. The retaliatory perpetrator may perceive symbolic intergroup threat and an attack against the ingroup for which they seek revenge, for example an increase in anti-Muslim incidents (e.g., shots fired at a mosque) after the Paris terror attack. The mission perpetrator can have links to extremist groups and seek to enforce their worldview, for example organised racist attacks by Neo-Nazis.

The Sussex Hate Crime Project in the UK (Paterson et al., 2018) examined hate crimes towards Muslims and LGBT communities in the UK. The project involved 20 different studies (experiments, surveys, interviews) with over 2,000 LGBT and 1,000 Muslim participants. The aim was to gain knowledge of victimisation and hate crimes. Over 70% of participants in both groups reported a high rate of hate incidents within three years (see Figure 10.12), in particular online and in the media.

Hate crimes can have direct effects on the individual and indirect effects on the community. Direct effects include poorer physical and mental health of victims of hate crime compared to victims of similar non-hate motivated crimes (e.g., poorer sleep, anxiety and depression, social withdrawal, feelings of anger, threat and vulnerability). Hate crime conveys hostility and intolerance not only to the victim, but also to the community of which the victim is a member. The entire stigmatised group can be negatively affected by individual attacks (Perry & Alvi, 2012). Indirect experiences of hate crimes increase feelings of vulnerability and empathy in the community, which in turn increase feelings of anger, anxiety, and shame, which then lead to specific behaviours as responses to specific emotions (anger leads to action, anxiety to avoidance, shame to retaliation). Identification with the community was associated with greater anger and motivation to combat hate crime (Paterson et al., 2018).

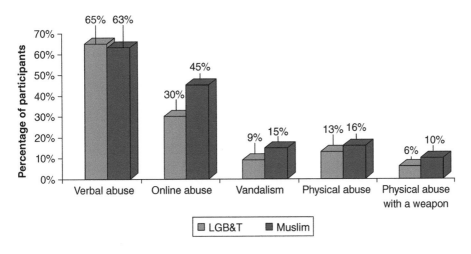

Figure 10.12 Percentage of participants who have been a victim of a hate crime. Adapted from Paterson et al. (2018)

Being a victim of hate crime can not only lower people's well-being (e.g., post-traumatic stress disorder, anxiety, and depression) and lead them to withdraw socially from society, it can also reduce trust in the police and decrease the reporting of future hate crimes. Feddes and Jonas (2020) conducted a survey among 391 participants from the LGBT community in the Netherlands. Of the participants ($N = 61$), 16% reported having experienced hate crime in the past year, for example, being on the receiving end of hate speech, being pushed or hit, experiencing hostility or personal threat, or being sexually intimidated. Participants who had been victims of hate crime reported lower life satisfaction and higher stress and depression than those who had not experienced hate crime. They also reported feeling less confident in the police, perceived the police as less fair and less engaged in the community, and had lower intentions to report hate crimes in the future. The association between hate crime experiences and lower intentions to report future hate crimes to the police was mediated by lower trust in the police.

Intergroup biases influence decision-making in courtrooms. For example, crimes committed by racial minorities (versus majorities) can receive harsher sentence recommendations by jurors (Sommers, 2007). Conservative political identity is associated with opposition to hate crime penalty enhancement (Cramer et al., 2017). Labelling assaults as hate crimes can reduce beliefs in defendant guilt, for example, for hate crimes based on gender in the USA (Plumm & Terrance, 2013).

This section has demonstrated how theories of intergroup relations (e.g., social identity, intergroup emotions, intergroup contact) can be applied to real-world issues to understand and tackle diversity challenges in schools and work teams, mental health stigma, and hate crime.

EXERCISE 10.4

Reducing Hate Crime

Hate crime is an extreme form of societal prejudice. Chapters 9 and 10 have introduced ways to reduce prejudice (e.g., intergroup contact and imagined contact). How can these interventions reduce hate crimes? What is problematic in such attempts? Can you find other ways to reduce hate crimes, for example in governmental reports or in research that you can find on GoogleScholar?

10.7 SUMMARY

Diversity is increasingly part of everyone's life, offering exciting experiences such as meeting people from different social and cultural backgrounds. On the one hand, these experiences may involve fascinating surprises and change the way we think, feel, and act. Diversity provides opportunities to learn about other people's cultures and your own culture, even leading to greater creativity. Going through the acculturation process can be both interesting and difficult, involving growth but also rejection. On the other hand, relations with people from groups that are different from the groups to which we belong can bring challenges as well as prejudice and discrimination, and even result in hate against groups stigmatised by society. Such conflict between our ingroups and outgroups can be based on real competition for resources during times of crisis (e.g., jobs, money), symbolic and existential threat (e.g., preserving the values of one's nationality), or even just through mere social categorisation.

This chapter has equipped you with the major classic and contemporary theories and research to understand intergroup and intercultural processes and to apply them to real-world issues, such as workplace diversity, mental health, and hate crime. For example, social identity processes play a role in collective action and social movements aimed at achieving social change for disadvantaged groups. You have learnt about the importance of the different concerns majority and minority groups bring into intergroup interactions, and the role of culture when researching intergroup relations and recommending solutions to educators, practitioners, and policy-makers. The theories discussed have successfully informed real-world interventions, for example the Time to Change campaign to reduce mental health stigma in England.

10.8 REVISION

Please select the correct or best answer to each of the multiple-choice questions below:

1   What was the main conclusion from the results of the minimal group paradigm?

    a   Prejudice is a result of the competition for limited resources between ingroups and outgroups.

    b   Prejudice is a result of categorising people into groups based on arbitrary criteria.

    c   Prejudice results from a mix of competition for limited resources and categorising people into groups based on arbitrary criteria.

2   What does the intergroup emotions theory explain best?

    a   Stereotype content.

    b   Ingroup favouritism.

    c   Outgroup derogation.

3   What is a consequence of thinking about your own death?

    a   You form stronger ties with your ingroup members and support the ingroup's worldview.

    b   You see the bigger picture of the world and are kinder to outgroup members.

    c   You cut ties with people and focus more on your own health.

4   What is a good explanation for crowd behaviour?

    a   People calculate the costs and benefits of acting in a crowd. When they cannot reach their goal, they become violent.

b People lose their identity in a crowd (deindividuation) and lose control over their emotions. They are irrational and impulsive.

c People create a new identity and crowd behaviour develops as a function of intergroup dynamics.

5 Which of these following statements regarding mental health stigma is correct?

a Health professionals are immune to mental health stigma.

b Mental health stigma is more severe in non-Western cultures.

c Mental health stigma is mainly prevalent in Western cultures.

Answers: 1b, 2c, 3a, 4c, 5b.

10.9 FURTHER READING

Foundations

Nadler, A. (2016). Intergroup helping relations. *Current Opinion in Psychology, 11*, 64–68. https://doi.org/10.1016/j.copsyc.2016.05.016

This paper applies theories of intergroup relations to prosocial behaviour between groups.

Richeson, J. A., & Shelton, J. N. (2007). Negotiating interracial interactions costs, consequences, and possibilities. *Current Directions in Psychological Science, 16*, 316–320. https://doi.org/10.1111/j.1467-8721.2007.00528.

This paper reviews the literature on how interracial interactions can be stressful.

Derks, B., Scheepers, D., & Ellemers, N. (Eds.). (2013). *Neuroscience of prejudice and intergroup relations*. New York: Psychology Press.

This book provides an overview of the social neuroscience of intergroup relations.

Advances

Major, B., Mendes, W. B., & Dovidio, J. F. (2013). Intergroup relations and health disparities: A social psychological perspective. *Health Psychology, 32*(5), 514–524. https://doi.org/10.1037/a0030358

This paper applies theories of intergroup relations to explaining health inequalities.

Cadamuro, A., Birtel, M. D., Di Bernardo, G. A., Crapolicchio, E., Vezzali, L., & Drury, J. (2021). Resilience in children in the aftermath of disasters: A systematic review and a new perspective on individual, interpersonal, group, and intergroup level factors. *Journal of Community & Applied Social Psychology, 31*(3), 259–275. https://doi.org/10.1002/casp.2500

This paper presents an integrated model of individual, interpersonal, and intergroup factors for resilience in children in the aftermath of disasters.

Applications

Haslam, S. A., & van Dick, R. (2010). A social identity approach to workplace stress. In D. De Cremer, R. van Dick, & K. Murnighan (Eds.), *Social psychology in organizations* (pp. 325–352). New York: Taylor & Francis.

This chapter applies the social identity approach to real-world problems.

Social Movements

Black Lives Matter: https://blacklivesmatter.com/

Me Too: https://metoomvmt.org/

Videos

Social identity: https://sk.sagepub.com/video/social-psychology-social-identity

Elaborated social identity model: https://sk.sagepub.com/video/group-dynamics-the-elaborated-social-identity-model

Social movements: https://sk.sagepub.com/video/mass-appeal-collective-behavior-and-social-movements

10.10 REFERENCES

Abrams, D., & Hogg, M. A. (1990). An introduction to the social identity approach. In D. Abrams & M. Hogg (Eds.), *Social identity theory: Constructive and critical advances* (pp. 1–9). Hove: Harvester-Wheatsheaf.

Allport, G. W. (1954). *The nature of prejudice*. Reading, MA: Addison-Wesley.

Anderson, C., Robinson, E., Krooupa, A., & Henderson, C. (2020). Changes in newspaper coverage of mental illness from 2008 to 2016 in England. *Epidemiology and Psychiatric Sciences, 29*, E9. doi:10.1017/S2045796018000720

Arndt, J., Vess, M., Cox, C. R., Goldenberg, J. L., & Lagle, S. (2009). The psychosocial effect of thoughts of personal mortality on cardiac risk assessment. *Medical Decision Making, 29*(2), 175–181. https://doi.org/10.1177/0272989X08323300

Behavioural Insights Team. (2012). *EAST: Four simple ways to apply behavioural insights*. www.bi.team/publications/east-four-simple-ways-to-apply-behavioural-insights

Benet-Martínez, V., & Haritatos, J. (2005). Bicultural Identity Integration (BII): Components and psychosocial antecedents. *Journal of Personality, 73*(4), 1015–1050. https://doi.org/10.1111/j.1467-6494.2005.00337.x

Berry, J. W. (1997). Immigration, acculturation, and adaptation. *Applied Psychology, 46*(1), 5–34. https://doi.org/10.1111/j.1464-0597.1997.tb01087.x

Berry, J. W., Phinney, J. S., Sam, D. L., & Vedder, P. (2006). Immigrant youth: Acculturation, identity, and adaptation. *Applied Psychology, 55*(3), 303–332. https://doi.org/10.1111/j.1464-0597.2006.00256.x

Bigler, R. S., & Hughes, J. M. (2010). Reasons for skepticism about the efficacy of simulated social contact interventions. *American Psychologist, 65*(2), 131–132. https://doi.org/10.1037/a001809

Birtel, M. D., & Crisp, R. J. (2012). 'Treating' prejudice: An exposure-therapy approach to reducing negative reactions toward stigmatized groups. *Psychological Science, 23*(11), 1379–1386.

Birtel, M. D., & Mitchell, B. L. (2023). Cross-cultural differences in depression between White British and South Asians: Causal attributions, stigma by association, discriminatory potential. *Psychology and Psychotherapy: Theory, Research and Practice, 96*(1), 101–116. https://doi.org/10.1111/papt.12428

Birtel, M. D., & Oldfield, G. (2022). Affective, cognitive, and behavioral mental illness stigma in health care: A comparison between general ward nurses and the general population. *Stigma and Health, 7*(4), 380–388. https://doi.org/10.1037/sah0000416

Birtel, M. D., Reimer, N. K., Wölfer, R., & Hewstone, M. (2020). Change in school ethnic diversity and intergroup relations: The transition from segregated elementary to mixed secondary school for majority and minority students. *European Journal of Social Psychology, 50*(1), 160–176. https://doi.org/10.1002/ejsp.2609

Birtel, M. D., Wood, L., & Kempa, N. J. (2017). Stigma and social support in substance abuse: Implications for mental health and well-being. *Psychiatry Research, 252*, 1–8. https://doi.org/10.1016/j.psychres.2017.01.097

Blair, I. V., Ma, J. E., & Lenton, A. P. (2001). Imagining stereotypes away: The moderation of implicit stereotypes through mental imagery. *Journal of Personality and Social Psychology, 81*(5), 828–841. https://doi.org/10.1037/0022-3514.81.5.828

Blascovich, J., Mendes, W. B., Hunter, S. B., Lickel, B., & Kowai-Bell, N. (2001). Perceiver threat in social interactions with stigmatized others. *Journal of Personality and Social Psychology, 80*(2), 253–267. https://doi.org/10.1037/0022-3514.80.2.253

Brewer, M. B., & Miller, N. (1984). Beyond the contact hypothesis: Theoretical perspectives on desegregation. In N. Miller & M. Brewer (Eds.), *Groups in contact: The psychology of desegregation*. New York: Academic Press.

Carvalho-Freitas, M. N. de, & Stathi, S. (2017). Reducing workplace bias toward people with disabilities with the use of imagined contact. *Journal of Applied Social Psychology, 47*(5), 256–266. https://doi.org/10.1111/jasp.12435

Cialdini, R. B., Borden, R. J., Thorne, A., Walker, M. R., Freeman, S., & Sloan, L. R. (1976). Basking in reflected glory: Three (football) field studies. *Journal of Personality and Social Psychology, 34*(3), 366–375. https://doi.org/10.1037/0022-3514.34.3.366

Cichocka, A., Marchlewska, M., Golec de Zavala, A., & Olechowski, M. (2016). 'They will not control us': Ingroup positivity and belief in intergroup conspiracies. *British Journal of Psychology, 107*(3), 556–576. https://doi.org/10.1111/bjop.12158

Corker, E., Hamilton, S., Robinson, E., Cotney, J., Pinfold, V., Rose, D., Thornicroft, G., & Henderson, C. (2016). Viewpoint survey of mental health service users' experiences of discrimination in England 2008–2014. *Acta Psychiatrica Scandinavica, 134*(S446), 6–13. https://doi.org/10.1111/acps.12610

Corrigan, P. W., River, L. P., Lundin, R. K., Penn, D. L., Uphoff-Wasowski, K., Campion, J., . . . & Goldstein, H. (2001). Three strategies for changing attributions about severe mental illness. *Schizophrenia Bulletin, 27*(2), 187–195. https://doi.org/10.1093/oxfordjournals. schbul.a006865

Corrigan, P. W., & Watson, A. C. (2002). Understanding the impact of stigma on people with mental illness. *World Psychiatry, 1*(1), 16–20.

Cramer, R. J., Laxton, K. L., Chandler, J. F., Kehn, A., Bate, B. P., & Clark III, J. W. (2017). Political identity, type of victim, and hate crime-related beliefs as predictors of views concerning hate crime penalty enhancement laws. *Analyses of Social Issues and Public Policy, 17*(1), 262–285. https://doi.org/10.1111/asap.12140

Crisp, R. J., Birtel, M. D., & Meleady, R. (2011). Mental simulations of social thought and action: Trivial tasks or tools for transforming social policy? *Current Directions in Psychological Science, 20*(4), 261–264. https://doi.org/10.1177/0963721411413762

Crisp, R. J., & Turner, R. N. (2009). Can imagined interactions produce positive perceptions? Reducing prejudice through simulated social contact. *American Psychologist, 64*(4), 231–240. https://doi.org/10.1037/a0014718

Crisp, R. J., & Turner, R. N. (2011). Cognitive adaptation to the experience of social and cultural diversity. *Psychological Bulletin, 137*(2), 242–266. https://doi.org/10.1037/a0021840

Cuddy, A. J., Fiske, S. T., Kwan, V. S., Glick, P., Demoulin, S., Leyens, J. P., ... & Ziegler, R. (2009). Stereotype content model across cultures: Towards universal similarities and some differences. *British Journal of Social Psychology, 48*(1), 1–33. https://doi.org/10.1348/014466608X314935

Dixon, J., Durrheim, K., & Tredoux, C. (2007). Intergroup contact and attitudes toward the principle and practice of racial equality. *Psychological Science, 18*(10), 867–872. https://doi.org/10.1111/j.1467-9280.2007.01993.x

Dixon, J., Levine, M., Reicher, S., & Durrheim, K. (2012). Beyond prejudice: Are negative evaluations the problem and is getting us to like one another more the solution?. *Behavioral and Brain Sciences, 35*(6), 411–425. https://doi.org/10.1017/S0140525X11002214

Drury, J., & Reicher, S. (2009). Collective psychological empowerment as a model of social change: Researching crowds and power. *Journal of Social Issues, 65*(4), 707–725. https://doi.org/10.1111/j.1540-4560.2009.01622.x

Feddes, A. R., & Jonas, K. J. (2020). Associations between Dutch LGBT hate crime experience, well-being, trust in the police and future hate crime reporting. *Social Psychology, 51*(3), 171–182. https://doi.org/10.1027/1864-9335/a000409

Festinger, L. (1954). A theory of social comparison processes. *Human Relations, 7*, 117–140. https://doi.org/10.1177/001872675400700202

Fischer, A., Halperin, E., Canetti, D., & Jasini, A. (2018). Why we hate. *Emotion Review, 10*(4), 309–320. https://doi.org/10.1177/1754073917751229

Fiske, S. T. (2018). Stereotype content: Warmth and competence endure. *Current Directions in Psychological Science, 27*(2), 67–73. https://doi.org/10.1177/0963721417738825

Fiske, S. T., Cuddy, A. J. C., Glick, P., & Xu, J. (2002). A model of (often mixed) stereotype content: Competence and warmth respectively follow from perceived status and competition. *Journal of Personality and Social Psychology, 82*(6), 878–902. https://doi.org/10.1037/0022-3514.82.6.878

Foa, E. B., & Kozak, M. J. (1986). Emotional processing of fear: Exposure to corrective information. *Psychological Bulletin, 99*, 20–35. https://doi.org/10.1037/0022-3514.82.6.878

Gaertner, S. L., Dovidio, J. F., Nier, J. A., Banker, B. S., Ward, C. M., Houlette, M., & Loux, S. (2000). The Common Ingroup Identity Model for reducing intergroup bias: Progress and challenges. In D. Capozza & R. Brown (Eds.), *Social identity processes: Trends in theory and research* (pp. 133–148). London: Sage. https://doi.org/10.4135/9781446218617.n9

Gaertner, S. L., & Dovidio, J. F. (2000). Reducing intergroup bias: The common ingroup identity model. Psychology Press.

Gaertner, S. L., Mann, J., Murrell, A., & Dovidio, J. F. (1989). Reducing intergroup bias: The benefits of recategorization. *Journal of Personality and Social Psychology, 57*(2), 239–249. https://doi.org/10.1037/0022-3514.57.2.239

Glick, P., & Fiske, S. T. (1996). The ambivalent sexism inventory: Differentiating hostile and benevolent sexism. *Journal of Personality and Social Psychology, 70*(3), 491–512. https://doi.org/10.1037/0022-3514.70.3.491

Golec de Zavala, A. G., Cichocka, A., Eidelson, R., & Jayawickreme, N. (2009). Collective narcissism and its social consequences. *Journal of Personality and Social Psychology, 97*(6), 1074–1096. https://doi.org/10.1037/a0016904

Greenberg, J., Landau, M. J., Kosloff, S., Soenke, M., & Solomon, S. (2016). How our means for feeling transcendent of death foster prejudice, stereotyping, and intergroup conflict: Terror management theory. In T. D. Nelson (Ed.), *Handbook of prejudice, stereotyping, and discrimination* (2nd ed., pp. 107–148). Abingdon: Routledge. https://doi.org/10.4324/9780203361993-11

Greenberg, J., Pyszczynski, T., & Solomon, S. (1986). The causes and consequences of a need for self-esteem: A terror management theory. In R. F. Baumeister (Ed.), *Public self and private self.* Springer Series in Social Psychology (pp. 189–212). New York: Springer. https://doi.org/10.1007/978-1-4613-9564-5_10

Gronholm, P. C., Henderson, C., Deb, T., & Thornicroft, G. (2017). Interventions to reduce discrimination and stigma: The state of the art. *Social Psychiatry and Psychiatric Epidemiology, 52*(3), 249–258. https://doi.org/10.1007/s00127-017-1341-9

Guillaume, Y. R. F., Dawson, J. F., Priola, V., Sacramento, C. A., Woods, S. A., Higson, H. E., Budhwar, P. S., & West, M. A. (2014). Managing diversity in organizations: An integrative model and agenda for future research. *European Journal of Work and Organizational Psychology, 23*(5), 783–802. https://doi.org/10.1080/1359432X.2013.805485

Henderson, C., Robinson, E., Evans-Lacko, S., Corker, E., Rebollo-Mesa, I., Rose, D., & Thornicroft, G. (2016). Public knowledge, attitudes, social distance and reported contact regarding people with mental illness 2009–2015. *Acta Psychiatrica Scandinavica, 134*, 23–33.

Henderson, C., Robinson, E., Evans-Lacko, S., & Thornicroft, G. (2017). Relationships between anti-stigma programme awareness, disclosure comfort and intended help-seeking regarding a mental health problem. *The British Journal of Psychiatry, 211*(5), 316–322. https://doi.org/10.1192/bjp.bp.116.195867

Hewstone, M., & Brown, R. (Eds.). (1986). *Contact and conflict in intergroup encounters*. Basil Blackwell.

Hofstede, G. (2011). Dimensionalizing cultures: The Hofstede model in context. *Online Readings in Psychology and Culture*, *2*(1). https://doi.org/10.9707/2307-0919.1014

Hofstede, G., Hofstede, G. J., & Minkov, M. (2010). *Cultures and organizations: Software of the mind*. New York: McGraw-Hill.

Hogg, M. A. (2000). Subjective uncertainty reduction through self-categorization: A motivational theory of social identity processes. *European Review of Social Psychology*, *11*(1), 223–255. http://dx.doi.org/10.1080/14792772043000040

Hogg, M. A., & Williams, K. D. (2000). From I to we: Social identity and the collective self. *Group Dynamics: Theory, Research, and Practice*, *4*(1), 81–97. https://doi.org/10.1037/1089-2699.4.1.81

Hopkins-Doyle, A., Sutton, R. M., Douglas, K. M., & Calogero, R. M. (2019). Flattering to deceive: Why people misunderstand benevolent sexism. *Journal of Personality and Social Psychology*, *116*(2), 167–192. https://doi.org/10.1037/pspa0000135

Hundschell, A., Razinskas, S., Backmann, J., & Hoegl, M. (2022). The effects of diversity on creativity: A literature review and synthesis. *Applied Psychology*, *71*(4), 1598–1634. https://doi.org/10.1111/apps.12365

Kitayama, S., Park, J., Boylan, J. M., Miyamoto, Y., Levine, C. S., Markus, H. R., ... & Ryff, C. D. (2015). Expression of anger and ill health in two cultures: An examination of inflammation and cardiovascular risk. *Psychological Science*, *26*(2), 211–220. https://doi.org/10.1177/0956797614561

Klein, R. A., Cook, C. L., Ebersole, C. R., Vitiello, C., Nosek, B. A., Hilgard, J., ... & Ratliff, K. A. (2022). Many Labs 4: Failure to replicate mortality salience effect with and without original author involvement. *Collabra: Psychology*, *8*(1), 35271. https://doi.org/10.1525/collabra.35271

Kosslyn, S. M., Ganis, G., & Thompson, W. L. (2001). Neural foundations of imagery. *Nature Reviews Neuroscience*, *2*(9), 635–642. https://doi.org/10.1038/35090055

Kotter, J. (1996) *The 8-step process for leading change*. www.kotterinc.com/8-steps-process-for-leading-change/

Krendl, A. C., & Pescosolido, B. A. (2020). Countries and cultural differences in the stigma of mental illness: The east–west divide. *Journal of Cross-Cultural Psychology*, *51*(2), 149–167. https://doi.org/10.1177/0022022119901297

Larkings, J. S., & Brown, P. M. (2018). Do biogenetic causal beliefs reduce mental illness stigma in people with mental illness and in mental health professionals? A systematic review. *International Journal of Mental Health Nursing*, *27*(3), 928–941. https://doi.org/10.1111/inm.12390

Larson, J. E., & Corrigan, P. (2008). The stigma of families with mental illness. *Academic Psychiatry*, *32*(2), 87–91. https://doi.org/10.1176/appi.ap.32.2.87

Lauber, C., & Rössler, W. (2007). Stigma towards people with mental illness in developing countries in Asia. *International Review of Psychiatry*, *19*(2), 157–178. https://doi.org/10.1080/09540260701278903

Lazarus, R. S., and Folkman, S. (1984). *Stress, appraisal, and coping*. New York: Springer.

Lee, Y.-T. & Jussim, L. (2010) Back in the real world. *American Psychologist, 65*(2), 130–131. https://doi.org/10.1037/a0018195

LeVine, R. A., & Campbell, D. T. (1972). *Ethnocentrism: Theories of conflict, ethnic attitudes, and group behavior.* Hoboken, NJ: John Wiley & Sons.

Li, C. R., Lin, C. J., Tien, Y. H., & Chen, C. M. (2015). A multilevel model of team cultural diversity and creativity: The role of climate for inclusion. *The Journal of Creative Behavior, 51*(2), 163–179. https://doi.org/10.1002/jocb.93

Link, B. G., Cullen, F. T., Struening, E., Shrout, P. E., & Dohrenwend, B. P. (1989). A modified labeling theory approach to mental disorders: An empirical assessment. *American Sociological Review, 54*(3), 400–423. https://doi.org/10.2307/2095613

Link, B. G., & Phelan, J. C. (2013). Labeling and stigma. In C. S. Aneshensel, J. C. Phelan, & A. Bierman (Eds.), *Handbook of the sociology of mental health* (2nd ed., pp. 525–541). Springer Science + Business Media. https://doi.org/10.1007/978-94-007-4276-5_25

MacInnis, C. C., & Page-Gould, E. (2015). How can intergroup interaction be bad if intergroup contact is good? Exploring and reconciling an apparent paradox in the science of intergroup relations. *Perspectives on Psychological Science, 10*(3), 307–327. https://doi.org/10.1177/1745691614568482

Mackie, D. M., & Smith, E. R. (2002). *From prejudice to intergroup emotions: Differentiated reactions to social groups.* New York: Psychology Press.

Maddux, W. W., Lu, J. G., Affinito, S. J., & Galinsky, A. D. (2021). Multicultural experiences: A systematic review and new theoretical framework. *Academy of Management Annals, 15*(2), 345–376. https://doi.org/10.5465/annals.2019.0138

Major, B., Mendes, W. B., & Dovidio, J. F. (2013). Intergroup relations and health disparities: A social psychological perspective. *Health Psychology, 32*(5), 514–524. https://doi.org/10.1037/a0030358

Major, B., & O'Brien, L. T. (2005). The social psychology of stigma. *Annual Review of Psychology, 56*(1), 393–421. https://doi.org/10.1146/annurev.psych.56.091103.070137

Markus, H. R., & Kitayama, S. (1991). Culture and the self: Implications for cognition, emotion, and motivation. *Psychological Review, 98*(2), 224–253. https://doi.org/10.1037/0033-295X.98.2.224

Markus, H. R., & Kitayama, S. (2010). Cultures and selves: A cycle of mutual constitution. *Perspectives on Psychological Science, 5*(4), 420–430. https://doi.org/10.1177/174569161037555

Marques, J., & Yzerbyt, V. (1988). The black sheep effect: Judgmental extremity towards ingroup members in inter- and intra-group situations. *European Journal of Social Psychology, 18*, 287–292. https://doi.org/10.1002/ejsp.2420180308

Martiny, S. E., & Rubin, M. (2016). Towards a clearer understanding of social identity theory's self-esteem hypothesis. In S. McKeown, R. Haji, & N. Ferguson (Eds.), *Understanding peace and conflict through social identity theory: Contemporary global perspectives* (pp. 19–32). Cham, Switzerland: Springer International.

McDevitt, J., Levin, J., & Bennett, S. (2002). Hate crime offenders: An expanded typology. *Journal of Social Issues, 58*(2), 303–317. https://doi.org/10.1111/1540-4560.00262

Miles, E., & Crisp, R. J. (2014). A meta-analytic test of the imagined contact hypothesis. *Group Processes & Intergroup Relations, 17*(1), 3–26. https://doi.org/10.1177/136843021351057

Mirza, A., Birtel, M. D., Pyle, M., & Morrison, A. P. (2019). Cultural differences in psychosis: The role of causal beliefs and stigma in White British and South Asians. *Journal of Cross-Cultural Psychology*, *50*(3), 441–459. https://doi.org/10.1177/0022022118820168

Mummendey, A., & Otten, S. (1998). Positive–negative asymmetry in social discrimination. *European Review of Social Psychology*, *9*(1), 107–143. https://doi.org/10.1080/14792779843000063

Page-Gould, E., Mendes, W. B., & Major, B. (2010). Intergroup contact facilitates physiological recovery following stressful intergroup interactions. *Journal of Experimental Social Psychology*, *46*(5), 854–858. https://doi.org/10.1016/j.jesp.2010.04.006

Paterson, J. L., Walters, M. A., Brown, R., & Fearn, H. (2018). *The Sussex Hate Crime Project: Final report*. Brighton: University of Sussex. Available at: www.sussex.ac.uk/webteam/gateway/file.php?name=sussex-hate-crimeproject-report.pdf&site=430.

Perry, B., & Alvi, S. (2012). 'We are all vulnerable': The *in terrorem* effects of hate crimes. *International Review of Victimology*, *18*(1), 57–71. https://doi.org/10.1177/0269758011422475

Plaut, V. C. (2010). Diversity science: Why and how difference makes a difference. *Psychological Inquiry*, *21*(2), 77–99. https://doi.org/10.1080/10478401003676501

Plumm, K. M., & Terrance, C. A. (2013). Gender-bias hate crimes: What constitutes a hate crime from a potential juror's perspective? *Journal of Applied Social Psychology*, *43*(7), 1468–1479. https://doi.org/10.1111/jasp.12105

Putnam, R. D. (2007). *E pluribus unum*: Diversity and community in the twenty-first century. Rhe 2006 Johan Skytte Prize Lecture. *Scandinavian Political Studies*, *30*(2), 137–174. https://doi.org/10.1111/j.1467-9477.2007.00176.x

Ramos, M. R., Bennett, M. R., Massey, D. S., & Hewstone, M. (2019). Humans adapt to social diversity over time. *Proceedings of the National Academy of Sciences*, *116*(25), 12244–12249. https://doi.org/10.1073/pnas.1818884116

Reicher, S. D., Spears, R., & Postmes, T. (1995). A social identity model of deindividuation phenomena. *European Review of Social Psychology*, *6*(1), 161–198. https://doi.org/10.1080/14792779443000049

Riek, B. M., Mania, E. W., & Gaertner, S. L. (2006). Intergroup threat and outgroup attitudes: A meta-analytic review. *Personality and Social Psychology Review*, *10*(4), 336–353. https://doi.org/10.1207/s15327957pspr1004_4

Rüsch, N., Angermeyer, M. C., & Corrigan, P. W. (2005). Mental illness stigma: Concepts, consequences, and initiatives to reduce stigma. *European Psychiatry*, *20*(8), 529–539. https://doi.org/10.1016/j.eurpsy.2005.04.004

Saguy, T., Tausch, N., Dovidio, J. F., & Pratto, F. (2009). The irony of harmony: Intergroup contact can produce false expectations for equality. *Psychological Science*, *20*(1), 114–121. https://doi.org/10.1111/j.1467-9280.2008.02261

Sam, D. L., & Berry, J. W. (2010). Acculturation: When individuals and groups of different cultural backgrounds meet. *Perspectives on Psychological Science*, *5*(4), 472–481. https://doi.org/10.1177/1745691610373075

Schuhl, J., Lambert, E., & Chatard, A. (2019). Can imagination reduce prejudice over time? A preregistered test of the imagined contact hypothesis. *Basic and Applied Social Psychology*, *41*(2), 122–131. https://doi.org/10.1080/01973533.2019.1579719

Schulze, B., & Angermeyer, M. C. (2003). Subjective experiences of stigma: A focus group study of schizophrenic patients, their relatives and mental health professionals. *Social Science & Medicine, 56*(2), 299–312. https://doi.org/10.1016/S0277-9536(02)00028-X

Sherif, M., Harvey, O., White, J. B., Hood, W. R., & Sherif, C. W. (1961). *Intergroup conflict and cooperation: The Robbers Cave experiment [1954].* Norman, OK: University of Oklahoma Book Exchange.

Singelis, T. M. (1994). The measurement of independent and interdependent self-construals. *Personality and Social Psychology Bulletin, 20*(5), 580–591. https://doi.org/10.1177/0146167294205014

Smith, E. R., & Mackie, D. M. (2015). Dynamics of group-based emotions: Insights from intergroup emotions theory. *Emotion Review, 7(4)*, 349–354. https://doi.org/10.1177/175407391559061

Sommers, S. R. (2007). Race and the decision making of juries. *Legal and Criminological Psychology, 12*(2), 171–187. https://doi.org/10.1348/135532507X189687

Stephan, W. G., & Stephan, C. W. (1985). Intergroup anxiety. *Journal of Social Issues, 41*(3), 157–175. https://doi.org/10.1111/j.1540-4560.1985.tb01134.x

Stephan, W. G., Ybarra, O., & Morrison, K. R. (2009). Intergroup threat theory. In T. D. Nelson (Ed.), *Handbook of prejudice, stereotyping, and discrimination.* New York: Psychology Press.

Tajfel, H., Billig, M. G., Bundy, R. P., & Flament, C. (1971). Social categorization and intergroup behaviour. *European Journal of Social Psychology, 1*(2), 149–178. https://doi.org/10.1002/ejsp.2420010202

Tajfel, H., & Turner, J. C. (1979). An integrative theory of intergroup conflict. In W. G. Austin & S. Worchel (Eds.), *The social psychology of intergroup relations* (pp. 33–47). San Francisco, CA: Brooks/Cole.

Tausch, N., Becker, J. C., Spears, R., Christ, O., Saab, R., Singh, P., & Siddiqui, R. N. (2011). Explaining radical group behavior: Developing emotion and efficacy routes to normative and nonnormative collective action. *Journal of Personality and Social Psychology, 101*(1), 129–148. https://doi.org/10.1037/a0022728

Thornicroft, G., Sunkel, C., Aliev, A. A., Baker, S., Brohan, E., El Chammay, R., ... & Winkler, P. (2022). The Lancet Commission on ending stigma and discrimination in mental health. *The Lancet, 400*(10361), 1438–1480. https://doi.org/10.1016/S0140-6736(22)01470-2

Time to Change. (2020). *Our impact.* www.tnlcommunityfund.org.uk/media/insights/documents/turtl-story-impact-report-20192020.pdf

Trawalter, S., Richeson, J. A., & Shelton, J. N. (2009). Predicting behavior during interracial interactions: A stress and coping approach. *Personality and Social Psychology Review, 13*(4), 243–268. https://doi.org/10.1177/1088868309345850

Triandis, H. C. (1995). A theoretical framework for the study of diversity. In M. M. Chemers, S. Oskamp, & M. A. Costanzo (Eds.), *Diversity in organizations: New perspectives for a changing workplace* (pp. 11–36). Thousand Oaks, CA: Sage. https://doi.org/10.4135/9781452243405.n2

Triandis, H. C., & Gelfand, M. J. (1998). Converging measurement of horizontal and vertical individualism and collectivism. *Journal of Personality and Social Psychology*, *74*(1), 118–128. https://doi.org/10.1037/0022-3514.74.1.118

Turner, J. C., Hogg, M. A., Oakes, P. J., Reicher, S. D., & Wetherell, M. S. (1987). *Rediscovering the social group: A self-categorization theory*. Oxford: Basil Blackwell.

van Knippenberg, D., De Dreu, C. K., & Homan, A. C. (2004). Work group diversity and group performance: An integrative model and research agenda. *Journal of Applied Psychology*, *89*(6), 1008–1022. https://doi.org/10.1037/0021-9010.89.6.1008

van Knippenberg, D., & Schippers, M. C. (2007). Work group diversity. *Annual Review of Psychology*, *58*, 515–541. http://dx.doi.org/10.1146/annurev.psych.58.110405.085546

van Zomeren, M., Postmes, T., & Spears, R. (2008). Toward an integrative social identity model of collective action: A quantitative research synthesis of three socio-psychological perspectives. *Psychological Bulletin*, *134*, 504–535. https://doi.org/10.1037/0033-2909.134.4.504

Vezzali, L., Birtel, M. D., Di Bernardo, G. A., Stathi, S., Crisp, R. J., Cadamuro, A., & Visintin, E. P. (2020). Don't hurt my outgroup friend: A multifaceted form of imagined contact promotes intentions to counteract bullying. *Group Processes & Intergroup Relations*, *23*(5), 643–663. https://doi.org/10.1177/13684302198524

Wright, S. C., Aron, A., McLaughlin-Volpe, T., & Ropp, S. A. (1997). The extended contact effect: Knowledge of cross-group friendships and prejudice. *Journal of Personality and Social Psychology*, *73*(1), 73–90. https://doi.org/10.1037/0022-3514.73.1.73

Yadav, S., & Lenka, U. (2020). Diversity management: A systematic review. *Equality, Diversity and Inclusion: An International Journal*, *39*(8), 901–929. https://doi.org/10.1108/EDI-07-2019-0197

11
BEHAVIOUR CHANGE
MILICA VASILJEVIC

Contents

11.1 AUTHOR'S PERSONAL JOURNEY

Source: © Milica Vasiljevic

I was born in a country that no longer exists. My early childhood was spent in a country lauded for its multiculturalism, diversity, multilingualism, and equality. That is until the country imploded in one of the most violent conflicts that Europe has seen in recent times. My family is a great example of how the country was typically described; my parents came from different Republics that made up the Former Yugoslavia, they were from different ethnic groups, and they spoke different mother tongues. My early years, when I learnt how to switch seamlessly between languages depending on the context, and how to fit in with the rich diversity surrounding me, planted in me an interest in studying people's thoughts and behaviours. I was fascinated by how different people and cultures united and lived harmoniously. But when I was seven years old, the country was thrown into a violent civil conflict. Former friends, colleagues, family members in a blink became enemies. My parents and I escaped the violent conflict and became refugees, staying with my grandparents. One of the earliest memories of being a refugee was a conversation that some neighbours were having in front of the block of flats where my grandparents lived. Skopje is always extremely hot in the summer and in July 1991 this was no different. We were sitting on the balcony with my parents and grandparents and some of the neighbours started discussing the war in Croatia, and the destruction of my home town Vukovar. Suddenly one of the neighbours started talking about my family and said: 'Why do they not go back to where they came from? What on earth are they looking for here?' I became interested in why people would wish ill on their fellow human beings, even though at the time I knew little about the group and intergroup processes at play.

This all came to make much more sense when, through a series of competitive scholarships, I found myself studying Experimental Psychology at the University of Oxford. Somehow, during the course of my degree, I naturally tended to gravitate towards the courses on social psychology. Seminal studies such as the Robbers Cave Experiment by the Sherifs, the minimal group paradigm by Tajfel, and conformity and obedience studies by Asch and Milgram seemed to offer the best explanations for the human behaviours that tended to puzzle me. But, even more so, social psychology seemed to offer elegant theoretical solutions for behaviour change with the early fieldwork by Kurt Lewin. This led me to complete a PhD at the Centre for Group Processes and Intergroup Relations at the University of Kent, where I developed and evaluated the efficacy of a prejudice-reduction intervention aimed at decreasing prejudice across multiple groups at the same time. My penchant for evaluating behaviour change interventions led me to the University of Cambridge and the first multidisciplinary research unit on behaviour change, funded by the Department of Health and Social Care in England. There I started investigating how changing different aspects of people's environments (such as labelling on foods and alcohol, and changing the size of products) impacts population-level health-related behaviours. I am still working on such interventions, and I am very excited to be able to share with you some of these insights on behaviour change in this chapter.

11.2 INTRODUCTION

In the previous chapters you learnt about the common methods and methodological innovations used by social psychologists. You also learnt about some of the seminal theories and key studies in diverse areas of social psychology, including interpersonal relationships, group processes, intergroup relations, attitudes, and social influence. Reading through the chapters in this book, you have probably gathered that social psychologists are concerned with understanding and predicting the thoughts, feelings, and behaviours of

> **Key concept – Behaviour:** How people act in response to an internal or external stimulus.

people. These insights are then used to develop models and theories of **behaviour**, which are in turn used to develop interventions to **change behaviour**.

This last chapter is concerned with the social psychology of behaviour change. In the Foundations section of the chapter, you will learn more about seminal theories of behaviour change, including the Theory of Planned Behaviour (TPB), the Health Belief Model, Integrative Self-Control Theory, Habit Theory, and other theories and models that

> **Key concept – Behaviour change:** Any alteration or adjustment of behaviour that affects a person's functioning, brought about by interventions or occurring spontaneously.

have been crucial in moving this field forward. In the Advances section, we will turn our attention to more recent developments in this field, including nudge theory, and integrative frameworks and models of behaviour change, such as the Behaviour Change Wheel. We will also discuss future directions in the field of behaviour change. The chapter concludes with an overview of recent applications in this field, including nudge interventions in the food domain, digital interventions, as well as how to raise public support for the most effective and promising behaviour change interventions and policies.

11.3 LEARNING OBJECTIVES

By the end of this chapter, you will be able to:

- Describe and evaluate the contribution of different behaviour change theories to our understanding of human behaviour and behaviour change;
- Compare and contrast the social-cognitive theories of behaviour change with more recent theorising, including the Reflective-Impulsive Model and Integrative Self-Control Theory;
- Explain the tenets of the 'nudge' ('choice architecture') framework of behaviour change;
- Critically analyse ethical considerations that have been put forward relating to nudging people towards a certain behaviour;
- Understand and be able to use integrative frameworks of behaviour change, such as the Behaviour Change Wheel;

- Critically consider the future avenues for behaviour change research and practice;
- Understand different applications of behaviour change theories and be able to use behaviour change frameworks in your own research and study of behaviour change.

11.4 PART 1: FOUNDATIONS

Our journey into understanding behaviour change begins with an overview of the seminal theories and models that have shaped this exciting area of research. We start by examining some of the classic theories then move on to more recent integrative theories and models of behaviour change.

11.4.1 Theory of Planned Behaviour (TPB)

The Theory of Planned Behaviour (TPB) (Ajzen, 1991) is one of the most enduring and cited theories in psychology. The TPB developed from and extended the Theory of Reasoned Action (TRA) (Fishbein & Ajzen, 1975). You have already come across both of these theories in Chapter 6 where Chris Jones and Lambros Lazuras vividly described the tenets of both the TPB and TRA using football analogies. To recap, the Theory of Reasoned Action (TRA) proposes that the likelihood of engaging in a particular behaviour is dependent on the behavioural *intentions* that a person holds towards the behaviour, which is predicted by a person's *attitudes* towards performing the behaviour and the person's beliefs about what others may think about them performing said behaviour (*subjective norms*; for a further discussion on norms see also Chapter 7). Intentions have been defined as the instructions that people give themselves to enact particular behaviours. The construct is most often measured via self-report by asking people to indicate their level of agreement with statements such as: '*I intend to* cycle to work every day/eat more fruits and vegetables every day.'

The TPB extended the predictive validity of the TRA by adding the construct of *perceived behavioural control* to the model, thereby acknowledging that even in instances when a person holds positive attitudes towards a particular behaviour and perceives favourable social norms, thus bolstering their intention to engage with the behaviour, the person may still fail to engage in the behaviour due to a lack of perceived control (such as the lack of essential skills or resources). Therefore, the greater the person's perceived control over the behaviour, the more likely it is that their intention will be carried out. For example, I may be holding positive attitudes towards healthy eating, and I may also receive plenty of support from my family and friends to make my diet healthier (positive social norms). This translates into me intending to cut out pre-cooked junk foods from my diet. However, due to a lack of cooking skills and free time (perceived behavioural control) my good intentions may not translate into effective behaviour change towards healthier eating. A graphical representation of these pathways can be seen in Figure 6.10, Chapter 6.

A central tenet of the TRA and TPB is that behaviour enactment and change rely on conscious awareness and deliberation. Both theories assume that behavioural intentions require some form of conscious decision-making, especially for novel or high-consequence decisions.

The theories also acknowledge that when a behaviour has become routine or habitual, behavioural intentions may also be activated automatically (Ajzen & Dasgupta, 2015). For a broader discussion of automaticity, see Chapter 5 on social cognition.

While both the TRA and TPB have proven popular with researchers, the theories have also faced criticisms. One of the biggest criticisms levelled at these theories is that there is a considerable gap between people's intentions and their actual behaviours (known as the **intention–behaviour gap**). In a now seminal review, Webb and Sheeran (2006) searched for the most robust experimental studies examining whether increasing people's intentions can lead to effective behaviour change. They found 47 experiments on this topic and extracted relevant information from them to conduct a meta-analysis, an analysis combining the data from all these studies. They found that even when experimental manipulations increased people's intentions to engage with a particular behaviour, translating these intentions into actual behaviour had a small-to-modest effect at best. This finding suggests that there are other constructs that are important for enacting behaviour change. Despite the great popularity of the TPB, researchers working in this field have therefore turned their attention to alternative theories that may better explain how we can instigate successful behaviour change.

> **Key concept – Intention–behaviour gap:** The often-observed mismatch between people's intentions and their actual behaviours.

GUEST PERSONAL JOURNEY

Paschal Sheeran

I *really* wanted to leave my home town at 18 and, despite my parents' wishes, went to University College Dublin (UCD) funded by a government grant and summer work. I took philosophy, psychology, and maths in the first year, intending to do philosophy or maths. However, all of the smart, attractive people were doing psychology so I followed their lead. After graduation, I worked on building sites in the UK. Injured by a fall from a London bus, I returned to UCD to complete a Master's in applied psychology. My big break came when I saw a newspaper ad for a research assistantship in Scotland, working with Charles Abraham on a social psychology of HIV/AIDS

Source: © Pascal Sheeran

project. It seemed inconceivable that one could get paid to do research and have as much fun as Charles and I did. Charles encouraged me to do a PhD, so I started one at the University of East London and then moved to the University of Sheffield, where I stayed for 20 years. In 2013, my family and I moved to the University of North Carolina-Chapel Hill to see the sun.

(Continued)

My interest in behaviour change accrues from my own inability to concentrate and get things done. Plus, I've been a foreigner for most of my life and have learned to care much more about how people act towards me than what they think. I enjoy trying to figure out how to help people do the things they want to do, especially when I get to work with fun, talented colleagues (please stand up, Peter Gollwitzer and Alex Rothman!) and grad students. It's a borderline miracle that I don't work in IT or at a grocery store and instead get to be a social psychologist! The trick (that worked for me at least) is finding situations (people, places, events) that will propel you.

11.4.2 Social Cognitive Theory (SCT)

Social Cognitive Theory (SCT) (Bandura, 1986) arose from the earlier Social Learning Theory (SLT) by Bandura (1977). At its core, SCT highlights the importance of observational learning, cognitive processes, and social experiences in determining behaviour. Both SCT and SLT advocate that (a) people learn by watching other people enact behaviours, and (b) behaviours are learned in social contexts. Social Cognitive Theory additionally stipulates that the maintenance of behaviours over time requires environmental reinforcement and individual self-regulation, which are thought to work reciprocally. You have already come across the SCT in Chapter 4 of this book, where you were introduced to the Bobo Doll experiment (see Key study 4.2), which showed that children can learn to model aggressive behaviours by observing an adult person behaving aggressively towards the doll.

Self-efficacy (people's subjective estimate of the amount of personal control they expect to have in any given situation) and *outcome expectancies* (people's beliefs about the possible consequences of their actions) are two core constructs in the SCT. The concept of self-efficacy is similar to the concept of perceived behavioural control posited in the TPB. The SCT further proposes that self-efficacy and outcome expectancies operate together with *goals* (see Chapter 5 for more information on goals) and *socio-structural factors* in determining behaviour and behaviour change. Socio-structural factors refer to the impediments (barriers) or opportunities (facilitators) that are present in people's living conditions, personal circumstances, and political, economic, or environmental systems. Thus, unlike the TRA and TPB, this theory takes a broader view as to how behaviour is predicted, by taking into account wider sociocultural factors beyond the individual engaging in a particular behaviour. In Figure 11.1 you can see a graphical representation of the constructs proposed to predict behaviour change in the SCT.

Goals and behaviours are thought to be directly and indirectly affected by self-efficacy and outcome expectancies. Thus, to change behaviour, the SCT proposes that people go through the process of *goal* formation and subsequently engage in attempts to execute these goals. In the SCT, goals are divided between those that are proximal (short-term) and those that are distal (long-term). For example, I may have a long-term (distal) goal to lead a more environmentally friendly and sustainable lifestyle. To achieve this distal goal, I would need to set myself short-term (proximal) goals such as switching from fossil fuel to renewable

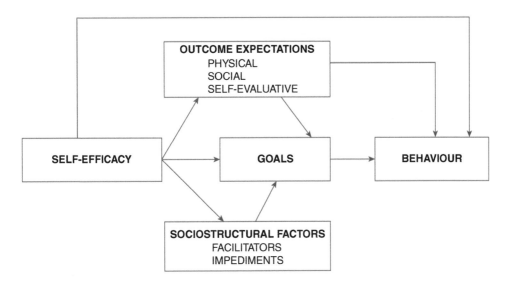

Figure 11.1 A graphical representation of the components proposed to predict behaviour in the Social Cognitive Theory (SCT)

Source: Bandura (2012)

energy in the home, ditching the car for more active modes of transportation, as well as reducing my meat consumption. The proximal goals are the building blocks of our long-term goal pursuit and behaviour change. Proximal goals are akin to the construct of *intentions* used in other social cognitive approaches such as the Theory of Planned Behaviour (TPB).

According to Bandura, forming goals is a necessary – but not sufficient – condition for encouraging goal pursuit and behaviour change. Outcome expectancies and perceived socio-structural factors determine whether a formed goal is pursued. For example, if I think that the potential negative outcomes and socio-structural barriers of my decision to ditch the petrol car (inefficient and underdeveloped national grid for electric charging, increased electricity costs) outweigh the potential positive outcomes and socio-structural facilitators (reduced reliance on fossil fuels, cleaner air), I may decide that goal pursuit and behaviour change in this instance are not viable and abandon my goals. On the other hand, self-efficacy is thought of as a crucial condition for formed goals to be pursued and result in successful behaviour change.

Empirical studies testing the tenets of SCT have found that people with higher self-efficacy and more positive outcome expectancies are better able to translate their goals/intentions into action and change their behaviours in diverse domains, such as work performance, technology use, education, health-related behaviours, and so on (to learn more about this, check out reviews by Stajkovic & Luthans, 1998; Talsma et al., 2018; Tang et al., 2019). Furthermore, studies that have developed and tested the impact of interventions to increase self-efficacy and/or improve outcome expectancies have also found encouraging results (e.g., Stacey et al., 2015; Unrau et al., 2018).

The theory has, however, also come under criticism. For example, the individual components of the SCT, seen in Figure 11.1, are thought to be poorly specified, with much less currently known about the impact of some components (such as the impact of socio-structural barriers and facilitators) than others (such as self-efficacy). Even for components where we have sufficient evidence of impact, we know that there is a discrepancy in how these constructs are measured and used across studies and different sub-fields. Self-efficacy, for example, is operationalised and measured in different ways across studies. Therefore, individual components of the theory seem to perform well when tested, but much less is known about the theory as a unified whole. Finally, a systematic review of the use of social cognitive theory to promote healthy eating and physical activity found no difference in effectiveness between studies that applied SCT more extensively in intervention development and those that didn't (see Prestwich et al., 2014). This finding suggests that the tenets of SCT are not sufficient for behaviour change enactment and there are therefore other components not specified by the SCT that are important for behaviour change.

11.4.3 Health Belief Model and Protection Motivation Theory

The Health Belief Model (HBM) (Hochbaum, 1958; Rosenstock, 1966, 1974) and Protection Motivation Theory (PMT) (Rogers, 1975, 1983) are two of the earliest models that were developed by social psychologists to examine failures of people to participate in preventive health behaviours. Both models provide some of the earliest theorising on how 'fear appeals' work. Fear appeals are persuasive messages that attempt to arouse fear by communicating the potential risk and harm to individuals if they do not heed the message's recommendations (see Dillard, 1994; Maddux & Rogers, 1983). The best real-world illustration of fear appeals are the warning messages that can be seen on tobacco packaging.

In a nutshell, both the HBM and the PMT propose that behaviour change can be accomplished by inducing threat and simultaneously providing information on how to counteract that threat (coping appraisal). The PMT includes features of the TPB and SCT by proposing that intentions are an important part of behaviour change following a fear appeal message, whereas the HBM omits the pathway between intention to behaviour change and proposes that fear appeals can modify behaviour directly.

Both models have found a faithful following among researchers working in applied fields. In terms of impact, comprehensive meta-reviews of experimental tests of fear appeal theories show that they work best when they also communicate effective coping strategies (Kok et al., 2018; Peters et al., 2013; Tannenbaum et al., 2015).

11.4.4 Model of Action Phases (Implementation Intentions)

The Model of Action Phases (MAP) (Gollwitzer, 1990; Heckhausen & Gollwitzer, 1987) was developed in response to the robust finding that setting goal intentions does not necessarily translate into actual behaviour change. The MAP successfully distinguishes between two important facets of goal pursuit in behaviour change: *goal setting* (intention formation) and *goal enactment* (intention realisation). The previous theories and models of behaviour change reviewed above (TPB, SCT, PMT) were primarily concerned with the goal setting or intention formation phase of behaviour change. The goal setting or intention formation phase of behaviour change is our decision to pursue a particular goal (e.g., *'I intend to use a more active travel mode to commute to work'*). According to the MAP, one of the core weaknesses of these earlier models was the sole focus on the motivational phase of forming intentions for behaviour change, while disregarding how our intentions translate into action.

The MAP further contends that failures in behaviour enactment, even in instances when intentions were formed, can be partly explained by the lack of specific plans as to 'when', 'where', and 'how' one needs to act. Thus, the intention realisation phase is a crucial component of the MAP that goes beyond the more traditional models of behaviour change. To realise our intention/goal, Gollwitzer (1999) proposed that we need to form *implementation intentions*: plans that specify when, where, and how we will initiate a goal-directed response and involve creating an *if* (critical situation) and *then* (goal-directed response) contingency. To take our earlier example, according to the MAP, it is not sufficient just to say that 'I intend to use a more active travel mode of commuting to work'; in order for this intention to be successfully translated into action, I will also need to set myself specific implementation plans, such as: *'I intend to use the bike to travel to work each day regardless of the weather conditions when I encounter my cycling helmet and rain coveralls next to the front door.'*

Implementation intentions can thus be thought of as commitment tools that guide the person to enact the intended behaviour when certain contextual conditions or cues are encountered. Importantly, these contextual conditions/cues can be external or internal to the individual. Thus, one can be cued by seeing the helmet and coveralls to take the bike to work, as in the example above (external context), or one can have an implementation intention of *'I will take a walk outside as soon as I feel restless'*, and therefore, in this case, will be cued by internal feelings of restlessness to go and take a walk (internal context).

Another important feature of implementation intentions is that they have been shown to operate outside conscious awareness and in an automatic fashion (for a refresher about automaticity, see Chapter 5). Therefore, when a relevant contextual cue is encountered, the execution of the intended behaviour can proceed effortlessly, swiftly, and without conscious deliberation. Once our implementation intentions are formed, we don't need to consciously think about when, where, and how we need to execute the intended behaviour; we can rely on the contextual cues to help us to guide our behaviours.

A meta-analysis of 94 studies on this topic found that implementation intentions had a medium-to-large positive effect on goal attainment ($d = .65$) (see Gollwitzer & Sheeran, 2006). While most of the studies in this meta-analysis were conducted in laboratory settings, more recent field tests have also demonstrated the potential of implementation intentions interventions in modifying people's behaviours in the real world (Milkman et al., 2011). Importantly, studies have also shown that implementation intentions are more effective when the cue–response link is stronger, providing support for the notion that implementation intentions can successfully modify behaviour because control of behaviour is delegated to specified situational cues that initiate action automatically (Webb & Sheeran, 2007).

More recent investigations have also demonstrated that the effectiveness of implementation intentions (II) can be enhanced if such interventions are coupled with mental contrasting (MC) interventions. In such combined MCII interventions, participants are encouraged to mentally contrast the imagined positive outcome ('What would be the best result of accomplishing this goal?') with the potential obstacles that may prevent goal attainment ('What might prevent me from accomplishing this goal?'). The participant is then asked to make a plan addressing these obstacles ('What may be an effective way to address this obstacle?'). Combined mental contrasting implementation intentions (MCII) interventions have been shown to change behaviour more effectively than either of the interventions in isolation (Adriaanse et al., 2010; Kirk et al., 2013).

Implementation intentions are one way in which we can set ourselves up for success with behaviour change challenges. We will now turn to other theories and models that have attempted to describe failures of self-control or self-regulation, thereby providing a basis for other interventions to counteract self-control challenges.

EXERCISE 11.1

Set an Implementation Intention for a Behaviour Change Challenge that is Personally Relevant to You

Think of a behaviour change challenge that is personally relevant to you at the present moment. The behaviour change challenge can be in any domain: for example, exercising more consistently, changing dietary habits to be more healthful, having more efficient work meetings, and so on. Once you have identified your behaviour change challenge, go through the process of setting an implementation intention for this behaviour change challenge. Write specific plans in the form of 'I will DO X, at TIME, in LOCATION'.

Once you have set-up your specific implementation intentions, try acting on them. Do this a few times over the course of a couple of days (you can set different implementation intentions or use the same one if it is still applicable). Once you have had a bit of practice, consider how helpful this technique was in getting you to engage with your behaviour change challenge. Is there a way in which you will need to enhance your implementation intentions? Can implementation intentions be useful for modifying some of your other behaviours that you are struggling with at present?

11.4.5 Integrative Self-Control Theory

Would you opt for £100 right now or £1,000 in a month? These and related questions are posed by researchers who are interested in self-control phenomena. It is also questions such as this one that were posed by Walter Mischel and colleagues in what are now famously known as the 'marshmallow test' studies (Mischel et al., 1989). Mischel and colleagues studied young children of preschool age in their nursery surroundings. The children were told that they would receive an immediate reward of either one marshmallow or one pretzel stick, and one tiny toy. Alternatively, they were told that if they could wait for 15 minutes without ringing for the experimenter to come back, they would instead receive the greater reward of two marshmallows or two pretzel sticks, and two tiny toys. This now famous paradigm enabled Mischel and his colleagues to study the phenomenon of 'delay of gratification' (i.e., do we prefer smaller immediate rewards or delayed larger rewards). Through a series of experiments, the researchers could show what strategies the children employed to successfully resist temptation or delay their gratification in the marshmallow test. For example, one successful strategy that went against the researchers' predictions was to remove the marshmallows from the children's sight or ask the children to busy themselves with other tasks or thoughts unrelated to the marshmallows. But, perhaps most importantly, Mischell and his colleagues were able to show in their longitudinal cohorts that performance in the marshmallow test had enduring long-term consequences. The children who were better able to delay their gratification (i.e., had greater self-control) years later performed better at school, their health and well-being was more adjusted, and they suffered from fewer behavioural problems, when compared to those children who struggled to delay their gratification.

In Integrative Self-control Theory (Kotabe & Hofmann, 2015), the motivation for **self-control** arises when we experience a conflict between our momentary desire and a somewhat incompatible higher-order goal we hold. For example, we may desire to eat a delicious cake that is in front of us, but this may be incompatible with our higher-order goal of eating healthily and maintaining a healthy weight. This incompatibility between our desire and higher-order goal is what we would term temptation. Both our *self-control motivation* (the degree to which we wish to control temptation) and *self-control capacity* (all the mental resources that a person can invoke in the self-control conflict) interact to determine the potential self-control effort we exert in this *self-control conflict* (temptation). The actual amount of self-control effort that we end up exerting depends on an interaction between our self-control motivation and self-control capacity at a given point in time. For example, we may be generally very highly self-control motivated to eat healthily and maintain a healthy weight, but in that moment our self-control capacity may be low due to workplace stress and/or lack of time to cook. Our self-control effort in this instance will therefore depend on an interaction of these two facets.

> **Key concept – Self-control:** Our ability to regulate our emotions, thoughts, and behaviours when faced with temptations.

Importantly, in every self-control conflict there will also be enactment constraints which can be anything in our environment that may undermine or promote the enactment of our desire or self-control goal. Enactment constraints are defined as environmental factors not under one's personal control (e.g., finite resources like time and money) and physical and social cues in our immediate external environments. Designing our immediate external environments to favour self-control goal enactments and constrain momentary desire should help facilitate the fulfilment of our long-term self-control goals. For example, if we were at a lunch function and everyone else was opting to eat cake for dessert, this may pose an enactment constraint that undermines our self-control goal to eat healthier. Conversely, if all the cake was gone or if the lunch function was set up in such a way as to favour healthier choices (e.g., by reducing the amount of cake available and increasing the amount of fruit available), then the enactment constraints in our environment would help us stay faithful to our self-control goal to eat healthily and override any momentary desire for an unhealthy snack (cake).

We discuss an example of an availability intervention aiming to modify the ratio of available healthier and unhealthier food options in the Applications section of this chapter, which provides a nice practical example of how environmental constraints can impact the enactments of our self-control goals. This avenue for self-control goal enactment is also in line with recently popularised choice architecture or nudge models of behaviour change that we will discuss in more detail in the Advances section of this chapter (see Marteau et al., 2012; Thaler & Sunstein, 2008).

Historically, interventions aimed at reducing self-control failures have taken the approach of modifying and increasing individuals' self-control capacity, most often via cognitive (re)-training tasks. Such interventions target the mental representations that people hold. One such intervention is goal setting, where people are encouraged to set mental representations of what they are hoping to achieve. A recent meta-analysis showed that setting goals exerts a small-to-medium effect on behaviour change, with goals that are challenging, public, and made within a group found to be more effective than those made individually in private (Epton et al., 2017). Another intervention strategy is self-monitoring, which is supposed to act when self-control conflicts arise. Self-monitoring is when people are trained and encouraged to intentionally and consistently observe their own behaviours with the aim of minimising any potential adverse consequences of self-control conflicts. Self-monitoring interventions have proven particularly effective in weight loss trials. Like goal-setting interventions, self-monitoring interventions exert a small-to-medium effect on behaviour change and seem to be more impactful when the monitoring is done publicly and when it's physically recorded (see Harkin et al., 2016).

More recent approaches aim to modify people's momentary temptations (desire) by either reducing the appeal of the momentary temptations (e.g., through evaluative conditioning, avoidance training, or attentional bias modification) or teaching people how to regulate their desires and cravings (e.g., via distraction, mindfulness, or acceptance-based interventions). Interventions aiming to reduce the appeal of momentary temptations have been tested mainly in laboratory settings and often without actual behavioural outcomes, since training in such types of interventions occurs mainly via computer-mediated tasks (Moran et al., 2023). More research into the effectiveness of such tasks to change behaviour is therefore needed. Finally, interventions that teach people how to regulate their desires have been found to be successful at modifying mental health-related behaviour. More recently, they have also shown some success in field studies beyond mental health, but further research regarding their efficacy for varied behavioural outcomes beyond mental health is still needed (Ruffault et al., 2017).

11.4.6 Reflective-Impulsive Model (RIM)

The Reflective-Impulsive Model (RIM) (Strack & Deutsch, 2004) is an integrative theory that proposes that behaviour and behaviour change arise from two broad systems of information processing: the reflective and the impulsive system. The RIM is based on earlier dual-model theorising (Fazio, 1986; Petty & Cacioppo, 1986). However, it goes beyond those models to explicitly delineate how behaviour and behaviour change are enacted by the interplay between the reflective and impulsive systems. The basics of **dual-models of information processing** have been described in greater detail in Chapters 5 and 6, so if you need a refresher of these concepts, do have another look at the seminal models described in these chapters.

> **Key concept – Dual-models of information processing:** Models that propose that we use two different modes of processing: an impulsive and a reflective system. System 1 (impulsive) is thought to be fast and intuitive, relying on automatic responses, while System 2 (reflective) is considered slower and analytical, requiring conscious effort for decision-making and behaviour enactment.

According to the RIM, behaviour may be enacted based on reflective (sometimes referred to as conscious) processing, which is thought to be based on deliberation and careful weighing of the available stimuli and information relevant for the decision task at hand. Alternatively, behaviour may be enacted based on the impulsive (non-conscious) system, which is thought to operate automatically and is fast, efficient, and not dependent on intentions. The reflective and impulsive systems are believed to operate in parallel, with the impulsive system thought to be activated always, while this is not the case for the reflective system. The reflective system is thought to require a great deal of cognitive capacity, whereas the impulsive system is not affected by disturbances of cognitive capacity, enabling it to become the default system in decision-making and behavioural enactment. The reflective system can draw inferences, which the impulsive system cannot. Such reasoning reserved for the reflective system is also implicated in behavioural decision-making, which leads to behavioural intentions (a concept with which we are already familiar from the earlier social cognitive theories we discussed above). The impulsive system is comprised of behavioural schemata that are defined as memory representations of situations, behaviours, and behavioural outcomes that are linked, based on past, frequent co-occurrence. For instance, smelling and seeing a loaf of bread in the oven would be associatively connected with eating the bread and feeling satiated due to the frequent co-occurrence of these representations. Behavioural schemata can be likened to habit-like structures (we will look at habits in the next subsection).

In terms of interventions evaluating the impact of tenets of RIM on behaviour change, many of the approaches have used evaluative conditioning, a technique discussed previously within Integrative Self-control Theory. While evaluative conditioning has been shown to be effective at changing evaluative associations, there is currently limited evidence that evaluative conditioning can change actual behaviours (for a recent meta-analysis, see

Aulbach et al., 2019). Another type of intervention used to test the RIM is approach/avoidance training, which has found mixed results in terms of behaviour change (see the review by Loijen et al., 2020).

11.4.7 Habit Theory

> **Key concept – Habit and habitual behaviour:** A habit is a behaviour that is done often and regularly, mostly without our full awareness. Habitual behaviour often occurs when we encounter a relevant contextual cue that triggers the behavioural response stored in memory.

The turn of the 21st century saw a renaissance in research and theorising surrounding the concept of **habits and habitual behaviours**. These concepts are not new and have certainly held interest for psychologists since long before the 21st century. William James, the forefather of psychology, was a great proponent of habit research and considered habits as important explanatory blocks in considerations of human behaviour and behaviour change (see James, 1890). Lay definitions consider habits as frequent, persistent, or customary behaviours. In psychology, this definition is made more precise by including details on the mechanisms by which habitual behaviours acquire their enduring persistence. Thus, habits are defined as behaviours that are prompted automatically when encountering relevant contextual cues based on learned cue–behaviour associations (see Wood & Neal, 2009).

Habit theory proposes that cue–behaviour memory associations are formed when there is a history of behavioural repetition in a consistent cue context. Going forwards this cue–behaviour memory association becomes activated whenever we encounter the contextual cue (Orbell & Verplanken, 2010). Habit cues can be varied and can include physical location (e.g., in the bathroom), previous behaviour in a scripted sequence (e.g., putting the jacket on), completion of a prior behaviour (e.g., arrival home from work), and so on. For example, if I always take my daily vitamin supplements after dinner, this will form a cue–behaviour memory association, whereby, upon finishing dinner, I will be automatically cued to reach for my vitamin supplements. The context-dependence of habits has been illustrated in work showing habit disruptions when people move house, for example (see Verplanken & Roy, 2016). In an elegant illustration of the habit-disruption hypothesis, those people who recently moved house were more likely to change their sustainable behaviours (e.g., reducing water, gas, and electricity usage, walking or cycling to work) following a sustainability intervention when compared to those who did not move house recently.

Once habits are established, habitual behaviour does not depend on momentary goals or motivational states. Just think about it: how often have you continued eating crisps even after feeling full, or how often have you continued watching the movie even after losing interest in it? These behavioural actions speak to the momentary goal-independent nature of habits. This notion was elegantly demonstrated in an experimental study by Neal and colleagues (2011), who gave either fresh or stale popcorn (experimentally inducing goals/motivation via changing the reward value of the popcorn) to participants either in a popcorn-eating cue context (cinema) or a non-popcorn-eating context (meeting room). While participants purportedly rated different movie clips, their popcorn consumption was tracked. The cinema contextual cue mattered only to those participants with strong popcorn-consumption habits, whereby they ate equal quantities of the fresh and stale popcorn when in the cinema. However, in the meeting room (non-popcorn-eating context), this effect was not apparent. In that context, both those with strong and weak popcorn-consumption habits consumed larger quantities of the fresh popcorn (see Figure 11.2). These results serve to demonstrate that habit was only cued in the relevant context (cinema), where it was independent of the reward value (freshness) of the popcorn.

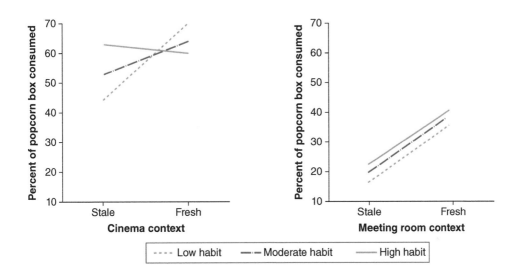

Figure 11.2 Percentage of popcorn eaten in (a) cinema and (b) meeting room context among participants with different levels of pre-existing popcorn-consumption habits

Source: Neal et al. (2011)

However, it is important to note that goals and motivational states, while not important in the enactment of habitual behaviours, may still be important in the earlier stages of habit formation. Thus, habitual behaviours, even though independent of momentary goals, may still serve higher-order motivational goals which lead to the formation of the habit in the first place. For more information on the interplay between goals and habitual behaviours, see Chapter 5 on social cognition.

> **Video:** Why we fail and how we stand up afterwards by Katherine Milkman [TEDx Talk] www.youtube.com/watch?v=zaf3yQ4OLdw

A final important feature of habitual behaviour is that it is automatically activated upon encountering the relevant contextual cue. It therefore doesn't require conscious deliberation or reflective processing, freeing up cognitive space for other tasks. This feature of automaticity is particularly useful for many behaviours that need to be carried out daily, such as brushing teeth, putting on clothes, driving, and so on. This is also the feature that has revived interest in habit formation and maintenance, leading many researchers to propose that habit interventions may be suitable for long-term positive behaviour change at the population-level. The behaviour change interventions that are inspired by habit theory most often examine the impact of interrupting the cue–behaviour links that lead to negative behaviours, and strengthening the cue–behaviour links that help a new habit to form that is beneficial for the person (see Verplanken & Orbell, 2022).

11.4.8 Other Theoretical Perspectives on Behaviour Change

More recently, some other theoretical perspectives on behaviour change have come to prominence. That is not to say that these theories or models are new, but that there has been a recent revival and a surge of interest in these types of perspectives. One of these theoretical perspectives is the use of social identity theory (SIT) (Tajfel & Turner, 1979) to explain how groups exert influence on people's behaviours and, even more interestingly, how our understanding of group and intergroup processes can be leveraged to design more effective behaviour change interventions. Encouragingly, these recent intervention studies have revealed that harnessing the power of people's group memberships and their identification with various groups can have profound effects on improving health and well-being (Jetten et al., 2012). We learnt in detail about the SIT and the novel interventions arising from tenets of this theory, such as Groups4Health, in Chapters 8 and 10, so if you would like a refresher on these topics go back to these chapters.

Another perspective that has gained renewed interest recently is the use of ecological models to explain and change behaviour. Ecological models propose that factors at multiple levels affect human behaviour. Therefore, to devise more effective behaviour change interventions we need to consider the complex interplay between individual, social, and environmental levels. For example, our decisions about whether to reduce our use of fossil fuels in the home and for transportation will depend on our individual values, beliefs, and goals, but also on the social norms exhibited by people in our social circles, the set-up of our environments (i.e., whether using alternative fuels is easy or difficult, e.g., whether heating the home with alternative fuel is possible and viable), as well as any relevant local policies or government mandates and laws.

These ideas are not new and can be traced back to early theorising by Kurt Lewin, one of the forefathers of social psychology, who is also widely regarded as the founder of ecological psychology. Ecological psychology began in 1936, when Lewin wrote about the importance of person–environment interactions in understanding human behaviour. Lewin was an early proponent of the idea that to understand human behaviour we have to dispense with the idea that the person and the environment are independent variables (Lewin, 1936). These early ideas were developed by Barker (1968), who conducted real-world studies in a Midwest town in the USA, observing how children's behaviours changed when they changed their environments (e.g., from school to a social club to the home setting, and so on). Based on these field observations, Barker argued that it is impossible to predict human behaviour without knowing the environmental setting or situation that the person is in.

KEY THINKER

Kurt Lewin

Kurt Lewin is considered as one of the fathers of modern social psychology. His research and theorising have contributed to a diverse set of domains that interest social psychologists, including leadership, group dynamics, and experiential learning. However, one area that is most closely associated with Lewin is his development of Field Theory (Lewin, 1951). Field Theory took tenets of Lewin's earlier theorising to propose that behaviour (B) is a function (f) of the state of the environment (E) and that of the person (P), as expressed in Lewin's now famous formula B = f(PE) (see Lewin, 1936). In Field Theory, he expanded on these ideas to suggest that behaviours arise from a person's psychological field (the sum of all forces and influences that can impact a person's behaviour, including situational, cultural, and social influences) and a person's life space (the person's

Source: © https://snl.no/Kurt_Lewin

unique construal of their feelings, thoughts, perceptions, goals, and experiences). Lewin is also recognised for the value he placed on applied work and field experimentation in real-world settings. He founded and directed the Research Center for Group Dynamics at the Massachusetts Institute of Technology (MIT), and as part of his centre he devised the 'change experiment' (more commonly known as sensitivity training) for intervening to counteract racial and religious prejudice. After his untimely passing at the age of 57, his legacy continued with his prominent students and mentees: Leon Festinger (see also Chapter 2), Roger Barker, Bluma Zeigarnik, and Morton Deutsch.

Ecological models have found the greatest application in health behaviour change. Reviews of this body of research show that most of the evidence to date has focused on one or two aspects of the model, favouring the personal aspect of ecological models (Golden & Earp, 2012). This illustrates a common bias in research on behaviour change, which often focuses on the individual as being more important in behaviour enactment, and this bias even extends to ecological models of behaviour change. Of course, some of this bias may stem from the inherent complexity in testing behaviour change interventions at multiple levels of influence (intrapersonal, interpersonal, organisational, community, and public policy).

On the other hand, the bias in focusing on individual-level behaviour change interventions, even among ecological models, may also arise from a classic finding in social psychology about the fundamental attribution error (FAE). The fundamental attribution error describes a common phenomenon whereby we tend to attribute others' behaviours to internal (underlying) causes rather than external, contextual factors in one's environments (see Jones & Harris, 1967). Therefore, the fundamental attribution error may explain why most behaviour change interventions have historically focused on changing behaviour at individual-level, with less of an emphasis on changing environmental and contextual factors. A good example of a successful implementation of the ecological model is interventions to stop smoking, which have been enacted at various levels of the ecological model since the 1960s when the adverse impacts of tobacco smoking became public knowledge.

11.5 PART 2: ADVANCES

The Foundations part of this chapter provided a discussion of the dominant behaviour change theories that have guided work in this area since the first publications on this topic at the end of the 19th century. While the seminal theories of behaviour change that we have discussed were developed by social psychologists, later theorising and applications of these theories have been done by large interdisciplinary teams made up of researchers working in diverse fields, such as psychology, economics, sociology, anthropology, law, computer science, and similar. In line with these developments in the field of behaviour change, in the Advances section we are going to turn our attention to a recently popularised framework of behaviour change, commonly known as 'nudge' or 'choice architecture'. We will discuss the tenets of nudge and its associated issues, including the research methods popularised by this framework and the ethical issues that are often invoked in relation to nudge interventions. We will then discuss some novel frameworks that have synthesised individual behaviour change theories and taxonomies of behaviour change interventions. We will finish the Advances section by looking at the future of behaviour change research and practice.

11.5.1 Nudge

You have probably heard about **nudge** (or **choice architecture**), and have witnessed some of the heated debates surrounding the potential ramifications of being nudged into a certain behavioural course of action. Nudge came to prominence with the publication in 2008 of the popular book, *Nudge: Improving Decisions about Health, Wealth, and Happiness* by Richard Thaler and Cass Sunstein. The book brought to the attention of the public and policy-makers a plethora of research showing the profound impact that unobtrusive cues in our environments have on our behaviours. Some

> **Key concept – Nudge or choice architecture:** An approach to behaviour change that is based on modifying people's environments to encourage a certain behaviour without constraining other response options.

iconic examples of such interventions discussed in the book are the houseflies drawn in the urinals of Schiphol Airport to improve hygiene, the chevrons painted on streets giving the illusion of speed in order to slow down drivers, and the musical-notes stairs in Sweden that were painted to encourage people to walk rather than take the lift. In the words of Thaler and Sunstein (2008, p. 6): 'Nudge is any aspect of the choice architecture that alters people's behaviour in a predictable way *without forbidding* any options *or significantly changing their economic incentives*' (emphasis added). Later discussions of nudge have also added that they are behaviour change techniques that are designed to guide people to make better choices (with the people themselves judging whether these choices are indeed better) (see Sunstein, 2016). With their emphasis on modifying people's environments or choice architecture, nudge techniques are regarded as **population-level interventions for behaviour change** rather than individual-level interventions.

> **Key concept – Population-level interventions for behaviour change:** Interventions that are aimed at communities or populations rather than being focused on individuals only.

KEY STUDY 11.1

Auto-enrolment in Pension Plans

A great example illustrating the power of nudge is to look at how changing the default options in pension plan enrolment can increase the number of people holding pension plans. In a study that has been cited over 4,000 times to date, Madrian and Shea (2001) showed that changing the default from opt-in (where workers need to self-enrol in a pension plan when they join an organisation) to opt-out (where workers are automatically enrolled into a pension plan upon joining an organisation, but they have the option to opt-out if they so wish) drastically increases the percentage of people who are enrolled in a pension plan. In this experiment, 86% of those who joined a US organisation after an opt-out mandate was brought in for pension auto-enrolment chose to keep their pension plan, compared to 49% of those who were hired during an opt-in mandate. These findings were recently used by the UK government to change the default policy regarding pension savings for workers in the UK, with the opt-out option being mandated across UK organisations. It has resulted in more people than ever having a pension plan.

The Origins of Nudge

Even though the popularity of nudging in the public domain is recent, the research and ideas covered in Thaler and Sunstein's (2008) book are based on a century of empirical work in psychology and economics. Although often referred to as a theory, nudge is much wider, and is more appropriately thought of as a framework of behaviour change. At its most basic, nudge or choice architecture approaches to behaviour change depart from traditional social-cognitive models of behaviour change (e.g., TPB, TRA, SCT, and Social Learning Theory) and are rooted in dual-process models of judgement and decision-making (similarly to Integrative Self-Control Theory, RIM, and habit theory). Nudge or choice architecture approaches harness the power of non-conscious (automatic) processes in behaviour enactment and behaviour change.

The experimental origins of nudge can be traced to the 1970s when two young psychologists, Daniel Kahneman and Amos Tversky, started conducting experiments to test the dominant hypothesis at the time that humans are rational utility maximisers who aim to arrive at the most rational behavioural choice when faced with daily decision-making tasks (Tversky & Kahneman, 1974). Unexpectedly and counter to contemporary wisdom at the time, their experiments showed that participants most often relied on shortcuts to make their decisions rather than carefully weighing up all alternatives, as proposed by the rational models of human behaviour favoured at the time. Kahneman and Tversky's now iconic experiments showed that people's attention is captured by easily accessible or available information at the point of making a behavioural decision. For example, the availability heuristic originally examined by Kahneman and Tversky has more recently been used to study instances of increased use of car travel in the wake of the 9/11 terrorist attacks. The salience of the attack led to significant reductions in air travel and associated increases in car travel, despite factual evidence that more injuries and deaths occur when travelling by car (Kunreuther, 2002). In addition to being the first researchers to examine and describe seminal heuristics, such as the availability, recency, and status quo bias (for more details on heuristics and biases see Chapter 5), Kahneman and Tversky were also the first to demonstrate the phenomenon of loss aversion, showing that considerations of losses are more impactful than considerations of gains when people make decisions in what actions and behaviours to engage in (Kahneman & Tversky, 1979). Loss aversion has, for example, been used to study people's unwillingness to purchase insurance despite living in areas of known catastrophe risk, such as California and Florida (Kunreuther & Pauly, 2006).

For this paradigm-shifting work, Daniel Kahneman won the Nobel Prize in Economics in 2002. His long-term collaborator, Amos Tversky, would have also been recognised with the prize, but Nobel Prizes are not awarded posthumously. You will have noticed that Kahneman won the Nobel prize in Economics despite being a psychologist. There is a simple reason for this – a Nobel prize in Psychology does not exist.

The seminal experiments by Kahneman and Tversky inspired a young economist by the name of Richard Thaler when all three of them were on a sabbatical at Stanford University in 1977–1978. Thaler adopted many of the learnings from Kahneman and Tversky's experiments, which were going against the mainstream economic theory of humans as rational agents. The collaborative work between Kahneman, Tversky, and Thaler is largely credited as the birth of Behavioural Economics, a new field of economics in which humans are considered to be fallible and under the influence of heuristics when making their judgements and decisions (see also Chapter 5). For his contributions to founding the field of Behavioural Economics, Richard Thaler received the Nobel Prize in Economics in 2017.

The impact of the work by Kahneman, Tversky, and Thaler has been far reaching, spurring on applied intervention field research in underdeveloped countries, especially among poorer communities. Taking into account the cognitive biases and heuristics that are often part and parcel of decision-making, behavioural scientists have developed interventions that target people's capacity to make decisions. For example, research has shown that people who are put under financial strain are also more likely to exhibit a strain in cognitive resources (e.g., depressed scores on a multitude of IQ tests) (see Mani et al., 2013; Shah et al., 2012).

For example, Mani and colleagues (2013) found that most sugar cane farmers in India, who rely on receiving most of their income once a year during harvest time, exhibited financial strain just before harvest time, with 88% of them pawning their belongings and 99% of them having some type of loan. This period also coincided with the farmers scoring on average 10 IQ points lower than when tested after harvest. To address the impact of such 'cognitive taxes', researchers have devised interventions to ease the cognitive burden on decision-makers. For example, in a study among farmers in rural Kenya who rely on harvest income for their livelihoods, farmers who were offered free home delivery of fertiliser just after harvest, when their finances are healthier, are more likely to buy fertiliser than if this offer is made when the fertiliser season is in full swing and their finances and cognitive deliberations are under strain (see Duflo et al., 2011). Insights from such applied field experiments have been recognised with the awarding of another Nobel Prize to Abhijit Banerjee, Esther Duflo, and Michael Kremer in 2019.

But what you are probably most familiar with is the widespread interest that was garnered by the publication of the popular book *Nudge* (Thaler & Sunstein, 2008) as mentioned above, which paved the way for the nudge (choice architecture) approach to permeate policy-making. Governments across the world became interested in the potential of using nudge interventions due to their purported simplicity, cost-effectiveness, and ability to harness knowledge of human decision-making with the aim of bettering societal outcomes. The British coalition government of 2010, led by Conservative Prime Minister David Cameron, was the first to examine nudge interventions, a move facilitated by the foundation of the Behavioural Insights Team (BIT) that at first sat within the Cabinet Office. Later nudge units followed across the world, including one in President Obama's administration, The White House Office of Information and Regulatory Affairs (OIRA) led by Cass Sunstein.

> **Video:** Saving Money and Saving Lives by Cass Sunstein [TEDx Talk] www.youtube.com/ watch?v=hmghRSbhSZY

11.5.2 'Sludge'

Think back to how easy or difficult it was for you to complete and file the forms for your student loans. Did you have to fill out multiple forms and read multiple instruction sheets accompanying these forms, and did you have to obtain various supporting documentation before you could file your forms? The time-consuming process and friction you may have experienced while completing these forms is an example of a 'sludge'. Sludge is a relatively new term that has been used to describe interventions that influence people's behaviours and make people worse off (as judged by themselves) (see Newall, 2023; Thaler, 2018). Sludge is an extension of what has sometimes been referred to as a 'dark nudge', to differentiate the popularised instances of government behavioural experts nudging people for the good, to those that private organisations may engage in and which do not always have better outcomes for the population as their goal. Thus, Ponzi schemes and the way gambling websites are designed would fall into this category of sludge interventions. While at present in the public domain we know much less about sludge than nudge interventions, research in this area will be important for moving forward our understanding of how nudges, and other interventions that intend to change behaviour by changing people's environments, exert their effects.

KEY STUDY 11.2

Fighting Against Sludge by Simplifying Procedures

One way in which researchers interested in behaviour change have tried to counteract frictional sludges is by simplifying procedures. Devoto and colleagues (2012) conducted a field randomised controlled trial in Morocco, testing an intervention that aimed to increase the uptake of piped water to low-income households. The water provider company had a specialised programme targeting low-income households but found that existing procedures were too burdensome (producing 'sludge') because they asked householders to fill out complex forms, provide a certified copy of their identification document, and file all these documents at a considerable distance from where they were residing. So the research team designed an intervention to counteract these contextual frictions by simplifying the forms, sending a member of the team to help people with filling out the form in their homes, verifying householders' identification by taking a photo of their ID during the home visit, and filing the application on their behalf, meaning that householders did not have to travel far away and could apply for getting piped water from the grid from the convenience of their own home. In the control group, householders could also apply for the same type of interest-free credit to obtain piped water, but in their case, they had to engage in the existing burdensome process of filing the forms without any assistance or simplification. After six months of the intervention, 69% of households that received the intervention had water piped directly to their homes, whereas only 10% of households in the control group were connected to the grid. This study reflects the great impact that simplifying interventions can have in counteracting sludge frictions in important behaviour change domains, such as direct access to clean water.

11.5.3 Randomised Controlled Trials (RCTs)

The cornerstone of behaviour change intervention evaluation is the **randomised controlled trial (RCT)**. RCTs are a subset of randomised experiments that boast stringent protocols for sample identification, randomisation, intervention roll-out, fidelity checks, and analysis plans. They were first popularised in clinical medicine, where the efficacy of a particular drug, com-

pared to a placebo, was commonly tested via RCTs. Experimental methods (see Chapter 1) have always been the preferred choice for testing the effectiveness of social psychological interventions, but more recently, with the rise of evidence-based policy-making and interest in what behavioural science can contribute to intervention development, the RCT, with its stringent protocols, has become the method of choice for those wishing to test the efficacy of different behaviour change interventions (Figure 11.3).

A good example of a successful use of RCT methodology for evaluating the efficacy of behaviour change interventions is that of the efficacy tests of the 'Scared

> **Key concept – Randomised controlled trials (RCTs):** A subset of randomised experiments that boast stringent protocols for sample identification, randomisation, intervention roll-out, fidelity checks, and analysis plans. The cornerstone of RCTs is the purely random allocation of participants into the intervention or control group, thus minimising the potential impacts of any extraneous variables that may confound the conclusions that can be drawn from the study.

Straight Programme'. This programme was developed in the USA with the aim of deterring juvenile delinquents and at-risk children from engaging in criminal behaviours.

Figure 11.3 Pyramid depicting the hierarchy of scientific evidence of different research methods. The top of the pyramid depicts research methods providing the highest quality of evidence combined with the lowest risk of bias

Source: https://www.sciencedirect.com/science/article/pii/S0002916522047554?via%3Dihubhttps:// www.sciencedirect.com/science/article/pii/S0002916522047554?via%3Dihub

The programme introduced at-risk children to serious criminals in custody, hypothesising that this would make it more tangible for them to understand the negative consequences of engaging in crime. Early observational studies purported to find an encouraging effect in reducing delinquency and crime, which also led to the roll-out of this programme in other countries. However, years later, when several RCTs were conducted testing the effectiveness of 'Scared Straight', the trials showed that the intervention programme was not just unsuccessful, in fact it had the opposite effect, and the children who were exposed to the programme were more likely to engage in crime (Petrosino et al., 2005).

RCTs in behavioural research have become more popular with the growing use of behavioural insights for addressing public policy problems. The Behavioural Insights Team (BIT), which came into existence during the Coalition government in 2010, was an early proponent of using the RCT methods for evidence-based policy-making. The BIT argued that behavioural interventions for public policy are particularly suited for this method of enquiry since relevant data on the public's adoption of different policies is already being collected routinely by public bodies (e.g., the National Health Service, Tax office, and so on), and that the RCT method can be adapted to be cheap and not too complex. A good example is one of the earlier RCTs conducted by the BIT on behalf of the HM Revenue and Customs (HMRC), a government department that wanted to increase levels of tax collection. The behaviour change intervention involved adding a simple social norm message (see Chapter 7 for social norms) to the usual letter sent to people who owed tax to the HMRC. The BIT sent people either the standard letter that was used before without mentioning social norms, or a letter containing different social norm messages. The letters with the social norm information said: '9 out of 10 people in Britain pay their tax on time.' In another of the RCT groups, people received letters that also said that most people in the recipient's local area, or postcode, had already paid their overdue taxes. The RCT showed that social norms were effective at increasing the proportion of those who paid their overdue taxes. This was particularly pronounced when the letters contained information about the local social norms of the recipients (see Behavioural Insights Team, 2012).

GUEST PERSONAL JOURNEY

Elizabeth Evans

After my undergraduate psychology degree, I was sure of one thing – no more studying. I wanted a reliable salary in a graduate job! But 18 months later I contacted a prospective PhD supervisor ... just in case. I have always wondered how eating-related problems develop: only research could satisfy my curiosity. I was lucky to obtain Master's and PhD funding to investigate (at Durham University) the development of children's problems with eating and body image. But then came crunch time: finding my first post-doctoral job! By this point I had two children and was tied to North-East England. Was an academic career possible without international moves? Fortunately, I lived close to good universities with brilliant health psychology teams. In my first research posts, I jumped headlong into a new research area: developing interventions to improve dietary and physical activity behaviours, which were evaluated in randomised controlled trials (RCTs) to see if they worked. It was such a learning curve – but it felt wonderful to put science to work, solving problems that other researchers merely described. Of course, with a few years' experience I learned that both activities are reciprocally informative: we should not intervene to change a behaviour we don't

Source: © Elizabeth Evans

understand, but mere understanding doesn't change things. Permanent jobs (and two more children) followed. With full control of my research agenda at last, I now combine my initial interest in understanding eating-related problems with my intervention evaluation skills to try to prevent problems with eating and body image developing in a diverse range of people and places.

11.5.4 The Ethics of Nudge

As much as nudge techniques enthused the public after the publication of Thaler and Sunstein's (2008) book, they also provoked fierce debates about the ethics of using nudge interventions. The principal arguments made against nudge or choice architecture interventions of behaviour change are that they undermine individual agency and autonomy, and may therefore be thought of as manipulative. Individual agency is defined as the control we have over our behaviours and actions, while autonomy is defined as the capacity to make an informed, uncoerced decision or choice. From the outset, nudge critics have been concerned that the central tenet of nudge interventions is reliant on non-conscious processes for decision-making. If nudge harnesses the power of non-conscious, automatic processes and doesn't rely on reflective processes, then critics have pointed out that nudge interventions may be manipulative and undermine people's individual agency and autonomy (for more detailed discussions, see Bovens, 2009; Osman, 2016).

A point in favour of nudging is that choice architecture is inevitable (for a detailed discussion, see Sunstein, 2015). Our external environments and the contexts in which we make decisions about our behaviours are always designed by some choice architect or another. This happens without us being fully aware of the decisions that went into designing our environments or 'choice architecture'. According to Sunstein and other supporters of nudge, then, it would be better for our environments to be designed by a benevolent choice architect, rather than a choice architect that has 'sludge' in mind. This argument to a certain extent alleviates some of the manipulatory concerns raised about nudge.

A good example of this inevitability can be found in how our supermarkets or cafeterias are arranged or organised. The products on offer must be displayed somehow, and for this there are 'choice architects' who decide where different products are positioned. In this case, the choice architects are the supermarket and cafeteria managers, as well as the managers within the larger organisational structures. Invariably, these choice architects display sweets at counter checkouts at children's eye-levels. These kinds of arrangements are based on our knowledge of the saliency of stimuli in our external environments and how to capture attention most successfully. The supermarkets and cafeteria choice architects therefore arrange the environments to harness this knowledge with the aim of boosting shareholders' profits. Thus, in Sunstein's (2015) argument, since our environments are designed by choice architects, it is best if choice architecture decisions are governed by certain principles and by a benevolent body, such as, for example, our governments, which should prioritise choices that will benefit individual members of the public and the collective social good.

Another argument in favour of nudging is that not all nudges work along the same principles, and therefore they may not present the same ethical objections regarding autonomy and individual agency. Since the first publication of the book *Nudge* (Thaler & Sunstein, 2008), there have been several attempts to differentiate between the different types of nudge interventions. Most scholars distinguish between the informational type of nudges, such as calorie and warning labels, and more intrusive nudges, such as defaults (i.e., interventions which rely on people sticking with pre-set options, such as auto-enrolment in pension plans). Both ethicists and philosophers of science are more in favour of informational nudges, or what is sometimes termed Type 2 nudges (or what we might call softer nudges). Rather than relying fully on automatic processing, as Type 1 nudges do, Type 2 nudges require the engagement of the more reflective parts of our cognitive systems, which implies that issues of agency and autonomy may be less apparent in examples of Type 2 nudges (Lin et al., 2017). Type 2 nudges are therefore different from Type 1 nudges, which require System 1 or automatic processing and decision-making (see Hansen & Jespersen, 2013; Sunstein, 2016).

The dichotomy of the two systems of thinking (conscious [System 2] and non-conscious [System 1]) proposed under dual-process theories is too simplistic of course. We now know that the two systems interact in decision-making and behaviour enactment (Melnikoff & Bargh, 2018). Furthermore, recent integrative reviews of nudge interventions have found that relying on System 1 thinking is not a necessary requirement for nudges to be effective, and that prior preferences matter for the effectiveness of nudges. This lends further support to the idea that rationality and autonomy may not be as important as initially suggested when nudge captured the public's imagination (De Ridder et al., 2022).

11.5.5 Behaviour Change Taxonomies

In the past decade, the behaviour change research community has made ongoing calls for better integration and understanding of how various theories of behaviour and behaviour change work, as well as how behaviour change interventions use and report tenets of different behaviour change theories. Such calls have resulted in concerted efforts to integrate and better understand the antecedents of behaviour and behaviour change, with the associated benefits for theoretically grounded and evidence-based intervention and policy development. These calls for better integration and specification stem partly from findings that evaluations of behaviour change interventions often do not report in sufficient detail the theoretical basis for the chosen intervention, and do not provide detailed descriptors of what the intervention entails. This is problematic for future replication studies, since researchers from other research groups may not be able to repeat the methods used by the original researchers (see the discussion of Open Science research practices in Chapter 1). It also precludes us from properly synthesising the plethora of available evidence, which in turn affects future development and iteration of theories and models of behaviour change. Understanding the active ingredients in behaviour change interventions is essential to help us move forward the science of behaviour change.

While over the years there have been numerous attempts at categorising and synthesising behaviour change theories and their proposed components, to date those with the widest application among researchers, policy-makers, and practitiones in the field of behaviour change are the COM-B model, as part of the Behaviour Change Wheel, the Theoretical Domains Framework (TDF), and the Behaviour Change Technique Taxonomy (BCCT) v1, all of which were developed by Susan Michie and colleagues.

The Behaviour Change Wheel (BCW) (Michie et al., 2011) brings together 19 existing frameworks of behaviour change identified via a systematic literature review. The BCW is presented as a multi-layered wheel, with the central layer containing the COM-B model delineating the main components of behaviour change: capability (C), opportunity (O), and motivation (M). These elements interact to affect behaviour (B) and are in turn hypothesised to be affected by the behaviour. Capability in the COM-B is defined as the individual's psychological and physical capacity to engage in a given behaviour (including the necessary knowledge and skills). Motivation is defined as all the brain processes that energise and direct behaviour, be it reflective or automatic. Motivation thus also includes habitual processes, emotional responding, and goal-directed or more analytical decision-making. The definition of opportunity includes all the factors that are external to the individual that make the behaviour possible or prompt it. The interactions between the different components of the COM-B model that are central to the Behaviour Change Wheel are graphically presented in Figure 11.4.

The second layer of the wheel beyond the COM-B contains nine different intervention functions that were gleaned from a systematic review of 19 existing behaviour change frameworks (e.g., education, persuasion, coercion, and so on). Intervention functions describe the myriad different functions that a behaviour change intervention can have. For example, a single intervention can have more than one function. A brief, doctor-led intervention to increase uptake rates of cervical screening, for example, can be made up of both education and persuasion functions. The outer layer of the wheel is made up of seven potential policy categories, such as guidelines, communications/marketing, legislation, and so on. The Behaviour Change Wheel then allows for differentiation between interventions (activities aimed at changing behaviours) and policies (actions performed by responsible authorities to support or facilitate interventions). Figure 11.5 shows the Behaviour Change Wheel.

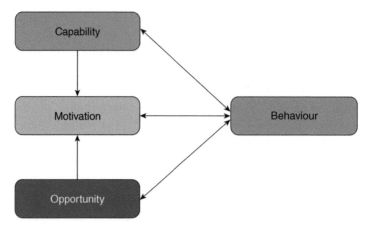

Figure 11.4 Graphical representation of the COM-B model proposed within the Behaviour Change Wheel by Susan Michie and colleagues (2011)

Source: Michie et al. (2011)

> **Video:** A 15-minute introduction to the Behaviour Change Wheel by Robert West
> www.youtube.com/watch?v=itp7Qo6L5Pc

The Behaviour Change Wheel and the COM-B model have been used to decide on the target behaviour which needs to be modified via an intervention. The choice and design of a suitable intervention is made after considering the intervention functions that are likely to be most effective at bringing about a change in the target behaviour. The intervention choice is then informed by and influences the likely policy categories that can be used to impact the target behaviour.

For the more successful development of behaviour change interventions and their implementation in practice, Michie and colleagues developed a Theoretical Domains Framework (TDF) (Cane, O'Connor, & Michie, 2012). The TDF integrates a multitude of behaviour change theories into a single framework consisting of 14 domains and 84 constructs relevant to behaviour change. Based on a COM-B analysis undertaken beforehand, researchers use the Behaviour Change Wheel and the COM-B model in conjunction with the TDF to decide on the most appropriate theoretical domains to target their intervention (see Table 11.1).

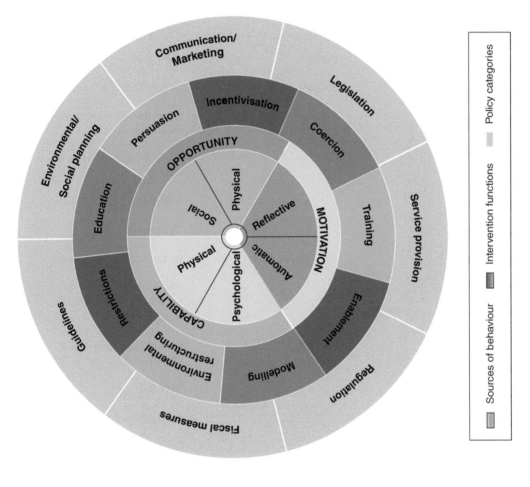

Figure 11.5 The Behaviour Change Wheel, with the COM-B model presented in the centre

Source: Michie et al. (2012)

Table 11.1 Mapping of the Behaviour Change Wheel's COM-B system to the TDF domains

COM-B component		TDF domain
Capability	Psychological	Knowledge
		Skills
		Memory, Attention and Decision Processes
		Behavioural Regulation
	Physical	Skills
Opportunity	Social	Social Influences
	Physical	Environmental Context and Resources
Motivation	Reflective	Social/Professional Role & Identity
		Beliefs about Capabilities
		Optimism
		Beliefs about Consequences
		Intentions
		Goals
	Automatic	Social/Professional Role & Identity
		Optimism
		Reinforcement
		Emotion

Source: Cane et al. (2012)

Once researchers and practitioners arrive at the most appropriate theoretical and behavioural factors needed to affect behaviour change for the target behaviour, they turn to deciding how best to devise their intervention. The Behaviour Change Techniques Taxonomy (BCCT v1) is a recently devised tool that provides a hierarchically structured taxonomy of behaviour change techniques (BCTs) used in behaviour change interventions (see Michie et al., 2013). A behaviour change technique (BCT) is the smallest observable and replicable part of a behaviour change intervention that, on its own, has the potential to bring about behaviour change. The Behaviour Change Techniques Taxonomy (BCCT v1) summarised 93 BCTs clustered within 16 higher-order categories.

The best way to illustrate how these integrative tools can be used for developing and implementing behaviour change interventions is to demonstrate it with an example study. In a recent study, we used the COM-B model and the TDF to devise a more effective intervention to increase Portuguese GPs' screening for harmful levels of alcohol use among their patients (Rosário et al., 2022). We identified several BCTs to be used in our training and environment-restructuring intervention to reduce any potential barriers to patient screening. For example, the barrier 'lack of knowledge and skills' among GPs (COM-B component: Capability; TDF domain: Knowledge and Skills) was addressed with the BCTs 'behaviour practice/rehearsal', 'demonstration of the behaviour', 'habit formation', 'information about health consequences', 'information about social and environmental consequences', and 'instruction on how to perform a behaviour'. These BCTs were part of our bespoke training, which was delivered to those GPs who had been randomly selected to receive the intervention. To address the barriers 'lack of time', 'lack of support', and 'lack of screening and counselling materials' (COM-B component: Opportunity; TDF domain: Environmental Context/Resources), we used the following BCTs: 'adding objects to the environment', 'imaginary reward', 'pros and cons', 'restructuring the social environment', 'social support', and 'verbal persuasion about Capability'. These BCTs were incorporated in our posters and leaflets, which were designed to help GPs and their practice staff to remember to deliver alcohol screening to their patients. As a result of this theory-driven behaviour change intervention, we found that the GP practices that were part of the intervention group were 136 times more likely to screen for hazardous alcohol consumption when compared to control practices that did not receive this intervention.

EXERCISE 11.2

Human Behaviour Change Project (HBCP)

Access the Human Behaviour Change Project (HBCP) via the following link: www.humanbehaviourchange.org/ Use the resources provided to tackle a behaviour change challenge of your choosing. You can train yourself on how to use the BCTT v1 and examine the current strength of evidence regarding various behaviour change techniques and their associated mechanisms of action. You can also investigate how the behaviour change challenge you have chosen is presented within the emerging Behaviour Change Intervention Ontology (BCIO).

Integrative tools such as the BCW, COM-B, TDF, and BCCT v1 have been important catalysts in advancing a more unified science of behaviour change. Such tools have made it possible for behaviour change researchers to start using shared concepts and ground the development of behaviour change interventions more firmly in theories and existing evidence of behaviour change. These and similar tools are crucial for helping us to devise and implement theoretically grounded behaviour change interventions, enhance the replicability of behaviour change interventions in the future, and improve the reporting of behaviour change interventions. This in turn will help us to synthesise evidence in systematic reviews which will iteratively feed into the further development and innovation of theories of behaviour change.

11.5.6 The Future of Behaviour Change: Where do we Go from Here?

Now that we have considered the different theories and models proposed to understand behaviour change, and have discussed the latest developments (including integrative frameworks of behaviour change), it is time to take stock and reflect on where we go from here. You will have gathered throughout this and the previous chapters that individual explanations of behaviour change have dominated research in this interdisciplinary area. Even when theories and models have attempted to incorporate the individual within the wider environmental context, most often our tests of those theories have focused on how we can modify the individual's behaviour (e.g., the training approaches to modify individuals' self-control). Inevitably, this means we have considered the wider context in which the individual operates much less. Some of this evidence is now starting to accumulate through the use of nudge or choice architecture interventions. However, progress in this area overall has been slow. Understanding how individuals and wider environments interactively impact behaviour and behaviour change is still beyond our grasp. The recent revival of ecological frameworks of behaviour change may help us to accomplish this in the future.

Many behaviour change theories do not specify how interventions should be designed and carried out, and there is no agreed nomenclature in the field of behaviour change. Thus, many of the components in behaviour change intervention studies are underspecified and fail to adopt an accepted naming system. This precludes us from learning about how interventions work (i.e., the parts and techniques) and impedes further theory development. The work arising from the use of integrative taxonomies like the Behaviour Change Wheel has started paving the way for a more unified science of behaviour change, but there is still more work to be done. The newly emerging Behaviour Change Ontology (BCIO), which is part of the Human Behaviour Change Project (HBCP), with its interface with artificial intelligence (AI) and machine learning (ML) tools, will further help us in this quest. Tools such as AI and ML are likely to be important not only in our development of a more integrated science of behaviour change, but also in the ways we design, deliver, and evaluate behaviour change interventions.

We also have a poor understanding of the long-term effectiveness of behaviour change interventions based on the theories we have discussed in this chapter. Most interventions have been tested with short follow-ups, sometimes extending to up to a year, but not much beyond. Future tests of behaviour change interventions should be designed to include longer follow-ups to allow us to gauge the effectiveness of such interventions in the long term. Longer-term follow-ups would also help us to extend our knowledge of the mechanisms that are important for the maintenance of behaviours initiated through behaviour change interventions.

More robust tests of the mechanisms of action in behaviour change intervention studies are also needed. At present, we have a poor understanding of why certain interventions work or don't work. Therefore, more concerted efforts to identify mediating and moderating variables of behaviour change interventions will be needed in the future.

11.6 PART 3: APPLICATIONS

In the Foundations part of this chapter, you learnt about the seminal theories of behaviour change which were developed by social psychologists. In the Advances section you learnt about more recent developments in the field of behaviour change, work that has been mostly carried out by large interdisciplinary teams (teams made up of research experts coming from diverse backgrounds, including psychology, economics, sociology, anthropology, political science, law and so on). In the Applications section you will learn about some recent applications in behaviour change carried out by interdisciplinary teams, including the effectiveness of nudge-type interventions, insights into how to increase the acceptability of behaviour change interventions, and leveraging the power of digital technology for behaviour change interventions.

11.6.1 Choice Architecture or Nudge-type Interventions Aimed at Improving Human and Planetary Health

The recent shift in highlighting the importance of the external environment in behaviour change has translated into a flourish of novel interventions aimed at modifying people's environments with the aim of improving human and planetary health. A popular framework categorising the different environmental features and cues that may impact people's behaviours is the typology of interventions in proximal physical micro-environments (TIPPME) (Hollands et al., 2017). The TIPPME categorises six intervention types that alter either the properties or the placement of objects or stimuli in the environment. For example, the presence (*availability*) and location of objects/stimuli within an environment (*position*) can be manipulated. Other types of interventions examine the properties of objects/cues that can be manipulated within a given environment (e.g., *functionality, presentation, size,* and *information*). In this section, we will discuss current evidence regarding the effectiveness and public support for size, availability, and information (labelling) interventions used to tackle health and environmental behaviour change.

Size Interventions

The size of the foods and drinks we consume has increased considerably over the years. For example, in the USA and elsewhere, there is evidence that food portions have steadily grown since the 1970s. This increase exceeds recommended portion guidance by public health

Figure 11.6 Example of wine bottles used in a study by Mantzari and colleagues (2022). Left: 37.5-cl bottle; right: 75-cl bottle

Source: Mantzari et al. (2022)

bodies and coincides with rising levels of obesity at the population level (see Wrieden et al., 2008; Young & Nestle, 2002). A good illustration of these steady increases in portion sizes are the French fries and Cokes sold in McDonalds that have been 'supersized' since the chain's inception in the 1950s. But food and non-alcoholic drink portions are not the only things, that have increased over the years. A recent Christmas edition of the *British Medical Journal* reported an archival analysis of the glassware used for wine consumption. It found that, over the last 300 years, our wine glasses have grown six-times larger, which may be one contributor to the increase in wine consumption at the population level (Zupan et al., 2017).

One proposed intervention of the TIPPME (Hollands et al., 2017) to tackle this issue is to reduce the size of food and drink portions, packaging, and tableware. In a review of the literature, Hollands and colleagues (2015) suggested that such a size-reduction intervention would equate to an approximately 12–16% decrease in average daily energy intake from foods consumed among UK adults. Interestingly, the effect of the size-reduction intervention seems to be more pronounced when foods are self-served rather than pre-served (Holden et al., 2016). These encouraging findings have also been replicated beyond the domain of food consumption. For example, in a study where households were randomised to buy either 50cl or 75cl bottles of wine over two 14-day intervention periods, households drank less and at a slower rate when they bought the smaller 50cl wine bottles (Codling et al., 2020). If you are hoping to reduce your alcohol consumption, remember this finding next time you are in the supermarket: it is worthwhile opting for the smaller wine bottle! Furthermore, the size effect has also been found to be effective in reducing meat consumption while at the same time increasing vegetable consumption, providing benefits for both human and planetary health since meat consumption is a known contributor to climate change (Reinders et al., 2017).

Availability and Proximity Interventions

Changing the availability (the range and/or number of options) of products, or their proximity (i.e., the distance at which they are positioned) to potential consumers, is another intervention covered by the TIPPME. Increasing the proportion of healthier options or positioning the healthier food choices closer to the consumer seem to encourage healthier selections (these findings have been supported by a recent systematic literature review by Hollands et al., 2019). More recently, studies have been conducted in other domains, including meat and alcohol consumption. Increasing the availability of non-meat vegetarian options decreased meat consumption and increased vegetarian-meal consumption by 8–15% in real-world university cafeteria settings (Garnett et al., 2019). Similarly, in a simulated online supermarket coupled with actual online purchasing, Clarke and colleagues (2023) found that increasing the availability of non-alcoholic drinks from 25% to 50% or 75% significantly reduced alcohol selection and purchasing. One of the proposed mechanisms by which availability and proximity interventions work are perceptions of social norms, although work testing social norms as a potential mediating mechanism in these types of studies is still at a very early stage.

Information Interventions

The TIPPME operationalises information interventions by adding, removing, or changing words, symbols, numbers, or pictures that convey information about the product or object or its use (Hollands et al., 2017). Examples of information interventions include calorie labelling on product packaging, health warnings on cigarettes packaging, traffic light nutritional labels, portion claims, and so on.

At its simplest, presenting the calorie content on product packaging labels effectively reduces the total amount of energy people consume. While the actual amount of this reduction differs between reviews, the current evidence points to average reductions of between 27 calories (4.6%) and 47 calories (7.8%) per meal (see Crockett et al., 2018; Zlatevska et al., 2018). These reductions may seem small, but it must be considered that calorie labelling interventions are intended to have a wide reach across the population, as in other interventions that are aimed at modifying people's environments. Furthermore, interventions like calorie labelling often have upstream impacts, such as encouraging industry reformulation, potentially leading to improvements in product healthiness.

One way we can make information labelling more effective is to use additional tools as opposed to just displaying the content of the product. A good example of such an enhanced information intervention is the warning labels that we are all familiar with on cigarette packaging. Decades of research show that warning labels on cigarette packaging discourage non-smokers from starting to smoke and encourage current smokers to stop smoking. This research has also shown that graphic pictorial warning labels are more impactful when compared to text-only warnings. These kinds of interventions have also been tested in other domains, including sugar-sweetened beverages (SSBs), snack foods, alcohol, and ready meals containing meat. Interestingly, these studies have also demonstrated that simple textual labels (denoting calorie content or textual warnings) are less effective at changing people's selection of the harmful products when compared to pictorial or graphic warning labels (see Hughes et al., 2023, Mantzari et al., 2018; Taillie et al., 2021).

KEY THINKER

Theresa Marteau

Source: © Theresa Marteau

Theresa Marteau graduated with a degree in Social Psychology from the London School of Economics and Political Science (LSE), before embarking on an MSc in Clinical Psychology at the University of Oxford, and later a PhD in Health Psychology at the University of London. She has made significant contributions to the field of health behaviour change by showing that communicating personalised risks for preventable diseases does not effectively change human behaviour. For example, her seminal experimental studies and systematic reviews demonstrated that personalised genetic risk information does not change people's preventive behaviours, as initially believed. These findings led Theresa to examine other more effective avenues for behaviour change, including interventions targeting people's environments (such as availability, size, and labelling interventions, as discussed in the section above). She founded and led the first policy research unit on behaviour change – the Behaviour and Health Research Unit (BHRU) at the University of Cambridge. Under the auspices of the BHRU, Theresa pioneered large-scale population-level studies testing the principles of 'nudge' in the health domain. For her contribution to the field of health behaviour change, she was appointed Dame Commander of the Order of the British Empire in the 2017 Queen's Birthday Honours List. More recently, she advised the UK government's Scientific Advisory Group for Emergencies (SAGE) on behaviour change matters during the COVID-19 pandemic.

11.6.2 Public Support for Behaviour Change Interventions and Policies

In addition to examining the impact of different behaviour change interventions, psychologists, working in multidisciplinary teams, have also made significant contributions to our knowledge regarding **public acceptability of policies**, or what makes interventions more acceptable to the public. This work is important because public support (acceptability) can predict which policy interventions can be successfully initiated and maintained. Understanding what features make policies more acceptable to the public can also help researchers to devise novel interventions that are more likely to be successful. Furthermore, this work can help us to devise better ways to communicate existing and novel behaviour change interventions so they can garner better support.

> **Key concept – Public acceptability of policies:** The level of positive or negative public attitudes towards a given policy.

Information interventions, especially those that denote a product's factual information (such as calorie labelling without any warnings), are often popular with the public because they go hand in hand with the expressed desire of the electorate for transparency in the products on offer and the right to know what we are buying (see Diepeveen et al., 2013; Reynolds et al., 2019). These interventions are also popular with industry since they are considered as softer interventions as compared to more drastic measures, such as changing the default products on offer, changing the ratio of available products on offer, or changing the size of the marketed products. Paradoxically, the interventions that seem to be more effective at changing people's behaviours, such as reducing the size of products or increasing the availability of healthier options, are less supported by the public (Adams et al., 2016). These findings mirror work on the **Nuffield intervention ladder,** which shows that the public is more supportive of the least intrusive, but also the least effective, policies (Nuffield Council on Bioethics, 2007). These findings in intervention support may stem from a classic finding in social psychology about the fundamental attribution error (FAE), whereby we tend to attribute the causes of others' behaviours (but not ours) to internal (underlying) causes rather than external, contextual factors in ones' environments (see Jones & Harris, 1967). This bias is so pervasive that even when we explicitly communicate the impact of external environmental influences on behaviours, people are reluctant to support interventions that modify their environments (for a review, see Reynolds et al., 2022).

> **Key concept – Nuffield intervention ladder:** Classification system that categorises interventions around the principles of *proportionality* (balancing out the degree of infringement on personal freedoms and the benefits that the public health intervention is expected to deliver) and *intrusiveness* (amongst several intervention options, the option which infringes least on the liberty of individuals or is the least coercive should be chosen). The ladder was introduced in 2007 by the Nuffield Council on Bioethics and has since become an influential framework in bioethics and public health policy.

GUEST PERSONAL JOURNEY

James Reynolds

Source: © James Reynolds

While at school I didn't really know what I wanted to do for a career. Psychology wasn't available as an A-level at my school back in 2005, but I was always interested in human behaviour and so eventually decided to take a gamble and apply to do psychology at university. While studying for my Psychology BSc at Sheffield Hallam University in the UK, I became really interested in health behaviours. The topic of my undergraduate research project – and subsequently my PhD – was cannabis use and how using it affects our cognition and behaviour. After my PhD, I became a post-doctoral researcher with Thomas Webb at the University of Sheffield. This allowed me to research people's use of self-regulation techniques to change their own health behaviours, such as quitting smoking or running marathons. After a year and a half at Sheffield I got my second post-doc at the University of Cambridge, working with Theresa Marteau in the Behaviour and Health Research Unit (BHRU). My time with the BHRU was split between evaluating interventions that aim to improve people's diets and investigating why the public support or oppose health policies. Although the latter topic was never something I had planned to do, or was even aware of, I quickly became invested in the topic. After getting my first lecturing job at Aston University, I applied for a European Research Council (ERC) Starting Grant to continue this work. I was successful and obtained a €1.5 million grant over five years to work on increasing public support for health policies. I now run a team of researchers investigating why the public support or oppose health policies. In addition to getting to work on really interesting psychological questions, social psychology has provided me with the possibility to make a real change in the world. I currently advise the World Health Organisation (WHO) on this topic, allowing me to meet and work with politicians and leading public health scientists around the world.

One important consequence arising from these findings is that researchers have attempted to raise the acceptability of more effective but less popular interventions (such as defaults, availability, and size). One way to increase public support for these less palatable interventions and policies seems to be to communicate the level of effectiveness of these interventions. Conversely, communicating evidence of intervention ineffectiveness seems to reduce public support for policies (Reynolds et al., 2020). Fairness considerations also seem to affect public acceptability of policies, with policies characterised as fairer to all groups and cross-sections of a society being deemed more acceptable (Toumpakari et al., 2023). Finally, communicating evidence of the multiple benefits arising from an intervention raises public support more when compared to communicating only one benefit or no benefit (see Mantzari et al., 2022).

11.6.3 Digital Behaviour Change Interventions

Many of you probably have smartwatches and other digital devices that can continuously monitor your daily footsteps, sleep duration, and vigorous exercise duration and intensity, together with your heart rate and stress levels. These are some examples of the sorts of health monitoring that our digital devices can log for us daily, but our digital devices are also capable of delivering behaviour change interventions. Some of you may already be receiving some simple messaging based on behaviour change principles, such as 'Your average daily footstep count is 6,000 steps which is below the recommended 10,000 daily footsteps. Try walking more today'. Digital devices can go even further, with behaviour change apps that have been developed and designed based on one of the theories and models of behaviour change that you have read about in this chapter.

As the above examples show, digital behaviour change interventions can range from the purely informational, through self-guided apps, to digitally delivered or guided human interventions. The reasons for the rise of digital behaviour change interventions are manifold. First, many of the face-to-face interventions that require trained practitioners or coaches are expensive to run and are therefore inaccessible to many. Prime examples of such behaviour change interventions are in the domains of mental health and well-being, and smoking cessation. Digital interventions in these domains have paved the way for more people to reach much-needed intervention services in a cost-effective way (Kyaw et al., 2023; Stanic et al., 2023). There are also contextual reasons when face-to-face intervention delivery is not possible, such as during the COVID-19 pandemic and the ensuing national lockdowns. Furthermore, many lifestyle decisions that require behaviour modification carry a certain level of stigma, as in the example of accessing mental health services (see Gulliver et al., 2010). Digital interventions can be accessed from the privacy of one's own home and in one's own time. Another advantage of digital interventions is their capacity to allow access to intervention support at any time and place. With greater and more affordable access to digital devices and the internet, the potential reach of digital interventions at the population level has also grown. In addition to these advantages, digital interventions have been found to be as effective or even more effective than traditional behaviour change interventions, making them a promising tool for the future (Pauley et al., 2023).

Despite their rise in popularity and the advantages digital interventions bring, they are not without problems. Every day circa 200 digital intervention apps in the health domain are launched (Aitken et al., 2017). However, the rapid development and launch of digital apps means they do not always work effectively. More importantly, they may not be sufficiently pre-tested and piloted before launch, and they may not include an

Figure 11.7 A person on an exercise mat looking at their smartwatch apps

Source: Karolina Grabowska/Pexels

evidence-based behaviour change component. While many of the earliest digital apps were developed by academic research teams and took longer to come to market, nowadays more diverse, and usually commercial, teams launch these apps. And while access to digital devices and the internet is growing, there is still a divide between users and non-users (with non-users disproportionately coming from disadvantaged backgrounds, and the divide being more pronounced in developing countries). Digital interventions also seem to be accepted more by female and younger users, potentially exacerbating any existing inequalities in engagement with behaviour change interventions (e.g., Titov et al., 2017). Issues of privacy and security also permeate decisions to engage with digital behaviour change interventions.

Their disadvantages notwithstanding, digital interventions are becoming an essential part of the toolkit for researchers, practitioners, and policy-makers wishing to design and implement effective behaviour change at the population-level. Factors that have been found to increase the effectiveness of digital interventions are: the personalisation/tailoring of the content, sending reminders, adopting user-friendly and technically stable app design, providing complementary personal support for the digital intervention, and the use of gamification (Jakob et al., 2022). Some of the more exciting recent developments in digital interventions include the just-in-time, adaptive delivery, context-sensing apps, which can be trained to recognise the user's contextual cues that may lead to engaging with unhealthy behaviours, and alert users to avoid them (see Key study 11.3).

KEY STUDY 11.3

'Just-in-time' Context-sensing App to Facilitate Smoking Cessation

In the domain of smoking cessation, such a just-in-time, context-sensing app was recently pilot tested by Naughton and colleagues (2023). A plethora of research shows that smoking cessation lapses are more likely when the person wishing to quit experiences a situational/environmental cue that triggers their craving to smoke a cigarette. In this recent pilot RCT, the researchers tested the feasibility of using Quit Sense, a theory-guided smoking cessation intervention app, which is trained to deliver 'context-aware' lapse-prevention support. The app is trained by the users themselves to deliver just-in-time adaptive intervention support using smartphone location sensing. That means that in the training phase, each smoker individually trains the app to recognise the environmental cues that lead to cigarette craving. In the intervention phase, the app is programmed to send prevention support messages when the mobile is in a geolocation identified as a cue context for smoking. In their pilot RCT, Naughton and colleagues (2023) were able to show that users who were randomised to the Quit Sense app were more likely to successfully quit when compared to the control group of participants, who received the current Stop Smoking services without the Quit Sense app.

EXERCISE 11.3

Evaluating the Behaviour Change Components of a Digital App

Either open an existing or download a new digital application (app) on your phone or tablet. The digital app may be in any domain: health, well-being, personal finances, tracking of time, and so on. Take a few moments to familiarise yourself with what the app does, and then list all the components that you can see of the behaviour change theories and frameworks that we have discussed in this chapter. How do you think the app is trying to engage with you as the end user? What behaviour change techniques and mechanisms can you recognise? Which techniques and mechanisms seem to work better, and which ones seem to work less well in relation to this app? Finally, if the app developer approached you, what would you advise them to do to improve the app's effectiveness for users?

11.7 SUMMARY

In this chapter we have learnt about classic and modern theories and models of behaviour change. We began by looking at initial social-cognitive theories of behaviour change (including the TPB and Social Learning Theory), which propose that intentions and self-efficacy (perceived behavioural control) can explain behaviour and behaviour change. Considerations of the sizeable intention–behaviour gap led us to more modern theories of behaviour change, including the Model of Action Phases, Integrative Self-control Theory, RIM, and habit theory. All these theories surmise that behaviour enactment and change rely heavily on automatic (non-conscious) processes.

These theories were taken further by multidisciplinary teams to develop more encompassing frameworks, such as the 'nudge' (choice architecture) framework, which was discussed in our Advances section. We discussed the methodological and ethical ramifications of nudge before embarking on a discussion of more recent integrative taxonomies of behaviour change and intervention components, such as the Behaviour Change Wheel and the Behaviour Change Techniques Taxonomy (BCTT v1). We concluded the chapter by looking at applications of these theories and frameworks. We examined size, availability, and labelling interventions in the domain of food, alcohol, and meat consumption, before discussing work on how we can increase public support for various behaviour change interventions (including the ones that are considered to be more controversial by the public). We finished the chapter by discussing digital behaviour change interventions, a field that is expected to grow exponentially in the future.

11.8 REVISION

1   Compare and contrast more traditional social-cognitive theories of behaviour change with nudge.
2   How can habit theory help us to change people's behaviours more successfully?
3   What are the ethical challenges levelled at nudging, and how concerned should behaviour change researchers and practitioners be about them?
4   How can the Behaviour Change Wheel be used for developing more effective behaviour change interventions?
5   What is the evidence of effectiveness and public acceptability for size, availability, and information interventions in changing human and planetary health?
6   Evaluate the promise of digital interventions to change people's behaviours.

11.9 FURTHER READING

Foundations

Webb, T. L., & Sheeran, P. (2006). Does changing behavioral intentions engender behavior change? A meta-analysis of the experimental evidence. *Psychological Bulletin, 132*, 249–268. https://doi.org/10.1037/0033-2909.132.2.249

This is a seminal review paper in which Thomas Webb and Paschal Sheeran examine and quantify the intention–behaviour gap. The intention–behaviour gap refers to the often-observed mismatch between people's intentions and their actual behaviours.

Mischel, W., Shoda, Y., & Rodriguez, M. L. (1989). Delay of gratification in children. *Science*, *244*, 933–938. https://doi.org/10.1126/science.2658056

In this classic paper Walter Mischel and colleagues describe the famous 'marshmallow studies', which examined delay of gratification and self-control among preschoolers.

Milkman, K. L., Beshears, J., Choi, J. J., Laibson, D., & Madrian, B. C. (2011). Using implementation intentions prompts to enhance influenza vaccination rates. *Proceedings of the National Academy of Sciences*, *108*, 10415–10420. https://doi.org/10.1073/pnas.1103170108

In this field experiment, Katherine Milkman and colleagues tested the effectiveness of an implementation intention intervention to increase flu vaccination rates among workers in a US organisation. The implementation intention prompts successfully increased vaccination rates compared to simple information leaflets containing the dates and venues of the vaccination clinics.

Advances

Marteau, T. M., Hollands, G. J., & Fletcher, P. C. (2012). Changing human behavior to prevent disease: The importance of targeting automatic processes. *Science*, *337*, 1492–1495. https://doi.org/10.1126/science.1226918

This article by Theresa Marteau and colleagues presents an early overview of nudge or choice architecture interventions in the domain of disease prevention. The paper highlights the importance of targeting automatic or non-conscious processes for effective behaviour change.

De Ridder, D., Kroese, F., & van Gestel, L. (2022). Nudgeability: Mapping conditions of susceptibility to nudge influence. *Perspectives on Psychological Science*, *17*, 346–359. https://doi.org/10.1177/1745691621995183

In this recent paper Denise De Ridder and colleagues discuss the impact of different types of nudges, and whether nudge interventions work in the same way for everyone. The paper also highlights that nudges do not necessarily rely fully on automatic or non-conscious processing.

Michie, S., Richardson, M., Johnston, M., Abraham, C., Francis, J., Hardeman, W., ... & Wood, C. E. (2013). The behavior change technique taxonomy (v1) of 93 hierarchically clustered techniques: Building an international consensus for the reporting of behavior change interventions. *Annals of Behavioral Medicine*, *46*, 81–95. https://doi.org/10.1007/s12160-013-9486-6

This paper by Susan Michie and colleagues introduces the behaviour change technique taxonomy (BCTT v1). Since its publication the taxonomy has been widely used by researchers and practitioners in the field of behaviour change.

Applications

Zupan, Z., Evans, A., Couturier, D. L., & Marteau, T. M. (2017). Wine glass size in England from 1700 to 2017: A measure of our time. *BMJ, 359*. https://doi.org/10.1136/bmj.j5623

This Christmas edition *BMJ* article by Zorana Zupan and colleagues summarises an archival study examining the size of wine glasses used from the 1700s to date. In an engaging manner, the article showcases that the glasses that we drink wine from today are approximately six times larger than those used in the 1700s.

Adams, J., Mytton, O., White, M., & Monsivais, P. (2016). Why are some population interventions for diet and obesity more equitable and effective than others? The role of individual agency. *PLoS Medicine, 13*, e1001990. https://doi.org/10.1371/journal.pmed.1001990

In this recent article Jean Adams and colleagues discuss the effectiveness and equitability of different dietary and obesity interventions. They show that interventions requiring higher individual agency are often less effective and less equitable, but more acceptable to the public.

Holden, S. S., Zlatevska, N., & Dubelaar, C. (2016). Whether smaller plates reduce consumption depends on who's serving and who's looking: A meta-analysis. *Journal of the Association for Consumer Research, 1*, 134–146. https://doi.org/10.1086/684441

This meta-analysis review by Holden and colleagues shows that the impact of size interventions may depend on how food is served and by whom. According to their meta-analysis, reducing the size of plates may not always lead to reductions in consumption.

11.10 REFERENCES

Adams, J., Mytton, O., White, M., & Monsivais, P. (2016). Why are some population interventions for diet and obesity more equitable and effective than others? The role of individual agency. *PLoS Medicine, 13*, e1001990. https://doi.org/10.1371/journal.pmed.1001990

Adriaanse, M. A., Oettingen, G., Gollwitzer, P. M., Hennes, E. P., De Ridder, D. T., & De Wit, J. B. (2010). When planning is not enough: Fighting unhealthy snacking habits by mental contrasting with implementation intentions (MCII). *European Journal of Social Psychology, 40*, 1277–1293. https://doi.org/10.1002/ejsp.730

Aitken, M., Clancy, B., & Nass, D. (2017). *The growing value of digital health: Evidence and impact on human health and the healthcare system.* IQVIA Institute for Human Data Science. Retrieved from: www.iqvia.com/insights/the-iqvia-institute/reports-and-publications/reports/the-growing-value-of-digital-health

Ajzen, I. (1991). The theory of planned behavior. *Organizational Behavior and Human Decision Processes, 50*, 179–211. https://doi.org/10.1016/0749-5978(91)90020-T

Ajzen, I., & Dasgupta, N. (2015). Explicit and implicit beliefs, attitudes, and intentions: The role of conscious and unconscious processes in human behavior. In P. Haggard & B. Eitam (Eds.), *The sense of agency* (pp. 115–144). New York: Oxford University Press.

Aulbach, M. B., Knittle, K., & Haukkala, A. (2019). Implicit process interventions in eating behaviour: A meta-analysis examining mediators and moderators. *Health Psychology Review, 13,* 179–208. https://doi.org/10.1080/17437199.2019.1571933

Bandura, A. (1977). *Social learning theory.* Englewood Cliffs, NJ: Prentice-Hall.

Bandura, A. (1986). *Social foundations of thought and action.* Englewood Cliffs, NJ: Prentice-Hall.

Barker, R. G. (1968). *Ecological psychology.* Stanford, CA: Stanford University Press.

Behavioural Insights Team. (2012). *Applying behavioural insights to reduce fraud, error and debt.* London: Cabinet Office.

Bovens, L. (2009). The ethics of nudge. In T. Grüne-Yanoff & S. O. Hansson (Eds.), *Preference change: Approaches from philosophy, economics and psychology* (pp. 207–219). Dordrecht: Springer Netherlands.

Cane, J., O'Connor, D., & Michie, S. (2012). Validation of the theoretical domains framework for use in behaviour change and implementation research. *Implementation Science, 7,* 1–17. https://doi.org/10.1186/1748-5908-7-37

Clarke, N., Blackwell, A. K., Ferrar, J., De-Loyde, K., Pilling, M. A., Munafò, M. R., … & Hollands, G. J. (2023). Impact on alcohol selection and online purchasing of changing the proportion of available non-alcoholic versus alcoholic drinks: A randomised controlled trial. *PLoS Medicine, 20,* e1004193. https://doi.org/10.1371/journal.pmed.1004193

Codling, S., Mantzari, E., Sexton, O., Fuller, G., Pechey, R., Hollands, G. J., … & Marteau, T. M. (2020). Impact of bottle size on in-home consumption of wine: A randomized controlled cross-over trial. *Addiction, 115,* 2280–2292. https://doi.org/10.1111/add.15042

Crockett, R. A., King, S. E., Marteau, T. M., Prevost, A. T., Bignardi, G., Roberts, N. W., … & Jebb, S. A. (2018). Nutritional labelling for healthier food or non-alcoholic drink purchasing and consumption. *The Cochrane Database of Systematic Reviews, 2018*(2). https://doi.org/10.1002/14651858.CD009315.pub2

De Ridder, D., Kroese, F., & van Gestel, L. (2022). Nudgeability: Mapping conditions of susceptibility to nudge influence. *Perspectives on Psychological Science, 17,* 346–359. https://doi.org/10.1177/1745691621995183

Devoto, F., Duflo, E., Dupas, P., Parienté, W., & Pons, V. (2012). Happiness on tap: Piped water adoption in urban Morocco. *American Economic Journal: Economic Policy, 4,* 68–99. https://doi.org/10.1257/pol.4.4.68

Diepeveen, S., Ling, T., Suhrcke, M., Roland, M., & Marteau, T. M. (2013). Public acceptability of government intervention to change health-related behaviours: A systematic review and narrative synthesis. *BMC Public Health, 13,* 1–11. https://doi.org/10.1186/1471-2458-13-756

Dillard, J.P. (1994). Rethinking the study of fear appeals: An emotional perspective. *Communication Theory, 4,* 295–323. https://doi.org/10.1111/j.1468-2885.1994.tb00094.x

Duflo, E., Kremer, M., & Robinson, J. (2011). Nudging farmers to use fertilizer: Theory and experimental evidence from Kenya. *American Economic Review, 101,* 2350–2390. https://doi.org/10.1257/aer.101.6.2350

Epton, T., Currie, S., & Armitage, C. J. (2017). Unique effects of setting goals on behavior change: Systematic review and meta-analysis. *Journal of Consulting and Clinical Psychology, 85,* 1182–1198. https://doi.org/10.1037/ccp0000260

Fazio, R. H. (1986). How do attitudes guide behavior? In R. M. Sorrentino & E. T. Higgins (Eds.), *Handbook of motivation and cognition: Foundations of social behavior* (pp. 202–243). New York: Guilford Press.

Fishbein, M., & Ajzen, I. (1975). *Belief, attitude, intention, and behavior: An introduction to theory and research.* Reading, MA: Addison-Wesley.

Garnett, E. E., Balmford, A., Sandbrook, C., Pilling, M. A., & Marteau, T. M. (2019). Impact of increasing vegetarian availability on meal selection and sales in cafeterias. *Proceedings of the National Academy of Sciences, 116,* 20923–20929. https://doi.org/10.1073/pnas.1907207116

Golden, S. D., & Earp, J. A. (2012). Social ecological approaches to individuals and their contexts: Twenty years of *Health Education and Behavior* health promotion interventions. *Health Education and Behavior, 39,* 364–372. https://doi.org/10.1177/1090198111418634

Gollwitzer, P. M. (1990). Action phases and mind-sets. In E. T. Higgins & R. Sorrentino (Eds.), *The handbook of motivation and cognition: Foundations of social behavior* (Vol. 2, pp. 53–92). New York: Guilford Press.

Gollwitzer, P. M. (1999). Implementation intentions: Strong effects of simple plans. *American Psychologist, 4,* 493–503. https://doi.org/10.1037/0003-066X.54.7.493

Gollwitzer, P. M., & Sheeran, P. (2006). Implementation intentions and goal achievement: A meta-analysis of effects and processes. In M. P. Zanna (Ed.), *Advances in experimental social psychology* (Vol. 38, pp. 69–119). https://doi.org/10.1016/S0065-2601(06)38002-1

Gulliver, A., Griffiths, K. M., & Christensen, H. (2010). Perceived barriers and facilitators to mental health help-seeking in young people: A systematic review. *BMC Psychiatry, 10,* 1–9. https://doi.org/10.1186/1471-244X-10-113

Hansen, P. G., & Jespersen, A. M. (2013). Nudge and the manipulation of choice: A framework for the responsible use of the nudge approach to behaviour change in public policy. *European Journal of Risk Regulation, 4,* 3–28. https://doi.org/10.1017/S1867299X00002762

Harkin, B., Webb, T. L., Chang, B. P., Prestwich, A., Conner, M., Kellar, I., … & Sheeran, P. (2016). Does monitoring goal progress promote goal attainment? A meta-analysis of the experimental evidence. *Psychological Bulletin, 142,* 198–229. https://doi.org/10.1037/bul0000025

Heckhausen, H., & Gollwitzer, P. M. (1987). Thought contents and cognitive functioning in motivational versus volitional states of mind. *Motivation and Emotion, 11,* 101–120. https://doi.org/10.1007/BF00992338

Hochbaum, G. M. (1958). *Public participation in medical screening programs: A socio-psychological study* (No. 572). Washington, DC: US Government Printing Office (US Department of Health, Education, and Welfare, Public Health Service, Bureau of State Services, Division of Special Health Services, Tuberculosis Program).

Holden, S. S., Zlatevska, N., & Dubelaar, C. (2016). Whether smaller plates reduce consumption depends on who's serving and who's looking: A meta-analysis. *Journal of the Association for Consumer Research*, *1*, 134–146. https://doi.org/10.1086/684441

Hollands, G. J., Bignardi, G., Johnston, M., Kelly, M. P., Ogilvie, D., Petticrew, M., ... & Marteau, T. M. (2017). The TIPPME intervention typology for changing environments to change behaviour. *Nature Human Behaviour*, *1*, 1–9. https://doi.org/10.1038/s41562-017-0140

Hollands, G. J., Carter, P., Anwer, S., King, S. E., Jebb, S. A., Ogilvie, D., ... & Marteau, T. M. (2019). Altering the availability or proximity of food, alcohol, and tobacco products to change their selection and consumption. *Cochrane Database of Systematic Reviews*, *9*. https://doi.org/10.1002/14651858.CD012573.pub3

Hollands, G. J., Shemilt, I., Marteau, T. M., Jebb, S. A., Lewis, H. B., Wei, Y., ... & Ogilvie, D. (2015). Portion, package or tableware size for changing selection and consumption of food, alcohol and tobacco. *The Cochrane Database of Systematic Reviews*, *2015*(9). https://doi.org/10.1002/14651858.CD011045.pub2

Hughes, J. P., Weick, M., & Vasiljevic, M. (2023). Impact of pictorial warning labels on meat meal selection: A randomised experimental study with UK meat consumers. *Appetite*, *190*, 107026. https://doi.org/10.1016/j.appet.2023.107026

Jakob, R., Harperink, S., Rudolf, A. M., Fleisch, E., Haug, S., Mair, J. L., ... & Kowatsch, T. (2022). Factors influencing adherence to mHealth apps for prevention or management of noncommunicable diseases: Systematic review. *Journal of Medical Internet Research*, *24*, e35371. https://doi.org/10.2196/35371

James, W. (1890). *Habit*. New York: Henry Holt.

Jetten, J., Haslam, C., & Alexander, S. H. (Eds.). (2012). *The social cure: Identity, health and well-being*. New York: Psychology Press.

Jones, E. E., & Harris, V. A. (1967). The attribution of attitudes. *Journal of Experimental Social Psychology*, *3*, 1–24. https://doi.org/10.1016/0022-1031(67)90034-0

Kahneman, D., & Tversky, A. (1979). Prospect theory: An analysis of decision under risk. *Econometrica*, *47*, 263–291. https://doi.org/10.2307/1914185

Kirk, D., Oettingen, G., & Gollwitzer, P. M. (2013). Promoting integrative bargaining: Mental contrasting with implementation intentions. *International Journal of Conflict Management*, *24*, 148–165. https://doi.org/10.1108/10444061311316771

Kok, G., Peters, G.-J. Y., Kessels, L. T. E., Hoor, G. A., & Ruiter, R. A. C. (2018). Ignoring theory and misinterpreting evidence: The false belief in fear appeals. *Health Psychology Review*, *12*, 111–125. https://doi.org/10.1080/17437199.2017.1415767

Kotabe, H. P., & Hofmann, W. (2015). On integrating the components of self-control. *Perspectives on Psychological Science*, *10*, 618–638. https://doi.org/10.1177/1745691615593382

Kunreuther, H. (2002). Risk analysis and risk management in an uncertain world. *Risk Analysis: An International Journal*, *22*, 655–664. https://doi.org/10.1111/0272-4332.00057

Kunreuther, H., & Pauly, M. (2006). Insurance decision-making and market behavior. *Foundations and Trends® in Microeconomics*, *1*, 63–127. https://doi.org/10.1561/0700000002

Kyaw, T. L., Ng, N., Theocharaki, M., Wennberg, P., & Sahlen, K. G. (2023). Cost-effectiveness of digital tools for behavior change interventions among people with chronic diseases: Systematic review. *Interactive Journal of Medical Research, 12*, e42396. https://doi.org/10.2196/42396

Lewin, K. (1936). *Principles of topological psychology*. London: McGraw Hill.

Lewin, K. (1951). *Field theory in social science*. New York: Harper.

Lin, Y., Osman, M., & Ashcroft, R. (2017). Nudge: Concept, effectiveness, and ethics. *Basic and Applied Social Psychology, 39*, 293–306. https://doi.org/10.1080/01973533.2017.1356304

Loijen, A., Vrijsen, J. N., Egger, J. I., Becker, E. S., & Rinck, M. (2020). Biased approach-avoidance tendencies in psychopathology: A systematic review of their assessment and modification. *Clinical Psychology Review, 77*, 101825. https://doi.org/10.1016/j.cpr.2020.101825

Maddux, J. E., & Rogers, R. W. (1983). Protection motivation and self-efficacy: A revised theory of fear appeals and attitude change. *Journal of Experimental Social Psychology, 19*, 469–479. https://doi.org/10.1016/0022-1031(83)90023-9

Madrian, B. C., & Shea, D. F. (2001). The power of suggestion: Inertia in 401 (k) participation and savings behavior. *The Quarterly Journal of Economics, 116*, 1149–1187. https://doi.org/10.1162/003355301753265543

Mani, A., Mullainathan, S., Shafir, E., & Zhao, J. (2013). Poverty impedes cognitive function. *Science, 341*, 976–980. https://doi.org/10.1126/science.1238041

Mantzari, E. & Marteau, T. M. (2022) Impact of sizes of servings, glasses and bottles on alcohol consumption: A narrative review. *Nutrients,*14, 4244. https://doi.org/10.3390/nu14204244

Mantzari, E., Reynolds, J. P., Jebb, S. A., Hollands, G. J., Pilling, M. A., & Marteau, T. M. (2022). Public support for policies to improve population and planetary health: A population-based online experiment assessing impact of communicating evidence of multiple versus single benefits. *Social Science & Medicine, 296*, 114726. https://doi.org/10.1016/j.socscimed.2022.114726

Mantzari, E., Vasiljevic, M., Turney, I., Pilling, M., & Marteau, T. (2018). Impact of warning labels on sugar-sweetened beverages on parental selection: An online experimental study. *Preventive Medicine Reports, 12*, 259–267. https://doi.org/10.1016/j.pmedr.2018.10.016

Marteau, T. M., Hollands, G. J., & Fletcher, P. C. (2012). Changing human behavior to prevent disease: The importance of targeting automatic processes. *Science, 337*, 1492–1495. https://doi.org/10.1126/science.1226918

Melnikoff, D. E., & Bargh, J. A. (2018). The mythical number two. *Trends in Cognitive Sciences, 22*, 280–293. https://doi.org/10.1016/j.tics.2018.02.001

Michie, S., Richardson, M., Johnston, M., Abraham, C., Francis, J., Hardeman, W., ... & Wood, C. E. (2013). The Behavior Change Technique Taxonomy (v1) of 93 hierarchically clustered techniques: Building an international consensus for the reporting of behavior change interventions. *Annals of Behavioral Medicine, 46*, 81–95. https://doi.org/10.1007/s12160-013-9486-6

Michie, S., van Stralen, M. M., & West, R. (2011). The Behaviour Change Wheel: A new method for characterising and designing behaviour change interventions. *Implementation Science, 6,* 1–12. https://doi.org/10.1186/1748-5908-6-42

Milkman, K. L., Beshears, J., Choi, J. J., Laibson, D., & Madrian, B. C. (2011). Using implementation intentions prompts to enhance influenza vaccination rates. *Proceedings of the National Academy of Sciences, 108,* 10415–10420. https://doi.org/10.1073/pnas.1103170108

Mischel, W., Shoda, Y., & Rodriguez, M. L. (1989). Delay of gratification in children. *Science, 244,* 933–938. https://doi.org/10.1126/science.2658056

Moran, T., Nudler, Y., & Bar-Anan, Y. (2023). Evaluative conditioning: Past, present, and future. *Annual Review of Psychology, 74,* 245–269. https://doi.org/10.1146/annurev-psych-032420-031815

Naughton, F., Hope, A., Siegele-Brown, C., Grant, K., Barton, G., Notley, C., ... & High, J. (2023). An automated, online feasibility randomized controlled trial of a just-in-time adaptive intervention for smoking cessation (Quit Sense). *Nicotine and Tobacco Research, 25,* 1319–1329. https://doi.org/10.1093/ntr/ntad032

Neal, D. T., Wood, W., Wu, M., & Kurlander, D. (2011). The pull of the past: When do habits persist despite conflict with motives? *Personality and Social Psychology Bulletin, 37,* 1428–1437. https://doi.org/10.1177/0146167211419863

Newall, P. W. (2023). What is sludge? Comparing Sunstein's definition to others'. *Behavioural Public Policy, 7,* 851–857. https://doi.org/10.1017/bpp.2022.12

Nuffield Council on Bioethics. (2007). *Public health: Ethical issues.* Retrieved from www.nuffieldbioethics.org/publications/public-health

Orbell, S., & Verplanken, B. (2010). The automatic component of habit in health behavior: Habit as cue-contingent automaticity. *Health Psychology, 29,* 374–383. https://doi.org/10.1037/a0019596

Osman, M. (2016). Nudge: How far have we come? *Œconomia. History, Methodology, Philosophy, 6*-4, 557–570. https://doi.org/10.4000/oeconomia.2490

Pauley, D., Cuijpers, P., Papola, D., Miguel, C., & Karyotaki, E. (2023). Two decades of digital interventions for anxiety disorders: A systematic review and meta-analysis of treatment effectiveness. *Psychological Medicine, 53,* 567–579. https://doi.org/10.1017/S0033291721001999

Peters, G.-J. Y., Ruiter, R. A. C., & Kok, G. (2013). Threatening communication: A critical re-analysis and a revised meta-analytic test of fear appeal theory. *Health Psychology Review, 7,* S8–S31. https://doi.org/10.1080/17437199.2012.703527

Petrosino, A., Turpin-Petrosino, C., & Buehler, J. (2005). 'Scared Straight' and other juvenile awareness programs for preventing juvenile delinquency. *Campbell Systematic Reviews, 1,* 1–62. https://doi.org/10.4073/csr.2004.2

Petty, R. E., & Cacioppo, J. T. (1986). The elaboration likelihood model of persuasion. In Berkowitz, L. (Ed.), *Advances in experimental social psychology* (Vol. 19, pp. 123–205). New York: Academic Press.

Prestwich, A., Sniehotta, F. F., Whittington, C., Dombrowski, S. U., Roggers, L., & Michie, S. (2014). Does theory influence the effectiveness of health behavior interventions? Meta-analysis. *Health Psychology, 33,* 465–474. https://doi.org/10.1037/a0032853

Reinders, M. J., Huitink, M., Dijkstra, S. C., Maaskant, A. J., & Heijnen, J. (2017). Menu-engineering in restaurants – adapting portion sizes on plates to enhance vegetable consumption: A real-life experiment. *International Journal of Behavioral Nutrition and Physical Activity*, *14*, 1–11. https://doi.org/10.1186/s12966-017-0496-9

Reynolds, J. P., Archer, S., Pilling, M., Kenny, M., Hollands, G. J., & Marteau, T. M. (2019). Public acceptability of nudging and taxing to reduce consumption of alcohol, tobacco, and food: A population-based survey experiment. *Social Science & Medicine*, *236*, 112395. https://doi.org/10.1016/j.socscimed.2019.112395

Reynolds, J. P., Stautz, K., Pilling, M., van der Linden, S., & Marteau, T. M. (2020). Communicating the effectiveness and ineffectiveness of government policies and their impact on public support: A systematic review with meta-analysis. *Royal Society Open Science*, *7*, 190522. https://doi.org/10.1098/rsos.190522

Reynolds, J. P., Vasiljevic, M., Pilling, M., & Marteau, T. M. (2022). Communicating evidence about the environment's role in obesity and support for government policies to tackle obesity: A systematic review with meta-analysis. *Health Psychology Review*, *16*, 67–80. https://doi.org/10.1080/17437199.2020.1829980

Rogers, R. W. (1975). A protection motivation theory of fear appeals and attitude change. *Journal of Psychology*, *91*, 93–114. https://doi.org/10.1080/00223980.1975.9915803

Rogers, R. W. (1983). Cognitive and physiological processes in fear appeals and attitude change: A revised theory of protection motivation. In J. T. Cacioppo & R. E. Petty (Eds.), *Social psychophysiology: A source book* (pp. 153–176). New York: Guilford Press.

Rosário, F., Vasiljevic, M., Pas, L., Angus, C., Ribeiro, C., & Fitzgerald, N. (2022). Efficacy of a theory-driven program to implement alcohol screening and brief interventions in primary health-care: A cluster randomized controlled trial. *Addiction*, *117*, 1609–1621. https://doi.org/10.1111/add.15782

Rosenstock, I. M. (1966). Why people use health services. *Millbank Memorial Fund Quarterly*, *44*, 94–124. 10.1111/j.1468-0009.2005.00425.x

Rosenstock, I. M. (1974). Historical origins of the health belief model. *Health Education Monographs*, *2*, 328–335. 10.1177/109019817400200403

Ruffault, A., Czernichow, S., Hagger, M. S., Ferrand, M., Erichot, N., Carette, C., … & Flahault, C. (2017). The effects of mindfulness training on weight-loss and health-related behaviours in adults with overweight and obesity: A systematic review and meta-analysis. *Obesity Research & Clinical Practice*, *11*, 90–111. https://doi.org/10.1016/j.orcp.2016.09.002

Shah, A. K., Mullainathan, S., & Shafir, E. (2012). Some consequences of having too little. *Science*, *338*, 682–685. https://doi.org/10.1126/science.1222426

Stacey, F. G., James, E. L., Chapman, K., Courneya, K. S., & Lubans, D. R. (2015). A systematic review and meta-analysis of social cognitive theory-based physical activity and/or nutrition behavior change interventions for cancer survivors. *Journal of Cancer Survivorship*, *9*, 305–338. https://doi.org/10.1007/s11764-014-0413-z

Stajkovic, A. D., & Luthans, F. (1998). Self-efficacy and work-related performance: A meta-analysis. *Psychological Bulletin*, *124*, 240–261. https://doi.org/10.1037/0033-2909.124.2.240

Stanic, T., Avsar, T. S., & Gomes, M. (2023). Economic evaluations of digital health interventions for children and adolescents: Systematic review. *Journal of Medical Internet Research, 25*, e45958. https://doi.org/10.2196/45958

Strack, F., & Deutsch, R. (2004). Reflective and impulsive determinants of social behavior. *Personality and Social Psychology Review, 8*, 220–247. https://doi.org/10.1207/s15327957pspr0803_1

Sunstein, C. R. (2015). The ethics of nudging. *Yale Journal on Regulation, 32*, 413–450.

Sunstein, C. R. (2016). People prefer System 2 nudges (kind of). *Duke Law Journal, 66*, 121–168.

Taillie, L. S., Chauvenet, C., Grummon, A. H., Hall, M. G., Waterlander, W., Prestemon, C. E., & Jaacks, L. M. (2021). Testing front-of-package warnings to discourage red meat consumption: A randomized experiment with US meat consumers. *International Journal of Behavioral Nutrition and Physical Activity, 18*, 1–13. https://doi.org/10.1186/s12966-021-01178-9

Tajfel, H., & Turner, J. C. (1979). An integrative theory of intergroup conflict. In W. G. Austin & S. Worchel (Eds.), *The social psychology of intergroup relations* (pp. 33–47). Monterey, CA: Brooks/Cole. Reprinted in M. A. Hogg, & D. Abrams (2001). *Intergroup relations*. New York: Psychology Press.

Talsma, K., Schüz, B., Schwarzer, R., & Norris, K. (2018). I believe, therefore I achieve (and vice versa): A meta-analytic cross-lagged panel analysis of self-efficacy and academic performance. *Learning and Individual Differences, 61*, 136–150. https://doi.org/10.1016/j.lindif.2017.11.015

Tang, M.Y., Smith, D. M., McSharry, J., Hann, M., & French, D. P. (2019). Behavior change techniques associated with changes in postintervention and maintained changes in self-efficacy for physical activity: A systematic review with meta-analysis. *Annals of Behavioral Medicine, 53*, 801–815. https://doi.org/10.1093/abm/kay090

Tannenbaum, M. B., Hepler, J., Zimmerman, R. S., Saul, L., Jacobs, S., Wilson, K., & Albarracín, D. (2015). Appealing to fear: A meta-analysis of fear appeal effectiveness and theories. *Psychological Bulletin, 141*, 1178–1204. https://doi.org/10.1037/a0039729

Thaler, R. H. (2018). Nudge, not sludge. *Science, 361*, 431–431. https://doi.org/10.1126/science.aau9241

Thaler, R. H., & Sunstein, C. R. (2008). *Nudge: Improving decisions about health, wealth, and happiness*. New Haven, CT: Yale University Press.

Titov, N., Dear, B. F., Staples, L. G., Bennett-Levy, J., Klein, B., Rapee, R. M., ... & Nielssen, O. B. (2017). The first 30 months of the MindSpot Clinic: Evaluation of a national e-mental health service against project objectives. *Australian & New Zealand Journal of Psychiatry, 51*, 1227–1239. https://doi.org/10.1177/0004867416671598

Toumpakari, Z., Valerino-Perea, S., Willis, K., Adams, J., White, M., Vasiljevic, M., ... & Jago, R. (2023). Exploring views of members of the public and policymakers on the acceptability of population level dietary and active-travel policies: A qualitative study. *International Journal of Behavioral Nutrition and Physical Activity, 20*, 64. https://doi.org/10.1186/s12966-023-01465-7

Tversky, A., & Kahneman, D. (1974). Judgment under uncertainty: Heuristics and biases. *Science, 185*, 1124–1131. https://doi.org/10.1126/science.185.4157.1124

Unrau, N. J., Rueda, R., Son, E., Polanin, J. R., Lundeen, R. J., & Muraszewski, A. K. (2018). Can reading self-efficacy be modified? A meta-analysis of the impact of interventions on reading self-efficacy. *Review of Educational Research, 88*(2), 167–204. https://doi.org/10.3102/0034654317743199

Verplanken, B., & Orbell, S. (2022). Attitudes, habits, and behavior change. *Annual Review of Psychology, 73*, 327–352. https://doi.org/10.1146/annurev-psych-020821-011744

Verplanken, B., & Roy, D. (2016). Empowering interventions to promote sustainable lifestyles: Testing the habit discontinuity hypothesis in a field experiment. *Journal of Environmental Psychology, 45*, 127–134. https://doi.org/10.1016/j.jenvp.2015.11.008

Webb, T. L., & Sheeran, P. (2006). Does changing behavioral intentions engender behavior change? A meta-analysis of the experimental evidence. *Psychological Bulletin, 132*, 249–268. https://doi.org/10.1037/0033-2909.132.2.249

Webb, T. L., & Sheeran, P. (2007). How do implementation intentions promote goal attainment? A test of component processes. *Journal of Experimental Social Psychology, 43*, 295–302. https://doi.org/10.1016/j.jesp.2006.02.001

Wood, W., & Neal, D. T. (2009). The habitual consumer. *Journal of Consumer Psychology, 19*, 579–592. https://doi.org/10.1016/j.jcps.2009.08.003

Wrieden, W., Gregor, A., & Barton, K. (2008). Have food portion sizes increased in the UK over the last 20 years? *Proceedings of the Nutrition Society, 67*(OCE6). https://doi.org/10.1017/S0029665100590582

Young, L. R., & Nestle, M. (2002). The contribution of expanding portion sizes to the US obesity epidemic. *American Journal of Public Health, 92*, 246–249. https://doi.org/10.2105/AJPH.92.2.246

Zlatevska, N., Neumann, N., & Dubelaar, C. (2018). Mandatory calorie disclosure: A comprehensive analysis of its effect on consumers and retailers. *Journal of Retailing, 94*, 89–101. https://doi.org/10.1016/j.jretai.2017.09.007

Zupan, Z., Evans, A., Couturier, D. L., & Marteau, T. M. (2017). Wine glass size in England from 1700 to 2017: A measure of our time. *BMJ, 359*. https://doi.org/10.1136/bmj.j5623

INDEX